The New Tolkien Companion

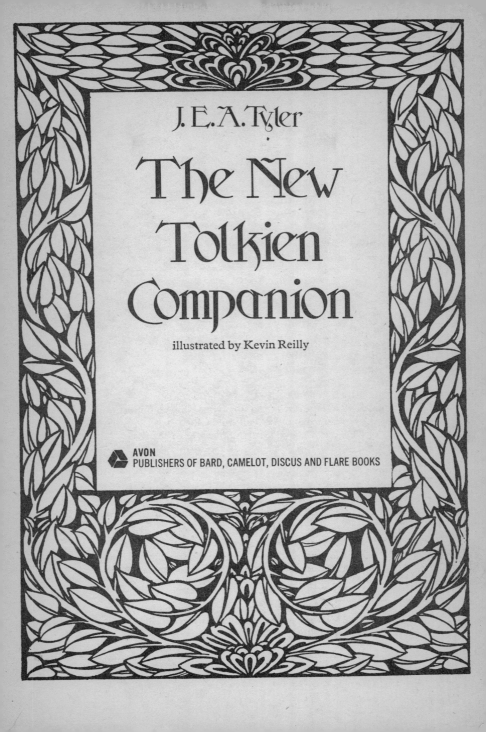

J. E. A. Tyler

The New Tolkien Companion

illustrated by Kevin Reilly

AVON
PUBLISHERS OF BARD, CAMELOT, DISCUS AND FLARE BOOKS

AVON BOOKS
A division of
The Hearst Corporation
959 Eighth Avenue
New York, New York 10019

First Avon Printing, March, 1977
First revised Printing, February 1980

AVON TRADEMARK REG. U.S. PAT. OFF. AND IN
OTHER COUNTRIES, MARCA REGISTRADA, HECHO EN
U.S.A.

Printed in the U.S.A.

COM 10 9 8 7 6 5 4 3 2

For Susan

Elen síla lúmenn' omentielvo,

ACKNOWLEDGEMENTS My gratitude to Messrs. George Allen & Unwin Ltd and to the Estate of the late Professor J. R. R. Tolkien, for permission to quote from the following volumes:

The Hobbit © George Allen & Unwin Ltd 1937, 1951, 1966

The Lord of the Rings © George Allen & Unwin Ltd 1968, comprising
  The Fellowship of the Ring © George Allen & Unwin Ltd 1954, 1966
  The Two Towers © George Allen & Unwin Ltd 1954, 1966
  The Return of the King © George Allen & Unwin Ltd 1955, 1966

The Adventures of Tom Bombadil © George Allen & Unwin Ltd 1961

The Road Goes Ever On text © George Allen & Unwin Ltd 1961 and J. R. R. Tolkien 1967; music © Donald Swann 1967

Foreword to the Second Edition

Throughout the entire history of the philological sciences there have been few feats of literary translation to equal that performed by Professor John Ronald Reuel Tolkien, of Oxford, England, between the years 1932 and 1953. During this period Tolkien laboured, if not unceasingly, then with as much intensity and devotion as his other (considerable) scholastic duties permitted, on the translation, annotation and general reorganization of a collection of extremely ancient bound volumes which had entered his benevolent custodianship some years before he took up his Chair at Merton College, where he lectured in Anglo-Saxon and associated subjects.

Tolkien's work in the fields of Early English Literature and Comparative Mythology had prepared him for working with antique manuscripts, but the Annals of the Shire, four volumes transcribed from copies of the original tomes compiled by the renowned Hobbits Bilbo and Frodo Baggins, were written during the Third Age of Middle-earth long ago; and they were far older than the Celtic, Germanic and Icelandic manuscripts with which Tolkien was then accustomed to deal. Nevertheless, he set himself to the deciphering of one of the four volumes, the Red Book of Westmarch, and by 1936 he had successfully completed the translation – and the preparation for publication – of the first (much smaller) section of the Red Book.

The resulting book, called by its publishers *The Hobbit*, but by its translator *There and Back Again* (in deference to the known preferences of its author), appeared in 1937 and was a runaway success, as these events are termed in the publishing world. Yet no one (beyond a small *coterie* of academics at Oxford) was then aware that it contained translated historical narrative, as opposed to inventive children's fairy tale fiction in the Andrew Lang tradition. For, reluctant to reveal his true role as translator, Tolkien had instead tacitly assumed the pose of 'author' and did not abandon this until the publication, seventeen year later, of the sequel to *The Hobbit*. But in the Prologue to *The Lord of the Rings*, as the sequel is known, he made it abundantly clear that the entire work consisted chiefly of translated historical narrative from the pen of Frodo Baggins (heir of that Hobbit who had written the earlier, smaller section), with some amendments by contemporary sources and additions by later hands. *The Lord of the Rings* was then revealed as an historical document of great age and immense significance.

With that generally understood, the scale and excellence of Tolkien's philological, historical and above all literary achievement at last became clear. Yet the merits of his translation lie not so much in the skill of his solutions to technical problems with language and script as in the peerless way he overcame these difficulties without ever relinquishing his perception of the text as a work of real literary merit on the part of its long-dead authors. He kept faith with what the Hobbit-scholars of long ago had to say, though his own interest lay more closely in the languages they had used.

> I desired to do this for my own satisfaction, and I had little hope that other people would be interested in this work, especially since it was primarily linguistic in inspiration . . .

The inspiration was therefore academic but the effort required from Tolkien was positively Herculean. It is worth noting in this context that, within the space of thirty years, he was able to complete to his own satisfaction work on only *one* of the four volumes which had come into his possession: The Red Book of Westmarch. Sadly, he was unable to finish the larger work (three volumes compiled by Bilbo Baggins and called by him *Translations from the Elvish*) before his death in 1973. By far the single greatest reason for this lies in the fact that, from the day *The Lord of the Rings* was first published, commercial demand from a public overwhelmed by the beauty and strangeness of the ancient world as revealed by Tolkien's labours put an intolerable strain on his time; and being, after all, a perfectionist, he was afterwards constantly employed in further revision and amending of detail, and had little energy to spare for further undertakings.

So *The Lord of the Rings*, until recently, remained the lynchpin of Tolkien's translated work. Few will argue if I describe it as one of the most commercially successful books of all time. So powerful is its attraction, even for those not overly concerned with linguistics or history or other arcane subjects, that it is still widely believed – even by those who have read Tolkien's frequent disclaimers – to be an original work, a marvellous invention on the part of a distinguished and gifted scholar.

Yet while *The Lord of the Rings* remains the longest single segment of what may be termed the Ring Epic, it is no longer its sole pillar. For in 1977 *Translations from the Elvish* was at last published (thanks to diligent editorial work on the part of Professor Tolkien's son, C. J. R. Tolkien) under the title *The Silmarillion*, and almost immediately it emulated the commercial success of its predecessor, being instantly seized, and devoured, by those hundreds and thousands of cognoscenti (I am one) for whom the name *Tolkien* has long been synonymous with a vast and splendid vision, poignant, terrible and deeply devout. As a result it has already come to form a second foundation of the Epic. Indeed, it may be said to take pride of place, by reason of its ancientry alone.

A brief outline of the respective ages of the original manuscripts – or rather, of the sources from which they were originally drawn – now becomes necessary.

The Hobbit and *The Lord of the Rings*, though published first, were composed in the late Third and Early Fourth Ages, and describe events which took place in the closing years of the Third Age; whereas *The Silmarillion*, also composed in the late Third Age, draws almost exclusively on source-material from the First Age. Yet it was published last of all three works: chiefly for reasons of commercial acceptance.

The Silmarillion, physically, is a smaller text than *The Lord of the Rings*. Yet it is highly compressed, a compendium of stories, poems and myths grouped around a single mighty theme, rather than a personal narrative; and it should not, strictly speaking, be compared to the larger work, certainly not on literary grounds. For it belongs to an older tradition of tale-telling. It is bardic in form, a cycle of stories, each of which, if narrated in the style of *The Lord of the Rings*, would furnish an epic of similar proportions. And it covers a truly vast expanse of time, from the Beginning of the Universe to the ending of the Third Age. The only personalities who appear throughout the text are themselves Divine, or at least formerly Divine; which may give an indication of the 'High' tone employed throughout. The homeliness of Hobbit-life, an enchanting 'lesser' aspect of the Ring narrative, is altogether missing.

The Silmarillion is a remote, exalted voice which speaks to us from the depths of the Elder Days, a composite made up of many individual voices of their day: Elf-minstrels, loremasters of Men, and other great, but long-dead persons.

That apart, *The Silmarillion* is rich in information of the sort which initially led this compiler to attempt the construction of the first incarnation of *The Tolkien Companion* – merely on the strength of the material contained in *The Lord of the Rings* and its accessory volumes. It was my opinion that the plethora of unfamiliar names and words with which those works abound necessitated the assembly of some form of index or concordance. This I attempted to do. And so matters might have stood, had *The Silmarillion* never been published, as at one time seemed depressingly possible. Yet after all it *did* appear; and none were more delighted than I, even though, in my case at least, its publication clearly meant the instant outdating of the original *Tolkien Companion*. For much that was only outlined in *The Lord of the Rings* is the very subject-matter of *The Silmarillion*, with the inevitable result that many entries in the previous *Companion* have required extensive modification, while new entries – 1,800 of them – have had to be created.

The result is this revised edition. Within its pages, as in the earlier volume, I have listed in alphabetical order almost all of the 'foreign' names and words that are mentioned anywhere in the Ring Epic and in *The Silmarillion*, which pre-dates it. The Ring Epic may be said to include by definition not only *The Hobbit* and *The Lord of the Rings* but also *The Adventures of Tom Bombadil* and *The Road Goes Ever On*. (Both of these volumes contain notes by Tolkien on his translations and the former has a selection of rustic Hobbit-verses of slightly later date than the Tale of the Ring.) In addition, by using the same principles of decipherment as he did, though, of course, far more hesitantly, I have attempted to give meanings to many words in the Elvish, Dwarvish and Mannish tongues which were never translated by Tolkien (most of these come from the Ring Epic proper, since *The Silmarillion* is well furnished with an index containing many useful translations, and in addition an Elvish vocabulary of real value; I have, of course, incorporated these translations into the entries which follow).

I have also taken the opportunity to correct any errors which appeared in the earlier edition. These, thankfully, were not many, and were chiefly of the typographical or computational sort. Perhaps my grossest error was to postulate an Eldarin origin for Sauron of Mordor, Lord of the Rings; but in defence of this supposition I can plead that the existence of the Maiarin race was, before publication of *The Silmarillion*, generally unknown – at least, to me. No reference to this people had appeared in any *published* translation of Tolkien's; and as I had confined myself to researching published material and no other, there was, it seems to me, no conceivable way in which I could have known this fact; or, having known it, have incorporated it into my own text without departing from my own circumscriptions. That aside, I should like to take this opportunity of expressing my gratitude to those purchasers of *The Tolkien Companion* who took the trouble to write to me and point out various errors which had (as is inevitable in works of this sort) escaped my attention. Most gratifying of all was the fact that, of those who wrote, most seemed to regard *The Tolkien Companion* as a not unuseful work in its own right and were kind enough to tell me they had found it a valuable adjunct to the Epic. I could have wished for no higher praise.

J.E.A.T.
Iden Lock, August, 1978

Compiler's Note

Standard cross-referencing practice has been followed throughout. That is to say, SMALL CAPITALS have been used at various points to indicate suggested lines of further research within this Companion, according to the subject at hand. Simple *italics* for individual 'foreign' words are merely intended to emphasize their linguistic qualities.

References to *The Lord of the Rings* are by Book, Chapter and Appendix number. I have chosen this system because of the difficulty of reconciling the many different existing paginations of this work. References to all other works by Tolkien are by title and page number.

In order to preserve, so far as is possible, an uncluttered prose style – and so aid 'readability – I have endeavoured to provide all inessential references and extraneous comments in the form of end-notes; these may be found at the end of each 'chapter' (i.e. letter of the alphabet).

Similar motives have prompted my policy towards abbreviation. Generally speaking, I dislike begrudging any word its proper length, and furthermore I believe that a mass of abbreviations and numbers serves the interest only of those who enjoy reading railway time-tables. I am not one of these persons. Where I have abbreviated it has been for the purpose of identifying the original language from which any given word has been translated. These are as follows:

Adûn. = Adûnaic, the earliest speech of Western Men.
Khuz. = Khuzdul, the secret ancestral language of the Dwarves.
Sind. = The Sindarin or Grey-elven tongue.
Q. = The Quenya or High-elven tongue.
West. = Westron: the Common Speech of Middle-earth.

A peculiarity of the alphabetical sequence is the complete absence of entries beginning with either *j* or *x*. This is because none of the languages listed used these consonants in this form during the period under review.

Accursed Years One of the many names given by tradition to the period of Sauron the Great's first dominion over Middle-earth. Other names – the Black Years, the Dark Years, The Days of Flight – betray equally bitter memories of the latter part of the Second Age, when Númenor grew in power while Men and Elves of Middle-earth groaned under Sauron's tyranny or fought desperate wars for their very existence.

Sauron established this early dominion by means of the Rings of Power. These were forged in Eregion, not by the Lord of Mordor but by the High-elves of Celebrimbor's House, seduced for this purpose in the days when Sauron's treacheries were not readily apparent. Under his tutelage, the Elven-smiths grew skilful at this craft and succeeded in forging, first lesser Rings with limited powers, then the Nine, the Seven and the Three.

The One Ring was forged by Sauron himself – and from the moment he first put it on and spoke the Ring-spell, his power in Middle-earth waxed, until many of the Free Peoples were defeated or enslaved. The Accursed Years had numbered nearly two thousand before the Last Alliance of Elves and Men took Sauron's Ring, cast down the Dark Tower and laid his first realm in ruin, thus ending the Age.

Adamant A poetic invention for an imagined hard substance.

Adan (*pl. Edain*) 'Man', (pl.) 'The Second People' (Sind. from Q. *Atan, Atani*) In its most ancient form, the name for the race of Men (as opposed to the 'First People', the Elves). Later this title, in its Sindarin form (above), was applied more specifically to the Men who belonged to the Three Houses of the Elf-friends, who came across the Blue Mountains into Beleriand during the Elder Days, and fought alongside the Eldar in the long wars against Morgoth the Enemy; and it is in this later, Grey-elven form that the name is most often encountered.

Of the forging of this most ancient friendship, and of the trials undergone by the 'Second People' in their defence of Beleriand against Morgoth, *The Silmarillion* has much to say. Arriving piece-meal in tribal groupings the Three Houses first established independent chiefdoms and kingdoms in Beleriand; then, as one by one these peoples encountered the evil of Morgoth, they joined with the Eldar and held lands in fief from the Elven-kings. Thus for the most part they shared the fate of the Elves, and were nigh on annihilated before the greatest of their heroes, Eärendil, son of Tuor of the Third House and Idril, daughter of Turgon King of Gondolin, sailed west over Sea to reach the Undying Lands and bring the aid which succoured Middle-earth, so ending the Elder Days.

At the ending of the First Age, in return for their sacrifices in the wars, the Edain were granted land 'West-over-Sea' – the Isle of Elenna, most westerly of mortal lands. Using Eärendil's Star as their beacon, the greater part of them then set out for their future home. They named their new realm *Númenor*.

The Elves then called this people *Dún-edain*, 'Men-of-the-West'. And the Númenoreans began to grow more kingly and proud, and more like to the Eldar themselves, with whom they lived in friendship for the greater part of the Second Age; for they had also been rewarded with longer life than other Men, though not with that immortality they always desired. Yet Númenor withered and fell at last, and few survived: only the Faithful, led back to Middle-earth by Elendil the Tall. Like the Elves, they were a dwindling people.

See also MEN; NÚMENOR.

Adanedhel 'Elf-man' (Sind.) An admiring name given by some of the Elves of the city of Nargothrond to the Man Túrin Turambar, son of Húrin of the Third House and Morwen Eledhwen of the First House of the Edain.

Adorn A river in Rohan. It rose in the White Mountains and fell westward into the Isen.

Adrahil A Lord of the fiefdom of Dol Amroth; the father of Imrahil and of the Lady Finduilas, who became the wife of Denethor, twenty-sixth Steward of Gondor.

Aduial (Sind. from Q. *Undómë*) Eventide, twilight, 'Star-opening'. The root of the word, *-uial*, occurs in the Grey-elven name for Lake Evendim: *Nenuial*.

Adûnaic The language that the Dúnedain of Númenor adopted in the days of their power. It was largely based on their early native Mannish speech before this became influenced by Eldarin modes of thought. It perished in the Downfall of Númenor. The survivors, or Faithful, of that land spoke either the Grey-elven (Sindarin) tongue, or the Common Speech of Middle-earth, which had itself partly been derived from the ancient Adûnaic.

The word *Adûnaic* ('The-Speech-of-the-West') is itself an example of that Númenorean tongue, as are the names of all the Kings and Princes of Númenor after Tar-Calmacil (except Tar-Palantir) – and the name of the Downfall itself, *Akallabêth*.

See also NÚMENOR; SPOKEN TONGUES.

Adûnakhor (**Ar-Adûnakhor**) 'Lord-of-the-West' (Adûn., Q. *Herunúmen*) In its Númenorean form, as it appears here, the royal title assumed by the nineteenth King of Númenor, the son of Calmacil. It was ill-omened for two reasons: firstly, this was the first time a Númenorean ruler had taken a royal title in a Mannish tongue, as opposed to the older practice of assuming Eldarin names; and secondly, the particular title 'Lord of the West' had hitherto been given only to the Elder King, Manwë Súlimo, Lord of the Valar and chief of the Ainur, the Holy Ones. Adûnakhor's choice of name was therefore both insolent and blasphemous; though the popularity he gained from the Númenoreans by so choosing may have seemed sufficient recompense.

Adurant 'Double-course' (Sind.) A river of Ossiriand. It was the southernmost of the six tributaries of the Gelion, a fast-running mountain stream whose source was high in the Blue Mountains. Adurant reached the lowlands in two branches, which joined together some miles further on to enclose the 'Green Isle' of Tol Galen.

The Adventures of Tom Bombadil A collection of assorted Hobbit-poems taken from various sections of the Red Book and published, together with explanatory notes, under the title of the most well-known of the verses.

'The Adventures of Tom Bombadil' A Hobbit-poem about the semi-legendary (to some Hobbits) dweller 'down-under-hill' in the

Old Forest on the eastern borders of the Shire. It dates to the early Fourth Age. The poem, together with many others, has been published as a separate supplement to the available translation of the Red Book of Westmarch; it appears under the same general title (see previous entry).

Aeglos See AIGLOS.

Aegnor 'Fell-fire' (Sind. [originally *Aikanáro*, Q.]) The fourth of the sons of Finarfin of the House of Finwë, one of the princes of the Noldor who came back to Middle-earth during the Elder Days to make war upon Morgoth for the recovery of the Silmarils. At the beginning of the Long Peace, he and his brother Angrod took the northern part of the Dorthonion highland; they held it in feoff from Finrod, their elder brother, as the northernmost bulwark of the Elves' domains against the evil of Morgoth. In the four hundred and fifty-fifth year since the return of their father's people to Middle-earth, Morgoth, long quiescent in Angband, unleashed sudden war upon the Noldor: the Battle of Sudden Flame, in which the hills of Dorthonion in the north were literally kindled in the fire of his onslaught. In that desperate fight Aegnor and his brother Angrod were among the first to fall.

'A Elbereth Gilthoniel' The opening line (and title) of the beautiful Hymn sung by the Eldar of Middle-earth to Elbereth, or *Varda* (Q.), in her aspect as *Fanuilos*, the divine or demiurgic intercessary. In the Hymn she is pictured as standing on the slopes of Mount Everwhite (*Oiolossë*, Q.), arms raised, listening to the cries for aid of Elves and Men. The full text, in the Grey-elven (Sindarin) tongue, is:

> *A Elbereth Gilthoniel,*
> *silivren penna míriel*
> *o menel aglar elenath !*
> *Na-chaered palan-díriel*
> *o galadhremmin ennorath,*
> *Fanuilos, le linnathon*
> *nef aear, sí nef aearon !*[1]

Although the language is Sindarin, it is unlikely that this verse is of Grey-elven origin. For it was the Exiles, the High-elves who dwelt among the Sindar in Lindon, in Lórien and in Rivendell, who most longed for the solace of the Vala Queen Elbereth, with whom they had once dwelt in bliss. The style of the poem bears hallmarks of Quenya inflection, especially in the High style of the language chosen and in the reverential second person singular used throughout.

Note: compare with the High style of Quenya used in *Namárië*, the Lament of Galadriel in Lothlórien (Book II Chap. 8). For a fuller account of the meaning of the Hymn, see Notes and Translations to the Song Cycle *The Road Goes Ever On*.

Aelin-uial 'Meres of Twilight' (Sind.) The name given by the Elvenfolk of Doriath, Thingol's kingdom in Beleriand, to the region of eerie marshes which bordered their forested land in the south-west, where the river Aros flowed into the Sirion. Here lay a flood-plain, and here the renewed waters of the Sirion diverged, temporarily, into wide fens before gathering together once more into the great Falls of Sirion. The Meres were part of the defensive circle of enchantment woven about Doriath by its Queen, the Lady Melian, after the rebellion of Morgoth.

Aeluin 'Blue-mere' (Sind.) A small lake in eastern Dorthonion. See TARN AELUIN.

Aerandir 'Sea-wanderer' (Q.) A mariner of the Edain, one of those three who accompanied their lord Eärendil on his renowned journey from Middle-earth to the Undying Lands, at the end of the First Age. As all know, that journey brought about the mustering of the Valar and the overthrow of Morgoth. Aerandir, however, never set foot on the shores of Aman the Blessed; for he and his two companions, Falathar and Erellont, were bidden by Eärendil to remain in the boat Vingilot while he himself continued the journey on foot. After the deliberations of the Valar the three were given a new ship, and sent speedily back to Mortal Lands. Their fate was not that of Eärendil.

Aerie A poetic invention in the Hobbit style, supposedly a name of Elvish origin. It occurs in the poem 'Errantry' (part of *The Adventures of Tom Bombadil* collection in the Red Book) and refers to an imaginary Elf-kingdom.

Aerin A woman of the Edain, a kinswoman of Húrin of the Second House, who dwelt in Dor-lómin during the First Age. The fall of Dor-lómin in the wars brought about occupation of that land by a lesser race of Men, Easterlings brought thither by Morgoth and planted as a colony. Aerin, despite her lineage, was wedded perforce to one of these, named Brodda. She is remembered in the tales of Men as one who secretly lent aid to Morwen the mother of Túrin Turambar; later it was this woman Aerin who revealed to Túrin whither his mother had departed, and so unwittingly brought home to him the import of his deeds. Túrin, in his rage, slew Brodda at his own board and fled into the night. Of Aerin's eventual fate *The Silmarillion* does not speak.

Aftercomers A translation of the Grey-elven word *Hildor*.

Afterlithe The name given in the Shire Reckoning to the month of July, being the seventh month of the year. In Bree, the name used for this month was *Mede*.

Afteryule The name given in the Shire to the first month 'after Yule' of the year. The Bree name was *Frery*.

Agarwaen 'Bloodstained' (Sind.) Part of the riddling name assumed by Túrin Turambar when he dwelt in Nargothrond for a while during the wars against Morgoth. The full name was *Agarwaen son of Úmarth* ('The Bloodstained, Son of Ill-fortune').
    See also ÚMARTH.

Aglarond 'Halls-of-Glory' The Sindarin name for the Glittering Caves of Helm's Deep. The existence of this name shows that these remarkable natural wonders were known in Gondor long before the Men of Éothéod took possession of the land, which then became known as Rohan. The Rohirrim themselves paid scant courtesy to the beauty of the Caverns, using them as store-houses to supply the chain of fortresses collectively known as Helm's Gate: the Hornburg, the Deeping Wall and the Deeping Tower. Thus the gorge of Aglarond formed the strongest fortress in all Rohan, and the caves and their wonders went unseen by folk of other races – until the Fourth Age, when a colony of Dwarves led by Gimli, Glóin's son, settled there.

Aglon See PASS OF AGLON.

Aha The Quenya or High-elven word for 'rage', but more properly, the title of the Tengwa (or 'letter') number 11 – which represented the sound of hard *h*. (*Aha* replaced the more ancient title *harma*, 'treasure'.)

Aiglos 'Icicle' (Sind.) Also spelt *Aeglos*. The Spear of Gil-galad, last of the High-elven Kings in Middle-earth. He used this weapon throughout his long wars with Sauron; at the Battle of Dagorlad (3434 Second Age) the Spear was indefatigable. It was destroyed with Gil-galad on the slopes of Orodruin, in final combat with Sauron.

Ainulindalë 'Music-of-the-Ainur' (Q.) The Myth of the Creation, as set down long ago in the First Age by the earliest of the Noldorin loremasters, Rúmil of Tirion, in the Undying Lands. It is by far the most ancient of all creation myths.

The Ainulindalë appears in its entirety as the first part of the collection of similar legends and traditions known as *The Silmarillion*; no need therefore exists for a repetition or summary in these pages. Of particular interest, however, is the demiurgic role played in the Creation by the Ainur, or Holy Ones, some of whom afterwards dwelt in Arda (the World) and were known as *Valar* and *Maiar*. Their part was active in all aspects of the Creation – save their own creation – yet the Ainulindalë stresses throughout that, in so doing, the Ainur were but following a Theme already chosen by the Creator. Their rôle in the Beginning is one of embellishment, of refinement, of preparation and amendment. They have no part of the basic Design; they are but agents. And yet their role is nonetheless very great. It is the Ainur who make the World, who cause new stars to shine, who set waters on the face of the earth and who raise mountains on the edges of the seas. They build great lamps to bring Light to Arda, and when these lamps are thrown down (by one of themselves, a renegade) they cause Trees to grow – which also bring Light. They cause beasts to thrive, and birds to multiply. Only from the creation of intelligent Life do they hold back, for here their agency ceases.

This 'demiurgic' role is of interest when contrasted with the later legends of Men, who, although they have not altogether forgotten the part played at the Beginning by the Holy Ones, have for long minimized or overlooked it. The Powers are seen, or remembered, only in their lesser (and later) role of intercessaries (see FANUILOS); and the story of their own Beginnings is nowadays a matter for poets rather than theologians. But the Ainulindalë is far older than the oldest tales of Men.

Ainu (pl. *Ainur*) 'Holy One' (Q.) The name given in High-elvish tradition to the Spirits brought into being by Ilúvatar (God) before the Beginning, who participated in the Creation and who made and ordered the World (Arda), in preparation for the arrival of the Erusën, the Children of God. As is told in the AINULINDALË, many of them afterwards came to Arda and dwelt here, whereafter they were known as the VALAR and MAIAR.

Akallabêth 'The Downfall [of Númenor]' (Adûn.) A moral and historical work in the keeping of the Stewards of Gondor. It detailed

the arising, eventual seduction and inevitable fall of the Númenoreans, and the swallowing up of that land under the Sea.

Alcarin (Tar-Alcarin) Seventeenth King of Númenor, who ruled
at the height of its true power, before the renunciation of Eldarin
traditions and speech. His name, in High-elven form, means 'the
Glorious'.

Alcarinquë 'Glorious' (Q.) One of the stars created by Varda
(Elbereth).

Alcarondas The great warship which bore the last Númenorean
King, Ar-Pharazôn, on his last sea-journey, from Númenor to the
Undying Lands.

Alda The Quenya or High-elven word for 'tree', but more
properly the title of Tengwa number 28, representing the
sound *ld*. In Sindarin-inflected languages, this letter stood
for the sound *lh*. Naturally enough, the name for 'tree' was much
used in Elvish speech, and *alda* forms a root for many words and
names of Quenya origin. The Sindarin form of the same name was
galadh (e.g., *Galadhremmin Ennorath* 'Tree-woven-[Lands-of-]
Middle-earth').

Aldalómë This is a poetic gathering-together of words into a single
concept, typical of Quenya (the High-elven tongue). It means 'Tree-
shadow' and, as used by Treebeard the Ent (Book III Chap. 4),
refers to the ancient black heart of his forest.
See also ALDA above.

Aldamir From 1490–1540 Third Age, the twenty-third King of
Gondor and the second son of Eldacar. His elder brother was killed
in the war that temporarily deposed his father from the throne of
Gondor (see KIN-STRIFE), and so Aldamir came to rule after Eldacar.
He was killed in battle.

Aldarion (Tar Aldavion) The sixth King of Nûmenor. In him the
male descent of Elros Tar-Minyatur failed, and on his death
Nûmenor turned to its first ruling Queen, his daughter Tar-Ancalinë.
See also LORDS OF ANDÚNIË.

Aldaron 'Lord of Trees' (Q.) One of the Elves' most ancient names
for OROMË THE GREAT of the Valar.

Aldëa The name given in KINGS' RECKONING to the fourth day of the
week. Although the Númenoreans took the Elvish week and left it

largely intact, they changed the older name of this day – *Aldúya*, given in honour of the Two Trees of Valinor – so that it referred only to the White Tree. *Aldëa* was later used in Middle-earth (when the Dúnedain week became adopted by most of the Westron-speaking people). However, the Dúnedain themselves used the Sindarin equivalent *Orgaladh*. The Hobbits called this day *Trewesdei* (later *Trewsday*).

See also ALDA.

Aldor the Old From 2570–2645 Third Age, the third King of Rohan and second son of Brego, son of Eorl the Young. At the feast given by Brego to celebrate the building of the King's Hall Meduseld, Aldor's elder brother Baldor publicly vowed to walk the 'Paths of the Dead'. He did not return. A sorrowing Brego died the following year and Aldor became King.

During his long (75-year) reign, the Rohirrim consolidated their newly acquired territory of Calenardhon, moving both north and westward, driving out the last of the Dunland people who dwelt in the valleys of the White Mountains, and re-occupying older fortresses such as Dunharrow and the Hornburg. It was thus around this time that the Rohirrim earned the chief hatred of the Men of Dunland, who swore a blood-feud against them.

Aldudénië 'Lament-of-the-[Two] Trees' (Q.) A song of mourning, now lost, made in the Elder Days by one of the Vanyar, named Elemmírë; it tells of the poisoning of the Two Trees of Valinor by Morgoth.

Aldúya The ancient Eldarin name for the fourth day of the week, from which the Númenorean ALDËA was derived. It is in the High-elven (Quenya) form and can be translated as 'Trees'-day', being named in honour of the Two Trees of Valinor.

Alfirin A small golden flower which grew in the fields of Lebennin, south of the White Mountains in the realm of Gondor. The name, which is of Sindarin form, translates as '[Only-too-]mortal-growing-thing', and contains strong echoes of Elvish sorrow for the flower's short life.

Almaren The name given by the Valar to their first earthly dwelling. Where the light of the great lamps Illuin and Ormal met and blended at the broadest part of the World, there lay a green isle in the midst of a lake. This was Almaren. It was destroyed in the early conflicts between the Valar and the renegade Ainu, Melkor; after which the Valar left Middle-earth and went to dwell in Aman, afterwards called the Undying Lands.

Alphabet of Daeron The name given, in Grey-elven (Sindarin) lore, to the *certhas* (runes) devised in Beleriand in the First Age by Daeron, minstrel and loremaster to King Thingol Greycloak of Doriath. Although runes had been used by the Sindar from earliest times, Daeron's runic system was a significant departure from the older unfinished forms, for it was greatly influenced and enriched by the *Tengwar* script of the High-elves (whose return to Middle-earth in the First Age had an overwhelming effect on Grey-elven culture as a whole).

The Dwarves held Daeron's runes in such high esteem that the House of Durin in Moria later adopted the alphabet for its own, after which these *certhas* became known as the *Angerthas* ('Long-rune-rows [of]') *Moria*. These runes were subsequently further adapted by the Moria Dwarves to their own specialized needs. Much later, the Dwarves of Erebor further modified the Angerthas in a manner that reverted somewhat to the original (Elvish) forms.

Alphabet of Fëanor The alphabet of 'letters', or *Tengwar*, devised by the Noldor (High-Elves) long ago in the Undying Lands and later brought back with them to Middle-earth in their exile. The Tengwar of Fëanor were so-called because their creation was ascribed to him, although it was acknowledged that the Fëanorean letters owed much to the older Alphabet of Rúmil, unknown in Middle-earth.

From the High-elves in Middle-earth, knowledge of the Fëanorean letters then spread among the Grey-elves, whose runes of Daeron (see ALPHABET OF DAERON) were greatly influenced by the more cursive Tengwar – a system based upon brushes and pens rather than on carving and inscription. Eventually the Sindar wholly adopted the Fëanorean Tengwar according to their own 'open' mode. The West-door of Moria was inscribed in this fashion, with certain Tengwar being accorded proper vowel functions, replacing the older system in which the vowels were represented only by diacritic marks (generally placed above the preceding consonant).

As can be seen, the Sindarin substitution of vocalic letters for the

diacritic *tehtar*, or 'signs', expands the originally consonantal group
of Tengwar into a full alphabet. This system was known as the Mode
of Beleriand. The same inscription, in the older, High-elven usage,
would have been written thus:

Both forms of Tengwar continued to be fully phonetic: that is,
letter values were assigned according to mode and point of articulation. Thus the Tengwar could theoretically be used by all races –
though the Dwarves never adopted them, always preferring the
'Long Rune-rows' of Moria. By the end of the Third Age the letters
of Fëanor (in the older mode) were known to all men of learning in
the West.

Note: the Alphabet of Fëanor was divided into four series of six
separate grades of Tengwar, with twelve 'additional' letters. There
were a number of 'signs' (*tehtar*) to modify groups of consonants
with vowel-values. Each of these letters had its own 'title', or name,
in the Quenya tongue (the initial sound of which was invariably the
same as the letter concerned).

See also TENGWAR; Appendix E.

Alphabet of Rúmil The *Tengwar* ('letters') of Rúmil: the oldest
form of Eldarin cursive writing, known only to the Eldar of the
Undying Lands. Although unknown in its original form in Mortal
Lands, this system deeply influenced the later ALPHABET OF FËANOR,
which was to become widespread in Númenor during the Second
Age and in Middle-earth during the Third. As the name implies, the
invention of this writing-system is credited to the Noldorin Elf Rúmil
of Tirion.

Alqualondë 'Swans'-haven' (Q.) High-elven city of Eldamar, built
during the Elder Days by Olwë prince of the Telerin Elves, after the
belated arrival on the shores of the Undying Lands of that remnant
of his people which he led. The Haven was so named because the
Teleri reached Aman with the aid of great swans; these towed their
enchanted ships the last stage of the Great Journey, from Eressëa to
Eldamar. It lay to the north of Tirion.

See also KINSLAYING AT ALQUALONDË.

Altariel See GALADRIEL.

Aman the Blessed The ancient name given by the Valar (in their own tongue) to the UNDYING LANDS.

Amandil (Tar-Amandil) Third King of Númenor, the grandson of Elros Tar-Minyatur.

Note: the name *Amandil* ('Lover-of-the-Uttermost-West') contains the reverential *Aman*.

Amandil of Andúnië The father of ELENDIL THE TALL and last Lord of Andúnië, westernmost city of Númenor. He was also the last leader of that remnant of the Númenoreans who remained loyal to the traditions of the Eldar, and who as a result called themselves 'the Faithful'. Andúnië, a haven on the western shore of the land, was their chief city until the days of Ar-Gimilzôr; and Amandil was its lord in the days when Ar-Pharazôn was King of Númenor.

Although Amandil's chosen calling was that of the sea – his son Elendil and his grandsons Isildur and Anárion were also great mariners – in his latter days he counselled the king on matters of policy. This was a privilege afforded him because of his lineage – scarcely less royal than Pharazôn's, for Amandil was descended in direct line from the Lady Silmariën and therefore from Elros Tar-Minyatur, the founder of Númenor. But when Pharazôn made his renowned expedition to Middle-earth in 3261 Second Age, at the end of which he returned bearing Sauron the Great as a 'prisoner', Amandil's stock at court declined even as Sauron's waxed, and soon afterwards he withdrew from the king's presence and went to Rómenna in the east of Númenor, there to guide his exiled people through the long period of persecution which followed.

After many years word reached Amandil of the building of the Great Armament. By now he was an old man. Counselling his sons to be alert for some great disaster, he resolved to attempt to emulate the feat of his forefather Eärendil, and sail into the West to plead for the cause of the Dúnedain. He never returned.

Note: the *Palantíri*, the marvellous 'seeing-stones' which had been made during the Elder Days by Fëanor, were given by the Eldar of the Undying Lands to Amandil during the years of persecution. These, of course, were carried back to Middle-earth by Elendil and his sons and helped for centuries to unite the realms of Arnor and

Gondor. Similarly, Amandil's Silver Rod (of the Lordship of Andúnië) was carried back to Middle-earth to become Elendil's Sceptre of Kingship – and last emblem of Númenor, whose own royal sceptre, that of Ar-Pharazôn, had perished in the Inundation.

Amarië (of the Vanyar) An Elf-maiden, the beloved of Finrod son of Finarfin, afterwards called Felagund. They were sundered when Finrod, together with his kindred, left the Undying Lands in pursuit of Fëanor, and never came back to Aman, where Amarië waited, while his life endured.

Ambarona A Quenya embellishment, Entish in style, applied by Treebeard to Fangorn Forest.[2]

Amlach of Estolad An Adan of the Third House, and moreover a grandson of Marach, who had led this people across the Blue Mountains into Beleriand. His name is recorded because he was one of those who opposed a proposed early league between this House of Men, and the Elves. Virulent and scornful were his arguments, throwing confusion into the hearts of his fellows. But then came an eerie occurrence: Amlach returned to the council – or appeared for the first time, as he indignantly claimed – and denied that he had spoken in this way, or indeed at all. It became apparent that spies and deceivers were among them – which caused Amlach at least to change his purpose, for he disliked being impersonated in this way. He went north, in defiance of his own original arguments, and entered the service of Maedhros son of Fëanor. His fate is not recorded.

Amlaith of Fornost From 861–946 Third Age, the first King of Arthedain, and eldest of the three sons of Eärendur who quarrelled over the kingship of Arnor, thus dividing the realm into three: Arthedain, Cardolan and Rhudaur. *Fornost Erain* ('Northern-fortress [of the] Kings') became Amlaith's chief city, while Elendil's beautiful and ancient capital of Annúminas was deserted and soon fell into ruin.

Amon Amarth 'Mount Doom' (Sind.) An epithet for ORODRUIN, first used in Ithilien during the later part of the Second Age – when the volcano erupted to signal Sauron's initial assault upon the survivors of Númenor 'before they should take root'. 'Mount Doom' it remained ever after.

Amon Dîn 'The Hill of Silence' (Sind.) A beacon-hill which lay on a north-eastern shoulder of the White Mountains overlooking Druadan Forest. The hill formed the first of a long-established chain of such beacons between Gondor and Rohan.

See also BEACON-HILLS.

Amon Ereb 'Lonely Hill' (Sind.) A mountain in East Beleriand, an outlier of Andram, the 'Long Wall'. On its slopes during the very first clashes between the Elves and the forces of Morgoth, there fell a lord of the Green-elves, Denethor son of Lenwë, whose people had come late into Beleriand and who had been latterly dwelling across the Gelion, in Ossiriand. Later, after the great defeats in the north, Amon Ereb was maintained for a while as a bastion in defence of Ossiriand and the south.

Amon Ethir 'Hill of Spies' (Sind.) An artificial mound, built by the Elves of Nargothrond at the direction of their king, Finrod Felagund, one league from the gates of their city; from its summit Elves kept watch in days of war.

Amon Gwareth A rocky, precipitous knoll which rose from the exact centre of the Hidden Vale of Tumladen in West Beleriand, rather in the manner of the Rock of Orthanc rising from the Ring of Isengard in later days. On the summit and sides of this hill Turgon son of Fingolfin built his city of Gondolin.

Amon Hen 'The Hill of the Eye' (Sind.) More properly, the Hill of the Eye of the Men of Númenor, for it was one of a group of three tall hills straddling the Anduin and the Falls of Rauros, maintained by the Men of Gondor as outposts (of their Númenorean realms-in-exile). The other two hills were Amon Lhâw, 'The Hill of the Ear', on the eastern bank, and Tol Brandir, the Tindrock, which no man or beast had ever climbed, in the centre of the stream. The summits of Lhâw and Hen had High Seats, where Men of Gondor could keep close watch on their frontiers.

Amon Lhâw 'The Hill of the Ear' (Sind.) See AMON HEN above.

Amon Obel A tall hill rising from the middle of the Forest of Brethil on the borders of Doriath in Beleriand. Upon this hill the people of the Second House of the Edain, the Haladin, built a settlement, called Ephel Brandir. They thus commanded the ways of the forest for many years.

Amon Rûdh 'Bald Hill' (Sind.) A solitary, towering hill, which rose abruptly from the moors to the west of Doriath, dominating the lands that lay round about. We are told it rose sheer in places, a rocky crown above green slopes. Here in antiquity the Dwarf Mîm, who in his time had much to do with Túrin Turambar, made his habitation. As a matter of fact the halls of Mîm were but the surviving delvings of his people, the *Noegyth Nibin* (or 'Lesser-Dwarves' in the Grey-elven terminology). This race of Dwarves had been the first to enter Beleriand, but had suffered at that time from the enmity of the Grey-elves, who knew them not and suffered no strangers in their lands. Afterwards the unfortunate persecution ceased, and the 'Lesser-Dwarves' were let alone. Amon Rûdh was one of the oldest of their early settlements; but in the days of the Wars against Morgoth, only Mîm still dwelled there.

See also SEREGON.

Amon Sûl 'The Hill of Winds' (Sind.) The name of the tower built by Elendil on the summit of *Weathertop*[3], southernmost and tallest of the Weather Hills in Eriador. After the division of Arnor into three separate states (in 861 Third Age), Weathertop commanded the Great East Road from Cardolan into Rhudaur, and since it lay on the frontiers of both kingdoms, possession of the tower early became a source of dispute. Its importance was increased by the fact that Amon Sûl also contained the only remaining *palantír* of the North (the other two were in the possession of Arthedain).

After the realm of Angmar arose in the north, the Weather Hills became an eastern outpost of Cardolan and Arthedain in alliance against the Witch-king. In 1409 Third Age a great army advanced out of Rhudaur – which was wholly under the dominion of Angmar – to surround Weathertop and raze the tower of Amon Sûl. The *palantír* was carried in retreat to Fornost (but was later to be lost with Arvedui).

Of the tower in its youth, little is known save that Elendil watched there for the Elf-host of Gil-galad, coming from Lindon in the days of the Last Alliance. With the ending of the North-kingdom (1974 Third Age), the strategic importance of the Weather Hills declined and the many fortifications fell into ruin. The lands round about became desolate.

Amon Uilos The Sindarin form of the Quenya word OIOLOSSË, meaning 'Mount Everwhite'. This mountain's oldest name was *Taniquetil* (Q.) 'High-white-peak'.

Ampa The Quenya word for 'hook', but more properly the title of the Fëanorean Tengwa number 14, which represented the sound *mp* in Quenya; it was modulated in other tongues to a *v* sound.

Amras See AMROD AND AMRAS below.

Amrod and Amras The two youngest of the seven sons of Fëanor, twin brothers, who were alike in appearance, and in all they thought and did. They were born in the Undying Lands, but fell into evil when the Silmarils were stolen and the Two Trees poisoned; for they, together with all their brothers and many more of the Noldor besides, swore the great oath which doomed the House of Fëanor, and afterwards came, after grievous deeds, to the shores of Middle-earth, where ever after they made their abode.

At the beginning of the War of the Great Jewels many battles were fought, and in these Amrod and Amras took a leading part; but after the commencement of the Long Peace they removed to East Beleriand, into open country to the east of Doriath. (It is said they were great hunters, and spent most of their time at the chase.) But the Long Peace came to an end, and in the Battle of Sudden Flame the northern Elf-kingdoms were overthrown and the hinterland realm of the twin brothers became a frontier of war; they therefore retreated into the south, with Caranthir their brother, and maintained an insecure foothold there for many years.

But as time passed, the position of the Eldar and the Edain in Middle-earth became truly desperate. In these troubled times they turned on each other, and at the forefront of this strife – which was for the possession of the Silmaril won long before by Beren and Lúthien – were the surviving sons of Fëanor: Maedhros, Maglor, Amrod, Amras. In an assault upon the Havens of Sírion both twin brothers were slain. Soon afterwards Eärendil took the Silmaril for ever out of Middle-earth.

Amroth An Elf-prince of the Woodland realm of Lothlórien and later of the Elf-havens of Belfalas, where his name lingered.

He was a Silvan Elf, that is, an Elf of the Eastern race of Wood-elves, possibly of Nandorin origin. And he dwelt in the forests of Lórien, where his high house was on Cerin Amroth, the mound named after him. But in the middle years of the Third Age, when Lórien was again troubled by things from the world outside, he determined to take ship over Sea to safety with his beloved, the Elf-maiden Nimrodel. He waited for her long at the Havens but she never came to him, having been lost in the crossing of the White Mountains. So, when a storm broke the moorings of his ship and hurled it far out to sea, Amroth, in his grief and uncertainty, dived into the raging waters in an attempt to reach the shore. In this way he also was lost to Elvenkind.

See also LAY OF NIMRODEL.

Anach See PASS OF ANACH.

Anadûnê One of the names given at its founding to the land of Númenor; it is in the Adûnaic tongue (though influenced by Eldarin) and means 'Westernesse'.

Anar 'Fire-golden' (Q) The Sun. According to the traditions of the Vanyar (the 'Fair-elves' of Eldamar), the Sun was in origin the last golden fruit of the dying Tree Laurelin, brought forth by the prayers of the Vala Yavanna at the same time as the last silver flower of the Elder Tree, Telperion. Aulë made great vessels to bear the Sun and the Moon aloft, and Varda (Elbereth) set them in the sky and fixed their courses. The Noldor believed that the Sun, which they called *Vása*, 'Heart of Fire', was also a sign of the coming of the Second People, Men, and of the eclipse of the Firstborn in Middle-earth.

In Sindarin, *Anor*.

See also *The Silmarillion*, pp. 99–101.

Anardil From 324–411 Third Age, the sixth King of Gondor.

Anarion (Tar-Anarion) The eighth King of Númenor.

Anárion The younger son of Elendil the Tall and brother of Isildur. The brothers, both of whom had been born in Númenor before its Fall, ruled as conjoint Kings of Gondor from shortly after its founding (in 3320 Second Age) until Anárion perished at the Siege of the Barad-dûr (3430). The rule subsequently passed to his son Meneldil, from whom all later Kings of Gondor were descended.

As the realm was originally ordered, Anárion was given the fief of Anórien (named after him), which he ruled from his high city of Minas Anor. When Sauron suddenly attacked Gondor, in 3429 Second Age, Anárion took command of the Southern Army and was successful in confining the Enemy to the further (eastern) shore of the Great River. Isildur, meanwhile, went to his father in the North and together they rallied the Dúnedain and forged the Last Alliance with Elves. Anárion perished before the end of the war, slain at the Siege of Barad-dûr.

See also ISILDUR; LINES OF DESCENT.

Anarríma 'Net-of-Fire' (Q.) One of the constellations created by Varda (Elbereth) to bring light to Middle-earth for the comfort of the Elves, at their Awakening.

Anarya 'Sun's-day' (Q.) The second day of the week in both the Elvish calendar and the Númenorean system of Kings' Reckoning (the system which was eventually used by most of the Westron-speaking people of Middle-earth). The Sindarin form of the word, *Oranor*, was used by the Dúnedain; while the Hobbits (who had early taken their calendar from the Dúnedain) used a translation of *Anarya: Sunnendei*, which later became shortened to *Sunday*.

Anborn A scout for the Rangers of Ithilien, led by Faramir during the War of the Ring.

Anca The Quenya or High-elven word for 'jaws', but more properly the Tengwa number 15, which represented the sound *nk*.

Ancalagon the Black The greatest of all dragons of Middle-earth, and the leader of the host of winged fire-drakes – the first of their kind ever seen in Middle-earth – whom Morgoth unleashed upon the Host of the Valar in the final stage of the Great Battle which ended in his overthrow and casting-out. Ancalagon was slain, so the Elves say, by Eärendil, in battle in the upper airs, and crashed down upon Thangorodrim from a great height, destroying both it and himself in his fall.

Ancalimë (**Tar-Ancalimë**) First (ruling) Queen of Númenor, daughter of Tar-Aldarion. See LORDS OF ANDÚNIË.

Ancalimon (**Tar-Ancalimon**) Fourteenth King of Númenor.

Ancient Tongue The High-elven language, Quenya.

Ancient World References to the 'Ancient World' in Third Age literature can be taken to indicate the Mortal Lands before the ending of the Second Age, before the Fall of Númenor and the removal of the Undying Lands from the Circles of the World.

Andaith 'Long-mark' (Sind.) One of the *tehtar*, or 'signs', used in conjunction with the Fëanorean Tengwar to denote a 'long' vowel.

Ando The Quenya word for 'gate'; more properly the title applied to Tengwa number 5, used in the High-elven speech for the sound *nd*; in other tongues it more usually represented *d*.

Andor 'Land-of-Gift' (Q. or Valinorean) The most ancient name for that land subsequently known as NÚMENOR, given by the Valar; they gave the land itself to the Edain, as a reward for their sufferings in the War of the Great Jewels.

Andram 'Long-wall' (Sind.) A great escarpment or range of hills in Beleriand, hundreds of leagues long, which ran in a line roughly west-east, from Nargothrond to Ramdal ('Wall's-end'), separating north from south and forming a natural second line of defence against Morgoth.

Androth 'Long-delving' (Sind.) The inhabited caves of the Hills of Mithrim; where Tuor son of Huor of the Edain was fostered by the Sindar, following the death of his father in the Battle of Unnumbered Tears.

Anduin The Great River. It rose in northern Wilderland and flowed south for many hundreds of miles between Greenwood (Mirkwood) and the Misty Mountains. After passing the south-eastern end of the White Mountains and the western walls of the Ephel Dúath, the river bent west and eventually emptied into the Bay of Belfalas.

The Great River was aptly named, being, in the Second and Third Ages, the largest known river of Middle-earth. In many instances the Anduin formed the border between countries and provinces and, towards the end of the Third Age, much of it became a frontier of war between Sauron and the West. The Great River entered the Sea through a broad delta, the Ethir Anduin, south of Dol Amroth.

Andúnië The most westerly city of ancient Númenor, renowned for loyalty to the Eldar and to Eldarin principles and modes of speech. The haven was founded by the Faithful (as Lords of the House of Valandil later termed themselves), before Númenor began its slow fall from grace and departed from the ways of the Eldar. The Lords of Andúnië counted themselves descendants of Valandil (first Lord), through him, of Silmariën, and through her, of Elros Tar-Minyatur, first King of Númenor. The Silver Rod of the Lords of Andúnië survived the Downfall of Númenor and was carried to Middle-earth by Elendil (son of the last Lord, Amandil) to become the symbol of

High-kingship in the realms of Númenor-in-Exile: Arnor and Gondor.

See also LORDS OF ANDÚNIË; NÚMENOR.

Andúril The Sword of Aragorn, greatest heirloom of the House of Isildur, so named after its re-forging by the Elven-smiths of Rivendell for use in the War of the Ring. It had formerly been called NARSIL.

The name of the Sword means 'Flame-of-the-West' (Q.); this was engraved upon the blade and its sheath, together with many runes of virtue and designs of seven Stars (to symbolize the High-kingship), as well as a rayed Sun and a crescent Moon (for the twin realms of Gondor and Arnor).

Andwise 'Andy' Roper Son of Hobson 'Roper' Gamgee of Tighfield, in the Shire, and the uncle of Samwise Gamgee, to whom he imparted some of his rope-lore and tricks with knots.

Anfalas 'Long-coast' (Sind.) A region of Gondor comprising the long northern coastline of the great Bay of Belfalas.

Note: Anfalas is sometimes translated *Langstrand.*

Anfauglir 'Jaws-of-thirst' (Sind.) A name for the great Wolf of Morgoth, Carcharoth.

Anfauglith 'Gasping-dust' (Sind.) Alternatively *Dor-nu-Fauglith* 'Land-[buried] under-choking-ash'. The name given by the Eldar and the Edain of Beleriand to the former grasslands of Ard-galen, devasted and destroyed in the Battle of Sudden Flame by Morgoth and the hosts of Angband.

Anga The Quenya word for 'iron' (used in various place- and personal-names, such as *Angmar, Angbor* and *Carach Angren*). More properly, the title of Tengwa number 7, used, in Quenya, to signify a soft *j* sound; in Sindarin it represented a harder *g*.

Angainor A great chain and fetter forged during the Eldar Days by the Smith of the Valar, Aulë; it was used to bind the renegade Vala, Morgoth, on two occasions: at the conclusion of the Battle of the Powers and at the overthrow of Angband and the ending of the First Age.

Angamaitë and Sangahyando Great-grandsons of Castamir the Usurper and leaders of the Corsairs of Umbar. Together, they led the band of Corsairs who slew Minardil, twenty-fifth King of Gondor, during a raid on the port of Pelargir in 1634 Third Age.

Angband 'Prison-of-Iron' (Sind., from Q. *Angamando*) The lesser and more westerly of the two fortresses made in Middle-earth by Melkor (Morgoth) at the beginning of the First Age. The older, and far greater, stronghold was called UTUMNO ('The Pit').

Angband was in the far north-west of Middle-earth, being conceived and planned by Melkor as a western outpost of his domain, a first defence against the West. Like Utumno, it was protected from the south (and partly from the west) by a giant range of cruel peaks, called *Ered Engrin*, the 'Iron Mountains'. The raising of these mountains had been the first defensive work undertaken by Morgoth.

Like Utumno, Angband was in reality a giant delving in the ground, though in its beginning not all of it lay under the earth. In the Battle of the Powers, fought by the Valar against Melkor, the fortress of Angband gave them little trouble; they razed it rapidly and with haste, passing on to set a siege about the greater fortress of Utumno to the east wherein Melkor then dwelt, but in their haste they omitted to destroy all of Angband, or seek out its lowest pits; and so many evil creatures, by lying hid or buried, escaped their wrath. Among these who thus survived the first ruin of Angband was its lord, the Lieutenant of Morgoth, Sauron the Abhorred. Not for the last time did Sauron thus by unhappy chance escape annihilation at the hands of his enemies.

Many ages passed, ages of captivity for Melkor, who had utterly lost the war. The eerie ruins of Utumno and Angband in the north slumbered; but after a while, the evil creatures which had escaped the vengeance of the Valar bred anew, and came forth to plague the lands round about, especially those to the south and east. Indeed it was their presence in the wide lands of Middle-earth which first caused the Valar to fear for the Quendi, and for the later Children of God who were yet to come; and to preserve them from danger they summoned the Quendi to make the Great Journey into the West and there dwell for ever, free – as they thought – from peril.

A further age passed. Melkor was released and 'paroled'. But as is well known, his repentance was feigned; and after a time he hatched his plots anew for the discomfiture of the Valar and the Eldar. Poisoning the Two Trees of Valinor, and stealing the Silmarils, he fled back to Middle-earth, a renegade once more; in this hour he was first named *Morgoth*, and so he was called everafter.

His first act was to build himself a new stronghold in Middle-earth.

Utumno was ruined beyond hope of reconstruction, but Angband less so; and Morgoth chose this more westerly site as the place for his new domain. Old delvings were repaired; new mines and shafts and tunnels were dug and excavated – and all underground, for the Dark Lord meant to make this fortress of Angband even stronger than Utumno of old. But because the Iron Mountains, originally raised as a bulwark against the south, were also a hindrance to his own forces, he delved a great tunnel under the range, a boring which issued from the ground in the north-west of the plain of Ard-galen through a great door of iron, closely guarded.[4] As a final buttress against attack, he protected the lands between the doors of Angband and the Ered Engrin behind with an artificial range of jagged peaks: Thangorodrim, the Mountains of Tyranny.

Such was the fortress and realm of Angband in the days of its power. From here Morgoth now directed the war against the Eldar and Edain – a war which went at first against him, so that Angband became ringed on its southern marches by a chain of hostile Eldarin kingdoms – until the initiative inevitably passed to the Dark Power of the North. Then the hosts of Angband came forth, and overthrew the siege, and Angband became, not an encircled realm, but the seat of the greatest power in Middle-earth, and the ultimate source of all the miseries of that time. In its deepest pit Morgoth sat on his throne and wore the Iron Crown wherein were set the Silmarils.

Yet in the end Morgoth was overthrown, by the host of the Valar; and in his ruin Angband, his last stronghold in Mortal Lands, was also destroyed: totally, unto the last pit. And we are told that in that Breaking the world itself was changed, and the seas poured in. The lands round about became bitterly cold and desolate. Apart from this Northern Waste, little trace remained, two full Ages later, of the Dark Power that had broken endless hosts of Elves and Men. Only the evil colds of Morgoth lingered.

See also ICE BAY OF FOROCHEL.

Angbor of Lamedon Lord of Lamedon, a region in the southern vales of the White Mountains and a province of Gondor. During the War of the Ring Angbor's forces engaged the landing parties of the Corsairs at Linhir on the river Gilrain. They were still fighting when, unlooked for, assistance arrived from the north; for the Heir of Isildur came to Linhir on his way to Pelargir, and the host that he led swept the field of friend and foe alike. But Angbor mastered his fear and so met Aragorn II, who bade him gather his folk and reinforce besieged Minas Tirith as quickly as he might. Seven days later his forces reached the City.

Angerthas Daeron Originally an Elvish runic script, attributed to the legendary Daeron, bard and loremaster to the Elven-king Thingol of Doriath during the First Age. It was later adopted by the Dwarves of Durin's House for their own exclusive use, after which it became known as the ANGERTHAS MORIA. (At this point the Grey-elves seem to have given up the use of runes altogether, turning instead to their distinctive Sindarin adaptation of the High-elven *Tengwar*.)

See also ALPHABET OF DAERON, ALPHABET OF FËANOR.

Angerthas Moria The name given to the ALPHABET OF DAERON sometime after this runic system had become more closely associated with the Dwarves of Moria than with the Elves of Beleriand who had originated and developed it. In general, Dwarves employed several modifications to the Elvish *certhas* (runes), mainly in order to reproduce certain sounds in the Dwarvish tongue (Khuzdul) which did not occur in Elvish or Mannish modes of speech. Later the Dwarves of Erebor (the Moria-exiles) made further changes but, by chance or design, these changes to the Alphabet tended to revert to an earlier, Elvish mode. (See Appendix E II.)

Note: the inscription on the Tomb of Balin (Book II Chap. 4) is in these Moria-runes. It reads:

This epitaph may be rendered (in Khuzdul) thus: BALIN FUNDINUL UZBADKHAZADDŮMU, which can in turn be translated as '[Here lies] Balin/Son of Fundin/Lord of Moria'. As few examples of written Khuzdul survive, it may be worth noting that the -*u*, -*ul* suffix appears to indicate a genitive case, while the prefix *Uzbad*- can be safely taken to mean 'King' or 'Lord'. Compare with the High-elven writing and inscription on the West-gate of Moria (Book II Chap. 4).

Anghabar 'Iron-mine' (Sind.) As the name implies, this was a great iron mine to the north of Gondolin, in the Encircling Mountains, discovered and initially worked by the Elves of Gondolin – in particular, by Maeglin Ëol's son, who was skilled in smithcraft.

Anglachel 'Iron-flame' (Sind.) One of a pair of matching swords (the other was called Anguirel) made during the Elder Days by the Grey-elven smith Ëol from a strange metal found by him in the heart of a stone that had fallen from the sky. This metal, apparently akin to common iron, was nonetheless harder than both iron and steel, and it was black, reflecting no light. The sword found its way into King Thingol's hoard (in payment of a fee); and afterwards was given by Thingol, on request, to the great warrior-elf Beleg Cúthalion – against the advice of the Lady Melian, who foresaw disaster in the ownership of the weapon. And so it proved. Beleg was afterwards accidentally slain, with his own sword, by his great friend Túrin Turambar; after which the sword passed to the ownership of Túrin, who wielded it against the foes of the Eldar and Edain. In the Elven-city of Nargothrond it was reforged for him, and he renamed it *Gurthang*, 'Iron-of-death', possibly in an attempt to evade the foretold disaster.[5]

But there was no escaping the curse on the weapon. Under its new name the Black Sword took many lives that had been Morgoth's to command; but it also took innocent lives: and in due course, when Túrin at last despaired of his own life, it slew Túrin at his own request. In this final letting of blood the Black Sword broke into two shards, which were afterwards buried with Túrin.

Angle The Angle, as it was known to folk of Eriador, comprised all the land between the two tributaries of the Greyflood: Mitheithel and Bruinen. Early in the Third Age, when the Angle was part of the North-kingdom of Rhudaur, one of the three strains of Hobbits – the Stoors – dwelt there for a while. But when the climate grew colder as the land became infiltrated by evil from the neighbouring Witch-realm of Angmar, the Stoors deserted Eriador and many went to Wilderland, not to return until the founding of the Shire.

Angle The Angle of the Naith of Lothlórien, known as Egladil. It was a cool green lawn which lay between the waters of Anduin and Silverlode.

Angmar 'Iron-home' (Sind.) The principal force behind the fall of Arnor and Arthedain was the evil and implacably hostile realm of Angmar, which rose early in the second millennium of the Third Age. Angmar, whose lands lay beyond the Ettenmoors on both sides of the Misty Mountains, was ruled from its beginnings by a black Sorcerer known as the Witch-king, later revealed as Chief of the Ringwraiths and Sauron's most terrible Lieutenant.

His task, to purge the North of his Black Master's enemies, was greatly eased by the division of Arnor into three separate states – which had taken place some four centuries earlier, after the death of Eärendur in 861 Third Age. This had already left the Dúnedain in self-inflicted disarray; yet the Witch-king, now established in his great fort of Carn Dûm, was to be satisfied with no less than the utter destruction of his enemies. In wars that lasted seven hundred years he ruined: first Rhudaur, by subversion; then Cardolan, by invasion; and finally Arthedain itself, last memory of royal Arnor, by massive assault.

By early 1974 Third Age, King Arvedui, 'Last-king' of Arthedain, was in desperate straits. Though already reinforced by an Elf-host from Lindon, in his great need he had also sent to Gondor for aid from his Southern kin. That spring – though too late for Arvedui or Arthedain – a mighty host arrived from Gondor, led by Eärnur, son of King Eärnil. In alliance with Elves of Lindon and Rivendell, Eärnur utterly defeated the forces of Angmar (who were already feasting and revelling in Fornost, believing their victory complete). Nonetheless, the Witch-king escaped into the shadows, having accomplished his main purpose: the destruction of the North-kingdom. But the annihilation of his own realm so enraged him that he afterwards counted Eärnur of Gondor chief among his enemies.

See also ARVEDUI; Appendix A I(iii).

Angrenost 'Iron-citadel' (Sind.) An earlier name, given in Gondor, for the Ring of ISENGARD.

Angrim 'Iron-net' (Sind.) One of the First House of the Edain; the father of GORLIM THE UNHAPPY.

Angrist 'Iron-cleaver' (Sind.) A knife or dagger of Dwarf-make, forged by the great smith Telchar (who also wrought the sword NARSIL) during the First Age in the city of Nogrod. It later came into the possession of one of the Sons of Fëanor, Curufin the Crafty; and when this Elf made war upon his ally Beren of the Edain, in the course of the treacheries of those days, it was taken from him – by Beren himself – and later used in a task for which no other dagger in Middle-earth would have sufficed: in cutting a single Silmaril free from Morgoth's Iron Crown.

Angrod 'Iron-champion' (Sind. from Q. *Angaráto*) The brother of AEGNOR.

Anguirel See ANGLACHEL.

Anna The Quenya word for 'gift', but more properly the title of Tengwa number 23, often used as consonantal *y*.

Annael One of the Sindar: the Elf who fostered the boy Tuor son of Huor, in his secret dwelling in the Androth, the caves of Mithrim.

Annatar 'Lord-of-gifts' (Q.) A benevolent title assumed by Sauron the Great at the beginning of the Second Age, in furtherance of his policies of apparent friendliness towards the Eldar.

Annon-in-Gelydh 'Gate-of-the-Noldor' (Sind.) The concealed entrance to Nevrast: a tunnel in the eastern wall of the Echoing Mountains, on the borders of Dor-lómin. It was built by Turgon's people, in the days before the founding of Gondolin when they still dwelled in Nevrast.

Ann-thannath 'The-Gift-of-Words' (Sind.) A mode of verse and song among the Elves of Beleriand, difficult to render into Common Speech (Westron) because of its Elvish patterns of thought and inspiration. The Lay of Leithian was originally composed in this mode.

Annúminas 'The-Tower-of-the-Sunset' (Sind.) The first and only capital of Arnor. It was a beautiful city on the banks of Lake Evendim (Nenuial), built by Elendil after the fall of Númenor. Annúminas did not long survive the division of Arnor (861 Third Age), and was allowed to fall into ruin after the Heirs of Elendil removed to Fornost Erain, which then became the capital of Arthedain.

It is told that Elendil kept the chief *palantír* of the North at Annúminas. (Of the other two, one was at AMON SÚL while the other rested at the Tower Hills, West of the Shire, where Elendil could cast his sight 'West-over-Water'.)

Note: it is recorded that Annúminas was restored in the Fourth Age by King Elessar (Aragorn II).

Anod See ENTS.

Anor The Sindarin form of the Quenya word ANAR (The Sun).

Anórien 'Sun-land' (Sind.) One of the two oldest provinces of Gondor, as the Realm was originally ordered. It was named in honour of *Anor* (the Sun), and also after Anárion, son of Elendil, who ruled Gondor conjointly with his brother Isildur at the beginning of the Realm. Anórien contained most of the land west of the Great River and east of the White Mountains. Its chief city was Minas Anor, later renamed Minas Tirith.

Anto The Quenya word for 'mouth', but more properly the title of Tengwa number 13, used (in Quenya) to express the sound *nt* and (in Sindarin and Mannish) for *dh*.

Apanómar 'the After-born' (Q.) An early name for the race of Men, awarded by Elves (the 'Firstborn').

Appledore A common Bree name.

Ar(a) A royal prefix to the names of those later Kings of Númenor who took their ceremonial titles in ADÛNAIC, discarding the Eldarin prefix *Tar-* for nationalistic reasons.

Ar- meant 'ruler, king' in early Mannish tongues, which, of course, were themselves derived partially from 'proto-Quenya'; and, as an acknowledgement of their Númenorean (and Eldarin) ancestry, all Kings and Chieftains of the Dúnedain of the North (beginning with Argeleb I) also adopted this prefix in *their* names (e.g., Aragorn, Araphant, Arassuil).

Note: those Kings of Númenor who took *Ar-*prefixed names are all alphabetized in this *Companion* under the main part of their titles (e.g., ADÛNAKHÔR, INZILADÛN, PHARAZÔN, rather than Ar-Adûnakhoôr, Ar-Inziladûn, etc.).

See TAR-, also *The Silmarillion* p. 356.

Aradan 'Royal-man' (Sind.) See MALACH ARADAN.

Arador From 2912–30 Third Age, the fourteenth Chieftain of the Dúnedain of the North, and grandfather of Aragorn. He was captured and put to death by hill-trolls.

Araglas From 2327–2455 Third Age, the sixth Chieftain of the Dúnedain.

Aragorn I From 2319–27 Third Age, the fifth Chieftain of the Dúnedain, slain by wolves.

Aragorn II Born in Rivendell (2931 Third Age), the only son of Gilraen the Fair and Arathorn II, fifteenth Chieftain of the Dúnedain of Arnor. When his father died in battle only two years after Aragorn's birth, the boy in his turn became Chieftain.

His mother then took him to safety in Rivendell, where the young Dúnadan was fostered by Elrond himself. There he bore the name *Estel* ('Hope') to conceal his true lineage from the emissaries of Sauron who were scouring the North for the last Heir of Isildur. On his twentieth birthday, Elrond revealed his true name and ancestry, and the ancient hopes of his House, and he gave to Aragorn the heirlooms of his Line: the Ring of Barahir and the shards of Elendil's sword Narsil.

Then Aragorn went out into the world and took up his part in the fight against Mordor. He made many journeys and served many notable Lords (including King Thengel of Rohan and Ecthelion II, Ruling Steward of Gondor). And he became hardy and wisest of living men, having also the friendship of Gandalf the Grey. But because of the many burdens he carried, Aragorn also grew sad and stern of countenance; and he was clad ever in simple green and brown as a Ranger of the North.

And yet he was no less than the direct descendant – through Kings of Arnor and Arthedain, and Chieftains of the North – of Isildur, Elendil's son; and, through Elendil, of Elros Tar-Minyatur, first King of Númenor and brother of Elrond Halfelven of Rivendell. And the Halfelven were themselves of the kin of Lúthien Tinúviel, whose Line, it was said, should never fail. To re-establish the ancient Kingship of both Gondor and Arnor was Aragorn's sworn duty, and his one great hope. How he fared in this task is told elsewhere.

See also LINES OF DESCENT and the 'Tale of Aragorn and Arwen' in Appendix A I(v).

Aragost From 2523–88 Third Age, the eighth Chieftain of the Dúnedain of Arnor.

Arahad I From 2455–2523 Third Age, the seventh Chieftain of the Dúnedain, and the father of Aragost.

Arahad II From 2654–2719 Third Age, the tenth Chieftain.

Arahael From 2106–77, the second Chieftain. Arahael was the son of Aranarth and the grandson of Arvedui, 'Last-king'.

Araman 'Beyond-Aman' (Q.) The name given by the Eldar of the Undying Lands to a region of cold semi-desert which lay north of Eldamar, on the eastern side of the Mountains of Defence, and which extended into the Far North. We are told that this land grew wider as one journeyed north, for the Pelóri range bent to the north-westward, away from the sea-coast. Araman was uninhabited, as was the equally barren southern waste of Avathar.

Aranarth From 1974–2106 Third Age, the first Chieftain of the Dúnedain. The death of his father, King Arvedui, and the final destruction of Arthedain, caused the Heirs of Isildur to conceal their royalty and pass into the shadows as Rangers of the North. The line of succession, however, remained unbroken. Aranarth was the first of fifteen Chieftains before Aragorn II and the final restoration of the fortunes of the House of Isildur.

Aranel 'Star-king' (Sind.) One of the birth-names of DIOR ELUCHÍL.

Aranrúth 'Anger-of-the King' (Sind.) The sword of Thingol Greycloak of Doriath; it was probably of dwarf-make, and may have been forged for him by the smiths of Nogrod at the beginning of the wars of Beleriand.
  Note: in an extraneous source (see *The Silmarillion* p. 317), we are told that this weapon survived the sack of Doriath and ultimately came into the possession of the Kings of Númenor. Presumably – since there is no mention of Aranrúth in Third Age records – it was lost for ever, along with many other ancient Eldarin treasures, in the Inundation.

Arantar From 339–435 Third Age, the fifth King of Arnor.

Aranuir From 2177–2247 Third Age, the third Chieftain of the Dúnedain; the son of Arahael, Aranarth's son.

Aranwë 'Kingly' (Q.) An Elf of Gondolin, the father of VORONWË.

Araphant From 1891–1964 Third Age, the fourteenth King of Arthedain. During Araphant's reign, contact with Gondor, long broken, was renewed – as the Kings of both countries 'perceived that some single power and will was directing the assault from many quarters upon the survivors of Númenor'.[6] Little, however, came of the contact. Aid was sent to Araphant's son Arvedui (see ARTHEDAIN), but it arrived too late to save the North-kingdom from final destruction.

Araphor From 1409–1589 Third Age, the ninth King of Arthedain. In 1409, the last year of his father's reign, a mighty host came out of Angmar and entered the lands of Cardolan and Arthedain, razing the country and burning the Tower of Amon Sûl. King Arveleg of Arthedain was defeated and slain; but his son Araphor, though still a stripling, drove the forces of the Witch-king away and successfully defended Fornost on the North Downs. In this he had the aid of the Elves of Lindon. For most of his reign afterwards Eriador had peace, Angmar having been temporarily checked by Elves of Lindon and Rivendell (and, it is said, Lórien).

Arassuil From 2719–84 Third Age, the eleventh Chieftain of the Dúnedain.

Aratan 'Royal-man' (Q.) The second son of ISILDUR, slain, together with his father and two of his brothers (see also VALANDIL) at the Gladden Fields (Year 2, Third Age).

Aratar 'High-ones' (Q.) The innermost council of the VALAR, eight in number.

Arathorn I From 2784–2848, the twelfth Chieftain.

Arathorn II From 2930–33 Third Age, the fifteenth Chieftain of the Dúnedain, and father of ARAGORN II, the Renewer. In the prime of his life he married Gilraen the Fair, daughter of Dirhael, descendant of Aranarth, first Chieftain. Their only child was Aragorn; when the son was in his second year and the father in his sixtieth, the Chieftain was struck in the eye by an orc-arrow and perished, proving exceptionally short-lived for one of his race (as had indeed been foreboded some years before).

Araval From 1813–91 Third Age, the thirteenth King of Arthedain.

Aravir From 2247–2319 Third Age, fourth Chieftain of the Dúnedain.

Aravorn From 2588–2654 Third Age, the ninth Chieftain of the Dúnedain.

Araw The Sindarin form of the High-elven name *Oromë*, given to one of the great Valar, the Huntsman, who alone visited Middle-earth frequently in the Elder Days. In the Northern Mannish tongues he was known as Béma.

Of Araw, the Elves said that he stocked Middle-earth with noble animals of all kinds to further the pleasures of the Chase. The

Mearas, the remarkable royal horses of Rohan, were thought to have been descended from an animal brought by him from 'West-over-Sea' – as were the wild white cattle of the fields of Rhûn. These beasts were known (in Gondor) as the 'Kine of Araw'.

See also OROMË THE GREAT.

Archet A village of the Bree-land, peopled by Hobbits and Men. It lay upon the northern edge of the Chetwood, which stretched east from the Bree-country into the wilds beyond.

Arciryas A Prince of Gondor and younger brother of Narmacil II (slain in battle with the Wainriders in 1856 Third Age). He was also an ancestor of Eärnil II, the victor of the Battle of the Camp (1944), where the Wainriders were finally defeated.

Arda The Quenya word for 'region' or 'realm', but more properly the title of Tengwa number 26, representing the sound *rd* in the High-elven tongue and the softer *rh* in Grey-elven and Mannish usage.

According to the lore of the High-elves, *Arda* was the name given by The One to the World as He originally created it.

Ard-galen 'Green-region' (Sind.) The name given by the Elves of Beleriand to the vast, grassy plain north of Dorthonion and east of the Mountains of Shadow (the Ered Wethrin). North of Ard-galen lay the Iron Mountains which were the southern border of Morgoth's realm of Angband. Ard-galen was a region rather like Calenardhon (Rohan) in later days, *steppe* as we would call it today – in other words ideal cavalry country. But Morgoth's hosts came forth from Angband, and in the Battle of Sudden Flame the Elvish horse-archers, who had roamed freely there throughout the Long Peace, were overcome; and they were burned to death or driven forth for ever. The Green Region of the north became a desert of great size, wherein not a single plant grew; arid, lifeless and evil. It was then named *Dor-nu-Fauglith*, 'Land-[buried] under-choking-ash', and *Anfauglith*, the 'Gasping-dust'.

Árë The Quenya word for 'sunlight', but more properly the title of Tengwa number 31, after this 'additional' letter had altered its original name from *áze*. The value of the Tengwa likewise altered, from the *z* sound (for those languages which needed such a phonetic), to an *r* (*árë*), and later to *esse* ('name'), when the letter's value became further modified to represent the *ss* sound.

Aredhel The daughter of Fingolfin of the Noldor, sister of the Elven-kings Fingon and Turgon, and wife of the Grey-elf Eöl the Smith. Aredhel was also the mother of Maeglin the Traitor.

She was born, like all the Noldor of those days, in Eldamar, and she joined her brothers and her father in their support of the rebellion of Fëanor, and thus shared their exile. Together with Fingolfin's host, she made the perilous crossing of the Helcaraxë (the northern ice) into Middle-earth, and afterwards dwelt with her youngest brother Turgon, in his first kingdom of Nevrast by the Sea and later in Gondolin, the Hidden City. But long before, in Eldamar, she had been called *Ar-Feiniel*, the White [Royal] Lady, for she was dark-haired and pale, we are told, and dressed always in the palest colours; but she had a passion for adventure, fulfilled in former days only by hunting.

It was this restlessness of hers which proved her undoing; for, as is told in *The Silmarillion*, she wilfully decided to go and visit the Sons of Fëanor, her old friends, ignoring – or overlooking – her brother's admonitions concerning her safety. As a result she lost sight of the escort that had been told off to guard her, and came, by various paths, into the dreary forest of Nan Elmoth, wherein she was caught and taken to wife by the 'Dark Elf', Eöl the Smith.

Aredhel bore Eöl a son, named by his father *Maeglin* but by his mother *Lómion*. After some years, both he and she decided to escape from the dour life they were forced to lead, and in so doing made their way to Gondolin – where Turgon, overjoyed to see them, granted them sanctuary and honour. But, as all now know, they had been pursued: by Eöl, who was taken when trying to enter the Hidden City. And in the course of the interview which followed, the crazed Eöl attempted to slay his son Maeglin with a poisoned shaft. The point instead struck Aredhel, who died from the venom. Eöl was executed for this crime. Maeglin survived.

 Árë nuquerna A reversed form of the above letter (Tengwa number 31), incorporated into the writing system as letter number 32.

Ar-Feiniel See AREDHEL above.

Argeleb I From 1349–56 Third Age, the seventh King of Arthedain and the first to claim lordship over all the former lands of Arnor – in token of which he took his royal name with an *Ar-* prefix (see AR-). Argeleb's hopes for a reunited North-kingdom led to defiance and ultimately invasion from Rhudaur, where the Dúnedain were few and the Line of Isildur extinct. In fact, it was later learned that Rhudaur was in secret alliance with the evil realm of ANGMAR at this time.

In the war that followed, Argeleb fortified his eastern frontier (see AMON SÛL), but fell in battle with Angmar and Rhudaur. His son Arveleg I succeeded him and, for a time, drove away the forces of Angmar from the Weather Hills.

Note: the ruined fortifications described in Book I Chap. 10 were those constructed by Argeleb (except the Tower of Amon Sûl, raised long before by Elendil himself).

Argeleb II From 1589–1670 Third Age, the tenth King of Arthedain. It was this ruler who, embroiled in endless wars with Angmar, freely gave permission for the Hobbits Marcho and Blanco, together with their following, to cross the Baranduin and settle in the fertile lands beyond. All that he asked of the Hobbitry in return was: 'that they should keep the Great Bridge in repair . . . speed his messengers, and acknowledge his lordship'.[7] So the Hobbits first came to the Shire, as they called their new land. Three hundred years later the North-kingdom came to an end and the Shire-dwellers soon forgot (except in tradition) that there had ever been a King.

Argonath 'Pillars-of-the-Kings' (Sind.) The mighty carven stones on either side of the Anduin – where it flowed through a chasm into Nen Hithoel. They were erected by Rómendacil II of Gondor (*c.* 1340 Third Age), to mark the Realm's northern frontier and to forbid all but legitimate travellers from passing further. The Argonath were fashioned in the likenesses of Isildur and Anárion: 'still with blurred eyes and crannied brows they frowned upon the North. The left hand of each was raised palm outwards in a gesture of warning; in each right hand there was an axe; upon each head there was a crumbling helm and crown.'[8]

Argonui From 2848–2912 Third Age, the thirteenth Chieftain of the Dúnedain of Arnor.

Arien One of the female MAIAR, a fire-spirit, who was chosen by the Valar to guide the Sun, ANAR, on its celestial course.

See TILION; also *The Silmarillion* pp. 99–101.

Arkenstone The greatest and most prized possession in the hoard of the Dwarf-kings of Erebor, lost to their House when the dragon Smaug pillaged the Lonely Mountain (2770 Third Age).

The Arkenstone was a great white gem of brilliant translucency, mined from 'The-Heart-of-the-Mountain' – as the jewel was itself afterwards called by the Dwarves of Durin's House. Unexpectedly recovered from the Dragon by the Hobbit Bilbo Baggins in the year 2941, it was later used by him in an attempt to secure peace between Dwarves, Men and Elves before the Battle of Five Armies. It was afterwards laid to rest with Thorin Oakenshield, who was mortally wounded in that battle.

Armenelos (**the Golden**) 'Royal-fortress-of-the-Heavens' (Q.) The chief city of Númenor, where the kings of that land dwelled throughout the latter part of the Second Age. It stood near the centre of the island, near the feet of the Meneltarma, the highest mountain of Númenor. Originally, Andúnië in the west of Númenor had been the capital, but the regions about Meneltarma had been hallowed at the founding of the land, and Elros Tar-Minyatur, the first king, had built a tower and a citadel upon a hill, not far from the royal tombs, which had always been at the feet of Meneltarma. As time passed Andúnië lost the supremacy, and Armenelos grew, and became the royal residence.

Arminas and Gelmir Two Elves of Finarfin's House, more specifically of the people of Angrod, who came from Círdan bearing a message of warning to the King of Nargothrond (Orodreth: his elder brother Finrod was dead). The message was not heeded, and, as is told in *The Silmarillion*, Nargothrond fell shortly afterwards.

Arnach A shortened form of the name *Lossarnach*, the province of Gondor which lay to the south of the White Mountains between the rivers Sirith and Erui, one day's journey from Minas Tirith. The word is of (pre-Adûnaic) Mannish form, and its meaning is not recorded.

Arnor The more northerly of the two Númenorean realms-in-exile, founded by Elendil the Tall in the year 3320 Second Age, after he and his House escaped the wreck of Númenor and returned to Middle-earth with the remnant of the Dúnedain.

Though it was the elder and more prestigious of the twin states, the fortunes of Arnor did not mirror those of its sister-realm, the South-kingdom of Gondor. Whereas for over a thousand years

Gondor grew ever more powerful and glorious, the North-kingdom allowed itself, comparatively early in its history, to be dissolved into three separate states – a factor which led to its subsequent conquest and eventual destruction.[9]

Elendil himself wielded the High-kingship of both realms from his Northern capital of Annúminas; he was thus also accounted first King of Arnor. Upon his death (in 3441 Second Age), the High-kingship, and the rule of Arnor, passed to his elder son Isildur – who never reached Annúminas to take up the Sceptre, perishing instead at the hands of the Orcs while on the northward journey (Year 2, Third Age). The kingship of Arnor (but not the High-kingship of both realms) then passed to Isildur's fourth son Valandil – who, being only a child, had remained in Rivendell and thus escaped the massacre by the Gladden where his father and three elder brothers were slain. Valandil was accounted Arnor's third King.

On the death of Eärendur, tenth King, in 861, Arnor ceased to exist as a single Realm – after his three sons quarrelled over the succession. As a result, the proud Kingdom was divided into three separate states: Arthedain, Cardolan and Rhudaur.

It was not until almost five hundred years later that the first attempt was made to reconstitute Arnor as a single Kingdom, when Argeleb I of Arthedain, noting that the Line of Isildur was extinct in Cardolan and Rhudaur, thus claimed lordship over both. Cardolan wavered, but Rhudaur fiercely rejected the claim; it was later learned that Rhudaur was in secret league with the Witch-realm of Angmar, even then arising to the north of the Ettenmoors and preparing for the long wars which would eventually destroy the North-kingdom. But before its final destruction one other attempt was made to re-establish the Kingdom of Arnor – indeed, to re-join both Arnor and Gondor under the ancient High-kingship.

Following the death of King Ondoher of Gondor in 1944 Third Age, King Arvedui of Arthedain, who had married Ondoher's daughter Fíriel some four years previously, claimed the throne of Gondor. Isildur, he said, had not intended that Arnor and Gondor be divided for ever. Moreover, the sons of Ondoher had died with him in battle; whereas the Northern Succession to which he, Arvedui, was Heir, stood in line unbroken from Isildur, and before that from Elendil himself. But Gondor ignored this claim, and awarded the Crown instead to a victorious general, Eärnil.

Eärnil of Gondor was a wise King and, although the realm of Arthedain might seem a small thing to a ruler of all Gondor, he made a point of assuring Arvedui that he did not 'forget the royalty of Arnor, nor deny our kinship . . . I will send to your aid when you have need, so far as I am able.'[10] Thirty years later, to honour his pledge, he sent his son Eärnur north with a great fleet, but the Army of Gondor was too late to save the North-kingdom. Arvedui perished in the wastes of the North and with him passed the Kingship of Arthedain, and of Arnor.

Note: the original realm of Arnor constituted all Eriador between the Misty Mountains and the river Lhûn, excluding the lands of Hollin (Eregion) and Rivendell (Imladris). In contrast, its successor-state of Arthedain contained only the north-western region of old Arnor, as far east as the Weather Hills and as far south as the Great Road.

See also ARTHEDAIN; GONDOR; REALMS IN EXILE; and Appendix A I(iii).

Arod A fleet-footed horse of Rohan who bore the Elf Legolas and the Dwarf Gimli throughout the War of the Ring.

Aros A river of Beleriand, which formed the southern border of Thingol Greycloak's Kingdom of Doriath. It rose from two sources high in the precipices of southern Dorthonion and flowed southwards; below the confluence of these source-streams, the Aros was fordable only at the Arossiach, where the road from Nan Dungortheb and Dor Dínen crossed into Himlad. To the south-east of Doriath the Celon joined its waters to the larger river, after which the renewed Aros bent westward and flowed through the southern marches of Thingol's land before forming a confluence with the still greater river Sirion, north of the marshes of Aelin-uial.

Arossiach 'Fords-of-Aros' (Sind.) See AROS above.

Artamir The elder son of King Ondoher of Gondor. Along with his father and younger brother Faramir, he fell in battle with the Wainriders (in 1944 Third Age), thus giving ARVEDUI of Arthedain cause to claim the crown of Gondor.

Arthad One of the twelve faithful comrades of Barahir of the Edain, who dwelled with him in Dorthonion after its capture by Morgoth during the War of the Great Jewels, and who shared his adventures and sufferings. He was later slain, as a result of the betrayal of the outlaws by one of their number, Gorlim the Unhappy.

Arthedain The meaning of the name, 'The-Kingdom-of-the-[Dún]Edain', indicates the lineage of this realm, last of the Númenorean North-kingdoms to perish and State-apparent to the lordship of ancient ARNOR.

Arnor, being divided into three on the death of Eärendur, tenth King, did not survive beyond the ninth century of the Third Age; yet the smaller realm of Arthedain lingered on, often in desperate straits, for a further thousand years. This was no doubt due to the fact that the Line of Isildur was strictly maintained there.

The primary act of Arthedain's first King, Amlaith, eldest son of Eärendur, was to remove the capital from Elendil's city of Annúminas to the more strategic site of Fornost Erain (Norbury of the Kings) on the North Downs. As the senior kingdom of the three, Arthedain kept possession of two of the three Seeing-stones (*palantíri*) of the North: the Stones of Emyn Beraid (Tower Hills) and of Annúminas. For many years Arthedain was at peace – apart from disputes with Rhudaur and, less often, Cardolan. But with the establishment of the evil realm of Angmar (*c.* 1300 Third Age), this last Kingdom of the Dúnedain of the North became gravely imperilled.

In wars that lasted over seven hundred years, Arthedain, sometimes in alliance with Cardolan, fought bitterly against encroachment by Angmar and Rhudaur. After Cardolan was ravaged in 1409 the Kings at Fornost fought on, often with aid from Elvenfolk of Lindon and Rivendell, until the final disaster in 1974 – when the Witch-king of Angmar captured Fornost and drove King Arvedui north to perish in the icy wastes of Forochel. With him died the last Númenorean Kingdom in the North of Middle-earth.

Note: for a fuller account of the history of Arthedain (and Arnor), see Appendix A I(iii).

See also REALMS IN EXILE.

Arvedui 'Last-king' (Sind.) From 1964–74 Third Age, the fifteenth and, as his name signifies, last King of Arthedain, longest surviving state in the old realm of Arnor.

At his birth the following words were spoken of him by the royal counsellor: '*Arvedui* you shall call him, for he will be the last in Arthedain. Though a choice will come to the Dúnedain, and if they take the one that seems less hopeful, then your son will change his name and become king of a great realm.'[11] (See MALBETH THE SEER.)

On the death of King Ondoher of Gondor, together with his sons Artamir and Faramir (in 1944 Third Age), Arvedui claimed the crown of Gondor. By this time a man of full age though not yet King of Arthedain, Arvedui made this claim as the husband of the only surviving child of Ondoher (Fíriel, whom he had married four years

previously) *and* as the Heir of Elendil, whose son, Isildur, said
Arvedui, 'did not relinquish his royalty in Gondor, nor intend that
the realm of Elendil should be divided for ever.[12] But Gondor made no
reply to this, and the Crown was granted to a victorious general instead.

In 1974 Third Age, in the tenth year of Arvedui's reign, the power
of the neighbouring Witch-realm of Angmar arose again and, before
the winter was over, the Witch-king descended once more upon
Arthedain and captured Fornost. Together with a handful of loyal
guards, Arvedui escaped in the nick of time into the far North, seeking aid from the snow-dwellers of the great ice-bay of Forochel. In
the spring Círdan the Shipwright, hearing of the King's plight, sent
a ship north to rescue him. But the winter was not quite yet ended,
and the Elf-ship bearing Arvedui was driven back into the pack-ice
by a wild storm which rose unlooked-for in the night. So perished
Arvedui Last-king, and with him the Kingdom of Arthedain.

Note: in available translations from the Shire Records there exists
an odd discrepancy concerning the dates of the various events which
brought an end to Arvedui and the realm of Arthedain. In Appendix
A I(iv), King Eärnil II of Gondor is said to have learned about the
impending invasion of Angmar in the autumn of 1973 Third Age;
yet although he 'sent his son Eärnur north with a fleet, as swiftly as
he could,' according to 'The Tale of Years' (Appendix B) this force
did not reach Lindon until 1975, probably in spring.

Appendix B also gives 1975 as the year of Arvedui's death. Yet,
if the information in Appendix A I(iii) is also correct, this must mean
that the fugitive King remained with the Snow-men of Forochel for
just over a year – which is plainly as erroneous an assumption as
presuming that Eärnur was over a year at sea.

The probable origin of this problem lies in the fact that 'The
Tale of Years' was compiled (by the Tooks) from a number of varying sources, whereas the (abridged) sections on Arnor and Gondor
in the Appendices were originally copied from existing records.
At any rate the compilers seems to have misrepresented the events
of the year 1974 as occurring in two separate years, 1974 and 1975.
In this *Companion*, therefore, the year 1974 has been taken as the
date of Arthedain's fall, Arvedui's death, the arrival of Eärnur's fleet
and the subsequent Battle of Fornost, in which Angmar was also
thrown down for ever.

See also Appendix A I(iii) and (iv).

Arvegil From 1670–1743 Third Age, the eleventh King of Arthedain.

Arveleg I From 1356–1409 Third Age, the eighth King of Arthedain, son of Argeleb I. When his father was slain by invading forces of Angmar and Rhudaur in 1356, Arveleg rallied the Dúnedain and, aided by an Elf-host from Lindon, drove away the invaders from the fortified line of Weather Hills (see AMON SÛL). For fifty years Arveleg maintained the eastern ramparts against Angmar, falling in the invasion of 1409, in a final unsuccessful defence of Amon Sûl. Angmar was later driven back by Elven-forces from Lindon and Rivendell.

Arveleg II From 1743–1813 Third Age, the twelfth King of Arthedain.

Arvernien The southernmost part of West Beleriand, a region of fair woods (see NIMBRETHIL), bordered on the east by the Mouths of Sirion, and on the west and south by the Great Sea and the Bay of Balar. Its south-western promontary was Cape Balar. Here Eärendil the Mariner built the ship Vingilot, of birch-wood from the forests of Arvernien.

Arwen Evenstar The daughter of Elrond Halfelven and Celebrían, daughter of Galadriel. She was born in the year 241 Third Age in Rivendell; and so great was her loveliness that in her, it was said, the likeness of Lúthien Tinúviel had returned to earth.

To the children of Elrond was appointed the Choice of the Half-elven: to become of mortal kind and die in Middle-earth, or to take ship into the West with Elrond when the time came for the Three Rings to pass away.

For many years Arwen Undómiel ('Evenstar') dwelt among her mother's kin, in Lothlórien, to the east of the Misty Mountains. It was here that she fell in love with Aragorn II of the Dúnedain, and so made her Choice. Thus the Doom of Lúthien was indeed shared by Arwen Evenstar.

See also LÚTHIEN TINÚVIEL and the 'Tale of Aragorn and Arwen' in Appendix A I(v).

Ascar 'Rushing' (Sind.) The northernmost of the six tributaries of the Gelion, in Ossiriand. It was afterwards called *Rathlóriel* ('Golden-bed'), because of the treasure of sacked Doriath that was lost in its waters.

Asëa aranion In the Valinorean tongue, 'King's-leaf'; known in Gondor as kingsfoil and in the north as *athelas*.

Asfaloth The swift white steed of GLORFINDEL, Noldorin Elf of Rivendell. `

Ash[y] Mountains The *Ered Lithui*, northern rampart of Mordor, which ran east from the Black Gate into the southlands of Rhûn. Upon a spur which jutted south from the inner wall stood Barad-dûr, the Dark Tower of Sauron.

Asta, Astar 'month' (Q.) The name given by Númenorean lore-masters to the new unit of calendar-computation devised by them early in the Second Age and subsequently incorporated into the Kings' Reckoning system – which was eventually adopted by many of the people living in the Westlands of Middle-earth during the last half of the Third Age.

The *asta* was equal to one-twelfth of the solar year, which the Númenoreans divided into ten *astar* of 30 days each and two of 31. in both the later Stewards' Reckoning and the New Reckoning of the Fourth Age, all the *astar* had 30 days; however, in all three reckoning-systems there were also 3 to 5 additional days which did not fall into any *asta*.

Astaldo 'Valiant' (Q.) A title of the Vala TULKAS.

Astron In the Shire Reckoning, the fourth month of the year, roughly equivalent to our April. In Bree this month was known as *Chithing*.

Atalantë 'The Downfallen' (Q.) The High-elven equivalent of the Adûnaic word *Akallabêth*, applied to the land of Númenor after its inundation.

Note: the close resemblance between this Quenya word and the name *Atlantis* – particularly noteworthy because both are names of vanished, inundated civilizations – may be considered a fit subject for comment. (See also AVALLONË.) For if the linguistic and historical identification of Atalantë with Atlantis is sustainable, then the Fall of Númenor – and, by cross-dating, all other events spoken of in this *Companion* – can actually be dated in modern historical terms. The Atlantis myth comes down to us from the Athenian, Plato; who had it (he said) from the writings of an earlier Greek sage, Solon – who had reportedly heard the story in Egypt, during his travels in the sixth century BC.

In the Egyptian's story, as reported by Solon, the fall of Atlantis was dated positively to a period 15,000 years earlier. Therefore, if the connection is accepted between *Atalantë* and *Atlantis*, and if the other details of the story are likewise taken at face value, the fall of Atlantis/ Númenor took place in, or can be computed to, the middle of the last ice age. Which in turn can be made to mean that the period described in *The Silmarillion*, wherein Morgoth first established his power in the north of Middle-earth, corresponds very closely and significantly with the *onset* of this last glaciation. More cannot be said of this matter.

Atanamir (Tar-Atanamir) 'Jewel-of-Men' (Q.) The thirteenth King of Númenor and one of the first openly to protest the Ban of the Valar, which was held by Númenoreans to deny Men the Gift (or Doom) of immortality. As a result, messengers were sent from the West to Númenor, to soothe their spirits and explain the Ban of the Valar. But Atanamir was not soothed, and rejected the counsel given him. Númenor later split into factions, a situation which eventually brought about civil war and the final fall of the Land of the Star.

Atanatar I From 667–748 Third Age, the tenth King of Gondor.

Atanatar II Alcarin ('The Glorious') From 1149–1226 Third Age, the sixteenth King of Gondor. When he inherited the realm from his father Hyarmendacil I, Gondor was at the peak of her might. The succession of the four imperial 'Ship-kings', culminating in the mighty Hyarmendacil, had scattered the enemies of the Dúnedain and no foe dared to contest the will of the Men of the West.

Atanatar II, unlike his renowned forbears, did little to maintain the power that had passed to him, preferring to squander the tremendous wealth of Gondor in idle pursuits and ostentatious luxury, so that in his time men said 'precious stones are pebbles in Gondor for children to play with'. The commencement of Gondor's slow decline can thus be attributed to Alcarin, though in his day such an eventuality seemed unthinkable. During his reign the Crown of Gondor, once a simple Númenorean war-helm, was replaced by a jewelled crown of *mithril* and other precious metals. Such was Atanatar Alcarin's concept of kingship.

Atanatári 'Fathers-of-Men' (Q.) One of the oldest Elvish names for Men, and used only of the very first of the Edain to enter Beleriand. It was a title of ceremony rather than a figure of speech.

Atani See ADAN.

Atendëa The leap-year in the Númenorean calendar (Kings' Reckoning). The name means 'double-middle', so called because the extra day was allowed for by doubling Mid-year's Day (*loëndë*).

Athelas This was a plant of great healing virtue brought to Middle-earth, it is said, by the Númenoreans of the Second Age. It grew sparsely in the North and only in places where the Men of Westernesse had passed. The plant was certainly known in Númenor, where the Valinorean name *asëa aranion* was used; but in Gondor, where this 'kingsfoil' grew abundantly, its healing properties were unknown and the leaves were esteemed only for their refreshing scent.

See also Book IV Chap. 8.

Aulë the Smith One of the great Valar; the Lord of all material things, or of things made by craft; oldest and greatest of loremasters and the most skilful of all artisans; the Maker of the Dwarves. Aulë was the Spouse of Yavanna Kementári, the Vala who made all things that grow or have ever grown upon the earth, and together they did much to shape the face of the world in its Beginning, as is told in *The Silmarillion*.

Avallónë The Haven of the Eldar in Tol Eressëa, the 'Lonely Isle' off the shores of Valinor, founded long ago by the Teleri when they dwelt for a while in that island before completing the Great Journey to Aman the Blessed. It was built anew by those returning Exiles who came back from Middle-earth at the end of the First Age. Avallónë was said to be visible to 'the farsighted' from the summit of the holy mountain Meneltarma in Númenor.

Note: few of those reading this *Companion* will have overlooked the close resemblance between the names *Avallónë*, which is a Quenya (Elvish) word, and *Avalon*, a Celtic (Mannish) name meaning, it is said, 'Isle of Apples'. Both are indeed traditionally applied to faraway islands in the West, unreachable save by those appointed to make the journey. In (Celtic) British mythology, King Arthur is said to have been borne away in a barge draped with black samite to the Isle of Avalon, there to recover from the grievous (mortal) wound sustained by him at the Battle of Camlann. Is this a dim memory of a far older tradition? Or does Arthur of Britain live still in Tol Eressëa within sight of Valinor?

See also ATALANTË.

Avari 'the Unwilling' (Q.) The name given in Elvish tradition to those of the ancient Quendi of Middle-earth who, when summoned by Oromë the Vala to make the Great Journey to Valinor, refused;

and dwelt in Middle-earth ever after. They were sometimes known
as the East-elves.

See also ELVES.

Avathar 'Shadows' (Q.) Like ARAMAN, this was the name of a
barren wilderness on the eastern shores of Aman, a narrow, bleak,
cold region between the Mountains of Defence (the *Pelóri*) and the
Sea. Araman lay to the north of Eldamar, Avathar to the south.

Azaghâl A Dwarf-king of the First Age, Lord of Belegost in the
Blue Mountains. He marched in alliance with the Eldar and the
Edain to the Battle of Numberless Tears. In one of the most heroic
deeds of that dreadful fight, Azaghâl contained the first onslaught of
the Dragon Glaurung by means of the valour (and armour) of his
warriors, defeating the Worm (who might otherwise have slain many
more of the Eldar and the Edain) at the cost of his own life.

Azanulbizar This vale – known to the Elves as Nanduhirion and to
Men as the Dimrill Dale – lay below the East-gate of Moria between
two outstretched arms of the Misty Mountains. It was a sacred place
to the Dwarves of Durin's House for many reasons, not least for the
grievous loss of life which the Dwarves suffered in the Battle of
Azanulbizar against the Orcs of AZOG (2799 Third Age). The numbers
of the slain were so great that the Dwarves were unable to lay their
dead in stone as was their custom; instead, they were compelled to
burn the bodies of their kin. (See BATTLE OF AZANULBIZAR.)

The valley contained many places greatly revered by Dwarves of
Moria, whose Kingdom had, in the days of its power, included these
lands beyond the Gate. Here were to be found *Kibil-nâla* (the source
of the Silverlode river), *Kheled-zarâm* (the Mirrormere) and Durin's
Stone, an ancient pillar which marked the place where Durin the
Deathless himself first gazed into the lake to see a crown of stars
reflected round his head. Durin founded the Kingdom of Moria in
the caves overlooking the vale and its lake; it was later Dwarves who
bored westward until they reached the far side of the Misty Mountains and the lands of southern Eriador.

Ázë A Quenya word for 'sunlight,' but more properly,
the title of the Fëanorean Tengwa number 31, in its earliest
form. See ÁRË.

Ӡ **Ázë nuquerna** The reversed form of Tengwa number 31, allotted the number 32 in the Fëanorean system. Its use was identical to that of *ázë*.

Azog A chieftain among the tribe of Orcs which occupied the deserted Dwarf-realm of Moria in the 28th century of the Third Age. Azog's murder and decapitation of the Dwarf Thrór, Heir of Durin, was the event which signalled the commencement of the War of the Dwarves and Orcs, in which the Dwarves had the victory 'through their strength, and their matchless weapons, and the fire of their anger, as they hunted for Azog in every [orc-] den under mountain.'[13] Azog was slain at the Battle of Azanulbizar (in 2799 Third Age) by Dáin Ironfoot. His orc-head was then set on a stake, with a purse of small money – which Azog himself had insolently offered as weregild for the death of Thrór – stuffed into his mouth.

Note: Azog's son, the equally formidable Bolg of the North, led the Orcs at the Battle of Five Armies (2941 Third Age).

Notes
1 Book II Chap. 1.
2 Book III Chap. 4.
3 Merely a rendering of *Amon Sûl* into the Common Speech.
4 Some may find it significant that, in the religious imagery of the Mannish West, 'Hell' is invariably pictured as a subterranean region of extreme temperature, with known gateways to the surface of the earth, from which the hosts of evil issue forth to plague the lives of living Men, and through which the damned are dragged, never to return to the light.
5 Cf. Aragorn's renaming of Narsil.
6 Appendix A I(iv).
7 Prologue I.
8 Book II Chap. 9.
9 Parallels are numerous. Supreme examples are the division of the later Roman Empire (into East and West), and the parcelling-out of the Empire of Alexander by Alexander's generals.
10 Appendix A I(iv). In some editions of *The Lord of the Rings* the translation *royalty* has been misprinted *loyalty*.
11 *Ibid.*
12 *Ibid.*
13 Appendix A III.

Bag End The ancestral dwelling of the well-to-do Hobbit family of Baggins, originally built into the Hill of Hobbiton (in approved Hobbit manner) by Bungo Baggins, father of Bilbo. It was the 'manor-hole' of the villages of Hobbiton and Bywater, and was certainly more magnificent than common village *smials*. The desirability of such a residence caused great friction between Bilbo and his cousins, the Sackville-Bagginses: on one notable occasion he returned from a long absence to find them actually in possession of the place, his death having been conveniently presumed.

After Bilbo's return from his Journey to the East (2942 Third Age), rumours quickly spread around his neighbourhood that the tunnels of Bag End were stuffed with sacks of treasure. Needless to say, such stories were wild exaggerations of the (fairly) modest wealth Bilbo had earned as reward for his services to the Dwarves of Erebor (see *The Hobbit*). The luxurious hole was eventually sold to the persistent Sackville-Baggins by Frodo, Bilbo's heir, before his own flight from the Shire in the year 3018. However, after his return the following year, Bag End once more became Frodo's residence; and upon his final departure in 3021, his entire estate, including his home, passed to Samwise Gamgee, whose heirs dwelt there ever after.

Baggins A Hobbit squirearchy and an ancient family of repute in the Shire. There was said to be a strong Fallohidish strain in the Baggins clan – but Hobbits said that of all families (such as Tooks and Brandybucks) who were noted for 'adventurous' tendencies. The most illustrious members of this family were of course Bilbo and his heir Frodo.

Bagshot Row A street on the Hill of Hobbiton which ran alongside the Party Field. Number Three was the residence of Hamfast Gamgee and his son Samwise, gardeners to the Baggins family.

Bain son of Bard From 2977–3007 Third Age, the second King of Dale – following the death of the Dragon Smaug and the rebuilding of that city at the feet of the Lonely Mountain. His father was Bard the Bowman, slayer of the Dragon.

Balan See BËOR (THE OLD).

Balar The great Bay of Balar lay in the south of Beleriand, forty-five leagues wide at its widest point. In the mouth of the bay there lay a tiny islet, the Isle of Balar, said to be the remnant of the greater island of Tol Eressëa.

Balbo Baggins An illustrious member of the Baggins family of the Shire, wedded to Berylla Boffin. He was Bilbo's great-grandfather.

Balchoth 'Mighty-horde' (Sind.) The name which was given in Gondor to a fierce clan of Easterlings who, in the latter part of the Third Age, forcibly occupied the ancient realm of Rhovanion, south and east of Mirkwood. Princes of this land had traditionally been friendly with Gondor (Eldacar had been born there), but they were no match for the invading Balchoth, who were given to evil ways and were wholly under the sway of the Dark Lord.

In 2510 Third Age they abandoned their petty pillaging of the lower vales of Anduin and crossed the River in strength, seeking to invade Calenardhon, the sparsely peopled northern province of Gondor. In this they had the aid of Orcs and other fell races. During the ensuing battle, the northern army of Gondor was driven back and all seemed lost, when the horsemen of Éothéod suddenly charged from the North – in response to a belated plea for aid from Cirion, the Ruling Steward of Gondor. In a classic cavalry pursuit, the Riders of Éothéod routed the Balchoth and hunted them to the death across the fields of Calenardhon. In gratitude (and in desire to have a strong ally to his north), Cirion ceded the province to the Riders. In Gondor this new realm was then known as *Rohan*.[1]

See also BATTLE OF THE FIELD OF CELEBRANT.

Baldor The eldest son of Brego, second King of Rohan. Baldor's rashness brought about both his father's untimely end and his own lonely death.

The Rohirrim, newly settled in the former province of Calenard-

'hon, had chosen a green hill at the feet of the White Mountains on which to build the Kings' Seat; this 'Golden Hall' they named *Meduseld*, and Brego held a great feast there to celebrate its completion. In front of the assembled company, Baldor then vowed to walk the 'Paths of the Dead'. He duly passed the Dark Door in Dunharrow and was never seen again by any men of Rohan. His father died of grief the following year (2571 Third Age) and Baldor's brother Aldor became king in his stead.

See also PATHS OF THE DEAD.

Balin son of Fundin A great and noble Dwarf of the House of Durin and a lifelong follower of the Kings of Erebor. Gentle, though no less proud than others of his race, Balin nonetheless became a great warrior and adventurer of his day, fighting at the Battle of Azanulbizar (where his father Fundin fell).

He was afterwards one of the Companions of Thráin son of Thrór, and was journeying with him when Thráin was taken by the forces of Dol Guldur (2845 Third Age) and later slain. Balin then became a follower of Thráin's son Thorin Oakenshield, and was one of the Thirteen Dwarves (and one Hobbit) who entered Erebor, re-establishing the Dwarf-kingship 'under the Mountain'.

Some years later, Balin became restless with peace and luxury and resolved to lead an expedition to Moria, most ancient of all Dwarf-realms in Middle-earth and long lost to Dwarf-kind. Few details are known of their fate (see Book II Chaps. 4–5) save that the colony perished with Balin in 2994 Third Age, five years after he had declared himself 'King of Moria'. He was buried in the Chamber of Mazarbul.

See also ANGERTHAS MORIA.

Balrog 'Demon-of-Power' (Sind., from Q. *Valarauka*) In their origins, as a part of the Thought of Ilúvatar, these were MAIAR of the following or service of Melkor, the mightiest of the Ainur. Like Arien (who was however of Aulë's people) they were spirits of fire. Their lord was afterwards called Gothmog. In far-off days they took service with Melkor, and were swiftly corrupted to his purposes, appearing ever after to Elves and Men as daemonic beings of great size, armed with fire and fire-enshrouded, who bore also swords and maces and whips. Only the mighty among the Eldar could withstand them, and then only by the power that was within them that came from Valinor; for no ordinary weapons or warriors could slay these evil creatures. Gothmog, indeed, is named as the Balrog who slew Fëanor himself, at the Battle-under-Stars in the North. He also slew

Fingon son of Fingolfin, at the Battle of Numberless Tears. And this fell being took the leading part in the last assault on Gondolin – but was finally slain by Ecthelion, Captain of Gondolin, in single combat in the courtyard before the King's Tower; though Ecthelion also fell. The Balrogs took part in all the major assaults of Morgoth during the War of the Great Jewels, and were slain or destroyed in the fall of Angband. Save one; for one at least of these daemonic Powers survived the breaking of Thangorodrim and fled to the safest place it knew – the very roots of the Misty Mountains, greatest in Middle-earth.

And yet this hiding-place was not secure enough. In 1980 Third Age by mischance the Dwarves of Moria were delving deep under Caradhras for *mithril* and thus accidentally released the entombed Balrog, which slew two of their Kings: Durin VI and (the following year) his son Náin I. The Dwarves then fled from Moria, never to return while the Third Age lasted. Inside the dark halls of Khazad-dûm the Balrog walked and even the Orcs feared its presence. It was finally slain by Mithrandir.

Bamfurlong A locality in the Shire, not far from Maggot's Farm in the Marish of the Eastfarthing.

Ban- In original – as opposed to translated – Westron (the Common Speech) spoken by the Hobbits of the Third Age, the root *ban-* meant 'half'. Thus the Westron name for one of the Hobbit race was *banakil*, 'halfling'. The name *Banazîr*, 'halfwise', was the original Westron version of *Samwise*, as it is commonly translated from the Red Book.

Bandobras 'Bullroarer' Took One of the tallest 'Halflings' in Shire-history and the most notable Hobbit up to the period of the War of the Ring. Being four feet five and able to ride a horse, this adventurous Took was given the admiring nickname of 'Bullroarer'. He was also the first Hobbit in history to fight (and win) a battle: that which occurred at Greenfields in 2747 Third Age, after marauding Orcs led by Golfimbul of Mount Gram had invaded the North-farthing. Bullroarer slew the leader and the remaining Orcs fled in dismay.

Banks A common Hobbit-name, found in both Bree and the Shire.

Ban of the Valar 'The Ban', a mighty prohibition laid upon the founders of Númenor (the Edain) by the Valar, Guardians of the World. While the Númenoreans were allowed to explore the Seas to the east of their island – and to return to Middle-earth – the Ban specifically restricted them from sailing out of sight of their own shores towards the West. This was to ensure that none of the (mortal) Edain ever reached the Undying Lands, which then lay within sight of keen-eyed watchers upon the Meneltarma, highest mountain in Númenor.

At first the Edain respected the Ban, confining their exploratory voyages to the eastern reaches of the Great Sea, including the shores of Middle-earth; but as their power grew, they became ever more jealous of the immortality of the Elves.

Eventually the growing resentment of the Ban became a Númenorean obsession. The few remaining 'Faithful', who still followed the Eldar and used the Elvish tongues, were increasingly persecuted; while most of the Númenoreans, and almost all the later kings, continued to look westward with envy and yearning. In the end the proud and deranged King Ar-Pharazôn was seduced by Sauron into breaking the Ban – by carrying battle into the Western Seas, in an attempt to take immortal life from the Valar by force. As a result, the whole world was altered, the Seas devoured Númenor, and the Undying Lands were withdrawn for ever from all further temptation.

Barad-dûr 'Dark Tower' (Sind.) Ancient fortress of Sauron's might. It crouched upon a great south-pointing inner spur of the Ashy Mountains, with its 'towers and battlements, tall as hills, founded upon a mighty mountain-throne above immeasurable pits; great courts and dungeons; eyeless prisons sheer as cliffs, and gaping gates of steel and adamant . . .'[2]

First constructed early in the Second Age (and completed with the power of the Ring, which rendered its foundations impregnable), the Barad-dûr was the mightiest stronghold of the Age – and of the Age which followed, recalling somewhat of the ancient might of Thangorodrim, fortress of Sauron's master, Morgoth, in the Elder Days.

The Dark Tower was destroyed twice, the first time being at the end of the Second Age after a seven-year siege by the victorious Army of the Last Alliance. But its huge foundations survived: for they were built with the power of the Ring and, while it remained in the World, they could not be unmade. Late in the Third Age, Sauron, again arisen, secretly waited for many years in his lesser fortress of Dol Guldur in Mirkwood while the Dark Tower was raised once more. Finally, in 2951 Third Age, Orodruin again burst into flame and the Dark Lord openly returned to Mordor.

Note: in the Black Speech, the Barad-dûr was known as *Lugbúrz*, which is also thought to have meant 'Dark-tower'.

Barad Eithel 'Tower of the Well' (Sind.) A tower built on the borders of Ard-galen by Fingolfin son of Finwë, at the beginning of the wars against Morgoth. It was in fact the chief stronghold of the neighbouring lands, Fingolfin's kingdom of Mithrim and his son Fingon's of Dor-lómin. The Barad Eithel was Fingon's stronghold at the commencement of the Battle of Numberless Tears: the place outside whose walls the Elf Gelmir son of Guilin was so cruelly put to death in order to enrage the defenders of the Tower. The device succeeded, and Fingon sortied from Barad Eithel – to meet his death in the battle. The tower then came into the possession of Morgoth.

Barad Nimras 'White Tower' (Sind.) A coastal fortress raised by Finrod son of Finarfin to guard the havens of Brithombar and Eglarest by sea. It was an out-work of Nargothrond, Finrod's kingdom, but was garrisoned by Elves of the Falas, whose lord, Círdan, was an ally of Finrod's. It was captured the year after the Battle of Unnumbered Tears by the armies of Angband, and thrown down.

Baragund One of the Edain of the First House; the younger brother of Belegund, and son of Bregolas the brother of Barahir; Baragund was thus the cousin of Beren Erchamion. He was the father of Morwen Eledhwen, who wedded Húrin of the Third House.

Together with all his kind, Baragund dwelled in Dorthonion, which this House of Men held in fief from the sons of Finarfin. But after the great defeat on Ard-galen, in the Battle of Sudden Flame, the Northern-kingdoms were for the most part swept away; and the Men of Dorthonion were nigh on annihilated. Only Barahir still held out, with twelve comrades, including both Baragund and Belegund and his own son Beren. Three years later, after many desperate adventures, the band of outlaws was betrayed by one of their number – GORLIM THE UNHAPPY – and all save one were slain, including Baragund and his brother.

Barahir A chieftain of the First House of the Edain; the father of Beren Erchamion. While he was still a boy, Barahir's people removed from Estolad, which had been their first dwelling in Beleriand, to Ladros (Dorthonion), which they held in alliance with the Noldor. But after a while Morgoth unleashed war upon the Eldar and the

Edain, and in the Battle of Sudden Flame he threw off the yoke of the siege upon his land. Dorthonion was overrun, and the Elves were driven back. In that battle Barahir saved the life of the Elven-king Finrod, and as a result Finrod gave him his ring, with pledges of friendship to Barahir's House and kin. Three years afterwards Barahir, who with twelve faithful companions (see also BARAGUND above) were all that remained of the Edain of Dorthonion, was slain in an ambush. Of the twelve, only his son, Beren, survived.

See also RING OF BARAHIR.

Barahir From 2395–2412 Third Age, the eighth Ruling Steward of Gondor.

Barahir Prince of Ithilien in the Fourth Age. Like his grandfather Faramir, Barahir was a scholar, and the 'Tale of Aragorn and Arwen' is ascribed to him. See Appendix A I(v).

Baran (of Estolad) The elder son of Bëor of the Edain; he assumed the chieftainship of the First House following his father's departure to take service with Finrod Felagund.

Baranduin 'Golden-brown-[long] River' (Sind.) The Elves' name for this great stream, one of the three principal rivers of Eriador. The Hobbits of the Shire knew it as the Brandywine (orig. *Bralda-hîm*, 'Heady-ale', more formally *Branda-nîn*, 'Border-water').

The Baranduin long served as a natural eastward defence of the Shire; so far as the Hobbits knew, it was crossable at only one point: the Bridge of Stonebows, the Great Bridge at the north end of the Buckland. (This arched bridge, built in the early years of the North-kingdom to speed the King's messengers between east and west, was known to the Hobbits as the Brandywine Bridge.)

The lesser river Withywindle ('Winding-willow-river') flowed into the Baranduin at the southerly edge of the Buckland; from here the enlarged river passed into the Overbourn marshes and then out of knowledge of the Hobbits at Sarn Ford. It eventually reached the Sea in a great estuary south of Harlindon.

Barazinbar The Dwarvish (Khuzdul) name for the great peak of the Misty Mountains known to Men as the Redhorn and to Elves as *Caradhras*, 'Red-peak' (Sind.) It was the most northerly of the three mountains under which lay the vast and ancient Dwarf-kingdom of Khazad-dûm – and under Barazinbar itself lay the fabulous *mithril* mother-lode. For many reasons, the exiled Dwarves of Moria were only too familiar with the shining buttresses and cruel eastern face of the mountain. The Dwarvish names for the other two were Zirak-zigil and Bundushathûr (Silvertine and Cloudyhead to Men, *Celebdil* and *Fanuidhol* to Elves).

See also MORIA.

Bard (I) of Esgaroth From 2941–77 Third Age, King of Dale; otherwise known as Bard the Bowman, for his deed of slaying the great dragon Smaug when it attacked the lake-town of Esgaroth (in 2941 Third Age). Bard subsequently led an army to the Lonely Mountain (Erebor), in alliance with Elves of Mirkwood, to exact compensation from the Dwarf-expedition which had stirred up the Dragon in the first place (see *The Hobbit*). A disastrous confrontation with the Dwarves was avoided by the timely arrival of an enemy hostile to all: the Goblins of the North. Bard's forces helped secure a victory against these Orcs in the ensuing Battle of Five Armies, after which he rebuilt Dale and became its first King since Girion. His son Bain ruled after him.

Bard II The son of Brand son of Bain, and thus the great grandson of Bard the Bowman. He was fourth King of Dale restored. After his father fell in battle at the doors of Erebor during the War of the Ring, Bard jointly led the combined forces of Men and Dwarves which raised the siege of the Lonely Mountain and drove the Easterlings away.

Bardings (from *Bardingas* 'Sons-of-Bard') The followers of King Bard ("the Bowman') of Esgaroth and his descendants; Men of Dale.

Bar-en-Danwedh 'House of Ransom' (Sind.) The bitter name given to the dwellings of the Dwarf Mîm upon Amon Rûdh: by Mîm himself, after his capture by Túrin Turambar.

Barliman Butterbur During the time of the War of the Ring, the Innkeeper of *The Prancing Pony*, chief hostelry of the Bree-land. His family had, in fact, owned and run this important Inn for generations.

Barrow-downs A line of grey-green slopes lying east of the Shire, between the Old Forest and Bree. They were a source of dread to Shire- and Bree-dwellers alike – and rightly so. And yet they were also the site of the most ancient memorials to Men of Middle-earth, having been revered by the ancestors of the Edain, before this people crossed the Blue Mountains into Beleriand during the First Age.

The hills were crowned with old stone circles and isolated dolmens, and with numerous 'barrows', or stone-chambered burial-mounds.

There, the early Men had buried the noble among their dead. Their descendants, in the Dúnedain kingdoms of Arnor and Arthedain, therefore revered the mounts (which they knew as *Tyrn Gorthad*, 'Mounds-of-Dread'), and later princes of Arthedain and Cardolan inhumed their own royal dead there in similar mounds. But after the final fall of the North-kingdom, evil spirits from faraway Angmar entered the mounds and animated the long-dead corpses. These Barrow-wights walked in the hollow places among the stone-rings and the Downs became a place of dread in nearby lands.

Barrowfield The burial-field which flanked the main road approaching Edoras, the capital of Rohan. There, all the Kings of the Mark were buried, together with their royal accoutrements, in long 'barrows', or grave-mounds. The First Line, (of nine Kings from Eorl the Young to Helm Hammerhand), lay buried in a row of nine mounds upon the west of the road; the Second Line, beginning with the barrow of Fréaláf Hildeson, stood to the east. There were seventeen mounds raised altogether during the Third Age.

Barrow-wights The Undead; according to ancient Mannish belief, certain evil spirits possessed the power to inhabit and animate the bodies of the Dead. See also BARROW-DOWNS.

Battle of Azanulbizar (2799 Third Age) Also known as the Battle of Nanduhirion. One of the great battles of the Third Age: a decisive confrontation between traditional enemies, and the conclusive battle of the War of the Dwarves and Orcs.

Losses on both side were heavy for, although the Dwarves had righteous anger and superb weaponry on their side, the sky was cloudy and no sun appeared over the darkling vale of Moria to hinder the light-hating Orcs of AZOG, gathered in ranks on the slopes above the ancient gates of the Dwarf-realm. The warriors of Thráin, Thrór's son, charged repeatedly but their initial assaults were repulsed with great loss. Indeed, many of the mighty among them had fallen before – almost too late – reinforcements finally arrived, from the Iron Hills. These were led by Náin, son of Grór. Náin was killed by Azog, but his own son Dáin (Ironfoot) slew the great Goblin and hewed off his head. The few surviving Orcs fled south.

But the numbers of Dwarvish dead were almost beyond counting; and much to their grief (for it went against custom), the Dwarves were forced to heap the bodies of their Fallen and burn them in a great fire, rather than leave them to wolf and worse. Accordingly, in

Dwarf-lore, a 'Burned Dwarf' was one of those warriors who fell at Azanulbizar. They were greatly honoured in memory.

Note: for a fuller account of the Battle, and the macabre events which caused it, see Appendix A III 'Durin's Folk'.

Battle of Bywater (November 3rd, 1419 Shire Reckoning, i.e. 3019 Third Age) The final battle of the War of the Ring, and the first to be fought in the Shire for nearly three hundred years (when Bandobras Took defeated an Orc-band, at the Battle of Greenfields in the Northfarthing).

Note: for a detailed account of the Bywater affair, see Book VI Chap. 8.

Battle of Dagorlad (3434 Second Age) The greatest battle of the Second Age, in which the forces of Sauron the Great were put to flight or utterly destroyed by the Last Alliance of Elves (led by Gilgalad) and Men (led by Elendil the Tall). It was a stupendous conflict: even a full Age later, the area north of the Black Gate was still widely known as 'Battle Plain'. The many graves of Men, Elves and Orcs there were eventually swallowed up by marshland.

After the victory of Dagorlad, the armies of the Last Alliance passed through the Black Gate, entered Mordor and laid siege to the Barad-dûr for seven years – before Sauron finally emerged to be overthrown, in a deadly combat which cost the lives of both Gilgalad and Elendil.

Battle of Dale (3019 Third Age) More properly, the second Battle of Dale (the first being known as the Battle of Five Armies), in which Men of Dale and Dwarves of Erebor were initially defeated by Easterlings of Sauron's rule. Kings Dáin Ironfoot of Erebor and Brand of Dale were both slain; but their forces withstood the siege that followed – and their sons, Thorin (III) Stonehelm and Bard II, later drove the attackers away from Dale, which was subsequently rebuilt.

Battle of Five Armies (2941 Third Age) Sometimes referred to as the first Battle of Dale. Its more popular name stems from the fact that no less than five separate armies participated, though not, of course, on five separate sides.

The Five Armies included: Elves, led by Thranduil of Mirkwood; Men, led by Bard of Esgaroth; Dwarves, led by Thorin Oakenshield and Dáin Ironfoot; a Goblin-host, led by Bolg son of Azog; and a Wolfe-horde which marched with the Orcs to plunder Erebor. A full account of this extraordinary battle – which so nearly developed into a disastrous conflict between Dwarves on the one hand, Elves and Men on the other – can be found in the Hobbit Bilbo Baggins' account of his journey to the East, titled by him *There and Back Again* (*The Hobbit*). A short summary must suffice here.

Having disturbed the dragon Smaug from his long sleep in the gutted halls of Erebor, the thirteen Dwarves of Thorin's party were able, in the Worm's absence, to re-enter the Lonely Mountain and take possession of the vast wealth inside. In the meantime, Smaug – angry with the lake-dwellers of Esgaroth for aiding the Dwarves – flew south to raze and burn their town; but in this attack, the Dragon was slain by Bard the Bowman, descendant of kings.

Gathering the surviving Lake-men together, Bard then promptly marched north to Erebor to demand compensation for damage to the lake-town (and a reward for slaying the Dragon). His Men were soon joined by an Elf-host of Mirkwood, with other grievances against the Dwarves. But Thorin – who now called himself Thorin II – had secretly sent to the Iron Hills for aid: and he refused to parley with these armies at his Gate, biding his time till Dáin Ironfoot's forces arrived – as he knew they would, after hearing of his need (not to mention the unguarded wealth of Erebor).

The Dwarves of the Iron Hills duly appeared and all seemed set for a tragic battle between the three armies when suddenly, from the North, there came a vast Goblin-host, in alliance with an army of Wolves. The Orcs had also heard of the death of the Dragon and had come to sack the Mountain. In the face of this new threat, Elves, Men and both Dwarf-forces joined together in a desperate alliance – and finally, with the aid of the Eagles and of Beorn the skin-changer, the Orcs and Wargs were defeated.

King Thorin II Oakenshield was mortally wounded and was later buried with the Arkenstone on his breast and the elf-sword Orcrist at his side; his kinsman, Dáin Ironfoot, then became King under the Mountain. Less haughty than Thorin, he wisely gave the Men and Elves their just compensations and became a great and wise King, finally falling in the (second) Battle of Dale (3019 Third Age).

Battle of Fornost (1974 Third Age[3]) The final battle of the Dúnedain and their allies against Angmar, in which the Elven forces of Círdan of Lindon and the host of Eärnur of Gondor defeated the Witch-king of Carn Dûm, destroying his army and the power of Angmar for ever. This victory was, however, too late to save King ARVEDUI or his kingdom of ARTHEDAIN.

Eärnur of Gondor was the son of King Eärnil, who had already promised to send to the aid of Arvedui if and when he could. So when word finally reached Eärnil that the Witch-king was about to assail Arthedain for the last time, the King kept his word – but before Gondor could assemble a sending force and reach the North-kingdom, Arvedui was dead. Nonetheless, Eärnur's expedition arrived in due course at Lindon, where Círdan then assembled a host of Elves, together with the surviving Dúnedain of the North. When all was ready, they crossed the river Lhûn and marched east.

By this time, however, the Witch-king was already in occupation of the Arthedain capital of Fornost. When he advanced contemptuously to meet his foes, the cavalry of Gondor circled round the Hills of Evendim to his north and fell upon his right flank. Frantically fleeing east and north, the retreating forces of Angmar were then attacked simultaneously by the pursuing cavalry and by another host of Elves, from Rivendell, led by Glorfindel. In this way, the forces of Angmar were so thoroughly routed that none of them survived. Angmar never arose again and the Witch-king was driven from the North.

Battle of Greenfields (2747 Third Age) See BANDOBRAS 'BULL-ROARER' TOOK.

Battle of Sudden Flame A translation of the Grey-elven words *Dagor Bragollach*; being the name given to the Fourth Battle of Beleriand, in which Morgoth overthrew the Siege of Angband and made deep inroads into the kingdoms of his enemies, slaying Fingolfin the High King and overrunning many leagues of territory. It took place in the 455th Year of the Sun, and was the foreshadow of the still greater defeats to follow.

The Battle itself is carefully described elsewhere.[4] So grievous is that tale that few will wish for a recapitulation in these pages. It is worth noting, however, that the name of the Battle refers to the unusual stratagem employed by Morgoth to wreak confusion amongst his foes: for his first onslaught was a great out-pouring of fume and fire from Angband, which kindled the grass of Ard-galen and set the North literally ablaze. (Ard-galen was afterwards called Anfauglith, the Gasping Dust.)

Battle of the Camp (1944 Third Age) One of the many battles fought in defence of the realm of Gondor, after the waning of its power had led to repeated assaults from Easterlings.

The latest of these invaders, known as Wainriders (see EASTER-

LINGS), had already been waging war with Gondor for almost a century by the year 1944. Then King Ondoher fell in battle with them north of the Black Gate, and the northern wing of the Wainriders streamed into Ithilien (the lands of Gondor between the Great River and the Mountains of Shadow).

There, believing Gondor defeated, they camped and feasted, before preparing to despoil the lands across the River, where Minas Anor lay virtually defenceless. But unknown to their chiefs the Captain of the Southern Army of Gondor, Eärnil, had meanwhile defeated the Haradrim, the Wainriders' southern allies. Force-marching north, Eärnil came against the camp where the Wainriders were revelling, and easily routed them. They were driven north in confusion and terror, and many of them were swallowed up in the Dead Marshes.

As a reward for this victory, Pelendur, Steward of Gondor, offered the crown of Ondoher to Eärnil (although it had already been claimed by ARVEDUI of Arthedain). Eärnil accepted and became as wise a King as he was great a warrior.

Battle of the Crossings of Erui (1447 Third Age) The decisive battle of Gondor's civil war – the Kin-strife – in which the hitherto-deposed King, Eldacar, defeated the forces of the usurper Castamir in a great fight at the fords of the river Erui, in Lebennin.

Much of the valour of Gondor perished on that evil day, but Castamir also died at Eldacar's own hand, and the rightful Line was thus restored. However, the sons of Castamir escaped the holocaust and later came to Umbar, where they established a lordship independent of Gondor; and, for ever after, the Corsairs of Umbar were a peril to Gondor and a constant menace to her coastal fiefs.

Battle of the Crossings of Poros (2885 Third Age) This crucial victory by the armies of Gondor against her ancient foes, the Haradrim of the South, was won with the timely aid of her new-found allies, the Riders of Rohan. Folcwine of the Mark thus fulfilled the OATH OF EORL – though his twin sons, Fastred and Folcred, were slain in the battle. They were buried together upon the shores of the river Poros in a single mound.

Battle of the Field of Celebrant (2510 Third Age) An historic battle of Gondor, in which near defeat at the hands of an implacable enemy was exchanged for an overwhelming victory and a new ally.

When a massive invasion of the BALCHOTH suddenly crossed the river Anduin in 2510, Cirion, twelfth Ruling Steward of Gondor, quickly moved to deploy his Northern Army into the area. But as this force marched up from the south, it was cut off, and pushed north in disarray over the river Limlight. There, it was assaulted by a host of Orcs of the Mountains and forced towards the Anduin. All hope seemed lost when the sound of 'great horns of the North wildly blowing' was first heard in Gondor: Eorl the Young, of Éothéod, had answered an earlier summons for aid, late though it seemed. His Riders broke like a storm on the flanks and rear of the Balchoth and harried them to the death across the deserted fields of Calenardhon, the northern province of Gondor they had so often raided prior to their invasion. As a reward to Eorl and his people, Cirion ceded this sparsely peopled region to the Riders; they re-named it the *Riddermark*, the 'Mark-of-the-Riders' (although it became known in Gondor as *Rohan*).

Seee also BALCHOTH.

Battle of the Gladden Fields (Year 2, Third Age) Following hard on the heels of the great victories at the end of the Second Age – when the Barad-dûr was cast down and Sauron overthrown – came this military disaster, where much of the royal blood of Arnor was spilled.

It began when Isildur was marching north to take up the High-kingship of both Gondor and Arnor, having spent the two previous years in Gondor, instructing his nephew Meneldil, Anárion's son, in kingship. His party (which included his three eldest sons) was ambushed on the banks of the Anduin south of the river Gladden by a multitude of Orcs of the Mountains.

The Dúnedain were too few to effect much against so many and most were slain in defence of Isildur. (In fact only three Men ever returned.) When all was lost, Isildur jumped into the Great River, hoping to swim to safety, for the Ring on his finger had the power of rendering him invisible. And so he might have escaped – but, of its own accord, the Ring slipped from Isildur's finger, betraying him to the Orcs, who then saw him and shot him with arrows. The Great Ring then sank into the mud at the river-bottom, to lie undiscovered for thousands of years.

Battle of the Hornburg (3019 Third Age) Sometimes called the Battle of Helm's Deep, for this great affray of the War of the Ring took place beneath the walls of that chain of fortifications in Western Rohan known as Helm's Deep (or Helm's Gate). The Hornburg tower was the strongest redoubt of that defensive complex.

The situation leading up to the battle was as follows: already weakened by internal subversion and treachery, Rohan was increasingly pinned between the rival powers of Mordor and the traitor Saruman, both inexorable foes. The more immediate threat came from Isengard, fortress of Saruman the White, who – in his eagerness to destroy the power of the Riders and so extend his own dominion east and south – struck too soon.

Saruman's first invasion came in February 3019, when his armies (of Orcs and Dunlendings) attempted to force the Fords of Isen, the river which bordered the Westfold of Rohan. At that time his forces were rebuffed, but the Rohirrim themselves suffered great losses, including King Théoden's only son Théodred. On March 2nd Saruman again struck at the Crossings – and this time the defenders, led by Erkenbrand lord of Westfold, were routed and scattered in the darkness. The Army of Isengard flooded into Westfold Vale, bringing fire and razing the countryside as they advanced south with terrible speed.

Earlier that same day a powerful force of Riders of the Mark, led by the aged King Théoden himself (and accompanied by Gandalf, Aragorn, the Elf Legolas and the Dwarf Gimli), had set out from Edoras, many leagues to the east, for the purpose of reinforcing Erkenbrand. This force was still riding west on the following day when news came of the defeat at the Isen. On Gandalf's advice, Théoden's cavalry then turned aside and rode for Helm's Gate, a fortress of Rohan which lay in the northern vales of the White Mountains, some thirty leagues south of Isengard. It was the strongest place in all Rohan (save Dunharrow), and accordingly Théoden hoped to gather there all that survived of the Westfoldmen and so withstand a siege. But although he indeed found a number of defenders already on the walls and in the Hornburg when he reached Helm's Gate, the invading army that had followed him was far larger than his worst expectations.

About midnight, the enemy reached the outer fortifications, and the Orcs and Dunlendings began their fierce and repeated attempts to storm the Deeping Wall and its two embattled towers (the Deeping Tower and the Hornburg itself). So great were their numbers that they thought nothing of their immense losses and the Men of Rohan were sorely tried. The Isengarders also carried devilish devices, and shortly before dawn they used a 'blasting-fire' to breach the Deeping Wall and to carry it by assault. The defenders were swept away – or back into the Deep itself – and the Deeping Tower also fell to the enemy.

Most of the Rohirrim and their allies had meanwhile retreated to the Hornburg, and there they now awaited the dawn, for it was believed that all Orcs feared the Sun and fought less well under its light (though actually the Uruk-hai of Isengard were not much handicapped in this way, and the Men of Dunland were not affected at all). In any case, not even the Hornburg could long be held against the strength still arrayed outside its tall gates. Therefore, preferring to risk all in a final sortie, King Théoden chose to await the first rays of the Sun and then ride forth in a great charge. '. . . I will not end here, taken like an old badger in a trap,' were his words.[5]

So with the dawn came the King, mounted upon his horse Snowmane, surrounded by the Riders of his Guard, with his spear in rest and his shield blazing in the morning light. On his order, simultaneously, the great Horn of Helm rang out from the Tower, echoing and re-echoing in the chasm behind the Wall. The Isengarders were overthrown by this sudden sortie, and the Riders charged down the ramp and clove through them to reach the Dike. Behind them came the defenders of the caves in the Deep (whence many had fled when the Deeping Wall was taken), driving their enemies before them like chaff. And so the invaders found their siege broken and their assault brought to nothing; for the sortie utterly confused them, and the light of the Sun discomfited them, and above all they feared the ghostly horns which echoed without ceasing in their ears. In a state of complete rout, the Isengarders scrambled across the Dike in an attempt to reach the open coomb where they might again have the advantage: for they were still a great army.

But during the night, Erkenbrand of Westfold had force-marched across the Vale and the foothills, together with all the survivors of the second battle at the Isen; and he too now appeared on the west wall of the coomb, his forces extended in open skirmishing order. With Erkenbrand was Gandalf, mounted upon Shadowfax. And across the coomb, barring all escape, lay a great and sinister forest which had seemingly sprung up in the hours of darkness: rank upon rank of silent, watching trees, their roots buried deep in the grass, waiting. These were the HUORNS, the sentient trees of Fangorn Forest, who had crossed the Westfold Vale during the night, having been sent to the aid of Rohan by Treebeard. Above all, these strange creatures hated Orcs and desired to be revenged for many atrocities committed by the Isengarders in Fangorn during previous years.

Thus the Orcs were menaced on three separate sides, and the final charge of the Rohirrim completed their destruction. For, rather than face the spears of the Riders, they fled in panic under the shadow of the trees; there they died, caught and strangled one by one. So perished most of the Army of Saruman.

Note: the victory of the Hornburg had a further effect: by eliminating the threat from Isengard it freed the majority of the Rohirrim to ride to the aid of their ally Gondor, which was also then in great straits. In this way the Battle of the Hornburg came to be accounted one of the great clashes of the War of the Ring, second in scale only to the Battle of the Pelennor Fields, which took place a short time afterwards. In this greater conflict the Riders of Rohan also played a crucial part.

Battle of the Pelennor Fields (3019 Third Age) The greatest battle of the Third Age. For a full account of this epic encounter – in which Mordor's first real assault upon Gondor during the War of the Ring was thrown back with great loss – readers are advised to refer to Book V Chaps. 4–6; here a shorter description, aided by diagrams, may be of interest.

The chief defence of Minas Tirith lay in its indomitable city walls and great Gate, through which no enemy had ever passed. In addition, the farmlands around the city – the Fields of Pelennor – were further fortified. Begun by the far-sighted Steward Ecthelion II some eighty years before the War of the Ring, this outer defence consisted of a great perimeter wall, called the *Rammas*, and a pair of forts situated at the point where the main road out of the City ran along a causeway through Osgiliath and across the River.

However, by the time of the War, the forces of Gondor were grown too few to defend the Rammas with any hope of success; and Sauron's first assault carried his armies directly across the River, through Osgiliath, and – despite the heroic efforts of the defenders of the Causeway Forts – through the Rammas and into the Fields of the Pelennor. Those who manned the forts and the wall were forced, therefore, to make a speedy retreat across some ten miles of open land to the safety of the city. This withdrawal covered by Faramir's rearguard, was supported by a sortie from Minas Tirith, with the entire remaining strength of Gondor's cavalry (under Imrahil) thrown in to prevent the enemy overrunning the retiring defenders (see Diagram 1).

Nightfall found the city of Minas Tirith besieged on three sides by the army of Minas Morgul, first finger of the Hand of Sauron. For two nights and one dark day, the enemy remained just outside the city walls, digging fire-pits and bringing up great siege engines

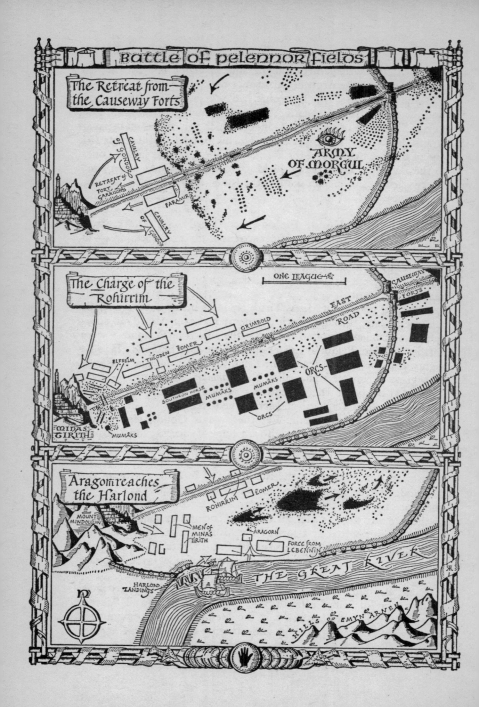

to test the defences with a gruesome and demoralizing hail. Finally, just before dawn on the third day of the Siege, they brought forward the great battering-ram, *Grond* (named after the Mace of Morgoth). Wielded by Trolls and shielded by Orc-archers, this weapon soon demolished the City Gate, and the Lord of the Nazgûl, mounted upon a great black horse, then prepared to enter where no enemy had ever passed before.

At this point the Battle of the Pelennor Fields began. Hardly had the Black Captain passed the Gate when, from the North, came the sound that no one, defender or besieger alike, had expected to hear: the battle-horns of Rohan, wildly blowing. By a strategem, the Rohirrim had avoided the forces of Sauron stationed on the South Road to block such reinforcements, and were even then breaking on the northern flank of the besiegers like surf upon a ridge of black sand. Sweeping all before them, the Riders soon cleared the entire northern half of the Pelennor (see Diagram 2), cramming the enemy to the south of the Causeway Road. Théoden's cavalry scattered the Orcs, drove the guards of the war-engines into the fire-pits and routed the Southron horsemen – though the King himself was then slain by the Nazgûl-lord.

Yet events might still have gone badly for Gondor; for in their fierce onset, the Rohirrim had not kept a broad front but had penetrated where they might, leaving great areas unfought, especially around the individual war-beasts of Harad. The forces of Morgul, now led by Gothmog (the Black Captain had been slain and Théoden avenged), were preparing their counter-attack when, to the dismay of Gondor, black sails were sighted upon the Anduin, heading for the Harlond landings. But the ships that bore the black sails were filled with fresh forces from Lebennin and the southern fiefs, brought thence by Aragorn, the Heir of Isildur; and the leading ship flew a standard bearing the White Tree and Seven Stars, emblems of the ancient royalty of Gondor.

And so the forces of Morgul were caught between the Wall, the City, the River and the Rohirrim (Diagram 3). The Rohirrim, now mainly unhorsed, continued to cut their way south; the men of Lebennin with Aragorn at their head strode north; and a sortie from Minas Tirith charged east. Only to the River could the forces of Sauron flee – and there they fought and died, or perished in the waters.

See also MOUNDS OF MUNDBURG.

Battle of the Powers The third of the Wars of Arda, in which the

Valar, after many ages during which they had not contested the rule of Mortal Lands with Melkor the Evil Ainu (Morgoth as he was afterwards named), came swiftly back and overthrew him for the sake of the Quendi (the Elves), who had at last awoken in Middle-earth and were in peril thereby.

It is said in the traditions of the Elves (who actually remembered little or nothing of that battle) that the first of Melkor's strongholds to be destroyed was his north-western fastness of Angband, then newly-built and commanded by Sauron, a Maia and a servant of Melkor. Then the Valar, who were led in the battle by Oromë and Tulkas, pressed forward to besiege Utumno, Melkor's older and greater stronghold. For long years this siege continued; and in the tumult the shape of the northern lands was changed – not for the first time, nor for the last. Eventually Utumno was broken for ever and Melkor was taken, a prisoner, back to Valinor, there to be in-carcerated in the Halls of Mandos for a period of three Ages.

Yet in thus imprisoning Melkor and thereby hoping for his repent-ance, the Valar made a similar mistake to that which Ar-Pharazôn (much later) committed with Sauron. (An underestimation of the enduring power of evil is indeed an abiding factor in the affairs of Arda.) For after the required three Ages had expired, Melkor was released – and there, in Valinor, he was able to work the greatest evil he ever committed. He poisoned the Two Trees and stole the Silmarils, fleeing back to Middle-earth to re-establish his realm of Angband (for Utumno had been utterly destroyed in the Battle of the Powers); and within a count of years the Valar were again forced to take the field against him. This was the second Battle of the Powers, the GREAT BATTLE which brought about their dark adversary's final downfall and expulsion from the circles of the World.

Battle of Unnumbered Tears A translation of the Grey-elven *Nirnaeth Arnoediad*, being the name given in the traditions of the Eldar and the Edain to the Fifth and final Battle of Beleriand, in which Morgoth the Enemy finally and for ever overthrew the Elf-kingdoms and the realms of Men, and made himself Master of Middle-earth for the first time since the Years of the Trees. It took place in the 470th Year of the Sun, and was the greatest defeat ever suffered by Elves or Men in their long wars against Morgoth or Sauron.

Like all the Battles of Beleriand, this great conflict is described elsewhere[6]. Few will wish to have that tale of grief retold in these pages, for many Elves and Men (and Dwarves) of renown were slain:

Fingon the High King, the son of Fingolfin, son of Finwë (the first to die because of the Silmarils); Gelmir son of Guilin of Nargothrond; Azaghâl the Dwarf-king of Belegost, defeater of the Dragon Glaurung; Huor of the Edain, together with most of the Men of Dor-lómin; and many more besides. All the Elves of Mithrim were slain. Only Turgon King of Gondolin – now High King of the Noldor – escaped, with most of his people. Indeed, this was the first battle of the long war to which Turgon had brought his host; but it availed the Elves and Men not at all.

Morgoth's victory was now all but complete. Nowhere in Middle-earth, save in Doriath, Gondolin and Nargothrond, was there a realm or an organized people to withstand him; but Thingol of Doriath took little part in this war (though despite his renunciation of the works of the Noldor he was enmeshed in their destruction before the end), and Morgoth's armies swept where they would throughout Beleriand. Nargothrond and Gondolin fell. The War of the Great Jewels was over. What little hope remained now lay in the West.

Battle Pit The mass grave for those ruffians of Saruman who perished at the BATTLE OF BYWATER. It had previously been a sand-pit.

Battle Plain A translation of the Sindarin word *Dagorlad*.

Battles of Beleriand The name given in the lore of the Eldar and the Edain to the five great battles fought against Morgoth the Enemy in the War of the Great Jewels during the First Age of Middle-earth. The first three of these battles were won by the Eldar; the last two were decisive victories for Morgoth, and cost the Elves the war.

The First Battle took place in the Dark Year, after the poisoning of the Trees and the flight of Morgoth to Middle-earth, but before the rising of the Moon or Sun. Seeking to eliminate the Sindar from Beleriand, Morgoth sent out two great hosts, one hunting south-west, the other south-east. For months they swept all before them. But Thingol had sent to Ossiriand for help, and the Elves of Doriath and Ossiriand fought a great battle against the Orcs in East Beleriand, and crushed them; though DENETHOR of Ossiriand was slain. However the western battle was lost by the Sindar, and the Elves of the Havens were driven to the edge of the Sea. Thingol strengthened Doriath in expectation of more battles to come – but before either side could make further moves the northern sky was lit by a great burning: Fëanor and the High-elves of his House had returned to

Middle-earth to regain the Silmarils. And Thingol of Doriath took no further direct part in the War.

The Second Battle is called the 'Battle-Under-Stars', the *Dagor-nuin-Giliath*, for it was fought directly after the First Battle; and the Moon had not yet appeared in the skies of Middle-earth. Fëanor, having landed at Losgar, swiftly occupied Mithrim; and his encampment was attacked by Orcs from Angband. They were heavily defeated, and the Noldor pursued them northwards, as far as the gates of Angband. There, on the plain, Fëanor, who was leading the pursuit, was mortally wounded by Gothmog, Lord of the Balrogs of Angband. Nevertheless it was accounted a victory for the Eldar.

The Third Battle is named *Dagor Aglareb*, the 'Glorious Battle'; and it was fought in the 60th Year of the Sun. As its name implies, it was an overwhelming victory for the Eldar. A sudden assault from Angband was contained and trapped north of Dorthonion, on the plains of Ard-galen; and not an Orc of that army ever returned to Morgoth's domain. This was the last and greatest of the victories won by the Eldar; and it was followed by the Long Peace, which lasted for four hundred years.

The Fourth Battle was the 'Battle of Sudden Flame', the *Dagor Bragollach*. Long years of peace had lulled the Eldar – now reinforced by new allies, the Edain – into a false sense of security. In the Year of the Sun 455 Morgoth took advantage of this by unleashing all his might in one, crushing blow. And his armies were aided by rivers of fire, which ran ahead of them and kindled the plain of Ard-galen, and even the north- and eastward-facing slopes of the mountain ramparts of Mithrim and Dorthonion. Ard-galen was transformed into a charred desert; and the Siege was overthrown. Many of the realms opposed to Morgoth were swept away; and hereafter the survivors were on the defensive. It was too late, moreover, for the Eldar and Edain to reverse the momentum of their fortunes.

Fifteen years after the Dagor Bragollach was fought the Fifth and last Battle of Beleriand, which the Elves called *Nirnaeth Arnoediad*, 'Unnumbered Tears', or the Day of Lamentation. They do not term it a battle, for indeed it was a disaster beyond their worst foretellings, a catastrophe, a massacre. Morgoth was utterly victorious and the Elf-kingdoms and the realms of Men were extinguished. And yet it had been intended to be a victory for the Eldar; indeed, the day was planned to begin with the enemies of Morgoth manoeuvring on the plains of Anfauglith (Ard-galen), in order to decoy Morgoth into a trap. But Morgoth was fully informed of their intentions (see ULDOR THE ACCURSED), and himself sprang his enemies' trap, before they were ready. Treachery within the ranks of the allies nullified their abundant heroism; and Fingon, High King, was slain. Only the host of Gondolin made a successful retreat from that field. The last military hope of the Elves and the Edain was destroyed for ever. Henceforward Morgoth was Lord of Middle-earth. The War of the Great Jewels had been fought – and lost.

Battles of the Fords of Isen (3019 Third Age) Two fierce clashes, only days apart, which took place during the War of the Ring between the Rohirrim of Westfold and the armies of Saruman the White, lord of Isengard. Both battles were fought at the strategic Fords of Isen, chief crossing-point into Rohan from the north. The first occurred on February 25th, when Théodred, son of King Théoden and Second Marshal of the Mark, was slain – although the Rohirrim were rallied by Erkenbrand, lord of Westfold, and the Isengarders were held off at the river. Nevertheless, the Orcs and Wild Men attacked again, on March 2nd, and in the torrent Erkenbrand was swept away. The Army of Isengard poured into Rohan, but was afterwards crushed before the walls of Helm's Deep (see BATTLE OF THE HORNBURG).

Battle-under-stars A translation of *Dagor-nuin-Giliath*; see BATTLES OF BELERIAND.

Bauglir One of the names given to Melkor by the Elves of Middle-earth. It means 'the Gaoler' in the Grey-elven tongue.

Bay of Belfalas 'The Windy Bay of Bel', greatest bay in western Middle-earth, lying between Cape Andrast and Umbar.
   See also *Note* under BELFALAS.

Beacon-hills From time immemorial Gondor used every means of communication available to her in order to safeguard and unite the realm. The most useful aids were, of course, the *palantíri*, the Seeing-stones of Númenor. But with the waning of the Third Age, many of these Stones became lost to the Dúnedain, and Gondor was forced to revive older, more primitive means of swift communication with her provinces and allies.
   The chain of seven hills in the eastern range of the White Mountains, running through the province of Anórien from Minas Tirith to the Firienwood, on the borders of Rohan, might have been placed there specifically for Gondor's purposes. A beacon lit atop one could be made out from the next, and so on; in this way a warning – of invasion or any other sudden peril – might be passed between Rohan

and Gondor in the time it took to kindle seven baskets of pitch-soaked firewood.

The seven beacon-hills of Anórien were: Halifirien (the most northerly), Calenhad, Min-Rimmon, Erelas, Nardol, Eilenach, and Amon Dîn (the southernmost).

Note: two of their names, *Eilenach* and *Rimmon*, were in a forgotten pre-Westron tongue, the language of the Men of the White Mountains during the Dark Years. The remainder were in the Sindarin nomenclature of the Dúnedain (e.g., *Nardol* 'Fire-head').

'Beater' and 'Biter' Translations of Orc-names given in antiquity to the famous Elf-swords *Glamdring* ('Foe-hammer') and *Orcrist* ('Orc-cleaver'). The weapons were discovered by members of Thorin Oakenshield's expedition to Erebor, in 2941 Third Age, in a Troll's lair. (See *The Hobbit*, Chap. 4.)

Beechbone The translation of the (unknown) name of an Ent of Fangorn – sadly a fatality in the Ents' assault upon Isengard during the War of the Ring.

Belecthor I From 2628–55 Third Age, the fifteenth Ruling Steward of Gondor.

Belecthor II From 2811–72 Third Age, the twenty-first Ruling Steward of Gondor. The last White Tree of Minas Tirith died with him and, ominously, no sapling could then be found to replace it. The dead Tree was left standing.

Beleg Strongbow One of the mightiest of the Grey-elves of Beleriand in the Elder Days, chief of the Marchwardens of Thingol's Hidden Kingdom of Doriath and friend and companion of Túrin Turambar.

Beleg was named *Cúthalion* ('the Strong Bow') in the speech of the Grey-elves. He was Thingol's chief captain (for all the strength of Doriath was arrayed on its frontiers), fought at the Nirnaeth Arnoediad, and took a part in many of the deeds of those times. Among these was the Hunting of Carcharoth, in company with Beren and Thingol himself. In later years Beleg was bidden by Thingol to seek out and safeguard Túrin Húrin's son, who was Thingol's ward. Beleg indeed found Túrin, and afterwards fought at his side in a little-known campaign in the lands of the upper Teiglin, during the years following the Battle of Numberless Tears. At the onset of this quest, Thingol had given to Beleg an ancient sword of power from his armoury, named ANGLACHEL. Now Beleg wielded the weapon more often than his great bow, for the war was close work.

But, as is told in *The Silmarillion*[7], the refuge of the guerillas (for such they were) was betrayed, as such refuges often are. Beleg was badly wounded and left for dead in the attack which followed – and Túrin was taken alive by the Orcs, who bore him away northward towards Angband. But Beleg recovered, and, with the aid of a refugee Elf named Gwindor, hunted down the Orcs who had captured Túrin. Then Beleg went stealthily to release the unconscious Túrin; but in severing Túrin's bonds the black sword Anglachel slipped, and its point struck Túrin's foot – he awakened, and forthwith slew Beleg in the dark, thinking him an Orc. Túrin grieved greatly for his friend, and made a song afterwards, named *Laer Cú Beleg*, the Song of the Great Bow. Beleg's sword, Anglachel, he took for himself, and bore it until his life's end.

Beleg From 946–1029 Third Age, the second King of Arthedain.

Belegaer 'Great-Sea [of the West]' (Sind.) The name given in Beleriand to the sea which lay between the shores of Valinor and the coastlands of Middle-earth.

Belegorn From 2148–2204 Third Age, the fourth Ruling Steward of Gondor.

Belegost 'Mighty-fortress' (Sind.) The name given by the Elves to the Dwarf-city of *Gabilgathol*, built by the Khazâd (the Dwarves) early in the First Age – a full Age before the extinguishing of the Light of the Trees in Valinor and the return of Morgoth – in the east of the Blue Mountains, north of Mount Dolmed. (It was known to Men as *Mickleburg*.[8])

From here, and from their twin city of *Nogrod* (Tumunzahar, the 'Hollow-Peak'), the Dwarves mounted journeys and trading expeditions into Thingol's Beleriand. They were thus the first new 'speaking-peoples' encountered by the Sindar,[9] for an Age and more had still to pass before Men would awake and likewise cross the Blue Mountains into Beleriand. It was soon afterwards that Thingol sought the counsel of the Dwarves of Belegost, and they aided him in the planning and building of Menegroth, the 'Thousand Caves' of Doriath; for this service they were paid in pearls.

Intercourse between the Dwarves of Nogrod and Belegost and the High-elves, however, was less happy. The Noldor, indeed, for the most part despised the 'Stunted People', as they called them, and

Caranthir the son of Fëanor, who held the easternmost regions of Beleriand, the nearest to the Dwarf-kingdoms, was haughty in his dealing with them. (Here perhaps lies the beginning of the subsequent enmity between the peoples – another fruit of the Oath taken by the Sons of Fëanor at the outset of their rebellion.) However, mounting danger drew the Dwarves and the Eldar closer together, and a satisfactory trading partnership was eventually arranged, to the mutual profit of both parties.

The first name of any King of Belegost to be recorded in the histories of the Eldar is that of Azaghâl; he it was who brought his sturdy people to the Nirnaeth Arnoediad, and who fought faithfully in alliance with the Sons of Fëanor. It was his people who defeated the Dragon Glaurung, though Azaghâl himself was killed in the fight.

But the defeat of the Eldar in the War against Morgoth brought about a further sundering of the two peoples, Elves and Dwarves. It is told that it was Dwarves from Nogrod who slew King Thingol in his own halls, and who tried to steal the Nauglamir, which had been made long before by their forefathers for Finrod of Nargothrond. The Dwarves of Belegost, however, did not side with their kinsmen in this deed, or in the grievous deeds which followed. Yet the deeds themselves had been performed, and henceforth deep distrust was to come between these two ancient 'speaking-peoples'. And the Dwarves were likewise caught in the ruin of Beleriand: for when Morgoth was overthrown, and Angband broken, the shape of the lands was changed, and the Sea flowed in to cover Beleriand, and a great gulf was made through the Blue Mountains, casting down Mount Dolmed and drowning the cities of Nogrod and Belegost, though they lay on the eastern side of the mountains. But the survivors went to Moria in after years, swelling its numbers, and true to the tradition of their forefathers, soon struck up another agreeable relationship with the Noldor – which came to nothing, or nearly nothing, in the end.

Belegund One of the Edain of the First House, the son of Bregolas brother of Barahir, and elder brother of Baragund; Belegund was also the father of Rían wife of Huor (of the Third House) and thus the grandfather of Tuor and great-grandsire of Eärendil the Mariner. (His younger brother Baragund was the grandsire of Túrin Turambar.)

Belegund and his brother were among the twelve companions of Barahir on Dorthonion, outlaws who waged guerilla warfare against the forces of Morgoth in the years immediately following the Dagor Bragollach; as is told in *The Silmarillion*, both were among those of their band slain by Orcs after their betrayal by Gorlim the Unhappy.

See LINES OF DESCENT.

Beleriand 'Country of Balar' (Sind.) The land of the Grey-elves during the Elder Days, and the most westerly Elven-realm anywhere in Middle-earth – until its sudden destruction at the end of the First Age. Like Númenor, it was swallowed under the Sea.

The manner of its founding was as follows: in the Beginning of Days, from across the Blue Mountains, there came the Three Kindreds of the Eldar, the 'West-elves', moving ever West into the wide and beautiful lands that lay beyond.

The Eldar were following the ancient call of the Valar, who had long before summoned all Elvenkind to attempt the Great Journey West across the Sea to Valinor. Two of the Kindreds eventually completed the Journey, leaving Beleriand and taking ship into the Uttermost West, where they dwelt for untold years in bliss and everlasting life. However, most of the third Kindred, afterwards called *Sindar* (Grey-elves), fell so deeply in love with the lands west of the *Ered Luin* (Blue Mountains) that they lingered on the coasts and in the forests, unmoved by the hereditary Sea-longing and taking instead a keen delight in the beech-forests, willow-meads and mountains of their new country. Thingol Greycloak, father of Lúthien Tinúviel, was their King.

As is told elsewhere, many of the Grey-elves' long-sundered Noldorin Kindred – 'High-elves' of Eldamar – rebelled against the Valar and came back to Middle-earth in exile towards the end of the First Age. In their attempts to recover the stolen Silmarils by force from the renegade Vala Morgoth, these High-elves received aid from their Grey-elven kin in Beleriand and (later) from Men. But all were, in the end, completely defeated: the High-elven fortresses of Nargothrond and Gondolin (established at the beginning of the Wars of Beleriand) were destroyed after years of bitter fighting, and Beleriand, beloved home of the Grey-elves, became infested by evil things from Angband.

It is also told that the Valar, finally taking pity on the plight of the Elves and Men of Middle-earth, came in the end to their aid; that Morgoth the Enemy was overthrown; that his evil realm in the North was destroyed, and that Beleriand itself was overwhelmed in the same cataclysm and cast under the waves. At the beginning of the Second Age, all that remained of Beleriand was Lindon (the former country of Ossiriand), divided into the two capes of Forlindon and Harlindon. At that time, Havens were established there for those of Elvenkind who wished finally to heed the call of the Valar and sail West over Sea. Throughout the Second Age these lands of Lindon were ruled by Gil-galad, last High-elven king in Middle-earth.

Note: for a fuller account of the lands and peoples of Beleriand, see *The Silmarillion, passim,* but especially pp. 118–24; for information concerning the origin of the name, see p. 319.

Belfalas The name given to both the greatest bay in western Middle-earth and a coastal province of Gondor – a cape which thrust into the Bay of Belfalas from north of the Anduin delta. The chief city of the province was the sea-washed tower of Dol Amroth, with its ancient Elf-havens on the shores below.

Note: it is possible that the *Bel-* ingredient in this name is an echo of Beleriand, which in the Third Age lay under the Sea.

Belladonna Baggins The well-to-do and reputedly eccentric wife of Bungo and mother of Bilbo Baggins. She was a child of Gerontius, 'the Old Took'.

Bell Gamgee Wife of Hamfast Gamgee ('the Gaffer'), and the mother of Samwise, the youngest of her three sons.

Belmarie A poetic invention in the Hobbit style, supposedly a name of Elvish origin. It occurs in the poem 'Errantry', which is included in *The Adventures of Tom Bombadil,* and it refers to a fanciful Elf-kingdom.

Belthil 'Holy-light' (Sind.) The name given by King Turgon of Gondolin to the Image he wrought of the Tree Telperion; it stood in the Tower of the King, together with its sister-tree, Glingal, the Image of Laurelin the Golden. Both image-trees were destroyed in the sack of Gondolin.

Belthronding The name given by Beleg the Elf to his great bow, his skilful use of which brought him the admiring appellation *Cúthalion,* 'Strongbow'.

Béma The name given in the Northern Mannish tongue to the Vala *Araw* (Sind.), whose High-elven name was *Oromë.*

See *Silmarillion* p. 363.

Bent World A term for the planet Earth, in its later (and current) aspect as a spherical body – as opposed to the 'Straight World' of remote antiquity.

Bëor (the Old) The name given by his people to Balan, chieftain of the First House of the Edain, after he had abdicated his chieftainship (in favour of his son Baran), in order to go to Nargothrond and serve the Elven-king Finrod. He was the first of the Edain to take service with one of the Noldor. (*Bëor* means 'vassal' in the Mannish tongue spoken at that time.) Bëor, or Balan, was indeed the leader of the first Mannish people ever to enter Beleriand; and from the moment he first spoke with Finrod, his allegiance to the Eldar seems never to have been in doubt. For this reason he was renowned among the High-elves and members of his House were afterwards treated with great honour by all the Eldar. He was a forefather of all the heroes and Elf-friends among the Edain. Bëor died in his 94th year, forty-four years after he had changed his name and his allegiance.

Beorn In the late Third Age, Beorn was the chieftain of the clan of Northern Men whose traditional duty it was to maintain the safety of the trade routes from Eriador to Mirkwood, particularly over the high pass of the Misty Mountains and across the Ford of Carrock. Bilbo Baggins attributed many strange characteristics to Beorn (see *The Hobbit*, Chap. 7); whatever the truth of these stories, he was certainly a Man of great (oddly bear-like) strength, fiery temper and a suspicious nature. Like all his clan (called *Beornings*), he hated Orcs even more than strangers – and thus later came to play a vital role in the Battle of Five Armies, where his opportune arrival and berserk rage helped to crush the Goblin army. He personally slew Bolg, the chief of the Orcs.

The Beornings were akin to the Éothéod and to the Men of the Vales of Anduin; their language was a Northern dialect related to the language of Dale.

Note: these people were, by repute, bakers of extraordinary talent. Their honey-cakes were much praised by travellers who used the high pass and the Ford of Carrock.

Beornings See BEORN above.

Bereg The name of one of the great-grandsons of Bëor the Old, a leader of a fragment of the First House of the Edain who were afraid to settle in Beleriand and who returned over the Blue Mountains into Eriador, so vanishing into the limbo of history.

Note: this people may have been remote ancestors of the Men of the White Mountains, and of their degenerated descendants, the Dunlendings.

Beregond From 2763–2811 Third Age, the twentieth Ruling Steward of Gondor – and one of the mightiest soldiers in her history: in 2758–59, while still the heir to the Stewardship, he defeated a long-prepared attack by the Corsairs of Umbar and simultaneously sent aid to Rohan, which was then suffering grievously from the effects of the Long Winter and Dunlending invasion.

Beregond During the War of the Ring, a man-at-arms in the Third Company of the Guard of the Citadel of Minas Tirith – and the comrade and guide of Peregrin Took. He was devoted to Faramir (son of Steward Denethor II) for whom he 'risked all, to save him from death'.[10] For his decisiveness and courage, Beregond was afterwards honoured by the King and appointed Captain of Faramir's personal Guard.

Beren Erchamion The memories of Men reach far back into the Elder Days, beyond the rise of Númenor, into times when the 'Fathers-of-Men', the Edain, fought in Beleriand as allies of the Elves in their wars against the Dark Power of the North. Though a younger race than Elves, the heroic Edain gained the respect and admiration of the Elder Kindred, proving valiant, loyal, and frequently capable of rising to great heights of nobility.

Noblest of all was Beren, son of Barahir, a chieftain of the First House of the Edain. His name is indissolubly linked with that of the Lady Lúthien Tinúviel, most beloved of Elvenkind. For that reason the Tale of Beren and Lúthien was long preserved in the records of Elven-lore – the chief source being the Sindarin 'lay' composed in Beleriand by Grey-elven minstrels before the Elder Days had passed. The Lay of Leithian ('Release from Bondage') is a long work – so long that only Elrond himself was said to have remembered it in full. A short, translated section may be found in Book 1 Chap. 11; a fuller account, in prose form, can be read in *The Silmarillion* pp. 162–87.)

The Lay tells of Beren's father Barahir, and of his friendship with the Elven-king Finrod of Nargothrond, whose life he saved at the Battle of Sudden Flame. To Barahir, Finrod gave his ring, as a token of gratitude towards Barahir's house and kin. Barahir was slain shortly afterwards, by Orcs, who captured this ring; and his son Beren avenged him, gaining the ring of Finrod. He then fled the wreck of Dorthonion, crossing the forbidding Mountains of Terror and fighting off the attacks of monstrous spiders, before reaching safety in the hidden forest of Neldoreth, in Doriath.

There, wandering through the beech-glades in sorrow and weariness he beheld, dancing 'to music of a pipe unseen',

> *Tinúviel the elven-fair,*
> *Immortal maiden elven-wise*[11]

As is the way with Elves of the Wood, Lúthien swiftly fled when a mortal – the first she had ever seen – appeared; until Beren called her by her elven-name, *Tinúviel*, 'Nightingale'.

> *And doom fell on Tinúviel*
> *That in his arms lay glistening.*[11]

Lúthien was the daughter of Thingol Greycloak, King of this land of Doriath into which Beren, fleeing from peril, had chanced to wander. Beside the waters of the Elven-river Esgalduin they plighted their troth.

Many were the hardships they endured together in the years that followed. Beren was taken by the forces of the Enemy, and imprisoned. But Lúthien rescued him, and together they recaptured the greatest prize of all, one of the three stolen Silmarils. This they took as a bride-piece from Lúthien to her father. But Beren was slain in the hour of triumph by the Wolf Carcharoth, guardian of the Gates of Angband; and he died in the arms of Lúthien who, in her grief, also chose to accept mortality and die in Middle-earth, so that she might follow him. They were both reborn by the Grace of the Valar, and lived out mortal lifespans elsewhere in Beleriand.

Yet their Line continued through their son Dior Eluchl to Elwing; and handed down with the ancestry was the Silmaril, greatest heirloom and trophy of the House of Thingol. Given by Elwing to her husband Eärendil the Mariner, it was used by him to pass the Shadows and so come to the Uttermost West – where he enlisted the aid of the Valar on behalf of Elves and Men after their defeat by Morgoth. As a sign to all the oppressed peoples of Middle-earth, the Silmaril, affixed to his ship, was then set in the heavens to shine for ever as a symbol of Hope.

Note: the surname *Erchamion* ('One-handed') refers to Beren's mutilation by the Wolf Carcharoth, whereby the hand which held the Silmaril was bitten off and swallowed.

Beren (of Gondor) From 2743–63 Third Age, the nineteenth Ruling Steward of Gondor, and the father of Beregond, chief war-captain of the day. It was this Beren who gave the keys of Isengard – then an ancient but deserted fortress of Gondor – to Saruman the Wise, thinking to have the great Wizard's aid in defending the northern provinces and allied territories (especially Rohan, gravely weakened by invasion, hardship and famine).

Beryl An emerald, traditionally an Elf-token.

Bifur, Bofur and Bombur Three of the thirteen Dwarves who, in 2941 Third Age, undertook the Quest of the Dragon of Erebor – as companions of Thorin Oakenshield (and Bilbo Baggins). Unlike the other Dwarves of the company, these three (though descended from Dwarves of Moria) were not of Durin's Line.

'Big People' Hobbit-parlance for Men.

Bilbo Baggins Altogether one of the most remarkable Hobbits of his or any other day. It is a tribute to the gentle nature of this kindly old Hobbit that he is as much remembered for his scholarship and skill in making songs, as for his proven courage, gallantry, 'adventurous' tendencies and great generosity.

Bilbo's hitherto-hidden skills of authorship came to light when, after returning from his epic Journey to the East (2941–2 Third Age), he sat down in his comfortable ancestral hole and proceeded to write, in a somewhat untidy hand, a clear if self-deprecating account of the events leading up to the Battle of Five Armies and the restoration of the Dwarf-kingship of Erebor. In these events Bilbo himself, of course, played a most prominent part, earning great credit with Dwarves, Wizards and Elves (not to mention the modest fortune pressed upon him for his future comfort).

During the course of these adventures, Bilbo gained possession of the One Ring. This curious incident – so unlike the other events of the expedition, though not unrelated to them – is described in great detail in Chapter Five of Bilbo's book, *There and Back Again* (translated from the Red Book of Westmarch as *The Hobbit*). It is almost as if Bilbo had wished to establish his claim to the Ring as being beyond all doubt, so precise is his accounting of the scene in the dim lower caverns of the orc-mines, with the Ring in his pocket like a leaden weight as he fought for his life with words and wit. In any event, after the Ring later passed out of his possession, Bilbo changed his mind about the accuracy of this part of the tale. But he never altered the manuscript he had written some sixty years before; so it is only in Frodo's narrative that we later hear of Bilbo's long remorse concerning this single (but significant) untruth.

At all events, the old Hobbit slipped quietly away to Rivendell in his eleventy-first (111th) year, leaving his estate – and the Ring – to

Frodo. There, dwelling in peace with Elrond and the High-elves, he spent long study amongst the Elvish Books of Lore. The total of his very considerable labours in this field has yielded some of the most remarkable scholarship in all Hobbit history. Thus Bilbo's 'Translations from the Elvish'[12] is a typically modest title for the three large, red volumes crammed with so much of the history of the First Age, when Men and Elves were like brothers and Hobbits apparently did not exist at all.

Bilbo travelled very little after his retirement to Rivendell, and in company with the Three Rings, he finally passed over Sea at the ending of the Third Age, his years in Middle-earth then totalling one hundred and thirty-one. Bilbo was thus the longest-lived Hobbit in history, always generous to a fault and long remembered for his wryly humorous personality as well as for his valiant deeds and other accomplishments. His adoption of the orphaned Frodo Baggins was an act of great philanthropy, well repaid. Unlike most Hobbits, neither Bilbo nor Frodo ever married, and their descendants were accounted those of Samwise. Both Bilbo and Frodo dwell now over the Sea.

Bilbo Gamgee Tenth child and fifth son of Master Samwise of Bag End.

Bill (the pony) A gaunt, half-starved animal purchased in Bree by Barliman Butterbur, innkeeper of *The Prancing Pony*, on 30th September 3019 Third Age, to replace others stolen from Meriadoc Brandybuck during the previous night. His poor condition was due to the treatment meted out by his previous owner, who sold the pony for the exorbitant price of twelve silver pennies. However, under the loving care of Samwise Gamgee, Bill flourished and proved of great value to the Company as a pack-animal, although he was later parted from them outside the doors of Moria. Yet despite Sam's gloomy apprehensions, the pony eventually succeeded in making his way back to Bree, where he was stabled and fed for a time at *The Prancing Pony*. He was later reunited with Samwise.

Bill Ferny A Man of Bree – and, by all accounts, a shifty, unpleasant sort of person, remembered with distaste. Ill-favoured from birth, Ferny later became involved with the machinations of Isengard (in a mean sort of way). He did his best to hinder the Company of the Ring at *The Prancing Pony*, later falling foul of the Bree-folk and working more openly for Saruman as warden of the Buckland Gate. His fate is not recorded.

Bindbale Wood A wood near Rushock Bog in the Northfarthing of the Shire.

'Biter' See 'BEATER' AND 'BITER'.

Black Breath An evil radiance or essence given off by the Nazgûl. It was said that close proximity was enough to render the victims feverish and delirious with dark, despairing dreams, leaving them with no will to live. Few remedies were sufficient. Only the healing herb kingsfoil could cure it – and then only in the hand of the rightful King.

See also RINGWRAITHS.

Black Captain An epithet used in Gondor for the fell Lord of Minas Morgul, leader of the Nine Riders, King of the Nazgûl – in his aspect as a warlord of irresistible cruelty, power and terror. In the North, Men knew him as the Witch-king of Angmar. A sorcerer, a Ringwraith and a Spear in the Hand of Sauron, he was most greatly to be feared.

See also WITCH-KING.

Black Foe (of the World) A translation of the Grey-elven word Morgoth, first applied to the renegade Vala Melkor, by Fëanor, after the theft of the Silmarils.[13]

Black Gate A translation of the Sindarin word *Morannon;* the main entrance to the land of Mordor. The Black Gate was a massive construction designed to fit the natural shapings of the earth and erected by the labours of countless slaves, on the orders of Sauron the Great during the Second Age. It was situated where the Ashy Mountains and the *Ephel Dúath* joined hands south of the great field of ancient Dagorlad. There, a defile (Cirith Gorgor) leading between the two mountain walls was stopped, at its mouth, by a vast wall of stone stretching from cliff to cliff; this wall was pierced by a single gate with two great doors of iron. Set upon guardian-hills to either side of the Morannon – and high above the wall – there rose two high towers: the 'Towers of the Teeth', Narchost and Carchost, which had originally been built by Gondor in days of power, to watch over Mordor and prohibit the entry of evil things. But the watch failed and the Towers were filled with sleepless eyes and sharp iron.

Black Land A translation of the Sindarin word *Mordor*.

Black Númenoreans During the first thousand years of Númenor's rise to power, many of the Dúnedain who dwelt there chose to return to Middle-earth – for although the Western Seas had been forbidden to them by the Ban of the Valar, great territories lay still unconquered in Middle-earth.

Although these returning Númenoreans were only explorers or harbour-builders, those who followed them in later days were of a different sort: restless and given to domination over lesser Men. Many coastal areas of Middle-earth were seized by these so-called 'Black Númenoreans' and brought under their subjection. And among them there rose nine powerful princes and lords, the friendship and alliance of whom was cultivated by Sauron the Great. He gave a Ring of Power to each of these Nine great lords. Although seeking to serve only themselves, they thus fell into his trap and became Ringwraiths, enslaved for ever.

The Second Age passed, Sauron fell and the Black Númenoreans dwindled, mingling their blood with that of lesser races. In 933 Third Age, Umbar, the oldest of their coastal fiefs, fell for the first time to Gondor; and the followers of Elendil erected there a great monument in memory of Ar-Pharazôn's triumph over Sauron the Great. But in the course of the many wars of the Age, Umbar was taken again by the enemies of Gondor and remained for many years afterwards an independent state, bitterly hostile to Gondor and a refuge for her foes.

Note: the Black Númenoreans were also referred to (in Númenor) as 'King's Men'.

See also CORSAIRS OF UMBAR; RINGWRAITHS.

Black Pit The literal translation of the Sindarin word *Moria:* an Elvish term for the mighty Dwarf-city under the Misty Mountains, also known as *Hadhodrond*. It was not an admiring name, for Elves did not go underground of choice. The Dwarves knew their own dolven halls as *Khazâd-dûm*, the 'Mansion-of-the-Khazâd' (*Khazâd* was the name for their own race).

Black Riders The Nazgûl, the Nine Ringwraiths, undying servants of Sauron, Lord of the Rings. They were so-called because they were invariably mounted on beasts of black colour, whether horse or other fell creature.

See also RINGWRAITHS.

Blackroot A translation of the Sindarin name *Morthond*, given to the river which emerged from the White Mountains high in the Blackroot Vale and flowed south to the Sea.

Black Shadow The name given in Gondor to the sickness which emanated from the Ringwraiths. See BLACK BREATH.

Black Speech This unpleasant tongue developed out of Sauron's desire, early in the Accursed Years, to devise a single language for use by all his servants. (For Trolls spoke as they would, while the many tribes and bands of Orcs differed in their speech from den to den, and the Men of Sauron's rule all spoke their own languages.) But the minds of his numberless henchmen were not fitted to hold such a concept and, after Sauron's first overthrow at the end of the Second Age, this ancient tongue was forgotten by all but the Ring-wraiths.

Few specimens are extant: it is not a language that scholars willingly record. The only known example lies in the Ring-inscription, as traced secretly by Isildur before the heat of Sauron's hand faded and the fiery letters dimmed. The actual letters of the inscription are Eldarin but the tongue used is clearly the ancient Black Speech:

> *Ash nazg durbatulûk, ash nazg gimbatul,*
> *ash nazg thrakatulûk agh burzum-ishi krimpatul*
> ('One Ring to rule them all, One Ring to find them,
> One Ring to bring them all and in the darkness bind them')[14]

The word *nazg* ('ring') can also be found in the ancient name *Nazgûl* 'Ringwraiths'; and *burzum* is obviously related to the Orcs' name for the Barad-dûr: *Lugbúrz* ('Dark-tower').

Sauron revived the use of this language on his second arising in the Third Age – but only he and his most immediate lieutenants used it in its original form. Other versions were greatly debased.

Black Sword (of Nargothrond) A translation of the Grey-elven name *Mormegil*, being the admiring title bestowed upon the warrior Túrin Turambar by folk of West Beleriand, during the years in which he fought for the Elven-city of Nargothrond. Túrin was so-called because of the sword Gurthang (see ANGLACHEL) which he bore.

Black Years An epithet for the ACCURSED YEARS, or the period from the middle of the Second Age to the dawning of the Third, when Sauron the Great of Mordor enslaved much of the Western lands of Middle-earth. The Black Years ended with his first overthrow (3441 Second Age). Called by the Elves the Days of Flight.

Bladorthin As the Dwarves of Erebor recorded, Bladorthin was a ruler or king of Elves[15] who ordered a sheaf of new spears from the smiths of Erebor in the days before the coming of the Dragon. Unfortunately, he died before delivery of the weapons and his heirs did not choose to honour the agreement. The spears were therefore kept in hoard by the Dwarves of the Lonely Mountain.

Blanco See MARCHO AND BLANCO.

Blessed Realm An Elvish term for the Undying Lands or Uttermost West. The oldest recorded name for Valinor was *Aman* (the Blessed).

Blooting The Bree word for the eleventh month of the year, roughly corresponding to our November. The Shire word was *Blotmath*.

Blotmath (pronounced 'Blommath') See BLOOTING above.

Blue Mountains A translation of the Sindarin name *Ered Luin* (pl.). Of old, this high, windy range marked the westernmost boundary of Eriador and the easternmost of Beleriand, the land of the Grey-elves in the West of Middle-earth. The Ered Luin were first crossed by the Eldar, as they passed West on their way to the Sea far back in the First Age.

But the Elder Days ended in a cataclysm which drowned the lands and shook the mountains to their foundations; and the Ered Luin then seem to have been divided into two separate ranges by the inrushing Sea. Icy colds gripped the northern chain and lingered there ever after. During the Third Age few folk dwelt in these mountains, save only a handful of Dwarves who maintained settlements and mines in the eastern foothills.

Note: also called *Ered Lindon*, the 'Mountains of Lindon', (by the Noldor).

Boar of Everholt In the latter days of King Walda of Rohan, the great Boar of the Firienwood (on the borders of Gondor and Rohan) was accounted a worthy and daunting prey for any huntsman. But Walda was slain by Orcs and his son Folca vowed to pursue no wild beast while there remained a single Orc alive in Rohan. When the last den had been exterminated, Folca rode away to hunt the Boar of Everholt. He slew the beast but died later of the tusk-wounds it gave him.

Bob A Hobbit of Bree and the ostler in charge of the stables at *The Prancing Pony* Inn.

Boffin See BOPHÎN.

Bofur See BIFUR, BOFUR AND BOMBUR.

Bolg An Orc-captain, the son of AZOG and leader of the Goblin-army at the Battle of Five Armies, where this large and savage Orc was slain by the (even larger) Beorn.

Bolger A fairly prosperous Hobbit-family, with pretensions to aristocratic status: nearly all their children were given prestigious names.

See also FREDEGAR BOLGER.

Bombadil See TOM BOMBADIL.

'Bombadil Goes Boating' A Bucklandish piece of whimsical verse, dealing with a river-expedition undertaken by the semi-legendary (to the Hobbits) figure of Tom Bombadil. It can be found as part of the collection entitled *The Adventures of Tom Bombadil*.

Bombur An immensely fat Dwarf who, with his kinsmen Bifur and Bofur, accompanied Thorin Oakenshield on the Quest of the Dragon of Erebor. After the successful conclusion of that expedition, and the prosperity that followed, Bombur grew so enormously wide in the belt that he became unable to walk; and it took six stout young dwarves to carry him from couch to table, and back again.

See also BIFUR, BOFUR AND BOMBUR.

Book of Mazarbul A diary or chronicle kept by the Dwarves of Balin's expedition to Moria (2989–94 Third Age). The latter entries, recording the death of Balin and the entrapment of the colony, were written by the Dwarf Ori, an old comrade of Balin's and one of the original thirteen Dwarves of Thorin Oakenshield's company. The Book somehow survived the destruction of the Moria-expedition.

Book of the Kings This volume comprises the main history of Gondor and Númenor, with some reference to the Line of Isildur in Arnor. From it was derived much of the information concerning Gondor's history that is found in the Red Book (under Appendix A I).

Bophîn In original – as opposed to translated – Westron (the Common Speech of the Westlands), the name *Bophîn* is the proper form of the Hobbit surname translated as *Boffin*. Its original meaning is unknown.

Bór An Easterling chieftain who, together with his people, came across the Blue Mountains into Beleriand in the year following the Battle of Sudden Flame. His sons were Borlad, Borlach and Borthand. Unlike the Easterling clan of Ulfang the Black, Bór's people remained faithful to the Eldar, with whom they took service. Of Bór's fate *The Silmarillion* does not speak; his sons, however, died bravely at the Nirnaeth Arnoediad.

Borgil The red 'War-star' (Sind.), as known to the Elves; probably the planet Mars.

Borin A Dwarf of the House of Durin and one of Gimli's ancestors. He was born in the Grey Mountains (*Ered Mithrin*), whither many of Durin's folk removed after the settling of the Lonely Mountain (*Erebor*). But when the Dragons made war upon the Dwarves of the Ered Mithrin, Borin accompanied King Thrór back to Erebor.

Borlach One of the sons of BÓR.

Borlad The eldest son of BÓR.

Boromir An Adan of the First House, first Lord of Ladros in Dorthonion, held in fieff from the Elves of Finiarfin's house. He was the great-grandson of Bëor the Old and grandsire of Barahir.

Boromir From 2477–89 Third Age, the eleventh Ruling Steward of Gondor, and one of its mightiest Captains. It was he who defeated the first incursions into Ithilien of the race of *uruks*, black Mordororcs of great strength. Boromir drove them out after much fighting, but not before the ancient city of Osgiliath was finally destroyed and its bridge broken. Boromir himself received a Morgul-wound in that war which shortened his life: he died twelve years after his father Denethor I.

Note: Boromir of the Fellowship of the Ring was named after this great warrior. The name is of mixed Quenya and Sindarin form, and translates as 'Jewel-of-War'. (See following entry.)

Boromir It was a sign of the decline of Gondor, and of the increasing need of her peoples for captains of war rather than for men of learning that, towards the end of the Third Age, there were many among the ruling families who esteemed the craft of arms higher than all other skills. Such a man was King Eärnur, last King of Gondor –

and so also was Boromir, son of Steward Denethor II, brother of Faramir, and Captain of the armies of Gondor until his death during the War of the Ring (3019 Third Age).

Like Eärnur, Boromir took no wife, delighting chiefly in battle and in trials of arms. He was a brave and honourable warrior, the champion of his people, and was much esteemed for these qualities in Minas Tirith. As the elder son of Denethor II, Boromir was Heir to the Stewardship of the Tower and so, when both he and his brother were visited by the same prophetic dream, he would suffer none but himself to journey north to Imladris (Rivendell), seeking to unravel the hard words contained in the dream.

After a journey of many months, he succeeded in finding the House of Elrond, where he joined the great Council (Book II Chap. 2), and became part of the Fellowship of the Ring. The manner of his departure from the Fellowship – and of the last battle he fought – is recounted in Book III Chap. 1.

Boron The grandson of Bëor the Old (of the First House of the Edain) and father of Boromir of Ladros.

Borthand One of the sons of BÓR the Easterling.

Bounders Border-watchers of the Shire, a volunteer force employed to 'beat the bounds' and prevent incursions by undesirables. Their numbers varied according to need.

Bowman 'Nick' Cotton Third son of Tolman Cotton, Hobbit of the Shire; he was the brother of Rose Cotton (later Rose Gamgee).

Bracegirdle A prosperous family of Hobbits of the Shire, a branch of which lived in Hardbottle village.

Braldagamba In original (as opposed to translated) Westron, this (postulated) word would mean 'heady-buck' – a possible pun in the Hobbit style on the (jocular) Hobbit-name for the river Baranduin: *Bralda-hîm* ('heady-ale'). Such a jest would, of course, have made play on the similarity of this name with that of the clan which had colonized the strip of land on the river's eastern bank, *Brandagamba* (Brandybuck).

Bralda-hîm 'Heady-ale', in original Hobbit Westron (see BRALDA-GAMBA above). It was a popular term for the river Baranduin, and has been translated from the Red Book as 'Brandywine'. Both names indicate the same punning reference to the hue of the river's waters and its resemblance to the colour of strong drink.

Brand From 3007-19 Third Age, the third King of Dale restored, son of Bain son of Bard the Bowman. Assailed by Easterlings of Sauron's rule during the war of the Ring, Brand died at the Second Battle of Dale, defending the gates of Erebor. He was succeeded by his son Bard II.

Brandagamba 'March-buck', an original Westron name (translated from the Red Book as 'Brandybuck').

Branda-nîn 'Border-water', the genuine Hobbit (Westron) name for the river Baranduin, which served the Shire-folk as an eastward frontier.

See also BRALDA-HÎM.

Brandir the Lame One of the Edain of the Second House, the Haladin. In the terrible years following the Nirnaeth Arnoediad, Brandir inherited the leadership of his people – who still dwelt in the Forest of Brethil – upon the death of his father Handir. Being a man of defensive inclination, he fortified Amon Obel with a stockade and palisade of wood (the Ephel Brandir); and he forbade open acts against Morgoth's forces, for he hoped to ride out the storm by lying hid in the forest.

His plans were upset by the arrival in the midst of the Haladin of a great warrior, Túrin son of Húrin – whom at first the Haladin did not recognize. Brandir tended Túrin with his own hands. It was not long afterwards that Nienor the sister of Túrin, spell-enslaved by the Dragon Glaurung so that she did not even know her own name, came also among the Woodmen of Brethil; and Túrin, who had last seen her as a little girl and knew her not, fell in love with her, and she with him; but Brandir the Lame also loved Níniel, as she was then called.

Soon afterwards the Dragon again came to that region of Beleriand. Túrin, who had by now wedded 'Níniel', went out against the Dragon; but Brandir, who wished, as told above, to avoid trouble and war, would not aid him in this quest; so Dorlas and Hunthor alone of the Haladin went with Túrin, and Brandir was shamed before his people.

In the fight with the Dragon Túrin was victorious; but Glaurung, in his death-throes, struck him down, so that he was left for dead. Brandir, who did not know that Glaurung was also mortally stricken, believed that all was lost and Turambar dead; and he still loved Níniel. He attempted to escape with her but she became fey, and rushed towards the place of battle. There she had her last encounter with the dying Dragon: the spell the Worm had laid on her was lifted, and she, realizing for the first time that she was carrying her own brother's incestuous child, cast herself into the waters of Teiglin and perished – while Brandir watched, helpless to prevent her.

Then the lame chieftain, sorrowing, made his way back to Ephel Brandir, and told his people some of what had befallen. And while they were digesting this news, Túrin himself – who was not dead as Brandir believed – came back. Then he and Brandir quarrelled, for Túrin believed that Brandir had in part brought about Níniel's death. They came to blows, and Brandir was slain.

Brandybuck The (translated) name of one of the most prominent Hobbit-families of the Shire. After the Oldbucks had colonized the strip of land east of the river Baranduin (*c.* 740 Shire Reckoning), Gorhendad Oldbuck changed the family name to *Brandybuck*, and the strip of land became known as the Buckland. Gorhendad also commenced the tunnelling of the great ancestral *smial*, Brandy Hall, into the side of Buck Hill. This mansion later grew to such an extent that most of the Brandybuck clan were eventually able to dwell there (though in somewhat crowded conditions). The chief of the clan was thereafter known as the Master of Buckland (or of the Hall), and his authority was widely respected.

See also BRANDAGAMBA.

Brandy Hall See BRANDYBUCK above.

Brandywine A translation of the Hobbits' (jesting) name for the river BARANDUIN.

Brandywine Bridge The Hobbits' name for the ancient Bridge of Stonebows, which crosssed the Baranduin north of the Buckland.

Bree A small inhabited region of central Eriador, 'like an island in the empty lands round about. Besides Bree [village] itself, there was Staddle on the other side of the hill, Combe in a deep valley a little further eastward, and Archet on the edge of the Chetwood.'[16]

The Bree-land was notable for being settled by both Men and Hobbits. Men of Bree claimed that the original village was extremely ancient; at the end of the Third Age, it was certainly the oldest surviving settlement of Hobbits, far older than the Shire.

The village of Bree consisted of about one hundred proper stone houses (for Big Folk) and a smaller number of hillside *smials* (for Hobbits), the whole enclosed by a dike and thorny hedge. The main meeting place was *The Prancing Pony* Inn, the most important hostelry of the district, where travellers and inhabitants nightly exchanged gossip and tales over mugs of Bree-ale provided by the gregarious innkeeper. The village was situated near the crossing of two ancient highways, the East Road and the North Road. But by the end of the Third Age, few travellers came up the Greenway (as the North Road was called), and even fewer came down from the desolate northlands. Bree's importance therefore declined steadily in these latter years.

Bree-land The countryside surrounding the village of Bree. Though the Men of its four villages (Bree, Archet, Staddle and Combe) maintained that the whole area was an ancient settlement dating back to the First Age, it is more likely that the original founders were Men from Dunland and from the vales of the White Mountains, fleeing north in the Second Age to escape the tyranny of Sauron (see ACCURSED YEARS). But in the Third Age war swept over all of the lands of Eriador; defenceless apart from the usual dike and hedge arrangement, Bree was actually protected by the Rangers of the North throughout the last third of the Age – although the Bree-dwellers themselves were unaware of this until after the War of the Ring.

Bree Reckoning The calendar system used by the Bree-folk, not dissimilar to the Shire Reckoning. Year One corresponded to the first settlement of Hobbits in Bree (1300 Third Age), just as Year One of the Shire Reckoning indicated the crossing of the Baranduin by Marcho and Blanco and their following (1601 Third Age).

Bregalad 'Quick-beam' (Sind.) The 'short' name of an Ent of Fangorn Forest, so called because on one remote occasion he reportedly said 'yes' to an older Ent before the latter had finished his question. Bregalad was thus noted for his (relative) speed of decision. He was of rowan-kind and was much attached to rowan-trees.

Brego From 2545–70, the second King of Rohan, son of Eorl the Young. When he came to the kingship, Brego completed the work begun at the Battle of the Field of Celebrant by driving the last remnant of Easterlings out of that part of Rohan known as the Wold. Later, he built the great hall of Meduseld in Edoras; at the feast to celebrate the completion of that 'Golden Hall' his elder son Baldor vowed to pass the 'Paths of the Dead'. Baldor never came back and the grief-stricken Brego died the following year. His second son Aldor then became King.

Bregolas One of the Edain of the First House; the son of Bregor and brother of Barahir; he was also the father of Belegund and Baragund. He was slain, fighting beside the Elf-lords Angrod and Aegnor, in the defence of Dorthonion during the Battle of Sudden Flame. Three years later his sons were also dead, slain together with his brother Barahir in an ambush.

Bregor One of the Edain of the First House; the father of Bregolas and Barahir.

Breredon A village of Buckland in the Shire.

Brethil 'Silver-birch' (Sind.) See FOREST OF BRETHIL.

Bridgefields The meadows in the Eastfarthing of the Shire which approached the Bridge of Stonebows (the Brandywine Bridge).

Bridge Inn The chief hostelry of the Bridgefields district in the Shire.

Bridge of Mitheithel This was an ancient stone bridge of three great arches which crossed the river Hoarwell, or Mitheithel, some miles west of Rivendell. It was often called the Last Bridge because further south the Hoarwell grew too deep and wide to be crossed or forded.

Bridge of Stonebows The bridge over the Baranduin, probably built in the early years of the Kingdom of Arnor to speed communications between Lindon and the eastern lands of Eriador. After the settling of the Shire (in 1601 Third Age), the Hobbits knew it as the Brandywine Bridge, or the Great Bridge.

Brilthor 'Glittering-torrent' (Sind.) The name given in Ossiriand to the fourth of the six tributaries of Gelion.

Brithiach 'Gravel-fords' (Sind.) A ford across the upper waters of Sirion, on the northern border of the Forest of Brethil.

Brithombar 'Dwellings of Brithon' (Sind.) The more northerly of the two Havens founded early in the First Age by those Telerin Elves who were led by Círdan, the *Falathrim* ('Coast-elves'). It stood at the mouth of the river Brithon. Its sister-haven was EGLAREST at the mouth of the Nenning. It was rebuilt with the aid of the Noldor, after this High-elven people had returned to Middle-earth to make war on Morgoth. Both Havens held throughout the War, but fell at last in the year after the Nirnaeth Arnoediad. The surviving

Falathrim escaped to the Isle of Balar, where they remained until the ending of the First Age.

Brithon 'Gravelly' (Sind.) A river of West Beleriand. At its mouth stood the Haven of Brithombar (see preceding entry).

Brockenborings A maze of old tunnels and *smials* in the west of the hills of Scary in the Shire.

Brockhouse A fairly common Hobbit-surname, found in both the Shire and Bree.

Brodda An Easterling warrior in the service of Morgoth, who held lands in Dor-lómin as reward for his aid during the Nirnaeth Arnoediad. He forcibly wedded Aerin of the Edain, and was afterwards slain at his own table by Túrin Turambar.

Brown Lands A desolate wilderness which lay between the southern eaves of Mirkwood and the hills of the Emyn Muil, west of the Black Gate. According to Ent-tradition, these lands had once been rich and fruitful, as the homes and gardens of the Entwives, established early in the Second Age.

> After the Darkness was overthrown the land of the Entwives blossomed richly, and their fields were full of corn. Many men learned the crafts of the Entwives and honoured them greatly; but we [Ents] were only a legend to them, a secret in the heart of the forest. Yet here we still are, while all the gardens of the Entwives are wasted: Men call them the Brown Lands now.[17]

It was in the days of the Last Alliance that war swept across the fertile gardens and fields, destroying the crops and uprooting the trees. Nothing grew there during the Third Age.

Brownlock A Hobbit-family of the Shire.

Bruinen The river Loudwater, which ran south from the Misty Mountains, embracing the uplands of Rivendell before it fell away south-west through Eriador, to meet the Hoarwell (Mitheithel); the conjoined rivers were known as the Gwathlo (Greyflood).

The Great East Road crossed the Loudwater at the Ford of Bruinen, close to the hidden valley of Rivendell. There, Elrond controlled the river, and it could be made to rise in flood and bar the Ford should need arise.

Brytta From 2798–2842 Third Age, the eleventh King of Rohan, much loved by his people, who called him *Léofa* ('Beloved'), because of his kindness and liberality.

Bucca of the Marish The first Thain of the Shire (appointed in 1979 Third Age) – and incidentally, the founder of the Oldbuck family, later the Brandybucks. The Thainship remained with the Oldbucks until the colonization of the Buckland, whereupon the office passed to the chief Took.

Buck Hill The most prominent hill of the Buckland, near the village of Bucklebury; it was extensively tunnelled into one gigantic *smial* called Brandy Hall.

Buckland A strip of wooded country, nominally part of the Shire, though it lay on the eastern banks of the Baranduin, between the River and the Old Forest. The Buckland was in fact a 'colony' of the Shire, settled in about 2340 Third Age (*c.* 740 Shire Reckoning) by Gorhendad Oldbuck (who later changed his name to Brandybuck). The Bucklanders were nearly all originally Marish folk from the East farthing, and, being largely of Stoorish ancestry, were familiar with rivers and boats.

Because of the uncomfortable stories associated with the Old Forest, which crouched on the eastern borders of the little land, soon after settling there the inhabitants planted a great hedge, the High Hay, to protect Buckland from the East. Indeed, because of the nearness of the 'Outside World', the Bucklanders were habitually more cautious than other Hobbits, locking the Buckland Gate (and their own front doors) at night. They were therefore regarded with some suspicion by more insular (and complacent) Shire-dwellers.

The affairs of Buckland were administered from Brandy Hall, the great ancestral *smial* of the Brandybuck family. The head of the family – and chief Hobbit of the region – was known as the Master of Buckland.

Buckland Gate The entrance to Buckland from the north, along the Great East Road.

Bucklebury The chief village of Buckland, near Buck Hill. The Bucklebury Ferry plied across the Brandywine between the village and the Marish of the Eastfarthing.

Budge Ford A ford across The Water, linking Whitfurrows with the village of Scary in the Eastfarthing of the Shire.

'Bullroarer' The admiring nickname bestowed upon BANDOBRAS 'BULLROARER' TOOK.

Bunce A Hobbit-family of the Shire.

Bundushathûr The Dwarvish (Khuzdul) name for the southern-most of the three great peaks of Moria, known to Men as Cloudyhead and to the Elves as *Fanuidhol*.

Bungo Baggins The father of Bilbo Baggins and the husband of Belladonna Took, whom he wedded in 2880 Third Age (1280 Shire Reckoning). It was this well-to-do Hobbit who constructed the ancestral manor-hole of Bag End in the side of the hill of Hobbiton.

Burrows A Hobbit-family of the Shire.

Butterbur See BARLIMAN BUTTERBUR.

Bywater A village in the Westfarthing of the Shire, astride the Great East Road near the Pool of Bywater and not far from Hobbiton-on-the-Hill, with which it formed a single community.

Notes

1 In the story of the Balchoth, one is reminded of the Huns of a far later time; this fierce Easterling people also terrorized the eastern borders of an ancient Empire, before crossing a mighty river (the Rhine) in pursuit of pillage, there to be defeated by an alliance of Empire soldiery and northern Horsemen. The Horsemen (the Visigoths) were settled within the bounds of the Empire, while the Huns vanished from history shortly afterwards.
2 Book VI Chap. 3.
3 See Note under ARVEDUI.
4 *Silmarillion* pp. 150–4.
5 Book III Chap. 7.
6 *Silmarillion* pp. 188–97.
7 *Silmarillion* p. 206.
8 Interestingly enough, this word has also been applied to a far later city of Middle-earth – Constantinople. *Mickleburg* was its name among Germans of the north and west.
9 Incorrect; the first Dwarves to enter Beleriand were the 'Lesser-dwarves', the *Noegyth Nibin:* Mîm's people.
10 Book VI Chap. 5.
11 Book II Chap. I.
12 Now published under the title *The Silmarillion*.

13 This cannot be, although the authority is no less than *The Silmarillion* itself (p. 79); for Fëanor at that time had never heard – and therefore did not know – the Grey-Elven tongue (*Morgoth* is a Sindarin word). In all probability he named Melkor 'Dark Foe of the World' in *Quenya*, and the phrase was afterwards translated into Sindarin as *Morgoth*.

14 Book II Chap. 2.

15 Probably of the Nandor.

16 Book I Chap. 9.

17 Book III Chap. 4.

Cabed-en-Aras A sheer-sided ravine of great depth, through which ran the swift river Teiglin. It lay on the marches of the Forest of Brethil. Here Túrin Turambar slew the Dragon Glaurung, by ascending the sides of the gorge and so coming up underneath the Worm's guard; here also Nienor Níniel slew herself, after which this grim place was renamed *Cabed Naeramarth*, the 'Leap of Dreadful Doom', by the Woodmen of Brethil.

Cabed Naeramarth See preceding entry.

Cair Andros The island of Cair Andros lay in the middle of the Anduin, some leagues north of Minas Tirith where the provinces of Anórien and North Ithilien faced each other across the Great River. When the lands on the eastern side fell under Sauron's control, about 2900 Third Age, Túrin II, twenty-third Ruling Steward of Gondor, fortified the island to protect Anórien from raids and invasion.

The name *Cair Andros* means 'Ship of long-foam', for the island was shaped like a great ship, with a high prow facing upstream, against which the waters of Anduin broke with force.

Calacirian See CALACIRYA.

Calacirya 'Light-cleft' (Q., from the older form *Kalakirya*) The Realm of the Valar, Guardians of the World, was hidden from the shorelands of Valinor by a great range of mountains called the Pelóri, through which there was only one pass: the great ravine of the Calacirya.

In ancient times, the lands of the Valar were illuminated by the radiance of the Two Trees, Telperion and Laurelin the Golden,

which stood on a mound not far from the Calacirya. The Light of the
Two Trees flowed through this pass and into the coastal lands
beyond, where dwelt the Eldar and all those who had passed 'over
Sea'. The region of Eldamar thus illumined was called Calaciryan –
from the older form *Kalakiryande*, 'The-Region-of-Calacirya'. (It
was sometimes spelt *Calacirian* in verse of Elvish form.)

Calaquendi 'Light-elves' (Q.) The name given in the lore of the
Eldar to all those of Elven race who dwelt, or had ever dwelt, in
Aman the Blessed. These included all the VANYAR and the NOLDOR,
and a part of the TELERI (but not the SINDAR, a subdivision of the
Telerin race who lingered throughout the First Age in Beleriand).
Those of the Calaquendi who returned to Middle-earth – for what-
ever cause – were sometimes also called 'High-elves' (*Tareldar*) by
the dwellers therein. See also AMANYAR; MORIQUENDI; ÚMANYAR.

Calembel The chief town of the province of Lamedon in Gondor.
It was situated upon a low hill commanding the ford across the river
Ciril.

Calenardhon 'Green-region' (Sind.) A northern province of
Gondor. It lay north of the White Mountains, between the rivers
Anduin and Isen, and extended as far north as the Limlight and the
Forest of Fangorn. Calenardhon was an ancient land, once peopled by
the Dunlendings and Men of the upper vales of the Mountains. (It
was, in fact, this folk who constructed the old refuge of Dunharrow
and the secret tunnels and passages which lay under the Dwimorberg.)
In the days of its power, Gondor defended this land with two strong
fortresses: the Hornburg at the entrance to the gorge of Aglarond,
and Angrenost, at the feet of the Misty Mountains.

But as the Third Age slowly passed, the province of Calenardhon
became depopulated by war and by plague. In the year 2510 it was
suddenly overrun by the invading Balchoth, and many of its remaining inhabitants perished. The army of Gondor, marching north to
defend the province, was assailed by hordes of Orcs and Balchoth,
and only the last-minute appearance of the Riders of Éothéod saved it
from defeat. In gratitude, Gondor ceded her depopulated province
to the Riders, who called their new land the *Riddermark*.

See also ARD-GALEN; ROHAN.

Calendar of Imladris The system of reckoning used by the Elves
of Rivendell; the only Elf-calendar known (or recorded) by the compilers of the Red Book. The Elves always preferred to reckon, where-

ever possible, in sixes and twelves, and their *yén* or (long) 'year' was equivalent to 144 (solar) years, or *loa*, which were divided into six full 'seasons' and some extra days. These seasons were named *tuilë, lairë, yávië, quellë, hrivë* and *coirë* (spring, summer, autumn, fading, winter and stirring). The *loa* began on the last day of *coirë* (this day had a special name, *yestarë*).

To correct inherent inaccuracies in the system, the Eldar inserted three 'middle-days', or *enderi* between 'autumn' and 'fading'. Every twelfth year these extra days were doubled to give an average *loa* of 365 days. This is obviously a somewhat inaccurate system, but to the Eldar – 'who had, as Samwise once remarked, more time at their disposal'[1] – it presumably sufficed.

See also Appendix D.

Calenhad 'Green-hump' (Sind.) One of the chain of seven beacon-hills between Minas Tirith and the Firienwood, linking Gondor and Rohan. It lay west of Min-Rimmon and east of the Firienwood.

See also BEACON-HILLS.

Calimehtar A prince of Gondor, younger brother of King Rómendacil II. His grandson was Castamir the Usurper.

Calimehtar From 1856-1936 Third Age, the thirtieth King of Gondor. His father, King Narmacil II, was slain in battle by the Wainriders, and the son avenged this death by a great victory over these formidable peoples in 1899, upon the ancient battlefield of Dagorlad. This victory was achieved with the aid of rebels from Rhovanion, who had been enslaved in the invasion which took Narmacil's life.

Calimmacil A prince of Gondor, son of Arciryas and nephew of Narmacil II. It was through this blood-link with the royalty of Gondor that Calimmacil's grandson, the victorious general Eärnil II, claimed – and was subsequently awarded – the crown of Gondor (in 1945 Third Age).

Calma The Quenya word for 'lamp', but more properly the title of the Fëanorian Tengwa number 3, representing the sound *ch* (later *k*) in Quenya and Sindarin.

Calmacil (**Tar-Calmacil**) The eighteenth King of Númenor.

Calmacil From 1294-1304 Third Age, the nominal eighteenth King of Gondor, though his son Minalcar (later crowned in his own right as RÓMENDACIL II) ruled as Regent in Calmacil's name.

Calmatéma In the Fëanorian system of writing (the *Tengwar*), the title given to the 'series' of letters which utilized the sounds *k*, *g*, *kh*, *gh* (the velar stops and back spirants). These sounds were represented by letters 3, 7, 11, 15, 19 and 23 in Westron (Series III), and by 4, 8, 12, 16, 20 and 24 in Quenya (Series IV).

See also Appendix E II(i).

Camellia Baggins The (Sackville) wife of Longo Baggins, Hobbit of the Shire. Their only son Otho was the first of the Sackville-Bagginses. (Otho later wedded Lobelia Bracegirdle.)

Camlost 'the Empty-Handed' (Sind.) The bitter name assumed by BEREN ERCHAMION when he returned to the halls of King Thingol Greycloak – without the Silmaril. In truth, his right hand still held the Jewel, but the hand itself at that time lay within the belly of the Wolf Carcharoth.[2]

Captain of Despair An epithet used in Gondor for the Chief Nazgûl, the Lord of Minas Morgul.

Captain of the Haven (of Umbar) The title of the Harbourmaster or Governor of the Havens of Umbar during the time of the Corsairs. He was responsible for the efficiency of the harbour and the ships berthed there.

See also CORSAIRS OF UMBAR.

Captain of the White Tower The (traditional) title of Gondor's war-leader; in the days after the passing of the Kings, the title was normally held by the Heir to the Stewardship. Boromir, son of Denethor II, bore this rank.

Carach Angren 'Iron-jaws' (Sind.) The Isenmouthe; the gate and wall which guarded the road from the plateau of Gorgoroth in Mordor to the valley of Udûn, which lay behind the Black Gate. Together with the fortress of Durthang which overlooked it, the Isenmouthe was built by Gondor early in the Third Age, to guard Mordor and prevent the re-entry of evil creatures there. After Sauron's return, these fortifications were used by him to prevent *escape* from the Black Land.

Caradhras 'Red-peak' (Sind.) The Elvish name for the northernmost of the three great peaks that rose above the ancient Dwarf-realm of Moria. (The other two were Celebdil the White and Fanuidhol the Grey.) Because of its cruel reputation, and the blood-like tinge which habitually lit its northern face, this mountain was known in the Westron speech as the Redhorn. The Dwarves called it *Barazinbar*.

The high pass over Caradhras, from Hollin in Eriador to the Dimrill Dale on the far side, was known as the Redhorn Gate.

Caragdûr 'Dark-fang' (Sind.) The name given by the Elves of Gondolin to the steep northern face of the hill Amon Gwareth, on which their city was built.

Caranthir the Dark The fourth of the Sons of Fëanor, by repute the most quick-tempered and fell (most like his father, as some said). He returned with his father and his other brothers to Middle-earth in the year before the rising of the Moon, as is told in *The Silmarillion*,[3] and took part in the Battle-under-Stars in Mithrim and Ard-galen, afterwards taking Thargelion, the most easterly portion of Beleriand, as his realm. He was thus the first of the High-elven lords to encounter the Dwarves, who dwelt at that time beyond the Ered Luin in their cities of Nogrod and Belegost. As a result, all trade between Dwarves and Elves passed first through Caranthir's lands, affording him and his people considerable profit. But the main focus of his interest lay of course in the North, and to guard against the evil of Morgoth, Caranthir fortified the mountains about Lake Helevorn (for this eastern sector of the front was the most difficult to defend).

It is told that all of the Sons of Fëanor were prickly, and though valiant, not the easiest of allies. Caranthir exemplified this touchiness. The annals of the times are replete with stories of misunderstandings and missed opportunities, many of which can be laid to the door of the brothers – or to their Oath – and most of all perhaps to Caranthir. For example, he at first underrated the valour of the Edain, so indirectly contributing to the grievous losses sustained by the Haladin when first they came to Beleriand; and he hated the sons of Finarfin (though we are not told why), and thereby did much to sow dissension between the Noldor and King Thingol, who was of course related to Finarfin's kindred.

Caranthir held his lands – named now *Dor Caranthir* ('Caranthir's Land') – for many hundreds of years, and did his part in the War; but in the Battle of Sudden Flame, whereby Morgoth overthrew the Siege of Angband, the front held by the Eldar and the Edain was broken, and Thargelion was invaded. Caranthir, with the remnant of his people, fled south, to the land of the brethren Amrod and Amras, and there he dwelt until the Nirnaeth Arnoediad.

In that grievous battle Caranthir played a valiant part; but it is also told that it was the allies he brought to the fight, Men of Eastern

race (not Edain), who were in great part responsible for the defeat
sustained by the Eldar on that day: for Caranthir's 'allies' were
secretly in Morgoth's pay (see ULDOR THE ACCURSED) and it was their
sudden betrayal at the height of the battle which brought ruin upon
the rearguard, and so upon the whole Eldarin army. Afterwards
Caranthir, together with his brothers Curufin and Celegorm, lived a
hunted life in Beleriand, with no realms to rule, making no war upon
Morgoth but seeking still for some way to fulfil the Oath sworn long
before. And in their wandering days they fell into evil thoughts, and
committed evil actions. It came to their ears, after a while, that a
Silmaril had been recovered from Morgoth and lay hid in Menegroth;
and they resolved to recover the Jewel, by any means possible – as
indeed they were bound to do, by their Oath. Thingol Greycloak of
Doriath, to whom the Jewel had indeed been given (by Beren and
Lúthien), was already dead, slain in his own hall; but Thingol's heir
Dior Eluchíl ruled in Menegroth, and was the new Keeper of the
Silmaril. Him it was whom the three brothers, Celegorm, Curufin
and Caranthir now attacked, by stealth and in the dead of winter.
But they were unsuccessful in their objective (for the Silmaril was
carried to safety by Dior's daughter Elwing the White); and, though
they succeeded in slaying the Heir of Thingol – and in destroying
Doriath – all three were killed.

Caras Galadhon 'The City of the Trees' (Sind.) Chief dwelling-
place of the Elves of Lothlórien, where:
> . . . there rose to a great height a green wall encircling a green hill
> thronged with mallorn-trees . . . Their height could not be guessed,
> but they stood up in the twilight like living towers. In their many-
> tiered branches and amid their ever-moving leaves countless lights
> were gleaming, green and gold and silver.[4]

The mightiest of the *mellyrn* bore several great platforms, or *flets*,
the highest of which held 'a house, so large that almost it would have
served for a hall of Men upon the earth.'[5] There, during the Second
and Third Ages, dwelt the Lady Galadriel and her husband Celeborn
the Wise.

Note: the name *Caras Galadhon* is probably of Silvan (East-elven)
origin.

Carc An ancient raven of the Lonely Mountain, father of Roäc,
Thorin Oakenshield's messenger before and during the Battle of
Five Armies (2941 Third Age).

Note: the name is not translated in the tongues of Elves or Men,
and is probably of onomatopoeic origin.

Carcharoth 'The Red Maw' (Sind.) Called also *Anfauglir*, ('the Jaws of Thirst'). The Wolf of Angband, Guardian of the Gates of Morgoth's Realm in the North; the Slayer of Beren and of Huan the Hound of Valinor; and, for a time, the Keeper of a Silmaril.

We are told that this great beast was in origin a cub of the brood of the werewolf Draugluin; but that Morgoth, fearing the power of Huan – of whom it was said that he should not die until he had encountered the greatest wolf of the world – took the cub, and nourished it in evil ways, until it outgrew all others of the wolf-race. Then Carcharoth was sent to guard the gates of Angband.

On a time Beren and Lúthien came by evil roads to that place, and there Carcharoth challenged them, but was overcome by the power of Lúthien; then for a while he slept. But they, having secured a Silmaril from Morgoth's Iron Crown,[6] were hindered in their escape by the Wolf, who was now undaunted by spells and who attacked them. Beren attempted to ward him off with the power of the Jewel, but the Wolf was not easily affected by such prohibitions, and bit off Beren's hand which held the Silmaril, swallowing it. Then the pain of the Jewel – which endured no evil, and burned wicked flesh – drove him mad, so that he fled in anguish and rage, and gave no thought afterwards to his duties, or indeed to anything but the terrible pain in his belly.

After a time of thus raging hither and thither throughout northern Beleriand, Carcharoth came on a time to the fences of Doriath, and broke through the ring of enchantment set upon that land. In the northern part of the Forest of Neldoreth he was caught by hunters from Menegroth – who included Beren and Huan – and there, in the ensuing battle, Carcharoth slew Beren and the Hound of Valinor, but was himself slain by Huan before he died. His great corpse was then disembowelled, and the Silmaril recovered.

Carchost Carchost ('Fang-fort') and Narchost '(Fire-fort') were the names originally given to the two Towers of the Teeth which guarded the Black Gate into Mordor. Both were originally built by Gondor to prevent entry to the Black Land, early in the Third Age, after Sauron's first overthrow.

Cardolan In 861 Third Age, at the death of King Eärendur, the realm of ARNOR was divided into three, owing to quarrels among his sons. The separate states which emerged were Arthedain, Rhudaur and Cardolan ('Land-of-Red-Hills'). The kingdom of Cardolan included all the lands of Eriador between the rivers Baranduin and Mitheithel-Gwathlo as far north as the Great East Road. The hill tower of Amon Sûl thus lay on the border between Cardolan and the easternmost of the three kingdoms, Rhudaur. Possession of this strategic point later became a source of conflict between the two states.

The story of Cardolan is sad, as are the histories of all three North-kingdoms. Often at war with Rhudaur, which early fell into evil ways under the influence of the Witch-realm of Angmar, Cardolan none-theless managed to survive until the great invasion of 1409, when forces of Angmar and Rhudaur marched across the border and surrounded Amon Sûl (Weathertop). The tower was burned, Cardo-lan's ally Arthedain was forced to retreat, and the surviving Dúnedain of Cardolan were driven to take refuge in Tyrn Gorthad (the Barrow-downs) and in the Old Forest. The last prince of the kingdom was slain in this war.

The Great Plague which came from the East in the year 1636 Third Age decimated the remaining population of Cardolan, and the kingdom was never re-established.

Carl Cotton The youngest son of Tolman Cotton (Farmer Cotton), Hobbit of the Shire. He was known within the immediate family circle as 'Nibs'.

Carn Dûm The chief city of the Witch-realm of Angmar. It was situated near the northernmost peak of the Misty Mountains, to the immediate south of the great Northern Waste. From this fortress the Witch-king planned and carried out his long – and ultimately successful – assault upon the surviving Dúnedain kingdoms of the North.

Carnimírië 'Red-jewels' (Q.) A rowan-tree of the Forest of Fan-gorn, much beloved by the Ent Quickbeam (Bregalad). Many rowans were destroyed by Orcs of Saruman, arousing the anger of this (relatively) impulsive Ent (see Book III Chap. 4).

Carnen The Red River, which flowed from a source in the western range of the Iron Hills to join the Celduin (River Running) north of Dorwinion. The enlarged river emptied into the great inland Sea of Rhûn.

Carnil 'Red-star' (Q., from *carnë-êl*) The star Betelgeuse, created for the lightening of Middle-earth by Varda (Elbereth).

Carrock A huge boulder, carven with stairs and a high seat, which lay in the river Anduin some miles north of the Ford which bore its name (etymologically related to the Sindarin word *Carach*, 'fang').

Castamir the Usurper From 1437–47 Third Age, the twenty-second King of Gondor. His accession to the throne was brought about by the great civil war, the Kin-strife.

King Eldacar was the son of Valacar, who had wedded Vidumavi, a fair lady of Rhovanion – but one of a lesser race than the Dúnedain accounted themselves. To these disaffected princes and nobles, it was unthinkable that one of mixed blood (and of shorter lifespan) should inherit the crown. Therefore, when Eldacar suceeded his father in 1432, there was rebellion in Gondor.

Led by Castamir, the Captain of the Fleets, the rebels besieged Eldacar in Osgiliath, finally driving the young King from the burning city in 1437. Castamir then ordered the execution of Eldacar's son, Ornendil, and put the city to the sack. Though a cruel and haughty man, he commanded the allegiance of the fleets, and of the southern fiefs: thus he proclaimed himself King.

But the Usurper's initial support quickly faded when it was seen that he neglected the land. A seaman, his main concern was for the Fleet, and he soon made preparations to remove the royal seat to Pelargir, the ancient haven near the Mouths of Anduin. In 1447 Third Age – when Castamir had ruled for a mere ten years – Eldacar, who had been gathering support in the land of his mother's kin, Rhovanion, marched south with a host at his back, gaining forces as he moved ever southwards. His armies finally met those of Castamir at the Crossings of the river Erui, in Lebennin. There, the rightful King personally slew Castamir, but the Usurper's sons escaped and took refuge at Pelargir. They later sailed away to Umbar and founded there a refuge for the foes of Gondor.

See also CORSAIRS OF UMBAR.

Causeway Forts Twin fortified towers guarding the road from Osgiliath to Minas Tirith, at the point where it ran through the Rammas Echor into the fields of the Pelennor.

Caverns of Helm's Deep See AGLAROND.

Caverns of Narog See NARGOTHROND.

Caves of the Forgotten According to a legend of the Dúnedain, the Caves of the Forgotten are grots in the eastern sides of the Pelóri, wherein lie buried the hosts of Ar-Pharazôn – and the last King of Númenor himself – who assailed Aman the Blessed and so brought destruction upon the Ancient World.

Celduin The River Running, which flowed out of the lake of Esgaroth to join the Carnen (Red River) north of Dorwinion. The enlarged river emptied into the inland Sea of Rhûn.

Celebdil 'Silver-tine' (Sind.) One of the three great peaks of the Misty Mountains, below which lay the ancient Dwarf-realm of Moria; the other two were Caradhras (the Redhorn) and Fanuidhol (Cloudyhead). The Dwarves knew the mountain as *Zirak-zigil*.

High in its peak – and remembered only in Dwarvish tradition – was the legendary Endless Stair, which climbed in unbroken spiral from the lowest Deep of Old Moria. This titanic work was constructed in the days of Moria's glory by stonewrights of Durin the Deathless. At the head of the Stair, carved into the living rock, was set a chamber and high ledge known as Durin's Tower.

Celeborn 'Silver-tree' (Sind.) A Grey-elven lord and a kinsman of King Thingol Greycloak. He later wedded the Lady Galadriel, afterwards becoming Lord of Lothlórien, where he dwelt until the beginning of the Fourth Age. He was the mightiest of the Grey-elven princes to remain in Middle-earth after the fall of Beleriand.

At the beginning of the Second Age Celeborn dwelled in Lindon (last remnant of Beleriand), later travelling to Eregion with Galadriel, most noble of the High-elven Exiles. When Eregion fell, Galadriel and Celeborn – and his kinsman Thranduil – passed east over the Misty Mountains to establish realms among the Silvan Elves of the forests far away. Thranduil took the northern part of Greenwood the Great for his kingdom; Celeborn and Galadriel passed further south to the ancient Elf-realm of Lórien (known also as *Laurelindórenan*).

There they dwelt through the Ages that followed: their power and wisdom – and the grey-feathered arrows of the Wood-elves – keeping all foes at bay. When Galadriel finally returned over Sea at the end of the Third Age, Celeborn abandoned the woods of Lothlórien and dwelt for a while in Rivendell, together with the sons of Elrond. No record remains of the date when he finally grew weary of Mortal Lands and sailed west from the Grey Havens, taking with him 'the last living memory of the Elder Days in Middle-earth.'[7]

Note: this name is also applied to the White Tree of Eressëa (a seedling of the Tree of Tirion, Galathilion) in records of the First Age.

Celebrant 'Silver-course' (Sind.) The Silverlode River. Rising from icy sources in the Dimrill Dale, it flowed through Lothlórien to join the Anduin at Egladil, southernmost point of the Naith of Lórien.

The Nimrodel stream was one of its tributaries. Its source in the Dimrill Dale was known to Dwarves as *Kibil-nâla*.

Celebrían (Sind., from the older form *Celebrîande*; meaning not known) The daughter of Celeborn and Galadriel, the wife of Elrond and the mother of Elladan, Elrohir and Arwen Evenstar.

In the year 2509 Third Age, while travelling from Rivendell to Lórien, Celebrían was waylaid by Orcs of the Mountains, who captured and tormented her until a swift rescue was accomplished by her sons. Though her poisoned wound was healed by Elrond, she lost all desire to stay in Middle-earth and passed over Sea the following year.

Celebrimbor 'Silver-fist' (Sind., from Q. *Telperinquar*) At the end of the First Age, a number of the High-elves (the Noldor) who had survived the War of the Great Jewels were forbidden by the Valar to return to their ancient home in Valinor. Chief among these Exiles were the princes and queens of the Royal Houses of Fëanor, Finarfin and Fingolfin.

Celebrimbor was the last lord of the House of Fëanor and the greatest of all Eldarin craftsmen to survive the War. He was the son of Curufin the Crafty, and therefore a grandson of Fëanor, and he dwelt with his father's people in Himlad after the return to Middle-earth – until the Battle of Sudden Flame, which broke the northern Elf-kingdoms and overthrew the Siege of Angband. Then Curufin and Celegorm and Caranthir and their sons and people were driven south and west in disarray. The people of Caranthir joined with kin of the brethren Amrod and Amrast in the south; while Celegorm and Curufin and their sons and people passed south-west, to the Kingdom of Nargothrond, then ruled by Finrod Felagund of the House of Finarfin. They came as vassals, but they were driven by need; and between the Houses of Fëanor and Finarfin there was not a little ill-feeling. Therefore the dispossessed brothers, together with their following, instead of being grateful for the sanctuary afforded them, bethought them of one day seizing this strong, Dwarf-delved domain under the hills from its rightful lord; but they bided their time.

Their time soon came, as is recorded in *The Silmarillion*.[8] There came a day when Beren son of Barahir came to Nargothrond, at the outset of his quest (for a Silmaril), invoking the pledge of friendship made years before to his father by Finrod King of Nargothrond. Finrod agreed to honour his words with deeds, and prepared to join with Beren on the quest; and at this time the Sons of Fëanor,

Celegorm and Curufin, made their move. They played skilfully upon the fears of the Elves of Nargothrond, so that Finrod was forced to abdicate his kingship before setting out – in favour of themselves. But after a while, tidings came back to Nargothrond of Finrod's heroism, and of his death, and then the Elves of Nargothrond turned upon the brothers, for they were ashamed of all that had been done, and perceived for the first time that the ambition and unscrupulousness of the Sons of Fëanor lay behind Finrod's fall. They cast out Curufin and Celegorm – and in that hour Celebrimbor the son of Curufin grew ashamed of his father's deeds, and repudiated them and him, and remained in Nargothrond when Curufin and Celegorm – now entirely without a following – were cast out.

It is not stated in available records how Celebrimbor came to survive the wreck of Nargothrond or the battle on Tumhalad. In all probability he, and the remnant of the Noldor which he now led – the last of the house of Curufin – afterwards went to dwell in the coastlands, or where they might; and took no further part in the War. So the Age passed.

It is also not known for certain whether the ban laid by the Valar on the return of the most prominent of the Exiles applied to Celebrimbor; at all events, in 750 Second Age he led his folk across the Blue Mountains to the lands west of Moria, where it had been reported that *mithril*, a metal most beloved of Elves, had been discovered under the mountains. There they established a realm called Eregion (Hollin), built their city of Ost-in-Edhil,[9] and engaged in trade with the Dwarves of Moria. The friendship that grew up there was the closest that had ever been known between the two races – and Celebrimbor himself etched the designs in the Hollin-door of Moria as a token of their mutual esteem (see Book II Chap. 4).

· Nonetheless the Smiths of the Noldor were ever thirsty for knowledge and craft-secrets; and, exploiting this desire, Sauron the Great (even then arising again in Middle-earth), seduced the Elves by revealing to them the techniques of Ring-making. Under his tutelage they grew in their craft, making first the lesser Rings, then the Nine and the Seven. The Three Elf-rings were created by Celebrimbor alone – and the One Ring was forged in secret by Sauron himself, 'to bring them all and in the darkness bind them'.

But the instant Sauron put on the Ring, far away in the heart of the volcano Orodruin, Celebrimbor became aware of the spell and hid the Three that he had made. Sauron's forces afterwards invaded Eriador and in 1697 Second Age they razed Eregion – though they were unable to enter Moria. Celebrimbor was slain and the Noldor were driven out.

See also WAR OF THE ELVES AND SAURON.

Celebrindal 'Silver-foot' (Sind.) See IDRIL CELEBRINDAL.

Celebrindor 'Land-of-Silver' (Sind.) From 1191–1272 Third Age, the fifth King of Arthedain.

Celebros 'Silver-foam' (Sind.) A stream of the Forest of Brethil, whose source may have lain on Amon Obel. It flowed westwards, down through the steep woodlands, until finally it fell into the swift Teiglin in a fall called Dimrost, the 'Rainy-stair'.

Celegorm the Fair The third Son of Fëanor, born in Eldamar during the Years of the Trees. During that time he came to be accounted among the following of Oromë the Vala; and Celegorm learned much of the lore of living creatures. He was the most wood-crafty of all the High-elves, being called also The Huntsman of the Noldor.

But – as is told in many stories – Celegorm, together with his six brothers, took the Oath of Fëanor and came back to Middle-earth in a great fleet of ships to make war upon Morgoth, who had stolen the Silmarils. In the first battle fought by the Noldor against Angband, Celegorm played a singular part; for it was he who, passing first of all across the Mountains of Shadow, was in a position to bear down victoriously on the flank of an orc-host: that same host which had previously laid siege to the Havens of the Falas (see BATTLES OF BELERIAND) and which, hitherto undefeated, was coming north to the aid of their comrades fleeing from the Noldor. After this battle Celegorm, together with Curufin, his closest friend and ally among the brethren, took up his abode in Himlad, the region between the Aros and the Celon; and there they dwelt for many centuries, until the Battle of Sudden Flame which overthrew their realm.

Celegorm is also renowned as being the master of the Hound of Valinor. This was Huan, who aided the quest of Beren and Lúthien, and who afterwards slew the great Wolf Carcharost. Long before, in the time of the Trees, Huan had been given by Oromë, his first master, to Celegorm, as a sign of friendship; and he had followed Celegorm faithfully ever after, even to Middle-earth, where it was decreed he should meet his fate. But Huan forsook Celegorm in order to aid Beren and Lúthien, twice frustrating evilly motivated attempts by the brethren Celegorm and Curufin to abduct and imprison Lúthien. And although he returned briefly to Celegorm's service, he later rejoined Beren and Lúthien and fell at last in battle at Beren's side.

However, Celegorm, since the Dagor Bragollach and the destruction of the realm that he and his brother had ruled, had now fallen into evil patterns of thought. In him, and in the brethren Caranthir and Curufin, the Oath they had taken indeed had wrought most grievous effects. And if they could work no destruction upon Morgoth – or indeed do anything at all to fulfil their Oath – they turned their counsels and their arms against their own kin. For in the growing darkness of their hearts they had lost the ability to distinguish friend from foe.

It has been told (see CELEBRIMBOR) how they came to dominate the counsels of Nargothrond, and how they successfully forced Finrod Felagund, that city's rightful king, to abdicate in favour of themselves. It was at that time that Lúthien, fleeing from Doriath, came among the Elves of Nargothrond; but Celegorm and Curufin imprisoned her – though not harshly, for Celegorm desired her. But it was at this time that Huan the Hound of Valinor first lent his aid to Lúthien, and he helped her escape from Nargothrond; and when, in a later time, she was again threatened with capture by Celegorm, Huan, who had meanwhile returned to the service of his master, now left this service for ever; and he would not let Celegorm approach, and indeed saw him never more.

It was soon afterwards that Celegorm and Curufin, and Caranthir their brother, fell into the greatest evil of all. For they, learning of the Silmaril which was lodged in Menegroth, determined, according to their vow, to take it for themselves (see CARANTHIR). And for the second time there was battle and murder in the halls of Menegroth in Doriath (Thingol was already dead). In that fight Celegorm was slain by Dior Eluchíl, Thingol's heir.

Celepharn From 1110–91 Third Age, fourth King of Arthedain, father of Celebrindor.

Celon 'Falling-water' (Sind.) A tributary of the river Aros; the eastern border of Himlad. Its source was in the Hills of Himring.

Celos A river of Lebennin (a large province of Gondor), running from the southern slopes of the White Mountains to the Great River. It was not a major stream, being a tributary of the larger Sirith, which it joined some twenty-five leagues north of Pelargir.

Note: this name is also spelt *Kelos*. Its meaning is probably similar to *Celon* above.

Cemendur From 158–238 Third age, the fourth King of Gondor.

'Ceorl' A formal mode of address in Rohan, used by one of high rank to a person of lesser status. (The word has descended into modern usage as 'churl'.)

Cerin Amroth The name given in Lothlórien to the dwelling-mound of the Elven-prince Amroth.

> Upon it, as a double crown, grew two circles of trees: the outer had bark of snowy white, and were leafless but beautiful in their shapely nakedness; the inner were mallorn-trees of great height, still arrayed in pale gold. High amid the branches of a towering tree that stood in the centre of all there gleamed a white flet.[10]

Cermië (Q.) The seventh month in Kings' and Stewards' Reckoning and the fourth in the New Reckoning, being roughly equivalent to our July in all three systems. The Dúnedain called this month by its Sindarin name, *Cerveth*. The Hobbits of the Shire knew it as *Afterlithe*, while in Bree it was called *The Summerdays*.

Certar The Quenya word for 'runes', referring in particular to the ALPHABET OF DAERON. They were known to the Sindar as *certhas* (or *Círth*, the name for the system as a whole).

See Appendix E.

Certhas See CERTAR above.

Cerveth See CERMIË.

Chalcedony A mineral composed of pacted silica, usually banded, translucent, of a waxy lustre and extremely beautiful.

Chamber of Mazarbul The Chamber of Records of Old Moria, situated on the seventh Level, near the twenty-first Hall of the North End. In it were originally kept many chests containing inscribed stone tablets and ancient books of the Dwarves. But following the flight from Moria by the Dwarves – after the coming of the Balrog in 1980 Third Age – the Chamber was plundered by Orcs. None of the original records survived at the time of the War of the Ring.

The Chamber of Mazarbul was later used by Balin son of Fundin as a throne-room after his expedition entered Moria (2989 Third Age). Following his death, the remnant of his colony fought to the last in this chamber, falling finally in defence of Balin's tomb.

Chambers of Fire A translation of the Sindarin words *Sammath Naur;* more properly, a massive tunnel delved into the cone of the volcano Orodruin to gain access to the vast furnaces of the Mountain: the Cracks of Doom. Here Sauron forged the One Ring.

Chetwood A sizeable stretch of wooded area commencing on the north-eastern borders of the Bree-land and running for two days' march into the wild country beyond.

Chieftains of the Dúnedain For the three thousand years following the establishment of the Númenorean realms-in-exile, Gondor and Arnor, both kingdoms were under almost constant assault by foes of the Men of Westernesse. In Gondor, though the Line of Elendil ultimately failed, the Realm survived and the Dunedain of the South were then ruled by the House of the Stewards. But in Arnor, even though both the kingship and the state were destroyed, the Line of Isildur Elendil's son endured against all odds.

In 1974 Third Age, with the passing of Arvedui 'Last-king' – and the realm of Arthedain, last remnant of ancient Arnor – the surviving Dúnedain of that land forsook open royalty and passed into the shadows as simple Rangers of the wild. The Heir of Isildur was then known as Chieftain of the Dúnedain of Arnor – as an affirmation that, one day, the North-kingdom would be re-established. The first to take the title was Aranarth, son of Arvedui.

There were fifteen Chieftains before Aragorn II and the renewal of Arnor's royalty. Their names were: Aranarth, Arahael, Aranuir, Aravir, Aragorn I, Araglas, Arahad I, Aragost, Aravorn, Arahad II, Arassuil, Arathorn I, Argonui, Arador and Arathorn II. Though their self-imposed tasks of watchfulness and guardianship went largely unthanked (and unnoticed), the Chieftains of the Dúnedain never lost pride in their lineage – or hope in the eventual restoration of the fortunes of their House.

Each Chieftain was brought to manhood in Elrond's house, where also were kept the Heirlooms of the Line of Isildur: the Sceptre of Annúminas, the Ring of Barahir, the shards of the sword Narsil and the silver circlet, the Elendilmir, worn by the Kings of Arnor.

Children of Eru A translation of the Eldarin words *Erusēn* and *Eruhíni:* Elves and Men. Also called the Children of Ilúvatar or *Híni Ilúvataro* (Q.).

Children of the Sun Men.

Chithing The fourth month of the Bree-reckoning, corresponding to *astron* in Shire-usage.

Chubb A somewhat prosperous family of Hobbits in the Shire.

Chubb-Baggins A family of Shire Hobbits. The first Chubb-Baggins was Falco, son of Bingo (Baggins) and Chica (Chubb).

Círdan the Shipwright One of the mighty among the Grey-elves of the First, Second and Third Ages of Middle-earth; successively Lord of the Falathrim of Eglarest and Brithombar; Lord of the Isle of Balar; Lord of Lindon and Guardian of the Grey Havens – whence, from time to time, Elven-ships set sail into the West, never to return.

In his origins he was a noble Telerin Elf, of the kindred of the Sindar, whose people lingered in Beleriand when the remaining Eldar crossed for the first time into the West; they did so because of the pleas of the Maiarin Sea-lord Ossë. There, while at the same time Elwë Thingol was founding his realm of Doriath deep in the heart of the forests, they dwelt on the coasts; for they were enamoured of the Sea, and Ossë desired that they should live on the borders of his domain; and they were afterwards called the Falathrim, the 'Coast-elves'. The chief of these was Círdan. He was therefore of the Falathrim, of the Sindar, and of the Teleri all at once. His chief city was Eglarest, though at that time his people also founded the Haven of Brithombar. (These were the two most ancient harbours of the Elves in Middle-earth.)

Throughout the War of the Jewels Círdan remained for the most part in the Falas, guarding the coasts (with aid from Finrod of Nargothrond; see BARAD NIMRAIS) against any assault from Angband that might arrive by sea; though on one occasion at least he took the field of battle with a host, and that was seven years after the Battle of Sudden Flame, when he led a seaborne force to the aid of Fingon the High King, beleaguered in Hithlum and in desperate straits, playing a decisive part in that slender victory. But twenty-eight years afterwards there came the Day of Lamentation, the Battle of Numberless Tears, in which the hosts and the kingdoms of the Noldor were thrown down for ever; and in the aftermath of that terrible defeat the armies of Morgoth laid seige to the Havens of Eglarest and Brithombar, and took them, and destroyed them. Círdan and the remnant of his people then went aboard the last ships and fled to the offshore Isle of Balar, where they lay hid for the rest of the war.

During the Second and Third Ages of Middle-earth, Círdan the Shipwright – who dwelt after the ruin of Beleriand in Lindon, at the Grey Havens founded in Year One, Second Age – was held to be the wisest of the Eldar; to him Celebrimbor gave one of the Three Rings, Narya the Great, Ring of Fire. At the end of the Second Age he marched with Gil-galad in the Army of the Last Alliance and, together with Elrond, Herald of Gil-galad, he stood at the side of the last King of Lindon during the final combat with Sauron on the slopes of Orodruin, watching in sorrow as Gil-galad fell.

In about the thousandth year of the Third Age, Gandalf the Grey arrived at the Grey Havens; Círdan then surrendered the Ring Narya to the Wizard – for he knew whither Mithrandir came and when he would depart. In the years that followed, Círdan aided the Dúnedain of the North-kingdoms as often as he might; indeed, he led the forces of Lindon which crossed the Lhûn (in 1974 Third Age) and overthrew the Witch-king of Angmar at the Battle of Fornost, a military feat recalling the battle in Hithlum long before.

But Círdan was still the Keeper of the Havens, the Elves' Shipwright, and his heart dwelt by the Sea. It is told that he remained at the Havens until the end, sailing west himself on the last ship to leave Middle-earth.

Ciril A river of Lamedon in southern Gondor. It rose in a high vale of the White Mountains, flowed south past the hill-town of Calembel, and joined the Ringló some fifteen leagues below the Ethring Ford.

Note: this name is sometimes spelt *Kiril*.

Cirion From 2489-2567 Third Age, the twelfth Ruling Steward of Gondor. It was during his long Stewardship that Gondor was threatened by the Easterlings known as the Balchoth, who dwelt at that time south and east of Mirkwood. Fearing invasion, Cirion sent north for aid from the Horsemen of Éothéod, northern folk friendly to Gondor. Before his messages could arrive, however, the Balchoth swarmed across the Great River and began to pillage the northern province of Calenardhon. Cirion dispatched the Northern Army of Gondor to hold the invaders, but disaster struck and the Dúnedain were soon in desperate straits.

It is told elsewhere (see BATTLE OF THE FIELD OF CELEBRANT) how the Men of Éothéod arrived in the nick of time and destroyed the Balchoth. In his wisdom, Cirion chose to repay the Riders of Éothéod by granting them the province they had saved (in exchange for an Oath of Alliance).

Cirith Gorgor 'Haunted Pass' (Sind.) A defile or gorge at the juncture of the Mountains of Shadow and the Ered Lithui which served the Dark Lord as the main entrance to Mordor. Across the mouth of this defile lay the Morannon, the Black Gate, blocking all entrance to the pass and to the deep vale of Udûn which lay beyond.

Cirith Ninniach 'Rainbow Pass' (Sind.) The steep gorge in the Shadowy Mountains (Ered Wethrin) through which ran the (unnamed) stream which fed the Firth of Drengist.

Cirith Thoronath 'Eagle Pass' (Sind.) The highest pass in the Encircling Mountains; it lay to the north of Tumladen and Gondolin. This was the route taken by those few of the Noldar and the Edain who escaped the sack of Gondolin. Here fell Glorfindel, in battle with a Balrog.

Cirith Ungol The Spider's Pass. This high route across the Mountains of Shadow from Minas Ithil (Minas Morgul) to Gorgoroth consisted, in fact, of two passes: one clearly marked and one secret.

The main route, the Morgul Pass, ran past the gates of that evil city; the secret, more tortuous path climed up endless broken steps, past yawning chasms, until it reached a cleft between two jagged peaks at the very summit of the Ephel Dúath. There the Spider had her lair.

See also SHELOB THE GREAT.

Cirth 'Runes' (Sind.) See ALPHABET OF DAERON; CERTAR; Appendix E.

Ciryaher From 1015–1149 Third Age, the fifteenth King of Gondor. He was remembered as the most powerful of all the rulers of that realm. In the year 1050, after conquering the Harad, he changed his name to *Hyarmendacil*.

Ciryandil From 936–1015 Third Age, the fourteenth King of Gondor (and father of Ciryaher, later known as Hyarmendacil I). Ciryandil ('Ship-lover') was the third of the line of 'Ship-kings' of Gondor. Sea-minded like his father Eärnil I, he continued Eärnil's policy of extensive fleet construction. He later fell in battle against the Haradrim, and his son took mighty revenge.

Ciryatan (Tar-Ciryatan) 'Ship-builder' (Q.) The twelfth King of Númenor, and the first to commence active exploitation of the coastal lands of Middle-earth. There he built great havens and forts, levying tribute from the lesser Men who dwelt in that part of the world.

Ciryon The third of the four sons of Isildur; killed at the massacre of the Gladden Fields (Year 2 Third Age).

Citadel of the Stars The literal translation of the Sindarin word *Osgiliath;* the name of the great city of Gondor astride the river Anduin, and the oldest seat of the Kings of that realm.

The city was burned during the Kin-strife (in 1437 Third Age) and, though resettlement was later attempted, Osgiliath never recovered its former eminence. It was finally deserted a thousand years later and afterwards became desolate.

City of the Corsairs The City of Umbar.

City of the Trees A translation of the Sindarin name *Caras Galadhon*.

'Closed Door' A translation of *Fen Hollen* (Sind.).

Cloudyhead The name given in the Common Speech (Westron) to the mountain known as Fanuidhol (or *Bundushathûr*, in the Dwarvish speech); one of the three Mountains of Moria. The other two were the Redhorn (Caradhras) and the Silvertine (Celebdil).

Coirë The season of the year known, in the Elves' calendar system, as 'stirring'. It was judged the last of the six seasons observed by the Elves, falling between winter (*hrivë*) and spring (*tuilë*).

See also CALENDAR OF IMLADRIS.

Cold-drake A species of Dragon, found in the Grey Mountains and in the wastes beyond, and not of the usual fire-breathing sort. In the year 2589 Third Age, Dáin I, of the Dwarves of the Ered Mithrin (Grey Mountains) was slain, together with his son Frór, by a beast of this kind; this caused his folk to abandon the mountains and return to Erebor.

Coldfells The Ettenmoors north of Rivendell; a notorious haunt of Trolls.

Combe A village in a deep valley of the Bree-land.

Common Speech The Westron; the language spoken most widely among the peoples of the westlands of Middle-earth throughout the Third Age. (It is represented by English in the various translations from the Red Book that have so far been published.[11]) The Common Speech or Westron was an ancient Mannish tongue, much modified by Elvish words and inflexions, and further altered in later years by assorted influences from other tongues of those Men whom the Dúnedain of Númenor found on their return to Middle-earth.

In the Third Age, the Westron became a *lingua franca* of the Westlands, being spoken (at least as a second tongue) by most folk who dwelt there, including the Elves. It is true that the Rohirrim always preferred their ancestral tongue, which was itself related to an early ancestor of the Westron, Adûnaic (the speech of the Edain before the Second Age); and it is also true that the language spoken by Men of the upper Anduin and the towns of Dale and Esgaroth was derived from similar origins. But these peoples also knew the Common Speech, and used it fluently at need, and the Men of Bree and of Eriador – and the Halflings of the Shire – spoke the Westron as their native language; indeed, few of these peoples knew any other.

But in Gondor many preferred an Elvish tongue, though not all of them used the Grey-elven (Sindarin) language as a daily speech. Only the Dúnedain themselves spoke Sindarin freely (for matters of learning their loremasters also used the High-elven Quenya). Yet all folk of Gondor could speak the Westron – unlike the men of Dunland and the Wild Men of Druadan Forest, who spoke only ancient tongues which owed little or nothing to the Common Speech. Another unrelated language was Khuzdul, the ancient Dwarf-tongue which no other race succeeded in learning. But unlike the more primitive Dunlendings and Wild Men, the Dwarves of Erebor and of the Ered Luin also spoke the Westron freely and fluently (and preserved Khuzdul primarily for their own secret purposes).

Note: for additional information concerning Languages and Peoples of the Third Age, see Appendix F.

See also SPOKEN TONGUES.

Company of the Ring See FELLOWSHIP OF THE RING.

Coranar 'Sun-round' (Q.) The solar year, as recorded by the Elves. This period was more usually called a *loa*. The long Elvish 'year', the *yén* (pl. *yéni*) was, in fact, equivalent to 144 *loa*.

Cormallen 'Ring-of-Gold' (Sind.) See FIELD OF CORMALLEN.

Cormarë 'Ring-day' (Q.) This day, equivalent to September 22nd in the old style, was declared a feast day in the New Reckoning of the Fourth Age. It was, of course, Frodo's (and Bilbo's) Birthday.

Corollairë 'Evergreen-Mound [of the Two Trees]' (Q.)
See EZELLOHAR.

Corsairs of Umbar Chief among the foes of Gondor during the later Third Age were the assorted brigands, pirates and seaborne raiders known to the Dúnedain as the Corsairs of Umbar. The fierce hostility of the Corsairs to the South-kingdom was deep rooted, being partly inherited and partly based on the determination of successive Kings of Gondor – especially the four 'Ship-kings' – to brook no enemy or independent lordship within striking distance of their might.

Lying to the south, along the coasts of the Harad, the ancient fortress and harbour of Umbar was one of the earliest Númenorean settlements in Middle-earth – the original Haven having been established sometime after the year 600 Second Age. The original inhabitants of this great cape and port were of that race later known as BLACK NÚMENOREANS, utterly opposed to the Faithful, and themselves followers of the latter Kings of Númenor.

When that land sank beneath the Sea at the end of the Second Age, these 'King's Men', corrupted by Sauron during the Black Years, became hostile to Gondor – until 933 Third Age, when Eärnil I, the second 'Ship-king', captured the Havens of Umbar and drove out the renegades. (It may well have been the growing sea-power of Umbar which prompted Tarannon Falastur, first 'Ship-king', to strengthen Gondor's fleets in the first place, some years before.) The Black Númenoreans attempted to retake Umbar for many years – indeed, in alliance with the Men of Harad, they besieged it – but they were decisively defeated and scattered by Ciryaher (Hyarmendacil I) in the year 1050 Third Age.

Some four hundred years later, in 1447, Umbar fell from Gondor's control when the sons of Castamir the Usurper sailed from Pelargir with the remaining rebel fleets of Gondor and seized the ancient haven as a refuge. The Corsairs, as they were afterwards known, raided Gondor's coasts ceaselessly until 1810, when King Telumehtar (Umbardacil) retook the port and slew the last of Castamir's Line.

Soon afterwards, the power of the Harad arose again and Umbar changed hands once more, as the Haradrim made the haven – and its naval strength – an adjunct of their own kingdoms. Raiding and piracy continued; and, in 2758 Third Age, the greatest force that had ever sailed from Umbar attacked the coasts of Gondor (in three fleets with black sails), striking as far north as the mouth of the Isen. Beregond son of Beren (nineteenth Steward) repulsed the Corsair invasions but there was great loss and destruction. After some years of quiescence, the Corsairs again sent a fleet against Gondor, in the War of the Ring; but, as is told elsewhere, the black sails ascended the Anduin no further than Pelargir before defeat overtook them. But Umbar remained inviolate and, while the Age lasted, the Corsairs' ships were an ever-present threat to the fiefs of the South.[12]

Cotman The ancestor of the Cotton family of Hobbits of the Shire. *Note:* his original (as opposed to translated) name was *Hlothram*, 'Cottager'.

Cotton A family of Shire-hobbits.

Council of Elrond A meeting held in Rivendell, the house of Elrond, in the year 3018 Third Age, to debate the lore of the Rings and to decide the ultimate fate of the One Ring borne by Frodo the Hobbit. All of the Free Peoples – Elves, Men, Dwarves and Hobbits – were represented. Much of great import was discussed, and the true extent of the danger in which all Peoples then lay was, for the first time, openly revealed.

After arduous debate, the decision was taken by those assembled to mount a quest into Mordor, with the object of destroying the Ruling Ring. It was the Hobbit Frodo Baggins who took this Quest upon himself.

See also Book II Chap. 2.

Council of the North-kingdom Founded early in the Fourth Age by King Elessar (Aragorn II), this was a group of advisers enrolled to give counsel concerning the reconstituted realm of Arnor. Included in this Body were the Mayor and Thain of the Shire and the Master of Buckland.

Court of the Fountain The Place of the Fountain was a courtyard in the Citadel of Minas Tirith, where the White Tree grew. From the Court, steps led to the Tower of Ecthelion, highest point in the City.

Craban (pl. *Crebain*) 'Crow' (Sind.) An unfriendly species of black crow found in the hills and woods of Dunland and Fangorn, and easily recruited by enemies of Men and Elves as watchers and spies.

Cracks of Doom The huge fissures in the floor of the *Sammath Naur*, the 'Chambers of Fire' tunnelled into the side of the cone of the volcano Orodruin. In these vast natural furnaces burned the only fire in Middle-earth hot enough to destroy the Ruling Ring. No other flame, not even the ancient fire of the Dragons, was fierce enough for this purpose. Hence the Quest of the Ring-bearer.

Cram A type of waybread, or biscuit, baked by Northern Men for journeys in the Wild. By all accounts it was somewhat uninspiring to eat, but it stowed away easily and was rich in food-content.

Crebain See CRABAN.

Crickhollow The location of a house owned by the Brandybuck family and used by them to shelter guests who found the life of Brandy Hall somewhat crowded. It lay some distance north of Bucklebury, not far from the High Hay.

Crissaegrim 'Cloven-peaks' (Sind.) The southern and southward-facing faces of the Encircling Mountains: a sheer wall of great height, overlooking the vale of Dimbar in the north of Beleriand. Here the great Eagle, Thorondor, and all his kin besides, made their lofty eyries, beyond the reach of friend and foe alike.

Crossings of Erui A ford or watering-place across the river Erui in Lebennin, south of the White Mountains in the land of Gondor. In the year 1447 Third Age, the major battle of Gondor's civil war, the Kin-strife, was fought on this site with much loss of life on both sides.

Crossings of Isen The fords across the river Isen north of Helm's Deep, where the road from Isengard to Anórien ran beside the river for some leagues before crossing the shallowest point and turning south-east.

See also BATTLES OF THE FORDS OF ISEN.

Crossings of Poros The Poros river marked the boundary between South Ithilien, in Gondor, and the debatable lands known as South Gondor, frequently invaded by Men of Harad. Where the Harad road crossed the river – before branching west to Pelargir and north to the hills of Emyn Arnen – there lay a series of shallow fords. This was the traditional invasion route from the Southlands, and a traditional first point of defence.

In 2885 Third Age, Gondor, aided by Rohan, won a great victory over an invading army of Haradrim at these Crossings.

Crossings of Teiglin The most southerly ford across the swift river Teiglin, before this stream became too torrential, and its sides too precipitous, for crossing. These fords lay some three miles west of the most westerly eaves of Brethil, at a point where the old southern road from Tol Sirion and Mithrim to Nargothrond left the safety of the Forest and wandered out on to the plain of Talath Dirnen.

Cuiviénen 'Water of Awakening' (Q.) The name given in the traditions of the Eldar to the ancient lake, somewhere in the unknown East of Middle-earth, beside whose waters the Quendi 'awoke', far back in the deeps of time.

The Grey-elven form of this name was *Nen Echui*.

Note: see *The Silmarillion* (pp. 48–9) for a more precise account of the location of Cuiviénen.

Culúrien 'The-Red-and-Gold' (Q.) One of the many names given by the Valar and Eldar to LAURELIN THE GOLDEN, one of the Two Trees of Valinor.

Curse of Mandos The dreadful pronouncement of doom made upon the Noldor by the Vala Mandos, in Araman, after the rebellion of Fëanor and the Kinslaying at Alqualondë. It was the inevitable corollary to the Oath of Fëanor, and proved a truer collection of prophecies. (The full text, as recalled and recorded by the Noldor, can be found in *The Silmarillion*, p. 88.)

Curufin the Crafty The fifth son of Fëanor, and indeed that one of the seven brethren most like to their father in temperament and abilities. (His name is but an adaption of Fëanor's own birth-name *Curufinwë*.) He was born in Valinor, and like all the Sons of Fëanor took the dreadful Oath that carried Fëanor and his host and the hosts of his allies back to Middle-earth. There Curufin held lands in league with his brother CELEGORM, with whom he had most in common; and throughout the War he fought and schemed at Celegorm's side. For this reason the tale of his life and deeds is essentially the same as Celegorm's and may be found under the entry of that name.

Nevertheless it may be stated here that, apart from Fëanor himself, of all the Noldor who came back to Middle-earth in those days, Curufin seems to have been the most 'evil' (if *evil* is a word that can safely be applied to any of the Eldar.) Certainly his were the most evil deeds, though it was perhaps his inheritance of character combined with the driving force of the Oath they had all taken which was ultimately responsible. Next to Fëanor himself, Curufin was the greatest craftsmen of the Noldor – and great service he could have rendered; but in latter days chose instead to scheme and plot and wage war against those whose interests were in common with his own. He was slain in the attack on Doriath, together with Celegorm and Caranthir.

Curufinwë 'The Skilful' (Q.) The birth-name of the Noldorin prince FËANOR given by his father Finwë.

Curunír 'Man-of-Skill' (Q.) An honorary title applied by the Elves and the Dúnedain to the wizard SARUMAN THE WHITE. The valley in which he later settled, at the feet of the Misty Mountains, was known to Men of Gondor as Nan Curunír, The Wizard's Vale.

Cúthalion 'Strongbow' (Sind.) See BELEG CÚTHALION.

Notes

1 Appendix D.
2 The whole episode is described in pp. 162–87 of *The Silmarillion*.
3 pp. 106–7.
4 Book II Chap. 7.
5 *Ibid.*
6 Appendix D. p. 181.
7 Prologue: *Note on Shire Records*.
8 Appendix D. p. 170.
9 Whereabouts not known.
10 Book II Chap. 6.
11 In English-speaking countries. It is worth noting that *The Lord of the Rings* has been translated – successfully, we are told – into more than a dozen languages.
12 Cf. the history of Carthage, founded by Phoenicians, destroyed by Rome and afterwards re-occupied by the piratical (Germanic) Vandals. This colony eventually was destroyed by Byzantium, and the ancient harbour taken over by Moorish pirates.

Daeron A Grey-elf of the First Age; according to Elvish tradition, the minstrel and loremaster of Thingol King of Doriath. His is a shadowy figure (his name actually means 'shadowy', or perhaps 'hidden') on the borders of several tales of those days, chiefly that of Beren and Lúthien. For Daeron is said to have loved Lúthien, and to have twice betrayed her to her father in the matter of Beren of the Edain. The minstrel afterwards went away into the East and became lost to the knowledge of the Elves.

His chief memorial remains his systemizing and re-ordering of the ancient Grey-elven runic alphabet (the *certhas*), the use of which then gradually spread among other races. Daeron's Runes may be considered the oldest known form of common writing originated in Middle-earth.

See also ALPHABET OF DAERON.

Note: although Daeron's fate is not specifically recorded, in later Ages certain ruins on the coastlands of Middle-earth – at the mouth of the river Greyflood – bore, on some maps, the name *Lond Daer*. *Lond* means 'harbour, haven'; does the *Daer* element (which by itself means 'shadows') incorporate some faint echo of the name of the greatest of all Elvish minstrels? And if so, does this mean that Daeron in the end sailed over Sea? No records tell.

Dagnir 'Victor' (Sind.) One of the twelve faithful Edain of Dorthonion who remained in that land with BARAHIR after the Dagor Bragollach, and waged a guerilla war upon the occupying armies of Angband. All were slain within three years – except Beren son of Barahir.

Dagnir Glaurunga 'Bane of Glaurung' (Sind.) Part of the epitaph engraved upon the grave-stone of Túrin Turambar at Cabed Naeramarth. It was Túrin who had slain the greatest Worm of the Age, the fire-drake Glaurung of Angband, who had ravaged the north and sacked Nargothrond, and who had been defeated only once before.[1]

Dagor Aglareb 'Glorious Battle' (Sind.) The third of the BATTLES OF BELERIAND. It was fought in about the 60th Year of the Sun and, as its name implies, was the greatest victory ever won by the Eldar over the forces of Angband. It began as an assault on all fronts by Morgoth, a broad southward push against the Eldarin kingdoms of the North; while separate hosts of Orcs and Trolls burst through the Pass of Sirion in the west, and through Maglor's Gap in the east, the main army of Angband came up against the northern walls of the Dorthonion highland. There they were contained, and afterwards taken on both flanks, by the Elves. They broke, and, in retreating across the endless leagues of Ard-galen, were exposed to the cavalry of the Eldar, and annihilated. Their comrades who had penetrated into Beleriand were afterwards 'mopped up' piecemeal.

Dagor Bragollach The BATTLE OF SUDDEN FLAME.

Dagorlad The flat, barren plain which lay before the Gates of Mordor, and the location of the greatest battle of the Second Age, between the forces of Sauron and the armies of the Last Alliance. (See BATTLE OF DAGORLAD.)

Note: the word, of Sindarin form, means 'Battle-plain', or 'Plain-of-Victory' (from the Quenya root, *Dacil*, 'Victor'; Sind. *Dagnir*).

Dagor-nuin-Giliath The 'Battle-under-Stars' (Sind.), second of the BATTLES OF BELERIAND, fought in the year before the rising of the Moon by the newly-returned Noldor of the House of Fëanor against a sudden – and badly-timed and -planned – assault from Angband. It was a swift and crushing victory for the High-elves, but Fëanor himself was mortally wounded.

Dáin I A King of Durin's Folk; a ruler of the Dwarves of the Grey Mountains (Ered Mithrin), and a descendant of Thráin I – who had founded the kingdom of Erebor, under the Lonely Mountain, after the Dwarves fled from Moria. It was under Thráin's son Thorin I that most of Durin's Folk left Erebor for the unexplored riches of the Ered Mithrin further north. There, for some three hundred years, their wealth grew ever more great, until rumours of it eventually reached the ears of the Dragons of the Northern Waste and Withered Heath. In 2589 Third Age one of these slew King Dáin and his second son Frór at the very doors of their Hall. Soon afterwards, most of the Dwarf-colony deserted the Grey Mountains and many returned to the Lonely Mountain, where their skills soon rendered them even more prosperous than before. Dáin's heir, Thrór, became King under the Mountain.

Dáin (II) Ironfoot The mightiest warrior and one of the wisest kings of Durin's folk.

He was born in the year 2767 Third Age, the son of Náin son of Grór, King of the Dwarves of the Iron Hills in the far North-east. Thus he was only thirty years of age – and considered still a stripling by his people – when called upon to fight at the Battle of Azanulbizar, the greatest and final clash in the War of the Dwarves and Orcs. The army of the Iron Hills arrived late on the battlefield, and Dáin's father Náin soon fell at the hands of AZOG. Dáin then slew the great Orc with his axe. He later led his folk back to the Iron Hills, where he became King.

In the year 2941, the Dwarves of Thorin Oakenshield's party, beseiged in the Lonely Mountain by hosts of Men and Wood-elves, sent for Dáin for aid; he duly arrived with a great force of mail-clad Dwarves who played a prominent part in the BATTLE OF FIVE ARMIES. In that great fight Thorin Oakenshield, heir of Durin, was slain, and Dáin, as Thorin's true heir, was then made King under the Mountain. He proved a wise and benevolent ruler, having the friendship of the Men of Dale and Esgaroth and the respect of the Elves of Mirkwood.

But during the War of the Ring, even Dáin's great wisdom and mighty axe were insufficient to prevent an invasion of Dale and Erebor by Easterlings of Sauron's rule. The combined forces of Men and Dwarves failed to stem the tide and were driven back to Erebor. There, Dáin Ironfoot, standing over the body of his fallen ally King Brand, continued to wield his famous axe until, in his turn, he fell – in the 252nd year of his life.

Dairuin One of the Edain of the First House; a companion of Barahir in Dorthonion; slain (as were all save Beren) by treachery and ambush.

Daisy Gamgee The eighth of the thirteen children of Samwise Gamgee, named after his eldest sister.

Dale A city-state established by Northern Men during the Third Age on the southward slopes of Erebor in Wilderland; it was traditionally friendly with the Dwarf-kingdom under the Mountain.

The township prospered through this long association: in exchange for works of metal and stone, the Men of Dale traded foodstuffs, cloth and other essentials necessary to the Dwarf-community. For many years the two settlements lived in peace and mutual prosperity (like the realms of Eregion and Moria long before). But when Smaug the Golden, greatest Dragon of his time, came against the Lonely Mountain (in 2941 Third Age), the nearby town of Dale was burned and its people dispersed. Most of them made their way south to swell the numbers of the lake-community of Esgaroth, becoming fishermen and boatmen.

In the last third of his own narrative, *There and Back Again*, Bilbo Baggins gives a careful account of how the Dwarves retook Erebor, how the Dragon was slain by Bard of Esgaroth (descended from King Girion of Dale), and how Dale and Erebor were re-established in peace and prosperity. However, in the War of the Ring, Dale – always vulnerable to invasion from the East – was captured by armies of Easterlings sent by Sauron to clear the route from Rhûn to Mirkwood and the Misty Mountains. Brand son of Bain, son of Bard the Bowman, was slain, and his son Bard II became King and drove the enemy away. In the Fourth Age which followed, Dale prospered.

Damrod A scout for the Rangers of Ithilien, who were led by Faramir in their guerilla attacks against the Harad Road at the time of the War of the Ring.

Dark Door The ancient entrance from the foot of the Dwimorberg Mountain in Dunharrow to the maze of tunnels and passages under the White mountains. Delved in the Black Years by a forgotten race, these underground passages later became known as the 'Paths of the Dead'. In the furthest glen of the Haunted Mountain,

> there stood a sheer wall of rock, and in the wall the Dark Door gaped . . . like the mouth of night. Signs and figures were carved about its wide arch too dim to read, and fear flowed from it like a grey vapour.[2]

Dark Elves A translation of the Quenya word *Moriquendi*, being in origin the Eldarin term for all those of Elvenkind who never came to Valinor, Eldamar or Eressëa – as opposed to the *Calaquendi*, the 'Light-elves' (and also the *Sindar*, who, though they did not go to Aman while the First Age lasted, afterwards journeyed there, as the Sea-longing took them, and were thus reunited with the remainder of the Eldar; as a result they are not accounted among the 'Dark-elves'.) Included in the category of *Moriquendi* are two Telerin peoples: the *Nandor* and the *Laiquendi*; and all the *Avari*, the 'Unwilling', separated from the Eldarin kindreds at the Beginning of Days. But an extraneous source[3] tells us that this term 'Dark-elves' underwent a shift of meaning during the First and Second Ages, and often carried overtones that did not strictly refer to the ancient (and somewhat blurred) dichotomy between Light-elves (of Aman) and Dark-elves (of Middle-earth). Indeed, the whole question of Elvish nomenclature is extremely complicated (and is best understood by reference to the diagram on p. 309 of *The Silmarillion*). The extent of the problem can be easily understood when one considers that, of three *Eldarin* kindreds, the *Vanyar* went to Aman and dwelt there everafter; the *Noldor* went to Aman and returned in Exile to Middle-earth; and the *Teleri* became split into many subdivisions, some of whom went to Aman, some of whom remained in Beleriand – the *Sindar* – and some of whom abandoned the Great Journey while still east of the Misty Mountains – the *Nandor*, though later a further subdivision of the latter – the *Laiquendi* – came into Beleriand after all, and dwelt in Ossiriand. The Vanyar and the Noldor and the first kindred of the Teleri are all Calaquendi; the Nandor, the Laiquendi and the Avari are all Moriquendi; while the Sindar, Nandor and Laiquendi form a separate category altogether, the *Úmanyar* 'Not of Aman'.

Dark Enemy (of the World) A translation of the Sindarin name *Morgoth*. (See Note 13 on p. 92 of this *Companion*.)

Dark Lord Sauron the Great, Lord of the Rings, Ruler of Mordor.

Dark Power of the North The realm of ANGBAND during the First Age. See also MORGOTH THE ENEMY.

Dark Tower A translation of the Grey-elven word *Barad-dûr*.

Dark Years See ACCURSED YEARS.

'Daro!' A Sindarin imperative, meaning 'Descend!'

Days of Flight See ACCURSED YEARS.

Daystar The Sun.

Dead Marshes An area of low-lying, swampy ground west of Dagorlad, between the Emyn Muil and the Black Gate. The change of climate brought about by Sauron's resettlement of Mordor in the middle years of the Third Age caused the marshland outlying the

Nindalf to expand until it enveloped the burial-places of the Men and Elves slain at the Battle of Dagorlad. It was said that, at night, when the will-o'-the-wisp lights flickered above the meres, one who looked into the noisome pools would see the phantom faces of those dead warriors. This was thought to be a malevolent enchantment of the Dark Lord.

See also Book IV Chap. 2.

Dead Men of Dunharrow See PATHS OF THE DEAD.

Deadmen's Dike The name given in Bree and the northlands of Eriador to the green mounds and grass-grown earthworks which had once been *Fornost Erain*, Norbury of the Kings, capital city and fortress of Arthedain before its fall.

Déagol 'Secret' The translated name (orig. *Nahald*) of the Stoor, or River-hobbit, who, when fishing on the Anduin about the year 2463 Third Age, accidentally discovered in the mud of the riverbed a shiny golden ring. This was, of course, the Ruling Ring, lying where it had slipped from the finger of Isildur, thus betraying him nearly an Age before.

Unfortunately for the finder of the Ring, he was accompanied on this outing by a friend, Sméagol (Gollum), who murdered Déagol for the precious object and buried his body far from home. It was never found.

Death Down After the battle of Hornburg (3019 Third Age), in which the Rohirrim defeated the Army of Isengard, the heaps of dead Orcs were too great for burial or for burning, causing concern to those charged with repairing the damage of the battle and disposing of the dead. However, during the night, the HUORNS of Fangorn secretly gathered the carrion together in one great pit which they covered by a vast cairn of stones. This mass grave was called the 'Death Down' ever after in Rohan. No grass grew there.

Deathless Lands Aman the Blessed.

Deep-elves A rendering of the name *Noldor* into the Common Speech.

Deephollow A village of the Shire, north of the Overbourn Marshes and close to the Brandywine river.

Deeping Coomb The name given in Rohan to the coomb or bay in the northern White Mountains, to the south of the Westfold Vale. Through it ran the Deeping Stream.

Early in the Third Age, Men of Gondor built a mighty fortress (the Hornburg) at the point where the coomb narrowed into a gorge. Much later, the entire upper reaches of the coomb were strengthened by similar fortifications added by Men of Rohan. Chief of these was the Deeping Wall, which sealed off the mouth of the gorge. Below the wall lay Helm's Dike, a vast earthwork through which the Deeping Stream ran in a green gully to water the Vale below.

Deeping Wall The fortified wall which ran from the Hornburg tower across the mouth of Helm's Gate, the entrance to the gorge of Aglarond in western Rohan. Twenty feet tall, it was wide enough for four men to walk abreast along the parapet, and was so constructed that the top leaned out over the base, forming a completely smooth, unscalable façade. At the further end of the wall stood another bastion, the Deeping Tower, though this was not as strong, nor as tall, as the Hornburg.

Deldúwath 'Deadly-Nightshade' (Sind.) One of the many perjorative names given to the former land of Dorthonion, after its capture by Morgoth in the years following the Battle of Sudden Flame.

Denethor (of Ossiriand) An Elf-lord of the First Age, of the kindred of the *Laiquendi* ('Green-elves' as the Noldor called them; they were a subdivision of the Nandor) of Ossiriand. He was the chieftain who had led this kindred across the Blue Mountains into the lands beyond, the last of the Telerin peoples ever to do so. It is told that it was Denethor's father Lenwë who first forsook the main Telerin host, and led his people, the Nandor, into regions unknown (or unrecorded); but as the Years of the Trees in faraway Aman wore away, evil things awoke in Middle-earth and the eastern lands became perilous. Lenwë's son Denethor therefore gathered up his people and crossed the Ered Luin into Beleriand, there to seek the friendship of the Sindar, long-sundered kinsmen of the Nandor. This he did, and was granted the Land of the Seven Rivers as his abode – Ossiriand as it was called.

This crossing was followed by centuries of peace, for in those days evil things did not yet come into Beleriand, where Thingol ruled in power and splendour. But as events over the Sea moved towards their climax and Morgoth came fleeing back to Middle-earth, his armies went boldly on to the offensive, and fast-moving columns invaded Beleriand from north and east. Thingol was hard put to it, and an eastern host which had broken through from the north might have wreaked untold damage, had it not been for the Green-elves of Ossiriand, led by Denethor son of Lenwë. In this First Battle of Beleriand, Denethor played an heroic part, but was overmastered in the end by the iron weaponry of the Orcs and died on Amon Ereb, in a last stand that immortalized the valour of his people in the annals of the Elves.

Denethor I From 2435–77 Third Age, the tenth Ruling Steward of Gondor. During his rule, the evil breed of *Uruk-hai*, great Orcs of Mordor, first appeared in Ithilien.

Denethor II From 2984–3019 Third Age, the twenty-sixth and last Ruling Steward of Gondor. Like most of his House he was of true Númenorean blood: proud, wise, powerful of will and a man who took his many responsibilities in deadly earnest.

Being possessed of the foresight of his race, Denethor perceived early in his rule that the final assault of Mordor would come in his time. Therefore, he kept his own counsel in most matters, being naturally masterful and one who brooked no vacillation. Nevertheless, the power of Gondor was so diminished by the time he came to the Stewardship that he could do little more than watch, and wait, and occasionally harass the Harad Road to prevent Southron forces marching north to swell Sauron's power.

In 2976 Third Age, this proud and lonely man had married the lady Finduilas, daughter of Adrahil, Prince of Dol Amroth. But her heart grew sad in the great stone city of Minas Tirith, so far from the Sea that she loved, and she died twelve years later, having borne Denethor two sons: Boromir and Faramir. With her passing, the Steward grew ever more withdrawn, given to silent vigils and long thought in the high Tower of Ecthelion.

Being a man of iron will, he dared to use the *palantír* (Seeing-stone) of that Tower, to gain intelligence concerning the Enemy's moves against Gondor. His strength of mind was too much for Sauron to overcome by this means, yet the Dark Lord was still able to direct the visions shown in the stone: thus Denethor was fed endless images of the power of Mordor opposed to him. In the end this broke his mind, with grievous consequences for Gondor.

His unfortunate prejudice against Gandalf the Grey is accounted for by the knowledge, acquired early in his life before coming to the Stewardship, that the Wizard desired – indeed, was planning – the accession of Aragorn, last Heir of Isildur, to the throne of Gondor. As this would have supplanted his own House, Denethor, unwilling to perceive the benefits that such an event would bring, grew deeply suspicious of the Grey Wanderer – seeing him as a bitter rival if not an actual enemy. So it was that pride and despair combined in this great man to cause deep depression, followed by madness, followed by death itself. The tragic manner of his ending is told in Book V Chap. 7.

Déor From 2699–2718, the seventh King of Rohan.

Déorwine The chief of the house-carls of Théoden, King of Rohan, during the time of the War of the Ring. He fell in the Battle of the Pelennor Fields (March, 3019 Third Age).

Derndingle A natural bowl-shaped dell deep in the heart of Fangorn Forest; the traditional meeting-place of the Ents of that land.

Dernhelm The name assumed by Éowyn, niece of King Théoden of Rohan, when she rode in the host of Rohan to battle at the gates of Gondor. (See Book V Chap. 3.)

Derrilyn A poetic invention in the Hobbit style, supposedly a river-name. It can be found in Bilbo's poem 'Errantry', No. 3 in the selection of such Hobbit-verse found under the collective title of *The Adventures of Tom Bombadil*.

Derufin See DUILIN AND DERUFIN.

Dervorin This noble of Gondor was the son of the Lord of Ringló Vale (which lay between Lamedon and Lebennin, south of the White Mountains). During the War of the Ring he personally led three hundred footmen of his father's household to help defend the city of Minas Tirith; the remainder of his folk stayed behind to protect the southern fiefs against an expected invasion by the Corsairs of Umbar.

Desolation of Smaug See following entry.

Desolation of the Dragon This was the general name for the area surrounding the Lonely Mountain and ruined township of Dale, during the years of Smaug's dominion in Erebor (2770–2941 Third Age). The land was so described because every village, house and blade of grass had been scorched and destroyed by the roving Dragon on his frequent forays from Erebor.

Desolation of the Morannon The desert that lay before the Black Gate, where:

   . . . nothing lived, not even the leprous growths that feed on rottenness. The gasping pools were choked with ash and crawling muds, sickly white and grey, as if the mountains had vomited the filth of their entrails upon the land about. High mounds of crushed and powdered rock, great cones of earth fire-blasted and poison-stained, stood like an obscene graveyard in endless rows, slowly revealed in the reluctant light.[4]

Diamond Took A Hobbit-maid descended from Bandobras Took, and a member of the North-Took clain. She married Peregrin Took early in the Fourth Age and bore him one son, Faramir (who later married Goldilocks, daughter of Samwise, thus uniting the Gamgee/Gardners and the illustrious Tooks).

Dimbar 'Sad-dwelling' (Sind.) The vale of Dimbar was a narrow, enclosed land in the north of Beleriand. It was perhaps ten leagues across at its widest point (in the north) and twenty long, being shaped like a spearhead between the arms of the Sirion and one of its tributaries, the Mindeb. On the far banks of both rivers lay the forests of Doriath and Brethil, silent and impenetrable. Across Dimbar, from west to east, ran an old road, from the Brithiach to the valley of Nan Dungortheb (keeping close to the skirts of Doriath) and so, given good fortune, to Himlad. Overshadowing Dimbar from the north reared the Crissaegrim, the southern faces of the Encircling Mountains.

Dimholt A gloomy copse of dank trees upon the Hold of Dunharrow in Rohan. It stood between the inner Glen of the Dark Door and the Firienfeld (the open field of the Hold).

Dimrill Dale The name given in the Common Speech to the deep valley known to the Dwarves as *Azanulbizar* and to the Elves as *Nanduhirion*.

Dimrill Gate The ancient Gate of Moira, high in the mountain-wall which overlooked the vale of Azanulbizar and the lake of Kheled-zâram. It was so named to distinguish it from the western gate: the Doors of Durin.

Dimrill Stair The eastern descent of the high pass known as the Redhorn Gate – which ran from Hollin in Eriador to the Dimrill Dale on the eastern side of the Misty Mountains.

Dimrost The Rainy Stair. See CELEBROS.

Dior Eluchíl The son of Beren of the Edain and Lúthien Tinúviel daughter of Thingol Greycloak of Doriath; called *Aranel* 'the Beautiful' (during his childhood), and afterwards *Eluchíl* ('Thingol's

Heir'). He was born in Ossiriand, in the Land of the Dead That Live, on the isle of Tol Galen, in the days after the Quest of the Silmaril, and dwelled at Lanthir Lamath. He took to wife a kinswoman of Thingol named Nimloth. Their children were Eluréd, Elurín and Elwing the White.

It is told elsewhere[5] how the possession of the Silmaril brought disaster upon Thingol, and how he came to be slain in his own halls of Menegroth by jealous and greedy Dwarves, and how the Silmaril itself was captured by these Dwarves (of Nogrod), and borne away eastwards. Then the Dwarf-army was caught and destroyed by the Elves of Ossiriand, led by Beren. At that time Dior left Ossiriand and went to Menegroth, to become the Heir of Thingol. But there was still a store of tragedy hoarded up within the fate of the Silmaril. Not long afterwards, Beren and Lúthien departed from Mortal Lands for the second – and final – time, and the Jewel then passed to Dior's keeping. And again shortly afterwards, the Sons of Fëanor heard of the Silmaril, and came against King Dior of Doriath with war, to wrest it from Dior's keeping (see CARANTHIR). The assailants were slain, but Dior likewise fell in battle, and his wife Nimloth was killed, and his two young sons, Eluréd and Elurín, were abducted and left to starve. Only Elwing escaped; and the Silmaril.

Also the name of the ninth Ruling Steward of Gondor, who ruled from 2412–35 Third Age.

Dirhael One of the royal Dúnedain of the North-kingdom in the late Third Age. He was indirectly descended from Aranarth, first Chieftain, and his daughter Gilraen was the mother of Aragorn II, last Chieftain.

Dís The only Dwarf-woman mentioned in surviving records, possibly because the Dwarves were exceedingly jealous of their women and went to great pains to conceal their whereabouts (if not their actual existence). She was the sister of Thorin Oakenshield and the mother of Fíli and Kíli, and was thus of Durin's Line.

Dispossessed The NOLDOR; specifically, the HOUSE OF FËANOR.

Dol Amroth 'Amroth's Hill' (Sind.) This towering coastal hill-fortress was the chief bastion of Gondor's power in the Bay of Belfalas throughout the Third Age. Though the castle itself (*Tirith Aear* 'Seaward Tower') was actually constructed to protect the provinces of Anfalas and Belfalas from sea-borne raiding, it also had other, older associations. For below its rocky promontory lay long-deserted Elf-harbours (*Edhellond*), where elves of Lórien, sailing down Morthond to the Sea, had rested and refitted their ships before undertaking the great voyage West. For this reason it was widely believed (in Gondor) that folk of Dol Amroth had elven-blood in their veins. Indeed, the name of the hill itself recalls the Silvan Elf-lord AMROTH, who was tragically drowned off these coasts in the middle years of the Age.

Of all the Dúnedain, the Princes of Dol Amroth were accounted second in rank only to the Heir of the Steward himself. At the time of the War of the Ring, Dol Amroth was ruled by Prince Imrahil, son of Adrahil.

Dol Baran 'Brown-head' (Sind.) The southernmost of all the foot-hills of the Misty Mountains.

Dol Guldur 'The Hill of Sorcery' (Sind.) For nearly two thousand years this evil fortress was the most feared place in Middle-earth, save only Mordor itself.

Built in the early years of the Third Age upon a stony height in the southern fastness of Greenwood the Great, Dol Guldur soon acquired a fearsome reputation. Dark clouds hung over it and evil beasts began to terrorise the forest, which was then renamed Mirkwood. The Council of the Wise (the Wizards and the Chief Eldar) assumed that one of the Ringwraiths had occupied it; even then they did not dream that Sauron was gradually taking shape once again.

For it was the Lord of the Rings himself who had settled in Dol Guldur. To prevent his enemies striking before his own power was fully reborn, he carefully concealed his identity, so the people of the Forest knew the Power of Dol Guldur only as 'the Necromancer'. In 2063 Third Age, increasingly perturbed at the growth of evil in southern Mirkwood, Gandalf the Grey secretly entered the Tower; but Sauron managed to retreat into the East without revealing himself. Nearly eight hundred years later the Wizard again entered Dol Guldur: this time he found the dying Dwarf Thráin in the dungeons, and discovered that the Necromancer was indeed Sauron.

Gandalf subsequently summoned the White Council and strongly urged an attack on the fortress. But, swayed by the arguments of Saruman the White (who wished only to further his own purposes), they did nothing. By this time the Necromancer's plans were nearly complete. So, in 2941, when the White Council finally agreed to attack, Sauron simply withdrew and soon afterwards openly declared himself in Mordor. The Nazgûl then occupied the Tower, and it remained a place of great fear until the Elves of Lórien finally over-threw the fortress at the very end of the Third Age.

Dolmed 'Wet-head' (Sind.) The tallest of the Blue Mountains. It was a great spur projecting westwards from the middle of the range. During the First Age this was Dwarf-country: to the north lay their city of Belegost, and to the south Nogrod.

Dome of Stars The palace in the City of Osgiliath where the sages of Gondor kept one of the three *palantíri* (seeing-stones) of the Realm. The other two were at Minas Ithil and Minas Anor. During Gondor's civil war, the Kin-strife, the City was burned and the Dome of Stars destroyed: the *palantír* was lost in the waters of Anduin.

Doom of Mandos See CURSE OF MANDOS.

Doom of Men Archaic tradition contains many parables and legends which serve to illustrate and emphasize the basic differences between Elves and Men. Of these distinctions, by far the most sig-nificant was the Elves' possession of immortaility – which was ultimately to create an unbridgeable gulf between them and the *Atani*.

Yet we are told[6] that the Valar soon perceived that the Gift of Immortality bestowed on the Elder Children was no gift at all in a Middle-earth that was itself mortal. Elves might be bound to the Circles of the World, but they could die by mischance, or be killed. As a refuge from the Mortal Lands, the Valar therefore provided the shorelands of Valinor: the Undying Lands, wherein Eldar and Valar might dwell for ever.

But when it came to His younger children, Men, Eru was careful to create them of the same stuff as Middle-earth itself, as Mortals – dying and leaving the Circles of the World for ever. The mortality He gave them was then called the Gift of Men. But over the years, Men grew more powerful, and kingly, and noble. And some – notably the Númenoreans – thought themselves like to the Eldar in all ways, except one. Not perceiving the mercy implied in the Gift, they cursed their inheritance, calling it the Doom of Men. They feared death; and from that fear came the seeds of their long decline from Númenor to Middle-earth.

Doom of the Noldor See CURSE OF MANDOS.

Doomsman (of the Valar) Mandos.

Doors of Felagund The threefold gateway of Nargothrond.

Dora Baggins Eldest daughter of Fosco Baggins, Hobbit of the Shire. She was reportedly a prolific letter-writer. Bilbo, somewhat unkindly, left her a waste-paper basket in his Will.

Dor Caranthir 'Caranthir's Land' (Sind.) See THARGELION.

Dor Cúarthol 'Land of Bow and Helm' For a while (after the Dagor Bragollach but before the Nirnaeth Arnoediad), the name given to all the lands between the rivers Teiglin and Mindeb, including Dimbar. The reason was that this region had become infested with guerillas of the Edain under the dual leadership of Túrin Húrin's son and Beleg Cúthalion, the Strongbow, Marchwarden of Doriath. In those days Túrin wore, and was known as, the DRAGON-HELM (OF DOR-LÓMIN); and Beleg, of course, was famous for the skill with which he wielded his great bow, Belthronding.

Dor Daedeloth 'Land of the Shadow of Horror' (Sind.) A name among the Eldar and the Edain for ANGBAND.

Dor Dínen 'Silent Land' (Sind.) Like Dimlad, a narrow fenced-in land between Doriath and Dorthonion. It was said that no creatures lived there. It lay between the upper waters of Esgalduin and Aros, spear-shaped, with the forest of Doriath to the south. The road from Dimbar, having passed through Nan Dungortheb, crossed the Bridge of Esgalduin (also called the Old Bridge or *Iant Iaur*) a league north of Doriath and turned north-east through Dor Dínen, reaching the Arossiach after perhaps two days' journey (for one on foot). After the Dagor Bragollach this region of Beleriand fell under the dominion of Morgoth.

Dor-en-Ernil 'Land-of-the-Princes' (Sind.) One of the southern fiefs of Gondor. It lay between the rivers Ringló and Gilrain.

Dor Firn-i-Guinar 'Land of the Dead That Live' (Sind.) The name given in the lore of the Sindar and the Green-elves to that region of southern Ossiriand that lay about the waters of Adurant, including the island of Tol Galen – after Beren Erchamion and Lúthien Tinúviel came to dwell there, towards the end of the First Age. Both, of course, had been granted a second (mortal) lifespan by the Grace of the Valar.

Dori With his companions Ori and Nori, one of the twelve Dwarves who accompanied Thorin Oakenshield on the Quest of the Lonely

Mountain (in 2941 Third Age). All three were of Durin's Line – but only remotely related to Thorin. Dori and Nori remained in Erebor after its conquest; Ori accompanied the ill-fated expedition of Balin.

Doriath 'Land of the Fence' (Sind.) In origin, the name given by the Sindar to the former Forest of Eglador, after this region of Beleriand had become enclosed and defended by the 'Girdle of Melian': a web of enchantment woven by the Maia Melian, wife of Elu Thingol, and set around the borders of the forest to protect their realm from intrusion or attack. The Realm of Doriath, as it was in the days of Thingol's lordship, consisted of the two forests of Neldoreth and Region, with the Esgalduin flowing between. In the centre of the land Thingol built Menegroth, the 'Thousand-caves', and there afterwards for many long years, he dwelt, impregnable in his silvan citadel, the 'Hidden King' of the 'Fenced Land'.

Doriath endured throughout the greater part of the First Age, as is told in *The Silmarillion*, protected by the enchantments of the Lady Melian. Only twice were these defences breached: by Beren of the Edain, and by the Wolf of Angband, Carcharoth. But in later years the Silmaril brought thither by Beren enmeshed Thingol, Melian and the land of Doriath within the web of its destiny; and Thingol was slain, by Dwarves, in his own treasury. With the passing of the King Melian withdrew her power, and the Girdle was relaxed, and a further army of Dwarves broke through the forest to reach Menegroth and there avenge their kinsmen. It was not long afterwards that Doriath fell for ever; for Melian had by this time departed into the West, and the land became undefended save by elven-swords, and the Sons of Fëanor made sudden war upon Dior Thingol's Heir – in order to wrest the Silmaril from the Grey-elves' possession. In that onslaught many Elves died, on both sides, and the realm of Doriath was cast down, and never arose again.

Dorlas One of the Edain of the Second House, the Haladin of the Forest of Brethil. He was the leader of a small band of woodmen who were attacked by Orcs not far from the ravines of the Teiglin, and subsequently rescued by Túrin son of Húrin, who was at that time seeking for Finduilas, daughter of Orodreth king of Nargothrond; for she had been taken prisoner by Orcs in the sack of that Elven-city, and he still hoped to deliver her. Dorlas it was who told Túrin of Finduilas' fate; after which Túrin allied himself to the Woodmen of Brethil and made war upon the Orcs and their allies.

It was three years later that the Men of Brethil were again attacked by Orcs – this time from captured Nargothrond, sent against the

Edain by the Dragon Glaurung. This time Túrin did not go to the war – and it was Dorlas who spoke scornfully to him, causing Túrin to change his mind and take the field. A year later Glaurung himself came against the Woodmen, and this time Túrin needed no prodding. He determined to fight the Dragon, and asked for volunteers to help him. Dorlas was the only one bold enough to stand forward – yet this man's courage, when put to the test, failed him at the last; and he withdrew from the expedition even before they had espied the Dragon. Afterwards he was slain by Brandir, his former chieftain – whom he himself had publicly derided for lack of courage.

Dor-lómin 'Echoing Land' (Sind.) The southern region of Hithlum, a plain some thirty leagues wide at its broadest point, and fifteen leagues long, enclosed on three sides by mountains: in the west, the Echoing Mountains; in the south-east, the Ered Wethrin, the 'Shadowy Mountains'; and in the east, the Mountains of Mithrim. It was first occupied after the Second Battle of Beleriand, by Fingon son of Fingolfin, who for many years held the land subject to his father. But in the years between the Dagor Aglareb and the Dagor Bragollach, the race of Men came for the first time into Beleriand, and the most numerous of their three Houses – the Third House, now led by Hador Lórindol – went into the service of the Noldor of Fingolfin's house, and were as a result given the land of Dor-lómin in fief; though their main military strength was maintained further north and east, on the marches of Hithlum. For three generations the Edain of Hador's House held Dor-lómin, and wrought great deeds in the service of the Eldar, foremost among the Edain; but at the Nirnaeth Arnoediad all were at last slain – save Húrin the son of Galdor son of Hador, who was taken alive. Hithlum, and Mithrim, and Dor-lómin, fell at last under the dominion of Morgoth, and were never regained by the Eldar and the Edain.

Dor-nu-Fauglith See ANFAUGLITH.

Dorthonion 'Pine-tree-land' (Sind.) The original name for the forest-clad uplands of northern Beleriand, famous in story and song. This highland was seventy leagues by twenty leagues, extremely mountainous, and thickly wooded with coniferous trees, particularly pines, as the ancient name of this country tells us. (Another form is *Orod-na-Thôn*, 'Pine-Mountain'.)

The land – more particularly Ladros, the eastern portion of Dorthonion, on the edge of the plains of Ard-galen – was first occupied by the First House of the Edain; but as the years progressed

Morgoth's power waxed, and after the great Battle of Sudden Flame Dorthonion was abandoned – by all save BARAHIR – and fell into evil. Even the very trees became malevolent (see also FANGORN). At about this time Dorthonion began to be known as *Taur-na-Fuin* ('Forest-under-Night') and *Deldúwath* '(Deadly-Nightshade'). But the memory of the pine trees upon the windswept highlands of Dorthonion continued to provide Treebeard the Ent with one of the wistful images used in his lament for the vanished country of Beleriand (see Book III Chap. 4).

Dorwinion 'Land of Maidens' (Sind.) A country to the north-west of the Inland Sea of Rhûn. The highly praised wines of this region were much desired by the Wood-elves of Mirkwood, and part of the wine crop was regularly shipped up the Carnen/Celduin to Esgaroth and beyond.

Downs Smooth, treeless uplands, often of chalk or limestone overlaid with turf.

Dragon-helm (of Dor-lómin) The chief heirloom of the House of Hador in the First Age, called also the Helm of Hador. It was probably made for that renowned chieftain of the Edain after he and his people, the Third House, had come to dwell in the land of Dor-lómin as allies of the Noldor, though whether or not it was of Elven craftsmanship (which might seem likely, judging by the esteem with which this piece of armour was held) is not recorded. Surprisingly, it was not captured by the agents of Morgoth in the years which followed the Nirnaeth Arnoediad and the fall of Dor-lómin, for its whereabouts was kept hidden, by Morwen wife of Húrin the Steadfast. Later she sent the Helmet to Doriath, for at this time it belonged by rights to Túrin Húrin's son, as the Heir of Hador; and he was now dwelling in Doriath with Thingol. Now Túrin, in the event, fled from Doriath (see SAEROS) without the heirlooms of his house, but it was afterwards brought to him in his self-imposed exile (on Amon Rûdh) by Beleg Cúthalion, the strongbow of Doriath and chief of Thingol's marchwardens – and Túrin's comrade. Then Túrin put on the Helm of his fathers for the first time and went to war. So successful were he and Beleg in their prosecution of this war that the country in which they fought was named the 'Land of Bow and Helm', and Túrin in pride adopted the second of his many *noms-de-guerre*, calling himself *Gorthol*, the Dread Helm. Yet when all was said and done he was unwise thus to advertise his presence – and his existence – to Morgoth[7]. For after a time Orcs came against him, and they were betrayed (see MÎM), and in the ensuing fight Túrin was captured, and Beleg was left for dead, and the treasures and weapons of the outlaws were taken or despoiled by the Orcs. No further mention of the Helm of Hador is made in the annals of the Age.

Dragons Of all the many evil creatures ever to appear in Middle-earth, among the most ancient, as well as the most awesome, were the Great Worms. However, though it has been told that once there were many Dragons in the world, few of their names have been recorded. GLAURUNG was the most feared Worm of the Elder Days, and ANCALAGON THE BLACK was the first lord of the kindred of flying dragons; but there were many other lesser worms whose titles and names were never learned by the Eldar, and therefore never recorded.

The Great Worms were divided into three distinct breeds: the *Uruloki*, a fire-breathing sort, of high royalty, who however were unable to fly (Glaurung was one of these); their evolved kindred who could fly (Ancalagon and SMAUG THE GOLDEN were of this sort); and many lesser 'cold-drakes' whose power lay in speed and size alone. Most wielded great powers of enchantment; and all were immensely strong, quick-witted, intellectual, greedy – and callous almost beyond belief.

It has been said that the whole race of Dragon-kind was lured into evil ways by Morgoth the Enemy long before the Elder Days had passed. Even if this were not so, the Dragons' natural vices would have soon brought them into conflict with that other race of Middle-earth whose traits most closely resembled their own; for the Dwarves of those far-off days were even less renowned for philanthropy than their more recent descendants. And their wealth was very great (even as Dwarves reckoned such things). Both races fought for possession of the same hoards. Usually, the Dragons won.

Yet Dragons had other enemies, especially during the First Age, when many of them served the Dark Power of the North in the wars against Men and Elves. (The High-elven city of Gondolin was overcome in the end by a terrible host of Dragons aided by Orcs.) With the passing of Morgoth and the end of the Age, most of these Dragons were slain, and only the strongest and most cunning survived.

At least two royal Dragons still existed during the Third Age: Scatha of the Grey Mountains and Smaug the Golden – who attacked the Lonely Mountain in the year 2770, driving away the Dwarves of that realm and taking their amassed wealth for himself.

Smaug and Scatha were both slain by Men, and in each case there was a further dispute between the parties involved as to the disposition of the hoard – a well-known characteristic of Dragon-treasure.

Draugluin 'Blue-wolf' (Sind.) The chief of the werewolves (or 'wargs') of Angband, the forefather of Carcharoth. He was slain by the Hound of Valinor, Huan, on the drawbridge of Tol-in-Gaurhoth (Tol Sirion).

Drengist See FIRTH OF DRENGIST.

Drogo Baggins The father of Frodo Baggins. Drogo and his wife Primula (Brandybuck) were tragically drowned while boating on the Baranduin. Frodo, their only child, was later adopted by his cousin Bilbo.

Druadan Forest A large, brooding wood which huddled against the north wall of the White Mountains in the land of Anórien. Though it lay within ten leagues of Minas Tirith, this eerie place was shunned by Men of Gondor; for in its depths dwelt a strange, forgotten race of men, if Men they were. These were the WOSES, the 'Púkel-men' who had long before inhabited the seaward lands south of the Isen. It is not known when the Púkel-folk first came to Druadan, but even at the end of the Third Age a few still lingered there, wary and fearful.

In the early days of Gondor, the Dúnedain took little notice of these 'Wild Men' of Druadan. Indeed, they made a great road directly through the Forest for their wagons, which brought quarried stone from Min-Rimmon to Minas Anor. This road was later abandoned and forgotten.

Drúwaith Iaur 'Old Púkel-land' (Sind.) The coastal lands south of the river Isen; the ancient home of the WOSES, who later migrated inland to Druadan Forest.

Dry River The entrance to Tumladen and Gondolin through the wall of the Encircling Mountains; in archaic times it had been a river, which had drained the former lake of Tumladen.

Duilin and Derufin The sons of Duinhir, Lord of Morthond Vale. The Men of that land (in western Gondor) were accounted fine bowmen; accordingly, Duinhir and his two sons led five hundred of their best archers to help defend the city of Minas Tirith during the War of the Ring. Both Duilin and Derufin were slain as they courageously attacked the war-oliphaunts of Harad at a crucial stage during the Battle of the Pelennor Fields (March, 3019 Third Age).

Duilwen A river of Ossiriand; one of the tributaries of Gelion.

Duinhir See DUILIN AND DERUFIN.

Dumbledors A piece of comic invention in the Hobbit style. The Dumbledors were insects, vanquished by the hero in Bilbo's poem 'Errantry', which can be found in *The Adventures of Tom Bombadil*.

Dúnadan (pl. *Dúnedain*) 'Man-of-the-West' (Sind.) The Dúnedain, or Men of Westernesse, were the Númenoreans and their descendants, the 'Kings-of-Men': survivors of the disaster which overtook rebellious Númenor at the end of the Second Age.

In return for their endeavours in the cause against Morgoth the Enemy during the First Age, the *Edain* of Middle-earth had been rewarded with the great gift of the Island of Elenna in the middle of the Western Seas. Accordingly, at the beginning of the Second Age, most of them sailed away from Middle-earth to their new land. They named this realm *Númenor*, 'Heart-of-the-West' (Q.), and thenceforth they were known to the Elves as *Dúnedain*, 'Men-of-the-West'. For three thousand years they grew ever more powerful and lordly, but in the end most of them were corrupted by pride, by fear of death – and by design of Sauron; and Númenor fell at last.

Yet the Dúnedain did not all perish in the Downfall. Those BLACK NÚMENOREANS who had already settled the coastlands of Middle-earth during the years of Sauron's dominion lived on; while the FAITHFUL of Númenor, who alone endured the Deluge and survived it, then returned to Middle-earth where they founded the Realms in Exile: Arnor and Gondor.

During the Third Age, the Black Númenoreans died out, or were dispersed in wars and invasion. But the loyal Dúnedain, the descendants of Elendil the Tall and the Lords of the Faithful, somehow contrived to keep a foothold in Middle-earth – though grievously reduced in number by long years of war, pestilence and increasing assault by forces of Sauron.

An account of the sad fate which nevertheless overtook the sundered Dúnedain Kingdoms of the North may be found elsewhere (see especially ARNOR and ARTHEDAIN). Here it must suffice to say that only Gondor, the South-kingdom, survived throughout the Third Age and into the Fourth. Yet the Dúnedain of the South habitually married late, or not at all; and as the years passed, the race slowly dwindled and the lifespan of the 'Kings-of-Men' grew less (though originally three times that of lesser Men).

The ancestors of the Dúnedain, the Edain, had been accounted by Elves as the noblest of all races of Men. Indeed, the royal Houses of the Edain had been enriched by Elven-blood through two notable unions of Elves and Men during the Elder Days. And even at the end of the Third Age the kinship between the two races could still be seen in the dark hair, grey eyes and noble bearing of the Men of Westernesse, and in their gifts of wisdom and foresight. And though some of the race may have become corrupted, the true descendants of the Dúnedain never forgot the ancient kinship with Elves, and esteemed Elven-lore above all other learning. Of all Men of Middle-earth, only the Dúnedain knew and used an Elven-tongue as their daily speech. Many spoke the Grey-elven (Sindarin) language, and their sages studied the yet more ancient Quenya tongue of the High-Elves. The Dúnedain also had great scholars, and from them were derived various systems of reckoning and writing which later became widespread in Middle-earth.

But they themselves had learned this lore from the Elves long before. And from the Elves the Men of Westernesse also derived the lineage of their Kings. In fact, the first Ruler of Númenor was himself Half-elven: Elros Tar-Minyatur, brother of Master Elrond of Rivendell and son of Eärendil the Mariner. Yet by the time of the War of the Ring, the last direct descendant of that ancient Line, Aragorn son of Arathorn, could only claim the title of Chieftain of the Dúnedain of Arnor. For if the Dúnedain had once known greatness and a power beyond the measure of their foes, their days declined – as all things must in Middle-earth – and their strength was much diminished.

See also GONDOR; NÚMENOR.

Dungortheb 'Dreadful Death' (Sind.) See NAN DUNGORTHEB.

Dunharg The original (as opposed to translated) name in Rohan for the old fortified plateau known as *Dunharrow*, 'Dark-burial-place'.

Dunharrow (For translation see above entry) The most ancient and mysterious of the ancient sites which the Rohirrim found when they explored the new land ceded to them by Gondor in the late Third Age.

Unlike all other fortifications in Rohan, Dunharrow, in the vale of Harrowdale, had not been built by Gondor. Long before the Númenoreans came back to Middle-earth, before Sauron established his dominion in the Accursed Years, a forgotten race of Men had laboured long in shaping this unassailable fortress, temple or tomb complex.

Harrowdale was a steep valley through which the river Snowbourn ran down from the White Mountains to water the Eastfold. On the eastern side rose three mountains: the Irensaga, the Dwimorberg, and the Starkhorn to the south. A winding road, of singular construction, climbed from the ford of the Snowbourn to a mountain-meadow high above the valley, upon the knees of the Dwimorberg. Across this plateau marched a double line of menhirs, running like an avenue towards the mountain-wall, through the Dimholt and into the secret glen beyond. In the time of the Rohirrim, men shunned this place.

Dúnhere The lord of Harrowdale in Rohan. He fell at the Battle of the Pelennor Fields (March, 3019 Third Age) and, like all Rohan's dead in that fight – save the King – he was buried with the fallen of Gondor.

Dunland A fair green country of hills and glens in the region known as Enedhwaith, south of the river Swanfleet (Glanduin) and west of the Misty Mountains. It was inhabited by scattered settlements of hillmen, wary, secretive and hostile to strangers. Though Hobbits and Dwarves had once also dwelt there, only these hill-folk, the DUNLENDINGS (see following entry), remained at the time of the War of the Ring.

Dunlendings The hill-folk of Dunland. Though a dispirited, backward race at the time of the War of the Ring, the Dunlendings were actually the degenerate descendants of the Men who in the Second Age had inhabited the vales of the White Mountains – where they built both the Dunharrow and the Paths of the Dead under the Dwimorberg. (See AMLACH).

But during the years of Sauron's power these peoples were diminished. Many of them left the mountains and emigrated north into Eriador (where the Men of Bree were thought to be descended from them). Others remained, dwindling slowly in the White Mountains until first Gondor, then Rohan, drove them from their ancient valleys.

By the time of the late Third Age, the largest surviving group dwelt in the hills of Dunland, which lay north of the Isen and west of the Misty Mountains. Wild and uncouth, the Dunlendings were nonetheless fierce fighters when roused: and their chief enemies were the Men of Rohan, whom they called *Forgoil* ('Strawheads').

In the great Dunlending invasion of 2758 Third Age, these peoples, led by the renegade Wulf (son of Freca) overran the Mark. Many of the Rohirrim died in that invasion – which coincided with the Long Winter and with a great assault of the Corsairs upon Rohan's ally Gondor, so that help from that quarter was delayed. But in the end Wulf was slain and, with the spring thaw, the Dunlendings were finally driven out again, even from the Ring of Isengard, which they had occupied some fifty years earlier.

Durin (I) the Deathless 'Durin is the name that the Dwarves use for the eldest of the Seven Fathers of their race, and the ancestor of all the kinds of the Longbeards.'[8] Far back in the Elder Days, at the strange beginnings of that people, he awakened and came to Azanulbizar, the great vale on the east of the Misty Mountains. There, he looked into the lake of Kheled-zâram (the Mirrormere) and saw, reflected around his head, a crown of seven stars, though it was daytime. In the caves above Kheled-zâram he then made his dwelling, founding the great realm of Khazad-dûm (Moria).

Durin lived so long that the became widely known as 'the Deathless' and, even after his eventual passing, 'five times an heir was born in his House so like to his Forefather that he received the name of Durin[9] – for the Dwarves believed that it was in fact the Deathless who had been reincarnated. For this reason the principal monuments of Dwarf-lore were named after him.

Durin III During the sixteenth century of the Second Age, the Ruler of Khazâd-dûm and the Dwarf-king most renowned for friendship with the Elves. He was given the chief of the Seven Rings.

Durin VI From 1731-1980 Third Age, the King of Moria. He ruled at the time of the final great exploratory delving under Barazinbar (Caradhras) for the *mithril*-lode. In these excavations, miners accidentally released the BALROG which slew Durin – and, the following year, his son Náin I. As a result, the Dwarves of Durin's Line abandoned Moria and went into exile.

Durin's Bane The BALROG, as referred to by the exiled Moria-Dwarves.

Durin's Bridge Between the First and Second Halls of Old Moria lay a great abyss, so deep that none of Durin's Folk was ever able to sound its depths. Spanning it was a slender bridge of stone which could only be crossed in single file. The bridge was built during the

First Age as a defence against any enemy that might enter Moria far enough to capture the Great Gates and First Hall.

Durin's Crown The name given by the Dwarves to the halo of seven stars first seen by Durin the Deathless as he gazed into the Mirrormere (Kheled-zâram).

Durin's Day The Dwarves' New Year's Day; the first day of the last new crescent moon of autumn, when the Moon *and* the Sun appeared in the sky simultaneously.

Durin's Folk The most ancient and (at one time) most numerous and powerful of the Seven Houses of the Dwarves was that founded by Durin the Deathless. Dwarves of this House were known to the Elves as the Longbeards, for their beards – always symbolic of age and wisdom among Dwarves – were longer than any competing growths, were invariably forked, and were worn thrust into the belt.

Though their vast ancestral halls of Khazad-dûm (Moria) held out long against would-be dispossessors, in the end this greatest of all Dwarf-strongholds was taken from Durin's Folk, in 1981 Third Age and they became a wandering people. From Moria they came to the North, to Erebor (where Thrain I founded a new Dwarf-kingdom 'under the Mountain'); to the Ered Mithrin (Grey Mountains), from whence they were later driven by attacks from depredatory Dragons; and to the Iron Hills, where a cadet branch of the Line established itself in comparative security. Yet Erebor was also taken from them, when the great Dragon Smaug drove the Dwarves from the Halls under the Lonely Mountain in the year 2770 – and for a time many of the Heirs of Durin wandered in Eriador in exile and (relative) poverty. Although they later recovered much of what had been lost to the Dragon (see *The Hobbit*), their race was much depleted, and the Dwarves of Durin's Line were never to regain their old glories. And the lost realm of Moria remained forbidden to them while the Third Age lasted.

See also Appendix A III 'Durin's Folk'.

Durin's Stone An ancient, weathered pillar on the greensward near Lake Kheled-zâram (the Mirrormere) in the vale of Azanulbizar. It marked the place where Durin the Deathless first looked into the lake and saw, reflected around his head in the cool waters, a crown of seven stars shining as a symbol of royalty – even though it was daytime and there were no stars in the sky.

Durin's Tower One of the mightiest feats of engineering performed by the Dwarves of Moria at the height of their powers, early in the Second Age, was the building of the Endless Stair and its tower:

> From the lowest dungeon to the highest peak it climbed, ascending in unbroken spiral in many thousand steps, until it issued at last in Durin's Tower carved in the living rock of Zirakzigil, the pinnacle of the Silvertine.[10]

Durthang 'Dark-oppression' (Sind.) At the end of the Second Age after the first overthrow of Sauron, the victorious people of Gondor resolved that no evil creature should re-enter the neighbouring land of Mordor. They therefore built several mighty fortresses inside the Black Land to control any movement there.

One of the greatest of these was the castle of Durthang, high upon the rock-wall overlooking the Isenmouthe and the pass from Gorgoroth to Udûn behind the Black Gate. As Gondor's power waned, around the middle of the Third Age, the castle – like all other Mordor-keeps – was taken by the Nazgûl, and it became an orc-hold.

Dwalin One of the twelve Dwarves who accompanied Thorin Oakenshield on the Quest of the Lonely Mountain. After the recovery of Thorin's inheritance, he remained in Erebor, content to live in peace – unlike his brother Balin, who led a misguided expedition to recover the ancient Dwarf-realm of Moria.

Dwarrowdelf The translated Westron name (orig. *Phurunargian*) which meant 'Dwarf-delving' and was applied by Men to the great underground city of Moria.

Dwarves The Children of Aulë the Smith of the Valar, of all 'speaking-peoples' the only race not created by the direct will of God – though, as is told in *The Silmarillion*,[11] Eru intervened in the hour of their Making and commanded that the Seven Fathers remain asleep until after the appearance in Middle-earth of the Elves, whom he had long before ordained to be the first to walk the world. Then the Seven Fathers awoke for the second time, and went abroad, and commenced the works of their hands; and after a time spent in these labours, like all peoples they wandered ever westward, until they crossed the Blue Mountains into Beleriand, and there encountered the Elves – and so entered the records of the Ages. They called themselves *Khazâd*, but the Elves called them *Naugrim*, the 'Stunted People', and *Nogothrim*,[12] which means 'Dwarf-folk', and *Gonnhirrim*, 'Stonemasters'; and other names besides. But there was seldom great love between Elves and Dwarves, and as the First Age wore away, and the tragedies of that time unfolded, enmities arose between the races, the memory of which lingered into later days and was never entirely eradicated. Yet both peoples have this in common: that both have been belittled in the tales of Men of later days, and are now figures of folklore and fun, and the subject of jokes made by the ignorant. Yet once it was otherwise.

Of the three Elder races – Elves, Dwarves and Men – it was undoubtedly the Dwarves who exhibited the greatest love for the lands of Middle-earth and the treasures to be found there. For the Elves were, from the beginning, destined to find their long home on further shores, away from Middle-earth to the West. And although Men loved the creations of the world after their own fashion, they continually aspired to greater things, desiring to be like the Elves and not realizing the true value of the Gift they already possessed. Not so the Dwarves. Their love of possession for its own sake was balanced by the delight they took in ever more majestic and skilful feats of craftsmanship. From their beginnings they throve, the miner's chisel and smith's forge bringing them riches, power and great influence over the affairs of the Elder Days.

Of their origins the Dwarves told little to strangers; the small amount which is recorded in the Red Book comes from the tales of Men of Dale, who dwelt near them for many years and had commerce with them. But *The Silmarillion* is richer by far in tales of the Dwarves' origins, and of their deeds during the Elder Days. The first of their race to enter the lands of the Elves in the west were the *Noegyth Nibin*, the 'Lesser-Dwarves', who mined and delved in Beleriand long before the coming of the Noldor from the deeps of the Sea. It was this people who excavated the Caves of Narog – in their own tongue *Nulukkizdîn* – but they were fugitives from their own people, we are told, and the Sindar did not love them, and there was persecution of this people by the Elves of the woods; a persecution which only ceased when more Dwarves, of the true race of the Khazâd, came into Beleriand in after years.

These second-comers were altogether a more impressive people; indeed, long before their crossing of the Ered Luin into Beleriand, they had already created for themselves many vast and populous cities in the east of Middle-earth, the most ancient of which was Moria, but the most westerly of which were the twin cities of Nogrod and Belegost, delved in the eastern side of the Blue Mountains. The Dwarves of these cities indeed had much to do with the Elves during the First Age, both good and evil. They fought on occasion with the Eldar against Morgoth (see AZAGHÂL), and traded with Caranthir's people, and made roads into Beleriand, and delved the halls of Thingol, and performed many works of craft and smithwork on behalf of the Eldar – yet somehow there was never the same kind of abiding affection between the peoples which is the most cherished memory of Elves and Men. And on occasion the Dwarves marched against the Eldar, being seduced from their good sense by their lust for riches. It was Dwarves of Nogrod who murdered Thingol Greycloak of Doriath, and Dwarves of that same city who sacked Menegroth and stole the Nauglamír, made long before by their forefathers; and it was a Dwarf who betrayed Túrin Turambar.

But these were the doings of the Naugrim of Beleriand and the Ered Luin. To the south-east, on the far side of the Misty Mountains, there stood the great Gates of a city already of vast dimensions and legendary repute – Moria, Khazâd-dûm, the ancestral Halls of Durin, eldest and most royal of all the Seven Fathers of the Dwarves.

The Golden Age of Moria lay still in the future but even in the First Age it was already the greatest of all Dwarvish accomplishments. The almost endless dolven Halls, Deeps, Levels, roads, chambers and pits were lit with glittering crystal lamps; the walls, cut with marvellous skill from the living rock with scarcely a chiselmark, shone with banners, helms, shields, proud spears of steel and corslets of silver set with gems. Far below, in the Deeps, patient miners worked with pick and basket, while masons above busily extended old roads or carved new, lofty chambers to the glory of Durin's name. At the great Eastern Gate, mail-clad guards watched over the Vale of Azanulbizar and the lovely lake of Kheled-zâram.

Such was the splendour of Moria in those days. Its power was too great to overcome and it remained inviolate throughout the tumults of the First Age – while Nogrod and Belegost were ruined when Beleriand was drowned under the Sea. Thus many dispossessed Dwarves of those cities flocked to Khazad-dûm, swelling its numbers and its craft. And so the realm grew ever more rich and powerful while outside was ruin and a Change of the World.

Although Dwarves had always been wealthy, the discovery of *mithril* under the roots of Barazinbar early in the Second Age made the inhabitants of Moria fabulously rich. The Smiths of the High-elves (who did not share the ancient prejudices of their Grey-elven kin against Dwarves) eagerly founded a settlement near the west-wall of Moria, to engage in trade for this metal, most prized by all Elves.

And the friendship that existed between Elves of Eregion and Dwarves of Moria was the greatest that has ever been between the two peoples. Yet, when war swept over the lands of Eriador, the Moria-dwellers, fearful for their treasures, shut the doors of the city. Thus Khazad-dûm survived the War of the Elves and Sauron, and the long dominion of the Lord of the Rings over Middle-earth during the Accursed Years of the Second Age.

Nevertheless Moria fell at last. In 1980 Third Age the miners were once more tunnelling down into the roots of Barazinbar, seeking the full extent of the *mithril*-lode. At the heart of the vein slept an evil spirit from the Realm of Morgoth. Somehow it had escaped from the ruin of Thangorodrim at the end of the First Age – and had been slumbering in the very depths of the mountain ever since. The Balrog slew Durin VI and, the following year, his son Náin I; then the Dwarves of Durin's House fled from Moria, never to return while the Third Age lasted.

Many of those who escaped made their way into the North, to Erebor, the Lonely Mountain, where Náin's son Thráin I founded the first Kingdom 'under the Mountain' (1999 Third Age). But his own son Thorin I, desiring to rule a kingdom of his own, passed still further into the north, to the Grey Mountains, taking with him the greater part of Durin's Folk. There his people once again began to amass great wealth – until their ancient enemies, the Dragons, heard of this and made war upon them, driving the Dwarves from these mountains and back to Erebor in the year 2590.

Yet while the expedition to the Grey Mountains had ultimately failed, the days of the Dwarves did not seem so very hard, for Erebor had already been made rich and fair, and the skill and industry of the returning Dwarves of Durin's Line soon produced even greater results. Both Erebor and the Dwarf-dwellings in the Iron Hills prospered – until the year 2770, when the greatest Dragon of his time, Smaug the Golden, learned of the treasure under the Lonely Mountain, and came against King Thrór with consuming fire and great wrath. All of the Dwarves were scattered or slain, the nearby town of Dale was ruined and the surrounding country became a scorched, barren desert. Inside the Great Hall of Thrór, Smaug slept upon a vast pile of wealth and weapons.

Dispossessed yet again, the remaining Dwarves dispersed: some to the Iron Hills, some to Eriador and some to the meagre mines of the Blue Mountains, there to scratch a living as blacksmiths and iron-masters. In the end, Thrór could stand the shame no longer and, in his unreason, resolved to go to Moria. His murder by Orcs there and the bitter six-year war which followed brought about the last mustering of the Dwarves of the Seven Houses. In the year 2799, grim, mail-clad warriors bearing spears, mattocks, and their beloved axes, marched to Azanulbizar to give final battle against the Orcs of the Misty Mountains. There, many of the Dwarves – and almost all of the Goblins – were slain. (See BATTLE OF AZANULBIZAR; WAR OF THE DWARVES AND ORCS.)

Nevertheless, towards the very end of the Third Age, the fortunes of the Dwarves of Durin's House unexpectedly revived. In the excellent account he titled *There and Back Again*, the Hobbit Bilbo Baggins tells of the manner in which Smaug the Dragon came to be slain and the Dwarves of Erebor came to regain their inheritance – despite the fact that the old enmity between the Dwarves and the Elves (and in this case, Men), nearly led to a disastrous reversal of their fortunes. Bilbo himself took a significant part in these events; as a result, the Dwarves of the Lonely Mountain thereafter showed great friendship towards Hobbits whenever the two peoples met. More significantly, from this point onwards through the remainder of the Age, the Dwarves of Durin's Line continued to ally themselves with all Free Peoples.

Of the reasons for the Dwarves' fabled feud with the Elves, little is said in the Red Book, but much in *The Silmarillion*. Each race attributed blame to the other. To Men it might seem likely that the Dwarves' legendary avarice had played the stronger part in fomenting disagreements between the two peoples. Yet the Dwarves might well have been justified, in their own eyes, in taking exception to the somewhat distant manner employed by Elves in their dealings with them (for there was often trade between the peoples). Perhaps, more than anything else, the rift was simply due to cultural differences: for Dwarves were quite unable to perceive any particular merit in trees, in skies and in hunting under the stars; while the very contemplation of dwelling underground filled Elves with abhorrence – though they did so on many occasions, and often employed Dwarves in the delving of these subterranean kingdoms and fortresses.

At all events, while Elves were often unfriendly, it was the Dragons of Middle-earth who were traditionally the Dwarves' most deadly enemies. And in this, the Dwarves' own fabulous wealth was their undoing: rumours of some Dwarf-hoard would, nigh and again, reach the ears of one of these fiery beasts and he would rise up in wrath (and greed), coming against the Dwarf-settlement with fire and claw. Sometimes the Dragon would perish, pierced through by sharp spears and finally dispatched with axe-strokes; more frequently the Worm would conquer, destroying his foes with great gouts of flame and then systematically exterminating the survivors. That attended to, the Dragon would gather all the wealth and weapons into one vast bed, to lie there in watchful sleep till slain by adventurers or dead of old age. As Dragons were extremely difficult to slay (and hardly ever died of old age), a course of events such as this frequently meant permanent exile for the hapless Dwarves – unless some great warrior could be paid to slay the Worm. As *exile* also usually meant *penury*, the treasure more often remained where it lay.

However, the prerequisite great warriors certainly existed even if their services could not often be employed. The emerging race of Men was a race of Heroes and some of them went in for dragon-slaying on their own account. And here lie the origins of unfriendly relations between Dwarves and Men; for Dwarves were never slow to claim their own – and a warrior, having won a Dragon-hoard at great cost, was understandably reluctant to yield it up. Many early kingdoms of Men were founded on such hoards – and this did not improve relations between them and the original owners.

Whatever their relations with Men and Elves – and these were not always bad – Dwarves, like other races, regarded Orcs with unpitying hate. The Orcs, of course, coveted Dwarf-treasure as much as anyone else (not least for the matchless weaponry to be found there); and, as both races habitually dwelt underground, battle and cruel deeds between them were a common occurrence. The Dwarves defended their treasure with grim determination but, as the forces of evil grew in numbers and strength, many of their ancient mansions were taken from them. Even so, the Orcs never managed to enter Moria until the Dwarves were driven out by an enemy of far greater power, late in the Third Age.

And even in those fading days, something of the old fire of the Naugrim of the First Age still lingered in the hearts of the Dwarves. But, like the Elves, they had long been a dwindling people, and ceaseless plundering of their ancient works had left them too long without secure dwellings. As a result, few of their records survived, and thus little further is known of their history or lore. For they were a secretive people and few of other race ever succeeded in learning their ancient tongue, *Khuzdul* ('The-Speech-of-the-Khazâd') – apart from such words as the Dwarves themselves still used openly.

Dwarves were small, stout and bearded, wore heavy boots and great hoods over their leather jerkins and mail hauberks. They fought with axes and laid their dead under stone engraved with elf-runes, long adapted to their own language. They were grasping, industrious, fierce, jealous, brave, loyal – and unflinching in labour or adversity. With metal and stone and with all things of craft, they were wondrously skilled. But like the Elves, their days in Middle-earth are long past, and the proud race of the Khazad is now little more – and often less – than a folk-memory to Men of later days.

See also Appendix A III 'Durin's Folk'.

Dwarvish *Khuzdul*, the secret language of the Dwarves.

Dwimmerlaik A name used in Rohan for a ghost or unclean spectre.

Dwimorberg The 'Haunted Mountain' of the Ered Nimrais (the White Mountains). It rose behind the ancient Hold of Dunharrow. Under it, a dark road ran from the Hold (in Rohan) to the Vale of Morthond (in Gondor).

Dwimordene 'Haunted-valley' The name used among Northern Men for the (to them) legendary land of Lothlórien.

Notes
1 By Azaghâl, King of Belegost, at the Nirnaeth Arnoediad. See *Silmarillion* p. 193.
2 Book V Chap. 2.
3 *Silmarillion* p. 323.
4 Book IV Chap. 2.
5 *Silmarillion* pp. 232–3.
6 *Silmarillion* pp. 47–53.
7 *Silmarillion* p. 205.
8 Appendix III.
9 *Ibid.*
10 Book III Chap. 5.
11 *Silmarillion* pp. 43–6.
12 An alternative plural is *Noegyth. Nogothrim* appears to have a collective sense, though true collective plurals, in Sindarin, carry an – *ath* suffix (e.g. *Remmirath, Periannath*).

Eä 'Let it Be' (Q.) According to High-elven tradition, this is the Word spoken by God (Eru) when he caused the material universe to come into Being at the Creation; afterwards the name of the Universe itself.

Eagles The greatest birds of Middle-earth; in origin a direct manifestation of the Thought of Manwë, Lord of the Valar – or so the Eldar believed – in the same way that all things that grow upon the earth were in origin a manifestation of the thought of Yavanna Kementári – and all evils traceable to Melkor.

The Eagles of Manwë were not evil, nor was any other race ever able to dominate them. In the youth of the world, before evil stirred (or so the Eldar said), they dwelt in the treetops; but after the rebellion of the Noldor and the Darkening of Valinor, Manwë, Lord of the Valar, who desired through his messengers to learn what was passing in Mortal Lands, commanded the children of his thought to leave their arboreal dwellings, and henceforth live among the crags and peaks of the mountains, the loftiest of all dwellings of Middle-earth. So the Eagles came for the first time to their eyries.

In those far-off days they were greater in size than their descendants: Thorondor, their first King, who dwelt with his people in the Crissaegrim and the Encircling Mountains, is said to have had a wingspan of thirty fathoms, or 180 feet. Many times the great power, speed and courage of the Eagles led by Thorondor were of use to the Eldar (and to Manwë) in the turmoils of the First Age; but after the drowning of Beleriand, the Eagles removed further east, to the Misty Mountains where they afterwards dwelt among the high peaks. Among them was a House of princes, descendants of old Thorondor, who were greater in size than Eagles of other families, having prodigious wingbreadth and powerful talons. These, when not used for hunting, were employed against Orcs: for there was a great feud between the Eagles and the Goblins of the Misty Mountains in the later Third Age, especially after the Orcs attempted to re-establish themselves in the high passes during the years which followed the Battle of Azanulbizar (2799 Third Age).

By the time of Thorin Oakenshield's expedition across the Mountains, in 2941 Third Age, the Orcs of the Misty Mountains were firmly in control of the passes and, in alliance with the wolves of Wilderland, were already beginning to trouble the lands of the upper vales of Anduin. By chance, Thorin's party was assailed by a host of these Goblins – and was in great danger when the Eagles, observing the commotion from afar, swept down to rescue the members of the expedition from a fiery fate (see *The Hobbit*, Chap. 6). In this way an alliance was formed with the great birds for the first time, resulting in the Eagles' valuable assistance at the Battle of Five Armies later that same year.

The Eagles continued to preserve their friendship with Gandalf the Grey, who had accompanied the Dwarves' expedition, though it was many years before they were again called upon to lend their strength and speed to the common cause against Sauron. Gwaihir the Windlord, King of the Eagles, himself rescued Gandalf from imprisonment in Saruman's Tower of Orthanc in the year 3018 and, the following year, from the peak of the mountain Celebdil after the Wizard's epic struggle with the Balrog. For the final battle with Sauron at the Black Gate (Book V Chap. 10), the Eagles sent all their host; and Gwaihir, together with his close kin Landroval and Meneldor, rescued Frodo and Samwise from imminent death at the feet of the volcano Orodruin, after the Ring had been destroyed and Sauron cast down (Book VI Chap. 4).

The Great Eagles were noble birds, fleet and swift, proud and independent – and often cruel and merciless to their foes. Yet they were true allies, and on many occasions their aid staved off certain defeat for the armies of Elves and Men. For these services they were richly rewarded by their friends. They afterwards returned to their high fastness among the peaks of the Misty Mountains and dwelt there evermore.

Eärendil 'Sea-lover' (Q.) The strange tale of Eärendil the Mariner, who 'sailed out of the mists of the world into the seas of heaven with the Silmaril upon his brow',[1] is perhaps apocryphal, as are many

Elven-legends; yet it appears in the most venerated records of both Elves and Men, and in roughly the same form.

Eärendil was the son of Tuor of the Second House of the Edain and Idril, daughter of Turgon, King of High-elven Gondolin in the First Age. Their child was born in Gondolin before its fall and, escaping the sack, was brought to manhood on the shores of Beleriand, which for a while remained free of the Shadow. He later wedded the Elf-maiden Elwing the White, daughter of Dior, son of Lúthien Tinúviel, thus uniting the remnants of the peoples of Gondolin and Doriath.

The legend of Eärendil tells us that he dwelled for a while in Arvernien, on the shores of the Bay of Balar. On the death (or departure) of his father and mother, he became lord of this last Elven-people; it was at this time that he wedded Elwing.

We are told that Eärendil had long harboured a twofold purpose in his heart: to sail the Sea, seeking for his beloved parents, and to come to the Undying Lands and there beseech the aid of the Valar against Morgoth. From his boyhood a love of the Sea had filled him,[2] and so, in his manhood, he determined at last to implement these desires. With the aid of Círdan the Shipwright he built the ship Vingilot, from birchen planks of the wood of Nimbrethil. Then he set sail.

Three times he attempted to pass the Shadows which barred the way West – and three times a wind of wrath arose and drove his ship back. In the end, defeated, he turned back.

> *There flying Elwing came to him,*
> *and flame was in the darkness lit;*
> *more bright than light of diamond*
> *the fire upon her carcanet.*
> *The Silmaril she bound on him*
> *and crowned him with the living light,*
> *and dauntless then with burning brow*
> *he turned his prow . . .*[3]

. . . and the all-piercing radiance of the Silmaril – the only one of the Three Great Jewels to be recovered by the Eldar – enabled Eärendil to pass the Shadows and so come to the shores of Eldamar.

There he was received by Eonwë, Herald of the Valar, and was prepared for his further journey into the hidden land beyond the Pelóri, highest mountains in the world. Eärendil duly passed through the Calacirya, the 'Light-cleft' now dark and forlorn, into Valimar. There his embassy was heard by the Valar, who were persuaded to send a force to the aid of Elves and Men of Middle-earth oppressed by Morgoth and his servants.

Eärendil's fate is not known for sure, though it is certain he never again came to Middle-earth. The most hallowed tales maintain that he was bidden to sail the evening sky for ever, in a ship made of *mithril* and elven-glass, with the Silmaril affixed to his prow, shining as a beacon-star and a symbol of Hope to all dwellers in Middle-earth. Other legends say that the Ship was set in the Firmament by the hands of Elbereth herself, and that Eärendil dwelt ever after in Valinor, as a reward for his great journey.

Whichever tale is true, the seed of Eärendil lived on in Middle-earth. For Elros and Elrond, the *Peredhil* or Half-elven, each founded great dynasties of Men and Elves, which ruled for the remainder of the time allotted to these peoples. Elros became first King of Númenor, and Elrond was the mightiest Chief of Elves and Men during the Third Age. And both were the sons of Eärendil the Mariner.

Also the name of the fifth King of Gondor, who ruled from 238–324 Third Age.

Eärendil's Star The Evening Star. See EÄRENDIL.

Eärendur 'Sea-lover' (Q.) One of the Lords of Andúnië in Númenor, a descendant (through the Lady Silmariën) of Elros Tar-Minyatur, and a forefather of Elendil the Tall. Also the name of the tenth King of Arnor, who ruled 777–861 Third Age. In the year of his death, the ancient realm was divided into three lesser states in order to satisfy the ambition of his (three) sons, who had quarrelled over the rightful succession.

See also ARNOR; ARTHEDAIN.

Eärenya (Q.) The sixth day of the Númenorean *enquië* or 'week'. The Númenoreans, who were great mariners, desired to add a further day to the ancient Elvish *enquië* which they had previously used; *Eärenya* means 'Sea-day', and it was inserted between the former fifth and sixth days to produce a seven-day week – which was eventually adopted by almost all the Westron-speaking peoples of Middle-earth. This day was known to the Dúnedain of Middle-earth in its Grey-elven form, *Oraearon;* the Hobbits called it *Meresdei* (later *Mersday*).

Eärnil I 'Sea-lover' (Q.) From 913–36 Third Age, the thirteenth King of Gondor and the second of the four 'Ship-kings' who expanded the realm during the first millenium of the Age. Eärnil was the nephew of

Tarannon Falastur, 'Lord-of-the-Coasts', who had died childless; and he came to the throne with Falastur's great victories to consolidate. In particular, Eärnil purposed to extend Gondor's sway further south, as far as the Cape of Umbar, which was then occupied by a colony of BLACK NÚMENOREANS, old enemies of the Dúnedain of Gondor. To this end, Eärnil rebuilt the ancient Númenorean haven of Pelargir, on the lower reaches of Anduin, where he amassed a great fleet; and he took Umbar, which then became a fortress of Gondor. He was later lost at sea.

Eärnil II From 1945–2043 Third Age, the thirty-second King of Gondor and one of the greatest warriors in her history. Though he came to the throne by merit rather than royalty, Eärnil proved sure of hand, true of word and a mighty ruler.

He was Captain of Gondor's Southern Army at the time when the Wainriders' Confederacy made their last and greatest assault upon Gondor (1944 Third Age). King Ondoher and both his sons were slain in battle with these Easterlings, and the Wainriders poured into North Ithilien. There they camped and prepared to march across the Anduin – where Minas Anor lay defenceless. But in the meantime Eärnil had defeated the southern arm of the invaders in a bloody affray at the Crossings of Poros. Wheeling about, he force-marched north and came against the camp of the Wainriders with great strength. His army utterly defeated the Easterlings and drove them northwards out of Ithilien in confusion and terror.

For this deed Eärnil was granted the Kingship of Gondor, after an interregnum of one year in which the Councillors of the Realm endeavoured to decide what was to be done: for there was no close relative who might claim the Crown, and all remembered the Kinstrife. Some held that the kingship should be given to Arvedui, King of Arthedain; others opposed his claim. At all events, Eärnil was given the Crown, as the nearest relative (he was descended from Narmacil II). But he acknowledged Arvedui as his kinsman and promised to send to the aid of Arthedain if and when he could. It was some thirty years before he felt himself able to do so, however – although when he heard of the final preparations for Arthedain's destruction (in 1973 Third Age), he sent his own son Eärnur north with a great fleet. This force destroyed the evil realm of Angmar, though it arrived too late to save either Arvedui or Arthedain. Eärnur later succeeded his father.

Eärnur 'Sea-lover' (Q.) From 2043–50 Third Age, the thirty-third King of Gondor and the last to sit upon the Throne of that realm until the Restoration of the Kingship at the end of the Third Age.

He was the son of the warrior-king Eärnil II, and resembled his father in his great command of the martial skills. But whereas Eärnil also developed the qualities of wisdom, gentleness and restraint, his son did not, eschewing marriage and living only for the joys of battle; he was also burdened with a rash temperament. Yet for all that Eärnur was a mighty soldier, and his father appointed him Captain of the army which was sent to the aid of Arthedain in the far North.

In 1974 Third Age this army arrived by ship at the Harlond in the Gulf of Lune. It included many tall Men, brave banners and stout horses, for Eärnur himself proposed to lead the cavalry of Gondor in the forthcoming battle against the Witch-king of Angmar – who had already conquered Arthedain before any help could arrive. In alliance with an Elf-host of Lindon, led by Círdan, the Army of Gondor crossed the Lune and advanced towards Fornost. The forces of Angmar came up against them rashly, for the Witch-king did not fear the Dúnedain or the Elves; but Eärnur's cavalry wheeled north around the hills of Evendim and fell upon the right flank of the enemy. Angmar's forces broke and scattered, and Eärnur pursued them north-eastwards across Eriador. He overtook the Witch-king west of the river Mitheithel – and at the same instant reinforcement arrived from Rivendell, led by the Elf-lord Glorfindel. Angmar was utterly overwhelmed and the Witch-king was driven from the North.

Yet the son of Eärnil had made a great enemy. The Witch-king remembered the frustration of his plans and resolved to be avenged. Therefore, when Eärnur became King, in the year 2043, he received a challenge from the Nazgûl-lord of Minas Morgul (who was none other than the Witch-king himself). Eärnur was minded to accept the challenge but was restrained from doing so by the wise Steward, Mardil. But seven years later the Lord of Minas Morgul renewed the taunt, and Eärnur rode precipitately forth with a small escort to the gates of the Tower of Sorcery. He was never seen again by any man of Gondor.

Eärnur left no heir; therefore, after his death had been presumed, Mardil the Steward took office in the King's name – though neither he nor his Heirs, the Ruling Stewards, ever called themselves King or sat upon the great Throne. And for nearly a thousand years, the Crown of Gondor lay between the hands of King Eärnil, where he slept upon a stone bed in the Houses of the Kings.

See also Appendix A I(iv).

Eärrámë 'Sea-wing' (Q.) The name of the ship built in Arvernien by Tuor of the Edain at the end of the First Age, in which he and his wife Elwing the White sailed into the West – and were lost to the knowledge of dwellers in Middle-earth.

Eärwen 'Sea-maiden' (Q.) The daughter of Olwë of the Teleri and wife of Finarfin of the Noldor; she was the mother of Finrod, Orodreth, Angrod, Aegnor and Galadriel, and through her her children were able to claim kinship with Thingol Greycloak of Doriath in Middle-earth; for Olwë her father was Thingol's brother.

East-elves The people of the great forests east of the Misty Mountains; Silvan elves.

See also AVARI ELVES.

Eastemnet A low-lying area of Rohan between the rivers Entwash and Anduin.

Easterlings In the Third Age, this was the name given among folk of Gondor and Rohan to the various races and peoples from the lands of Rhûn and beyond. Most notable of these were the BALCHOTH and the WAINRIDERS, whose incursions into Western Lands during the latter part of the Age often threw Gondor and her allies into great danger.

Yet all peoples of Middle-earth had originally come from the East; in fact the Edain themselves were merely the *first* Men to do so. But by the time of the great Easterling invasions of the Third Age, these same Edain had long returned from Númenor and their mighty realms stood in the path of this new drive westward. The North-kingdoms of the Dúnedain were shielded by the position of Mirkwood and the Misty Mountains, but the Men of Dale were exposed to assault – and Gondor herself was constantly threatened by the existence of a great natural route across the wide plains between southern Mirkwood and the northern fences of Mordor.

The earliest Easterling invasions took the form of mass migrations rather than military expeditions, and their forces were easily driven off; but later incursions were better organized and far more formidable – the Wainriders, for example, moved their people and baggage in huge *wains*, or carts, while their nobility fought from chariots. They were also stronger and more numerous than previous invaders, and were better armed. From 1851–1941 Third Age they attacked Gondor repeatedly, forcing her to waste resources she desperately needed.

In 1856 King Narmacil II fell in battle with the Wainriders, and

Gondor withdrew all her forces behind the Great River. Rhovanion, one of her traditional allies, was enslaved by the Easterlings – but rose in revolt in 1899. Seizing his chance, Narmacil's son Calimehtar then crossed the Anduin in force and brought the Wainriders to battle on the old Field of Dagorlad. The victory he won there brought Gondor relief from the Easterling attacks for some time. And it was not until the year 1940 that the Wainriders reappeared – in great strength, and in alliance with other peoples, passing north and south of Mordor in their last and greatest invasion. As is told above (see EÄRNIL II), King Ondoher fell in battle during the first assault of this new campaign and only a fortunate victory by the Southern Army saved Gondor from being overrun.

Five hundred years later, another fierce Easterling people had made their way west as far as the brown meads south of Mirkwood. These were the Balchoth, a cruel clan completely under the sway of Sauron, and they terrorized the lands on both sides of the Great River. In 2510 Third Age, discontented with sporadic raiding, a great host of Balchoth crossed the Anduin on many boats and rafts – aided by Orcs of the Mountains. This sudden invasion was only thrown back because of the foresight of Cirion, twelfth Steward, and because of the valour of the horsemen of the North, led by Eorl the Young (see BATTLE OF THE FIELD OF CELEBRANT). But not even the combined strength of Gondor and Rohan could continually stem the westward flood, and the Easterlings threatened their eastern frontiers while the Third Age lasted.

Note: examination of the annals of the First Age (*The Silmarillion*) reveals that Easterling tribes and clans appeared in the west of Middle-earth during the Elder Days: not many years, in fact, after the migration of the Edain. For the most part these 'swarthy men' assisted Morgoth, though BÓR and his sons fought for the Noldor, and proved faithful.

See also ULDOR THE ACCURSED.

Eastfarthing One of the four quarters, or 'farthings', of the Shire.

Eastfold Vale The area of Rohan bordered by the White Mountains, the Mering Stream, and the rivers Entwash and Snowbourn. South of the Mering Stream, the land was called Anórien, and was accounted part of Gondor. Through the vale ran the chief road from Edoras to Minas Tirith.

East Lórien Throughout the last half of the Third Age, the evil power of DOL GULDUR dominated the southern reaches of Mirkwood.

Therefore, after overthrowing the dark fortress at the end of the War of the Ring, Celeborn of Lothlórien took all of this forest region, cleansed it, made it part of his realm and called it East Lórien.

East Vale A translation of the Grey-elven name *Talath Rhúnen;* see THARGELION.

Echoing Mountains A translation of the Grey-elven name *Ered Lómin,* being the name of the western mountain-wall of the lands of Hithlum and Dor-lómin.

Echoriath 'Encircling Mountains' (Sind.) A node or massif of tall peaks which buttressed the land of Dorthonion on the west, originally part of the Ered Wethrin but separated in later days from this range by the vale of the upper Sirion, and from the Ered Gorgoroth in the east by the Pass of Anach. In earliest times the Encircling Mountains had contained a deep lake amidmost – perhaps as a result of volcanic action and the formation of a caldera, which afterwards filled with water. But this lake drained away (see DRY RIVER), and what was left was the deep, hidden vale of Tumladen, with the hill of Amon Gwareth in its centre. Upon this hill, and protected by the Encircling Mountains, Turgon of the Noldor in after days built his city of Gondolin.

Echuir The Sindarin word for 'stirring', as applied to the final 'season' of the Eldarin *loa* or year. The Quenya term was *coirë.* See CALENDAR OF IMLADRIS.

Ecthelion of the Fountain One of the Captains of Gondolin, whose particular duty was the guarding of the innermost gate of the seven which protected Gondolin from the world beyond the Encircling Mountains. He was one of Turgon's chief lieutenants, and fought at Turgon's side during the Nirnaeth Arnoediad. But he is chiefly remembered as the Elf who slew – and was himself killed by – the Lord of Balrogs, Gothmog, in the last fight in defence of the city of Gondolin.

Ecthelion 1 From 2685–98 Third Age, the seventeenth Ruling Steward of Gondor. He rebuilt the high White Tower of the Citadel in the city of Minas Tirith.

Ecthelion II The father of Denethor II and, from 2953–84 Third Age, the twenty-fifth Ruling Steward of Gondor. Because of Gondor's growing need for men of worth, he initiated the practice of taking foreigners into his service – and some he rewarded with great honour. (One of these was none other than Aragorn II himself, in another guise.)

Edain See ADAN.

Edhellond 'Elf-havens' (Sind.) An ancient harbour of the Silvan Elves in the lee of Dol Amroth, on the coast of Belfalas. Throughout the Third Age, the tradition remained in Dol Amroth that Elves from Mirkwood and Lórien would ride the Morthond from their Forests to the Sea, resting at the Edhellond before taking ship into the West. (Folk said there was Elf-blood in the veins of the people of Amroth's Hill.)

Edoras 'The Courts' The capital of Rohan, situated at the feet of the White Mountains near the river Snowbourn. It was built in the late Third Age, after the fashion of the North – as a hill-fortress with stockade and dike. Crowning the hill was the magnificent King's Hall, Meduseld, completed by Brego, second King of the Mark, (Edoras was not a true stronghold, and the Kings of Rohan used Dunharrow, in the mountains further south, as a place of refuge in time of war.)

Edrahil An Elf of the city of Nargothrond, chief of those loyalists who refused to forsake their King Finrod Felagund, and who accompanied him to his death in Tol-in-Gaurhoth. It was at Edrahil's suggestion that Finrod, instead of casting the crown of Nargothrond away, gave it instead to his younger brother Orodreth, against his return. But Finrod – and Edrahil – never returned from the north, and Orodreth later became King of Nargothrond by right.

'Edro!' A Sindarin imperative, meaning 'Open!'

Egalmoth From 2698–2743 Third Age, the eighteenth Ruling Steward of Gondor.

Egladil 'Angle' (Sind.) That part of Lothlórien which lay between the confluence of the Anduin and the Silverlode.

Eglador 'Land of the Forsaken' (Sind.) The earliest of all Elven-names for the land of DORIATH.
    See also EGLATH.

Eglantine Took The wife of Paladin and mother of Peregrin Took.

Eglarest The southernmost of the two Havens of the Falathrim on the shores of Beleriand, founded by CÍRDAN THE SHIPWRIGHT early in the First Age. It lay at the mouth of the river Nenning (its sister-haven was BRITHOMBAR; at the outflow of the Brithon). Círdan himself dwelt there throughout most of the war against Morgoth, but in the year following the Nirnaeth Arnoediad, both Havens were assaulted by great armies from Angband, and fell at last, and were never rebuilt. Círdan and the survivors of the Falathrim went to dwell on the Isle of Balar, and afterwards, when the Age was ended and Beleriand drowned and broken, to the Grey Havens of Mithlond on the shores of Lindon.

Eglath 'Forsaken Ones' (Sind.) The name assumed by those of the Teleri (the Third Kindred of the Eldar) who would not depart from Middle-earth at the Beginning of Days, but instead lingered in Beleriand, seeking for Elwë (Thingol) their lord, who had been lost to them for many years. They were afterwards called the *Sindar*, the 'Grey-elves' (by the returning Noldor).

Eilenach One of a series of seven beacon-hills between Gondor and Rohan. Eilenach Beacon was atop a hill in the midst of the Forest of Druadan, at the southern end of the chain.
See also BEACON-HILLS.

Eilinel The wife of GORLIM THE UNHAPPY, slain in Dorthonion by soldiers of Sauron after the Dagor Bragollach.

Eithel Ivrin 'Ivrin's Well' (Sind.) A spring and cataract beneath the southernmost buttresses of the Shadowy Mountains in West Beleriand; it was the source of the river Narog. Also called the 'Falls of Ivrin' and the 'Pools of Ivrin'.

Eithel Sirion The source of the great river Sirion, on the eastern slopes of the Ered Wethrin (the Shadowy Mountains) on the borders of Ard-galen. Here was built the BARAD EITHEL.

Ekkaia The name given in the lore of the Eldar to the Outer or Encircling Sea of Arda – the ocean which encompassed all the lands of the earth in the days before the removal of Valinor from the 'circles of the world'.

Êl, Elin, Elenath The Sindarin word for 'star'. (*Elenath* was the collective plural.)
See ELEN, ELENI, ELENION; GIL, GILIATH; also *Silmarillion* p. 358.

Elanor A small, golden winter flower found in the forest-glades of Lothlórien. Its name means 'Sun-star'.

Elanor Gamgee Called 'Elanor the Fair', the eldest child of Sam Gamgee, born to Sam and Rose in the last year of the Third Age. Like a number of the children born then, she had golden hair, which was previously most unusual in a Hobbit-maid. After her father was made a Counsellor of the North-kingdom (Year 13 Fourth Age, 1434 Shire Reckoning), she was appointed Maid of Honour to the Queen of Gondor and Arnor.

In her thirty-first year, Elanor married Fastred of Greenholm and four years afterwards the couple moved to Undertowers, beneath the Tower Hills on the borders of the Westmarch. There the family long continued to dwell – and to preserve the Red Book, given by Samwise to Elanor in the year 61 Fourth Age, on his way to the Grey Havens and the Western Shores.

See also RED BOOK OF WESTMARCH.

Eldalië 'Elven-folk' (Q.) The ELDAR.

Elbereth 'Star-queen' (Sind.) The title or name by which the Grey-elves knew that Lady revered (by the High-elves) as *Varda* the Exalted, spouse of the Lord of the Valar himself.

To the High-elves Varda had three aspects: as the Exalted (spouse); as *Tintalle*, the 'Star-kindler', ruler of the Firmament, and as the divine or demiurgic intercessary, *Fanuilos*.

The Sindar (Grey-elves) of Beleriand called her *Gilthoniel*, 'the Kindler', which corresponded closely with her other name, Elbereth (the Quenya equivalent of *Elbereth* was *Elentári*); and both titles were often spoken together when invoking her aid or blessing.

Two hymns or ceremonial addresses to Elbereth occur in the text of the Red Book, and can be found in Book II Chaps. 1 and 8. The former example (see 'A ELBERETH GILTHONIEL') is in the Sindarin tongue; the latter, Galadriel's Lament in Lórien, is in the ancient High-elven Quenya and is the longest extant example of that language recorded anywhere. The verse is examined elsewhere (see 'NAMÁRIË'), but it is worth noting here that it pleads for a specific boon in terms which, though formal, are almost 'personal'. For Galadriel of Lothlórien was the most royal of Elven women living in Middle-earth during the Third Age, being of the House of Finarfin of Eldamar; and she had therefore once lived in the Undying Lands where Elbereth herself reigned.

Elbereth was said to dwell, together with her spouse, Manwë, the 'Elder King', in a lofty palace upon the summit of Mount Oiolossë, highest of the Pelóri of Valinor and therefore of all mountains. In the

Second and Third Ages the High-elves who made pilgrimage to the *Emyn Beraid* ('Tower Hills') to gaze into the *palantír* of the Tower were sometimes rewarded with a vision of Elbereth standing on the mountain, dressed in raiment of snowy white, listening to the cries of Elves and Men for aid and succour.

See also *The Road Goes Ever On*, pp. 58–66.

Eldacar I From 249–339 Third Age, the fourth King of Gondor.

Eldacar II From 1432–37 and 1447–90 Third Age, the twenty-first King of Gondor. The ten-year interregnum was caused by the temporary triumph of disloyal elements (led by CASTAMIR THE USURPER) during Gondor's civil war, the Kin-strife.

Eldacar was born the son of Valacar, twentieth King, who held the Northmen of Rhovanion in great esteem, having lived among them (at the wishes of his father Rómendacil II). Indeed, Valacar took to wife one of their race, the Lady Vidumavi, and from their union was born Eldacar (who was named Vinitharya in the land of his birth). But the Dúnedain of the South were suspicious and angry at this 'mingling' of their race of 'Kings-of-Men' with what they saw as lesser blood; and when Eldacar succeeded his father in the year 1432, there was rebellion and civil war.

However, Eldacar showed all the tenacity of the Dúnedain in refusing to be thus arbitrarily deposed; and he held out against the rebels for five years, eventually enduring a bitter siege in his capital city of Osgiliath. But the besiegers, led by Castamir, the Captain of Ships, finally drove him out, leaving the greatest city of Gondor in flames. Eldacar then retreated into the North, to Rhovanion, where he waited and planned.

As is told elsewhere, Castamir, who had crowned himself King after the fall of Osgiliath, then began to lose – or squander – much of the support he had originally commanded. For he had shown himself to be a cruel and despotic man (having executed Ornendil, Eldacar's son, when Osgiliath fell into his hands). In 1447 Eldacar marched south once more, gathering supporters daily, until at last he met the armies of Castamir at the Crossings of Erui. There was a great battle; Castamir was slain by Eldacar's own hand, and the Line of the Kingship was restored.

Thus Eldacar proved that, for all his 'mixed' blood, he was as noble a king and as courageous a soldier as Gondor could wish for. Indeed, he showed no signs of premature age, reigning for over forty years more in wisdom and majesty.

Eldamar 'Elven-home' (Q.) The ancient home of the Elves in the Undying Lands; that part of Aman allotted to the Calaquendi and all those who also passed 'West-over-Sea'. It comprised the shoreline of the Blessed Realm and all the middlemost lands on the eastern side of the Pelóri, but not the 'Lonely-isle' of *Eressëa*, which lay some little distance offshore; it was in fact at Eressëa that Elven-ships first docked, after the long journey out of Middle-earth.

In its beginning, Eldamar was lit in part by the ancient stars, and in part (especially in that region known as Calacirian) by the radiance of the Two Trees. On the eastern side of the great Pass through the Mountains of Valinor stood a high green hill, Túna; and on this hill the Vanyar and the Noldor built their city of Tirion, the chief city of the High-elves in Eldamar, whose silvery lights were reflected in the waters of the Shadowmere beneath. To the east lay the great Bay of Eldamar, and on the horizon stood the 'Lonely-Isle', *Tol Eressëa*, the abode of the Teleri for many 'long-years' before they too completed the journey to Aman and built a city on the shorelands of Eldamar (ALQUALONDË).

Such was Eldamar in ancient days. But in the Second and Third Ages, like Valimar ('Home-of-the-Valar', the lands to the west of the Pelóri), Eldamar lay under perpetual twilight. For although it had once been illuminated, in part, by the ancient Two Trees, the Trees were poisoned before the ending of the Elder Days, and the light of Valinor and Eldamar then became that of a land 'West of the Moon, East of the Sun', the unending evening of the Isles of the West.

Eldar 'People of the Stars' (Q.) The name given in remote antiquity, it is said, by Oromë the Vala to all Elvenkind; subsequently used to distinguish the Three Kindreds who separated from the *Avari*, the Unwilling, and, following the call of the Valar, made the Great Journey from Cuiviénen into the Uttermost West, at the Beginning of Days – though not all the Eldar arrived in Aman at the same time. Yet from the very beginning the destiny of the Eldar (West-elves) was set apart from that of Men – and even from that of the Avari, fated to 'dwindle to a rustic folk of dell and cave, slowly to forget and be forgotten.'[5] For all Elves, immortality proved a burden rather than a blessing while they dwelled in mortal lands where death, by grievous mischance, might still occur. Therefore, far back in the Elder Days, the Three Kindreds were summoned by the Valar, Guardians of the World, to make the Great Journey, there to dwell with the Valar themselves in harmony and everlasting life, far removed from the dangers and fleeting mortality of Middle-earth.

The Three Kindreds of the Eldar were the *Vanyar*, 'Fair-elves', *Noldor*, 'Deep-elves' and *Lindar*, 'Singing-elves' – more commonly known as the *Teleri*, 'the Hindmost', for they were ever last on the Great Journey. The Vanyar were fated to pass west without hindrance, and so come to Valinor, where ever after they dwelt in bliss. The Noldor likewise completed the Journey without delay, and for long ages dwelt with the Vanyar and the Valar in Aman, though it has been told how their bliss became diminished. Then most of this people came back to Middle-earth in exile, and here most of them died and passed to the Halls of Waiting. The history of the Noldor is the most grievous of all the histories of the Eldarin kindreds.

The third Kindred, the Lindar or Teleri, alone dallied on the Journey from Cuiviénen to Valinor; indeed, so numerous and lengthy were the delays experienced by this people that several times they became dispersed along the route and so came to form the nuclei of several entirely new Eldarin groupings. (How those who journeyed became separated into Teleri and Nandor, then Teleri and Sindar – and how some of the Nandor were afterwards reunited with some of the Sindar while the foremost Telerin kindreds came, after many long years, first to Eressëa and then to Aman – is described in *The Silmarillion* and is best read there; alternatively, the reader may refer to the entry TELERI in this *Companion*.)

Little is known of the subsequent history of the Vanyar. They are the 'Highest' of High-elves. In Eldamar, they dwelt at first in Tirion, their city upon the hill of Túna in the Calacirian; but they later removed to Valimar, and they came back to Middle-earth only once in after years, to the Great Battle whereby the Host of the West overthrew Morgoth the Enemy and so brought an end to the Elder Days. Their first and only Lord was, and is, Ingwë. The Vanyar dwell still in Aman and do not return, and the troubles of Middle-earth concern them not at all.

Better chronicled is the history of the Noldor, the craftsmen and loremasters of the Elves, whose skills flowered in ancient Eldamar, until in the end they overreached themselves and brought grief and misfortune to both the Blessed Realm and Middle-earth.

Their first Lord was Finwë, but, as is told elsewhere,[6] this great prince was slain by Morgoth in defence of the Silmarils – the first of all Elves to be slain in Valinor, though, sadly, not the last – and the lordship of the Second Kindred then passed to his sons: Fëanor (son of Míriel); Fingolfin, and Finarfin (the sons of Indis of the Vanyar), though Fëanor was the chief. Few of those who went into exile before the Elder Days had passed ever returned to Valinor, except by way of the Halls of Mandos, where each lingered according to the extent of his share of the crimes that the Noldor had committed, or had caused to be committed. The Noldor were 'High-elves'—as this term was understood in Middle-earth.

The history of the Teleri is more complicated. Their first Lords were the brothers Olwë and Elwë, and it is also said that at Cuiviénen they were the most numerous of the Three Kindreds of the Eldar. For this reason perhaps they were slowest on the march, and became separated, not only from the First and Second Kindreds, but also from each other, so that the wake of the Journey across Middle-earth was sown with various Telerin peoples, hindmost of the Hindmost. In the process the two Lords Olwë and Elwë also became separated from each other. The foremost Telerin people, led by Olwë, came in the end across the Sea; but at first only as far as Tol Eressëa (later they completed the migration). But Elwë never again saw his brother in life, for he lingered in Beleriand and there founded a separate Kingdom, of the Eldar in Middle-earth. His subjects were called the *Sindar*, 'Grey-elves', by the returning Noldor. All Telerin kindreds were dark-haired, like the Noldor. And except those who were slain in the Wars – or who never came at all into Beleriand and so dwindled – eventually also passed West, and dwell now in Eressëa.

At the beginning of the Second Age of Middle-earth the only Eldar left in Mortal Lands were the Sindar and a remnant of the Noldor. At this time their High King was Gil-galad, son of Fingon, son of Fingolfin, son of Finwë of the Noldor. But Celeborn and Thranduil, Lords of the Sindar, ruled realms elsewhere, in the eastern forests; and Círdan of the Teleri kept still his ancient lordship over the Elves of the coastlands and the Havens. But already they were a dwindling people, and from time to time ships would set sail from the Havens.

Throughout the long, slow years of the Third Age, the Eldar continued to decline in both power and numbers. The remaining High-elves dwelled mostly with Elrond in Rivendell, or with Círdan the Shipwright in Lindon, or wandered the Westlands in travelling companies; while those of the Sindar who still lingered in Middle-earth dwelt with Celeborn and Galadriel in Lothlórien, or with Thranduil in Mirkwood.

But with the great events of the War of the Ring in the closing years of the Third Age, the ban long imposed upon the Exiles was lifted at last, and all of the remaining Eldar set sail out of the Seas of Mortal Lands into the Uttermost West, taking with them the Three Rings, last symbols of their Dominion in Middle-earth.

They were a race high and beautiful, the older Children of the world . . . the People of the Great Journey, the People of the Stars . . . and their voices had more melodies than any mortal voice that now is heard. They were valiant, but the history of those that returned to Middle-earth in exile was grievous; and though it was in far-off days crossed by the fate of the Fathers, their fate is not that of Men. Their dominion passed long ago, and they dwell now beyond the circles of the world, and do not return.[7]

See also ELVES; QUENDI; Appendices A I(i); D; E II; F; also *The Silmarillion* (passim, but esp. pp. 305–6, 309).

Eldarin The generic name given to the languages spoken by the Eldar. The only two of these recorded in Middle-earth were the High-elven *Quenya* ('the Speech') and the Grey-elven *Sindarin*. Of the two, Quenya was by far the more ancient, being the oldest of all written languages. It was flowing, flexible and highly modulated, and was said (by the Eldar) to have been influenced by the speech of the Valar.

The Sindarin language was related to Quenya, and both were descended from a common ancestral tongue spoken in Middle-earth far back in the Elder Days. But during the long years when the Three Kindreds were sundered (see ELDAR), the Grey-elves remained in Mortal Lands and their language therefore changed to a far greater extent than Quenya, though the original kinship could still be discerned.

See also SPOKEN TONGUES; Appendix F I.

Eldarion The only son of King Elessar and Queen Arwen of Gondor and Arnor. He ruled after his father's passing in the year 120 Fourth Age.

Elder Children The ELVES.

Elder Days The First Age of Middle-earth.

Elder Kindred The ELVES.

Elder King The title bestowed upon Manwë, Lord of the Valar.

Eldest of Trees TELPERION.

Eledhwen 'Elf-sheen' (Sind.) See MORWEN ELEDHWEN.

Elemmírë 'Jewel-star' (Q.) The name of one of the stars created by Elbereth to bring light to Middle-earth, and so aid the newly-awakened Quendi (the Elves), at the beginning of the Elder Days. Also the name of an Elf of the Vanyar, the minstrel who made the Lament for the Two Trees, the *Aldudénië*.

Elen, Eleni, Elenion (Q.) The High-elven word for 'star', descended (like its Grey-elven equivalent, *Êl, Elin, Elenath*), from the very ancient Elven word-element *el*. It can be found in the personal title *Elentári*, 'Star-queen', in many words and names of Quenya origin used by Men of Númenor and Gondor (e.g., *Elendil*, 'Star-lover', *Elenna*, 'Land-of-the-Star'), and also in the ancient High-elven name for the first day of the week: *Elenya*. The *Eldar* ('People-of-the-Stars') of course had many names for the Stars, but at the time of the War of the Ring, the word *Elen* was the most ancient still preserved in Middle-earth. Its collective plural was *Elenion*, of which the Sindarin *Elenath* was the closest equivalent.

Elendë 'Star-land' (Q.) Eldamar.

Elendil (Tar-Elendil) 'Star-lover' (Q.) The fourth King of Númenor, and the first to send exploratory ships back to the shores of Middle-earth.

Elendil the Tall From 3320–3441 Second Age, the first High-king of both Arnor and Gondor, and the founder of these Dúnedain Realms in Exile.

Elendil was born in Númenor before its fall, the son of Amandil, last Lord of the Faithful of Andúnië. The Faithful were those Númenoreans who held true to the ways of the Eldar and thus survived when their rebellious countrymen were destroyed in the Downfall of that land in the year 3319 Second Age. Elendil than led the Faithful back to Middle-earth in nine ships, bearing a seedling of the White Tree, and the seven *palantíri;* and upon their arrival, these are the words that he spoke:

Et Eärello Endorenna utúlien. Sinome maruvan ar Hildinyar tenn' Ambar-metta! ('Out of the Great Sea to Middle-earth I am come. In this place will I abide, and my heirs, unto the ending of the world.')

Although Elendil was the High-king of both realms, he chose to dwell in Arnor, the senior of the two kingdoms, which he ruled personally from his beautiful city of Annúminas, beside Lake Evendim; his sons, Isildur and Anárion, ruled Gondor conjointly.

For a while both Exile Kingdoms were allowed to grow in peace. But, unbeknown to Elendil, Sauron the Great had also escaped the ruin of Númenor and had secretly re-entered Mordor. Forced to wait there while he gathered his strength, the Dark Lord became enraged on discovering that 'Elendil whom he most hated, had escaped him, and was . . . ordering a realm upon his borders.'[9] In the year 3429 Sauron struck – with swift attack against Gondor. Lying within his easy reach, on the shoulders of the Mountains of Shadow, Minas Ithil was quickly taken; but Anárion successfully defended the line of the Anduin, while Isildur escaped into the North to rally Arnor.

One year later, Elendil formed the Last Alliance of Elves and Men with Gil-galad, Elven-king of Lindon. The combined Hosts were mustered in Arnor and, in the year 3434, with Elendil and Gil-galad at their head, they crossed the Misty Mountains and marched south. At the ensuing Battle of Dagorlad, Narsil, the Sword of Elendil, and Aiglos, the Spear of Gil-galad, scythed through their foes and, though losses were grievous, the Alliance prevailed. Sauron was driven back to the Barad-dûr and there endured a long siege. Seven years later he finally emerged to engage Elendil and Gil-galad in single combat on the slopes of the volcano Orodruin. Though Sauron was himself overthrown in that fight, Gil-galad and Elendil were both slain. The High-kingship then passed to Isildur.

Elendili 'Elf-friends' (Q.) Another name for the FAITHFUL of Andúnië.

Elendilmir The Star of Elendil; the 'crown' of Arnor (though the Sceptre of Annúminas was the chief emblem of royalty in the North-kingdom). It was a single white gem bound to the brow by a slender fillet of silver.

Elendur The eldest of the four sons of Isildur, slain at the Gladden Fields (Year 2 Third Age). Also the name of the ninth King of Arnor, who ruled from 652–777 Third Age.

Elenna 'Star-wards' (Q.) This great isle was the most westerly of all Mortal Lands, being just within sight of the Undying Lands. At the end of the First Age, Elenna was given to the Edain by the Valar as a reward for their aid in the wars against Morgoth the Enemy. Accordingly, they set sail at the dawn of the new Age and founded there the realm of Númenor, far removed from the turmoil of Middle-earth.

Elentári 'Star-queen' (Q.) The High-elven form of the Grey-elven name ELBERETH. This Lady was more usually known to the High-elves as *Varda* 'The Exalted'.

See also TAR-.

Elenwë 'Star-maiden' (Q.) The wife of Turgon of the Noldor. She died during the dreadful crossing of the Holcaraxë, the Northern Ice, at the beginning of the period of Exile.

Elenya 'Stars'-day' (Q.) The first day of the 'week' (*enquië*) in Elvish and Númenorean reckoning – and ultimately in the calendar of almost all Westron-speaking peoples of Middle-earth. The Sindarin name for the same day was *Orgilion*, which was the word used by the Dúnedain. The Hobbits used a translation of *Elenya: Sterrendei*, which later became simply *Sterday*.

Elerrína 'Star-crowned' (Q.) A name for OIOLOSSË.

Elessar 'Elf-stone' (Q.) The title taken by Aragorn II on his ascension to the throne of Gondor. Although the name had been foretold for the Dúnadan long before, the reason for it was not apparent until he received the green gem which had originally been given by Galadriel to her daughter Celebrían, and by Celebrían to her daughter Arwen Evenstar. Thus it came to Aragorn – when he passed through Lothlórien with the fellowship of the Ring (Book II Chap. 8); thenceforth he wore the jewel at all times.

After the Battle of the Pelennor Fields, the people of Gondor also gave Aragorn the title 'Elfstone', not knowing who he was or why the lords of the Realm treated him with deference – but perceiving the great emerald as a work of Elvish craft.

Elf-friend A possible translation of the name *Elendil* (which also means 'Star-lover'). More specifically a title awarded to folk of other race who proved friendly to Elves. The Edain of the First Age were known as the 'Three Houses of the Elf-friends'.

Elfhelm A Marshal of Rohan who fought in – and survived – the great Battle of the Pelennor Fields (March, 3019 Third Age). He led the right wing of Riders when Théoden's men broke through the unguarded Pelennor wall at its most northerly point and charged across the fields. There, his *éored* wrought great destruction among the Orcs and Men who manned the fire-pits and siege-engines near the city-walls of Minas Tirith.

Several days later, Elfhelm commanded the main body of the mounted Rohirrim who guarded the northern flank in Anórien while the Host of the West marched to offer battle at the Black Gate.

Elfhild The wife of King Théoden of Rohan. She died early in her life, while giving birth to Théoden's only son, Théodred – who was himself slain at the Isen during the War of the Ring. Théoden never remarried.

Elfstan Fairbairn The eldest son of Elanor 'the Fair', daughter of Samwise Gamgee. He was the founder of the Fairbairn family.

Elfwine The nineteenth King of Rohan and the son of Éomer and Lothíriel, daughter of Imrahil of Dol Amroth.

Ell A variable unit of measure, approximately equal to $1\frac{1}{2}$ yards.

Elladan and Elrohir The twin sons of Elrond. Like their father (and his brother, Elros Tar-Minyatur), they were *Peredhil* ('Half-elven') and therefore possessed the life of the Eldar – while Elrond himself remained in Middle-earth.

In 2509 Third Age their mother, Celebrían, was journeying across the passes of the Misty Mountains when her party was ambushed by Orcs. The brothers rode swiftly to their mother's aid – and succeeded in rescuing her – but they never forgot the days of torment she experienced at the Orcs' hands while in captivity. For this reason, their feud with the Orcs was bitter.

Both Elladan ('Man-of-the-Stars') and Elrohir ('Star-rider') rode with the Dúnedain of the North to Aragorn's aid during the War of the Ring and, with the Grey Company, passed the Paths of the Dead and fought their way to Pelargir. There they took ship with the host of Lebennin and Langstrand up the Anduin, in time to arrive at a crucial moment during the Battle of the Pelennor Fields. After the Passing of the Three Rings, they remained with the Dúnedain of Arnor. Like their sister Arwen – although for different reasons – both brothers elected to become of mortal-kind.

Elostirion The name of the tallest of the towers of *Emyn Beraid*, in which the chief or master *palantír* was kept. It was built by Gil-galad during the Second Age.

Elrohir See ELLADAN AND ELROHIR.

Elrond 'Star-dome' (Sind.) Son of Eärendil and brother of Elros Tar-Minyatur; Herald of Gil-galad; Bearer of the Great Ring Vilya, mightiest of the Three; and Master of Rivendell throughout the Second and Third Ages of Middle-earth.

The sons of Eärendil were Elros and Elrond, the *Peredhil* or Half-elven. In them alone the line of the heroic chieftains of the Edain in the First Age was preserved; and after the fall of Gil-galad the lineage of the High-elven Kings was also in Middle-earth only represented by their descendants.[10]

The lineage of the *Peredhil* was indeed impressively ancient. Eärendil the Mariner, their father, was the son of Tuor (of the Third House of the Edain) and Idril Celebrindal, daughter of Turgon, High-elven King of Gondolin. Their mother, Elwing the White, was the daughter of Dior, son of Beren (of the First House of the Edain) and Lúthien Tinúviel herself, daughter of Thingol Greycloak and the Lady Melian of the Valar.

At the end of the First Age therefore, both Elros and Elrond were appointed a Choice: to become Mortal, or to accept the life of the Eldar. Elros decided to stay with the Edain, and was thus chosen to be Númenor's first King. But his brother's heart lay with the Eldar of Middle-earth, and thus Elrond chose to be of Elven-kind. Therefore, the same Choice was later passed on to his own three children: Elladan, Elrohir and Arwen Undómiel.

The early years of the Second Age were peaceful, and at that time Elrond dwelt with Gil-galad in Lindon, north of the Lune. The fabled refuge of *Imladris* ('Riven-dell') was not established until the middle of the War of the Elves and Sauron, which began in the year 1693. After Sauron's invasion of Eriador, Elrond was sent by Gil-galad to the aid of the Elven-smiths of Eregion. Although he could not save Eregion, he rescued the survivors and retreated northwards with them to a hidden valley deep in the foothills of the Misty Mountains; there Elrond founded the 'Last Homely House' of his kin.

For the remainder of the Second Age Elrond, now an Elven-lord of power, defended Imladris against all who would overcome it. And during the War of the Last Alliance, which secured Sauron's overthrow at the end of the Age, he marched with the Host as the Herald of Gil-galad. Thus he 'beheld the last combat on the slopes of Orodruin, where Gil-galad died, and Elendil fell'.[11] But Gil-galad had already bequeathed Vilya, greatest of the Three Rings to Elrond; and thus it was saved from destruction when Gil-galad perished at Sauron's hand. (Vilya was the Ring of the Firmament; Narya and Nenya, the Rings of Fire and Adamant, were in the possession of Círdan and Galadriel.)

Throughout the Third Age Elrond dwelled in Rivendell, wielding Vilya in concert with the other two Rings, for their intended purposes: 'understanding, making, and healing, to preserve all things unstained.'[12] But he could hardly stand aside from the affairs of his kinsfolk, and when, during the middle years of the Age, the North-kingdoms of the Dúnedain began to break up, the surviving Men of those lands relied heavily on Master Elrond's aid. He gave them sanctuary when they needed it, and sent a force to the last battle at Fornost against the Witch-king (in the year 1974). And when the North-kingdom finally fell, Elrond took the Heirs of Isildur into his own house, where also were kept the treasures of Isildur's Line: the Ring of Barahir, the Shards of Narsil, and the Sceptre of Annúminas.

But the House of Rivendell was not a fortress, nor a camp of war. It was a place of learning, of merriment and of quiet, beside a running stream, deep in a forest-clad northern valley. There, with his children, his loremasters, and many of the Chief Eldar of Middle-earth as his counsellors, Elrond dwelt until the end of the Age. Then as is told in the Red Book, the Master of Rivendell, friend of Elves and Men, passed in his turn 'West-over-Sea'; and with him went the Three Rings of the Elves. Thus Elrond was finally reunited with his wife Celebrían (who had gone over Sea long before); but he was sundered at the last from his sons Elladan and Elrohir, and his beloved daughter Arwen.

See also LINES OF DESCENT.

Elros Tar-Minyatur The son of Eärendil the Mariner and twin brother of Elrond; from 32–442 Second Age, the first King of Númenor; and the founder of the Dúnedain royal line.

He was known to the Edain by the High-elven title *Tar-Minyatur*. (*Elros* means 'Star-foam'), and he reigned over the Land of the Star for more than four hundred years – for to him and his descendants the Valar granted a great lifespan. His son Vardamir succeeded him.

Elu Thingol See THINGOL GREYCLOAK.

Eluchíl 'Thingol's Heir' (Sind.) See DIOR ELUCHÍL.

Eluréd 'Thingol's Heir' (Sind.) The elder of the two infant sons of Dior Eluchíl. He was left to starve in the forest by the Sons of Fëanor, after the sack of Doriath, together with his younger brother Elurín.

Elurín See preceding entry.

Elvenhome In its literal sense, this word was often applied to the country of Beleriand during the Elder Days; however, it is also frequently used as a translation of the word ELDAMAR.

Elven-rings The Three Rings.

Elven-smiths Prior to the rebellion of the High-elves, or *Noldor*, and the return of this people in Exile during the First Age, Elvish craft in Middle-earth had chiefly taken the form of skills with speech, song and enchantment. But the 'hopeless war' which the Noldor then began against Morgoth compelled them to develop anew the art of smithying, and so forge their own weaponry.[13]

Naturally, this was of a uniquely Elvish nature, though at first many of the techniques were acquired from the Dwarves of the Blue Mountains. One notable feature of such elven-blades was the happy faculty of warning their owners of approaching evil creatures (such as Orcs and Trolls) by shining with a cold blue light. This characteristic was shared by the swords Glamdring and Orcrist, as well as knife Sting, worn by Bilbo Baggins throughout his adventure, and later by Frodo and, for a short while, Samwise, in theirs. But for the Orcs – who captured most of the Elvish weaponry in the First Age – such blades were objects of abhorrence. They burned with a fierce light painful to Goblin-eyes, and so most of the captured arms were destroyed or cast away.

During the Second Age, the craft of smithying was further developed by the Noldor of Fëanor's House, in Eregion (where they had access to metals mined by the Dwarves of Moria). There were forged the Great Rings, perhaps the supreme examples of Elvish craftsmanship after the Silmarils, and the *palantíri* – which had been made by Fëanor himself in the Undying Lands long before. Yet all such Elvish essays into high craftsmanship now seem ill-starred, and the fate of the Great Rings echoes that of the Silmarils: marvellous they were, but great peril was brought into the world with them – and remained until they were finally removed from the Circles of the World.

Elven-swords See preceding entry; also ANGLACHEL; RINGIL.

Elves (Trans. from *Quendi* 'the Speakers'). In the Beginning of Days, long before Good or Evil moved in Middle-earth, when only the wild beasts and ancient trees inhabited the forests and valleys, the first of the 'speaking peoples' awoke and gazed 'out of the Wild Wood in wonder at their first Dawn'.[14] These were the Elves, the Firstborn, the immortal Elder Race of Middle-earth, noblest of the Children of Eru.

No subsequent race has ever had such a profound effect upon Middle-earth; for though Men, the Secondborn of Eru, have in many places wrought havoc with the natural order, and have left deserts where great forests once grew, and foul waters where crystal streams once ran, all these changes are but matters of detail compared with the far-reaching (and far more beneficial) alterations in the character of Mortal Lands – and the *olvar* and *kelvar* which dwell herein – effected long ago by the Fathers of the Elves, in the days before the rising of the Moon or Sun. For the Elves were, materially and spiritually, more closely bound to Middle-earth than Men; and all that they did was done long ago; and as a result the long effects of the presence of Elves in Middle-earth are more deeply-rooted than the works of Men, though the full measure of them can no longer easily be discerned.

In those most ancient of all days the subsequent differences between the Elf-kindreds had not yet begun to manifest themselves, and for a timeless period the Firstborn roamed freely around the Waters of Cuiviénen, and in the eastern forests, learning, understanding, and, above all, speaking: to each other (most of all) and to those beasts and growing things (*kelvar* and *olvar*) whose thoughts the Elves most desired to know. Their role in the affairs of Middle-earth is therefore one of awakening and teaching, rather than creation, or (as in the case of Morgoth and, unfortunately, Men) sub-creation. The Elves were the Quickeners of intellect, and articulation; they did not, strictly speaking, 'invent' these gifts; but they stimulated them, in themselves and in others; and having awakened and taught to the full extent of their ability (and their destiny) they departed from Middle-earth, leaving the remaining 'speaking-peoples' with the same hereditary task. (How well their successors have done is not for this compiler to estimate.)

Yet the changefulness of Mortal Lands affected the Elves in time, and, as is told in many places, they came to be divided into two main branches: the East-elves (or *Avari*), who loved the forests and were content there; and the West-elves, who conceived an awareness of their destiny and awaited a manifestation of it. These latter were the ELDAR; the Three Kindreds who were summoned to dwell across the Sea in Eldamar, and who began the Great Journey into the West for that purpose. Thus, far back in the First Age, two of these Kindreds at last sailed out of Middle-earth to the Undying Lands, and dwelt there agelessly in peace and exaltation.

However, the lesser Elves remained in Middle-earth throughout the Elder Days; and with them lingered a part of the Third Kindred of the Eldar, the *Sindar* (Grey-elves), who had stilled the Eldarin Sea-longing and had chosen to pass their days in Mortal Lands rather than sail into the West. In this way the race of Elves became divided into three: *Avari*, Grey-elves and High-elves (the name for those Eldar across the Sea in Eldamar).

Yet not all the High-elves were content to remain in the Undying Lands; a great number of the *Noldor* (the Second Kingdom) returned in exile to Middle-earth before the end of the First Age, thus initiating a series of gradual but nevertheless important changes for other peoples of mortal lands. Naturally enough, the return of the Exiles most directly affected their Grey-elven kin, who quickly adopted much of their lore (including the *Tengwar*, the High-elven alphabet of cursive letters). The Grey-elves themselves – who were numerous and whose language, *Sindarin*, was the most widely spoken among all Elves – subsequently passed on some of the Noldorin culture they had absorbed to the Wood-elves (another name for the Nandor), with whom they often dwelt in latter years. Ultimately, this gradual cultural transfer reached other races altogether. Thus, for example, the Grey-elves' own runic system (see ALPHABET OF DAERON) eventually spread to the Dwarves, and even – in a greatly debased form – to the Orcs and other servants of the Dark Power.

However, the peoples most profoundly affected by Elvish lore were the *Edain:* the Three Houses of Men who came west into Beleriand before the Elder Days had passed, and who adopted the ways of the Elves they found there. And the Elves of Middle-earth gave this knowledge freely, for in Men the Firstborn had recognized the shapes of their future inheritors; and so they enriched the minds of the Edain with all that Elven-lore could endow, even while they themselves began to prepare for their own separate destiny.

For the Undying Lands of Eldamar and Eressëa, in the Far West, had been set apart from the Beginning of Days as a refuge for all Elven-kind: to be a final home, removed from the perils and mortality of Middle-earth. And deep within the breasts of most Elves slumbered the 'Sea-longing', an innate desire to pass West to Eldamar and dwell there for ever. It was of course the exiled High-elves who felt this call most keenly, for they themselves had already once dwelt beyond the Sea. Accordingly, with the ending of the First Age and the lifting of their exile, most of the Noldor returned once more into the Undying Lands, and with them went a great number of the Grey-elves.

After the passing of the Three Rings, two full Ages later, few indeed of the Eldar (whether High-elves or Grey-elves) still tarried in mortal lands – though the Elven-woods of Wilderland long remained peopled by the lesser kindreds. For in the hearts of the Wood-elves the Sea-longing seldom awoke, and for the most part this people never came to Eldamar. They lingered instead in Middle-earth and eventually declined altogether, sharing the fate of all those whose destiny it remains to dwell on the Hither Shores.

Note: today only dim memories of the Elder Race survive in the legends and traditions of Men, though once there was great friendship between the peoples. Folk-stories, garnered from all quarters of the world, afford glimpses into remote antiquity – but little more.

For example, most northern and western lands of Men have tales of 'sprites', 'piskies', 'Brownies', and other diminutive creatures of wisdom, enchantment and malice (see also ORCS). Indeed such creatures take many forms, and are given many names; and in many cases a confusion has obviously occurred between two or even three quite distinct races. Yet from time to time a shaft of light strikes through the murk. The ancient Irish, who have many exceedingly antique legends and traditions, believed that Ireland[15] had in the past been invaded by successive waves of races, not all of whom were of mortal fibre, and most of whom came from the (mystic) West. One of these, called in Irish *Tuatha de Danaan* (the 'People of Don') are said, quite specifically,[16] to have sailed out of the West to Ireland to fight the evil Fomorians, to have defeated them, and then to have been themselves defeated by a new invasion of evil creatures, the *Fir Bolg*. The Tuatha then sailed back into the Far West, and did not return. (Significantly, they are not remembered as tiny creatures of malice – feeding on saucers of milk and stealing babies, and all the rest of the debased folk-memory – but as tall, beautiful, high beings of Light, great warriors and magicians, immortal and wise.) Some Welsh legends echo this theme, though different names are, of course, used.

Indeed, the idea of a Golden Age before the Age of Men – when older beings of quite different origin and destiny walked the earth – is exceedingly widespread. The Greeks had their age of 'Titans' (who were not, in the original legend, gigantic beings, rather beings of *power;* it was only later that power became equated with gigantism). Interestingly enough, the fate of the Titan Prometheus (who tried to steal Fire from the Gods and was chained to a rock as a punishment, doomed to be savaged each day by an eagle) contains curious jumbled echoes of the destinies of Fëanor (who likewise challenged the 'Gods'), and his eldest son Maedhros, who, as is told in *The Silmaril-lion,*[17] was chained to a rock and left there (but was actually *rescued* by an Eagle). It seems that, in the course of time, what folklorists call 'telescoping' has occurred, and this explains why, in regions of comparative isolation – certainly of less cultural diffusion – such as the Celtic West and the Germanic north, the legends have been preserved in less adulterated fashion. Yet examples can be found everywhere. And while *vanar* and *alfar* of Scandinavian myth are undoubtedly a recollection of Elves and their divisions, even the *cherubim* and *seraphim* of (Judaic) Cabbalistic tradition obviously owe a great deal to dimly preserved memories of older, more potent races, in the divine 'hierarchy' somewhere between the true Demi-urges (Angels and Archangels) and Men. Finally, the populous pantheon of the ancient Sumerians of Mesopotamia is chock-full of beings who are neither Gods nor Men – as indeed are many other religious systems, hierarchies and pantheons. But as might be expected, it is in the remoter lands of west and north that the memories are most clearly preserved.

Elves of the Darkness The DARK ELVES.

Elves of the Falas The FALATHRIM.

Elves of the Light The CALAQUENDI.

Elves of the Twilight The SINDAR.

Elvish See ELDARIN.

Elwë Singollo See THINGOL GREYCLOAK.

Elwing the White The daughter of Dior Eluchíl, son of Beren of the Edain and Lúthien daughter of Thingol Greycloak of Doriath. She was born at *Lanthir Lamath* (the 'Echoing-Cataract') in Ossiriand, and took her name[18] from this fair place. When she was still a child, Thingol her grandsire perished and Dior then arose and went to take up the lordship of Doriath; his wife Nimloth and his children, Eluréd, Elurín and Elwing, went with him, and dwelled for a while in Menegroth.

But the realm of Doriath Renewed was not fated to endure. On a night of winter, as has been told elsewhere (see CARANTHIR) the sons of Fëanor came against Dior's realm with fire and sword, to wrest from his keeping the single Silmaril which Beren and Lúthien had recovered years before. In this task they were not successful, though they slew Dior, and Nimloth his wife, and Eluréd and Elurín their sons – and were themselves slain in the same battle. But Elwing escaped from Doriath, bearing the great Necklace (the NAUGLAMIR) in which was set the Silmaril, and came in the end to the coastlands near the Sirion delta, where for a while she and her people found refuge from the works of Morgoth Bauglir. Here Elwing came to the fullness of her beauty, and she wedded Eärendil the Mariner of

Arvernien, thus uniting the noblest House of the Noldor in Middle-earth with the fairest House of the Grey-elves: the Line of Thingol and Melian.

Her high destiny is well known. When her husband Eärendil despaired of reaching Aman and so fulfilling his Quest, Elwing is said to have taken the likeness of a great sea-bird[19] and flown out to Sea, bearing the Silmaril; to alight exhausted upon the prow of Eärendil's ship Vingilot. He then used the Jewel to pass the Shadows and so come to the West. We are also told that, while the ship rested on the strands of Valinor, Elwing wandered northward to the land of the Teleri in Aman, at Alqualondë (she was after all akin to the people of Olwë, who was her great-grandsire's brother); but afterwards, together with Eärendil, she came at last to Valimar. There she was offered the choice of all the Half-elven: to be for everafter of Elven- or Man-kind. She chose the former, for both herself and for Eärendil. She afterwards dwelt in a white tower on the edge of Belegaer, the Great Sea, between the land of the Teleri and the region known as Araman, and there she dwells still, the patroness of all sea-birds and bride of the Evening Star.

Emeldir 'the Manhearted' The mother of Beren and wife of Barahir; she led the retreat of the First House from Dorthonion, after the Dagor Bragollach. Most of the surviving menfolk of that House remained in Dorthonion, to contest it with Morgoth, and all save one – her son Beren – were slain.

Emyn Arnen The 'Royal Hills' which lay between the Anduin and the Mountains of Shadow, in the province of Ithilien. They were, in fact, an eastern spur of the White Mountains, divided from the main range in ages past by the wide river-plain of the Anduin. The Emyn Arnen marked the boundary between North and South Ithilien. In the Fourth Age, after the destruction of Minas Ithil (latterly Minas Morgul), the Princes and Lords of Ithilien dwelled in these hills.

Emyn Beraid The 'Tower Hills' which marked the western boundary of the Shire. They were crowned with three Elf-towers built by the High-elven Exiles after their return to Middle-earth far back in the Elder Days. The tallest tower contained a *palantír* (Seeing-stone) of singular sort; it 'looked' only over Sea, and had been set there in the late Second Age by Elendil the Tall, so that he might gaze from afar at Eressëa and Eldamar – and look (in vain) for his drowned homeland of Númenor. After Elendil's death, the High-elves took over the custodianship of this Stone, and made occasional pilgrimages to the Emyn Beraid to use it. (See Book I Chap. 3 and *The Road Goes Ever On*, pp. 65–66.)

Emyn Muil A knotted range of ridged hills, cloven by the Anduin and the deep gorge of the Argonath. To the east they fell away until the land became flat and featureless; on the western side of the Great River, the hills dropped sharply in a cliff or scarp above the plain of Rohan. This was Rohan's East Wall. South of the Emyn Muil, on the eastern bank of the river, the lands sloped down into the swamps of Nindalf and the Dead Marshes.

Enchanted Isles The name given to the chain of islands set in the Great Sea as a defence and a cloak for Aman, after the rebellion of the Noldor and the beginning of their Exile. At this time Aman was also hidden by other means. The Enchanted Isles were of unknown number, and their positions also were not known (if indeed these remained constant). Few, journeying out of Middle-earth, ever passed their net.

Encircling Mountains The ECHORIATH.

Encircling Sea EKKAIA.

Enderi The 'Middle-days' (Q.) which the Elves added to the middle of their year to produce a total of 365 days. See CALENDAR OF IM-LADRIS.

Endless Stair By all accounts, one of the most impressive feats of stonemasonry ever performed by the Dwarves of Moria was the construction of this marvellous spiral stair, which climbed, in many thousand steps, from the lowest Deep to the very pinnacle of the Silvertine (*Celebdil*, known to the Dwarves as Zirak-zigil). At the head of the Endless Stair a high, windy chamber was carved into the living rock of the peak: this was Durin's Tower, where Kings of the realm might gaze out over the Misty Mountains.

After the desertion of Moria by the Dwarves in the late Third Age, the Endless Stair and Durin's Tower became a legend even to the Dwarves. Though lost, they were not destroyed until the epic battle between Gandalf and the Balrog, in January of the year 3019.

Endóre The Quenya word for 'Middle-earth'. The later, Sindarin form of the same word was *Ennor* (cf. *Galadhremmin Ennorath* 'Tree-woven-[Lands-of-]Middle-earth').

Enedhwaith 'Middle-folk' The open heath-country which lay between southern Eriador and the Isen. It was bounded on the east by Dunland and the southern peaks of the Misty Mountains. Always sparsely populated, the region was desolated after the severe floods of 2912 Third Age. This flooding was the result of the thaw following the Fell Winter of the previous year, when hardship and famine overtook all the western lands.

Ennor See ENDÓRE.

Enquië, enquier The High-elven (Quenya) word for 'week', applied to both the six-day week of the Eldar and the (later) seven-day week of Kings' Reckoning. The Eldarin 'days' were: *Elenya* ('Stars'-day'), *Anarya* ('Sun's-day'), *Isilya* ('Moon's-day'), *Aldúya* ('The Day-of-the-Two-Trees'), *Menelya* ('Heavens'-day') and *Valanya* ('The-Day-of-the-Valar'). *Valanya* was sometimes known as *Tárion*. The Númenoreans, who were much concerned with the Sea, added *Eärenya* ('Sea-day') to the list as the sixth day of the *enquië*, thus producing a seven-day week. *Tárion* (or *Valanya*) then became the 'High' day in the Dúnedain reckonings. They also changed *Aldúya* to *Aldëa* ('The-Day-of-the-White-Tree').

Entish The language of the *Onodrim* or ENTS. See main entry below and also Appendix F I.

Engwar 'the Sickly' An Elvish term for Men.

Entmoot A ritual assembly of Ents which occurred infrequently, at times of great need. The traditional place for these meetings was evidently the Derndingle, deep in the heart of Fangorn Forest.

Ents If the Elves were the oldest 'speaking-peoples' of Middle-earth, then the *Onodrim*, or Ents were the most ancient race of all. They were as old as the trees they cared for: 'the fathers of the fathers of trees, remembering times when they were lords.'[20] Another form of their name is *Enyd* (sing. *Anod*), from which *Ent*, the word used in Rohan, was doubtless derived.

In their remote beginnings, far back in the Elder Days, before even the Elves were roaming the vast forests of that vanished time, the Ents were indeed virtually indistinguishable from actual trees. But, as Treebeard (FANGORN) once remarked (to Meriadoc and Peregrin), 'Elves began it, of course, waking trees up and teaching them to speak and learning their tree-talk.'[21] And so the great Onodrim awoke and found their true nature.

From the moment the Elves cured them of dumbness, the Ents eagerly learned the languages of 'the Speakers', which they used after their own fashion, strung together in polysyllabic phrases of almost endless adjectives and the (very) occasional noun; a language of long, slow observation and a tree-ish reluctance to jump to conclusions. For the Ents' nature was close to that of the trees they protected and herded; ageing only slowly, Ents and trees passed down the Ages together.

Physically, each of the Onodrim most resembled the family of trees from which he was descended. Their strength was immense: as tree-roots can tumble the strongest structure, given time, so could Ents display the same enormous force, all in a few seconds (see Book III Chap. 9). Their power was sometimes compared with that of Trolls, but Ents were indeed much stronger than these lumpish beasts, which were created by Morgoth the Enemy 'in the Great Darkness, in mockery of Ents, as Orcs were of Elves.'[22]

Their history is sad, as is the history of all other 'speaking-peoples' who no longer dwell in Middle-earth. Like the Elves, their flowering period was that wide expanse of time known as the Elder Days. For long years they walked the forests – which then stretched from Northern Eriador to Fangorn – tending their herds, and speaking with the Elves (very quickly) and with each other (very slowly). But the Ents gradually grew apart from the Entwives, and 'entings' became few. The Entwives grew less interested in trees and forests, being more concerned with grasses, flowers and shrubs, and all the lesser growing things. They made gardens to live in, where they grew ever more skilful at these pursuits, while the Ents continued to wander and saw the Entwives less and less often.

Towards the end of the First Age, the Entwives crossed the Great River eastwards to escape the Darkness rolling down from the North; their agriculture continued to bring them great honour from Men but, in the end, the wars they had sought to escape swept over their lands and dispersed them, leaving only Brown Lands and barren earth where their gardens had flowered.

By the time of the War of the Ring, at the end of the Third Age, the Ents had long hidden in their remaining woods – of which Fangorn was the chief survivor. There they wandered alone, dwindling, but still tending their beloved trees.

See also Book III Chap. 4; Appendix F I.

Entwade The fords across the river Entwash between the Eastemnet and Westemnet of Rohan.

Entwash A large, meandering river which flowed from sources in Fangorn Forest, across the plains of Rohan, to meet the Anduin in a broad, low-lying delta north of the province of Anórien.

Entwash Vale The fens of the lower Entwash, including the delta.

Entwood The name in Rohan for Fangorn Forest.

Envinyatar 'The Renewer' (Q.) A secondary title borne by King Elessar (Aragorn II) of Gondor.

Enyd The ENTS.

Eöl One of the greatest smiths of the Elder Days, of the people of the Sindar (Grey-elves); the spouse of Aredhel of the Noldor and father of Maeglin the Traitor. Of all the individual histories of Elves and Men of the First Age, his is among the most tragic.

Eöl dwelled in the darksome woods of Nan Elmoth, and he kept a solitary way of life, for we are told he was of retiring disposition and did not care overmuch for those of his kindred – and even less for the High-elves. Of all Elves who have ever walked the world, Eöl was perhaps closest of all to the Dwarves; he may indeed be said, in a sense, to have been a Dwarf dwelling within the body of one of the Eldar, if such a thing can be imagined. From the Dwarves of the Blue Mountains he learned much of smithying, but after a while came to acknowledge no lordship in the matter of craft. Of all the smiths of the Grey-elves he was the most eminent. Only Celebrimbor of the Noldor is named before him.

It is told in *The Silmarillion*[23] how the Noldorin princess Aredhel came to be wandering in Eöl's woods, and how he took her to wife, and made her dwell with him in his gloomy retreat; and how, after a time, a son, Maeglin, was born to them. But when Maeglin was still young in years, his mother took him and fled from Nan Elmoth, back to Gondolin where her brother Turgon still reigned over his Noldorin people. And Eöl followed them, and so came also to Gondolin.

Before Turgon's throne, in the Tower of the King, the last act of the drama was played out. Greeted at first in kindly fashion by Turgon, Eöl spurned the king's friendship and defied his law. Then he attempted to slay his son Maeglin, but slew instead his wife, Aredhel Ar-Feiniel, sister of Turgon. He was executed for this crime by being cast down a precipice.

But two at least of his works lived on, and played a part in the events of that age. The black sword Anglachel, made by Eöl from meteoric iron, came to Beleg Strongbow, and after him to the renowned warrior of the Edain, Túrin Turambar. And Eöl's son Maeglin dwelt everafter in Gondolin, and became one of its lords, and in the end betrayed it, and Turgon his protector, to the death.

Éomer Éadig From 3019 Third Age to 63 Fourth Age, the eighteenth King of Rohan, and the close friend and ally of King Elessar (Aragorn II) of Gondor and Arnor.

Éomer's father was Éomund, the Chief Marshal of the Mark during the early part of King Théoden's reign. Éomund married Théodwyn, youngest sister of the King, who bore him two children: Éomer and Éowyn. But Éomund was slain by Orcs in the year 3002 and, shortly afterwards, Théodwyn died – to the great sorrow of the King, whose own wife had died in childbirth many years before. Therefore Théoden took Éomund's children into his house, treating them as his own son and daughter. And after the King's only son Théodred was slain in the opening campaign of the War of the Ring, Éomer, already Third Marshal of the Mark, became Théoden's heir.

He rode with Théoden's host to the defence of the Westfold Vale and the Battle of the Hornburg, where he and Aragorn fought so fiercely in league that none dared to stand against them. From the Hornburg, he accompanied the King on his last ride down to Gondor; and, when Théoden fell in battle during the great charge of the Rohirrim, Éomer was named King of the Mark. Though headstrong, he proved a valiant ally to Gondor in her hour of need and later became a mighty king of Rohan. In 3021 Third Age Éomer wedded Lothíriel, daughter of Prince Imrahil of Dol Amroth; their son, Elfwine the Fair, succeeded him.

Éomund The Chief Marshal of the Mark during the early reign of King Théoden of Rohan; the father of Éowyn and Éomer, eighteenth King. Éomund was responsible for the safety of the east marches of Rohan, where Orc-raiders were a constant threat to the prized horses of the Mark. In 3002 Third Age, his rashness and famed hatred of Orcs finally cost him his life, when he unwisely pursued a small raiding party into ambush.

Eonwë One of the MAIAR, the Herald of Manwë; he was the mightiest warrior in the world – after the champions of the Valar, whom, of course, he served.

Éored The name given in the tongue of the Rohirrim to the standard Rohan military unit: the cavalry squadron. Each of these bodies of mounted Riders was commanded by a noble, or by one of Marshal's, rank; each was recruited and furnished by the lord's own household and was mounted, armed and equipped according to the style of fighting employed by the Riders of Rohan. These squadrons varied in size, according to the duration of the muster and the size of the household, though 120 men – the strength of the *éored* commanded by the Third Marshal, Éomer, during the opening stages of the War of the Ring (see Book III, Chap. 2) – seems a little small, in view of the apparent numbers of Riders available to King Théoden at a slightly later date (perhaps Éomer did not at that time support an over-large personal establishment, since this seems to be the chief criterion in the size of any particular *éored*).

At all events, the *éored* was the chief unit of military strength, for the Men of Rohan did not fight on their feet. In centuries of living their 'horse-life' (see EORL THE YOUNG) they had polished their equestrian skills until they had become the most formidable heavy cavalry anywhere in the west of Middle-earth – and thus of great use to the (largely foot-bound) forces of neighbouring Gondor. Their tactics were those of both light and heavy cavalry: reconnaissance, envelopment, attack and pursuit. They were armed with ash-wood spears, swords, and bows for long-distance work, and knew the craft of chain-mail manufacture, so they were not only well-armed, and -mounted, but well-armoured also. Their method of attack was, firstly, to thin the enemy ranks with arrow fire, then to surround – or at least outflank – the enemy, and, finally, to loose spears and charge home in a body, using their lance-points on the first encounters and afterwards drawing swords for the close work. Unless they were greatly outnumbered, or at some other disadvantage, there was no cavalry in the west of Middle-earth which could stand against them.

Although the *éored* was the basic unit, the Rohirrim often fought in larger armies, comprising many *éoredda* and formed into wings or columns under the command of senior Marshals. Six thousand men of the Mark charged behind Théoden at the Battle of the Pelennor Fields, but Théoden himself reckoned[24] he might have assembled, if he had chosen, an expeditionary force of 10,000 – in Napoleonic terms, the equivalent of three full cavalry brigades.

Eorl the Young The last Lord of Éothéod (from 2501–10 Third Age) and the first King of Rohan (2510–45). Eorl was first called 'the Young' by the Men of Éothéod because his father Léod died while the son was still a mere stripling; Léod was attempting to tame a wild horse when it threw him and his head struck a rock. Instead of killing the horse, as was expected, Eorl recaptured the steed, named him Felaróf and rode him till his life's end.

It is recounted elsewhere (see BATTLE OF THE FIELD OF CELEBRANT) how in the year 2510 Eorl's people received tidings that Gondor was in danger; and how Eorl led his Riders to the aid of Gondor's Northern Army, in desperate straits at the hands of the Balchoth. In return, Cirion, twelfth Ruling Steward of Gondor, gave to Eorl and his people the wide province of Calenardhon, which they renamed *Riddermark*, the Mark of the Riders. In token of this gift, Cirion in his turn received the Oath of Eorl, pledging the Riders' continued allegiance to Gondor.

Thirty-five years later, Eorl, still almost as fresh-faced and tow-haired as in his youth, was slain by Easterlings in a new assault upon Rohan. His son Brego succeeded him and drove away the enemy. Eorl was laid to rest – together with Felaróf – in the first mound to be erected in the Barrowfield.

Eorlingas 'The Eorlings', the Sons of Eorl. An honorific title assumed by the warriors of Rohan.

Éothain The second-in-command of the *éored* of Westfold Vale at the time of the War of the Ring. This *éored* was led by Éomer, then Third Marshal of the Mark.

Éothéod From 1977–2510 Third Age, the northern homeland of the Horse-lords, before they moved south to the area which became known as Rohan. The lands of Éothéod lay between the Misty Mountains, the *Ered Mithrin* (Grey Mountains), and north-western Mirkwood. Prior to their settlement of this region, the Riders of Éothéod had dwelt in the vales of Anduin, between the Great East Road and the Gladden Fields. But after the final destruction of Angmar, this virile and expanding people, feeling a need for new territory, then migrated north.[25]

Éowyn In many of the songs and lays made by minstrels of Rohan concerning the War of the Rings and the part played in it by the Rohirrim, great honour was given to a woman: the 'Lady of the Shield-arm', who, defending her fallen Lord, slew the Chief Nazgûl and brought his power to nothing (as had been indeed foretold many years before).

This was the Lady Éowyn, sister of Éomer and later the wife of Prince Faramir of Gondor. She was the daughter of Éomund, Marshal of the Mark, and Théodwyn, sister of King Théoden; but after their early deaths, both Éomer and Éowyn were taken into the King's

House and raised as his son and daughter. Éowyn grew tall and fair, with a graceful step – and a skill with horse and blade to match any Rider of the Mark. As proud and brave as her brother, she found it increasingly difficult merely to wait upon the King in his decline; and she brooded much upon what she saw as the fall of Rohan into mean dishonour.

Thus Éowyn determined to find honourable death as a 'shield-maiden' on the field of battle. Disguised as an ordinary Rider, she rode with the King's host to the Fields of the Pelennor – and to her own supreme act of heroism. Even so, the fell wound she took from the Nazgûl seemed likely to bring her the end she had desired. But Éowyn was eventually cured in the Houses of Healing, where she met Faramir, Steward of the Realm; and at last she gave up all thoughts of battle, heroism and death. She and Faramir plighted their troth in the year 3019 Third Age, after the Downfall of the Lord of the Rings and the final victory of the West. They later dwelt together in Emyn Arnen.

Ephel Dúath The 'Dark Outer-fences' of Mordor, known to Men of Gondor as the Mountains of Shadow.[26] In the Third Age this colossal range of jagged peaks and dolorous vales was the second largest in Middle-earth – only the *Hith Aiglir*, the Misty Mountains, were greater in size and length. The Ephel Dúath formed an impassable western and southern wall around the land of Mordor.

The main range marched southerly from the Black Gate, parallel with the Great River (and in some cases only twenty miles from it), far into the lands of the Harad. Thirty leagues south of the river Poros, the Ephel Dúath bent abruptly east, stretching for a further two hundred leagues before turning north-east again and dwindling into a low, sullen line of hills.

Ephel Brandir 'Brandir's Fence' (Sind.) The name given by the Woodmen of the Forest of Brethil (the Haladin) to the stockaded settlement built by them – at the instigation of their chieftain, BRANDIR THE LAME – on the crown of the hill Amon Obel, in the midst of the wood.

Eradan From 2080–2116 Third Age, the second Ruling Steward of Gondor.

Erchamion 'The Empty-handed' (Sind.) See BEREN ERCHAMION.

Erebor The Lonely Mountain; the chief ancestral Halls of Durin's Folk in the later Third Age, following their flight from Moria. As is told elsewhere (see DURIN'S FOLK; DWARVES), Erebor was founded in 1999 Third Age by Thráin I, son of Náin I who was slain by the Balrog in Moria.

As its name implies, the Mountain stood apart from other ranges, and was a notable landmark in the flat plain east of Northern Mirkwood. It was easily defended (except against Dragons), but – more important to Dwarves – it was also exceedingly rich in minerals and precious metals. Yet shortly after its founding, Erebor was curiously abandoned by the majority of Durin's folk – who passed into the North and established a second colony amid the Grey Mountains. But this colony eventually came to naught and, in 2590 Third Age, Thrór son of Dáin I led Durin's Folk back to the Lonely Mountain, which then began to prosper greatly.

However, in the year 2770, Smaug the Golden, hearing of the newforged wealth of Erebor, sacked the Mountain, occupying the Great Hall and driving the Dwarves into exile and (relative) penury. For two centuries the Dragon was unchallenged until, in 2941, the unlikely combination of thirteen Dwarves and one Hobbit led to the demise of the Worm and the return of the King under the Mountain.

In the War of the Ring, Erebor was again attacked – by Easterlings of Sauron's rule – but the combined forces of Dwarves of Erebor and Men of Dale successfully withstood a siege there until news came north of Sauron's overthrow. The heartened defenders, led by Thorin Stonehelm and Bard II of Dale, sallied forth and drove away the enemy. Ever after the Kingdom under the Mountain was in alliance with and under protection of Gondor.

Erech See STONE OF ERECH.

Ered Engrin The IRON MOUNTAINS.

Ered Gorgoroth The MOUNTAINS OF TERROR.

Ered Lindon A name given by some of the High-elves to the *Ered Luin*, the Blue Mountains. This was of course because they first espied these mountains from the land of Lindon, in eastern Beleriand.

Ered Lithui The 'Ashy Mountains' which provided Mordor with a northern rampart. The range ran east from the Morannon (parallel with the southern range of the Ephel Dúath), into the wide and desolate lands of southern Rhûn. Upon a south-westerly spur projecting from the inner wall stood the Barad-dûr, the Dark Tower of the Lord of the Rings.

Ered Lómin The ECHOING MOUNTAINS.

Ered Luin The BLUE MOUNTAINS.

Ered Mithrin The 'Grey Mountains', which ran eastwards from Gundabad (in the Misty Mountains) to the Withered Heath.

Ered Nimrais The 'White Mountains' of Gondor. Unlike other mountain-chains of Middle-earth, the Ered Nimrais did not form a single range; instead, from a central massif or knot, great spurs projected north, south, east and west, as far as Cape Andrast and the Sea. Upon the knees of the most easterly of these mountains, Mindolluin, the Men of Númenor built their white city of Minas Anor (later Minas Tirith).

Ered Wethrin The 'Shadowy Mountains' which formed the eastern boundary-wall of the lands of Hithlum, Mithrim and Dor-lómin, in the north of Beleriand.

Eregion 'Land-of-Holly' (Sind.) The land of the Noldorin Elven-smiths, in Eriador, west of the Misty Mountains, whose chief city was Ost-in-Edhil.[27] It was settled by the Noldor in 750 Second Age and destroyed by Sauron less than nine hundred years later.

The Elves of Eregion were master craftsmen of the House of Fëanor, and were led by Celebrimbor, Fëanor's descendant. They migrated to eastern Eriador after hearing of the discovery of a great *mithril*-lode under the Dwarf-realm of Moria; and so they founded their colony at Moria's western gate to trade with the Dwarves for this metal, dearly beloved by all Elves. The Dwarves were happy enough with this arrangement, and both races worked together for many years in friendship and prosperity.

In time, the skill of the High-elves of Eregion bid fair to rival that of Fëanor himself, and under the tutelage of Sauron of Mordor, it reached a pinnacle with the forging of the Rings of Power, the greatest work of Elven-craft since the creation of the Silmarils. But Sauron betrayed the Elven-smiths and himself forged the Ruling Ring in secret. Learning of this, the Noldor then hid the Three Elven-rings they had made, but war was launched upon them by Sauron, and in the year 1697 Eregion was overrun and ravaged. The Dwarves of Moria were safe behind their impregnable mountain-walls but the Noldor were driven out or destroyed. So ended the brief flowering of Eregion.

Note: the token of the Noldorin smiths was holly, which they planted freely and used to indicate the borders of their realm. Many of these ancient trees survived in Eregion when all other living things had passed away, and still stood in later Ages. For this reason Eregion was known simply as *Hollin* to Men of Eriador during the Third Age.

See also ELVEN-SMITHS; WAR OF THE ELVES AND SAURON.

Ereinion 'Scion-of-Kings' (Sind.) See GIL-GALAD.

Erelas A beacon-hill which stood on the north wall of the White Mountains, overlooking the vale of Anórien. It was fourth in the chain of beacons stretching between Gondor and Rohan.

See also BEACON-HILLS.

Erellont The name of one of the three valiant Men, mariners who were companions of Eärendil on his last voyage. See also AERANDIR.

Eressëa 'Lonely' (Q.) Shortened form of *Tol Eressëa*, 'the Lonely Isle'; the name given by the Calaquendi to the great ship-shaped isle which had once been rooted in the waters of Middle-earth, but which was set adrift by the agency of the Valar and used to enable the Three Kindreds of the Eldar to complete the Great Journey and so come to the far West.

It is said in the traditions of the Elves that it was the Sea-Maia Ossë who begged the Teleri – the last of the Kindreds to travel by this marvellous means – to stay their voyage while they were still some distance from the strands of Aman; for he loved the Teleri, and did not wish to be parted from them; and they, loving him, did as he asked, and the Isle was grounded in the Bay of Eldamar and stood there ever after. *Tol Eressëa* then became its name. For an age or more the Teleri continued to dwell there, but many still yearned to complete the Journey and so come to the source of the Light which lit the western horizon; and so, at their request, Ossë sadly taught them how to build ships, and the Teleri sailed away from Eressëa, to Aman. But, after years the lonely Isle was re-peopled with Grey-elves and returning Noldorin Exiles, who built anew the city of Avallónë – nearest of all cities to the Blessed Realm, and visible (to the Farsighted) from the summit of Meneltarma in Númenor. And from Eressëa these Elves would, from time to time, sail to Númenor, there to enrich the culture of the High Men who then dwelled in that now-vanished country. But at the Drowning of Númenor, the shape and nature of the World was altered, and Eressëa, and Aman, were removed for ever from the seas of the earth.

Erestor One of the Noldor of Rivendell: Chief of the Counsellors of Elrond's house.

Eriador 'Eriador was of old the name of all the lands between the Misty Mountains and the Blue; in the South it was bounded by the Greyflood and the Glanduin that flows into it above Tharbad.'[28] In the North lay the great ice-waste of Forochel and the bitter colds of the realm of Morgoth. But after millennia of war, famine and plague had depopulated the region, the various settlements of Men, Elves and Hobbits became increasingly isolated from each other – and eventually only the great ruins of Eriador were left to testify to its former glories.

Erkenbrand A Lord of Rohan and, at the time of the War of the Ring, the Master of Westfold Vale. He took command of the Westfold forces after Théodred, Théoden's son, fell in battle with the armies of Saruman, early in the year 3019 Third Age. Though it was at first feared that Erkenbrand, too, had fallen, he organized a well-ordered retreat and was able to bring the battered but unbroken Westfold Riders to the aid of the King at the Battle of the Hornburg.

Ernil i Periannath 'Prince of the Halflings' (Sind.); an honorific title awarded to Peregrin Took by the people of Gondor, who believed he bore the rank with which their natural courtesy endowed him.

'Errantry' A lengthy Hobbit-poem found in the Red Book of Westmarch – and almost certainly composed by Bilbo, since it shows kinship with the later work ('Eärendil Was A Mariner') recited by him in the Hall of Fire in Rivendell prior to the Council of Elrond.

With his head full of Elvish influence – though not, at that time, Elvish skill – Bilbo probably wrote 'Errantry' shortly after his return from Erebor, long before he came to know the Elves better. The references to Elvish 'lore' and 'names' (such as *Aerie, Belmarie*) would seem to show that the Hobbit was not at the time fully conversant with Elvish tongues or history. As has been remarked, these words are 'mere inventions in the Elvish style, and are not in fact Elvish at all.'[29]

The poem is cyclical, and may be recited therefore endlessly. Its subject, though whimsically treated, is obviously influenced by various older tales that Bilbo may have unconsciously absorbed during his earlier stay in Rivendell. Later in his life, of course, the worthy Hobbit returned to Elrond's house and studied Elven-legends in greater detail. In a desire to make use of the metrical devices he had invented years before, Bilbo then rewrote 'Errantry' in the form in which it appears in Book II Chap. 1. Some of the lines, indeed, are almost identical:

> *Of crystal was his habergeon,*
> *his scabbard of chalcedony;*
> ('Errantry')
> *of silver was his habergeon,*
> *his scabbard of chalcedony;*
> ('Eärendil Was A Mariner')

Eru 'The One' (Sind., from Q. *Ilúvatar*, 'Father-of-All') God. The Power whom the Valar themselves served, who created *Eä*, the Cosmos, and *Arda*, the World therein.

Erui One of the Seven Rivers of Gondor, flowing from its source high in the vale of Lossarnach to its confluence with the Anduin thirty leagues above Pelargir.

See also BATTLR OF THE CROSSINGS OF ERUI.

Erusën This ancient word translates as 'the Children-of-God' (*Eru*), and refers to Men and Elves, for whom the world (*Arda*) was created. *Eruhíni Iluvatáro* carries the same meaning.

Eryn Lasgalen For most of the Third Age this mighty forest east of the Misty Mountains was known as Mirkwood, although its original title was Greenwood the Great. This change of name was gradual, and was largely due to the evil influence of Dol Guldur in the south of the Forest. But after the end of the Third Age, the Elves of Lórien crossed the Great River and destroyed Dol Guldur; Celeborn of Lórien and Thranduil of Northern Mirkwood then met in the midst of the Forest and renamed it *Eryn Lasgalen* 'The Wood of Green-leaves' (Sind.).

Eryn Vorn 'Black Woods' (Sind.) The wooded Cape of Minhiriath, south of the Baranduin estuary.

Esgalduin 'Veiled-river' (Sind.) The Enchanted river of Doriath. It rose from two sources in the Mountains of Terror, and flowed south, then west; in the north dividing Nan Dungortheb from Dor Dínen, and in the south forming a boundary between the forests of Neldoreth and Region.

Esgaroth The Lake-town of the River Running, built upon stilts in the shallows of the Long Lake.

When the nearby town of Dale was destroyed by Smaug the

Dragon in 2770 Third Age, many of the Men who had dwelt there passed south to the Long Lake and swelled the numbers of the lake-colony. Most of the trade (in wine and food) between Dorwinion (near the Inland Sea of Rhûn) and the kingdom of the Wood-elves in Mirkwood then passed through the lake-dwellers' ken. Esgaroth, therefore, in addition to its fishermen, had merchants and riverboat-men, who charged modest fees for speeding this commercial traffic. As such, the town prospered under its Burgesses – until the arousal of the Dragon almost two hundred years later. Smaug flew south to raze the Lake-town, but though he caused great damage, the Dragon was himself slain by Bard of Esgaroth, heir of the Kings of Dale. A great part of the Lake-town inhabitants then returned to the mountains and rebuilt Dale, and Bard became their king. Esgaroth continued to prosper nevertheless.

Esmeralda Brandybuck The wife of Saradoc Brandybuck and the mother of Meriadoc, later Master of Buckland and a Counsellor of the North-kingdom.

Esse The Quenya or High-elven word for 'name', but more properly, the title of the Tengwa (or 'letter') number 31, one of the 'additional' Tengwar. It represented the sound *z*. See also ÁRE.

Estë 'Rest' (Q.) A Queen of the Valar, the spouse of Irmo (Lórien). She is the Healer, dressed in grey, who brings peace to the wounded and afflicted. She wakes only at nightfall, and sleeps by day on an island in the Lake of Lórellin, in her spouse's domain of Lórien, in Valimar. In the hierarchy of the seven Valier (Valar Queens), Estë is named fourth, after Nienna and before Vairë. Her spouse Irmo is one of the two *Fëantúri* (Mandos is his brother), and is the Master of Dreams and Visions.

Estel The Sindarin name for 'Hope', by which Aragorn II was known in his youth – before Elrond revealed to him his true name and lineage. See the 'Tale of Aragorn and Arwen' in Appendix A I(v).

Estolad 'The Camp' (Sind.) The name given by Men (in the newly-learned tongue of the Grey-elves) to the region of East Beleriand where the Edain first settled. It lay east of the river Celon, and south of the wood of Nan Elmoth, and was chosen on the advice of Finrod

Felagund of the Noldor. For at that time the Edain, new-come in the West, were dwelling in an encampment on Ossiriand, the land of the Green-elves – who did not at all desire their presence. The first tribe of the Edain to settle in Estolad were the house led by Bëor the Old (though Bëor himself afterwards went away to Nargothrond); a year or so afterwards, the encampment was swelled by the arrival of the most numerous of the Adûnaic peoples: the Third House, led by Marach Aradan.

However the conjoined Houses of Men were not to dwell long in this remote place. Hearing of their (long-foretold) presence in western Middle-earth, some of the princes of the Noldor (notably those Elves of the houses of Fingolfin and Finarfin) invited the newcomers to leave Estolad and hold lands further north, as the allies and friends of the High-elves. This they did. The First House went to Dorthonion, and the Third, the People of Marach, went to Dor-lómin. However, Estolad was not deserted, for many remnants of kindreds remained. This mongrelized tribe of Men lingered in Estolad for another century or so, but were finally driven out for ever in the years of Morgoth's triumph.

Ethir Anduin 'Mouths of Anduin' (Sind.) The delta of the Great River, where it flowed into the Bay of Belfalas in six broad streams.

Ethring The small township built on either side of the river Ringló in Gondor; there, the road from Morthond to Pelargir forded the stream.

Ethuil 'Spring' (Sind.) The first season of the Eldarin *loa* (year). The (older) Quenya name was *tuilë*. See CALENDAR OF IMLADRIS.

Ettendales See ETTENMOORS below.

Ettenmoors A wild and remote region of northern Eriador, haunted by Trolls; it lay north of Rivendell and south of the realm of Angmar.

Ever-cold A translation of the Sindarin name *Himring*.

Evereven A poetic reference to the Eternal Twilight of Valinor and Eldamar – used after Morgoth's poisoning of the Two Trees (in the First Age) had removed their Light from the Undying Lands.

Evermind A translation of the Northern Mannish word *simbelmynë*, being the name given in Rohan to the white grave-flowers of the Barrowfield near Edoras.

Exiles The High-elves of Middle-earth, the NOLDOR.

Ezellohar (Untranslated) One of the names in Elven tradition for the green mound which stood before the western gate of the city of Valimar (or Valmar), in Valinor. Another was *Corollairë*. Here grew – and for many Ages stood in glory – the Two Trees of the Valar, raised from the green earth of Ezellohar by the enchantments of Yavanna Kementári.

Notes

1 Book I Chap 11.
2 His name means 'Sea-lover' (Q.).
3 Book II Chap. 1.
4 Book VI Chap. 9.
5 Book II Chap. 7.
6 *Silmarillion* p. 79.
7 Appendix F.
8 Book VI Chap. 5.
9 Appendix A I(i).
10 *Ibid.*
11 Book II Chap. 2.
12 *Ibid.*
13 Although the Noldor had of course already made swords and other weapons, before their revolt (*Silmarillion* p. 69). This had been on the advice of Melkor (Morgoth), first of all to make weapons of war. Later some of the Elves had assistance from Dwarf-smiths of the Blue Mountains. But the weapons of the Laiquendi and Avari were mere wood, horn and bone, for at this time the uses of metal were unknown to them.
14 Book III Chap. 3.
15 i.e. the extreme West of the Old World.
16 In the *Book of Invasions*, chief source of these legends.
17 *Silmarillion* pp. 108–110.
18 Meaning 'Star-spray' (Sind.).
19 *Silmarillion* p. 247. This is one of the many apocryphal ingredients of the Eärendil myth.
20 Book I Chap. 7.
21 Book III Chap. 4. They were themselves made by Eru, at the prayer of Yavanna Kementári.
22 *Ibid.*
23 pp. 131–39.
24 Book V Chap. 3.
25 It is impossible to overlook extraordinary parallels between the cultures and histories of the Éothéod/Rohirrim and the Gothic

Germans of the late Roman period. Both were blond, northern races who emigrated south and eventually became the allies of an older empire; both were originally nomadic peoples; and both were the most formidable heavy cavalry of their day. History *does* repeat itself. See also Note 1 on p. 91 of this *Companion*.

26 Not to be confused with the 'Shadowy Mountains' (*Ered Wethrin*) of northern Beleriand.

27 Location unrecorded.

28 Appendix A I(iii).

29 *The Adventures of Tom Bombadil.*

Faelivrin An admiring name (which means, 'Ivrin's Daysheen' in the Sindarin tongue) given to FINDUILAS daughter of Orodreth, the Heir of Finrod, by Gwindor, a prince of Nargothrond.

Faerie The 'Perilous Realm', the land of the Elves – as reported in mortal tradition. It is essentially a poetic term, for mortals are entirely unacquainted with these regions, and their interpretations can only be mere approximations of an unimaginable (for mortals) state of existence. Thus, in Bilbo's *There and Back Again* (*The Hobbit*), the term *Faerie* (together with *Aerie*) is used as a fanciful name for imagined Elf-kingdoms, somewhere vaguely in the West.

Fairbairns of the Towers The descendants of Samwise Gamgee's daughter, Elanor 'the Fair', traced through her eldest son Elfstan Fairbairn. Early in the Fourth Age, her family moved to Under-towers, on the slopes of the Tower Hills in the Westmarch of the Shire. They were later made Wardens of Westmarch, and eventually assumed the custodianship of the famous Red Book – charged with the duties of compiling, copying and keeping safe one of the principal record-sources of the Third Age.

Fair Elves A translation of the Quenya name *Vanyar*, meaning the First (and Highest) Kindred of the Eldar; who came to Valinor in the Beginning of Days and dwelt there ever after, unlike the 'Deep-elves' and the 'Grey-elves', both of whom were also Eldarin Kin-dreds. The Vanyar had golden hair.

Fair Folk The Elves.

Faithful The Faithful of Númenor; the small group of Númenorean families who, despite increasing persecution, continued to hold to the ancient Elvish traditions and tongues throughout the gradual estrangement of their people from the Eldar and the Valar. They lived mainly in the province of Andúnië, on the most westerly part of the island.

Like most Númenoreans, the Faithful were great mariners; and in 2350 Second Age, after many journeys back to Middle-earth, they established their own haven there, at Pelagir, on the lower Anduin. When Númenor was eventually destroyed (in the year 3319), a number of the Faithful escaped the disaster and sailed back to Middle-earth in nine of their ships, bearing a seedling of the White Tree and the seven *palantíri*. Led by Elendil the Tall, son of Amandil, last Lord of Andúnië, they then founded the Dúnedain Realms in Exile, Arnor and Gondor, in the Westlands of Middle-earth.

See also LORDS OF ANDÚNIË; NÚMENOR.

Falas 'Coastland' (Sind.) A name for any coastal region (e.g. *Belfalas* 'The coasts of Bel', *Anfalas* 'Long-beach'), but in its earliest proper sense, for the shorelands of West Beleriand: the abode of the *Falathrim*, the 'Coast-elves' (see CÍRDAN THE SHIPWRIGHT), a Telerin kindred who dwelt in this region, mainly at their two fortified Havens of Eglarest and Brithombar, throughout much of the First Age.

Falastur 'Lord-of-the-Coasts' (Sind.+Q.) The imposing title adopted by Tarannon, twelfth King of Gondor (from 890–913 Third Age) and the first of that realm's four renowned 'Ship-kings'. His actual victories were comparatively modest in the light of the achievements of his immediate successors – Hyarmendacil in particular. But, as Captain of the Hosts, Tarannon succeeded nonetheless in extending the rule and reach of Gondor along the shorelands west and south of the Anduin, thus re-establishing the ancient Númenorean sea-power (to a limited degree). To commemorate these early conquests, he laid down Gondor's first permanent fleet and took the crown in the name of Falastur.

Falathar One of the three faithful companions of Eärendil. See AERANDIR.

Falathrim 'Coast-Elves' (Sind.) An Elven-people: the Eldar of western Beleriand, originally part of the main host of the Teleri who had come last of all to the coastal lands of Middle-earth, in the days of the Great Journey. There the last of the many sunderings of the Teleri took place, when this people passed over Sea, leaving behind two subdivisions of their kindred: the Eglath, who remained to search for Elwë their lord, lost years before in Nan Elmoth, and who subsequently became the Elves of Doriath; and the Teleri who then dwelt on the coasts, declining to depart with the main host because of their love for the sea-lands of Beleriand – and because of the entreaties of the Sea-Maia Ossë, who did not desire them to vanish out of his domain for ever. From these earliest days the Falathrim were led by CÍRDAN THE SHIPWRIGHT, and dwelt chiefly in the two ancient Havens of Eglarest and Brithombar. In the lore of the Elves, they are accounted 'Grey-elves' (*Sindar*), and *Úmanyar*, but not *Moriquendi*, for those that survived the turmoils of three Ages of Middle-earth came in the end into the Far West, to the long home appointed for all those of Eldarin race. Their last dwelling in Middle-earth was the Haven of Mithlond; and Círdan himself was the last of all Elves to leave the 'Hither Shores'.

'The Fall of Gil-galad' The name given in the Common Speech to an Elvish lay, composed in Lindon or Rivendell early in the Third Age (the original title is unknown), and now no longer extant. At least one copy was evidently kept in Rivendell, for both Aragorn and Bilbo – and, surprisingly, Sam Gamgee – had an acquaintance with the poem. Bilbo probably brought a copy away with him on his return from Erebor via Elrond's house, later translating it at Bag End – where the sharp-eared Sam doubtless picked up a few stanzas.

Gil-galad was no less than the last High-elven King of Middle-earth, and the Lay concerns his long fight against the power of Sauron through the Second Age. This culminated in the Last Alliance, the (first) overthrow of Sauron and the death of the mighty Gil-galad:

> *the last whose realm was fair and free*
> *between the Mountains and the Sea.*[1]

Fall of the Noldor A translation of the Quenya title *Noldolantë*; being the name of the long lay or song composed by Maglor the second son of Fëanor, in the time between the Fall of Morgoth and his own death, when he wandered, half-mad, on the wild coasts of Middle-earth. Its subject was the making of the Silmarils, the rebellion of Fëanor, the Curse of Mandos – and all the evil deeds which followed after, bringing ruin upon the Deep-elves. Maglor and Maedhros, the two eldest sons of Fëanor, were the only two of the seven brethren ever to repent in any measure of their Oath. Both killed themselves at the end of the First Age, but one copy at least of the *Noldolantë* survived (probably in Rivendell), and so came to be one of the chief source-references of the *Quenta Silmarillion*.

Fallohides One of the three breeds or clans of Hobbits. Unlike the other two, Harfoots and Stoors, the Fallohides were 'more friendly with Elves than the other Hobbits were, and had more skill in language and song than in handcrafts; and of old they preferred hunting to tilling.'² They were also noticeably fairer of colouring than other Hobbits, often taller, (sometimes) slimmer, and were frequently found in some leadership capacity, being characteristically more adventurous than others of their people. They were also the least numerous.

Note: Marcho and Blanco, who led the Crossing of the Baranduin and the founding of the Shire (1601 Third Age, Year 1 Shire Reckoning) were scions of this excellent stock.

Falls of Ivrin The EITHEL IVRIN.

Falls of Sirion The greatest fall or cataract on the river Sirion, where the marshes formed by the confluence of the Aros with the Sirion in flat country suddenly emptied over a precipice into a foaming basin – which was itself drained by means of underground courses, reappearing nearly ten miles downstream at the Gates of Sirion.

Falmari 'Elves-of-the-Crested-Waves'; (Q.) more familiarly 'Sea-elves'. A name given in Aman to those of the Telerin Elves who came first across the Sea, by way of Eressëa, to the Undying Lands, on whose shores they afterwards dwelt, at Alqualondë: the People of Olwë.

Fana 'Veil' (Q.) See FANUILOS.

Fangorn This Sindarin word meaning 'Beard-of-Tree' is used in the Red Book to mean both the great Forest which stood on the eastern side of the Misty Mountains, and the venerable Guardian Ent who ruled that strange country. 'Tree-beard' is, of course, an exact translation of *Fangorn*.

It is not clear whether the Forest was named after the Ent, or the other way about; however, it is certain that both were of exceedingly great age. Fangorn himself claimed that the Wood had seen over three Ages of the outside world. Indeed, both Treebeard's Forest and the Old Forest near the Shire were the last remaining enclaves of the great woods of the Elder Days, and both contained deep vales from which the Great Darkness had never been lifted. Treebeard put it another way:

Taurelilómëa-tumbalemorna Tumbaletaurëa Lómëanor[3]
('Forestmanyshadowed-deepvalleyblack
Deepvalleyforested Gloomyland')[4]

was the old Ent's particular expression for those dark regions. This translates (very approximately) as: 'there is a black shadow in the deep dales of the forest.'[5] It is delivered in a typically Entish agglomeration of Elvish (Quenya) words – for *Taurë*, *tumbo* and *lómë* are the original forms of the Quenya names for forest', '[deep]-valley' and 'many-shadowed' respectively.

Fantasie A poetic invention in the Elvish style which appears in Bilbo's poem 'Errantry'. See also AERIE; BELMARIE; FAERIE.

Fanuidhol 'Cloudy-head' (Sind.) The Elves' name for the southernmost of the three mountains of Moria. The word is derived from the ancient Grey-elven element *fan-*, *fanui-*'cloudy' (and from the older Quenya *fana-* 'veil').

Fanuidhol was known as Bundushathur to the Dwarves and Cloudyhead to Western Men.

Fanuilos One of the ceremonial titles of ELBERETH, in her aspect as divine or demiurgic intercessary. In this role she was often thought of as standing on the slopes of Mount Oiolossë, radiant with inner (divine) light, arms uplifted as she listened to invocations for aid from Men and Elves.

Note: the Quenya element *fana-* referred to the *fanar*, or 'veils', with which the Valar clothed themselves when dealing with Elves and Men. (These 'veils' were in essence their physical manifestations.) The full title *Fanuilos* means 'Bright [Angelic]-Figure-Ever-white', as the suffix *-los* refers to the brightness of fallen snow (*cf. Lossoth*, 'Snow-people').

See also *The Road Goes Ever On*, p. 66.

Faramir One of the two sons of King Ondoher of Gondor, slain – in battle with the Wainriders' Confederacy – in 1944 Third Age. The death of the King and his two sons in this battle resulted in the crown of Gondor being awarded to a victorious captain, who took the royal title Eärnil II. Also the name of the Prince of Ithilien, Lord of Emyn Arnen and Steward to King Elessar of Gondor and Arnor. Faramir was the son of Denethor II, twenty-sixth and last of the Ruling

Stewards – before the events of the War of the Ring brought about the return of the King and the transference of Gondor's rule. He succeeded his father during the Siege of Minas Tirith (March, 3019 Third Age), and he ordered the affairs of the City until the crowning of King Elessar in May, when he was given the princedom of Ithilien.

Faramir was also the younger brother of Boromir (of the Fellowship of the Ring), and was like him in many ways, though not all. For while Faramir took pleasure in music and lore, his brother thought only of battles and great deeds. Nevertheless the needs of that time were such that Boromir was esteemed the higher of the two, especially in the eyes of their father. In the event both Boromir and Denethor died in the War of the Ring, and Faramir was badly wounded. In this way he came to the Stewardship.

Despite his father's opinion, Faramir was in no way Boromir's inferior as a warrior, and he spent much of the war on especially dangerous duty in Ithilien, then occupied by forces of the Dark Lord. Immediately before Sauron's long-awaited assault on Minas Tirith, Faramir hurried back across the Anduin and took charge of the outer defences of the City. While leading the rear-guard in the final retreat from the out-wall on March 12th, he was struck by an arrow and fell in a dark swoon. For three nights he lay in peril until healed at last by the King's own hand.

Later, Faramir was well rewarded for his valour and loyalty, and the Office of Steward was given to him and his heirs in perpetuity. He afterwards wedded the Lady Éowyn of Rohan and they dwelt together in Emyn Arnen during the years of King Elessar's rule.

Faramir Took The only son of Peregrin Took, born in Year 9 Fourth Age (1430 Shire Reckoning) to the union of his famous father and Diamond of Long Cleeve. Peregrin named his only son *Faramir* in honour of the new Prince of Ithilien, whom Peregrin greatly admired. Faramir Took eventually married Goldilocks, one of Sam Gamgee's many children, thus uniting two of the Shire's most illustrious families.

Far Downs The green-grey, treeless uplands which sloped away to the Grey Havens on the western edge of the Shire.

Far Harad The southernmost reaches of Middle-earth. Little was mentioned of its people in the records of Gondor, since prolonged if intermittent warfare between the Haradrim and the Dúnedain of the South poisoned relationships between the two races. The lands of

Far Harad were said to be exceedingly hot, and the warriors were described as 'black men like half-trolls with white eyes and red tongues'.[6]

Farin A Dwarf of Durin's House. He was the son of Borin and uncle of Thrór, first of the second Line of Kings under the Mountain.

Farmer Cotton Tolman 'Tom' Cotton; in the last fifty years of the Third Age (and a good many of the Fourth), one of the most prosperous Hobbits of Bywater and its district.

Farmer Cotton's only daughter Rose became Sam Gamgee's wife in 3020 Third Age, the Great Year of Plenty. Thus were links renewed between the Cottons (who played a prominent part in the Scouring of the Shire) and the ascendant Gamgee family.

Farmer Maggot A well-known and important Hobbit-farmer of the Eastfarthing, renowned for the prosperity of his holdings (and the excellence of his mushrooms). Yet for all his respectability, Maggot was also considered a canny person with his ear close to the soil; and it seems certain that he was on terms of friendship and mutual respect with Tom Bombadil.

Faroth 'Hunters' (Sind.) See TAUR-EN-FAROTH.

Far West The meaning of the direction West carried a special significance for the inhabitants of Middle-earth. For this was the direction in which all things flowed – where Elves sailed when they grew weary of mortal lands, and where the Valar themselves dwelt, in the Uttermost West, in Valimar of the Twilight.

Men of Gondor faced West in Standing Silence at the commencement of each meal: 'we look towards Númenor that was, and beyond to Elvenhome that is, and to that which is beyond Elvenhome and will ever be.'[7]

'Fastitocalon' The age-old myth of the giant sea-beast which mariners mistake for an island (with disastrous consequences) is the subject of the Hobbit-poem 'Fastitocalon', which, together with 'Oliphaunt', is a good example of the Hobbits' taste for comic bestiary lore. The poem is published as No. 11 in *The Adventures of Tom Bombadil* (though originally it was not more than an anonymous scribble in the margins of the Red Book).

Fastred A Knight of Rohan; one of King Théoden's house-carls, who fell at the Battle of the Pelennor Fields (3019 Third Age) and was laid to rest among his fellows there, beside the Great River.

Fastred and Folcred The twin sons of Folcwine, fourteenth King of Rohan. Together they brought aid to Gondor in one of her southern wars, thus fulfilling the Oath of Eorl. Under the twins' leadership, the Rohirrim turned the Battle of the Crossings of Poros (2885 Third Age) against the invading Haradrim; however, both sons of Folcwine were slain in the battle, and their burial mound afterwards guarded the Crossings.

Fastred of Greenholm In her thirty-first year Elanor 'the Fair', eldest child of Sam Gamgee, wedded Fastred of Greenholm (a descendant of Holman the Greenhanded), and together they moved to the Westmarch of the Shire. They were later made Wardens of Westmarch and eventually became custodians of the Red Book, which their descendants (the Fairbairns) continued to maintain down the years.

Fathers of Men A translation of the Quenya word *Atanatári*.

Fatty Bolger FREDEGAR BOLGER.

Fatty Lumpkin A well-fed pony of great common-sense; a companion of Tom Bombadil.

Fëanáro 'Spirit-of-Fire' (Q.) See following entry.

Fëanor 'Spirit-of-fire' (Sind., after the Q. *Fëanáro*). The eldest of the three sons of Finwë (the only child of Finwë's first spouse Míriel), and after the death of his father the joint High King of all the rebelling Noldor; the greatest craftsman of all time, whose pride grew together with his fabled skills until, in the end, his mightiest accomplishment brought about his own downfall, and the downfall of the Elven-people he ruled – not to mention years untold of misery for the guiltless inhabitants of Middle-earth, whither he went in exile. Fëanor was the first of the royal Exiles to be slain in Middle-earth, and dwells still in the Halls of Mandos.

Much is said of Fëanor and of his deeds – and even more of the fruits of his deeds – in records of the First Age, and little more than encapsulation is needed within these pages. His real name was *Curufinwë* ('the Skill of [the House of] Finwë'); though he was known all his life as *Fëanáro* (his mother's name for him), and survives in records and tales as *Fëanor*. Born during the Eldest Days, in Tirion the Fair, he was a prodigy among Elves. Amazingly skilled at matters of craft, and with a formidable intellect which made him the foremost loremaster and inventor of his people, he embodied the dynamic principle of activism, and was constantly at work, learning, experimenting, storing, devising, practising, polishing and developing; until he had altogether redirected his inherent drives, away from 'passive' understanding and contemplation, towards 'active' subcreation of the highest order. So he is remembered for lore, and for skill, but not for wisdom. Nonetheless, he wrought many objects of wonder, and in all his chosen fields accomplished more than all his successors. Among the lesser marvels were the eight *palantíri* (the Seeing-stones which were so prized in Númenor and Middle-earth many thousands of years later). And Fëanor himself also perfected the ancient Eldarin *Tengwar*, the ALPHABET OF FËANOR which served his people and others ever after. Such were Fëanor's deeds of mind and hand in Eldamar while the White Tree and the Golden still shone.

It has been recorded that only Fëanor was ever able to make the substance *silima*, the crystalline material from which he later created the chief source of his overweening pride. For his greatest achievement of all was fashioning of the three *silmarilli*, the 'Jewels-of-silima', that captured the Light of the Two Trees of Valinor and preserved it within their depths, so that they shone with glory like stars and gladdened the eyes of all who beheld them.

But the glory and splendour of the Silmarils led to terrible events. The Great Jewels tempted even one of the Valar (who was already given over to evil). He slew Finwë, and stole the Jewels, and poisoned the Trees so that their Light was dimmed for ever and the Land of the Valar plunged into twilight. This fallen Vala – called (by Fëanor) *Morgoth* – then fled to Middle-earth with the Silmarils.

Instead of accepting this turn of events and thus following the example of the Valar (whose loss was far greater), Fëanor grew wroth, and in the folly of his pride he vowed to pursue Morgoth across the Sea to Middle-earth in order to regain the Jewels by force. A great number of the Noldor supported him – but the Valar prohibited the venture. Nevertheless, Fëanor had his way, for the Noldor rebelled, and many of that Kindred followed the banners of Fëanor and Fingolfin back to Middle-earth in a great fleet of ships. But even as they sailed away from the Blessed Realm, great shadows rolled across the face of the Sea behind them, barring their return.

In the event, the Exile of the Noldor in Middle-earth endured for many bitter years. Finally defeated in their long wars against Morgoth, they were only saved by the intervention of the Valar, who cast out the Enemy and destroyed his realm. Most of the Exiles were then allowed to return to Eldamar, but not all – and not Fëanor, for the leader of the rebellion had been slain, together with a great number of his kin, in the War for the Great Jewels that he had made: for Fëanor was mortally wounded at the Battle-under-Stars, and died in the arms of his sons before the rising of the first Moon over Middle-earth.

Note: in the Second Age the survivors of Fëanor's House were led by Celebrimbor, his grandson. In their time, they too reached a peak of craftsmanship which came to an end with the making of a peril hardly less deadly than that created by their Forefather in the days of his pride.

See also ELDAR; ELVEN-SMITHS; *Silmarillion* (passim).

Fëanturi 'Masters-of-Spirits' (Q.) Two of the great Valar: the brethren MANDOS and LÓRIEN.

Feast of Reuniting A translation of the Grey-elven words *Mereth Aderthad*, being the name given by Fingolfin the High King of the Noldor to the great feast he ordained for all the Eldar in Middle-earth, Noldor and Sindar alike, in the 21st Year of the Sun, First Age. It was celebrated at the Eithel Ivrin.

Feast of the Spring of Arda The celebration ordained by the Valar after the completion of the shaping of the World; it was held in Almaren. At this feast Tulkas, newly-come to Middle-earth, wedded Nessa the sister of Oromë.

Felagund 'Lord of Caves' (from orig. Khuz. *felak-gundu* 'Cave-hewer') The name given by the Dwarves[8] to the Elven-king Finrod son of Finarfin, after he had, with their aid, enlarged and occupied the ancient delvings of *Nulukkizdîn* in the gorge of the river Narog. This underground city was of course known to Elves and Men as *Nargothrond*.

Felaróf The steed of Eorl the Young. The first of the fabled *Mearas* of Éothéod and Rohan. The *Mearas* were a long-lived line of horses thought to be descended from the steeds of Béma (the Huntsman of the Valar); they would bear no one but the rightful King or his offspring, and would accept no bridle or stirrup.

First caught and bridled by Léod, Lord of Éothéod, Felaróf bolted, throwing Léod and causing his death. His son Eorl was expected to slay the horse, but instead he subdued the animal, named him and rode him thereafter. The horse understood the speech of Men – and proved as long-lived, being laid to rest with his master in the same mound of the Barrowfield (in 2545 Third Age).

Fellowship of the Ring The eight companions of Free Peoples who were chosen by Elrond to accompany the Ring-bearer on the Quest of Mount Doom. They were: Gandalf; Aragorn, Dúnadan of the North, and Boromir, Prince of Gondor (for Men); Legolas, son of King Thranduil (for the Elves); Gimli, son of Glóin (for the Dwarves); and four Hobbits – Meriadoc, Peregrin, Samwise, and Frodo, the Ring-bearer. The Fellowship set out from Rivendell on December 25th in the year 3019 Third Age.

Fell Winter In Third Age records, this term refers to the winter of 2911, which struck northern Eriador with great severity, causing many of its rivers to freeze. At that time packs of white wolves from the North invaded the Shire.

Fengel From 2903–53 Third Age, the fifteenth King of Rohan, son of Folcwine of the Second Line. He was grasping and unpleasant, especially towards his children; therefore, Fengel's son Thengel, of his own choice, spent much of his life in Gondor, where he won renown. Thengel was the father of Théoden.

Fen Hollen 'Closed Door' (Sind.) A solemnly guarded ornamental door or postern gateway in the sixth circle of Minas Tirith, upon the side facing Mount Mindolluin. It led to the Hallows, the final resting-place of Gondor's great, upon a high plateau between the City and the cliffs above.

Fenmarch The low-lying border country between the Mouths of Entwash and the White Mountains, north of the Mering Stream; the frontier of Rohan and Gondor. Most of the eastern part of Rohan's Eastfold was fen country, watered by the broad river Entwash.

Fen of Serech A region of marshy ground surrounding the confluence of the upper Sirion and the Rivil stream, in south-western Ard-galen, guarding the Pass of Sirion from the North. It was thus a natural defence of the Noldor against the evil of Morgoth, especially in latter days, and for this reason perhaps they never drained the marsh or reclaimed the ground, preferring to leave well alone.

Fens of Sirion The westerly fringe of the AELIN-UIAL marsh.

'Ferthu Théoden hal!' 'Hail to thee Théoden on thy going!'

Field of Cormallen The Field of the Ring-bearers where, on April 6th, 3021 Third Age, the Host of the West gave thanks for the downfall of the Dark Lord, and the Ring-bearers Frodo and Samwise were publicly honoured by the King. The occasion was distinguished (particularly for Samwise) by the first performance of the Lay of Frodo of the Nine Fingers and the Ring of Doom, which was composed especially for the event.

The Field of Cormallen was in North Ithilien, between the refuge of Henneth Annûn and the isle of Cair Andros.

Fields of Pelennor The rich and fertile townlands of Minas Tirith; that area (about three leagues in diameter at its widest) which was enclosed by the Rammas Echor, the out-wall of the City.

See also BATTLE OF THE FIELDS OF PELENNOR.

Fíli and Kíli The two Dwarf-sons of Dís, descended from the Line of Erebor. Both marched on the Quest of the Lonely Mountain, led by their uncle, Thorin Oakenshield; and both fell during the Battle of Five Armies (2941 Third Age), defending him from Orcs. Thorin was also slain and Dáin Ironfoot of the Iron Hills then became King under the Mountain.

Fimbrethil 'Slender-birch' (Sind.) Wandlimb the lightfooted; an Entwife of Treebeard's youth. She was lost with the other Entwives when their gardens were turned into Brown Lands during the wars of the Second and Third Ages.

Finarfin The third and youngest of the three sons of Finwë of the Noldor, brother of Fingolfin and half-brother of Fëanor. Though the youngest of the three brothers, he was accounted by the Eldar the wisest, for he alone forsook the march into exile, and repented of the rebellion, and thus returned from Araman to Eldamar with a great many of his people, to continue dwelling with the Valar, and with the 'Fair-elves', the Vanyar. Both Finarfin and his brother Fingolfin were akin to the Vanyar, for their mother Indis was of this people; and they and their descendants were for the most part golden-haired, like all the Fair Elves.

However, Finarfin's own children – Finrod, Orodreth, Angrod, Aegnor, and Galadriel – were not so wise as he, and they joined their hosts to that led by Fingolfin, and so came to Middle-earth in exile, and shared in the deeds of that time. But all save Galadriel were slain in the War of the Great Jewels.

Note: in records of the Third Age (as opposed to the far older *Silmarillion*) this name is occasionally written *Finarphir*. The reason is not immediately obvious – unless the intended spelling is actually *Finarphin* and a typographical error has resulted in the final *n* being replaced with an *r*. To confuse matters further, in early editions of *The Lord of the Rings* the Noldorin Elf Gildor Inglorion identifies himself as 'of the House of Finrod', but in later editions as 'of the House of Finarphir'[9], whereas throughout *The Silmarillion* the name of the father of Finrod and Galadriel is always written *Finarfin*. The latter spelling must be regarded as the more accurate.

Finarphir See note under preceding entry.

Findegil A scribe of the Court of Gondor during the second century of the Fourth Age. In the year 172 he was instructed to make a copy, exact in all respects, of the Red Book of the Periannath – which was itself a copy of the Thain's Book of the Shire, originally made at the request of King Elessar. Findegil's copy was formally presented to the descendants of Peregrin Took and was kept at Great Smials ever after.

Finduilas The name of the Elven-daughter of Orodreth, King of Nargothrond after the death of his elder brother Finrod Felagund. She was the beloved (he had named her *Faelivrin*) of the Elf-lord Gwindor, a prince of that same city; but Gwindor was captured during the Nirnaeth Arnoediad and afterwards enthralled in Angband. And when he escaped and later returned to Nargothrond he came accompanied by Túrin of the Edain. Though Gwindor still loved Finduilas, unhappily for him she fell in love with Túrin. The Elf nobly released her from her earlier promises and bade her go where love called, though he added a warning against the fate surrounding Túrin, and he told her who Túrin really was.

It was shortly after this that Nargothrond fell to the power of Morgoth. Most of the Elf-women and -children were captured – including Finduilas – and Gwindor was slain; but Túrin, pursuing the Orcs who had captured her, became further enmeshed in the net of his doom, and never caught up with her. To his grief he afterwards learned that she had been killed by the Orcs, not far from the Crossings of Teiglin. She was buried in a barrow nearby, the Haudh-en-Elleth ('Mound of the Elf-maid'); but her spirit passed into the West.

Also the name of a princess of Dol Amroth in the late Third Age, the daughter of Adrahil and later wife of Steward Denethor II of Gondor. She bore Denethor two fine sons, Boromir and Faramir, but died early, from loneliness and depression, in 2988 Third Age, four years after her husband had come into his Stewardship. Denethor never wed again.

Finglas 'Hair-leaf' (Sind.) Leaflock the Ent; one of the surviving Onodrim of the Elder Days still living in Fangorn at the time of the War of the Ring. As the years slowly passed, Finglas gradually began to resemble one of his flock, eventually retrogressing to total tree-hood.

Fingolfin The second son of Finwë of the Noldor, elder brother of Finarfin and (younger) half-brother of Fëanor. Fingolfin was accounted by the Noldor the bravest of the three sons of Finwë; but although there had been enmity between himself and Fëanor, like the latter, Fingolfin unwisely chose to avenge the death of their father and repay the hurts offered to their House, and he too rebelled against the Valar; for he had but lately vowed to Fëanor that he would follow where his half-brother led. With him into exile went all his House, including his two sons Fingon and Turgon and his only daughter Aredhel Ar-Feiniel.

The long story of the deeds of the Elves' first High King in Exile is stirring, yet ultimately tragic and wasteful. Abandoned in Aman by Fëanor after the Kinslaying at Alqualondë (in which, to his ever-lasting regret, he had played a part), Fingolfin was nevertheless un-daunted, and accomplished the daring and desperate feat of crossing the Northern Ice, the Helcaraxë, into Middle-earth; though not without severe loss. It is said that the first Moon to grace the night-skies of Arda shone coldly down upon the Elf-host of Fingolfin in the freezing wastes of the North. At this time, unknown to Fingolfin, the Battle-under-Stars had already been fought in Middle-earth, and Fëanor lay dying in Ard-galen. But Fingolfin marched now swiftly south, towards Mithrim, where the Sons of Fëanor and their hosts were encamped beside the lake; but perceiving that the appearance of the new Sun in the sky had put all creatures of Morgoth to flight, he wheeled his great army across the passes of Ered Wethrin and crossed the seventy leagues of Ard-galen to stand before the very gates of Angband. There for the first time the Elf-lord truly under-stood the reality of the Power to whom he and the other Noldor had so rashly opposed themselves; and it was it this moment that he first conceived the 'containment' stratagem which was hereafter to govern the methods by which the Noldor waged war against their Enemy. For Fingolfin had a warrior's eye, and had perceived that the might of Angband was too great – infinitely too great – ever to be over-thrown by assault or direct action. The only possible chance lay in decoying Morgoth's armies to destruction upon Ard-galen; and this in turn meant setting a leaguer, or siege line, around Angband, with the double aim of protecting Beleriand to the south and (eventually) of provoking Morgoth into some rash action.

It was indeed the only possible strategy (see WAR OF THE GREAT JEWELS); and for many years and centuries it succeeded in penning the power of Morgoth into the far North. But as a policy it was essentially defensive, and Morgoth was always allowed to plot in secret. Worse, the Siege could be actively pressed only from the south and west, which left vast areas in the north and east available to the Enemy for the discreet movement of armies. Nor was the Siege pressed on a tactical (i.e. close-range) level; fifty leagues of open steppe separated the Gates of Angband from the linked chain of Elven-kingdoms, leagues in which the vast if unwieldy hordes of Morgoth were ultimately able to prevail over the dwindling – and little-replenished – ranks of the Eldar. Worst of all, the Siege was effective – and the military force of the Eldar and their allies coherent – only so long as all held true and acted as one army. And this happened less often than Fingolfin envisaged. Yet for all these drawbacks Fingolfin's was the only possible strategy available to the Elves, and though he lived only to see it crumble away in ruin – dying as a result in fury and despair – for four centuries and more it served the Noldor well.

Fingolfin was proclaimed High King of the Noldor in the first Year of the Sun. In that same year he had looked on the doors of Angband, afterwards returning to Mithrim – to meet again Fëanor, as he had supposed. But Fëanor was dead. And memories were still fresh among Fingolfin and his people of the terrible crossing from Aman. For a while an alliance between the two hosts seemed less likely than a battle, but Fingon son of Fingolfin had meanwhile performed the heroic feat of rescuing Maedhros the eldest son of Fëanor from torment upon Thangorodrim, and Maedhros in humility and sincerity now offered the High-kingship to Fingolfin, his father's brother.

Fingolfin and his people now occupied Hithlum and Mithrim as their realm. His elder son Fingon held the neighbouring land of Dor-lómin; but Turgon the younger went across the Echoing Mountains to Nevrast, and with him went Ar-Feiniel his sister. These were but three of the realms founded by the Noldor in those days, the first twenty years of the Sun, for the Sons of Fëanor likewise founded kingdoms in a great barrier line across the north – a barrier against Morgoth. And Fingolfin was High King of all. In the 21st year after his setting foot in Middle-earth he held a great feast, the Feast of Reunion, to which all Elves, of whatever kin, were invited.

Four centuries passed, years not altogether free from war, for time and again Morgoth made trial of Fingolfin's strength and purpose – and each time the High King's strategy and warcraft destroyed his armies. After the Dagor Aglareb Fingolfin had drawn the bonds of the Siege tighter, and his forces now patrolled as far as the borders of Angband. Nonetheless Morgoth had by now finished preparing the gigantic blow with which he meant to break free of the constraints of Fingolfin for ever. He unleashed the Dagor Bragollach, the Battle of Sudden Flame, in which the Elves' cavalry was destroyed on the burning plains of Ard-galen, while their foot-soldiers were thrown back with loss into Hithlum and Mithrim. Their allies, the Edain, were likewise defeated and driven, for the most part, from the North. Perceiving the onset of the very disaster he had long feared – from the day he had first gazed on the real might of Angband – Fingolfin the High King rode forth in madness from the rags of his army and clove through the Orcs to reach the Gates of Angband. There, as is told in *The Silmarillion*,[10] he challenged the Enemy to single combat. But despite his courage, there could be only one result of such a fight. Fingolfin perished; and the High-kingship of the Noldor in Middle-earth then passed to his eldest son, Fingon.

Fingon (the Valiant) The elder son of Fingolfin of the Noldor, brother of Turgon and Aredhel Ar-Feiniel. Like his father, he was one of the mightiest – and, as his name implies, most valiant – of all the High-elves of Middle-earth; and in his time he succeeded to the High-kingship of all the Noldor in Exile. But he did so at a time when fortune had turned irrevocably against the Eldar in their war against Morgoth, and he had reigned as High King for only fifteen years when Morgoth unleashed the final battle, in which the ruin of the Elves and the Edain was at last accomplished. In this final battle, the Nirnaeth Arnoediad, Fingon died, slain by a Balrog.

During his later life in Middle-earth Fingon reigned in Mithrim, ceding his former principality of Dor-lómin to a House of the Edain, friendly to his kin. He is remembered above all as the Elf who achieved the epic feat of rescuing a kinsman (Maedhros son of Fëanor) from torment upon Thangorodrim. For this Fingon is named The Valiant. He never wedded, and was succeeded as High King of the Noldor in Exile by his younger brother Turgon King of Gondolin.

Finrod Felagund The Friend of Men, called also *The Faithful* and *Lord of Caves*; the founder of Nargothrond and Companion of Beren. His memory is exalted in the tales both of Elves, of whom he was one of the noblest to walk the earth, and Men, towards whom he always behaved as a benefactor. For the sake of one Man Finrod laid down his life in Middle-earth.

Finrod was the eldest son of Finarfin. His three brothers were Orodreth, Angrod and Aegnor; and his sister was Galadriel. The children of Finarfin – though not Finarfin himself – came back to Middle-earth in the Elder Days, as is told in *The Silmarillion*, and waged war upon Morgoth in company with the Houses of Fingolfin and Fëanor, though only half their people had followed them to Middle-earth. Finrod was the great friend of Turgon, and into the mind of both Elves came dreams (sent at the bidding of the Vala Ulmo), warning them against dark days to come, and putting into their minds the thought of the needs of that future time. And while Turgon founded the Hidden City of Gondolin, as is told elsewhere, Finrod, having learned, from his kinsman Thingol of Doriath, of the Dwarf-delved Caves of Narog in West Beleriand, founded there the city of Nargothrond. He was afterwards called *Felagund*, 'Cave-hewer' in the Dwarvish tongue.[11]

It was Finrod, first of all High-elves, who encountered the race of Men, though their arrival had long been prophesied among the Eldar. The Men he encountered were Edain, of the kindred of Balan (Bëor) – of the First House of the Edain as this people were afterwards known; and though Finrod is called 'Friend of Men', it was with this kindred of Men in particular that his fate was woven. Balan entered Finrod's service – the first of all the Edain to serve a prince of the Noldor. Barahir, his descendant, fought at Finrod's side at the Dagor Bragollach, and indeed saved his life. Barahir's son Beren thus had a claim on Finrod's aid, and Finrod honoured the pledge and accompanied Beren on his Quest, relinquishing his kingship to do so.

But this first attempt to steal a Silmaril was doomed to bitter failure. All the Companions of the Quest were caught and imprisoned, by Sauron the servant of Morgoth, in the tower of Tol-in-Gaurhoth (formerly Tol Sirion) which guarded the Pass of Sirion. There Finrod was slain, by a werewolf, defending his friend Beren from the monster. Thus he repaid the debt, and so passed into the West for ever. Finrod Felagund never wedded, and was succeeded at Nargothrond by his brother Orodreth.

Finwë The first King of the Noldorin Elves, and one of the four princes (the other three were Ingwë, Olwë and Elwë) who led the Eldar on the Great Journey out of Middle-earth into the Far West. He was the father of Fëanor, Fingolfin and Finarfin, and thus the founder of one of the most royal Houses of the Eldar. But he was killed, in Aman, by Melkor (Morgoth), and thus was spared the shame which afterwards came upon his House, when two of his sons rebelled against the Valar and returned to Middle-earth, to make vengeful war upon Melkor.

Alone of the High-elven kings of old, Finwë wedded twice. His first wife was Míriel of the Noldor, who bore him Curufinwë, afterwards called Fëanor. But this birthing so taxed her body and spirit that she died soon afterwards, and passed to the Halls of Mandos. Finwë then wedded one of the Vanyar, Indis the Fair, a kinswoman of Ingwë (who was High King of all the Elves of Aman). This second wedding did not please Fëanor, as is told elsewhere,[12] and by it was created a division in the House of Finwë that bore fruit in after years. Yet Finwë loved Fëanor best of all his three sons – or perhaps it was the memory of Míriel Serindë that he loved. At all events, when Fëanor first went against the will of the Valar, and was banished as a result from Tirion where Finwë ruled, Finwë himself quitted the city upon the hill of Túna and went to live in Formenos, the fortress to the north which Fëanor had built for himself; and Finwë's second son Fingolfin ruled the city of Tirion in his place. So it was that when Melkor came to take the Silmarils from Fëanor's armoury – having already left the Two Trees dying on the mount of Ezellohar – Finwë resisted him, but was struck down. And in the deeds which followed this murder (for such it was) Finwë's house was laid low, and two of his three sons were slain, even as he had been, and by the same foe, and for the same cause – the Silmarils.

Fire of Doom The volcanic furnace in the 'Chambers of Fire' (the *Sammath Naur*) in the cone of Orodruin; there, the One Ring was forged by Sauron.

Fíriel 'Mortal-woman' (Sind.) The daughter of King Ondoher of Gondor, and the wife of Arvedui 'Last-king' of Arthedain. After the death of Ondoher and his sons, Arvedui claimed the crown of Gondor – basing part of his case on his marriage to Fíriel. However, his claim was rejected, and the crown was instead awarded to a victorious general (albeit of royal blood), Eärnil II.

Fíriel is also the name of the central figure in one of the more reflective Hobbit-poems, 'The Last Ship', collected and published as No. 16 in *The Adventures of Tom Bombadil*.

Though rustic and given to obvious rhetorical jokes, Hobbit-verse occasionally bids fair to glimpse things deeper than were generally known in the Shire. Nevertheless, the obvious allegorical content of 'The Last Ship' indicates that in origin it is not, in fact, a Hobbit-poem at all. For Hobbits did not, as a rule, care for allegory, and verse-advice in the Shire normally took a more practical form. In its original form, therefore, this particular verse almost certainly came from Gondor.

In the poem, Fíriel is watching for the dawn, somewhere near the mouth of a river in Gondor. She runs through the grass to the river-bank just in time to hear the silvery notes of Elf-harps and singing:

> *like wind-voices keen and young*
> *and far bells ringing.*

Three Elf-kings and their retinue sail majestically past in a swan-ship, on their way 'over-Sea' to the Undying Lands. They summon Firiel to join them, but her feet sink in the clay of the river-bank and she realizes that she must remain behind and accept her (mortal) fate.

The poem dates from the early Fourth Age, from a time when Elves were indeed sailing West in greater numbers than before.

Note: the *-iel* suffix in names of Sindarin form usually indicates femininity; e.g., *Fíriel, Berúthiel, Galadriel*. The High-elven equivalent was *-ë, -ën;* e.g., *Telperiën, Vanimeldë, Silmariën*. (The Grey-elven suffix *-wen* meant specifically 'maiden'; e.g., *Morwen*, 'Dark-maid', and *Arwen*, 'Royal-maid'.)

Firienfeld In Rohan, the name for the guarded upland meadow where stood the mysterious Dunharrow.

Firienwood This small forest marked part of the border between the realms of Gondor and Rohan, nestling up against the knees of the White Mountains where the fens of Rohan's Eastfold blended into the pastureland of Anórien. The traveller from Edoras to Mundburg (Minas Tirith) passed along a road through the wood, while above him on his right rose the Halifirien, the northernmost of Gondor's seven beacon-hills.

Fírimar 'Mortals' (Sind.) One of the Elves' early names for the race of Men.

Firith The Sindarin word for 'fading', as applied to the fourth of the six 'seasons' of the Eldarin 'loa' or year. The Quenya term was *quellë* (or *lasse-lanta*).

See CALENDAR OF IMLADRIS.

First Age The assembly of a comparative chronology of the First Age – the 'Elder Days' of the Elves – has long carried virtually in-superable problems for the scholar, not the least of which has been

the absolute dearth of precise information of the kind which compilers need in order successfully to impose systems of dating upon
hitherto-undated epochs. Great events were known to have taken
place, but their accurate location within a time-scale *itself related to
the existing time-scales of Middle-earth* (such as *The Tale of Years*) has,
until now, been impossible to achieve.

However the recent publication, under the collective title *The
Silmarillion*, of several extremely important pieces of ancient literature, many of which provide exactly this kind of cross-datable information, has reversed the situation. By cross-dating – that is, by
comparison work – a perfectly adequate chronology of the six-
century period which we may term 'the Years of the Sun', i.e. the
late First Age, can now be compiled. But before the onset of this
period, the further back we go into the past the more the haziness
increases, until before long we find ourselves dealing with quantities
of elapsed time so vast that they make all Man-made dating systems
seem quite absurdly inappropriate. For this compelling reason the
following chronological table does not attempt to assign year-values
to, or within, these remote epochs, though brief summaries of the
great events they contain are included. All, however, may be assumed
to involve spans of years greater by far than the gulf of time which
lies between those days and ours.

I have deliberately chosen not to follow the example of Prehis-
torians who, as all know, assign year-values in reverse order, thus
leaving the 'ancient' end of their time-scale conveniently open-ended.
It is an effective system, provided it can be made to mesh smoothly
with the known dates at the beginning of the New Age (which, of
course, run in the proper, forwards, direction). In other words, Year
One of the Old Age must be made to precede – by one year – Year
One of the New Age. But when Year One (Old Age) is itself unsurely
located – as is the case here – then the entire *raison d'être* of the
reverse-dating system becomes undermined, and the system itself
becomes inapplicable; for obvious reasons. Unfortunately, the closing years of the First Age (i.e. all events postdating the fall of
Gondolin) are the least-known of all; in fact they can only be estir-
mated. And as a result the otherwise splendid system of reverse-orde-
dating must be rejected.

Luckily, the first Year of the Sun provides the necessary 'fixed
point' from which to commence a Chronology proper (without such
a fixed point no chronology at all would be possible, unless it was
open-ended at both ends and therefore 'floating'). For this year is the
earliest date belonging to our relative list (of course, it cannot be

located in absolute terms, but all the dates which follow are computed directly from it, until after the fall of Gondolin, when we enter an area of uncertainty). I am therefore obliged to commence the Chronology proper at this point. I have assigned succeeding year-values in ascending order, according to measurable elapsed time.

Although most of the given dates are believed accurate to within a very small margin, some are necessarily of a more tentative nature. I have enclosed these within parentheses.

THE FIRST AGE

The Spring of Arda. First war with Melkor, who is defeated. The Valar come to Almaren; raising of Illuin and Ormal. Return of Melkor and delving of Utumno, the Pit. Second War with Melkor: Almaren is destroyed and the Lamps are cast down. Founding of the West and raising of the Mountains of Defence. Beginning of the Great Darkness and founding of Angband.

The Years of the Trees. Yavanna Kementári makes the Two Trees of Valinor; beginning of the Count of Time. After many ages the Quendi awake in Cuiviénen. For the sake of the Quendi the Valar make war upon Melkor. Battle of the Powers and destruction of Utumno; Melkor is imprisoned. The Eldar make the Great Journey from Cuiviénen to Aman. Foundation of Doriath in Middle-earth. Birth, in Eldamar, of Fëanor. Dwarves appear in the Blue Mountains. Building of Menegroth. Birth, in Menegroth, of Lúthien. The Nandor come to Beleriand and are granted lands in the south-east. Release from Mandos of Melkor; he subverts the Noldor. Death of the Two Trees and slaying of Finwë. Theft of the Silmarils. Rebellion of Fëanor.

The Sunless Year. The Kinslaying at Alqualondë and Curse of Mandos. First Battle of Beleriand. Fëanor comes to Middle-earth; he burns the Telerin ships at Losgar, abandoning Fingolfin in Araman. Battle-under-Stars in the North: Fëanor is slain. Rising of Isil (the Moon). Fingolfin and his hosts cross the northern icefields into Middle-earth after great hardship. Capture of Maedhros son of Fëanor, by treachery. He is tormented upon Thangorodrim.

Years of the Sun.

1   Rising of Anar (the Sun). Concealment of Valinor. Awakening of the Atani (Men) in eastern Middle-earth. Fingon son of Fingolfin rescues Maedhros from Thangorodrim. Fingolfin proclaimed High King in Exile.

2–20   Foundation of the Noldorin kingdoms of Beleriand.

21   The Feast of Reunion.

(50)   Foundation of Nargothrond.

55   Dagor Aglareb; the Noldor set the Siege of Angband.

58   Turgon begins the building of Gondolin.

110   Turgon withdraws to Gondolin, abandoning Vinyamar.

155   Fingon son of the High King defeats an Orc-host north of
        Drengist.

255   First appearance of the Fire-dragon Glaurung; he is defeated
        by Fingon. Beginning of the Long Peace.

(305)   The first Men appear in Beleriand; they are encountered in
        Ossiriand by Finrod of Nargothrond.

(306)   Bëor enters the service of Finrod; the Haladin come to
        Beleriand.

(307)   The People of Marach (the Third House of the Edain) come
        to Beleriand. (310–400) The Edain for the most part take
        service with the Noldor. The Haladin come to Brethil, the
        folk of Bëor to Ladros (Dorthonion), and the House of
        Marach, last of all, to Hithlum and Dor-lómin. Extension of
        the power of Nargothrond.

310   Aredhel Ar-Feiniel goes wandering in Nan Elmoth.

(311)   Birth of Maeglin.

(330)   Escape from Nan Elmoth of Aredhel and Maeglin. Death, in
        Gondolin, of Aredhel and Eöl.

350   Death, in Nargothrond, of Bëor the Old.

370   The Haladin (Second House of the Edain) come to Brethil.

389   Birth, in Estolad, of Hador Lórindol.

(441)   Birth of Húrin son of Galdor, in Dor-lómin.

(442)   Birth of Huor.

455   Dagor Bragollach and ending of the Long Peace. Fall of
        Ard-galen and Dorthonion, and of the eastern marches ruled
        by the Sons of Fëanor. Death of Fingolfin the High King;
        of Angrod and Aegnor, sons of Finarfin; and of Hador
        Lórindol of the Edain. Finrod saved by Barahir of the Edain,
        who returns to Dorthonion to contest its ownership. Fingon
        proclaimed High King. Húrin becomes Lord of Dor-lómin.

457   Sauron captures Tol Sirion. Easterlings occupy Mithrim and
        Dor-lómin. Húrin and Huor come to Gondolin. Turgon
        sends messengers into the West, who do not return.

458   Death of Barahir on Dorthonion.

462   Morgoth attacks Hithlum. Death of Galdor. Húrin becomes
        Lord of Dor-lómin. Beren comes to Doriath. Birth, in
        Dor-lómin, of Túrin.

463 Beren begins the Quest of the Silmaril. He enlists the aid of Finrod of Nargothrond, who is cast out by his people. Death of Finrod Felagund. Beren is rescued by Lúthien.

464 Aided by Huan, they again attempt the Quest. Seizing of a Silmaril and wounding of Beren. They return 'empty-handed' to Doriath. Coming of the Wolf. Death of Carcharoth, Huan, Beren and Lúthien. She and Beren are granted a second (mortal) lifespan and thereafter dwell in Ossiriand. The Silmaril remains in Doriath, in the keeping of Thingol.

470 Nirnaeth Arnoediad. Death of Fingon the High King, death of Huor and annihilation of the Men of Dor-lómin; capture of Húrin. Ruin of the Noldor and the Edain. Fall of Dor-lómin and Mithrim. The Orcs invade Beleriand. Turgon of Gondolin proclaimed High King in Exile. Birth, in Mithrim, of Tuor son of Huor. Birth, in Dor-lómin, of Nienor daughter of Húrin.

471 Sack of Eglarest and Brithombar; a remnant of the Falathrim escape to the Isle of Balar, taking with them Gil-galad, Fingon's heir and son.

482–3 Túrin 'banished' from Doriath.

483–4 Amon Rûdh, and treachery of of Mîm. Capture of Túrin and death of Beleg Cúthalion. Túrin goes to Nargothrond.

487 Tuor is enslaved by Easterlings. Túrin now war-leader of Nargothrond (the Mormegil). He builds a bridge across the Narog.

490 Tuor escapes servitude and wages war in Mithrim.

494 He comes to Gondolin.

495 Sack of Nargothrond. Bewitchment of Túrin and loss of Nienor. Both separately come to the Forest of Brethil, and are given sanctuary by the Woodmen.

497 Túrin weds 'Niníel' in Brethil. Death of Glaurung and of Nienor 'Niníel'. Death of Túrin Turambar.

498 Release of Húrin Thalion from Angband. He comes to Nargothrond, and afterwards to Doriath. He reveals the location of Gondolin.

501 Tuor weds Idril Turgon's daughter, in Gondolin. Jealousy of Maeglin.

502 Birth, in Gondolin, of Eärendil. (About this time Thingol is murdered in Menegroth by Dwarves of Nogrod. The Silmaril is captured but recovered. Sack of Doriath and second loss of the Silmaril – which is again recovered, by

Green-elves of Ossiriand led by Beren. Dior becomes King of Grey-elves in Doriath. Second death of Lúthien and Beren.)

(508) Ruin of Doriath and death of Dior. His daughter Elwing flees to the Havens of Sirion with the Silmaril. Treachery of Maeglin.

509 Sack of Gondolin and death of Turgon. Death of Maeglin. Tuor, Idril and Eärendil, escorted by a remnant of the Elves of Gondolin, escape to the Sea. Gil-galad proclaimed High King in Exile.

(550) Voyage of Tuor and Idril.

(555) Birth in Arvernien of Elros and Elrond, sons of Eärendil and Elwing.

(568) The Sons of Fëanor attack the Havens and slay many Elves and Men. Abduction of Elros and Elrond.

(570) The Voyage of Eärendil and Elwing. The Embassy of Eärendil.

(572) The War of Wrath and final overthrow of Morgoth. Ruin of Angband and drowning of Beleriand. The two remaining Silmarils are stolen from the Valar by Maedhros and Maglor, eldest (and only surviving) Sons of Fëanor. The Silmarils are lost for ever. End of the First Age.

First Battle (of Beleriand) See BATTLES OF BELERIAND.

Firstborn The Elves.

First House (of the Edain) The House of Bëor (for geneological table see *Silmarillion* p. 307, also LINES OF DESCENT in this *Companion*).

First Kindred (of the Eldar) The VANYAR.

First Line (of Rohan) All the Kings of the Mark in direct descent from Eorl the Young to Helm the Hammerhand. See also BARROW-FIELD and SECOND LINE (OF ROHAN).

Firth of Drengist A narrow gap in the Echoing Mountains, between Lammoth and Nevrast, through which a torrential river (see CIRITH NINNIACH) flowed to the Sea. On the west of the mountains lay a long firth, or deep-water estuary. At the mouth of this Firth – a place called Losgar – Fëanor landed with his fleet, after his flight from Eldamar. Here also he burned those selfsame ships.

Fladrif One of the three elder Ents of Fangorn Forest. His name was translated by Treebeard as 'Skinbark', and he was said to be much attached to birch-trees. Many of his folk were destroyed by Orcs of Saruman in the late Third Age, and Fladrif then retreated into the high places of the mountains, where he remained ever after.

Flame Imperishable, Flame of Anor The SECRET FIRE.

Flame of Udûn The Balrog, as addressed by Gandalf during their epic confrontation on the Bridge of Khazad-dûm (Book II Chap. 5). The Sindarin word *Udûn* is translated 'Hell' or 'the Underworld', so this epithet means, literally, 'Hell-fire' – the dark, unclean flame which constituted both the intrinsic nature and the chief weapon of the daemonic Balrog.

See also UDÛN.

Flammifer of Westernesse The Star of Eärendil; it was so called by the Edain because it shone like a beacon and guided them across the Western Seas to Númenor.

Flet A tree-platform, much used by the *Galadhrim* or 'Tree-people' of Lothlórien. The Elves themselves called such platforms *telain* (sing. *talan*).

The Floating Log A tavern of the Shire; the chief Inn of Frogmorton and district.

Flói A Dwarf-warrior of Erebor and one of the companions of Balin son of Fundin in the ill-fated attempt to establish a colony in Moria. One of the first casualties of that expedition, Flói was killed by an orc-arrow in 2989 Third Age, during the clearing of the first halls. He was buried 'under grass' near Lake Kheled-zâram (the Mirrormere), as the Dwarves had not yet regained access to the main halls and therefore could not follow the custom of laying their dead in tombs of stone.

Flower of Silver ISIL (the Moon).

Foamriders The Teleri of Aman, as they are called in the *Lay of Leithian*. It is an approximate translation of *Falmari* (Q.).

Folca From 2851-64 Third Age, the thirteenth King of Rohan.

See also BOAR OF EVERHOLT.

Folcred See FASTRED AND FOLCRED.

Folcwine From 2864-2903, the fourteenth King of Rohan, and the strongest leader to arise since the evil days of the Long Winter. His first act was the re-conquering of the Dunlending-occupied lands of the Westmarch, between the rivers Isen and Adorn. Later, to honour the Oath of Eorl, Folcwine sent a force of cavalry to the aid of Steward Túrin II of Gondor. This force was captained by his twin sons Fastred and Folcred, who fell in battle at the Crossings of Poros (2885 Third Age).

Followers A translation of the Quenya word *Hildor*; the race of Men.

Folde The northern part of Rohan's Eastfold.

Ford of Brithiach The only crossing-place of the upper Sirion between Tol Sirion and the Andram; it lay downstream from the former confluence with the Dry River, and somewhat to the north of the northern eaves of Brethil.

Ford of Bruinen The Ford of Rivendell, where the Great East Road crossed the river Loudwater (Bruinen). It was protected by a high bank on the further (eastern) side. Like the enchanted stream of Mirkwood, the Bruinen was under the power of an Elven-lord and, upon his command, would rise to bar the Ford.

Ford of Carrock A fording-place across the upper Anduin in northern Wilderland; it was marked by the great rock of Carrock. The crossing was kept open by the Beornings who charged a (reportedly high) toll for this service. Further south, the Old Ford provided the only other crossing-point for many hundreds of miles in either direction.

Ford of Stones A translation of the Sindarin name *Sarn Athrad*; the ford across the Gelion where the Dwarf-road from the Blue Mountains crossed from Thargelion into East Beleriand.

Fords of Aros The Arossiach. See AROS.

Fords of Isen The chief crossing-point of the river Isen between its source in the Wizard's Vale and its confluence with the Adorn. Possession of the Fords (which lay some ten leagues south of Isengard) was a matter of conflict between the Rohirrim and the Dunlendings from the early days of the Mark.

See also THÉODRED.

Forelithe The sixth month of the Shire Reckoning, coming immediately before the Lithedays, the three-day Mid-year period. In Bree this month was itself termed *Lithe*.

Forest-between-the-Rivers See TAUR-IM-DUINATH.

Forest of Brethil The largest forest in West Beleriand. Properly speaking, it was but the western outlier of the far greater forests of Doriath (Neldoreth and Region), but the river Sirion flowed between, and although in early times Thingol had accounted Brethil as part of his realm, he was later persuaded to grant this land to a Mannish people: the Haladin, newly-come to Beleriand and already in grievous need of a permanent refuge from the evils of the time. Thingol, therefore, granted Brethil to the people of Haleth (the Haladin), on condition they guarded his western flank. The Haladin accepted these terms, and dwelt within the wood for the remainder of the First Age.

The adjacent Forests of Neldoreth and Region were composed largely of beech- and holly-trees; but Brethil was a birch forest, as indeed its name tells us. In shape, it was rather like the faraway forest of Lothlórien in the east of Middle-earth, for it lay between the converging arms of two rivers, the Sirion and the swift Teiglin. The forest measured perhaps twenty leagues across at its widest point, and narrowed like a spear-head the further one journeyed southwest. In the centre of the wood there rose a tall hill, Amon Obel, on which the Woodmen later built a stockaded hill-fort, Ephel Brandir. Fifteen leagues to the south of Amon Obel and five beyond the southern border of Brethil, stood the lonely height of Amon Rûdh.

Forest of Neldoreth See NELDORETH.

Forest of Region See REGION.

Forest River A river which rose in the Grey Mountains, flowed through northern Mirkwood and entered the Long Lake towards its southern end. It was the main highway of riverborne commerce between the Men of Lake-town and the Wood-elves of Thranduil's realm in Mirkwood.

Foreyule The last month of the Shire Reckoning (known as *Yulemath* in Bree and the Eastfarthing).

Forgoil 'Straw-heads' The name is Dunlendish and was applied as an epithet by the (dark) Dunlendings to the (blond) Rohirrim. It is the only example of this ancient language recorded in the Red Book.

Forlindon 'North-Lindon' That part of Lindon which lay north of the Gulf of Lune. In the Second and Third Ages it was peopled mainly by Elves.

Forlond The 'Northern-haven' of the Gulf of Lune.

Forlong the Old At the time of the War of the Ring, Forlong (then known, somewhat irreverently, as 'Forlong the Fat') was Lord of Lossarnach in Gondor. To the Siege of Minas Tirith (March, 3019 Third Age), he led two hundreds of his own folk. Although Forlong fought valiantly, in the end he was surrounded and cut down by Easterlings on the Pelennor Fields.

Note: the name *Forlong* is of pre-Númenorean origin, unlike most of the personal names used in Gondor – which were of Grey-elven (Sindarin) form.

Formen The Quenya word for 'north', but more properly the title of Tengwa number 10, which represented the sound *f*. It was also used to indicate (directional) North – or even 'right-hand region', since the Eldar numbered the compass-points W,S,E,N, and orientated all maps with W at the top.

Formenos(t) 'Northern-citadel' (Q.) The name given by Fëanor to the city he built in the north of Eldamar during the twelve years of his exile from Tirion. There he kept the Silmarils – until they were stolen. It was abandoned when Fëanor and his sons went into exile in Middle-earth.

Forn The name by which Tom Bombadil was known to Dwarvish folk. The Eldar knew him as *Iarwain Ben-adar* ('Old Fatherless').

Fornost Erain 'Northern-fortress of the Kings' (Sind.); the chief stronghold of Arnor and later the capital of Arthedain (from 861 Third Age). It was known as 'Kings' Norbury' in the Common Speech.

With the rise of the Witch-king of Angmar, and the fall of Rhudaur and Cardolan (see ARTHEDAIN), Fornost became the principal fortress of the remaining Dúnedain of the North. It survived until 1974 Third Age, when Angmar defeated King Arvedui, and the Witch-king captured the great burg on the North Downs. Although the Witch-king was himself defeated the following year (see BATTLE OF FORNOST), the North-kingdom never arose again and Fornost became desolate. Men of the westlands later feared to go near the ruin, and it became known as 'Deadmen's Dike'.

Forochel In the Third Age all that remained of Angband, the once great realm of Morgoth the Enemy, was the icebound bay and cape of Forochel, then inhabited only by the *Lossoth* or Snowmen of that region.

See also ICE BAY OF FOROCHEL.

Forodwaith 'Northern-folk' The lands of the far North, named after the Men who dwelt there during the First Age. Their Third Age descendants were the *Lossoth*, the 'snow-people' of Forochel.

Forsaken Elves See EGLATH.

The Forsaken Inn The last (most easterly) tavern on the Great East Road. It was one day's journey from Bree, on the edge of the Wild.

Forsaken People A translation of the Grey-elven word EGLATH.

Fourth Age Although the Third Age was generally held to have ended with the Downfall of the Lord of the Rings on March 25th, 3019, the Fourth Age proper did not begin until the Passing of the Three Rings, some two years later, on September 22nd, 3021. For purposes of record-keeping, however, the Fourth Age was officially begun (in the New Reckoning of the Reunited Kingdom) on the anniversary of Sauron's fall, being the equivalent of March 25th, 3021 in the older system.

It was the epoch in which Men came into their final inheritance, while all other 'speaking peoples' – Elves, Dwarves and Hobbits – correspondingly declined.

Fourth Battle (of Beleriand) The BATTLE OF SUDDEN FLAME.

Fram The son of Frumgar and a lord of the Men of Éothéod. His greatest feat – for which he was long remembered in the tales of the Rohirrim, descended from the Éothéod – was the slaying of the great Dragon Scatha, scourge of the Grey Mountains and bane of Dwarves. The Dragon-hoard thus recovered was largely Dwarvish in origin, and Fram found himself involved in a dispute over the possession of the treasure. He sent the Dwarves the teeth of the Worm, made into a necklace, accompanied by an insulting message; as a result, the Dwarves indignantly slew Fram, thus perpetuating the nascent hostility between their race and the Northern Men.

Note: the Horn of Buckland, given by Éomer of Rohan to Meriadoc of the Shire, was part of Scatha's Hoard.

Framsburg A hill-fort of the Éothéod, built near the sources of Anduin by Fram, Frumgar's son. It was subsequently abandoned when the Riders of Éothéod emigrated south to their new land of Rohan.

Frár A Dwarf of Erebor and a member of Balin's ill-fated expedition to Moria. In 2994 Third Age, five years after the colony had proudly proclaimed Balin 'Lord of Moria', Orcs attacked and, according to the Book of Mazarbul, Frár then fell in defence of the Second Hall.

Fréa From 2645-59 Third Age, the fourth King of Rohan. He was the fourth child of Aldor the Old, and was himself already aged when he came to the kingship.

Frealáf Hildeson From 2759-98 Third Age, the tenth King of Rohan and the first of the Second Line. He was born in 2726, the son of Hild, sister of Helm Hammerhand, ninth King (and last of the First Line).

During the Long Winter (2758-9), Rohan suffered grievously, not only from famine but from invasion by Dunlendings led by Wulf, son of Freca. Wulf captured Meduseld after slaying Helm's older son Haleth; and Helm himself perished (along with his younger son Háma) during the subsequent siege of the Hornburg. But Fréaláf and many others had meanwhile retreated into the Dunharrow; and with the thaw, he secretly descended from the mountains with a small band of comrades and recaptured Edoras, slaying Wulf and avenging his kin.

Fréawine From 2659-80 Third Age, the fifth King of Rohan.

Freca One of the chieftains of Rohan during Helm Hammerhand's reign. His possession of wide lands near the river Adorn gave Freca virtual independence of the King, and he grew contemptuous of Helm's authority. In 2754 Third Age, he deigned to attend one of Helm's councils, but only for the purpose of procuring a marriage between the King's daughter and his own son Wulf. Helm refused – for in addition to his other defects, (it was said that) Freca had much Dunlendish blood in his veins. Insults followed and Freca was slain by Helm's own hand. Freca's followers then made alliance with the Dunlendings and four years later invaded the Mark in great strength.

See also Appendix A II 'The House of Eorl'.

Fredegar Bolger Frodo Baggins' distant relative and close friend. Although he took no part in their journey, Fredegar greatly assisted Frodo's party by concealing their departure from the Shire as long as possible, thus (unknowingly) putting himself in great danger.

Later, during Saruman's occupation of the Shire, Fredegar rekindled his courage and organised a resistance movement in the Brockenborings, in the northern part of the Eastfarthing. When finally captured by Saruman's men, Fredegar was imprisoned in the Michel Delving lockholes until eventually released by his returning friends. He was harshly treated during this incarceration and lost both a great deal of weight and his (hitherto well-merited) nickname of 'Fatty'.

Free Fair The seven-yearly event held on the White Downs near Michel Delving in the Shire, during the three days of Lithe (Midsummer). Among the other attractions of the Fair was the election of the Mayor of Michel Delving, the Shire's most important official.

Free Folk, Free Peoples Elves, Dwarves, Ents, Hobbits and Men.

Frerin A Dwarf of Erebor; the younger son of Thráin II, and brother of Thorin Oakenshield and Dís (mother of Fíli and Kíli). With his father, brother, sister and grandfather (King Thrór), Frerin escaped the attack on Erebor made by Smaug the Golden in 2770 Third Age, afterwards going into exile with his family.

As is recounted elsewhere (see WAR OF THE DWARVES AND ORCS), the ignoble death of Thrór brought all Seven Houses of Dwarves together for a war of revenge upon the Orcs of Moria. In the Battle of Azanulbizar (2799), Frerin fell, together with his kinsman Fundin, during the first assault of the Dwarves upon the Orcs.

Frery See AFTERYULE.

Friend-of-Men One of the titles awarded (by Men) to the Noldorin prince FINROD FELAGUND.

Friend of the Noldor A Noldorin title for the Smith of the Valar, Aulë, who is said to have taught them great craft-lore in their earliest days in Valinor.

Frodo Baggins The tale of the Downfall of the Lord of the Rings is, of course, in essence the story of the Hobbit Frodo Baggins and his selfless undertaking of the Quest of Mount Doom on behalf of all the Free Peoples of Middle-earth.

That tale is told in great detail elsewhere (*The Fellowship of the Ring*, *The Two Towers* and *The Return of the King*) and in such superb style that it would be unnecessary (and impertinent) to attempt any précis of it here. In any case, it is assumed that readers of this *Companion* are already familiar with Frodo's odyssey – indeed, that admiration for his exploits has prompted them to take a deeper interest in the historical context in which his journey took place. This entry will therefore be confined to setting in order Frodo's biographical details and noting his literary accomplishments, which were considerable (if not undertaken with the same academic enthusiasm which prompted his cousin Bilbo to become the foremost Hobbit-scholar of his Age).

Frodo Baggins was born in 2968 Third Age (1368 Shire Reckoning) in Buckland, to Drogo, great-grandson of Balbo Baggins, and Primula, youngest child of Gorbadoc 'Broadbelt' Brandybuck, of Brandy Hall. When he was twelve, his father and mother were both drowned in a boating accident; and some years later Frodo was adopted by his cousin. At that time the renowned Bilbo Baggins, still unmarried and therefore without an heir to his considerable fortune, was ninety-nine years old, and had been living quietly for some forty years following his unexpected return from the East. So when Frodo was twenty-one, the kindly old Hobbit invited him to leave the Buckland and join him in his luxurious Hobbiton *smial*. Both Hobbits shared the same birthday, September 22nd, and were, in addition, related; so the arrangement worked very well – until the day of Bilbo's 111th birthday (and Frodo's 33rd, his 'coming of age'), when Bilbo departed from the Shire, leaving most of his belongings and property to his heir.

It is not recorded anywhere that Frodo ever felt anything other than deeply grateful towards the old Hobbit; and, for his part, Bilbo thought Frodo the best Hobbit in all the Shire – though he little realized how vital his judgement of character might someday prove. Frodo indeed took strongly after Bilbo, and outwardly continued his benefactor's reputation for eccentricity during the seventeen years he lived alone in Bag End. Like Bilbo, Frodo had a strong element of Fallohidish blood in his veins; and this distressingly adventurous tendency surfaced in the form of long, solitary walks across the Shire, and (some said) occasional encounters with Elves.

In short, he rapidly became thought of as the heir to 'Mad Baggins' in all respects. So when, in his fiftieth year, Frodo suddenly announced he was selling Bag End to return to the Buckland, there was some consternation in the neighbourhood but little real surprise. The Hobbiton folk, of course, had no idea of the real reasons for Frodo's quitting the Shire; and few of them ever learned of his subsequent deeds on their behalf. Indeed, so far as Hobbits were concerned, the War of the Ring was largely a matter of expelling from the Shire the undesirable elements which had occupied it following Frodo's departure. And their later gratitude was chiefly given to those (i.e., Meriadoc, Peregrin and Samwise) who took leading roles in stimulating this desirable turn of events.

Obviously, little more need be said here of Frodo's many adventures following the departure from Buckland in September of 1418 Shire Reckoning. His Quest achieved, Frodo returned to the Shire little more than a year after setting out. But he did not take a leading role in the Reconstruction that followed (apart from serving as Deputy Mayor for a short time); and as soon as he could, Frodo once more settled down to a quiet life in Bag End. At this point he commenced his writing, and for the next year or so occupied his days in composing his part of the Tale of the Ring – and reorganizing various (incomplete) volumes of Bilbo's, bequeathed to him for this very purpose.

Yet Frodo's own account was later found to be a work of great literary merit, and for this reason alone his contribution to the store of Shire-learning must be considered of great value. Particularly apt were his translations from Elvish speech, for his old skill with languages had never deserted him, being exceeded in the Shire only by Bilbo's. For Bilbo himself was a true scholar – and Meriadoc Brandybuck became an extremely competent etymologist and botanist – but Frodo eschewed all such academic bypaths and confined his writing to a single (extremely clear and moving) account of the War of the Ring, which he titled, modestly enough: *The Downfall of the Lord of the Rings and the Return of the King (as seen by the Little People; being the memoirs of Bilbo and Frodo of the Shire, supplemented by the accounts of their friends and the learning of the Wise).* This account forms the core of the Red Book of Westmarch, which is itself the most valuable surviving source of information concerning the Third Age.

Frodo, of course, passed over Sea only two years after returning to the Shire that he loved. As a Ring-bearer this was his privilege – yet his words to Sam Gamgee reveal some of the loss he must have felt in leaving:

I tried to save the Shire, and it has been saved, but not for me. It must often be so . . . when things are in danger: some one has to give them up, lose them, so that others may keep them.[13]

So Frodo departed Middle-earth for the Blessed Realm at the age of only fifty-two, on (his birthday) September 22nd, 1421 Shire Reckoning. He left to find not an alternative to death, but healing and peace of mind. In that 'far green country' he lives still.

Frodo Gardner The eldest son of Samwise Gamgee, and the heir to Bag End. In token of his father's famed skills, he took the name *Gardner;* the family rose to prominence during the Fourth Age.

'Frodo's Dreme' See 'THE SEA-BELL'.

Frogmorton An Eastfarthing village situated on the Great Road.

Frór The second son of Dáin I, Dwarf-king of the Grey Mountains colony. Together with his father, Frór was killed by a COLD-DRAKE at the gate of the Dwarves' Hall (2589 Third Age). Soon afterwards, Durin's people forsook the Ered Mithrin (Grey Mountains).

Frumgar The chieftain who led the Éothéod from their original home near the Gladden to their new Northern lands, following the overthrow of Angmar and the cleansing of those regions (1977 Third Age).

Fuinur 'Dark-lord' (Sind.) One of the BLACK NÚMENOREANS of the middle Second Age. He and another lord, Herumor, went to Middle-earth during the Accursed Years, and so fell under Sauron's dominion. Their names are recorded because they afterwards went to the lands of Harad, and became great among the Haradrim. In this way Sauron's will was set to work among the Men of the South: transmitted thence by two Men of the West.

Fundin The son of Farin of Durin's House, and the father of Balin and Dwalin. Together with countless other Dwarves, he fell in the Battle of Azanulbizar (2799 Third Age).

Further Shores A translation of the ancient Sindarin word *Haerast:* the coast of Aman the Blessed. See also NEVRAST.

Notes

1 Book I Chap. 11.
2 Prologue 2.
3 Book III Chap. 4.
4 Appendix FI.
5 *Ibid*.
6 Book V Chap. 6.
7 Book IV Chap. 5.
8 One of the exceedingly rare occasions on which a name in
 common use among the Elves and Edain was derived from a word
 of Dwarvish origin.
9 Gildor may have been akin to GELMIR of the Havens.
10 pp. 153–4.
11 See Note 8 above.
12 *Silmarillion* p. 65.
13 Book VI Chap. 9.

Gabilgathol 'Great-fortress' (Khuz.) The original Dwarvish name for the city under the Blue Mountains known to Elves as BELEGOST.

Galabas In the original (as opposed to translated) Hobbit tongue, *Galabas* was the name of an ancient Shire-village. The elements contained in the name are *galab* ('game') and *bas* ('village' or 'farm'). This name has been translated from the Red Book as *Gamwich*.

See also GAMGEE.

Galadhrim 'People-of-the-Trees' (Sind.) The Elves of Lothlórien – who were known as the Galadhrim to their northern kin because of their age-old practice of dwelling amid the branches of the great *mellyrn* (mallorn-trees) of their land. The chief settlement of the 'Tree-people' was *Caras Galadhon*, 'the City of the Trees'.

See also LOTHLÓRIEN.

Galadriel 'Radiantly-garlanded [crowned] -maiden' (Sind., from Q. *Altariel*)[1] During the Elder days, one of the most royal princesses of the Noldor of Tirion; the daughter and youngest child of Finarfin son of Finwë the King, and sister of Finrod, Orodreth, Angrod and Aegnor. Together with her brothers (but not her father) Galadriel was a leader of those rebellious Noldor who forsook the Blessed Realm in order to make war in Middle-earth upon Melkor (Morgoth). But alone of the children of Finarfin, Galadriel survived that ill-fated expedition. She afterwards repented and spent the long years of her continuing exile aiding the cause of the Free Peoples against Sauron the Great, Servant of Morgoth. At the time of the War of the Ring, two full Ages after her rebellion and departure from Eldamar, she was the mightiest of the Eldar remaining in Middle-earth, and the oldest and bitterest foe of the Dark Lord.

Yet for all her majesty and power, she had lingered perforce in mortal lands throughout two full Ages – she who had once been a Queen among Queens in Eldamar across the Western Seas. Galadriel's historic role in the rebellion of the Noldor is not fully recorded in the Red Book, but from *The Silmarillion* we know she took a leading part in persuading her people to leave the Undying Lands and cross the Seas to Middle-earth for a war of revenge and possession. And when, at the end of the First Age, most of the Noldor were pardoned by the Valar and allowed to return, she was one of the few singled out to remain in exile.

Sometime before this Galadriel had wedded Celeborn of Doriath, a lord of the Grey-elves and a kinsman of Thingol Greycloak himself. And when the Valar prohibited her return to Eldamar, Galadriel 'replied proudly that she had no wish to do so';[2] she and Celeborn journeyed to Harlindon, where they dwelt for many years. Sometime later they passed eastwards to Eregion, a colony of High-elven craftsmen, founded in 750 Second Age. For a while they lived with the Elven-smiths of that land, but eventually they passed further east across the Misty Mountains to Wilderland, where Celeborn made a realm among the Wood-elves of Laurelindórenan (Lothlórien).

For the remainder of the Second and Third Ages, Galadriel and Celeborn dwelled together in Lórien. The Golden Wood became a secret place, hidden even from the knowledge of the other Elves; for, while the Power that dwelt there could not be concealed, few indeed perceived its true source, or suspected that one of the mighty among the Noldor yet lingered in Middle-earth. In the event, the long years of sorrow and exile passed at last and, as a reward for all her work against Sauron, 'but above all for her rejection of the Ring when it came within her power',[3] Galadriel was finally allowed to leave Middle-earth and pass once more 'West-over-Sea'. She took ship with the Ring-bearers in the last year of the Third Age.

Note: it is recorded in the Red Book (by Frodo) that the Lady Galadriel was the Bearer of Nenya, the Ring of Adamant, one of the Three Rings of the Elves.

See also LOTHLÓRIEN; 'NAMÁRIË'.

Galathilion 'Radiant Holy-Moons' (Sind.) The Grey-elves' name for the White Tree of Tirion. This holiest symbol of the Calaquendi of Eldamar was itself a descendant[4] of Telperion, the Silver Tree of the Valar, Eldest of Trees, which, together with Laurelin (the Golden

Tree), had once illuminated the land of the Valar. Galathilion stood beneath the *Mindon Eldaliéva* (the Tower of Ingwë) in a high, open courtyard, but unlike Telperion, gave no light. Its immediate descendant was Celeborn of Eressëa.

Note: a representation of Galathilion was worked into the design of the West-gate of Moria by Celebrimbor of Eregion. See Book II Chap. 4.

See also NIMLOTH; WHITE TREE.

Galbasi In the original (as opposed to translated) Hobbit-tongue, *Galbasi* (later *Galpsi*) meant 'One-from-[the-village-of-]Galabas'. As *Galabas* is itself translated as *Gamwich*, *Galbasi* has been rendered as the Hobbit-name *Gammidgy*, or *Gamgee*, in English translations of the Red Book.

Galdor the Tall The elder son of Hador Lórindol of the Third House of the Edain, brother of Gundor and the maiden Glóredhel. He was the Heir of Hador, and when Hador perished at the Battle of Sudden Flame, Galdor became Lord of Dor-lómin and Chieftain of the Third House. Before this he had wedded Hareth daughter of Halmir, Chieftain of the Haladin (the Second House of the Edain); and shortly afterwards she had borne him the first of his two renowned sons, Húrin; and then, a year later, Huor.

Thirteen years after the birth of Huor war again broke out in the north – the Battle of Sudden Flame – and the Men of Dor-lómin were driven from Ard-galen, though not from the fortress of Eithel Sirion, which they garrisoned on behalf of the Noldor of Mithrim. But in the defence of the tower Hador Lórindol fell at last, and Galdor his elder son then became Lord of Dor-lómin. But after a short time Morgoth again unleashed war. Hithlum was attacked; and Galdor was slain by an arrow – like his father, in a final defence of Eithel Sirion. He had ruled for barely seven years. He was succeeded in Dor-lómin by his elder son Húrin.

Galdor An Elf of the Grey Havens, sent as an emissary by Círdan the Shipwright to Rivendell, where he took part in the Council of Elrond (3018 Third Age).

Galenas The name given in Gondor to the flowering herb known to Hobbits as 'Pipe-weed'; more properly, *sweet galenas*. In the South-kingdom this plant was esteemed only for the fragrance of its flowers, and its other properties were quite unknown.

Gálmód The father of Gríma Wormtongue, counsellor to King Théoden of Rohan. In the tongue of Rohan, his name means 'sournatured' – a tendency clearly passed on to his son.

Galpsi A later form of the (original) Hobbit-name *Galbasi*.

Galvorn 'Gleaming-black' (Sind.) A hard, black metal, actually an alloy, devised in the Elder Days by the great Grey-elven smith EÖL. As is told elsewhere, this 'Dark Elf' had much to do in his time with the Dwarves of the Blue Mountains, and as a result had acquired great skills in the craft of metalwork. He was not perhaps the equal of Fëanor or the smiths of the Noldor, but he became as skilled as any Dwarf. Strangely, all the metals Eöl devised or discovered were coloured black. *Galvorn* was of this hue, and it was stronger than iron yet at the same time far less brittle. (Eöl is said to have made his own personal body-armour from *galvorn*.) Black also was the colour of the sword Anglachel, though Eöl did not devise the metal itself, only the manner of its working.

Gamgee A rustic family of Hobbits of the Shire, who came to prominence as a result of the War of the Ring. They were descended from Hamfast of Gamwich. The name *Gamgee* is a translation of the (original) Hobbit-name *Galbasi* or *Galpsi*.
See also GALABAS; GALBASI.

Gamling the Old A Westfold-man of Rohan who dwelled with Erkenbrand's people during the years of the War of the Ring. Though deemed too old to bear arms when Erkenbrand marched to the Crossings of Isen (March 2nd, 3019 Third Age), he was later obliged to do so after forces of Saruman defeated Erkenbrand and laid siege to Helm's Deep, which he commanded until the arrival of the King.

Gammidge, Gammidgy Translated (as opposed to original) Hobbit-names corresponding to *Galbasi*, *Galpsi*. See also GALABAS; GAMGEE.

Gamwich An ancient village of the Shire, home of Hamfast, founder of the GAMGEE (Gammidgy) family. See also GALABAS.

Gandalf the Grey One of the chief *Istari* or Wizards of Middle-earth, also known as *Mithrandir*, the 'Grey Wanderer', friend of all Free Peoples. The greatest opponent of the Dark Lord in the Third Age, Gandalf passed through fire, earth, water and air – and was afterwards reborn – in fulfilment of the destiny long appointed for him: to be the chief architect of Sauron's Downfall.

By the labour and valour of many I have come into my inheritance. In token of this I would have the Ring-bearer bring the crown to me, and let Mithrandir set it upon my head, if he will; for he has been the mover of all that has been accomplished, and this is his victory.

(From the Coronation Speech of King Elessar [Aragorn II] May 1st, 3019 Third Age)[5]

It was, of course, one of the great ironies of the War of the Ring that few of the inhabitants of Middle-earth – including the worthy folk of Gondor, gathered to hear the words of their new King – could have appreciated the true significance behind Aragorn's tribute to Gandalf the Grey. In fact, very few people realized just who the old Wizard was or whence he had come. To most Western folk, Gandalf was 'just a Wizard' – a vain, fussy old conjuror with a long beard and bushy eyebrows, whose chief asset was his uncommon skill with fireworks. Indeed, many great Men of the South regarded him as little better than a pest, a homeless vagabond, a meddler in affairs of state and a herald of ill-news.

Yet the five *Istari* who came to Middle-earth during the early Third Age were, in actuality, messengers sent from Valinor to 'contest the power of Sauron, and to unite all those who had the will to resist him'.[6] And they were themselves of Valinorean race, although they came to mortal lands in the shapes of aged Men; for they were MAIAR, in their beginnings Ainur of lesser – though still potent – degree than the VALAR, whom the Maiar served. Yet while their powers were great, they were forbidden to reveal their true natures or to use their full strength in direct conflict with the Enemy.

But the Mortal Lands of Middle-earth have always held great perils for Immortals, whether Elves or Valar or Maiar; they could be slain and they could be tempted and seduced away from their appointed tasks. As told in the Red Book, at least one of the *Istari* fell from grace in such a manner (see SARUMAN THE WHITE), in circumstances grievous to Gandalf – who, while less proud, was more wise and perceived the nature of the trap, thus avoiding it himself.

Of Gandalf's great labours in Middle-earth, little can be recounted in these pages; for none can have known the full story of the trials the Wizard undertook on behalf of the Free Peoples, from the time of his arrival at the Grey Havens (c. 1000), to the day of his departure at the very ending of the Third Age. It is known, however, that he took many hideous risks. On two occasions he actually entered the dark stronghold of Dol Guldur in Southern Mirkwood: once, in the year 2063, when he first tried to ascertain the true identity of the Necromancer who ruled there, and again in 2850, when he finally discovered that the 'Necromancer' was indeed Sauron himself (who was already gathering the Rings of Power and seeking for the Ruling Ring). At a meeting of the White Council the following year Gandalf pressed urgently for an outright attack upon Dol Guldur but was overruled by his brother-wizard Saruman the White.

Yet Gandalf, though frustrated by Saruman, had by chance a further card to play. For, on his last entry into Sauron's fortress, he had come across the dying Dwarf Thráin II, son of Thrór, who had survived just long enough to give him the key of the secret door into Erebor and the map which accompanied it. And in 2941 the Wizard unexpectedly encountered Thráin's Heir, Thorin Oakenshield; together, they hatched a scheme for the recovery of the Lonely Mountain and the baulking of any plans Sauron might have for the Dragon Smaug. As is told in *The Hobbit*, Thorin's expedition (and Gandalf's scheme) succeeded, the Dragon which guarded the Mountain was slain, and a great threat to the lands of the East wasre moved.

Little more is known of Gandalf's plans and movements until the year 3001 Third Age, when he appeared at Bilbo Baggins' Farewell Party – an account of which opens the first chapter of *The Lord of the Rings*. The Wizard was already worried about the golden ring which Bilbo had picked up on his travels. Suspicion hardened into fear, and Gandalf later searched urgently for Gollum but was unable to find him, even with the help of Aragorn, Ranger of Eriador. Not until seventeen years later did the Wizard at last learn the truth concerning the ring – and by this time the 'heirloom' was in the possession of a new owner, Frodo Baggins.

The plan which Gandalf and Frodo made for the disposal of the Ring – and the events which later took place – are all carefully detailed in Frodo's own narrative and require no restatement here. The Wizard was the leading force behind the success of Frodo's mission. For although he did not himself enter Mordor, by his unceasing efforts Gandalf rallied the Free Peoples for long enough to give the Ring-bearer his only chance. The heroism was Frodo's (and Samwise's), but the strategy was Gandalf's; and by bringing to bear every last ounce of his will and determination, the Wizard successfully countered every move that the Dark Lord made. In this way

Sauron's plans were frustrated and his schemes were brought to nothing.

So it came to pass that on March 25th, 3019 Third Age, the Ring-bearer completed his mission and Sauron of Mordor was overthrown for ever – and Gandalf's long labours in Middle-earth came at last to their conclusion. 'The Third Age was my age', he later told Aragorn; 'I was the Enemy of Sauron; and my work is finished. I shall go soon.'[7] Two years later, on September 22nd, he returned across the Sea to the Undying Lands.

Note: Gandalf is the name by which the Wizard was known to Northern Men. To the Elves (and the Dúnedain) he was *Mithrandir* ('Grey-wanderer'); to the Dwarves, *Tharkûn;* and, in his youth, 'in the West that is forgotten',[8] *Olórin.*

See also WIZARDS and the introductory note under 'The Third Age' in Appendix B.

Gap of Rohan The open plain (fifty miles wide at its narrowest), which provided the only sizeable break in the massive chain of mountain-ranges stretching from the Northern Waste to Cape Andrast in the south. Of immense strategic importance, the Gap was guarded by the mighty fortress and tower of Isengard, built by Men of Gondor in the early days of the realm.

Gardner of the Hill A prominent Shire-family of Hobbits, descended from Samwise Gamgee (through his son Frodo Gardner).

Gate of Kings The pillars of the ARGONATH.

Gates of Sirion The great arched caverns in the south side of the Andram, through which the river Sirion flowed into the sunlight, having for the last ten miles or so followed its course underground. SEE FALLS OF SIRION.

Gates of Summer A festival of the High-elves of Gondolin: a celebration of the first day of the season *lairë* (Sind. *laer*), 'summer'.[9]

Gelion The largest river in East Beleriand; it was twice as long as the Sirion, though less broad a stream. The Gelion had two sources in the north, rising from the areas of mountainous terrain upon either side of Maglor's Gap. The joined stream flowed south for a hundred and fifty leagues before bending west for the Sea. No less than seven tributaries fed the Gelion during this journey, the Seven Rivers of the Land of Ossir: Ascar, Thalos, Legolin, Brilthor, Duilwen and Adurant (the most southerly). Yet below the confluence with Adurant the Gelion was scarcely wider than above Ascar. But it was fordable in only one place: Sarn Athrad, where the ancient Dwarf road from the Blue Mountains crossed westward from *Thargelion* ('Beyond Gelion') into Beleriand proper.

Gelmir A Grey-elven personal name which occurs twice in existing records of the First Age. In both cases it is borne by an Elf of the House of Finarfin; in the first instance by the son of Guilin of Nargothrond, who was cruelly put to death – at Morgoth's command – outside the walls of Eithel Sirion, as a torment and a challenge to the defenders of the fortress (of whom one was Gelmir's brother Gwindor); and in the second, by an Elf of the people of Angrod, who came to Nargothrond – then ruled by Angrod's elder brother Orodreth – to convey a message of warning from Círdan of the Havens, with whom this Elf then dwelt. This took place shortly before the sack of Nargothrond.

Gerontius Took 'The Old Took'; the twenty-sixth Shire-thain and the second longest-lived of all Hobbits (his great age of 130 years being exceeded only by Bilbo Baggins).

Ghân-buri-Ghân The old chieftain of the Wild Men of Druadan Forest at the time of the War of the Ring. In gratitude for aid rendered to Gondor during the War, King Elessar gave the Forest to the Wild Men 'to be their own for ever'.[10]
See also WOSES.

Gift of Men See DOOM OF MEN.

Gil, Giliath 'Spark' (Sind.) A Grey-elven term for '[the glittering appearance of a] star'. The direct Quenya equivalent was *tinwë*. See also ÊL, ELIN, ELENATH.

Gildor 'Star-land' (Sind.) One of the twelve companions of BARAHIR of the Edain; he was slain on Dorthonion. by treachery.

Gildor Inglorion A High-elf of the House of Finarfin; during the Third Age the leader of a Wandering Company of his Kindred, who dwelled mainly in Rivendell and made occasional pilgrimages to the Tower Hills for the purpose of gazing into the *palantír* which was kept there. At the end of the Age he passed over Sea with the Keepers of the Three Rings. See also FINARFIN (note).

Gil-estel 'Star of Hope' (Sind.) A Grey-elven name for the Evening Star, the Star of Eärendil.

Gil-galad 'Spark-of-bright-light' (Sind.) The last of all the High-elven kings in Middle-earth; the son of Fingon, son of Fingolfin, son of Finwë of the Noldor. He was born before the Dagor Bragollach, in Mithrim, but his father, after that disastrous campaign perceiving that Mithrim had now become a frontier of war, sent his young son *Ereinion* (as Gil-galad was named at birth; it means 'Scion-of-Kings') to dwell with Círdan the Shipwright at the Havens of the Falas. Twenty years later the young prince was among those few Elves who escaped the sack of the Havens, and together with Círdan and a few others came to the Isle of Balar, in the midst of the Bay of that same name, where he dwelt until the end of the First Age. He was already Heir to the new High King (Fingon's younger brother Turgon of Gondolin), for his father Fingon had been slain in the Nirnaeth Arnoediad – of which the sacking of the Havens of the Falas had been but an aftermath. Thirty-eight years later, Gondolin fell, and Turgon was slain, and Gil-galad Ereinion was then proclaimed High King of the Noldor. But he remained in Balar until the end of the Age, for the Noldor were now few, and for the most part in hiding. Only on the coasts, in hidden refuges, were there any Elves, Noldor or Sindar, for him to rule.

At the beginning of the Second Age Gil-galad gathered most of the Noldor under his rule in Forlindon ('North-Lindon'), west of the Blue Mountains; while Harlindon (the southern cape and its adjoining lands) was ruled by Celeborn of the Grey-elves. But after a while Celeborn departed for distant lands and the remaining Grey-elves of Harlindon joined Gil-galad north of the Gulf of Lune.

The first thousand years of his reign were peaceful, for the Dark Power of the North had been overthrown; and for a while 'the Elves deemed that evil was ended for ever'.[11] Yet it was not so. By the sixth century, Sauron, servant of Morgoth in the First Age, was awake again and plotting the overthrow of the Free Peoples – though he chose at this time to display a mask of friendship. For in those days Sauron was not yet evil to look upon, and his true nature was not universally realized; and when he later began his rapid ascent to power in Middle-earth, only Gil-galad's people were undeceived by his overtures.

Sauron nevertheless succeeded in gaining the confidence of the Elven-smiths of Eregion – and in due course betrayed them, as Gil-galad had feared. War followed. In 1695 Second Age the new Dark Lord, having conquered the Southlands, invaded Eriador with a great host of Orcs. Gil-galad, although fighting desperately to stem the tide, nevertheless contrived to send reinforcements to the besieged

Elven-smiths of Eregion, and for a while they held out. But in 1697 Eregion fell at last and all the survivors retreated northwards. Two years later, all Eriador had fallen to the Enemy and Gil-galad was hemmed in behind the Lhûn.

But before the Elves of Lindon could be swept away in a final assault, aid arrived from an unexpected quarter: Tar-Minastir, eleventh King of Númenor, sent a great naval force to Lindon. Sauron was defeated in battle and driven out of the Westlands. In this way the Men of Númenor renewed their ancient alliance with the Eldar of Middle-earth – but gained the hatred of Sauron the Great, who never forgot his defeat. Before the Age had passed he was to take terrible revenge for this (and later) reverses, and Númenor was drowned beneath the Sea.

But a remnant of the Númenoreans survived and returned to Middle-earth, where they established the Realms in Exile. Then Sauron made war upon them once more, for their South-kingdom lined his very borders, and he feared lest they grow too powerful. In their last need the Men of Westernesse made alliance once more with the Eldar of Lindon, and in the year 3431 Second Age, the Hosts of Elendil and Gil-galad were mustered in Eriador. So began the War of the Last Alliance, in which after many battles, Sauron's first realm was pulled down in ruin.

But Gil-galad, last High-elven King of mortal lands, also passed away in that War, falling in single combat with Sauron himself. Yet his realm had been soundly established and staunchly defended, and the foundations laid by him proved sure enough to withstand his own passing. Thus Lindon was maintained throughout the turmoils of the Third Age, being in the end the longest to endure of all Eldarin realms of Middle-earth. It was finally deserted some time in the Fourth Age.

Note: it is recorded in the Red Book that Gil-galad was the original Keeper of the Elven-ring Vilya, the Ring of the Firmament. Before his death he passed on this Ring to his Herald, Elrond of Rivendell, who then became chief of the Eldar in Middle-earth.

See also 'FALL OF GIL-GALAD'; LAST ALLIANCE; LINDON; WAR OF THE ELVES AND SAURON.

Gilraen the Fair The daughter of Dirhael of the Dúnedain, the wife of Arathorn II, fifteenth Chieftain, and the mother of Aragorn II. See also the 'Tale of Aragorn and Arwen' in Appendix A I(v).

Gilrain (also spelled *Gilraen*) A river in Lebennin (a southern province of Gondor), which flowed south from the White Mountains to find the Bay of Belfalas north of the Ethir Anduin. The Serni flowed into it some miles above the river-mouth.

Gimilkhâd The younger of the two sons of the twenty-second King of Númenor, Ar-Gimilzôr (see also following entry). He was his father's favourite, and after Gimilzôr's death led that faction of the rebel Númenoreans called 'King's Men' – these were bitterly opposed to the repentant ways of Gimilkhâd's elder brother, Tar-Palantir, formerly known as Inziladûn. (Gimilkhâd's own son was Pharazôn, destined to usurp the Sceptre on the death of Palantir and afterwards to lead the Númenoreans into the abyss.) Gimilkhâd lived only 198 years, a remarkably low total for one of the royal Dúnedain.

Gimilzôr (**Ar-Gimilzôr**) The twenty-second King of Númenor and the fourth to take a royal title in the Númenorean (Adûnaic) tongue. His sons were Inziladûn, who reverted to a High-elven name, Tar-Palantir ('the Farsighted'), and Gimilkhâd.

See also preceding entry.

Gimli Elf-friend The son of Glóin of Erebor, descended from Borin, son of Náin II, of Durin's Line. His father was the brother of Óin; and both Óin and Glóin were part of Thorin Oakenshield's expedition to Erebor in 2941 Third Age, together with eleven other Dwarves, a Wizard and a Hobbit.

After the fall of the Dragon Smaug, the re-established Kingdom under the Mountain prospered greatly and Glóin became a Dwarf of great importance. In the year 3018 Third Age, he was therefore sent as an emissary to Elrond – for the Dwarves had received news which they wished to impart, and they desired the counsel of Elrond. To accompany him on the journey, Glóin took his son Gimli; and as a result, the younger Dwarf was enrolled in the Fellowship of the Ring, to represent his kinfolk in the enterprise.

Gimli's notable deeds during the War of the Ring are, of course, well documented elsewhere and need no mention here. But the unusual regard in which he was held by Elves is perhaps worthy of special remark – for Elves were not as a rule over-friendly towards Dwarves. While travelling with the Company of the Ring, Gimli became a firm comrade of Legolas, the son of King Thranduil of the Wood-elves of Mirkwood; and while in Lothlórien, the Dwarf also conceived a great love for the Lady Galadriel, afterwards considering himself her champion in all things. It seems certain that Galadriel herself was deeply moved by the Dwarf's devotion. She agreed to his bold request for a strand of her hair, which he took as 'a pledge of good will between the Mountain and the Wood until the end of days.'[12]

Gimli was named 'Lockbearer' and 'Elf-friend', and he survived the War to become Lord of the Glittering Caves of Aglarond, and a friend to Rohan and Gondor – as well as the Elves.

Note: one of the final entries in the Red Book states that Gimli Elf-friend sailed West over Sea in company with his friend Legolas after the Passing of Elessar in the year 120 of the Fourth Age. The recorder of this event is hesitant as to its truth, but nonetheless reports the tale.

Ginglith One of the lesser rivers of West Beleriand; it was a tributary of the Narog, rising some leagues south of the southern mountain-wall of Nevrast, and flowing south and then east for perhaps twenty-five leagues before joining the greater stream.

Girdle of Melian The name given in Grey-elven lore to the defensive circle of enchantment set about the borders of Doriath by the spouse of the Lord of Doriath, Melian of the Maiar. It failed when she herself withdrew from Middle-earth after the murder of her husband.

Girdley Island An island in the Baranduin, north of the Bridge of Stonebows, on the eastern border of the Shire.

Girion The last King of Dale – before the Dragon Smaug came flaming out of the north in 2770 Third Age, dispossessing the Dwarves of Erebor and destroying the lands round about. Girion was slain but his heirs escaped to continue his Line. Bard the Bowman of Esgaroth was of that descent.

Girithron (Sind.) The twelfth month of the year as recorded by the Dúnedain. The Quenya name was *Ringarë*.

Giver of Freedom A reverential name for Melkor, used by the Númenoreans (at the instigation of Sauron).

Gladden One of the main rivers of northern Wilderland. It flowed into the Anduin from a high pass in the Misty Mountains, one hundred miles north of the Dimrill Dale.

Gladden Fields A rendering into Common Speech of the Grey-elven name *Loeg Ningloron* ('Pools-of-golden-water-flowers'); being the name of the wet green lands about the mouth of the river Gladden, where this ran into the Anduin. Here many flowers grew, among them iris (gladden). See also BATTLE OF THE GLADDEN FIELDS.

Glamdring and Orcrist A matching pair of Elf-swords made by the Noldor during the War of the Great Jewels in the First Age. At that time, Glamdring ('Hammer-of-Foes') was borne by Turgon, King of the High-elven city of Gondolin. But both Turgon's sword and its mate Orcrist ('Cleaver-of-Goblins') were lost when Gondolin fell to the armies of Morgoth the Enemy. Both swords remained hidden for almost two full Ages, until they found their way into a Troll's hoard – from which they were afterwards rescued by Thorin Oakenshield and Gandalf the Grey.

Thorin claimed Orcrist for his own; and when the Dwarf fell at the Battle of Five Armies (2941 Third Age), this sword was laid upon his tomb. Gandalf bore Glamdring throughout the War of the Ring.

Note: Bilbo Baggins' short sword Sting was from the same Troll-hoard and was also a Gondolin-blade. It possessed similar Elvish qualities.

See also ELVEN-SMITHS.

Glanduin This river – called Swanfleet in the Common Speech – flowed westward from the Misty Mountains north of Dunland to find the Greyflood (Mitheithel) above Tharbad.

Glaurung The greatest Dragon of the First Age, and the first, though perhaps not the largest, of those beasts specially to be bred for warfare by Morgoth. He was the forefather of the *Urulóki*, the Fire-dragons, but luckily did not possess the power of flight, like some of his descendants. Even so, throughout his long career Glaurung wrought great woe among Morgoth's enemies, and in so doing served his Master well.

Glaurung first went to war two hundred years before the Dagor Bragollach, when he was still (relatively) young, and therefore both inexperienced and overconfident. In that battle, the assault of the Fire-drake was ignominiously beaten off, by Fingon of the Elves. Morgoth is said to have been angered at this insubordination on the part of the Worm, for he had intended to hold this weapon in reserve until the time should become ripe – and yet forewarned as they now were, the Elves proved quite unable, in the two centuries which passed before Glaurung was next unleashed upon them, to contrive means to deal with beasts of this sort. And in the Dagor Bragollach, and even more in the Nirnaeth Arnoediad which followed, the Worm of Morgoth (as they called him) wrought havoc, slaying many Men and

Elves before (on the latter occasion) being driven off the battlefield by a gallant host of armoured Dwarves from Belegost. Because of their comprehensive body-armour the Dwarves were able to withstand the fiery blasts, and attack Glaurung from close quarters; but their king, Azaghâl, was mortally wounded and the Dwarves fought no other foes that day.

But it was in the years which followed the Nirnaeth that Glaurung wrought his greatest evils. The creature played a leading part in the fulfilment of the grim destinies of the Children of Húrin: Túrin and Nienor. By bewitching them at separate times he ensured that the family was never re-united, for their paths always crossed; and he took away the power of memory from Nienor, so that she, unknowing, later came to wed her own brother: with terrible consequences for them both. The Dragon had already played the leading part in the sack of Nargothrond, and afterwards took what remained of the kingdom founded by Finrod as his share of the profits (Dragon-fashion, he turned upon his allies when the time came and seized the entire hoard for his own). Glaurung was later slain, by Túrin wielding the Black Sword Gurthang (Anglachel) at Cabed-en-Aras. Later dragons bred by Morgoth (see ANCALAGON THE BLACK) were winged as well as armed with fire, and potentially even more dangerous.

Glede A hot coal or burning ember.

Gléowine 'Joy-lover' The royal minstrel of King Théoden of Rohan. His last song was dedicated to the glorious death of the King upon the Fields of Pelennor.

Glingal The name given by King Turgon of Gondolin to the Image or replica of the Golden Tree of Valinor, Laurelin, that he wrought to grace his halls in exile. Its sister-tree (also an image, of the Silver Tree Telperion), was BELTHIL.

Glirhuin One of the Edain of the Second House (the Haladin of Brethil); he is said to have made a song prophesying inviolability for the 'Stone of the Hapless' – the name in Brethil for the grim monument above the Cabed Naeramarth, which marked the burial of Túrin Turambar, and of Morwen his mother, and the last known whereabouts of Nienor his sister.

See also TOL MORWEN.

Glittering Caves See AGLAROND.

Glóin From 2289–2385 Third Age, the King of the Dwarf-colony in the Grey Mountains. He was the son of Thorin I of Durin's Line.

Glóin son of Gróin A Dwarf of Durin's Line and one of the members of Thorin Oakenshield's renowned expedition to Erebor. As a result of the success of that undertaking, Glóin became wealthy and important in his own right; and, together with his son Gimli, he was later sent as an emissary to Rivendell, where he represented the King under the Mountain at the Council of Elrond (3018 Third Age).

Glóredhel The daughter of Hador Lórindol, Lord of Dor-lómin, and sister of the brethren Húrin and Huor. She wedded Haldir of the Haladin – her eldest brother Galdor simultaneously wedded Hareth the sister of Haldir, thus doubling the link between the Second and Third Houses of the Edain. Glóredhel later bore Haldir a son: Handir, whose own son was BRANDIR THE LAME (destined to be slain in Brethil by Túrin Turambar, a grand-nephew of Glóredhel of Dor-lómin and his own second cousin).

Glorfindel 'Golden-haired' (Sind.) Most scholars will agree that it would have been unreasonable in the extreme to have expected records of the First and Third Ages to be free from discrepancies. And yet close examination reveals that there are in fact very few. This is greatly surprising in view of the vast gulf of years which separates their respective periods of origin, and the many barriers which impede the accurate transmission of facts and events (not to mention spellings). All the same, noteworthy discrepancies of fact can actually be counted on the fingers of one hand;[13] and for the most part they are easily solved or reconciled (see for example FINARFIN [note]). Even in the last extremities of confusion, a careful student may often contrive to advance at least one theory with the merit of fitting all known facts – one which may claim to stand until a better can be contrived (or revealed).

The exception, the most puzzling discrepancy – indeed, amidst all this mass of material the only real puzzle of any kind – is the question attached to the Grey-elven name *Glorfindel*: to be precise, whether or not this name (which occurs several times in records originating as much as six thousand years apart) refers to one or two separate personalities.

In the narrative of Frodo Baggins, written, of course, at the end of the Third Age, Glorfindel is an Elf-lord of Rivendell, mighty among Elrond's counsellors, and leader of the host of Imladris. It is this Elf who meets and assists the Ringbearer and his companions on the East Road.[14] Afterwards, he is said (by Gandalf, who ought to have known) to come 'of a house of princes'.[15] Glorfindel of Imladris is quite clearly one of the mighty among the surviving Noldor of Middle-earth. It was he who was responsible for the defence of Rivendell during the years while Arthedain declined, who led a force to the Battle of Fornost, when his timely appearance completed the rout of Angmar begun by the cavalry of Gondor.[16]

On the other hand, in the earlier (but more recently published) *Silmarillion*, a golden-haired Noldorin prince of Gondolin, who also bears the name Glorfindel, is prominent throughout the last days of Gondolin and indeed makes possible, by his own heroism, the escape, from the doomed city, of Tuor, Idril his wife, and Eärendil their son.[17] This earlier Glorfindel is identified as a lieutenant of Turgon king of Gondolin; he is also said to have been the chief or leader of the House of the Golden Flower – presumably a noble Gondolin family. This great warrior fought at the Nirnaeth Arnoediad, and was a comrade of Ecthelion. Both were the chief servants of the king, Turgon.

Thus far the two identities, two full Ages apart though they be, can nevertheless be reconciled in one (long-lived) personality. It is therefore highly inconvenient to discover, as we do, that the earlier Glorfindel (of Gondolin) is quite definitely said to have perished in mortal combat with a Balrog, and to have been buried under a cairn in the mountains.[18]

There appear to be three possibilities. One, that Glorfindel of Gondolin indeed perished in battle as reported, and that he was afterwards re-born *in Middle-earth*. In which case this is only the second instance when any of the Eldar ever did so, for the spirits of their dead passed West as far as the Halls of Mandos (as they believed): later, and by the consent of Mandos, to be re-born – but in Valinor, not Middle-earth. Only Lúthien of Doriath lived out a second lifespan in mortal lands, so far as records tell.

But it is also possible that Glorfindel of Gondolin did *not* perish in the fight with the Balrog, and that he survived into the Third Age; in which case we must conclude that the account which so sorrowfully describes his heroism, fall – and burial – is inaccurate. Yet why should the original teller of the tale lie? Or was he himself the victim of a deception? In which case, what was the purpose of the subterfuge, and of the empty tomb?

The third possibility is as follows: that Glorfindel of Gondolin (First Age) and Glorfindel of Imladris (Third Age) are after all two distinct personalities. For all we know this name may not have been uncommon. And there is the matter of their lines of descent: a noble Elf of Gondolin would surely, like the king he served, have been a descendant of Fingolfin; whereas the golden hair of the later (Third Age) Glorfindel, *taken in isolation*, suggests rather kinship with the House of Finarfin (for golden hair was rare among the Noldor; only the kin of Finarfin are known to have possessed it).

Against all this, it must be considered highly coincidental that *both* were exiled princes of the Noldor, that *both* were golden-haired, and that *both* were named Glorfindel.

Undoubtedly there exists a slender chance that this taxing problem will be solved at a later date, that some unforseeable permutation of events and personalities still awaits revelation. But in the meantime any attempt on the part of this compiler to be 'decisive' on the subject of Glorfindel of the Noldor seems likely to meet with ignominy and disaster. Let him – or them – remain a mystery.

Goatleaf A Bree-family of 'Big People'.

Goblins A translation of the Grey-elven *yrch* (sing. *orch*). See ORCS.

Golasgil The lord of Anfalas (in Gondor) at the time of the War of the Ring.

Goldberry A Water-sprite of the Old Forest; the bride of Tom Bombadil and daughter of the 'River-woman' of Withywindle.

The Golden Perch The chief Inn of the village of Stock in the Eastfarthing of the Shire. Its beer was renowned.

Golden Wood The name in the Common Speech for the forest known as *Lórien* or *Lothlórien*.

Nowhere else in Middle-earth were the great *mellyrn* or mallorn-trees to be found. These trees bore long golden leaves on their boughs of silver bark, and so gave the Golden Wood its name.

Goldilocks Took The sixth child and second daughter of Samwise Gamgee. She wedded Faramir, son of Peregrin Took, in 1463 Shire Reckoning (Year 42 Fourth Age), thus linking the two most important families in the Shire.

Goldwine From 3680–99 Third Age, the sixth King of Rohan.

Golfimbul An Orc-chieftain, leader of the Goblins of Mount Gram (the location of which is not known, though it may have been near Gundabad in the Misty Mountains).

Golfimbul led a raid deep into western Eriador in 2747 Third Age, during the course of which he was slain by no less a Hobbit than Bandobras 'Bullroarer' Took (in what later became known as the Battle of Greenfields).

Gollum See SMÉAGOL-GOLLUM.

Golodhrim The Sindarin equivalent of the Quenya word *Noldor;* the collective term in use among the Grey-elves for the High-elves of the West who came back to Middle-earth during the Elder Days. The singular form was *Golodh* (normal pl. *Gelydh*).

Gondolin 'Hidden Rock' (Sind.; a punning mutation or rendering of the original Q. *Ondolindë*, 'Stone-song') The most beautiful, the most renowned and the longest to endure of all the Noldorin city-kingdoms founded in Middle-earth during the First Age. Completed in the second century of the exile of the Noldor, by Turgon son of Fingolfin the High King, it stood in splendour and secrecy for a further four hundred years, the last hope of the Noldor in mortal lands; but fell at last, through treachery, and was destroyed, never to rise again. The fall of Gondolin marked the final victory of Morgoth in the War of the Great Jewels; but its memory lived on, beyond that dark time, into the New Age.

Long before Elves awoke in Cuiviénen, in an age of the World forgotten by all save the Valar, a deep lake filled a valley in the Encircling Mountains in the north of Beleriand. The valley, which was circular, may originally have been formed by volcanic action, for there was a tall hill rising from its exact centre, an island in the enclosing lake, steep and precipitous. This valley afterwards became known as Tumladen, and the hill amidmost as Amon Gwareth – though by this time the lake had vanished, drained away through channels long dried up (see DRY RIVER) – and all that remained was the vale, green and fair, and the steep hill of Amon Gwareth. But it was Turgon of the Noldor who named these names, for no Elf before him ever walked in Tumladen or climbed the precipitous sides of the hill. Indeed Turgon himself could not have come there had it not been for the assistance of outside agency; for there was only one entrance to Tumladen through the Encircling Mountains, and that remained long hidden. For precisely this reason Turgon, who was utterly convinced of the need to prepare a well-thought-out 'last refuge' against foretold disaster, determined to build such a refuge in this hidden valley; yet as he also wished to dwell in a fair place, as much like faraway Tirion as he could contrive, so he planned carefully, and built with love. Fifty years after the first stone had been laid, at the beginning of his second century of exile, Turgon and his people secretly quitted Nevrast, where they had been living since the return to Middle-earth, and vanished into the mountains. From that day forward few Elves ever passed the outer doors (until the Nirnaeth Arnoediad, which then lay more than three and a half centuries in the future). Gondolin became the 'Hidden City', its whereabouts not known for sure, even by its allies. But within the impassable mountain-perimeter all that was fair in Elven-culture was preserved: consciously, and with reverence. And the city was made stronger and fairer than any other city that has ever been in Middle-earth, for Turgon never ceased to add to its strength, and its beauty. High towers were built, and mighty walls; yet the towers were slender pinnacles of grace and proportion; and the walls shone in the sunlight.

Centuries passed, the four hundred years of the Siege of Angband, by which Morgoth's movements were to some extent proscribed – although little else could be done, in all that time, to discomfit or damage him. Meanwhile the two most powerful Eldarin city-kingdoms – Nargothrond and Gondolin – lay far behind the Siege lines, enjoying an era of peace and splendour. But no one had foreseen the appalling speed with which the Siege would eventually be overthrown, nor the permanent confusion this defeat would wreak among the Eldar and their allies. Kingdom became sundered from kingdom during that perilous time, and though the north-west held out for a further fifteen years, the tide had now turned irrevocably against the Eldar. The last of all offensives to be mounted by them against Morgoth – to which Turgon brought the host of Gondolin, thus appearing among his allies and kin for the first time in over three hundred and fifty years – led only to the catastrophe of the Nirnaeth, in which the Eldar were overthrown for ever. Only the Gondolindrim held together as a body; they cut their way to safety, aided by the self-sacrificing heroism of the Men of Dor-lómin, led by Húrin and Huor.[19] This was the first and last time the host of Gondolin went to war; henceforward war would come to them.

In the case of Nargothrond, it was pride which led to the Elves' undoing (see TÚRIN TURAMBAR); but in the case of Gondolin, it was treachery – the treachery of Maeglin, Turgon's nephew, who had been treated with honour and lordship all his life, and who (to be fair) had served Turgon well for all that time. But when thirty or so years had passed since the Nirnaeth, Maeglin was captured by Morgoth; and rather than submit to torment, he revealed the entrance to the city, and moreover agreed to aid an attack from within its walls. Yet for some years Morgoth had known that Gondolin lay somewhere in the mountains to the west of Dorthonion, for this had been revealed to him by Húrin of the Edain, though unwittingly.

The sack of Gondolin came on the eve of the festival known as the Gates of Summer (the last day of *tuilë*); and it was brutal and annihilating, for Morgoth had long desired to strike this blow, and as he had no other foes in Middle-earth was as a result able to use as much force as he wished. No fortress could have withstood such an onslaught. Turgon fell, and Ecthelion was slain by, and himself slew, the mightiest of the Balrogs. But Tuor of the Edain killed Maeglin the Traitor, and then fled the city, together with his wife Idril, the daughter of Turgon, and their son Eärendil (in this they had the aid of GLORFINDEL). Behind them, Dragons set the city aflame, so that the sky over Tumladen was filled with the greatest burning it had known since the far-off days of the valley's making.

But the Line of Gondolin lived on, in Idril and Eärendil, and so in Elrond and Elros and all who come after (see LINES OF DESCENT). And even by its fall Turgon's city played a part in the final overthrow of Morgoth. For if Eärendil had not been carried in flight to the sea-lands, he might never have grown up beside the sea, never have become a seaman. He might never have made his historic voyage out of Middle-earth. Yet the idea of sending messengers into the West, to beg the forgiveness and aid of the Valar, was not in origin Eärendil's; for Turgon his grandfather had long held the belief that the only hope of the Noldor lay in the West, and this hope was fostered in his descendants also. Turgon was a pious ruler; and Gondolin had been intended to be a mirror in Middle-earth of Tirion the Fair (there were even Images of the Two Trees standing, or seeming to stand, in Turgon's halls). Perhaps for these reasons Gondolin was allowed to outlast all other Elven-cities of Middle-earth in the Elder Days. But it fell at last, and its fall was all the more terrible for being postponed.

Gondolindrim The Elves of the city of Gondolin; Noldor of the House of Fingolfin, the subjects of Turgon Fingolfin's son.

Gondor 'Stone-land' (Sind.) The South-kingdom of the Dúnedain in Middle-earth; one of the two Realms in Exile founded by Elendil the Tall after the Downfall of Númenor; and for many centuries the most powerful Kingdom anywhere in western Middle-earth. Unlike its northern sister-realm of ARNOR, the South-kingdom survived the turmoils of the Third Age and held out against increasing odds – until, with victory of the War of the Ring, Gondor was finally reunited with the North-kingdom, and the High-kingship of both realms was established once more.

At the founding of the realm, in 3320 Second Age, Gondor included most of the lands about the feet of the White Mountains, save only for the far western vales beyond the river Lefnui. Her chief provinces were the royal fiefs of Ithilien and Anórien, and her rule extended as far as the coastal regions of Anfalas and Belfalas. Her greatest cities were Minas Anor, the Tower of the Sun, on the eastern shoulders of the White Mountains; Minas Ithil, the Tower of the Moon, in the western vales of the Ephel Dúath; and Osgiliath, Citadel of the Stars, which lay in between, upon either side of the Great River. Elendil himself was the High-king of both Arnor and Gondor, but the South-rule he committed to his sons Isildur and Anárion; they dwelled in Minas Ithil and Minas Anor, and the Realm was administered from Osgiliath, where also was kept the chief *palantír* of Gondor.

In those days Sauron the Great was believed to have perished in the ruin of Númenor, and so the survivors of that same disaster did not hesitate to build their South-kingdom upon the very borders of his ancient Realm. But he, too, had survived. He returned in secret to Mordor, and, after little more than a hundred years, declared himself once more, and made war upon the Dúnedain: for he feared and hated the Númenoreans and their works. But Sauron struck too late (or too soon), and with too little strength for his purpose; he underestimated his foes and so was defeated in battle when the Last Alliance forged against him proved too strong for his power to withstand; he was driven back to the Barad-dûr and later overthrown altogether. So ended the Second Age.

A concise history of Gondor's fortunes in the Third Age can be found in Appendix A I(iv) and needs no elaboration here; a short summary must suffice.

For many years the South-kingdom grew steadily more powerful and splendid – until, by the eleventh century of the Third Age, its sway extended as far as the Greyflood and the Sea of Rhûn, and lesser states paid tribute. Yet this early period of intense activity was followed by an epoch of ostentation and luxury, in which most of the gains made by the 'Ship-kings' were allowed to slip away. Nevertheless, Gondor was slow in decline, and it was not until the middle years of the Age that assaults upon her frontiers began again in earnest. These came mainly from the East and South, and were often only driven back at great cost in toil and lives.

More ominously, the Line of Anárion (the hereditary ruling

dynasty of Gondor) now began to wither, and at last one of the Kings took to wife a woman of a lesser (but sturdier) race. This act later precipitated the civil war of Gondor, the Kin-strife, which destroyed much that was fair in the South Kingdom, and further sapped the dwindling strength of the Dúnedain. And although Gondor managed to resist her foes for many years, the Line of Anárion had failed altogether by the beginning of the third millennium.

The Dúnedain of the South were then ruled by their Stewards, a family also of high Númenorean race, who remained true to their trust and never claimed the Crown for themselves throughout the thousand years they ruled in place of the Kings. And led by the House of Húrin (the Line of the Ruling Stewards), the Dúnedain recovered somewhat, though they were never again able to prevent war from gathering on their borders. A protective system of alliances and defensible frontiers was established piecemeal, and in the end proved flexible enough to withstand the return to power of Sauron the Great – and his last attempt to drive the Dúnedain into the Sea.

During the War of the Ring, though all seemed lost for a while, the events of the time ultimately produced the means by which Gondor might not only be delivered from peril but reunited at last with her ancient sister-realm of Arnor, long sundered from her. And in that same war, the Dark Lord was cast down for ever, and a great threat removed from the Free Peoples of Middle-earth. The Re-united Kingdom of Gondor and Arnor lived on in the Fourth Age, last memory in Middle-earth of vanished Númenor; and the banner of Elendil flew again from the Tower of the Sun at the feet of the White Mountains.

See also REALMS IN EXILE.

Gonnhirrim 'Stone-masters' (Sind.) A name bestowed upon the race of Dwarves by the Elves of Beleriand. The more usual terms were *Noegyth, Naugrim* and *Nogothrim,* 'Stunted People' (doubtless the Dwarves themselves preferred *Gonnhirrim*).

Goodchild A family of Shire-hobbits related to the Gamgees. The mother of Samwise (and wife of Hamfast) was Bell Goodchild.

Gorbadoc 'Broadbelt' Brandybuck From 2910–63 Third Age (1310–63 Shire Reckoning), the Master of Buckland. He was the grandfather of Frodo Baggins (and the great-grandfather of Meriadoc Brandybuck). Gorbadoc was known as 'Broadbelt', doubtless due to his rampant waistline.

Gorbag An Orc-sergeant in the garrison of Minas Morgul.

Gorgoroth 'Dreadful Horror' (Sind.) A word in the Grey-elven tongue; in existing records, it is used for two separate locations, distinct in time and space. The first and earlier is *Ered Gorgoroth*, the 'Mountains of Terror' which were the southernmost edge of the Dorthonion plateau, where the Great Spider Ungoliant came after the poisoning of the Trees and ever after made a place of abhorrence and fear. The second instance is in the name of the 'Haunted Plain' of Mordor; the great plateau which occupied the north-western area of that country, a desolate, arid land, pocked with craters and fuming pits and riven with many deep crevasses. In the centre of the plain of Gorgoroth rose the smouldering cone of the volcano Orodruin.

Gorgûn One of the few words recorded in the aboriginal speech of the Wild Men of Druadan Forest (see WOSES). It is said to have meant 'Orcs'.

Gorhendad Oldbuck The founder of the Buckland. The Oldbuck family had long been prominent in the Shire when, in about 2340 Third Age (740 Shire Reckoning), they crossed the Brandywine eastwards and settled the strip of land between the river and the Old Forest. Gorhendad began the excavation of the Hill of Buckland, when he named Brandy Hall; at the same time he changed the family name to *Brandybuck*. He was later accounted the first Master of Buckland.

Gorlim the Unhappy One of the twelve brave companions of BARAHIR of the Edain in the last defence of Dorthonion. Gorlim was unhappy – notoriously so – because of the loss of his wife Eilinel, whom he believed a prisoner. He was captured by means of a cunning trick, and becoming the victim of one of the cruellest of all betrayals, was himself persuaded by Sauron the servant of Morgoth to betray Barahir and his companions. Then Gorlim was put to death. And in the ensuing attack upon their encampment, eleven of the twelve men, including Barahir but not his son Beren, were killed. Eilinel had been dead for nearly four years.

Gorthaur 'The Cruel' (Sind.) The Grey-elves' name (in the First Age) for SAURON THE GREAT.

Gorthol 'Dread Helm' (Sind.) One of the many *noms-de-guerre* assumed during his life by the warrior TÚRIN TURAMBAR. It refers to the Dragon-helm of Dor-lómin, the Helm of Hador, which Túrin wore in battle early in his career.

Gothmog The Lord of the Balrogs of Angband, and one of the most terrible servants of Morgoth during the First Age; in his earliest origins one of the lesser MAIAR, who afterwards became *Valarauka*, a Fire-demon of great power. It was this dreadful being who slew Fëanor at the Battle-under-Stars. Afterwards, Gothmog was made high-captain of the armies of Angband, and led the last assault on the Elves at the Battle of Numberless Tears, slaying at this time Fingon the High King. Thirty-nine years later Morgoth assailed the city of Gondolin, and in this attack the chief of his Balrogs again played a terrible part, for few indeed could stand before him. One who did was Ecthelion of the Fountain. Elf-lord and Fire-demon strove together in the courtyard below the King's tower – and both were slain. So ended Gothmog. His name survived in dark tradition, and was borne (in the Third Age) by the Lieutenant of the Tower of Minas Morgul, chief servant of the Witch-king. It is not recorded to which species this later Gothmog belonged. At all events, he was slain at the Battle of the Pelennor Fields, having, for the final (losing) stages of the battle, commanded the Army of Morgul.

See also BALROG.

Gram From 2718–41 Third Age, the eighth King of Rohan. He was the father of Helm Hammerhand.

Great Armament The name given to that assemblage of arms commanded by Ar-Pharazôn the Golden, last King of Númenor, for his assault upon Valinor and the Undying Lands. It was so great that it took nine years to assemble, from 3310–19 Second Age.

Great Battle The second Battle of the Powers; the attack upon Morgoth made at the end of the First Age by the Host of the Valar. Like Utumno of an earlier age, Angband was annihilated; and Morgoth was cast out – this time for ever.

Great Bridge The Shire-hobbits' name for the Bridge of Stone-bows, more commonly known as the Brandywine Bridge. (It had, in fact, been built by the Dúnedain of the North-kingdom long before the founding of the Shire.)

Great Darkness The term used by the Elves to mean the immense period of time between the overthrowing (by Melkor) of the Lamps of the Valar, Illuin and Ormal, and the Rising of the Moon and Sun towards the end of the First Age. Throughout this period darkness, broken only by starlight, reigned over Middle-earth, and for long

Melkor's rule – the spiritual Great Darkness – was uncontested by the Valar.

Great Eagles See EAGLES.

Great East Road One of the major highways of Eriador. It linked Lindon and the Grey Havens with Rivendell and the Misty Mountains, passing through the middle of the Shire and Bree. In the late Third Age the road was mainly used by Dwarves, who had mines in the Blue Mountains which were still in use.

Great Echo A translation of the Sindarin name *Lammoth*.

Great Enemy Morgoth.

Greater Gelion The more easterly of the two source-streams of the river Gelion, in East Beleriand. The Greater Gelion itself had two sources, on Mount Rerir and from Lake Helevorn.

Great Goblin An Orc-chieftain who led the tribe of Goblins which infested the high pass chosen by Thorin Oakenshield's expedition when they crossed from Eriador into Wilderland (in 2941 Third Age). His followers imprisoned the Dwarves and the Hobbit Bilbo, but their leader was slain by Gandalf the Grey. (See *The Hobbit*, Chap. 4.)

Great Gulf The name given in Eldarin tradition to the huge expanse of water created in the south of Middle-earth during the Eldest Days by powerful seismic forces—which the Elves attributed to the agency of the Valar. In fact the Gulf was created by the earth-movements brought about in turn by the Battle of the Powers in the North.

Great Jewels The *silmarilli* created by Fëanor of Eldamar in the First Age. Their theft (by Morgoth) brought about the Exile of the Noldor and the long wars which ravaged Middle-earth, when the Free Peoples were grievously reduced in number.
See also WAR OF THE GREAT JEWELS.

Great Journey The original Westward migration of the ELDAR. Far back in the Elder Days the Three Kindreds were summoned by the Valar (Guardians of the World) to journey from their homeland in the East across the western lands of Middle-earth to the shores of the Sea. From there, two of the Kindreds then set out on the further, greater journey: across the Sea to the Undying Lands.
See *The Silmarillion* pp. 52–4, 57–62.

Great Lake The lake in the centre of the World, as Arda was first shaped by the Valar. In the centre of the Lake stood the Isle of Almaren, first home in Arda of the Valar. Both Island and Lake – and much more besides – were destroyed by the renegade Vala Melkor, in the course of his second attack upon the Powers.

Great Lands Middle-earth.

Great Music The name given in the traditions and beliefs of the Eldar to that which took place before the Creation: the weaving of all possible sub-themes of Existence around a pre-ordained yet infinitely flexible Theme already chosen by Eru (God). This development of existential possibilities, analagous (in the legend) to musicians or choristers freely improvising within a fixed compositional mode – while all the time serving only the direct will of the Composer – was performed, or achieved, say the Elves, by the *Ainur*, the Holy Ones of God. When the Great Song (as it is also called) was complete for that time, two separate major Themes having been introduced and traced to their endings, Eru spoke; and the vision was made manifest. And then, according to the tradition,[20] the Ainur who had taken part left the dwelling of Eru and went down into the newly-created Universe (*Eä*), each to labour in making manifest his or her individual contribution to the Music. Among them was Melkor, who from the first had attempted to dominate all other contributions to the Great Music; now he, too, went down into Eä and laboured towards the fulfilment of his disharmonious counterpoint.

Great Ones The AINUR.

Great Place of the Tooks The chief household of Great Smials, where The Took kept his abode.

Great Plague In 1636 Third Age, a foul plague came out of the East and South and ravaged the Westlands of Middle-earth. Osgiliath in Gondor was particularly hard-hit. King Telemnar and all his children were struck down, and even the White Tree of Minas Anor perished (although a fortuitously preserved seedling then continued the Line of Nimloth). It was at this time that the Men of Gondor were forced to abandon their long watch on the neighbouring borders of Mordor.

From Gondor the plague then spread north-west to Eriador, where it devastated Cardolan (especially the region known as Minhiriath), and also caused great suffering in the Shire.

Great Rider OROMË.

Great Rings The Rings of Power; that is, the Nine Mortal-rings, the Seven Dwarf-rings and the Three Elven-rings – plus the Ruling Ring of Sauron. Other rings of various properties were made by the Noldor of Eregion, but these were 'only essays in the craft before it was full-grown, and to the Elven-smiths they were but trifles'.[21]

Great Sea A translation of the Sindarin name *Belegaer*; the Western Seas, which lay between Middle-earth and the shores of the Undying Lands.

Great Smials The chief burrowing-place or dwelling of the pre-eminent Took Family, in the Green Hills of Tuckborough. It was commenced in 2683 Third Age (1083 Shire Reckoning) by Thain Isengrim II.

Great Song See GREAT MUSIC.

Great Water The Sea.

Great West Road The main highway between Rohan and Gondor, running from Edoras in the north-west to Minas Tirith in the south-east.

Great Worms The Dragons of Middle-earth.

The Green Dragon The leading Inn of the village of Bywater in the Shire. It was patronized by Hobbits from both Hobbiton and Bywater.

Green-elves A translation of the Quenya name *Laiquendi*, being the name given by the exiled Noldor to the silvan Elves of Ossiriand, most rustic and wary of all the Eldar of Beleriand. These wore green, and shot with bows, and lived exclusively in the forests, and were by comparison with the Noldor – and even the Sindar – primitive in their culture, not knowing even the uses of iron. Yet for all this they were valiant, and, moreover, they were not Avari, but akin from afar to the Noldor, and closer still to the Sindar (Grey-elves). For the Laiquendi were of Telerin kind, as were the Sindar of Beleriand, being an offshoot of the *Nandor*. The latter represented the first sundering of the Eldar, for they were in origin the hindmost portion of the Teleri – themselves Hindmost of the Three Kindreds on the Great Journey – who had baulked at crossing the Misty Mountains into Eriador, and instead, led by a certain Lenwë, had turned back into the forests of Wilderland, to wander unrecorded paths for many centuries and millennia. They became the foremost of all woodland peoples, and by far the most woodcrafty of all the Eldar; but they still spoke their Eldarin language, though this changed greatly as the years waned. But as the Ages wore away of Melkor's imprisonment in faraway Valinor, evil things awoke once more in Middle-earth; and the forests of the Nandor grew dangerous. Then a portion of the Nandor, the vanguard, who by now had wandered further west, south of the dreaded Misty Mountains and so into Eriador,[22] turned their faces still westward, and, led by their chief Denethor, the son of Lenwë first chieftain of the Nandor, eventually came over the last mountain-range between them and the Sea and so entered Beleriand. In Ossiriand, the easternmost part of that ancient land, they then dwelt, with the permission of Thingol the King, and Denethor was their lord.

But war was on their heels. And although the newcomers fought for Thingol in the First Battle of Beleriand, Denethor was slain in that fight, upon the hill of Amon Ereb; and they were reduced in number; whereupon they withdrew into their green and secret country beyond Gelion, and suffered no strangers to enter, save those from Doriath, whom they still held in friendship. They took little part in the wars which followed, and when Beleriand was drowned and broken at the end of the First Age a remnant of Ossiriand was spared: it was named *Harlindon*. But what became of the Green-elves no records tell. They were accounted, together with the Nandor, among the *Moriquendi*, which means they are thought never to have completed the Great Journey into the West.

Greenfields A part of the Northfarthing of the Shire where, in 2747 Third Age (1147 Shire Reckoning), a band of Orcs was defeated by Bandobras 'Bullroarer' Took.

Greenhand A family of Shire-hobbits descended from Holman the Greenhanded of Hobbiton, through his son Halfred. They later removed from Hobbiton and founded their own settlement of Green-holm. Fastred, who wedded Elanor Gamgee in the early Fourth Age, was of this kin.

Greenholm See preceding entry.

Green Isle A translation of the Grey-elven name TOL GALEN.

Green Mound See EZELLOHAR.

Greenway The name given during the later years of the Third Age for the old North Road, where it ran through desolate regions of

Eriador. It was so called in the village of Bree because the paved stone of the ancient highway was grass-grown from lack of use.

Greenwood the Great The mightiest forest remaining in Middle-earth in the Third Age. It was over four hundred miles long and two hundred miles across at its widest point, where the old Forest Road threaded a path from Wilderland to the River Running. In the north-east dwelt Wood-elves of Thranduil's realm; in the south-west lived scattered settlements of woodmen.

Towards the end of the first millenium of the Third Age, Green-wood began to acquire an evil reputation: fell beasts stalked the gloom under the closely packed trees, and the trees themselves began to rot and wither and strive one against the other. It was not known until later that the evil came from the fortress of Dol Guldur in the far south-western reach of the forest. Greenwood then became known as *Taur e-Ndaedelos* ('Forest of Great Fear'), translated from the Red Book as *Mirkwood*. At the turn of the Fourth Age it was renamed *Eryn Lasgalen*, 'Wood of Green Leaves'.

Grey Company A company of thirty Rangers of the North who rode south to Aragorn's aid during the War of the Ring. They were led by Halbarad and also included Elladan and Elrohir, the sons of Elrond.

Grey-Elves The SINDAR.

Greyflood The river Gwathlo, as it was known to Men of Eriador. Properly speaking, the Greyflood was the name of the conjoined Mitheithel (Hoarwell) and Glanduin (Swanfleet), below Tharbad.

Grey Havens A translation of the Sindarin name *Mithlond*, being the name of the harbour and city founded by the Falathrim in Year 1 Second Age, as the chief haven of the Eldar in Middle-earth. Mithlond lay near the mouth of the river Lhûn (Lune) where this emptied into the Gulf of the same name. First Lord of the Havens was Círdan the Shipwright of the Falathrim, formerly Lord of Eglarest in West Beleriand, and after this haven had fallen to Morgoth, of the Isle of Balar, in the Bay of the same name.

Greymantle A translation of the Quenya name *Singollo* (orig. *Sindacollo*); its Sindarin form is *Thingol*. It was the surname or appellation of Elwë, Lord of the Teleri (jointly with his brother Olwë) on the Great Journey from Cuiviénen to Beleriand, who afterwards became King of Beleriand and Doriath, and was more usually translated 'Grey-cloak'.

See THINGOL GREYCLOAK.

Grey Mountains A translation of the Grey-elven name *Ered Mithrin*; a far northern range, running east from the Misty Mountains to the Withered Heath. The Grey Mountains were notoriously infested with Dragons.

Grey Wood The south-eastern reach of the Forest of Druadan (in Gondor).

Gríma Wormtongue.

Grimbeorn The son of Beorn and the Chieftain of the Beorning folk, who maintained the high pass over the Misty Mountains and the Ford of Carrock in the latter days of the Third Age.

Grimbold A Marshal of Westfold in Rohan at the time of the War of the Ring. He fought in both battles of the Fords of Isen and commanded the left wing of the Rohirrim in their great onset against the besiegers of Gondor (see BATTLE OF THE PELENNOR FIELDS). He fell in that last battle, far from his home in Grimslade, and was laid to rest in the 'Mounds of Mundburg', and so is commemorated in the Lay of that name.

Grinding Ice The HELCARAXË.

Grindwall A small hythe (harbour) on the north bank of the river Withywindle, outside the protection of the High Hay. It was guarded by a *grind* or fence which extended into the waters of the river.

Grishnákh The leader of those Orcs of Mordor who collaborated with the Uruk-hai of Saruman (led by Uglúk) in the attack upon the Fellowship near Parth Galen on February 26th, 3019 Third Age. He was described as 'a short crook-legged creature, very broad and with long arms that hung almost to the ground.[23]

Gróin A Dwarf of the House of Durin; the brother of Fundin and the father of Óin and Glóin.

Grond Originally, the Mace of Morgoth, also known as the 'Hammer of the Underworld'. The name was later given to the great battering-ram which broke the gates of Minas Tirith during the siege of Gondor. This ram was

> a hundred feet in length, swinging on mighty chains. Long had it been forging in the dark smithies of Mordor, and its hideous head,

founded of black steel, was shaped in the likeness of a ravening wolf; on it spells of ruin lay.[24]

Grór A Dwarf of Durin's Line; the youngest son of Dáin I and the grandfather of Dáin (II) Ironfoot. It was Grór who founded the Dwarf-realm in the Iron Hills in 2590 Third Age.

Grubb A family of Shire-hobbits related to the Bagginses through Laura Grubb, who wedded Mungo Baggins, Bilbo's grandfather.

Guarded Plain A translation of the Sindarin name *Talath Dirnen*; the name of the expanse of deserted land – chiefly heath and moor – which lay between the rivers Narog and Teiglin, to the north of the Realm of Nargothrond, whose northern march it was. Talath Dirnen was guarded by the Elves of Nargothrond.

Guarded Realm Valinor.

Guard of the Citadel The élite men-at-arms who were appointed to guard the Citadel of Minas Tirith and the Court of the Fountain. They were

> robed in black, and their helms were of strange shape, high-crowned, with long cheek-guards close-fitting to the face; but the helms gleamed with a flame of silver, for they were indeed wrought of *mithril*, heirlooms from the glory of old days. Upon the black surcoats were embroidered in white a tree blossoming like snow beneath a silver crown and many-pointed stars. This was the livery of the heirs of Elendil . . .[25]

(The) Guests A name for the (fleeting) race of Men, bestowed by the (ageless) Elves.

Guilin One of the Noldor of the First Age, of the kindred of Finarfin; an Elf-lord of Nargothrond. He is remembered as the father of the brothers Gelmir and Gwindor, one of whom was tortured to death during the Nirnaeth Arnoediad, the other of whom was taken alive in the battle and enthralled for many years in the pits of Angband. Guilin's fate is not known for certain.

Gulf of Lune The great firth which separated North and South Lindon. It was created by the drowning of Beleriand in the First Age, and lay over what had once been the Dwarf-cities of the Blue Mountains.

Gundabad Mount Gundabad, which stood at the meeting-point of the *Ered Mithrin* and the Misty Mountains. Traditionally the location of the chief Orc-stronghold of the North, it was sacked by the Dwarves during the War of the Dwarves and Orcs (2793–9 Third Age).

Gundor One of the Edain of the First Age, of the Third House; the younger brother of GALDOR THE TALL of Dor-lómin; the second son of Hador Lórindol. Gundor was slain, together with his father Hador, in a last defence of the tower of Eithel Sirion on the borders of Ard-galen, during the Dagor Bragollach. He did not wed, and left no sons to follow him.

Gurthang 'Death-iron' (Sind.) The name given by the warrior Túrin Turambar to the black sword formerly known as ANGLACHEL, after he had had it reforged in Nargothrond. The black sword had formerly belonged to the Elf-warrior Beleg Cúthalion, but in Túrin's hands it had taken Beleg's life – by 'accident'. Gurthang was to drink many more lives before, at the last, claiming Túrin's own. It was an accursed sword and thus matched its master perfectly.

Guthláf The Herald and banner-bearer of Théoden, King of the Mark during the War of the Ring. He fell in the Battle of the Pelennor Fields.

Gúthwinë 'Battle-friend' (Northern Mannish) The sword of Éomer, Third Marshal (later King) of the Mark.

Gwaeron 'Windy' (Sind.) The name – used only by the Dúnedain – for the third month of Kings' Reckoning (and the twelfth of the New Reckoning). In its Quenya form, this month was known as *Súlimë*.

Gwaihir the Windlord Lord of the Great Eagles of the Misty Mountains, a descendant of Thorondir. He became a friend of Gandalf the Grey when the Wizard healed him of a poisoned wound (probably caused by an orc-arrow). Several times in the closing years of the Third Age, Gwaihir repaid this debt: and during the War of the Ring the Eagles, led by Gwaihir and his brother Landroval, assisted Gandalf and the cause of the Free Peoples many times.

Gwaith-i-Mírdain 'People of the Jewel-smiths' (Sind.) The folk of Celebrimbor, Noldorin craftsmen who peopled the realm of EREGION in the Second Age. After the ending of the First Age these were the most skilful Elven-craftsmen anywhere in mortal lands; Celebrimbor their lord was the grandson of Fëanor. The summit of their craft was the making of the Rings of Power.

Gwathlo 'Shadow-flood' (Sind.) The river Greyflood in Eriador.

Gwindor of Nargothrond A prince of the Noldor, and a prominent war-leader of the city of Nargothrond; the brother of GELMIR and the elder son of Guilin. He was captured during the Nirnaeth Arnoediad – his brother Gelmir, captured twenty years before, had been cruelly executed before his eyes, as a (successful) provocation – and for fourteen years was enslaved in Angband. So broken was he by this treatment that he lost most of his former Elven-beauty and became physically withered, like an aged Man. Nevertheless his spirit remained unquenchable, and he contrived to escape from Angband, and after lonely wandering came into Dorthonion where he fell in with Beleg Cúthalion[26] – and indeed helped Beleg to effect the rescue of Túrin Turambar, who had recently been captured by Orcs. Afterwards Gwindor took Túrin with him to Nargothrond, where his companion was soon to win great honour and renown as war-leader: a position Gwindor himself had held before going to the Nirnaeth, there to fight (and lose) under the banners of Fingolfin's house (Gwindor was of Finarfin's kindred). To increase Gwindor's bitterness, his former beloved, the Elf-maiden Finduilas daughter of Orodreth, now gave her heart to Túrin the Man; but Gwindor, though he feared the worst, did not openly oppose the match. In the event, Nargothrond was destined to fall before aught else could occur; and Gwindor fought his last battle on the field of Tumladen. There he perished, in the arms of Túrin. Finduilas died shortly afterwards, a captive of Orcs. But Túrin escaped, for he was the bearer of the Curse upon the Children of Húrin, a curse which fell, not on him, but on those he loved.

Gwirith The Sindarin name – used only by the Dúnedain – for the fourth month of the Kings' Reckoning (and the first of the New Reckoning). The Quenya or High-elven name for this month was *Viressë*.

Notes
1 *Silmarillion* p. 360.
2 *The Road Goes Ever On*, p. 60.
3 *Ibid*.
4 The exact relationship is open to doubt; in *The Lord of the Rings* (Book VI Chap. 5) Gandalf, speaking to Aragorn, says, of Galathilion, that it was 'a fruit of Telperion, Tree of many names'. But in *The Silmarillion* (p. 59), we learn that the Tree of Tirion was *made* by Yavanna; of course, as she had also caused

the original Trees to grow, the references may not be contradictory. Certainly there was a recognized Line of Descent.

5 Book VI Chap. 5.
6 Appendix B 'The Third Age'.
7 Book VI Chap. 5.
8 *Ibid.*
9 A (conjectural) name for this festival is *Laerennyn* (Sind.).
10 Book VI Chap. 6.
11 Book II Chap. 2.
12 Book II Chap. 8.
13 Surely a tribute to the illustrious Editors.
14 Book I Chap. 11.
15 Book II Chap. 1.
16 Appendix A I(iv).
17 *Silmarillion* p. 243.
18 *Ibid.*
19 *Silmarillion* pp. 158–9.
20 *Ainulindalë* (*Silmarillion*) p. 20.
21 Book I Chap. 2.
22 From Elrond (Book II Chap. 2) we know that Eriador was thickly forested during the Elder Days – 'Time was when a squirrel could go from tree to tree from . . . the Shire to Fangorn east of Dunland'.
23 Book III Chap. 3.
24 Book V Chap. 4.
25 Book V Chap. 1.

Habergeon A hauberk or sleeveless mail-coat.

Hadhodrond This Grey-elven word, actually an Elvish name for the great Dwarvish city of MORIA, is a rare example of an Elvish attempt to reproduce a Dwarvish (Khuzdul) word phonetically. The Dwarves' name for Moria was of course *Khazad-dûm*, of which *Hadhodrond* ('Halls of the *Hadhod* [*Khazâd*, i.e. Dwarves]') was the phonetic equivalent.

Hador Lórindol One of the great Chieftains of the Edain of the First Age; the son of Hathol and great-grandson of Marach; and the father of Galdor the Tall, Gundor and Gloredhel. He was the first Lord of Dor-lómin.

He was born in the Year of the Sun 389, and, while still a young man, entered the service of Fingolfin the High King of the Noldor. As a reward for his services, and because of the love that Fingolfin bore him, he and his people were granted Dor-lómin in vassalage. There he gathered most of the Edain of the Third House, and within a generation he had made this northern land the most powerful and renowned of the realms of the Edain.

From the Elves' point of view, the enlistment of the most numerous and warlike of the Houses of the Edain made a great deal of sense. The land of Hithlum, Fingolfin's realm, was too vast for the Elves alone to defend; and by ceding its south-western part – Dor-lómin – to the Edain, while simultaneously retaining Hithlum itself and adjacent Mithrim, Fingolfin freed the Noldor from the necessity of having to garrison unnecessary territory. Better still, the strong arms of Hador's people were now in the 'front line' of the Siege. The most easterly and northerly of the outposts of Hithlum, the Tower of Eithel Sirion on the borders of Ard-galen, was also garrisoned by Hador's men.

For another forty years Hador ruled the Edain of Dor-lómin; but when he was sixty-six Morgoth, after long preparation, unleashed sudden war: the Battle of Sudden Flame as it was called, for the plains of Ard-galen were kindled and the running flames claimed many lives before the fighting had even begun. The Eldar and their allies were driven back to the ramparts of Hithlum, and withdrew, after loss, into their fortresses. But this withdrawal was only made possible by the courage and sacrifice of Hador: for at the cost of his own life, and of that of his second son Gundor, he defended the Elves' rearguard and so aided their escape. Twenty years later his grandsons Húrin and Huor were to perform a similar service, and at similar cost. Hador was succeeded as Lord of Dor-lómin by Galdor.

Note: the Edain of the Third House were for the most part golden-haired; Hador's Elven surname *Lórindol* actually means 'the Golden-headed'.

See also DRAGON-HELM (OF DOR-LÓMIN).

Hador From 2278–2395 Third Age, the seventh Ruling Steward of Gondor. He made the final correction to the (slightly imperfect) Stewards' Reckoning system of calendar computation, adding one day to the year 2360 to repair a minor accumulated deficit.

Haerast 'Further Shore' (Sind.) See NEVRAST.

Haladin The People of Haleth, the Second House of the Edain. They were the least warlike – though not the least doughty – of all the Edain peoples, and also the least numerous; but whereas the Men of the First and Third Houses could understand each others' speech, and therefore must once have shared a common ancestor (or at least a common pasture), the Haladin were in many ways different to them, though still accounted Edain. For in addition to speaking a tongue markedly unlike that of the Peoples of Bëor and Marach, the Men of the Second House were physically different: shorter and darker, though not as Easterlings are;[1] and, moreover, they had no great love for open lands and the pasturing of flocks, but sought rather for woods and forests[2] wherein to dwell and build their homes. But impelled by the same forces, they too set their faces west at an early time, and together with the other two Peoples of Men came over the Blue Mountains into Beleriand at the beginning of the fourth century after the first rising of the Sun. They might have lingered in Ossiriand, for that was a green, secret country much to their liking, but the Green-elves of that land did not desire this; and so the Haladin turned north, about the skirts of Dolmed, and passed into Thargelion. Here they dwelt for some years.

At this early date the Haladin were not yet a 'people' in the true sense of the word. They had only rudimentary social organization. Life was centred almost exclusively on the family group, or clan, and concepts of nationhood or even tribality did not exist. They had not acquired the custom of centralized rule. And they were, as a consequence, slow to unite. But when, in perhaps the twentieth year of their sojourn in Thargelion, their encampment was suddenly attacked by Orcs, the old, slow ways were instantly abandoned. One of their number, a head-of-family called Haldad, took the initiative and the command, gathering his people into the only defensive position that could readily be contrived.[3] And there, for weeks, the Haladin endured a siege without hope of succour. Haldad was killed, and the leadership of the newly united Haladin passed to his daughter Haleth, a forceful woman who did not disdain to wield sword and bow in the general defence of the stockade. But still the siege pressed closer – until, at the eleventh hour, the defenders were saved from annihilation by the arrival of the Elves of Thargelion, led by their lord Caranthir son of Fëanor. Hitherto this Elven-lord, the haughtiest of the sons of Fëanor, had altogether ignored the Haladin (as being of little worth); but now, seeing the heaps of slain and the grim faces of the besieged, he changed his mind (besides, he must have heard of other Elven-lords taking these Edain into their service, as allies and vassals). Caranthir then offered Haleth and her people honourable status as vassals within his own kingdom, but Haleth refused; for the lands of Thargelion had grown hateful to the Haladin. So they parted, and the survivors crossed over Gelion at the nearby ford (Sarn Athrad), and passed west, deep into Beleriand, following the footsteps of their kin.

But their immediate sufferings were not yet over: their route, had they known it, led through Estolad and Dor Dínen into the perilous land between the northern fences of Doriath and the Mountains of Terror; Nan Dungortheb, the Valley of Dreadful Death, the haunt of evil creatures of monstrous proportion and ferocious appetite. Many of the old and sick and wounded of the Haladin perished on this journey, and their will faltered, but Haleth led them forward – until Dimbar lay behind them.

Before them, between Teiglin and Sirion, lay wide, unoccupied lands. Beyond the Teiglin was a vast plain or moor, claimed by Nargothrond as part of its realm but thinly peopled for all that. Many of the Haladin, weary of narrow roads and looming heights, now passed out on to the plain and became a wandering people. But most remained with Haleth, and passed into the nearby Forest of Brethil, where they made a woodland realm – after first coming to an understanding with Thingol of Doriath, the suzerain of all Beleriand and especially of the lands bordering his kingdom of Doriath (see FOREST OF BRETHIL). Here the Haladin dwelt, until the ending of the Age; and their rustic domain was to outlast all other kingdoms and realms of that time.

From this time forward the Haladin never abandoned the idea of unity, so painfully learned. They continued to recognize chieftains, of whom, according to their own lore, Haleth was the first. Their dwellings lay deep within the Forest, on the slopes of the hill Amon Obel, and these were fortified in later days, after the woodland manner, with stockade and earthern wall. But so far as they could they eschewed the war. Nevertheless, the defeat of the Dagor Bragollach radically altered the strategic situation, and in the years following that faraway battle the people of Haleth found themselves for the first time in the forefront of the conflict. And now, for the first time, they made common cause with the Elves of neighbouring Doriath (on one notable occasion this alliance brought about the annihilation of an entire legion of Orcs marching through Dimbar). This was in the days of Halmir, whose own son and daughter were wedded to the daughter and elder son of the Lord of Dor-lómin (of the Third House). In this way the urgencies and exigencies of war brought the Haladin closer to others of the Edain, rather than the other way about. The lesson of unity had been well learned.

But now a time was approaching when all realms of the Eldar and Edain would fall into the greatest peril, if not kept secret and hidden. The Nirnaeth Arnoediad – to which a contingent from Brethil, led by Haldir, had gone, none of whom afterwards returned – ended for ever the days of open warfare and panoplied hosts. The North became ravaged by a new kind of fighting, deadly and merciless, demanding secret bases, high mobility, a knowledge of the country, and the determination to resort to 'ignoble' tactics – of the hit-and-run sort – if it meant damaging the enemy.[4] It was at around this time that BRANDIR THE LAME, grandson of Haldir who had been slain at the Nirnaeth, built the Ephel Brandir, atop Amon Obel. But no mere stockade of wood could have withstood the enemy who now approached – Glaurung the Dragon, new-come from the sack of

Nargothrond. The Haladin were preparing to flee when a certain warrior of the Edain (though not of their House), who was then dwelling with them in the Ephel, took the wrath of the Dragon upon his own head and went out to fight to save Brethil from the destroying flames. This of course was TÚRIN TURAMBAR; and meshed in his Doom were, among others, the Dragon, and all the People of Haleth, notably Brandir the Chief. As is well known, in the end the Dragon never came to Brethil, and the Haladin were able to return to their homes, though not unscathed by the episode.

Yet they were now, like all the Edain and Eldar, grievously reduced in number, and in such daily fear that they posed no further threat to Morgoth's dominion; and therefore they kept hidden as best they might. In this way a remnant survived the ending of the Age, and the inundation of their long home, afterwards gathering in Lindon. And in the 32nd year of the New (Second) Age, when most of the surviving Edain, of all Three Houses, set sail across the Sea to found Númenor, the People of Haleth went also, as part of that expedition.

Note: the name *Haladin* appears to mean 'Children of Halad'; *Halad* may be the name of a mythical progenitor.

Halbarad A Ranger of Eriador and the captain of the Grey Company. He led the Dúnedain to the aid of their Chieftain during the War of the Ring, but fell in the Battle of the Pelennor Fields (March, 3019 Third Age).

Haldad See HALADIN.

Haldan A chieftain of the Haladin of Brethil. See LINES OF DESCENT.

Haldar See preceding entry.

Haldir The son of Halmir of the Haladin. He wedded a noblewoman of the Third House (of Dor-lómin), Gloredhel daughter of Hador Lórindol, (while at the same ceremony his sister Hareth wedded the Heir of Dor-lómin, Galdor). The son of Haldir and Gloredhel was Handir. Haldir perished at the Nirnaeth Arnoediad, fighting in Fingon's rearguard, together with most of the force sent to that battle from Brethil.

Also the name (Third Age) of one of the Galadhrim (Tree-Elves) of Lothlórien, a marchwarden of the land.

Haleth The first real chieftain of the HALADIN, the daughter of Haldad and sister of Haldar. Both father and brother were slain in the defence of the stockade in Thargelion, after which Haleth, a woman of strong character and high courage, stepped into her father's shoes (he had organized the defence which had saved them) and took the leadership of the Haladin. She led them a dangerous road across northern Beleriand, but brought them to safety at last. Haleth then founded the settlement in the woods of Brethil, and dwelt there until her death, undisputed chieftainess of a House of Men. She was succeeded by her nephew Haldan. Everafter the Haladin called themselves, in her honour, 'the People of Haleth'.

Haleth (Third Age) The elder son of King Helm Hammerhand of Rohan. He was slain defending the King's Hall when the Dunlendings invaded the Mark in 2758 Third Age.

Halfast of Overhill Samwise Gamgee's 'cousin Hal'; the son of Halfred of Overhill, a village in the Westfarthing of the Shire.

Half-elven The PEREDHIL.

Halflings A translation of the Sindarin word *Periannath;* the name in the Common Speech for the Shire-folk – who spoke of themselves as *Hobbits,* a word derived from quite a different meaning.

Half-orcs An epithet used in Rohan for a particular race of creatures from Isengard – a fell breed with the height of true Men and all the ill-favoured characteristics of Orcs.

Halfred Gamgee The second son of Hamfast Gamgee and elder brother of Samwise. When a young Hobbit, he quitted Number 3 Bagshot Row and moved to the Northfarthing.

Halfred Greenhand The eldest son of the fabled Holman the Greenhanded of Hobbiton. In token of his father's prowess, Halfred adopted the surname *Greenhand.* His only son Holman, the last of that family, passed on the trade to Hamfast Gamgee.

Halfred of Overhill The younger brother of Hamfast Gamgee and son of Hobson 'Roper' Gamgee of Tighfield. Halfred had one son, Halfast, born after he went to live at Overhill, in the Westfarthing.

Halifirien The northernmost of the seven beacon-hills which lay along the feet of the White Mountains between Gondor and Rohan. The Halifiren Beacon overlooked the Firienwood, which stood at the border of the two countries, and a beacon burning there in time of war could have been seen as far away as Edoras.
    See also BEACON-HILLS.

Halimath The ninth month in the Shire Reckoning. (In Bree the same month was called *Harvestmath*.)

Halla The Quenya or High-elven word for 'tall', but more properly, the title of the *tehta* or 'sign' used for breathed *h*. The *tehtar* were diacritic marks which acted as vowel substitutes in the Fëanorian alphabet. *Halla* was a vertical raised bowless stem.

See also TENGWA, TENGWAR.

Hallas 'Long-leaf' (Sind.) From 2567–2605 Third Age, the thirteenth Ruling Steward of Gondor.

Hallow A sacred or holy place; also a name for tombs. The Tombs of the Kings and other great men of Gondor were built on a high plateau behind the city of Minas Tirith, and could be reached only through a guarded door, *Fen Hollen*, on the inside of the sixth wall of the city. The main avenue of the Hallows was named *Rath Dínen*, 'Silent Street'.

Halls of Waiting See following entry.

Halls of Mandos The name given in traditions of the Eldar to the Houses of the Dead, in the Uttermost West of Valinor; the place of Awaiting after Death, where the spirits of the departed go perforce, to sit awhile in meditation on their past lives before being released;[5] thereupon the souls of earth-bound Elves awaken once more in the Blessed Realm, but the souls of Mortal Men pass on, away from Arda for ever, to be gathered into the Thought of Eru. The Keeper of the Houses of the Dead is the Vala Námo, more often called Mandos (though this is properly the name of the Halls themselves). It is Mandos who decides how long shall be the time of Waiting.

Halmir See HALADIN.

Háma The younger son of King Helm Hammerhand of Rohan. In the winter of 2758–9 Third Age he was besieged in the Hornburg, together with his father and many of the King's followers. He led out a party of desperate men on a foray early in the new year and was lost in the snow. Helm himself died a short time afterwards. Also the name of the Captain of King Théoden's household and the Door-ward of Meduseld, the King's Hall in Edoras. He fell during the Battle of the Hornburg (March, 3019 Third Age) and was buried there in a separate mound.

Hamfast Gamgee The son of Hobson 'Roper' Gamgee and the father of the illustrious Samwise. For much of his life Hamfast was the most well-respected gardener of Hobbiton and district, being rightly renowned as much for his rural witticisms as for his superb potatoes.

He was born in 2926 Third Age (1326 Shire Reckoning), second son to a family of rope-makers in Tighfield. Young Hamfast, however, was more interested in the trade of his older 'cousin' Holman Greenhand, a gardener of note, who lived in Hobbiton by the Pool of Bywater. He became apprenticed to Holman and eventually succeeded him as the area's principal horticulturalist, being employed mainly in the extensive gardens of Bag End.

Hamfast married Bell Goodchild, who bore him six children, of whom Samwise was the youngest. Yet only Sam shared his father's love of the earth; he assisted in the gardens at Bag End until 'the Gaffer' retired, whereupon Sam in his turn took over the job. Old Hamfast enjoyed his retirement, living quietly in Number 3 Bagshot Row – apart from a minor upset in 1419 Shire Reckoning, when he was temporarily evicted – until finally, in the year 1428, at the age of 102, he died content. For in his later years the Gaffer had seen his favourite son acclaimed as a hero of the Shire, a leader of society and (best of all) as the greatest gardener of all time.

Also the name given by Samwise to his fourth son.

See also GAMGEE; RANUGAD.

Hamson Gamgee The eldest son of Hamfast Gamgee and elder brother of Samwise. Rather than follow his father's trade of gardening, Hamson moved back to Tighfield (where a branch of the family still lived), and pursued instead his uncle Andy's trade of rope-making.

Handir The father of Brandir the Lame of the HALADIN, the son of Haldir and Gloredhel of Dor-lómin. In his time he succeeded to the chieftainship of the Men of Brethil, but was slain in battle with Orcs while still in middle life. Brandir succeeded him.

Harad 'South' (Sind. from Q. *Hyarmen*) Properly speaking, this was the name given in Gondor to all those lands south of the river Harnen; a fuller title was *Haradwaith* [Lands of the] South-peoples'.

This area was divided (according to the reckoning of the Dúnedain) into Far and Near Harad, comprising a patchwork of petty kingdoms, all of which were frequently – indeed, almost continually – at war with Gondor during the Third Age.

Haradrim 'People of-the-South' (Sind.) The inhabitants of the lands of Harad; the Southrons, a fierce race of Men divided into a number of petty but warlike kingdom. Throughout much of the Third Age their armies repeatedly marched against Gondor; mostly they were defeated and driven back to their desert lands. Yet on only one occasion were the Haradrim totally overthrown by Gondor's might (see HYARMENDACIL I); and for over two thousand years they remained an unpredictable threat on the southern borders.

For all their (observed) warlike intentions and (ascribed) lust for gold, the Haradrim were nonetheless accounted true Men; and if they were at any time dishonourable or cowardly in battle, it has not been recorded. Yet their methods of warfare were unlike those of other folk: many horsemen they had, and troops of giant war-beasts, called *mûmakil* – on the backs of which rode their chieftains. Their soldiers were armed with spear and shield, helm and scimitar, all adorned with gold and much ornament (and they were also reported as being darker-skinned than the Dúnedain of Gondor, due no doubt to the long effect of the bright Sun in those distant lands). By all accounts, the Men of Harad were formidable warriors and determined opponents, and their enmity towards Gondor was deep-rooted.

The principal issue behind the initial outbreak of hostilities between the two countries was the possession of Umbar, which lay on the coast of Haradwaith some seventy leagues south of the river Harnen. Traditionally Black Númenorean land, it had been seized by Gondor in the tenth century of the Third Age; and in 1015, the Haradrim – stirred up by the dispossessed Black Númenoreans – attacked Umbar in great strength. Ciryandil, King of Gondor, was slain and both the Havens and City of Umbar were invested. But the besieged Dúndedain held out, and some years later the Southron Federates were heavily defeated by King Ciryaher – so heavily, in fact, that for several hundred years afterwards none of the Haradrim dared to cross the Poros, and the wide lands between that river and the Harnen became subject to Gondor.

But in the course of time Gondor's hold over the Harad was loosened and eventually broken. In 1540 a second King of Gondor was slain by the Southrons, and even though King Hyarmendacil II avenged this death, Gondor could no longer prevent the Haradrim from raiding her frontiers. Moreover, it seems clear that from this point onwards there was an increasing measure of co-operation between the Haradrim and the Corsairs of Umbar (for Gondor had not long held Umbar, having lost it again in 1448). In any event the Haradrim themselves were in possession of Umbar by the nineteenth century; furthermore, in 1944 they made an alliance for the first time with an Easterling people (the Wainriders). So the net around Gondor drew ever tighter.

Yet although Gondor was eventually forced to evacuate the debatable land of Harondor, for many centuries her strength still proved sufficient to defend her shortened borders. And though there was intermittent raiding by land and sea throughout this period, it was not until almost a thousand years later that any further full-scale assault came from south of the Poros. It was Sauron himself – or rather, his emissaries – who brought this about; for in 2885 their whisperings stirred up the Haradrim, who invaded South Ithilien by their traditional route. But the Southron Army was heavily defeated and driven south in disarray (see BATTLE OF THE CROSSINGS OF POROS).

Nonetheless the Haradrim were never again quiescent while the Third Age lasted. Their incessant border-raiding bled Gondor's strength at a time when Sauron the Great was once more openly returning to power in Mordor; and in due course Sauron brought the Men of Harad fully under his sway. And during the War of the Ring, a great force of Haradrim, supported by many of the huge *mûmakil*, fought for Sauron's part at the Battle of the Pelennor Fields. But in that great clash at Gondor's gate, they were defeated yet again, and their hopes of plunder dashed once more. Nevertheless, the warriors of Haradwaith were not so easily subdued, and in the first decades of the Fourth Age there was fighting again along the Harnen.

Harad Road The main route between the Harad lands and Gondor. In the latter years of the Third Age, this road – originally built by Men of Gondor – was mainly used by her traditional enemies, the Haradrim, to speed their forces northwards.

Haradwaith 'Lands-of-the-South-peoples' (Sind.) All the lands south of the river Harnen. See also HARAD; HARADRIM.

Haranyë 'Century' (Q.) The name given by early Númenoreans to designate the hunred-year cycle observed in their calendar system of KINGS' RECKONING.

Hardbottle A village of the Shire, home of the Bracegirdle family of Hobbits.

Harding A night of King Théoden's Household. He perished in the Battle of the Pelennor Fields (March, 3019 Third Age).

Harding of the Hill The great-grandson of Samwise Gamgee (through his son Frodo Gardner). The Gardners of the Hill lived in

Bag End following Sam's departure from the Shire in 61 Fourth Age (1482 Shire Reckoning).

Hareth The daughter of Halmir chieftain of the HALADIN; she wedded Galdor the Tall of Dor-lómin, the son of Hador Lórindol, thus uniting the Second and Third Houses of the Edain. Her own sons were Húrin and Huor.

Harfoots One of the three breeds or clans of Hobbits. They were the 'most normal and representative variety of Hobbit, and far the most numerous . . . the most inclined to settle in one place'.[6] Harfoots also maintained the archaic habit of dwelling in burrows (or *smials*) for longer than other Hobbits. Most Shire-hobbits were of Harfoot stock.

See also Prologue (1).

Harlindon 'South-Lindon' (Sind.) That part of the (Elvish) land of Lindon which lay south of the Gulf of Lune. See also LINDON.

Harlond The Sindarin word for 'Southern-haven', used as the place name for at least two separate harbours in Middle-earth: a haven in the Gulf of Lune, and the landings on the Anduin which served Minas Tirith as a river-port.

Harma The Quenya or High-elven word for 'treasure', but more properly, the title of Tengwa number 11, which represented the sound (hard) *ch*, as in *loch*. This sound later became 'softened' to simple *h* (e.g., from *Rochand* to *Rohan*), except at the end of words and before the sound *t*.

See also AHA.

Harnen 'South-water' (Sind.) The river which was accounted the frontier between South Gondor and the lands of Harad. It rose in the southern range of the Ephel Dúath (Mountains of Shadow) and flowed westwards to find the sea some two hundred miles south of the Anduin delta.

Note: on all currently available maps of Third Age Middle-earth, this river, though marked, is not named.

Harondor 'South-Gondor' (Sind.) The name given in Gondor to all the lands between the rivers Poros and Harnen. In the early Third Age the Dúnedain of the South claimed these barren desert lands as part of their realm.[7] Later, Harondor became a contested region between Gondor and the Harad.

Harrowdale The high vale in the northern White Mountains, above which lay Dunharrow, the most ancient stronghold in Rohan.

Harry Goatleaf One of the Big Folk of Bree, employed in the year 3018 Third Age as a watcher on the western gate. Like one or two other Bree-men, he was of inferior sort and easily corrupted. He later became a common footpad and his fate is not recorded.

Harvestmath See HALIMATH.

Hasufel A notable horse of Rohan; a handsome grey whose rider, Gárulf, was slain during the War of the Ring, in a battle between Orcs of Isengard and the *éored* of Éomer, Third Marshal of the Mark. Éomer later lent Hasufel to Aragorn and the horse served him well.

Hathaldir the Young One of the Edain of the First House; he was a companion of BARAHIR in the last campaign made on Dorthonion in the years following the Dagor Bragollach.

Hathol The Grandson of Malach Aradan of the Third House of the Edain; the father of Hador Lórindol of Dor-lómin.

Hauberk A mail-jacket designed to protect the neck and upper body.

Haudh-en-Arwen 'Howe [Burial-mound]-of-the-Maiden-Queen' (Sind.) The burial tumulus, in Brethil, of HALETH. Also known as *Tûr Haretha* ('Haleth's Mound') in the early form of Adûnaic spoken by the Haladin.

Haudh-en-Elleth 'Mound-of-the-Elf-maid' (Sind.) The burial barrow of Finduilas daughter of Orodreth King of Nargothrond, at the Crossings of Teiglin. She was slain by Orcs.

Haudh-en-Gwanûr 'The-Mound-of-the-Twins' (Sind.) The barrow which covered the remains of the brothers Fastred and Folcred of Rohan (Third Age). It stood by the river Poros. See BATTLE OF THE CROSSINGS OF POROS.

Haudh-en-Ndengin 'Hill-of-Slain' (Sind.; also known as *Haudh-en-Nirnaeth*, 'Mound-of-Tears') The great mound of corpses – of Elves and Men alike – built by the Orcs of Angband after the Nirnaeth Arnoediad, in Anfauglith. All the slain of that battle were piled unceremoniously there and left to rot.

Haudh-en-Nirnaeth See preceding entry.

Haunted Mountain A translation of the Northern Mannish word *Dwimorberg*; being the name given in Rohan to a peak of the White Mountains, which overhung Dunharrow.

Haunted Pass Cirith Gorgor.

Haven of the Swans A translation of the Quenya name ALQUALONDË; the chief city and haven of the Sea-elves of Aman (the Teleri).

Havens of Sirion The secret harbour near the Sirion delta, founded by Elves after the Nirnaeth Arnoediad and the fall of the Falas.

Havens of the Falas EGLAREST and BRITHOMBAR. See also FALA-THRIM.

Haysend A village of southern Buckland. It was located at the mouth of the Withywindle, where this river flowed out of the Old Forest and became part of the Baranduin (Brandywine).

Hayward A family of Buckland-hobbits, traditional keepers and patrollers of the High Hay.

Headstrong A family of Shire-hobbits related to the Brandybucks.

Heathertoes A family of 'Big People' of Bree.

Heavy-handed An early Elvish epithet for the race of Men.

Heirs of Anárion The ruling dynasty of Gondor, from the death of Elendil at the end of the Second Age to the passing of King Eärnur (2050 Third Age). Anárion was the younger son of Elendil the Tall, who founded both Arnor and Gondor in the year 3320 Second Age. From that date onwards, Anárion ruled Gondor conjointly with his elder brother Isildur, until his own death at the siege of Barad-dûr in 3440. When Elendil himself died, one year later, the lordship of Arnor was taken up by Isildur, and Gondor's rule was then given to Meneldil, Anárion's son. From Meneldil, the Kings of Gondor descended in line unbroken for nearly a thousand years.

But throughout the second millennium of the Third Age, the maintenance of the Line of Anárion became ever more difficult, and at last open dispute flared between rival claimants to the Throne. There then ensued the disastrous Kin-strife, the civil war of Gondor which nearly brought an end to the South-kingdom. Nevertheless, the Heirs of Anárion endured until the days of Eärnur, the thirty-third King; after him the last link with Elendil was broken. For Eärnur rode away to Minas Morgul and never came back, and he left no son to succeed him. Gondor was thereafter ruled by her Stewards (of the House of Húrin).

See also LINES OF DESCENT; Appendix A I(ii).

Heirs of Isildur The ruling dynasty of Arnor (and Arthedain). Although the North-kingdom itself dwindled in both size and strength and eventually passed away altogether, its ruling House was maintained against all odds in line unbroken – until, at the very end of the Third Age, the last Heir of Isildur was able to restore both the Kingship in Arnor and the ancient union with the South-kingdom of Gondor.

Isildur was the elder son of Elendil the Tall, High-King of Arnor and Gondor and founder of both the Realms in Exile. Upon his father's death Isildur assumed the High-Kingship and in Year 2 Third Age journeyed to Arnor to take up the Sceptre. But he never reached the North-kingdom, and his youngest son Valandil – whose three brothers were also lost with Isildur – then became King. All the Kings of Arnor and Arthedain (and the subsequent Chieftains of the North) were descended father to son from Valandil. The last Heir of Isildur in the Third Age was Aragorn II, sixteenth Chieftain of the Dúnedain; he later became ruler of the Reunited Kingdom of Gondor and Arnor.

See also LINES OF DESCENT; Appendix A I(ii).

Helcar 'Icy' (Sind.) The name given in the lore of the Eldar to the great Inland Sea of the north and east of Middle-earth, formed in ancient days by the destruction of the Mountain of Illuin. The Lake of Cuivíenen, the 'Water of Awakening' of the Elves, was a bay of Helcar.

Helcaraxë 'Jaws of Ice' (Q.) The Northern Ice. Where the coasts of Aman and Middle-earth approached one another, in the Far North of the World, the Sea had frozen, and cliffs and bergs of ice and uncounted smaller floes ground together everlastingly. Only once in recorded history was a crossing on foot ever successfully completed: that undertaken by the Noldor of the Houses of Fingolfin and Finarfin, after these rebelling High-elves had been treacherously abandoned in Aman by Fëanor. (See *The Silmarillion* p. 90.)

Helevorn 'Black-glass' (Sind.) The lake in the extreme north of Thargelion, about which Caranthir of the Noldor made his realm.

Hells of Iron A translation of the Sindarin name *Angband*.

Helluin 'Blue Ice' (Sind.) The Elves' name for the Dog Star.

Helm Hammerhand From 2741–59 Third Age, the ninth King of Rohan and the last of the First Line of the Mark. A strong man of great size, Helm received the nickname 'Hammerhand' when he slew a renegade chieftain, Freca, with but one blow from his fist. This act precipitated civil war in Rohan. A force of Dunlendings led by Freca's son Wulf invaded the Mark and Helm's elder son Haleth was slain defending the King's Hall. The King himself was defeated at the Isen and forced to seek refuge within the Hornburg.

Helm's misfortunes unhappily coincided with the Long Winter of 2758–9 Third Age, when the hardships already suffered by the besieged were exacerbated by famine and severe cold. Helm's younger son Háma perished, and the King, in his grief, took to clothing himself in white and stalking his enemies across the snow on moonless nights. One morning Helm failed to return from a sortie, and was found standing on the Dike, stiff and still as a statue, stone dead.

The line of the Kings of Rohan was recommenced with Fréaláf, son of Helm's sister Hild.

See also Appendix A II 'The House of Eorl'.

Helmingas The 'Sons-of-Helm';[8] a name adopted by the Men of Westfold in Rohan as a tribute to the great warrior-king Helm Hammerhand, who died in defence of the Westfold during the Long Winter.

Helm of Hador See DRAGON-HELM (OF DOR-LÓMIN).

Helm's Deep The general name for the complex of fortifications at the head of the Deeping Coomb in the northern White Mountains; the hold was originally built by Gondor but later strengthened by Kings of Rohan. The 'Deep' itself was the narrow and precipitous gorge of Aglarond, an ancient refuge and strong-place of the Westfold. To guard the entrance to the gorge (Helm's Gate), various defensive walls and towers were built, the chief of which was the Hornburg. It was in this fortress that the renowned Helm Hammerhand took refuge during the Long Winter of 2758–9 Third Age.

See also BATTLE OF THE HORNBURG.

Helm's Dike The great fosse or defensive ditch across the head of the Deeping Coomb; the outermost of the fortifications known collectively as Helm's Deep.

Helm's Gate The entrance to the gorge of Aglarond, guarded by the Deeping Wall and its towers. The gorge itself, together with its complex of fortifications, was known as Helm's Deep.

Henneth Annûn 'Window of the Sunset' (Sind.) An outpost of Gondor built in the contested province of Ithilien during the latter years of the Third Age. For by that time (over a century before the War of the Ring), it had at last become apparent that Gondor could no longer maintain a foothold in North Ithilien: Mordor-orcs roamed the country and the few remaining settlements there were heavily fortified. Therefore, foreseeing the type of warfare that Gondor would need to employ in order to make Ithilien a dangerous gain for the Enemy, Steward Túrin II constructed hidden refuges among the uplands and forests of that fair country.

Of these secret places, the longest-guarded and best-concealed was Henneth Annûn, a complex of natural caves and passages hidden behind a high waterfall which faced west over the Anduin vale. A secret passage led up to the caves from the forest below, and a further tunnel gave access to the rock platform at the head of the waterfall. The refuge was kept amply provisioned and provided an excellent base from which the Rangers of Ithilien were able to foray against the Enemy.

Hensday See HEVENSDAY.

Herblore of the Shire A notable treatise on botany (and significant contribution to Shire-scholarship), written by Meriadoc Brandybuck sometime during the early Fourth Age. Unfortunately, the work as a whole has not survived, save for a short extract which appears in the Prologue to *The Lord of the Rings*.

See also PIPE-WEED.

Herefara A knight of the Household of King Théoden of Rohan, slain on the Fields of the Pelennor (March, 3019 Third Age).

Herion From 2116–48 Third Age, the third Ruling Steward of Gondor.

Herubrand One of the house-carls of King Théoden of Rohan, slain in the Battle of the Pelennor Fields (March, 3019 Third Age).

Herugrim The name of the sword borne by King Théoden of the Mark. It was kept in a scabbard richly ornamented with gold and beryl-stones.

Herumor 'Black-lord' (Sind.) See FUINUR.

Herunúmen 'Lord-of-the-West' The Quenya equivalent of the Adûnaic title ADUNAKHÔR.

Hevensday A translation of the Quenya word *Menelya*, used as the fifth day of the week in the Shire Reckoning. In its original form this word was spelt *Hevenesdei*, but by the end of the Third Age it had evolved into *Hevensday* (or *Hensday*).

Hewer of Caves A translation of the Khuzdul words *felak-gundu*, rendered (in Sindarin) *Felagund*. See FINROD FELAGUND.

Hidden City Gondolin.

Hidden King Thingol Greycloak.

Hidden Kingdom Doriath.

Hidden Rock A translation of the Sindarin word *Gondolin*, itself a punning rendition of the older Quenya name *Ondolindë* ('Stone-song').

Hiding of Valinor A translation of the Quenya phrase *Nurtalë Valinóreva*, meaning the period after the raising of the Sun in which the Valar fortified and concealed their land.

Highday The seventh (and chief) day of the week in the Shire Reckoning, equivalent to *Valanya* (Q.) in Kings' Reckoning. An earlier form of the word was *Highdei*.

High-elves A translation of the Quenya term *Tareldar*; properly speaking, the title High-elves should apply to all the *Calaquendi* of Eldamar and Valimar. However, in translations from the Red Book, and following the usage of the Dúnedain, the term has been primarily used to indicate those of the *Noldor* (the Second Kindred) who returned to Middle-earth in Exile.

See also ELDAR.

High Faroth See TAUR-EN-FAROTH.

High Hay A great hedge built by the Hobbits of Buckland around their eastern border, in order to prevent the encroachment of the Old Forest. It extended nearly twenty miles in a loop from the Great East Road in the north to the confluence of the Withywindle and Baranduin (Brandywine) in the south. The Hay was carefully tended, several feet thick, and virtually impenetrable.

High Kings (of the Dúnedain) The title *High King* existed only in Middle-earth, and was first assumed by Elendil the Tall, son of Amandil of Andúnië, after the fall of Númenor and the return of the Faithful, whom he led, to Middle-earth. As it implies, the title refers to a sovereign supreme over other sovereigns, an upward extension of the feudal system. After Elendil this title was briefly borne by his elder son Isildur, but with Isildur's death lapsed for a period of three thousand years. It then was restored by Aragorn II (Elessar).

High Kings (of the Noldor) Although the Vanyarin lord Ingwë was always accounted High King over all Elves, the Noldor who returned to Middle-earth instituted a separate High-kingship, to mark their severance of all the old allegiances. The first High King to be proclaimed was Fingolfin; for although both he and his (older) half-brother Fëanor were the sons of Finwë (who did not go into exile), and were the two leaders of that revolt, no agreement was reached concerning the question of who was to be the final arbiter of all policy; and the hosts journeyed separately to Middle-earth. But shortly afterwards the problem solved itself with Fëanor's death, and Maedhros his son offered the High-kingship to Fingolfin, who bore it for more than four and a half centuries before perishing in the Dagor Bragollach. On Fingolfin's death, the title passed to his elder son Fingon; and when Fingon was slain, twenty years afterwards, at the Nirnaeth Arnoediad, his younger brother Turgon (of Gondolin) succeeded him – though by now the High-kingship was purely a nominal title, for the Elf-kingdoms were well-nigh destroyed. When Turgon himself also perished, in the fall of Gondolin, thirty-nine years after the Nirnaeth, the title passed to Fingon's son Ereinion Gil-galad.

Gil-galad was the longest to reign of all High-kings of the Noldor. He took the title before the ending of the First Age, as is told above, and did not relinquish it until his death, in combat with Sauron, at the end of the Age which followed. He therefore reigned for more than three thousand years. His death marked the extinction of the title, which was never resuscitated. Henceforth, the leadership of the remaining Eldar, both Noldor and Sindar, was given to Elrond of

Imladris, who at the great Battle of Dagorlad had been Gil-galad's Herald. (See following diagram.)

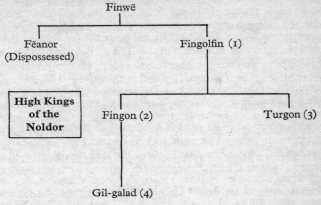

High Speech Quenya.

Hild The sister of Helm Hammerhand, ninth King of Rohan, and mother of Freáláf (Hildeson), tenth King.

Hildor 'Aftercomers' (Sind.) An Elvish name for the race of Men.

Hildórien The name given by the Elves to that region of the east of Middle-earth wherein the race of Men was said to have originated.

Hill of Erech See STONE OF ERECH.

Hill of Hearing A translation of the Sindarin words *Amon Llâw*. See AMON HEN.

Hill of Ilmarin Mount Oiolossë, in the Undying Lands – highest of the Mountains of Valinor (the Pelóri). Upon its summit, in the great palace of Ilmarin, dwelled the Lord of the Valar, Manwë, and his spouse, Elbereth.

Hill of Sight, Hill of the Eye Two common translations of the Sindarin name *Amon Hen*.

Hills of Evendim A separate range of hills in north central Eriador. They sheltered the beautiful Lake Evendim, or *Nenuial* ('Lake-twilight'), and guarded Elendil's City of Annúminas, which lay by the southern shores of the lake.

Himlad 'Cool plain' (Sind.) The northernmost part of East Beleriand, the land which lay between Aros, Celon and the Hills of Himring. Until the Dagor Bragollach Himlad was the realm of the brothers Celegorm and Curufin.

Himring 'Ever-cold' (Sind.) The tallest of the range of hills which formed the northern boundary of the land of Himlad (see preceding entry). Upon its summit Maedhros, eldest of the seven sons of Fëanor, built a great fortress, to guard against the evil from the north. This fortress fell in the Nirnaeth Arnoediad, and the lands it had guarded became infested by Morgoth's forces.

Hirgon An errand-rider of Gondor during the War of the Ring. He was sent from Steward Denethor to Théoden, King of Rohan, with the traditional token of impending war, the Red Arrow. Hirgon never returned to Minas Tirith, being slain in Anórien by ambushing Orcs.

Hírilorn 'Tree of the Lady' (Sind.) The name given by the Sindar of Doriath to the three-trunked beech-tree in which Lúthien Tinúviel was imprisoned by her father Thingol, in order to prevent her joining Beren on the Quest of the Silmaril; however, as is told elsewhere, Lúthien escaped from this arboreal prison, and followed Beren, and rescued him from Sauron's clutches.

Hirluin the Fair The Lord of Pinnath Gelin in the Langstrand of Gondor at the time of the War of the Ring. To the aid of Minas Tirith he led three hundred of his own green-clad men, but himself perished in the Battle of the Pelennor Fields.

Hisilómë 'Land of Mist' (Q.) The High-elves' original name for the land known to the Grey-elves as HITHLUM.

Hísimë 'Misty' (Q.) The eleventh month in the Kings' Reckoning, and the eighth in the New Reckoning of the Fourth Age. The Sindarin equivalent, used only by the Dúnedain, was *Hithui*.

Hithaeglir '[Chain of] Misty-peaks' (Sind.) The Grey-elven name for the great range of mountains known, in the Common Tongue, as the MISTY MOUNTAINS.

Hither lands, Hither Shores See NEVRAST.

Hithlain 'Mist-threads' (Sind.) A substance woven by Elves of Lothlórien and used by them for many purposes, especially the making of ropes. The name aptly describes the fine texture of these ropes, as reported by Samwise (himself having a family interest in the art of rope-making). They were grey in colour, light, and packed surprisingly closely. They were also extremely strong and, like many things of Elvish craft, served their bearers well in unexpected ways.

Hithlum 'Land of Mist' (Sind.) The most north-westerly of all the Noldorin realms of Middle-earth, founded by Fingolfin the High King after the Battle-Under-Stars, and ruled by him until his death in the Dagor Bragollach. Hithlum was a great, enclosed plain, fenced on the south, east and west by the ranges of Ered Wethrin and Ered Lómin, and open only to the north. It was fifty leagues wide at its widest point.

Together with its southern provinces, Dor-lómin and Mithrim, Hithlum was held by the Noldor and their allies until after the Dagor Bragollach, for the mountain-shield held back the advancing tide from Angband; even the death of Fingolfin did not bring about its fall. But fifteen years after the Dagor Bragollach came the terrible day of the Nirnaeth Arnoediad, and on that field well nigh all the strength of Hithlum was slain. This last of the northern realms then fell to Morgoth, for there were no Elves or Men left to defend it.

Hithui See HÍSIMË.

Hlothram In original (as opposed to translated) Hobbit-speech, the forename *Hlothram* meant 'Cottager'. This name has been translated from the Red Book as *Cotman*. See COTTON.

Hlothran In untranslated Hobbit-speech the element *hloth* meant a simple (i.e., two-roomed) cottage. The suffix -*ran* indicated a group or cluster of dwellings, and therefore the full word indicated a village of such cottages. It was a reasonably common Shire-name and has been translated from the Red Book as *Cotton*.

'The Hoard' This poem is No. 14 in the collection of such Hobbit-verses as have been assembled under the title *The Adventures of Tom Bombadil*. It is thought to have been modelled on fragments of tales, both Elvish and Númenorean, found by Hobbits in Rivendell – or passed on to them second-hand by others with some knowledge of the legends of the First Age.

The poem concerns the destiny of a hoard of Elvish treasure which is abandoned by the Elves and then passes to an ancient Dwarf, who increases its worth by his own labours, becoming so absorbed in his wealth and skills that he makes easy prey for the inevitable Dragon – which dispossesses him, taking the hoard for his own. Years later, the Dragon is slain by a Man, who founds his own kingdom on the

Dragon-hoard. But he grows old and heartless, and his gold becomes more to him than his realm or his people. He, in his turn, is over-thrown – and goes to his grave with the secret of the hiding-place of the Hoard.

Hoarwell The river Mitheithel, which rose in the Ettenmoors in northern Eriador and flowed south to join the Bruinen (Loudwater); just above Tharbad the enlarged Hoarwell merged with the Glanduin and the river was then known as the Greyflood (or Gwathlo).

Hobbiton One of the older villages of the Shire. It sprawled around the Hill of Hobbiton, near the Pool of Bywater, in the Westfarthing. Both Bywater and Hobbiton formed a single community.

Hobbitry-in-arms The Shire-militia, led by the Thain when oc-casion demanded. As occasion did so only infrequently, the Shire-muster was a rare enough sight, though most Hobbits had some skill with weapons and many were accomplished archers.

Hobbits (diminished form of *Holbytlan* 'Hole-builders') For a full account of the origins, histories and customs of this remarkable people – who play so notable a part in the great War of the Ring – readers of *The Tolkien Companion* are firmly advised to refer to available translations of the Red Book of Westmarch. For in addition to being the prime source of information about the Third Age of Middle-earth, this most venerable of Hobbit-chronicles is, of course, the chief surviving repository of all Hobbit-lore. Moreover, as the Red Book was written by Hobbits, and concerns the events of the War *as seen by* the most notable Hobbits of all time, not surprisingly it contains more revelations (intentionally or otherwise) about the Halfling folk than any other document in existence.

Accordingly, for an account of Hobbits' origins and customs, see the Prologue to *The Lord of the Rings*; for information concerning their language and names, see Appendix F.

See also KÛD-DÛKAN.

Hob Gammidge The son of Wiseman Gamwich of Tighfield, and the founder of the (Tighfield) Gamgees' rope-making business. He was known as 'Old Gammidgy'. Hob married Rowan, daughter of Holman the Greenhanded of Hobbiton, and their son Hobson con-tinued with the family trade.

See also GAMGEE; GAMWICH.

Hob Hayward A Hobbit of Buckland. (The Haywards were presumably the traditional keepers and patrollers of the High Hay – as their name signifies.)

Hobson 'Roper' Gamgee The son of Hob Gammidge and the grandfather of Samwise. He was the first of the family to take the name *Gamgee* (doubtless from his father's nickname of 'Gammidgy').
See also GAMGEE; GAMWICH.

Holbytla 'Hole-builder' An archaic word in the tongue of northern Men. The word *Hobbit* is thought to be a 'worn-down' version of this term.
See also Appendix F.

Holdwine The name given in Rohan to Meriadoc Brandybuck.

Holfast Gardner The son of Frodo Gardner and the grandson of Samwise Gamgee. He inherited Bag End from his father.

Hollin The name given among western Men to the High-elven realm of EREGION, built and destroyed during the Second Age. It was so named because holly was the token of the Elven-smiths of that land.

Hollowbold A translation into Mannish speech of the Dwarvish (Khuzdul) name *Tumunzahar*[9] (Sind. *Nogrod*), being the more southerly of the two great Dwarvish cities of the Blue Mountains.

Holman Cotton The son of Cotman of Bywater and Rose ('Greenhand'). He was known as 'Long Hom'.

Holman Greenhand The son of Halfred Greenhand and the grandson of the legendary Holman the Greenhanded of Hobbiton. Young Holman was Bilbo Baggins' first gardener at Bag End, and before he retired, he passed on his skills to his cousin Hamfast Gamgee (formerly of Tighfield), who taught them in turn to his own son Samwise.

Holman the Greenhanded The fabled Hobbit-gardener of Hobbiton, founder of the renowned Greenhand clan (through his son Halfred Greenhand).

Holy Mountain Oiolossë.

Horn A knight of the Household of King Théoden of Rohan, slain in the Battle of the Pelennor Fields (March, 3019 Third Age).

Hornblower A Southfarthing family of Shire-hobbits.

Hornburg The principal fortress of Helm's Deep, built early in the Third Age by Men of Gondor and later strengthened by Kings of Rohan. It commanded the entrance to the Deep, being situated upon a spur of rock which dominated the Deeping fortifications. The Hornburg consisted of a single tower or keep, surrounded by high walls of stone; its name stemmed from the fact that 'a trumpet sounded upon the tower echoed in the Deep behind, as if armies long-forgotten were issuing to war from caves beneath the hills.'[10]

See also BATTLE OF THE HORNBURG.

Horn-call of Buckland Although Hobbits of the Shire were generally rather complacent about possible dangers from 'outside', their kinfolk living in Buckland, on the far side of the river, did not as a rule share this sense of security. The High Hay was one indication of the greater precautions Bucklanders took against unauthorized entry; they also preserved the habit of locking their doors at night, and maintained an ancient general alarum, a swooping horn-call, only blown at times of urgent need.

House of Durin The descendants of Durin the Deathless, greatest of all Dwarves.

House of Elros The line of the Kings of Númenor, commenced by ELROS TAR-MINYATUR and ended with Tar-Palantir. (Ar-Pharazôn was a usurper, from a junior branch of this dynasty.)

House of Eorl The *Eorlingas*, 'Sons-of-Eorl'; the Line of the Kings of Rohan, descended from Eorl the Young, last Lord of Éothéod and first King of the Mark.

House of Hador The Third House of the Edain. See HADOR.

House of Húrin The Line of the Stewards of Gondor, descended from Húrin of Emyn Arnen, Steward to Minardil (twenty-fifth King) and a man of noble ancestry. The Stewardship later became largely hereditary and, after Steward Pelendur, the Rod of Office passed as a matter of course to the eldest son. The banner of the House was plain silver with no device or marking.

See also RULING STEWARDS.

House of Ransom A translation of the Sindarin words BAR-EN-DANWEDH.

House of the Golden Flower (of Gondolin) See GLORFINDEL.

Houses of the Edain The Three Kindreds of the Atani, the Elf-friends, who came across the Blue Mountains into Beleriand before the end of the First Age and fought Morgoth as allies of the Eldar. The First House was that led into Beleriand by Bëor the Old; the Second was the people known as the HALADIN. The Third was that kindred led into Beleriand by the chieftain Marach; this was the most numerous and hardy of all the Houses of the Edain, but it afterwards became known as the House of Hador, after its greatest chieftain, Hador Lórindol.

The First House, the People of Bëor, dwelt for a while in Estolad, but later journeyed for the most part into the far north, to Dorthonion, where in Ladros they made a realm in alliance with Angrod and Aegnor, of the House of Finarfin. They were savagely attacked during the Dagor Bragollach, and though they maintained a presence there for some few years afterwards (see BARAHIR), were eventually overwhelmed and driven out. The survivors came eventually to Brethil, where they sought sanctuary among the Haladin, and to Dor-lómin, where they were received by Hador's people. But Barahir, their last chieftain, and all who remained with him, were slain (save Barahir's son BEREN, who of all the First House is the most renowned in song and story).

The Haladin, as is told elsewhere, came by dangerous paths to Brethil, west of Doriath, and there founded a woodland realm. But though in later days many grievous affairs touched them, they remained unconquered by Morgoth. The most renowned of this Kindred of Men is the Lady HALETH, who led her people on the perilous journey, from Thargelion – where the Haladin had been well nigh wiped out – to West Beleriand.

The Third House was the most renowned in the wars with Morgoth. HADOR LÓRINDOL ('the Goldenhaired') was the first Lord of Dor-lómin, and the chief ally of Fingolfin the High King of the Noldor. Warriors of his House served the Noldor, and garrisoned the most dangerous outpost of all: the Eithel Sirion. Hador himself was slain during the Dagor Bragollach, in defence of this fortress, and GALDOR THE TALL, his elder son then took the lordship of his House. Galdor fell in battle seven years after his father, and was succeeded by HÚRIN THALION, his own elder son. And Húrin – the greatest warrior of all the Edain of the First Age – led the last stand of the Men of Dor-lómin at the Nirnaeth Arnoediad, in which his brother Huor was slain; but was himself captured and grievously used by Morgoth. At this time Dor-lómin fell to the enemy, and the survivors of the Third House were enslaved by Easterlings allied to Morgoth.

Most tragic of all the heroic Edain of the First Age was TÚRIN TURAMBAR. Túrin's grandfather Galdor had wedded Hareth of the Haladin; their sons were Húrin and Huor. Húrin wedded Morwen Eledhwen of the First House – and *their* children were Túrin and Nienor. The blood of all Three Houses therefore ran in Túrin's veins. (His story is told in many places and needs no recapitulation here.)

TUOR son of Huor was similarly descended, for his father had wedded Rían daughter of Belegund of the First House; she was the cousin of Morwen Eledhwen. But Tuor's story is happier than that of his cousins Túrin and Nienor: and through him the blood-lines of all Three Houses of the Edain, allied with the House of Fingolfin of the Noldor, were passed on, and survived the Wars, and became linked with the descent from Thingol and Lúthien, and (after the passing of two full Ages) with the Line of Finarfin, becoming the most royal Line of Descent of Middle-earth.

Houses of the Dead The HALLS OF MANDOS.

Hrívë (Q.) The fifth of the six 'seasons' of the ancient High-elven *loa* or year. *Hrívë* (Sind. *rhîw*) corresponded to winter (although the Eldarin *loa* actually concluded with a further 'season': *coirë*, 'stirring').

See also CALENDAR OF IMLADRIS.

Huan 'Mighty-Hound' (Sind.) The Hound of Valinor, the greatest and noblest dog ever to walk in Middle-earth, Companion of Beren and Lúthien, and Slayer of the Wolf Carcharoth. He was in his origins the Hound of the Vala Oromë; but far back in the Elder Days Oromë gave him to Celegorm of the Noldor; and Celegorm, when he came to Middle-earth in exile, brought the great animal with him.

As is well known, Huan served his second master faithfully for many hundreds of years. But the Hound was not fated to remain with Celegorm. For during the years which followed the Dagor Bragollach (and the dispossession of Celegorm), his path was crossed by Lúthien and Beren; as a result of these encounters Huan abandoned Celegorm, who had now fallen into evil ways, and allied himself to Beren and Lúthien – and indeed without his aid they could never have entered Angband, nor stolen a Silmaril in fulfilment of the vow made by Beren to Lúthien's father Thingol. During these adventures Huan slew many foes – among them the Werewolf-lord

Draugluin – and with his enchantments enabled his companions to escape detection. But at the ending of the quest, there came a meeting long prophesied – with the greatest Wolf of all, Carcharoth. Huan fought and slew the Wolf of Angband, but was himself mortally wounded in the fight, as indeed was Beren of the Edain.

Hunthor One of the Haladin; he was a companion of Túrin Turambar in the expedition against the Dragon Glaurung, but was killed – by accident – before he had been able to strike a blow.

Huor The younger son of Galdor of Dor-lómin and brother of HÚRIN THALION. Huor wedded Rían, daughter of Belegund (of the First House of the Edain); their son was Tuor, who wedded Idril Turgon's daughter. Huor himself did not live to see this, for he was slain, fighting valiantly alongside his brother, at the Nirnaeth Arnoediad. But through him the House of Hador was perpetuated, and linked with still mightier Houses, of the Eldar.

Huorns Sentient trees (or possibly regressed Ents) of Fangorn Forest, who dwelt only in the deepest dales of that land. Like the Great Willow of the Old Forest in Eriador, they were 'limb-lithe' and could move very swiftly from place to place, wrapped in tree-shadow. They were extremely dangerous – most of all to Orcs, whom they hated with an unbridled passion. Huorns were, however, under the control of true Ents.

Húrin Thalion The greatest warrior of all the Edain of the First Age, Lord of Dor-lómin after Galdor his father, brother of Huor, and father of Túrin Turambar and Nienor 'Níniel'. He was born in Dor-lómin, in the house of his father, some fifteen years before the Dagor Bragollach, in a time of peace. Both he and his younger brother Huor, represented a mingling of the chiefly lines of descent of both the Second and Third Houses of the Edain, for their mother was Hareth of the Haladin. But when Húrin was still barely come to full stature, Morgoth unleashed sudden war, and both the sons of Galdor went east to fight. As is told elsewhere, they escaped capture (or worse) and came by lofty paths to the Hidden City of Gondolin, the first of all Men to do so (though not the last), and so became known to Turgon the king. Thus the foundations were laid of an alliance which would outlast the Age.

Returning to Dor-lómin, to the house of Galdor their father, the brothers refused to reveal where they had been. (Nevertheless, before long, word came to Morgoth of the mysterious disappearance of these young princes of Men; and for the first time he paid attention to Húrin.) It was at about this time that Galdor was slain in a sudden attack upon Hithlum; but Húrin took the leadership and briskly repelled the invaders. He was now Lord of Dor-lómin. Eight years later he led the entire warriordom of his realm to the Nirnaeth Arnoediad, to fight on behalf of the High King in the set-piece battle which was intended to crush Morgoth's armies for ever. But it was the Eldar and the Edain who were destroyed on that dreadful day; and only by the valour of the Men of Dor-lómin, led by Húrin and Huor, was anything at all saved from the wreck. For they covered the retreat of the army of Gondolin. Huor and all the Edain who were in that rearguard were killed; but Húrin fought to the last. Then he was captured (by the special order of Morgoth) and brought, a prisoner, to Angband.

There is no need to dwell on the horror of that place, nor the steadfastness with which Húrin faced his chief Enemy. So high was his courage that Morgoth forbore to have him tortured, for he knew that this warrior of Men would defy him to the last. Instead, therefore, he cursed Húrin, and his children, and set him in a high place, chained to a chair of stone, to watch the world wheel by; while in the world beyond, Morgoth's forces went whither they would, reaping the last fruits of the Nirnaeth.

For twenty-eight years Húrin 'the Steadfast' (*Thalion*, a surname bestowed upon him by the Eldar, carries this meaning) endured his slow torment. Then he was released, to go where he might. This was not charity, for Morgoth hated him as much as ever; yet he knew that Húrin might yet betray a secret or two if left to wander. And so it proved. Húrin came to Gondolin – for whom he had fought to the last, beyond all hope for himself – and inadvertently revealed its whereabouts to Morgoth's spies. Then he went to Nargothrond and found it a ruin; and then to Brethil, where he learned of the fates which had overtaken his son and daughter – and found again his wife Morwen, whom he had not seen for nearly thirty years; and he held her in his arms before she died, of grief and long weariness. Then Húrin's bitterness was complete. Finally he journeyed to Doriath to reproach Thingol for the fate of his kin, but repented of his anger and departed, never again to be seen by any Elf or Man. Soon afterwards he slew himself, the last victim of the curse upon his line. Here indeed was a man who deserved a better fate.

Húrin of Emyn Arnen The founder of the House of the Stewards of Gondor (and the Steward to Minardil, twenty-fifth King).

See HOUSE OF HÚRIN; RULING STEWARDS.

Húrin I From 2204–44 Third Age, the fifth Ruling Steward of Gondor.

Húrin II From 2605–28, the fourteenth Ruling Steward of Gondor.

Húrin the Tall The Warden of the Keys of Minas Tirith and the chief official of that City (after the Steward). During the War of the Ring, he commanded the City while the Army of Gondor advanced to the Black Gate of Mordor.

Hwesta The Quenya (or High-elven) name for 'breeze', but more properly, the title of Tengwa number 12, which represented the voiceless *w* sound (as in *white*). In Sindarin (or Grey-elven) usage, this letter was employed to indicate the (harder) sound *chw*.

Hwesta Sindarinwa The title of Tengwa number 34, one of the additional (i.e., later) letters of the Fëanorian alphabet. Like letter 12 (see previous entry), it represented the sound of voiceless *w*, being an alternative for this letter used only by the Grey-elves – as the Sindar employed the older letter 12 to signify the typically Grey-elven sound *chw*.

Hyarmen The Quenya name for 'south', but more properly, the title of Tengwa number 33, which represented the sound *hy-* in those languages which required it. It also stood for (directional) South, even to those peoples who did not speak Quenya and had not learned the Tengwar.

Hyarmendacil I (born Ciryaher) From 1015–1149 Third Age, the fifteenth King of Gondor, the last of her four 'Ship-kings', and the mightiest war-leader in Gondor's history. Ciryaher's father, Ciryandil, was slain by the Haradrim, in 1015, at the beginning of the long siege of Umbar, which had been repossessed by Gondor some eighty years before. However, since Umbar could not be captured while Gondor commanded the seas, the new king awaited a propitious moment before attempting to raise the siege by counter-attack. By the year 1050 Gondor's strength was rebuilt, and Ciryaher crossed the Harnen with a great army; while at the same time, his fleets disembarked another host on the coasts of the Harad. The Haradrim were so severely defeated in the ensuing battle that for several centuries afterwards they posed no further threat to the South-kingdom.

To celebrate this victory, one of the greatest in Gondor's history, Ciryaher adopted the royal name *Hyarmendacil*, 'Victor-of-the-South'.

See also Appendix A I(iv).

Hyarmendacil II (born Vinyarion) From 1540–1621 Third Age, the twenty-fourth King of Gondor. Like his most illustrious forbear, he won a great victory over the Men of Harad (in the year 1551); and in token of this, Vinyarion took the royal name Hyarmendacil II.

Hyarmentir 'Guardian-of-the-South' (Q.) The name given in Eldamar to the second highest of all the Pelóri, the great mountain which stood far to the south, opposite the land of Avathar.

Notes

1 A historical parallel can perhaps be seen in the subdivisions of the Celts: the *Goidels* were shorter and darker than the *Gaels*, and their languages, though still related, were different.
2 It is of course possible that the Woodmen of Mirkwood (Third Age) were in some way descended from the Haladin.
3 *Silmarillion* p. 146.
4 In other words, classic guerilla warfare of the age-old sort.
5 The conditions obtaining in *Purgatory* (or even 'Limbo') would thus appear to incorporate a memory of this ancient tradition.
6 Prologue I.
7 Which may explain its name – or the other way about.
8 Cf. *Eorlingas*, 'Sons-of-Eorl'.
9 See also *Silmarillion* p. 335.
10 Book III Chap. 7.

Iant Iaur 'Old Bridge' (Sind.) The Bridge of Esgalduin. It was the place at which the traveller crossed from the dreadful valley of Nan Dungortheb into the more peaceful land of Dor Dínen. A league to the south lay the northern eaves of Neldoreth, protected from all evil by the unseen Girdle of Melian. The Elven-river Esgalduin, the river of Doriath, also possessed virtues which hindered the crossing of evil.

Iarwain Ben-adar The oldest of all names given to that enigmatic being known (to Buckland Hobbits) as 'Tom Bombadil'. It is Sindarin (Grey-elven) in form, being the name used by Elves of the West of Middle-earth during the Elder Days. Its meaning is equivalent to 'Old Fatherless'.

Iavas See YÁVIË.

Ibun One of the 'Lesser-Dwarves' (*Noegyth Nibin*) of Beleriand; he was a son of MÎM.

Ice Bay of Forochel An enormous bay which cut deep into the shores of northern Middle-earth.

An observation of the topography of this region, as depicted on various maps originally made in the late Third Age, suggests that at some time in the remote past the Sea broke through the land which then lay to the north of the Blue Mountains, and flooded far into the wastes of Forodwaith. If so, then such a dramatic change in the shape of the lands may well be connected with the destruction of Morgoth the Enemy at the end of the First Age – which is known to have had catastrophic consequences for that region. For the Great Battle in which Morgoth was overthrown by the Valar itself unleashed titanic forces which not only obliterated his evil fortress of Thangorodrim, but also inundated Beleriand, the land of the Elves in the West of Middle-earth. Even the Dwarf-cities of the Blue Mountains were destroyed in the cataclysm.

Is it therefore unreasonable to assume that, during the late Third Age, the waters of the Ice Bay lay over what had once been Morgoth's ancient realm of Angband? This is known to have been located in the Far North, and the icy colds of that region (which still lingered in the Third Age) were said to be an inheritance from his evil realm. And since Beleriand and Númenor were both drowned as a result of great wickedness, one may reasonably speculate that the first evil realm of Middle-earth was also plunged under the cleansing Sea.

Note: on all currently available maps of Middle-earth, the name of the Ice Bay is placed in a misleading location, indicating only its southernmost inlet.

See also LOSSOTH.

Idril Celebrindal The daughter of King Turgon of Gondolin; she became the wife of TUOR, one of the royal Edain – in one of the only three unions ever to take place between Elves and Men – and bore him a son: Eärendil. Together with her husband and her infant son, she escaped from Gondolin during its last hours, and came, after much wandering, to the small Elf-colony which was secretly being maintained in the south of Beleriand, near the Sirion delta. Here, in Arvernien, she dwelt thereafter with Tuor and Eärendil, until Tuor became old; and then, with him, Idril went aboard the ship Eärrámë and sailed into the West, to be lost to the tales of the Elves. But the Line of Gondolin was passed by her to her son Eärendil, and he passed it to his sons Elros and Elrond, and they to all who came after.

Note: her surname *Celebrindal* means 'Silver-foot' in the Grey-elven tongue.

Illuin The name given by Eldarin tradition to the more northerly of the two Lamps of the Valar, made at the Beginning of Arda to light the world. The other Lamp was *Ormal*, in the southern hemisphere; Illuin stood in the north; its form was that of a huge mountain, from the summit of which blazed the Lamp itself. This, like Ormal, had been wrought by the Smith of the Valar, Aulë. Both Lamps, together with their pillars, were destroyed by Morgoth (*Melkor* as he was then known), in a war against the Valar which broke out before even Elves had walked in Middle-earth. The resulting destruction was immense, and – not for the first time – the shape of the World was marred. Where hitherto the Mountain of Illuin had stood, there afterwards stretched a great lake or inland sea. Its name was Helcar.

Illuin and Ormal were never rebuilt, and the Valar, whose first dwelling in Middle-earth (Almaren) had also been destroyed, now removed to Aman in the West, where they founded Valinor. The 'Blessed Realm' was lit, not by Lamps, but by the Two Trees; but Middle-earth was illuminated during all this time by nothing save 'ancient starlight'. Only after the destruction of the Two Trees did the Valar again devise some method of bringing light to Middle-earth. And then they made, first the Moon, Isil, and afterwards the Sun, Anar. And both were set for ever beyond the reach of Melkor.

Ilmarë One of the Maiar. She was the Handmaid of Varda (Elbereth).

Ilmarin 'Mansion of the High Airs' (Q.) The name given by the Eldar to the high palace of the Valar King and Queen, Manwë and Elbereth; it stood atop Mount Oiolossë, highest of the Mountains of Valinor (the *Pelóri*).

Ilmen The Heavens.[1]

Ilúvatar 'Father-of-All' (Q.) The Creator. Called also *Eru*, 'The One' (Sind.).

Imlach One of the early Edain, of the Third House. He was a younger son of Marach, and the father of AMLACH.

Imlad Morgul 'Vale of Sorcery' (Sind.) One of the western valleys of the Mountains of Shadow, lying only twenty miles north-east of the bridges of Osgiliath. It was guarded by the evil tower of Minas Morgul and watered by the *Morgulduin* – once the Ithilduin, flowing gently down through Ithilien to the Anduin. The valley, the tower and the river were all renamed in Gondor after the fall of Minas Ithil to the Nazgûl (in 2002 Third Age).

It was said that the waters of the Morgulduin were deadly, and that the loathsome white flowers in the meadows of the valley produced noxious vapours; rottenness and decay filled Imlad Morgul. At the end of the Third Age the vegetation there was burned to the rock and the evil tower was thrown down for ever.

Imladris 'Deep-cloven-valley' (Sind.) The original Elvish name for the valley of Rivendell.

Imloth Melui A vale in the province of Lossarnach in Gondor; its woods and wild roses were locally renowned.

Imrahil The Prince of Dol Amroth; at the time of the War of the Ring, the chief nobleman of Gondor after the House of Húrin (the Line of the Ruling Stewards). He was the son of Adrahil and brother of the Lady Finduilas, wife of Steward Denethor II.

Imrahil was also a mighty warrior – and to the Siege of Minas Tirith he brought seven hundred sturdy Dúnedain of Belfalas, strengthened by a company of mounted men. (This latter force constituted Gondor's sole cavalry arm until the arrival of the Rohirrim.) He commanded the City when both the Steward and his heir, Faramir, were stricken during the Siege, and later fought gallantly in battle on the Pelennor Fields and before the Black Gate of Mordor. His daughter Lothíriel later wedded King Éomer of Rohan.

Note: although Imrahil was of unmixed Dúnedain lineage, his name was of Númenorean (i.e., Adûnaic) form – unlike most folk of Gondor, whose names were of Sindarin (Grey-elven) form.

See also DOL AMROTH.

Incánus The name given to Gandalf the Grey by the Men of Harad.

Indis the Fair A maiden of the Vanyar, and one of the only two of this 'Highest' of all Eldarin kindreds ever to be mentioned in records. She is said to have been akin to Ingwë the High King of all the Elves. Indis became the second wife of the King of the Noldor, Finwë, his first, Míriel Serindë, had passed away of exhaustion (and foreboding), after bearing the king's first son Fëanor. The wedding of Indis and Finwë was disliked by Fëanor, and mistrusted by some others, but she bore her husband two splendid sons; these were Fingolfin and Finarfin. The latter was golden-haired like his mother, and his House afterwards became renowned for this hereditary trait.

Ingold A warrior of Minas Tirith, leader of those who guarded the northern section of the Rammas (the out-wall of the Pelennor Fields) prior to the Siege of the City (March, 3019 Third Age).

Ingwë The King of the Vanyar, the 'Fair-elves' of Eldamar and Valinor, and High King of all the Quendi, whether in Aman or Middle-earth. He was born by the waters of Cuiviénen, at the Awakening of the Elves, and later led the First Kindred of the Eldar, the *Vanyar*, on the Great Journey from the east of Middle-earth to the Uttermost West, tarrying for no cause, first of all the Quendi to set foot on the shores of Aman the Blessed. There afterwards he dwelled, in Tirion, and later in the halls of Manwë and Varda upon the mountain Oiolossë, and was held first among all the Eldar. Ingwë returned to Middle-earth only once – when he led the Host of the Vanyar to the Great Battle which overthrew Morgoth.

Inland Sea As it appears on late Third Age cartography, this term refers to the Inland Sea of Rhûn. References from the First Age, however, apply to the (greater) Sea of Helcar.

(The) Inscrutable An Elvish epithet for the race of Men.

Inziladûn (Ar-Inziladûn) The twenty-third King of Númenor. Inziladûn deplored the schism which had come to divide the Númenoreans and the Eldar and, in token of this, changed his (Adûnaic) name to the (High-elven) *Tar-Palantir*, 'The Farsighted', shortly after his ascension to the throne.

But this act of contrition came too late to save Númenor from her Downfall. Palantir's daughter Míriel, who should have succeeded him, was prevented from doing so by rebellious elements. Instead, in the year 3255 Second Age, her cousin seized the Sceptre and became King, taking the (Adûnaic) royal name *Ar-Pharazôn*, 'The Golden'. Pharazôn was the last King of Númenor.

Inzilbêth (Ar-Inzilbêth) A beautiful Númenorean princess, of the Line of Andúnië. She was wedded – against her will – to the schismatic King Ar-Gimilzôr; and bore him two sons: INZILADÛN and Gimilkhâd.

Ioreth An elderly woman of Minas Tirith (formerly from the province of Lossarnach) who nursed the sick and otherwise aided the Healers during the Siege of the City (March, 3019 Third Age).

Irensaga A jagged peak in the northern White Mountains; it overlooked Harrowdale in Rohan, forming the northern wall of the Hold of Dunharrow.

Irmo The real name of the Vala better known as LÓRIEN. He was the Master of Dreams and Visions, the brother of MANDOS.

Iron Crown The crown in which Morgoth the Enemy mounted the three Silmarils which he had stolen from the High-elves of Eldamar and brought to Middle-earth in the latter part of the First Age, thus precipitating the War of the Great Jewels. At least one of the Silmarils was recovered – by Beren and Lúthien – but, as is told in *The*

Silmarillion,[2] the remaining two Jewels were taken from their keeper by the Valar, at the end of the Age, and the crown was reforged into a thrall's ring, which was then placed about his neck – for ever.

Iron Hills The location of one of the two main settlements of Durin's Folk in the latter years of the Third Age. These mountains lay about forty leagues east of Erebor and formed the only natural barrier between Mirkwood and the wide lands of the East.

The colony there was begun in the year 2590 Third Age, after attacks by Dragons had forced the Dwarves out of the Grey Mountains. Then Grór, son of Dáin I, led many of Durin's Folk to the Iron Hills – while his elder brother Thrór, Durin's Heir, led the greater part of them back to the Lonely Mountain, founded long before by Thráin I.

For a while the two Dwarf-kingdoms flourished. Although the Dwarves of the Iron Hills were a cadet branch of the Line of Durin, they were numerous and well armed, and while their wealth did not compare with that of Erebor, perhaps this very lack of treasure saved them from the unwelcome attentions of Dragons. For it was the Lonely Mountain, fabulously wealthy and full of Dwarves grown fat with prosperity, that Smaug the Golden, greatest Worm of his day, eventually chose as his dwelling-place in 2770.

For the 170 years that Smaug reigned in Erebor, the Iron Hills colony, led by descendants of Grór, boasted the only secure Dwarf-settlement in the west of Middle-earth. Yet despite their toughness and fierce disposition, even the Dwarves of the Iron Hills were no match for the forces which Sauron began to assemble in the East as the Age waned. And it was chiefly for this reason that, in the year 2941, Gandalf the Grey purposed to bring about the reinstatement of the Kingdom of Erebor and the destruction of the Dragon. (See *The Hobbit* and Appendix A III, 'Durin's Folk'.)

As is recorded elsewhere (see BATTLE OF FIVE ARMIES), after the death of Smaug there followed a crucial period when the Dwarves of Erebor were in dispute with both the Men of Esgaroth and the Elves of Mirkwood over the disposal of the Dragon-hoard. To back his claim with force, Thorin Oakenshield, besieged in the Lonely Mountain, sent secretly to the Dwarves of the Iron Hills (now led by Dáin Ironfoot, grandson of Grór). Over five hundred of these sturdy people set out to aid Thorin, fully prepared to give battle to Elves and Men on behalf of their kin. However, this grievous clash was averted by the (timely) arrival of an invading army of Orcs, the foes of all; and the mattocks and axes of the Iron Hills were put to better use on Orc-necks.

As Thorin Oakenshield was slain in this battle, Dáin Ironfoot, Durin's Heir, became the new King Under the Mountain. He ruled both Dwarf-realms with great wisdom until he fell at last in the War of the Ring.

Iron Mountains A translation of the Sindarin words *Ered Engrin*, being the name given by the Eldar to the great chain of mountains raised by Morgoth at the beginning of his realm in the north of Middle-earth, to protect it from attack (from South or West). Their full extent is not recorded, but it is known that they curved west-east in a great sickle, fencing in Utumno and Angband behind a hedge of grim peaks. The most southerly spur of this range (in later days) was Thangorodrim – beneath which lay the Gates of Angband.

Isen A river which rose in the southernmost vales of the Misty Mountains and flowed through the Gap of Rohan to find the Adorn some fifty leagues south-west of Isengard. The conjoined rivers flowed into the Sea between Enedhwaith and Drúwaith Iaur.

Isengard One of the mightiest fortifications of Middle-earth in the Third Age. The Ring of Isengard was a huge rock-wall, roughly circular in shape, which enclosed a shallow valley approximately one mile in diameter. This natural fortress lay within the greater valley of Nan Curunír, several leagues north of the Gap of Rohan.

During the early days of the South-kingdom, the rock-wall was cunningly refashioned by the Dúnedain, for they wished to make the Ring into a fortress of Gondor's might. At the centre of the enclosed valley they also constructed the Tower of Orthanc, in which they set one of the four *palantíri* (Seeing-stones) of the Realm.

At the time of its building, just before the ending of the Second Age, the Ring was named *Angrenost*, 'Iron-citadel' – which was also the meaning of the later, more widely used name, *Isengard* (a word in the tongue of the Rohirrim). A mighty fortress indeed, Angrenost was then accounted the northernmost bastion of Gondor's power – though it lay, in fact, beyond her borders. For many centuries it dominated the strategic Gap between the Misty Mountains and the White. But as the long years of the Third Age passed, Gondor retreated from her northern provinces. The impregnable Tower was locked and abandoned, and the Ring of Isengard became filled with wild folk from the hills and fells of Dunland.

For over fifty years the Dunlendings used the Ring as a base from which to harry the western frontiers of Rohan (though they were never able to enter the Tower). But in the end they were driven out – and then there came Saruman the White, Chief of Wizards, speaking soft words and asking for the Keys of Orthanc, for he desired (he said) to dwell there, as a friend of both Rohan and Gondor. This was in the year 2759, when Rohan was in sad disarray following the Long Winter and its attendant evils; accordingly, Saruman was freely granted permission to settle in Isengard and the Keys of the Tower were given up to him by the Steward of Gondor for the South-kingdom still retained jurisdiction over it.

For many years Saruman dwelt there quietly, while the Rohirrim slowly rebuilt their strength. But it was later seen how, from the first, the Wizard had desired above all to make himself a great lord of Men – and how, to this end, he had gained possession of the mightiest stronghold north of Minas Tirith (not to mention its Seeing-stone). In the year 2953, Saruman abandoned all pretence of custodianship and claimed Isengard for his own.

He repaired the ancient rock-wall and, underneath the valley enclosed by the Ring, he delved many pits and armouries, caves and dens, in which to house his new and formidable armies. Yet in the event, the Wizard launched his long-planned war upon Rohan before he was fully ready – and the unlikely alliance that was made against him proved too great for even the power of Isengard to withstand; and Saruman was cast out from the society of those he had once sought to dominate. In the last analysis, Isengard, though strong indeed, was less formidable than he had imagined.

After the War of the Ring, the rock-wall was cast down, but the Tower of Orthanc (which no power could destroy) was locked once more, and its Keys passed again into the keeping of the King of Gondor. Its *palantír* was then kept in Minas Tirith.

Isengrim Took (Isengrim II) From 2683–2722 Third Age (1083–1122 Shire Reckoning), the twenty-second Thain of the Shire. He commenced the excavation of a suitable dwelling-place for the aristocratic Took family, the splendid burrowings later known as Great Smials.

Isenmouthe See CARACH ANGREN.

Isil (Q.) The High-elven name for the Moon. According to tradition, both Moon and Sun (*Anar*) were set aloft by the Valar after the death of the Two Trees, to bring Light to Middle-earth. Isil was (and is) an aerial vessel, made by Aulë, and containing the last Flower of Silver, coaxed by Yavanna from the dying Tree Telperion. It is steered on its celestial course, say the Elves, by Tilion, one of the Maiar.

In Sindarin, *Ithil*.

See also *Silmarillion* (pp. 99–102).

Isildur From 3320 Second Age to Year 2 Third Age, the conjoint King of Gondor, and from 3441 Second Age to Year 2 Third Age, the second King of Arnor. He was the elder son of Elendil the Tall (founder of both Realms in Exile) and the brother of Anárion, who was slain at the gates of the Barad-dûr.

Isildur was born in Númenor, and when that mighty realm foundered under the Western Seas (in 3319 Second Age), he helped his father and brother to lead a remnant of the Dúnedain back to Middle-earth. There they founded the Númenorean realms-in-exile, Arnor and Gondor. Elendil became the High King of both realms, but chose to concentrate his rule in the North-kingdom of Arnor, while Isildur and his younger brother Anárion were given the South-kingdom of Gondor to rule conjointly. Anárion lived mostly in his city of Minas Anor on the knees of the White Mountains, and Isildur dwelled in Minas Ithil, the 'Tower of the Moon', which he had raised among the western vales of the Mountains of Shadow, the western border of Mordor.

But the Lord of Mordor had not perished in the ruin of Númenor (as all then believed), and so when Sauron finally launched a war against the Dúnedain of Middle-earth, the first stronghold to fall to his renascent power was Isildur's own city of Minas Ithil. In 3429 Second Age, the forces of Mordor came across the Spider's Pass and captured the Tower of the Moon in a surprise attack, sacking the city and burning its White Tree. But Isildur himself escaped and, leaving his brother to defend the line of the Anduin, he passed down the river to the Sea, raising the alarm and enlisting allies even as he went. And while Sauron attempted vainly to force the crossings of the Anduin, Isildur came at last to the havens of Lindon in the North, and brought the tidings to his father Elendil.

So began the war of the Dúnedain and the Elves against Sauron, of which the full tale is told elsewhere (see LAST ALLIANCE). Together with his father and their Elven-allies, Isildur marched south with a great army as soon as this could be mustered. In the final battle before the Black Gate, Sauron was defeated and driven back to the Dark Tower, where he was long besieged. There Isildur's brother

Anárion was slain, and there, in the following year (3341, the last of the Second Age), his father Elendil perished in personal combat with Sauron – who was overthrown. Isildur then became High King of both Arnor and Gondor.

However, before he passed away north through the Black Gate, Isildur had gained possession of the Ruling Ring of Sauron. This he took as weregild for the death of his kin – cutting the Ring from Sauron's own hand with the broken hilt-shard of Elendil's sword. Straight away the Ring began its work, for Isildur refused to destroy it (as counselled by Elrond and Círdan, who witnessed the scene); instead, he kept it as an Heirloom of Arnor – and thus ultimately nullified the victory so dearly bought.

For the first two years of the Third Age, Isildur remained in the South-kingdom, instructing his brother's son Meneldil in Kingship. Then, after planting a sapling of the White Tree in Minas Anor,[3] in memory of his brother, he marched away with a small escort of knights to take up the Northern Sceptre. Beside the Gladden Fields in Wilderland, this party was ambushed by a host of Orcs of the Mountains, and all but three were slain. Isildur almost escaped – only to be betrayed by his greatest treasure: he perished in the waters of the Anduin. His fourth son Valandil then became King of Arnor. See also HEIRS OF ISILDUR; RULING RING.

Isildur's Bane The name given among the Dúnedain of Arnor to the Ruling Ring of Sauron – which brought about the death of their last High King. See RULING RING.

Isilya 'Moon's-day' (Q.) The third day of the *enquië* or week in both the Elvish calendar and the Kings' Reckoning. The Sindarin name for the same day was *Orithil*; while the Hobbits of the Shire and Bree called it *Monendei* (later shortened to *Monday*).

Isle of Balar The great island in the mouth of the Bay of BALAR in Middle-earth, a remnant of ERESSËA. At the end of the First Age it became the dwelling of the Falathrim, led by CÍRDAN THE SHIP-WRIGHT. Gil-galad Ereinion, heir of Fingon the High King, was also fostered here.

Isle of Werewolves A translation of the Grey-elven name *Tol-in-Gaurhoth*, as the island of *Tol Sirion* was renamed after its fall to Sauron servant of Morgoth, two years after the Dagor Bragollach. Here Finrod Felagund met his death.

Istari The ancient Order of WIZARDS, actually MAIAR of Valinor. See also GANDALF THE GREY.

Isumbras Took (Isumbras I) In 2340 Third Age (740 Shire Reckoning), Isumbras became the thirteenth Thain of the Shire and the first Hobbit of the influential Took family to hold this office. (The Oldbucks, with whom the hereditary Thainship had previously resided, recrossed the Baranduin in that year and founded the Buckland, changing their family name to *Brandybuck*.)

Ithildin 'Star-moon' (Sind.) A metal developed during the Second Age by the Elven-smiths of Eregion; it was made from *mithril*, which the Elves obtained from the Dwarves of Moria. Ithildin was particularly suitable for the finest embellishments and hidden markings, for it did not shine unless illuminated by moon or stars, and even then only after the correct spells had unlocked its secret. The Doors of Durin (the West-gate of Moria) were inlaid with designs traced in this metal.

Ithilien 'Land-of-the-Moon' (Sind.) One of the two most royal and ancient fiefs of Gondor, founded by Isildur himself in 3320 Second Age. It lay in the narrow lands between the Mountains of Shadow and the Great River, bordered by the marshland of Nindalf in the north and the river Poros in the south. It was a fair land of trees, gentle hills and quick waters, and during the early years of the South-kingdom, many of the Dúnedain dwelt there in happiness and prosperity.

Yet beautiful though Ithilien was, its strategic position (on the eastern side of the Anduin) rendered the province especially vulnerable to attack from both the East and the South – particularly during the years of Gondor's decline, in the second half of the Third Age. Defenceless in the north, save for the partial shield of the marshes, the province was protected in the south only by the river Poros; and against direct attack from Mordor, the people of Ithilien were quite helpless. Nevertheless Gondor contrived to keep a foothold there throughout the wars and invasions of the Third Age, when her frontiers were left open to assault from all directions, as her might gradually diminished. But in the year 2002 the chief city of the province, Minas Ithil, fell to the Enemy, and only the hardiest of Gondor's people dwelt in Ithilien afterwards.

Indeed, a full century before the War of the Ring it was obvious to the Captains of Gondor that this fairest of her provinces must one day be abandoned to the Enemy. To ensure that Ithilien would not be taken without a fight, Steward Túrin II ordered the construction of secret refuges or bases from which a small but effective guerilla force of Rangers would be able to harass the foe. By the year 2901 most of the few remaining inhabitants of the province had fled, due to a sudden influx of Mordor-orcs; fifty years later Sauron himself openly returned to Mordor; Mount Doom erupted once more and Ithilien was at last evacuated – save for the Rangers, who then began to operate against the Enemy from the hidden bases (see HENNETH ANNÛN).

This period of Sauron's outright domination over Ithilien lasted some sixty years. Yet for the most part, he did not bother to amass any new force there (save only the growing armies of Minas Morgul, established long before). In fact, Sauron's chief purpose in capturing the province seems to have been in order to win control of the Harad Road which ran from the Crossings of Poros far in the south, northwards through Ithilien to the Black Gate of his own land. In the years immediately before the outbreak of the War of the Ring, this road was much used by his Southron allies – and their convoys suffered greatly at the hands of the Rangers. Finally, in March 3019, even the Rangers of Ithilien were withdrawn, to aid the city of Minas Tirith in its last need. But in the event Gondor was saved, and the Dark Lord cast down, and then Ithilien became free once more and was soon resettled. During the Fourth Age which followed it was again renowned as the loveliest of all the provinces of Gondor.

Note: in translations from the Red Book, *Ithilien* normally refers to North Ithilien, the fairest part of the province; this lay between the hills of Emyn Arnen and the northern marches. South Ithilien was the name given to the less well-populated and more barren land bordered by the Emyn Arnen, the Anduin and the Poros.

See also MINAS ITHIL.

Ivanneth The Sindarin form of the Quenya word *Yavannië*, the ninth month of the *loa* (year) in Kings' Reckoning. This name was used only by the Dúnedain.

Ivorwen The wife of Dirhael and mother of Gilraen the Fair, herself the mother of Aragorn II.

Ivrin The complex of springs and pools in the southern vales of the Ered Wethrin, which were the source of the river Narog. Called also *Eithel Ivrin*, and 'The Pools of Ivrin'.

The Ivy Bush An Inn of the Bywater district of the Shire, patronized (like its rival, *The Green Dragon*) by thirsty Hobbits from both Bywater and Hobbiton.

Notes

1 Though not in any spiritual or mystical sense. Its meaning carried something of the modern term 'space'.
2 P. 252.
3 The original White Tree of Gondor was in its origin a fruit of Nimloth (of Númenor), rescued from the destruction by none other than Isildur himself (*Silmarillion*, pp. 272–3).

Kalakirya 'Light-cleft' (Q.) See CALACIRYA.

Kalakiryan See CALACIRYA.

Kalimac The original (as opposed to translated) Bucklandish fore-name, of which the diminutive *Kali* carried the meaning 'jolly' or 'gay'. To preserve the full sense of the name, *Kalimac* has been translated from the Red Book as *Meriadoc* (abbreviated 'Merry').

Karningul The original (as opposed to translated) Westron name for that deep valley in eastern Eriador known to the Elves and the Dúnedain as *Imladris*. Both have a literal meaning of 'Deep-cloven-valley', translated from the Red Book as 'Rivendell'.

Kelos See CELOS.

Kelvar The Quenya words *kelvar* and *olvar* carried meanings almost identical to the modern *fauna* and *flora*, and were used in a similar sense.

Kementári 'Queen-of-the-Earth' (Q.) See YAVANNA KEMENTÁRI.

Khand A south-eastern country or province of Middle-earth, situated between the deserts of Near Harad and the wide fields of Rhûn, close to the southern marches of Mordor. It was peopled by a race of men known as *Variags*. Little more is said of this land or its people in the Red Book.

Khazâd (Khuz.) The Dwarves. Although the literal meaning of this word has never been learned, it is certain that *Khazâd* was the Dwarves' 'own name for their own race . . . since Aulë [the Smith of the Valar] gave it to them at their making in the deeps of time.'[1] It is one of the few Dwarvish words ever to become widely known to members of other races – since the Khazâd were secretive by nature and jealous of all their possessions, including their language (Khuzdul). *Khazâd* can also be found as an element in the Dwarves' name for the city which the Elves called Moria: *Khazad-dûm*, 'The-Mansion-of-the-Khazâd'. The once well-known battle-cries of this people – *Baruk Khazâd!* ('Axes of the Dwarves!') and *Khazâd ai-Menû!* ('The Dwarves are upon you!') – also include this ancient element.

See also HADHODROND.

Khazad-dûm 'The-Mansion-of-the-Khazâd' (Khuz.) The Dwarves' own name for the greatest accomplishment of their race: their vast city and realm under the Misty Mountains. It was more widely known as Moria, the Black Pit.

See HADHODROND; MORIA.

Kheled-zâram 'Mirror-mere' (Khuz.) The Dwarves' name for the beautiful dark lake which filled the Vale of Azanulbizar. This lake was one of the most revered places of the Dwarves – indeed, the entire valley was hallowed by numerous ancient associations for Durin's Folk.

Dwarvish legend states that Durin the Deathless, on his awakening far back in the Elder Days, came to the Vale and looked into the cool, still depths of the Mirror-mere. There he perceived, like a crown about his head, a reflection of seven stars in the water, though it was still daylight and the sun shone in the sky. This vision was accepted as an acknowledgement of Durin's incomparable royalty – he was the eldest of all the Seven Fathers of the Dwarves – and as a sign that he should found his kingdom there. The place where Durin gazed into the lake was later marked by an obelisk.

Kheled-zâram was shaped like a great spear-head, with its point thrust deep into the north of the mountain-spur which curved east and south to embrace the Vale. At its northern end, near the 'gore', one of the main passes across the mountains, the Dimrill Stair, descended beside the cascading waterfall which fed the lake.

See also AZANULBIZAR.

Khîm One of the 'Lesser-Dwarves' (the *Noegyth Nibin*) of Amon Rûdh; he was a son of MÎM. Khîm was slain by a member of the outlaw band then led by Túrin Turambar. See also BAR-EN-DANWEDH.

Khuzdul 'The-Speech-of-the-Khazâd' (Khuz.) A secret tongue of great age which the Dwarves revealed to no one (apart from a few battle-cries and place names which became generally known). It was not a language of everyday congress between Dwarves, being rather a tongue of lore, a memory of their ancient past; and, like the Quenya (High-elven) speech, it was preserved lovingly as a prized treasure, guarded from changefulness.

To the ears of the Elves – the first of the 'speaking-peoples' and the race with the most natural skill in such matters – Dwarvish speech seemed somewhat guttural. Indeed, the few examples of Khuzdul recorded in the Red Book reveal a strong Dwarvish predilection for spirants and glottal stops which doubtless affected the Dwarves' pronunciation of Elvish and Mannish languages. Conversely, Elves never learned the Dwarvish tongue, though on one or two occasions (see HADHODROND) they incorporated into their lexicon Sindarin phonetic approximations of Khuzdul sounds.

Note: because of the secrecy surrounding Khuzdul, the Dwarves normally spoke the languages common to those lands in which they lived and travelled. Thus, the Dwarves of Erebor, for example, regularly used the tongues of Northern Men. In fact all the personal names for Dwarves found in the Red Book are drawn from this language (of the Men of Dale).

Kibil-nâla In Khuzdul (the Dwarvish speech), this was the name given to the icy-cold source of the river Silverlode, rising from a natural well in the Vale of Azanulbizar.

Kíli See FÍLI AND KÍLI.

Kine of Araw As late as the Third Age, large white, horned cattle were often to be found in the lands near the shores of the Inland Sea. They were wild, noble animals, which were greatly prized as beasts of the Chase. Indeed, their forebears were said to be the legendary Kine of Araw, who was the Huntsman of the Valar. (*Oromë* is the Quenya form of his name.) For it was believed that far back in the Elder Days he had brought such beasts from across the Sea to further the pleasures of the Chase. (The horses of Éothéod – or, more particularly, the *Mearas*, Princes of Horses – were also thought to be descended from animals brought to Middle-earth by Araw.)

King of the Sea ULMO.

Kingsfoil The name given among rustic folk of Gondor to the healing herb *Athelas*.

King's Men The name given to their own party by the larger of the two Númenorean political factions: the group opposed to the Eldar and the Valar. The smaller faction, destined eventually to lose all influence in Númenor, were the FAITHFUL (as they called themselves).

Kings' Norbury The name given in the Common Speech to *Fornost Erain* (literally, 'Northern-fortress of the Kings'), the capital of Arthedain from 860–1974 Third Age. After it became desolate, the ruins there were known as 'Deadmen's Dike' – especially in Bree, only some one hundred miles to the south.

Kings-of-Men In the lore of the exiled Men of Westernesse, this title was applied by the Dúnedain to their own race, for they reckoned all Men as follows: High (the Men of the West, i.e., the Dúnedain themselves), Middle (the 'Men of Twilight' such as the Rohirrim and other Northern Men), and Wild (meaning the 'Men of Darkness', such as the Woses of Druadan or the degenerate Dunlendings).

From the very founding of their realms-in-exile, at the closing of the Second Age, it was an overriding concern of the Dúnedain to preserve the ancient Line of Númenor – and eventually this obsession, fervently pursued in Gondor, brought about a civil war which came near to destroying the very inheritance it was meant to protect. (See KIN-STRIFE.)

Later, many of the noble Dúnedain were forced by circumstance to 'dilute' their blood with that of lesser Men. However, it was long before this produced any discernible deterioration or lessening of life span – indeed, for a while the influx of fresh vigour greatly benefited the race of Númenor.

Kings' Reckoning The Calendar of the Dúnedain, largely derived from the far more ancient reckoning-system of the Elves (see CALENDAR OF IMLADRIS).

Originally developed by the Dúnedain of Númenor after the creation of their realm at the opening of the Second Age, Kings' Reckoning was subsequently brought back to Middle-earth at the closing of the Age – by the surviving remnant of the Dúnedain who founded the realms-in-exile of Arnor and Gondor. From there it gradually spread throughout the Westlands until, by the latter part of the Third Age, a modified version of this system had been adopted by almost all folk who used the Westron, or Common Speech.

The Elves of Middle-earth, who devised the first forms of calendar computation, seem to have based them primarily upon observed cycles of growth; and even their larger and smaller divisions of time were clearly chosen for ritual (as opposed to practical) reasons. Such a system – in which an Elvish 'year' or *yen* equalled 144 mortal years – was quite obviously unsuitable for Men; accordingly, the early Númenoreans devised a Calendar which, though deeply influenced by the Elvish system, was scaled more precisely to their own needs. Thus they eventually produced a workable system with significant alternations to the older computation of annual, seasonal, weekly and even daily cycles.

To begin with, they adopted the annual Eldarin cycle of 365 days, the *loa* ('growth'), though they retained the venerable Mannish custom of commencing this at Yule, or mid-winter (the Elves began their cycle at the opening of spring). The Númenoreans also abandoned two of the six Elvish 'seasons' ('fading' and 'stirring'), preferring to recognize only four: spring, summer, autumn and winter. In contrast to the Elven 'seasons' these were of unfixed length and merely indicated discernible (to mortals) changes in vegetation.

More significantly, the Dúnedain – desiring a simpler method of metering their 365-day year – redivided the *loa* into twelve months (*astar*) of nearly equal length (ten of 30 days and two of 31). The five special Eldarin days which belonged to no season were reduced to three and redistributed, and various accumulated deficits were adjusted at intervals. Later they added one day (*Eärenya* 'Sea-day') to the six-day Elvish *enquië* to produce a seven-day week; and at some time they also began reckoning the span of a day as being from sunrise to sunrise, rather than sunset to sunset, as the Elves did.

It was in this basic form that the system of Kings' Reckoning was observed by the Men of Westernesse during most of the Second Age. Naturally, their reverence for the Elves had led them to study the ancient Quenya tongue, and this they used for all season-, month- and day-names. (The Elves themselves, having no use for months, presumably never learned the names the Númenoreans gave to these, even though they were in their own Ancient Speech.)

The surviving Dúnedain of Númenor brought their Calendar back to Middle-earth after the Downfall (in 3319 Second Age). For the first two thousand years of the Númenorean realms-in-exile, the Kings' Reckoning was left virtually unchanged in both Arnor and Gondor; then the dwindling North-kingdom fell at last, and shortly afterwards Gondor's last King perished. Subsequently, in the year 2060 Third Age, Mardil the Good Steward introduced a revised Calendar. This was termed Stewards' Reckoning, although it was in reality mainly the old Númenorean system with the accumulated deficits of 5500 years re-adjusted. It was in this form that the Calendar was eventually adopted by most of the other Westron-speaking peoples of Middle-earth. (Curiously enough, many of these Westron-speakers used the *Quenya* names which the Dúnedain of Númenor had originally given to their months and incorporated for their seasons and days, whereas the Dúnedain themselves actually used the *Sindarin* equivalents for these.)

In any event, while almost all the other Westron-speaking folk adopted Stewards' Reckoning – and ultimately *New Reckoning* – only the Hobbits preserved the unrevised Kings' Reckoning, which they had taken up some time before settling the Shire, before the North-kingdom fell. The Hobbits' natural insularity preserved the ancient Númenorean system, which they modified only slightly, most notably in their numbering of years; thus the date when the Hobbits first crossed into the Shire, 1601 Third Age, was accounted Year One in their *Shire Reckoning*. Apart from a few minor innovations, the only other difference between Kings' and Shire Reckoning was in the calendar names which the Hobbits gradually evolved in place of the original Quenya names preserved elsewhere.

See also SHIRE RECKONING; Appendix D.

King Under the Mountain The title borne by the ruler of Erebor in northern Wilderland, last mansion of the Dwarves of Durin's Line in the Third Age. The Lord of Erebor was habitually addressed as 'King Under the Mountain', although the influence – if not the rule – of the Dwarves also extended over the valleys and nearby lands.

Kinslaying at Alqualondë The first and most evil of all the deeds committed by the rebelling Noldor; this act more than all others set the rebellion beyond the pale of forgiveness, and ultimately brought about the downfall of its perpetrators, of whom Fëanor was the chief. It was the fatal blow and (some have said) a greater evil than the poisoning of the Two Trees.

The two kindreds involved were the Noldor, led by Fëanor, and the Falmari, the 'Sea-elves' of Alqualondë – their city and haven on the northern shores of the Bay of Eldamar – whose King was Olwë. Fëanor, hastening north at the head of the fleeing Noldor, desired to use the ships of the Sea-elves to transport his host to Middle-earth; also he desired to enrol the Falmari in his rebellion. But Olwë refused both, so Fëanor attempted to take the ships by force from the quaysides of Alqualondë where they were moored. There followed a fight with the Sea-elves, and before long the Noldor had drawn their new-forged swords, and had begun to kill. The Falmari, now reinforced from the city, still fought on, but Noldor of other Houses now rushed forward to join in the battle, for they were still unaware that it had been Fëanor who had opened the hostilities; and with their added strength Fëanor prevailed over the mariners of Olwë. Many of these were slain; and not a few of the Noldor. Fëanor then seized the ships – and shortly afterwards betrayed even his own allies by sailing back to Middle-earth with his own host. He then destroyed the ships.

For this deed the Noldor were cursed by the Valar; and they forfeited whatever chance they might ever have had of gaining the friendship of Elwë Thingol, King of Beleriand, for Thingol was the brother of Olwë. The Noldor themselves had been bitterly divided over the Kinslaying ever since the truth about its cause had become known. Thus were the Noldor sundered from the Sindar, and from each other: to the clear profit of Morgoth. And the Kinslaying at Alqualondë was not the last time that Elves would slay Elves, though it was the last time in Aman.

Kin-strife The great Civil War of Gondor, which raged intermittently from 1432–48 Third Age, nearly destroying the Southkingdom of the Dúnedain and immeasurably weakening its internal resources. Among the immediate effects were the depopulation of whole provinces and the diminished respect in which Gondor was held by her traditional foes. More importantly, the ill-will engendered by the Kin-strife lingered between its factions long afterwards and played a part in the final extinction of the ruling Line of Anárion. And though Gondor was to regain her military strength in later years, she was never again able to rekindle the founding spirit inherited from Númenor.

And yet the origins of the civil war lay far back in the Númenoreans' own innate sense of their special destiny, and in the great (and justified) pride taken in their ancient lineage. Indeed, the Númenorean Kings were directly descended from the High-elves and from the heroic chieftains of the Edain of the First Age (through their first King, Elros Tar-Minyatur, son of Eärendil the Mariner). So the preservation of this blood-line undiffused by lesser stock became a severely maintained dictum in Númenor.

The Kings of Gondor, directly descended from the early Númenorean rulers, but dwelling in the lesser lands of Middle-earth, naturally strove to maintain their incomparable lineage untainted. And although for over a thousand years the blood of Elendil remained unmingled, nevertheless, by the time of the twentieth King, Valacar, the Line of Anárion had been 'diminished' in the eyes of many.

Valacar's father was the great warrior-king Rómendacil II, who had overwhelmed a vast horde of Easterlings with the aid of the Men of Rhovanion, welcome allies of Gondor. Partly in token of this, he sent his son to dwell for a while with the nobles of Rhovanion. But Valacar came under the spell of this fair Northern race and eventually married his host's daughter. From their union came Eldacar (called Vinitharya in the land of his birth). As is told elsewhere (Appendix A I(iv), 'Gondor and the Heirs of Anárion'), this union of the Heir to the Throne and a lady of 'lesser' race caused great friction in the South-kingdom. Therefore, by the time Valacar died and Eldacar became King (in 1432 Third Age), there was already open rebellion in many places.

Unfortunately for the King, the growing number of those opposed to him had the support of Gondor's invincible navy, battle-tested but idle at Pelargir for some time. Indeed, the Captain of the Fleets later emerged as the leader of the rebels; this was Castamir (a cousin of the King), who had easily gained the support of the people of Pelargir and the coastal provinces. Eldacar opposed this confederacy as far as he could, but was forced to take refuge in Osgiliath, where he was later besieged and finally driven out in the year 1437. He then escaped into the North, to take sanctuary in the land of his mother's people.

As might have been expected, the new 'King' proved unwise and arbitrary, cruel and vindictive. (See CASTAMIR THE USURPER.) It was not long before the very people who had originally supported his faction perceived their error in elevating such a man to the Throne. Indeed, after a mere ten years of Castamir's rule, Eldacar was able to return to Gondor – with an army which rapidly increased in number each day that he marched south. He met the Usurper at the Crossings of Erui (1447 Third Age). Castamir was then defeated and slain by Eldacar, who thus avenged the death of his elder son Ornendil, put to death by Castamir ten years before. But the Usurper's own sons and near kin escaped to Pelargir, where the Fleets still remained loyal to the rebels. The following year they departed to Umbar, where they established an independent lordship at permanent feud with Gondor.

To repopulate the devastated areas of his kingdom, Eldacar brought south many of the Northmen who had given him sanctuary. Contrary to the old fears, this did not instantly bring about the dwindling of the 'Kings-of-Men'. Eldacar himself lived to be 235 years old and was succeeded by his second son Aldamir in 1490.

Kiril See CIRIL.

Kirith Ungol See CIRITH UNGOL.

Kûd-dûkan In the original – as opposed to translated – speech of Northern Men, this conjoined word meant 'hole-dweller'. It has been translated from the Red Book as *holbytla* (pl. *holbytlan*), of which the diminished form, *hobbit*, is meant to represent *kuduk* (apparently the diminished form of *kûd-dûkan*).

See the Note at the end of Appendix F for a fuller explanation of the system of 'rendition' used in translating proper names from the Red Book.

Note
1 Appendix F II.

Ladros 'Fortified-plain' (Sind.) The name given by the Eldar and the Edain to the extreme north-eastern region of Dorthonion; a broad, shallow valley which opened on to the northern grassland and provided a natural route of access from the North into the highlands. Ladros was therefore of immense strategic importance to the Eldar, forming as it did a weakness in the wall of the Siege. Accordingly, Angrod and Aegnor, the two youngest sons of Finarfin, who dwelt in Dorthonion, were more than happy to grant this 'front-line' region to a House of Men, newly-come to Beleriand: the First House, descendants of Bëor the Old. The first Lord of Ladros was Boromir, grandson of Bëor.

For over a century the Edain held Ladros in alliance with the Eldar, but in the Year of the Sun 455 war again broke out in the North and for the first time the Edain felt the power of Angband. The Lord of Ladros, Bregolas the grandson of Boromir, was slain (together with Angrod and Aegnor of the High-elves) and the Orcs poured on into Dorthonion.

Ladybarrow An approximate translation of the Sindarin phrase *Haudh-en-Arwen* (actually 'Mound-of-the-Maiden-Queen'), the Grey-elven name for the burial-barrow or tumulus wherein lay Haleth, first chieftain of the Haladin. It stood in the Forest of Brethil. The name in the tongue of the Haladin was *Tûr Haretha* ('Haleth's Mound').

Laer See LAIRË below.

Laer Cú Beleg 'The Song of the Great Bow' (Sind.) The title given by Túrin Turambar to the Lament made by him in memory of his slain friend, the Elf-warrior Beleg Cúthalion of Doriath.

Laiquendi The GREEN-ELVES.

Lairë 'Summer' (Q.) The name of the second of the six Elvish 'seasons', and the second of the four observed in Kings' Reckoning and later systems used by Westron-speaking peoples. (In Elven usage, *lairë* was one of the longer 'seasons', containing 72 days.) The Sindarin form of this word was *laer*.

Lake Helevorn See HELEVORN.

Lake Nurnen See NURN, NURNEN.

Lake-town The town of ESGAROTH, upon the Long Lake in the north of Wilderland.

Lalaith 'Laughter' (Sind.) The name given by Húrin and Morwen of Dor-lómin to their first-born daughter, the younger sister of Túrin their son; she died in infancy. Morwen afterwards bore another daughter, Nienor.

Lambe The Quenya or High-elven word for 'tongue', but more properly, the title of Tengwa number 27, which represented the value of the sound *l*.

Lamedon A province of Gondor which nestled in the protective embrace of the White Mountains, between the river Ringló and the pass of Tarlang's Neck. Its chief settlement was the small town of Calembel, on a hill overlooking the Fords of Ciril (or Kiril), the principal river of the province.

Lammoth 'The Great Echo' (Sind.) A cold waste which lay to the west of the Ered Lómin, between mountains and sea-coast. As its name implies, it was a region where a single shout or cry awoke tumultuous echoes from the rocky countryside. According to Elvish tradition, these were the echoes of the voice of Morgoth, for it was in Lammoth that he was said to have been attacked by Ungoliant, and to have cried for help with such a loud cry that the terrible sound of his voice became imprinted for ever in the stone.

Lamps of the Valar See ILLUIN.

Lampwrights' Street A Westron translation of the Sindarin name *Rath Celerdain* ('The Street of the Lampwrights'). It was a busy thoroughfare in the city of Minas Tirith, encircling completely the first level and leading eventually to the Great Gate in the East Wall. The chief Inns of Minas Tirith were to be found there.

Land of Mist A translation of the Quenya name *Hisilómë* (Sindarin HITHLUM).

Land of Seven Rivers A translation of the Grey-elves' name for the country between Gelion and the Blue Mountains: OSSIRIAND. (The Noldor knew it as LINDON.)

Land of Shadow A Third Age epithet for Mordor – and more than mere imagery, for from his beginning Sauron the Great had proved a true master of Darkness, spinning it like a web and weaving it into shadow. Mordor's creatures needed the full skill of their night-eyes in the gloom that pervaded his land. The Darkness was very real, and as much an impediment to the foolhardy traveller as were Mordor's fauna, flora and other unpleasant phenomena.

Land of the Dead That Live A translation of DOR FIRN-I-GUINAR (Sind.).

Land of the Girdle Doriath. (See GIRDLE OF MELIAN.)

Land of the Star Númenor. Although the Kings of that Realm had no crown, they sometimes wore a diadem made of a plain silver band with a single glittering star on the brow. This represented both the Star of Eärendil – which had guided the Edain to their far western island at its founding – and the original name of Númenor itself, *Elenna* 'Star-wards' (Q.).
Note: this Star is also found as the chief marking in the heraldic emblem of Eärendil the Mariner, from whom all Kings of Númenor were descended, through his son Elros Tar-Minyatur, first ruler of the Land of the Star (from 32–442 Second Age).

Land of Willows NAN-TASARION (Nan-tathren).

Landroval A Great Eagle of the Misty Mountains; the brother of Gwaihir the Windlord (who, at the time of the War of the Ring, was himself the mightiest and swiftest of all the Eagle-lords).
See also EAGLES OF THE NORTH.

Langstrand 'Long-shore' A translation of the Grey-elven word *Anfalas*.

Lanthir Lamath 'Echoing Cataract' (Sind.) The house in Ossiriand of DIOR ELUCHÍL, near a waterfall of the same name. See also ELWING THE WHITE.

Largo Baggins The third son of Balbo Baggins and the great-grandfather of Frodo.

Lasse-lanta 'Leaf-fall' (Q.) An alternative name for *quellë* ('fading'), which was the fourth 'season' in the CALENDAR OF IMLADRIS and was also used in KINGS' RECKONING. In Elvish usage, this season had 54 days and was especially evocative to the Eldar (for reasons obvious to the tree-minded). The Grey-elven or Sindarin name for the same season was *narbeleth* ('sun-waning').

Lassemista 'Leaf-of-[shadowy]-Silver' (Q.) A tree-name in the ancient Elven High-speech (Quenya), used by the 'young' Ent Bregalad when mourning the untimely slaughter of many of his friends: the rowan-trees of Fangorn Forest.

Note: the name *Lassemista* provides the student of Elvish tongues with a significant glimpse of the venerable Elven intellect – as revealed by the structure and shades of meaning associated with the ancient Quenya root *mist*. We encounter it frequently throughout published records in a less-ancient form, modified (but not hidden) in the Grey-elven words *mithril, Mithrandir, Mitheithel*. In both Elven-tongues the element *mist-* (Q.), *mith-* (Sind.) appears to give an impression of 'greyness' enriched by a secondary feeling of 'silveriness' – and it also imbues 'silver' itself with a 'changeful' quality. Such subtle modifiers of meaning can only have been used deliberately to evoke a quality of 'shadowiness' (in the Elvish sense of 'illusory'). For Men the word *shadowy* has come to mean *elusive, mysterious* or perhaps *concealed*. Yet the Elves' use of it (in *mist-* and *mith-*) clearly carried a very different set of nuances which can only be summarized as 'Silvergrey-Shadowdim' (in a poor attempt to convey the original Elvish meaning).

Last Alliance The name given among Elves and Men to the Confederacy of the two Peoples which waged war against Sauron the Great from 3430–41 Second Age, overthrowing him and laying his first Realm in ruins. But though losses were heavy, and Gil-galad of the Elves and Elendil of the Dúnedain were both killed, the victory thus dearly purchased was, in the end, made fruitless by the survival of Sauron's Ruling Ring; and so the Dark Lord was able to grow and take shape once more. In a sense, therefore the War of the Ring was the final act of the Last Alliance – formed a full Age earlier – and its purpose was the completion of the same task.

The Alliance itself, between Elves of Lindon and Dúnedain of Gondor and Arnor, was formed in the year 3430, as a result of war which had broken out a year earlier, when Sauron of Mordor – whom all believed had perished in the ruin of drowned Númenor – unleashed a fierce and sudden attack upon the South-kingdom of the Dúnedain. Fortunately, his own strength had been diminished during the years of his captivity (in Númenor); while the Dúnedain Realms in Exile had been granted over a century in which to take root. Nonetheless, the first success was Sauron's: in 3429 he came over the Pass of Cirith Ungol and took Isildur's city of Minas Ithil; he burned the White Tree and then pressed forward to Osgiliath.

But Isildur escaped the sack of his city and fled down the Anduin to the Sea, spreading the alarm as he went; for all guessed that this was Sauron's last stroke against Númenor. Most of the folk of the coastal provinces flooded to the aid of Isildur's brother Anárion (who was defending the bridges of Osgiliath and his own city of Minas Anor), while Isildur himself journed by ship to the North, to his father Elendil.

It soon became apparent that the Dúnedain alone were too few to make an end of the Dark Lord. The might of Númenor had nearly achieved it in the past, but that power now lay under the Sea (at Sauron's contrivance) and allies must needs be sought elsewhere. Accordingly, Elendil turned to Gil-galad, High-elven King of Lindon and an ancient enemy of Sauron. One can be sure that Elendil had no need to remind the Elven-king of the aid afforded the Elves of Lindon by the Dúnedain long before (see MINASTIR); indeed, there was an ancient and honourable tradition of friendship and alliance between the Eldar and the Edain which reached back into the Elder Days and which had not altogether been eroded by the later heresies of the Númenorean Kings. So Gil-galad agreed to join with Elendil, the Last Alliance of Elves and Men was forged, and the following year (3431), the combined hosts of Lindon and Arnor began to be mustered in Eriador.

Three years later this Army crossed the Misty Mountains into Wilderland and marched south. Strategically this was a sound move. The Gap between the Misty Mountains and the White could have long been held against them – whereas by taking the eastern route, only the Morannon, the 'Black Gate' itself, stood between the Hosts and Sauron's own land of Mordor. That same year the armies met in a gigantic conflict upon Dagorlad, and Sauron was swept away, and the Last Alliance 'had the mastery: for the Spear of Gil-galad and the Sword of Elendil, Aiglos and Narsil, none could withstand.'[1]

Yet the victory was not complete, though many Elves and Men perished in the Battle of Dagorlad. Sauron retreated to his Dark Tower and there withstood a siege of seven years; for the Barad-dûr was too strong to be cast down from without, and Sauron could wait. But in the end, in the year 3441, he emerged, and the final combat of the Last Alliance was fought upon the slopes of Orodruin between the Dark Lord and his chief foes: Elendil and Gil-galad. The Elven-king was destroyed,[2] but by his death enabled Elendil to strike down Sauron before he, too, was slain.

With the overthrow of the Dark Lord, the Last Alliance should have achieved its purpose of freeing the inhabitants of western Middle-earth from his domination. Yet in the very hour of triumph this was cast away by a single (if excusable) act of wilfulness. Isildur, Elendil's son (whose beloved brother Anárion had been slain the previous year at the siege of Barad-dûr) stood beside his father during those last moments, and his grief overbore him. He cut the Ruling Ring from Sauron's hand with his father's sword Narsil, but although urged to destroy it (in the Cracks of Doom which were nigh at hand), he kept it as a weregild for his father and brother.

. . . . . *I will risk no hurt to this thing: of all the works of Sauron the only fair. It is precious to me, though I buy it with great pain.*[3]

In this way the ancient essence of Sauron's power survived his defeat, and the sacrifices of the Last Alliance were rendered in vain – though few saw Isildur's action or believed the victory anything but complete. Yet within two years the Ring's evil power had already claimed Isildur's own life: neither the first nor the last to be lost before the final destruction of the Ring, in 3019 Third Age, completed the overthrow of its Black Master.

Last Battle The Battle which many ancient legends of Men prophesy will be fought at the End of the World.[4]

Last Bridge The Bridge across the river Mitheithel in Eriador, so-called because it was both the southernmost bridge across the river and the easternmost on the Great East Road.

Last Homely House The House of Elrond in Rivendell. It was known to Elves as 'The Last Homely House East of the Sea'.

Last Mountain A translation of *Methedras*, literally 'Last-peak' (Sind.); the southernmost of the Misty Mountains.

'The Last Ship' The title of a Fourth Age Hobbit-poem found in the Red Book of Westmarch and published as No. 16 in *The Adventures of Tom Bombadil*. The significance of this piece of 'foreign' verse is discussed elsewhere (see FÍRIEL).

Last Shore An Elvish symbolic or poetic reference to the shores of Eldamar in the Uttermost West, beyond the furthest Seas.

Laura Baggins Bilbo's paternal grandmother (born Laura Chubb). Her husband was Mungo Baggins of Hobbiton; their son was Bungo who married the famous Belladonna Took.

Laurelin the Golden The name given by the Eldar of the Undying Lands to the Younger of the TWO TREES of Valinor; its other names were *Malinalda* and Culúrien. The Elder Tree was named Telperion.

Laurelin, which means 'Golden-song' in the Quenya tongue, bore shining golden leaves, the Light from which mingled with the Flowers of Silver of Telperion to illuminate the land of the Valar and certain parts of Eldamar. The Two Trees were the most ancient in the World, and were prized above all else by the dwellers in Valimar and Eldamar. But both were poisoned by Melkor (Morgoth) during the First Age. And although a seedling of Telperion survived (see GALATHILION) there were no known descendants of Laurelin – except the Sun (Anar), which was made, so the Elves say, from the last Leaf of Gold, coaxed from the dying Laurelin by Yavanna Kementari, Maker of the Two Trees.[5]

Laurelindórenan 'Land-of-the-Valley-of-Singing-Gold' (Q.) The full High-elven name for the Golden Wood of Wilderland in Middle-earth; in the Third Age this forest was called LOTHLÓRIEN.

The origin of this exceedingly ancient name is not altogether clear. One might have had no hesitation in assuming that it was given to the Golden Wood by the Eldar, as they passed westwards during the Great Journey – except that it contains the element *Laurelin*, which is of course also (and originally) the name of the Golden Tree of Valinor: a word the migrating Eldar would not then have known. The only other possibility is that *Laurelindórenan* is a name given to the Golden Wood by Galadriel, when she came there with Celeborn in the middle of the Second Age. Likewise *Lothlórien*, which contains the name of the Vala Irmo (*Lórien*), argues a knowledge of Valinorean affairs, and therefore a High-elven origin (although the *loth*- element, meaning 'blossom' or 'flower', is inconveniently Sindarin in form).

See also LÓRIEN.

Lay of Eärendil A poem made in the early Second Age (probably in Lindon) by an unknown minstrel, concerning the Voyage of Eärendil the Mariner, and what came of it. (It is quite unconnected, so far as is known, with *Earendil Was A Mariner*, a poem composed by the Hobbit Bilbo Baggins in the late Third Age.)

Lay of Leithian The story of Lúthien Tinúviel and Beren of the Edain; the original poetic account from which all subsequent extracts or translations have been drawn. (Nine of its verses appear, translated, in Book I Chap. 11, while further verse-extracts, together with a much longer prose rendition, may be found in *The Silmarillion* pp. 162–87.) It is, we are told, the second longest poem surviving from the Elder Days – though the title of the longest is not known for sure,[6] nor has the full text of the *Lay of Leithian* yet been published, except in the (much abbreviated) prose form mentioned above. All that remains to be said about this work is that it was originally composed in the Grey-elven or Sindarin language, and in the *ann-thennath* mode.[7] For long it was preserved only in the memories of living Elves, but thanks largely to the Hobbit Bilbo Baggins, it was eventually copied down in written form, and so has come to survive into our own day, as part of the collection of legends, poems and traditions assembled by Bilbo in Rivendell (under the 'working' title *Translations from the Elvish*), and ultimately published as *The Silmarillion*.

Leithian is a composite word which translates as 'Release-from-Bondage'; this is indeed the recurrent theme of the Tale of Beren and Lúthien: release from the bondage of the Quest, and of Beren's vow; release from the bondage of life in a darkened Middle-earth; release from the constraints of a Death that would have separated them for ever; and finally, release from the Circles of the World.

See also LÚTHIEN TINÚVIEL.

Lay of Lúthien See preceding entry.

Lay of Nimrodel An Elven-chant telling the story of the maiden NIMRODEL, who dwelt during the Third Age on the borders of Lothlórien, near the fair stream which later bore her name. The verse, a section of which is translated in the Red Book (Book II Chap. 5), was said to be of Silvan (Wood-elven) origin.

See also AMROTH.

Leaflock A translation of the name FINGLAS (Sind.).

Lebennin A province of Gondor; a wide green land which lay between the rivers Gilrain and Anduin and the lower reaches of the Erui. In the far south it was bounded by the Anduin delta and in the north by the eastern range of the *Ered Nimrais*, the White Mountains. Its chief city was the ancient port of Pelargir, on the Anduin.

Lebethron A variety of tree found in Gondor – and much prized by the woodwrights and carpenters of that land for the beauty and strength of its black wood.

Lefnui The chief river of the province of Anfalas in Gondor. It rose in a great western coomb of the White Mountains and wandered gently to the Sea, its mouth forming the 'heel' of Cape Andrast.

Legolas 'Green-leaf' (Sind.) It may seem curious that with all the mighty Elven-lords who dwelled in Rivendell at the time of the Council of Elrond, it should have been an Elf of Mirkwood who was actually chosen to join the Fellowship of the Ring. Legolas was the son of King Thranduil of Mirkwood, and thus an Elven-prince of Sindarin blood – but Elves far older and mightier than he could have been chosen for the Quest and would not have refused.

Yet all Elrond's choices were apt. Guided perhaps by Gandalf ('Even if you chose for us an Elf-lord, such as Glorfindel, he could not storm the Dark Tower, nor open the road to the Fire . . .'[8]), Master Elrond selected the Company of the Ring for reasons of fellowship rather than for strength or latent power. This Fellowship was to represent each of the Free Peoples – Hobbits, Men, Dwarves and Elves – and Legolas the Elf and Gimli the Dwarf, whose road home lay together, were both selected to journey 'at least to the passes of the Mountains, and maybe beyond'.[9] In the event both remained with the leader of the Fellowship until the end of the War of the Ring.

During these travels far from his home two profound experiences deeply affected the Elf. Like all of his race, Legolas was a lover of trees, and the venerable growths of Fangorn – most ancient of all forests still surviving in Middle-earth in those days – filled him with great wonder. More significantly, his journeys with Aragorn and the Grey Company brought him to the seaward lands of Lebennin, where he heard for the first time the crying of gulls, stirring within his breast the ancient and mystic 'sea-longing' of his people.

As is told in the Red Book, after the conclusion of the War of the Ring and the dawning of the Fourth Age, Legolas brought Elves of the Silvan race south from Mirkwood to the uplands of Ithilien, where they dwelled for a while in the fairest province of Gondor, with the permission and blessing of the King. One of the last notes in the Red Book states that after the Passing of King Elessar (Year 120 Fourth Age), Legolas at last followed the desire in his heart and sailed over Sea, taking with him his great comrade, Gimli Elf-friend, Dwarf of Durin's Line. 'And when that ship passed an end was come in Middle-earth of the Fellowship of the Ring.'[10]

Legolin A river of Ossiriand, a tributary of Gelion. Its source lay in the Blue Mountains.

Lembas (from orig. *lenn-mbass*) The Sindarin name for a kind of travellers' food or 'way-bread', baked by the Elves of Lothlórien. It resembled *cram* (the biscuit of the Men of Dale) in purpose but not in effect, being quite delicious and greatly sustaining, the more so if it was not mingled with other foods. It consisted of light-golden meal-cakes which kept fresh for many days if left in their mallorn-leaf wrappings.

The Quenya name was *coimas*, 'bread of life'.

Lenwë One of the Eldar of the Great Journey, of the Telerin Kindred; he was the leader of those of the Teleri – the last-comers, afterwards called *Nandor* – who baulked at the crossing of the Misty Mountains and thus became separated from all the other Eldar; and as a result never came to Aman. This was the second sundering of the Elves (the first had been the division between Eldar and Avari). Lenwë remained in Wilderland, but his son Denethor, together with a more adventurous remnant of the Nandor, wandered eventually into Eriador, and later still into Beleriand, where they became known as 'Green-elves'. But Lenwë's fate is not known.

Léod A Lord of the Men of Éothéod and the father of Eorl the Young, first King of Rohan. Like many Men of his northern land, Léod was a great horse-tamer, and one day he chanced to capture an animal which could not be tamed, eventually threw him, and thus caused his death. Léod's son Eorl hunted the stallion and caught him, claiming the animal's freedom as weregild for his father's death; this horse, Felaróf, was the first of the fabled *Mearas*.

See also ÉOTHÉOD.

Leofa 'Beloved' The nickname given in Rohan to King BRYTTA.

Lhûn (pl. *Luin*) 'Blue' (Sind.) See LUNE.

Light-elves The CALAQUENDI.

Lightfoot A horse of Rohan, the dam of Snowmane, steed of King Théoden.

Lilly Cotton The wife of Farmer Tolman ('Tom') Cotton and mother of Rose Cotton, who wedded the illustrious Sam Gamgee.

Limlight A river flowing eastwards from the northern marches of Fangorn Forest into the Anduin. It was accounted the northern border of Rohan.

Linaewen 'Lake-of-[small]-birds' (Sind.) the marsh-encircled lake in the middle of Nevrast.

Lindar 'The Singers' (Q.) The oldest name of the Third Kindred of the Eldar. See TELERI.

Lindir An Elf of Rivendell, possibly a minstrel. His name means 'One-who-sings' in Sindarin.

Lindon 'Country-of-Song' (Sind.) In origin, a name given by the exiled Noldor of Beleriand to the green, unknown country between the river Gelion and the Blue Mountains. This region was known to its inhabitants, the Green-elves, and to the Sindar, as OSSIRIAND. But the High-elves never crossed the lower Gelion, and the name *Lindon* reflects their (entirely occidental) impressions of this green, secret land, the sweet singing of whose inhabitants could be heard far across the river. (The Green-elves were a subdivision of the Nandor, who were a division of the Teleri, most musical of all Elves; see also FALMARI.) Consequently the Blue Mountains (Ered Luin), which the Noldor never crossed during their exile, became known to them as the *Ered Lindon*.

But at the end of the First Age most of Beleriand was drowned or broken in the upheavals of the earth brought about by the destruction of Angband in the North; and the Sea flooded in, even between Thargelion and Ossiriand, inundating the valley of the river Ascar and the middlemost peaks of the Mountains of Lindon. (See GULF OF LUNE.) *Lindon* then became the name given by all Elves to all the lands remaining west of the Blue Mountains. What had formerly been Thargelion became *Forlindon*, 'North Lindon', while that fragment of Ossiriand which had also escaped inundation was henceforth called *Harlindon*, 'South Lindon'. In the Second and Third Ages the Elven peoples of Lindon were a composite race made up of Noldor, Sindar, Green-elves and Falathrim, though most of the Noldor at first settled in Forlindon, under the rule of their last High King,

Gil-galad; while Celeborn, kinsman of Thingol of Doriath and mightiest of the surviving Sindar, ruled the Grey-elves and the other Teleri in South Lindon. But in after years, many of the Sindar migrated eastwards; and still later (c. 750 Second Age) a great number of the Noldor of Forlindon, led by Celebrimbor, also passed across the Blue Mountains, to settle in Eregion near the Dwarves' city of Moria. Gil-galad, however, remained in Lindon as High King, and ruled all the Elves, of whatever Kindred, who likewise did not desire to relinquish the sea-coasts.

For the first thousand years of the Second Age Lindon had peace and the Eldar prospered under the rule of Gil-galad. But by the middle years of the Age, Sauron, servant of Morgoth during the Elder Days, had arisen and was plotting the overthrow of the Elves of Middle-earth. To this end he seduced the High-elves of Eregion and, by means of the Rings of Power, betrayed them. So began the War of the Elves and Sauron, in which only Lindon held out against the reborn Dark Power. In the year 1695, the hosts of Sauron rolled into Eriador; within four years they had crushed Eregion and driven Gil-galad back to the Lune – and only aid from Númenor prevented the assault which would have swept the Elves of Lindon into the Sea.

Although there followed a long period of peace for the Westlands of Middle-earth, Sauron had not been destroyed; and when, at the end of the Age, he made war against the survivors of fallen Númenor, they entreated the help of Lindon. Thus Gil-galad led the Elven-folk of his land to join the Dúnedain of Arnor and Gondor in the Last Alliance against Sauron. In this war, Elendil of the Dúnedain and Gil-galad of Lindon were both slain; but Sauron himself was also cast down.

Ruled by Círdan the Shipwright, Lindon continued to endure throughout the Third Age which followed, though for many years her eastern border was threatened by Angmar. The arising of this evil 'Witch-realm' was the greatest peril faced by the peoples of Eriador during the Age, and the now-diminished Elven-hosts of Lindon gave frequent aid to the Dúnedain of Arnor in their long-fought war against the Witch-king. In the end, he was overthrown by a great feat of arms (the BATTLE OF FORNOST, 1975 Third Age), in which Elves of Lindon played a notable part.

After this last great endeavour, the people of Lindon withdrew altogether from the affairs of Men and lived quietly in their green land between the Mountains and the Sea. They took little part in the War of the Ring, and quietly maintained their realm into the Fourth Age. Lindon was thus the longest to endure of all Eldarin realms in

Middle-earth. Indeed, the Grey Havens were still maintained there after most of the Elves of Lindon had passed over Sea. Círdan himself is said to have lingered until the last ship set sail.

Lindórië 'Singer' (Q.) A Númenorean princess of the Line of Andúnië, sister of Eärendur and mother of Inzilbêth (wife of Ar-Gimilzôr, twenty-second King of Númenor).

Line of Anárion See HEIRS OF ANÁRION; LINES OF DESCENT.

Line of Isildur See HEIRS OF ISILDUR; LINES OF DESCENT.

Lines of Descent The Genealogical Tables originally provided with this entry have here been revised to incorporate the very extensive material made available for the first time with the publication of *The Silmarillion*. In order to avoid mere duplication of the four tables already available in that work (pp. 305–8), I have compressed these Lines of Descent into two charts, representing, in the first case, the ancestry of Aragorn and Arwen as it was derived from the Eldar; and in the second chart, the same Line of Descent traced from the Three Houses of the Edain. In addition I have shown those Lines of Descent from the Eldar and the Edain which, by Aragorn's day, had long been extinct.

These complicated family trees contain several notable features. Firstly, the ancestry of the *Peredhil* (Half-elven) brothers Elros and Elrond united the bloodlines of the (Noldorin) House of Fingolfin, the (Sindarin) House of Thingol, and all Three Houses of the Edain of Beleriand. Elros Tar-Minyatur passed on this lineage, through the Dúnedain of Númenor, Arnor and Gondor, to Aragorn. But Elrond his brother wedded Celebrían daughter of Galadriel and Celeborn (who was akin to Thingol, though the exact relationship is not known); *their* children – Elladan, Elrohir and Arwen Undómiel – were thus descended also from Finarfin of the Noldor. And the union of Aragorn and Arwen drew together all these ancient Lines of Descent.

The only Eldarin House which does not play a part in the composition of this royal lineage (which also, for good measure, includes a Maiarin strain) is, of course, that of Fëanor. For reasons too well known to require restatement here, this Line of Descent became accursed of the Valar, and dispossessed of the High-kingship. Six of Fëanor's seven sons perished without issue. Only Curufin passed on his clouded ancestry – to his son Celebrimbor. But though Celebrimbor lived until the middle of the Second Age, and laboured

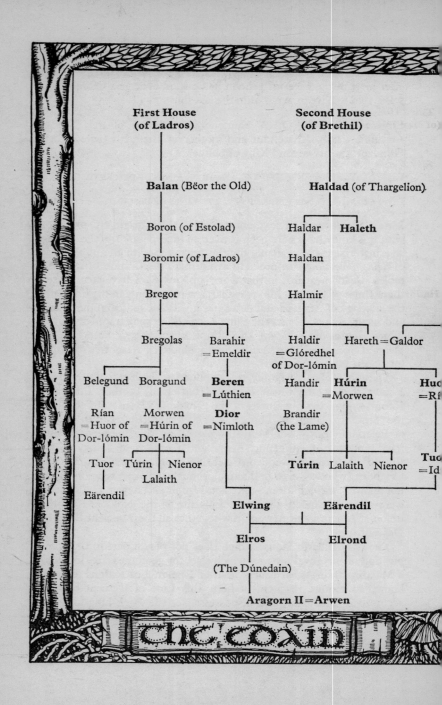

First House
(of Ladros)

Second House
(of Brethil)

Balan (Bëor the Old)   **Haldad** (of Thargelion)

Boron (of Estolad)   Haldar   **Haleth**

Boromir (of Ladros)   Haldan

Bregor   Halmir

Bregolas   Barahir   Haldir   Hareth = Galdor
                  = Emeldir   = Glóredhel
                                     of Dor-lómin

Belegund   Boragund   **Beren**   Handir   **Húrin**   Hu
                        = Lúthien   = Morwen   = Rí
Rían   Morwen   **Dior**   Brandir
= Huor of   = Húrin of = Nimloth   (the Lame)
Dor-lómin   Dor-lómin

Tuor Túrin Nienor   **Túrin** Lalaith Nienor   Tuo
      Lalaith   = Id

Eärendil

                        Elwing   **Eärendil**

                        Elros   **Elrond**

                        (The Dúnedain)

                        Aragorn II = **Arwen**

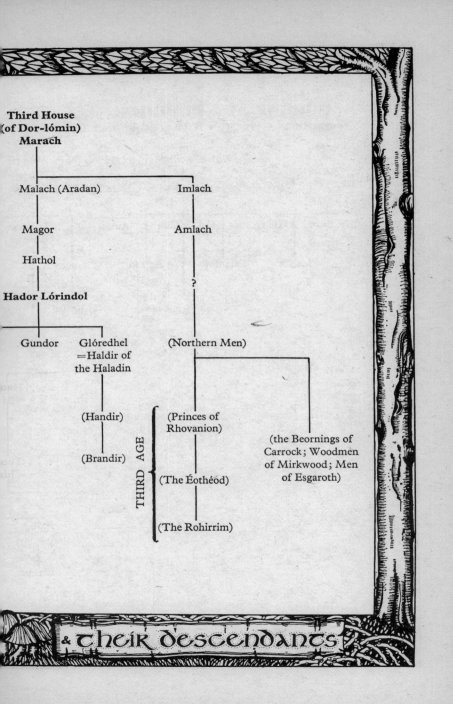

**Third House
(of Dor-lómin)
Marach**

Malach (Aradan)   Imlach

Magor   Amlach

Hathol   ?

Hador Lórindol

Gundor   Glóredhel   (Northern Men)
= Haldir of
the Haladin

(Handir)   (Princes of
Rhovanion)

THIRD AGE

(Brandir)

(The Éothéod)   (the Beornings of
Carrock; Woodmen
of Mirkwood; Men
of Esgaroth)

(The Rohirrim)

& THEIR DESCENDANTS

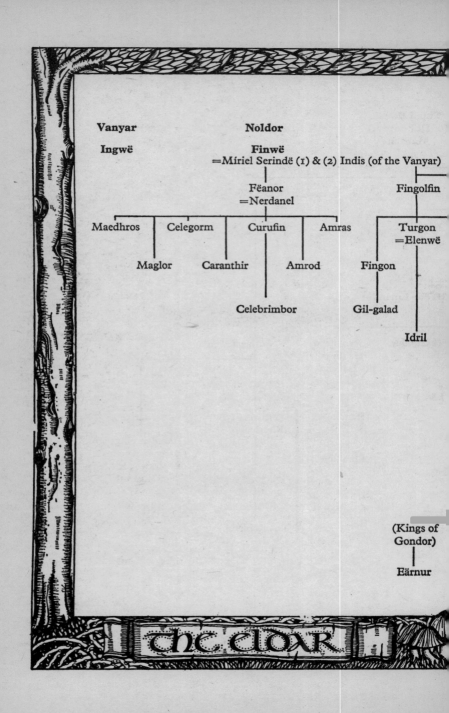

Vanyar   Noldor

Ingwë   Finwë
        =Míriel Serindë (1) & (2) Indis (of the Vanyar)

        Fëanor   Fingolfin
        =Nerdanel

Maedhros Celegorm Curufin Amras   Turgon
                      =Elenwë

   Maglor   Caranthir   Amrod   Fingon

        Celebrimbor   Gil-galad

                   Idril

                 (Kings of
                 Gondor)

                 Eärnur

The Eldar

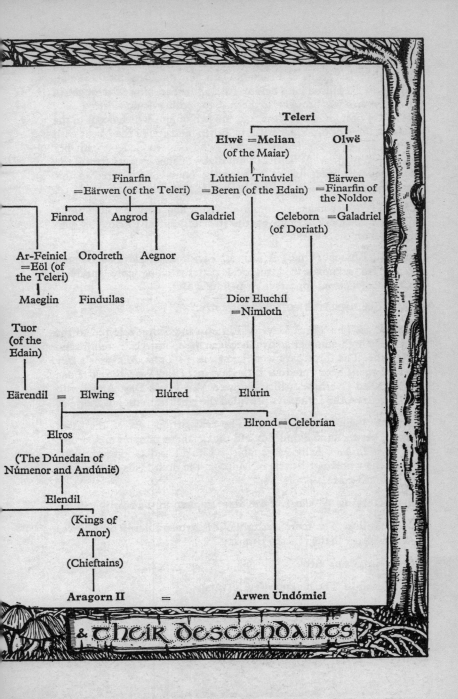

Teleri

Elwë =Melian   Olwë
(of the Maiar)

Finarfin   Lúthien Tinúviel   Eärwen
=Eärwen (of the Teleri)   =Beren (of the Edain)   =Finarfin of
the Noldor

Finrod   Angrod   Galadriel   Celeborn =Galadriel
(of Doriath)

Ar-Feiniel   Orodreth   Aegnor
=Eöl (of
the Teleri)

Maeglin   Finduilas   Dior Eluchíl
=Nimloth

Tuor
(of the
Edain)

Eärendil = Elwing   Elúred   Elúrin

Elrond =Celebrían

Elros

(The Dúnedain of
Númenor and Andúnië)

Elendil

(Kings of
Arnor)

(Chieftains)

Aragorn II   =   Arwen Undómiel

& their descendants

throughout that time to repair his ancestor's fault, he could escape neither the last fruits of Fëanor's Oath, nor the Curse of the Valar, laid upon his House long before. And all he had himself wrought in Middle-earth was brought, in the end, to nothing – and worse.

Also of note: in each of the four 'mixed' unions which occur in the Tables (three of the Eldar with the Edain, and one of the Maiar with the Eldar), it is the female partner who has wedded beneath her station, so to speak. Whether or not males of species were thought to be genetically incapable of crossing the bounds of kindred in this (descending) fashion, is a question that must remain unanswered.

Linhir The second most important town and port of Lebennin, a province of Gondor. It lay on the river Gilrain just below its confluence with the Serni.

Linnod 'Rhyme' (Sind.) A form of Elvish word-play, which conformed to acknowledged metrical patterns. The only surviving example of a *linnod* appears in Appendix A I(v).

Lithe See FORELITHE and following entry.

Lithedays The Three Days of Lithe in the Shire, referred to the three-day high-summer festival between the months of Forelithe and Afterlithe. The three days were known as – *1 Lithe, Mid-year's Day* and *2 Lithe*. There were four Lithedays in a Leap Year, the extra one being called Overlithe, which followed Mid-year's Day. Along with the Yuledays, the Lithedays provided the chief festivities of the year.

Lithlad 'Plain-of-Ash' (Sind.) The arid region east of the Dark Tower, between the Barad-dûr and the northern rampart of Mordor, the *Ered Lithui* ('Ashy Mountains'). Lithlad and Gorgoroth comprised the whole north-west of Mordor; the drab fields of Nurn lay to the south-east.

Little Delving A village of the Shire, located in the Northfarthing.

Little Gelion The more westerly of the two tributaries of the river Gelion. It rose in the Hills of Himring.

Little Kingdom Arda.

Little People The Periannath (Hobbits).

Loa 'Growth' (Q.) The term used by the Elves when referring to their (seasonal) 'year' of 365 days. In contrast, their ritual 'year', the *yen* (pl. *yeni*) was equal to no less than 144 *loa*.

The *loa* observed six primary divisions, based upon the cycles of growth perceived in natural vegetation – above all, in trees. In Quenya, these six 'seasons' were: *tuilë, lairë, yávië, quellë* (also called *lasse-lanta*), *hrívë* and *coirë*. Their equivalents in the Sindarin or Grey-elven tongue were: *ethuil, laer, iavas, firith* (or *narbeleth*), *rhîw* and *echuir*. These may be translated: spring, summer, autumn, 'fading', winter and 'stirring'. These 'seasons 'were of a fixed length, with *lairë* and *hrívë* containing 72 days each, while the other four each contained 54. An additional 5 days (which did not belong to any season) brought the total to 365. The primary deficiency resulting from this system of computation was corrected by adding three extra days every twelfth year. See also Appendix D.

Lobelia Sackville-Baggins If the available records of the period can be relied upon in this particular instance, then the long-standing feud between the Bagginses and the Sackville-Bagginses of the Shire was a truly regrettable affair in which most Hobbits sided with Bilbo and his heir, Frodo – presumably less for the justice of their cause than as a reaction against the unpleasant and shrewish nature of Lobelia Sackville-Baggins.

Lobelia had been born a Bracegirdle of Hardbottle, but had later married Otho, son of Longo Baggins and Camellia Sackville. Otho was an undistinguished Hobbit and Lobelia concentrated her affections upon their only son, Lotho (whose pimply countenance was reportedly a source of much unkind mirth among younger Hobbits). As Bilbo's nearest relatives (Otho was actually his cousin), the Sackville-Bagginses longed inexpressibly to dwell in his magnificent residence at Bag End. And when, in 2942 Third Age (1342 Shire Reckoning), the then heirless Bilbo disappeared while on an adventure in the East, Lobelia and her husband initiated proceedings to have him declared legally dead so that they might inherit his luxurious hole.

Bilbo himself relates (in the account he titled *There and Back Again*) how he most inconveniently returned just as his belongings were being auctioned off – riding up the Hill of Hobbiton with a pony laden with gold, and looking remarkably fit and unquestionably alive. The Sackville-Bagginses contested his identity for a while and the feud continued until Bilbo's disappearance in the year 3001 (1401 S.R.), when the disposal of his entire estate (which included the Desirable Residence) significantly omitted the S-Bs – save for a 'gift' of spoons. The prestigious *smial* was left to Frodo, whose relations with Lobelia remained strained until his eventual decision to leave the Shire, and sell the place to her. Lobelia was thus obliged to wait for almost eighty years from the time she had first believed Bag End to be hers.

Vindictive and grasping as she undoubtedly was, Lobelia was also indomitable, and she thus earned great respect from other Hobbits during the occupation of the Shire by agents of Saruman. On one occasion, after being insulted by one of these rogues, she attempted to savage him with her umbrella, although she was then quite old and only half his size. As a result, she was imprisoned in the Lockholes; and during her confinement there, her weakling son was murdered by Wormtongue, at Saruman's order.

Lobelia was released from her prison after the Battle of Bywater (1419 S.R.), emerging to great applause and cheering. She was touched by this but also stricken by the news of her only son's death, and she relinquished Bag End to Frodo in order to return to Hard-bottle, where she died the following spring. In her will, she left her money to help Hobbits made homeless during the occupation.

Lockholes Storage-*smials* or tunnels in the township of Michel Delving, converted into prisons by agents of Saruman during the occupation of the Shire in 3019 Third Age (1419 Shire Reckoning).

Loeg Ningloron 'Pools-of-golden-water-flowers' (Sind.) The GLADDEN FIELDS.

Loendë Midsummer's Day, the Mid-year's Day of Kings' and Stewards' Reckoning. There were three such 'extra' days (belonging to no particular month) in the old Númenorean Calendar of Kings' Reckoning, and five in the later revised system of the Stewards. In the Fourth Age the system was again revised so that the year began in spring instead of mid-winter; therefore, in this New Reckoning, *loendë* fell between the months which were equivalent to our September and October.

Lómelindi 'Dusk-singers' (Q.) The High-elven name for nightin-gales (the birds of Melian). See also TINÚVIEL.

Lómion 'Child-of-Twilight' (Q.) The secret name given by Ar-Feiniel, the White Lady of the Noldor, in her own (proscribed) tongue, to the son she bore Eöl, in Nan Elmoth. Eöl himself after-wards named the boy MAEGLIN.

Lond Daer 'Shadow Havens' (Sind.) The name given to the ancient ruins at the mouth of the river Gwathlo (Greyflood) during the Third

Age. (They are not shown on all maps.) Nothing whatever is known of these ruins, or their name; though there may be a connection with the name *Daeron*. As the ruins themselves appear to lie offshore, and as the name *lond* means 'harbour', one may conjecture that, at some time in the remote past, an ancient Elf-haven was inundated by the sea (a simple rise in sea-level would account for this; there is no necessary connection with any of the known inundations).

Lonely Isle A translation of the composite (Sindarin/Quenya) name *Tol Eressëa*.

Lonely Mountain A translation of the Grey-elven name EREBOR.

Longbeards The Dwarves of Durin's House. A noble growth was considered a sign of wisdom, age and maturity in all Dwarves, but the beards of Durin's Line exceeded all others; they were often forked and worn tucked into the belt.

Longbottom A village in the Southfarthing of the Shire where was grown most of the pipe-weed so much in demand elsewhere. The Southfarthing was more sheltered and sunny than other parts of the Shire, and 'leaf' (especially those favourite varieties known as 'Old Toby', 'Longbottom Leaf' and 'Southern Star') grew richly and abundantly there. The first recorded appearance of this curious herb was about the year 2670 Third Age (1070 Shire Reckoning) in the gardens of Tobold Hornblower, 'Old Toby' himself.

See also PIPE-WEED.

Longbottom Leaf See previous entry.

Long Cleeve A village in the Northfarthing, home of the North-tooks, who were descendants of Bandobras 'Bullroarer' Took, hero of the Shire and one of the great Hobbits of history.

Longholes A family of Bree Hobbits.

Long Lake A lake in northern Wilderland some miles south of Erebor and Dale; it was watered by the Forest River of Mirkwood and the river *Celduin* or 'River Running', which passed out of the southern end of the lake and wandered for many miles before empty-ing into the Inland Sea. The Long Lake was particularly notable for its Lake-town of Esgaroth, which was built upon stilts.

Longo Baggins The second son of Mungo Baggins of Hobbiton, and the uncle of Bilbo. He married Camelia Sackville, and their only child Otho was the first of the Sackville-Bagginses.

Long Peace The name given by the Eldar of Beleriand to the period of two centuries which followed the first appearance of the Dragon Glaurung, during which Morgoth lay quiescent in Angband and attempted nothing openly against his enemies. The Long Peace ended – shockingly – with the Battle of Sudden Flame; and henceforth war never ceased in Beleriand, until the end of the Age and the overthrow of Morgoth.

Long Wall A translation of the Sindarin name ANDRAM.

Long Winter The winter of 2758–9 Third Age, when snow fell thickly over the westlands of Middle-earth, and hardships were accentuated by the famine which followed. Both Gondor and (particularly) Rohan suffered additionally from attacks made against their realms at this time (see HELM HAMMERHAND).

Lóni A Dwarf of Erebor and a member of Balin's expedition to Moria (2989 Third Age). In the year 2994, Orcs attacked the colony and Lóni, together with his comrades Frár and Náli, fell defending the Bridge and the Second Hall.

Lord of All A title awarded to Melkor (at the instigation of Sauron) by the (heretical) later Númenoreans.

Lord of Caves See FINROD FELAGUND.

Lord of the Earth A title assumed by Sauron the Great[11] during the period of his ascendancy in Middle-earth during the Second Age – the Accursed Years, as they were called by his subjects.

Lord of the Nazgûl See MORGUL; RINGWRAITHS; WITCH-KING.

Lord of the Rings Sauron the Great of Mordor, Enemy of the Free Peoples and self-styled Master of Middle-earth – in his aspect as Ruler of the One Ring, which in turn ruled all the Rings of Power.

Lord of the West A translation of the Adûnaic title *Ar-Adûnakhôr*, adopted by the twentieth King of Númenor in preference to the traditional High-elven royal name (the Quenya equivalent was *Herunúmen*). This signalled both a return to the ancient Mannish tongue of the Edain and a deliberate renunciation of Eldarin mores and modes of speech. The title had previously been applied only to the 'Elder King' of the Valar, Manwë.

Lord of Waters The Vala ULMO.

Lords of Andúnië The Princes of the Faithful of Númenor, descendants of King Elros Tar-Minyatur through Valandil, son of the Lady Silmariën, daughter and elder child of Tar-Elendil, fourth King. They lived in Andúnië, westernmost province of Númenor, and held true to the traditions of friendship with the Eldar – when the later Kings (and most of the people) of Númenor departed from these ways, growing envious of the High-elves.

The Faithful were increasingly persecuted for their loyalties, but many endured – and in the end were the only Númenoreans to survive the Downfall of their land (in 3319 Second Age). These survivors reached the shores of Middle-earth in nine of their ships, bearing the Silver Rod, the seven *palantíri* and other heirlooms of their House. They were led by Elendil, son of Amandil, last Lord of Andúnië.

Note on the Númenorean Succession: the law allowing women to inherit the throne of Númenor was made after the sixth King, Tar-Aldarion, left only one child to succeed him; she became Tar-Ancalimë, the first ruling Queen. Before her time, the King had always been succeeded by his eldest son – and so the Lady Silmariën, although the elder child of Tar-Elendil (fouth King), became, not Queen of Númenor, but sister of the new King, Tar-Meneldur.

See also NÚMENOR.

Lórellin The name given in Eldarin tradition to the lake of the gardens of Lórien, in Valinor. Here the Vala Estë, spouse of Lórien (Irmo), slept by day.

Lorgan An Easterling chieftain, a subject and ally of Morgoth. He and his folk were awarded the land of Dor-lómin, after Morgoth's victory of the Nirnaeth Arnoediad had dispossessed the Edain (of the Third House) who had previously dwelt there. Tuor, son of Rían and Huor, was enslaved by this man, but escaped after three years' servitude.

Lórien The name given in Eldarin tradition to the Gardens, in Valinor, of the Vala Irmo, one of the two *Fëantúri* (his brother was Mandos). Irmo was usually called after the name of the Garden, *Lórien*. In memory of this fair place in the Blessed Realm, the High-elves (probably Galadriel) altered the original (now unknown) Nandorin name of the Golden Wood of Wilderland to this form. The more formal Quenya name for the Golden Wood was LAURELIN-DÓRENAN.

See also LOTHLÓRIEN.

Losgar A place near the mouth of the Firth of Drengist, probably its southern shore. Here, in the Sunless Year, Fëanor of the Noldor burned the fleet of ships which had carried himself and his host back from Aman to Middle-earth.

Lossarnach A province of Gondor. It nestled under the south-facing vales of Mount Mindolluin, to the south-west of the city of Minas Tirith.

Note: the name *Arnach* (*Lossarnach* means 'Snowy-*Arnach*') is of pre-Númenorean form (like *Erech, Rimmon, Eilenach*) and is in the language of the race of Men who made their homes in the high reaches of the White Mountains during the Dark Years of the Second Age.

Lossoth 'Snow-people' (Sind.) The Snowmen of Forochel, who dwelt on the shores of the great Ice Bay on the edge of the Northern Waste. According to a note in the Red Book they were:

a strange, unfriendly people, remnant of the Forodwaith . . . The Lossoth house in the snow, and it is said that they can run on the ice with bones on their feet, and have carts without wheels.[12]

Lost Isle Another name for the 'Lonely Isle' of *Tol Eressëa*.

Lótessë 'Flower-month' (Q.) The name of the fifth month of the year in Kings' Reckoning, as used in Númenor during the Second Age and by most Westron-speakers of Middle-earth in the latter part of the Third. *Lótessë* was unaffected by the changes made when Stewards' Reckoning replaced Kings' Reckoning in the last third of the Age; however, with the advent of New Reckoning, in the Fourth Age, it became the second rather than the fifth month of the new Calendar (adapted to begin the year in spring instead of winter). In all these systems, *Lótessë* had thirty days and was roughly equivalent to our May.

The Sindarin form of the name, *Lothron*, was used by the Dúnedain; the Hobbits' name for this month was Thrimidge (used in both the Shire and Bree).

Lothíriel The daughter of Imrahil, Prince of Dol Amroth, and wife of Éomer, eighteenth King of Rohan. They wedded in the last year of the Third Age, and their son, Elfwine the Fair, eventually succeeded Éomer.

Lothlann 'Wide-and-empty' (Sind.) The name given by the Eldar of Beleriand to the great steppe which lay east of Ard-galen and north of Maglor's Gap. It was conquered by Morgoth during the Battle of Sudden Flame.

Lothlórien 'Dream-flower' (Sind.+Q.) The composite word which was the most widely used name, in the Third Age at least, for the Golden Wood of Wilderland, called also *Lórien* and *Laurelindórenan*. This ancient forest stood upon both sides of the river Celebrant, to the west of Anduin, and was believed by some of the Wood-elves (Nandor) of Mirkwood to be the land where all their kindred had once dwelt, before migrating north (probably in the Second Age).

While Lothlórien was not the most ancient forest in Middle-earth, it was unquestionably the most singular: for only there were to be found the great *mellyrn*, the mallorn-trees which gave the Golden Wood its name. Golden were the leaves of those trees and their boughs were silver-grey; and they grew to a height beyond the measure of all other living things. And the people of Lothlórien were as singular as their trees, for they did not dwell on the ground, but in the woven branches of the mighty *mellyrn*, on high platforms (or *telain*). For this reason the Elves of the Golden Wood were called the *Galadhrim*, 'Tree-people', and they were the noblest of all Silvan Elves.

During the Elder Days, the Galadhrim dwelled happily in their golden forest and nothing disturbed the world outside, until the end of the First Age – when many of their remote kinfolk suddenly returned to Middle-earth in order to make war upon Morgoth the Enemy. Although this long, 'hopeless' war was primarily waged far away to the north-west, it is known that the ensuing Great Darkness of the victorious Morgoth reached even as far south as Fangorn, so the forest of Lórien must then have been entirely surrounded by Evil. Yet it did not founder in that dark tide, which ultimately brought ruin and a change of the world – when many fair Elf-kingdoms were swept away along with the Evil in the cataclysm that ended the Age.

The Second Age brought many changes for the Elves who remained in Middle-earth, particularly for the Grey-elves, whose ancient homelands had been for the most part inundated at the Breaking of Thangorodrim. Chief among the Grey-elven lords were Thranduil and Celeborn, both kinsmen of Thingol Greycloak, who had once been the greatest King of Elves upon Middle-earth. Some time in the first third of the Age, Thranduil passed east to Greenwood – whither many of the Elves of Lórien had migrated in the

Elder Days – and he founded a realm there in the north of the forest. But Celeborn, the mightier of the two, came to the forest of Lórien, and the Galadhrim (to whom the Eldar were as Kings) received him gladly and welcomed his folk, and eventually even adopted the Grey-elven tongue (which they ever after spoke with an 'accent').

Celeborn's Queen was of even nobler race. Though she was called *Galadriel* by the Sindar, her High-elven name was *Altariel*, and she was the sister of Finrod Felagund, fallen King of Nargothrond. Galadriel was thus the most royal of all the surviving High-elven Exiles, and therefore of all Elves then living in Middle-earth. More-over, she brought with her to Lórien one of the Three Elven-rings: Nenya, the Ring of Adamant. And though she was unable to wield Nenya while Sauron possessed the Ruling Ring, her own power was too great to be overthrown, and so Lórien survived the Accursed Years, when Sauron extended his dominion.

In the Third Age the forest of Lórien became a source of strange rumour; its borders were shunned by folk of other race, and even the Wood-elves of Greenwood were sundered from their southern kinfolk. For although Galadriel and Celeborn took part in the high Councils held by the Wizards and the Chief Eldar, the Wise kept secret the true nature of the place which came to be known as *Lothlórien* ('[land of the] Blossoms-of-Dreaming'). The Lord and Lady and their court dwelt deep in the heart of the forest, in a great arboreal city: *Calas Galadhon*, 'the City of the Trees', where grew the tallest and most beautiful *mellyrn* of the land. And the power of Galadriel, focused through the Ring of Adamant, laid a change on the Golden Wood, so that it was set apart from the stream of time, ageing far more slowly than other lands.

It was at the end of the first millennium of the Third Age that the power of Sauron grew once more, and there arose in the southern heights of Greenwood a dark tower of evil repute, 'though the Shadow in the Forest . . . was not yet known for what it was.'[13] *Dol Guldur*, this tower was called, for the Wise then believed it to be inhabited by one of the Nazgûl (who had escaped when their Master was overthrown at the end of the Second Age). It was at this time that the forest began to be populated with evil things, and the name of Greenwood was changed to *Taur e-Ndaedelos* ('Forest of Great Fear'), which has been translated from the Red Book as *Mirkwood*. Both Thranduil's realm to the north and Celeborn's to the west became islands of refuge as the power of Dol Guldur spread through-out the forest of Mirkwood and into the adjacent lands. Nonetheless, it was not until the end of the second millennium that the situation grew perilous. In the year 1980 a Balrog appeared in Moria and the following year the Dwarves of that realm were driven away in exile. There were then two evils to be feared and Lothlórien lay in between them. Accordingly, many of the Galadhrim then decided to journey to safety across the Great Sea, forsaking Middle-earth altogether. (As is told elsewhere – see AMROTH – this was the choice taken by one of the last Silvan Princes of the land.)

Yet Lórien endured throughout the Third Age, even though the peril from Dol Guldur grew greater as the years passed, and there was often deadly strife with Orcs and other fell creatures under the fair boughs of the *mellyrn*. It is recounted in the Red Book how members of the Fellowship of the Ring, fleeing from Moria, were sheltered in Caras Galadhon, and were greatly assisted by the Lord and Lady of Lórien. Shortly after their departure, the Golden Wood suffered the heaviest assaults it had yet experienced from Dol Guldur: in March 3019, Orc-hosts crossed the Great River and assailed the Galadhrim in three separate waves – but all were beaten back and in the end, the Elves of Lórien themselves took the offensive, crossing the Anduin eastwards and destroying Dol Guldur.

Nonetheless, with the victory of the War of the Ring, the great days of Lórien came at last to an end. For Galadriel's long exile in Middle-earth was rescinded by the Valar as a reward for her labours against Sauron (and for her rejection of the Ruling Ring). At the end of the Third Age she took ship into the West, together with the Bearers of the other Rings of Power; and shortly after her passing, Celeborn also deserted the Golden Wood. In the Fourth Age only a few of the Galadhrim still 'lingered sadly . . . and there was no longer light or song'[14] in Lothlórien.

See also EAST LÓRIEN; LAURELINDÓRENAN.

Lotho Sackville-Baggins The weedy and ineffectual only son of Otho and Lobelia Sackville-Baggins. Due to an unfortunate facial complaint, his nickname (among younger Hobbits) was 'Pimple'. Nonetheless, after the death of his father in 3012 Third Age (1412 Shire Reckoning), Lotho became the nominal head of the clan, and was afterwards singled out for manipulation from afar by Saruman – who was already beginning to take an interest in the Shire.

The family had always been well-to-do, and had owned much property in the Southfarthing, including farms and leaf-plantations. The foolish Lotho was easily inveigled into purchasing more of the same, far more than he could possibly afford, and as much of the money for these purchases came from Isengard, he was quickly caught on one of the oldest of all hooks. By the time of the War of the Ring the Hobbit was so indebted to Saruman that he was helpless to prevent the Wizard's agents from entering the Shire and following their master's will, while ostensibly working for 'Pimple'. In this way Lotho was the key to Saruman's control of the Shire – though once this had been accomplished, of course, Saruman had little need of him. Lotho was eventually murdered by Gríma Wormtongue, on the orders of 'Sharkey', in 1419 Shire Reckoning.

Lothron See LÓTESSË.

Loudwater A translation of the Grey-elven word *Bruinen*, which was the name of the river whose two source-streams marked the ancient boundaries of Rivendell, in Eriador.

Lugbúrz 'Dark-tower' (Black Speech) The name given by Orcs and other fell creatures to the ancient Fortress of Sauron. The Dark Tower was known to the Elves and the Dúnedain as *Barad-dûr*, which carried the same meaning.
Note: the word *Burzum* (Black Speech) almost certainly meant 'Darkness'. (See also RING-INSCRIPTION.)

Lugdush An Orc of Isengard, one of the Uruk-hai. During the War of the Ring he was part of a raiding company led by Uglúk across northern Rohan as far as the Great River. The raid was partly successful, and the returning Uruk-hai had reached the very borders of Fangorn before being caught by the Riders of Rohan. All the Orcs perished in the subsequent battle.

Luinil 'Blue-star' (Sind., from *luin-êl*). One of the stars wrought by Elbereth (Varda) for the lighting of Middle-earth at the time of the Awakening in Cuiviénen.

Lumbar (meaning not known) As preceding entry.

Lune A rendering in the Common Speech of the ancient Grey-elven word *Lhûn* (pl. *Luin*), 'Blue'. The word appears in these three different forms in the names of several features of western Eriador, including the great river (*Lhûn*), which arose in the far north, and the great Gulf of Lune, where the river finally reached the Sea. To the north and south of the Gulf rose the *Ered Luin*, 'Blue Mountains'.

Lúthien Tinúviel The Elven-daughter of Thingol Greycloak of Doriath and the Lady Melian of the Maiar. She is remembered as the most beautiful maiden ever to walk the earth; and she was the most beloved of all her Kindred. Yet she chose to relinquish her Elven immortality, and to share the destiny (the Gift) of Men: for the sake of a Man: Beren son of Barahir of the Edain, whose life and death were woven with hers. Thus Lúthien was lost to Elvenkind, and dwells now beyond the West, apart from all her kindred, save one.

The days of Lúthien lie now in the deep past, and not all of her story is known or recorded. She was born in Menegroth, in Doriath, in the middle of that epoch of the First Age known as the Years of the Trees; and her father Elwë (Thingol), was the highest and noblest of all the Elves remaining in Middle-earth, and the mightiest ruler. Moreover, Lúthien's mother was Melian of the Maiar, a Handmaiden of the *Valier* (Queens of the Valar) Vána and Estë, and akin to the great Yavanna Kementári, who of all the Valier was accounted second only to Elbereth (Varda). Lúthien's ancestry therefore included strains of the Valar, Maiar and Eldar; it was the most illustrious Line of Descent that has ever been in Middle-earth.

For years uncounted Lúthien grew slowly to womanhood ('As the stars above the mists of the world was her loveliness, and in her face was a shining light'[15]); while across the Sea in the Undying Lands her kindred, the Falmari (Telerin Elves whose king was Lúthien's father's brother Olwë) came at last ashore in Aman, and made for themselves a maritime realm in northern Eldamar. During this forgotten time Middle-earth slept under starlight and Melkor lay imprisoned in the Halls of Mandos. But all things pass, and all epochs wane. The age-old peace was doomed to wither away, in rebellion and war. High-elves came back to Middle-earth to wage war on Melkor (Morgoth), who himself had already returned, to Angband which he had rebuilt. And even before Melkor's flight from Aman his will had crossed the Sea and stirred his servants into life. Middle-earth became evil; and Beleriand was invaded. Thingol withdrew into Doriath, which Melian had already surrounded with a Girdle of enchantment, through which none could penetrate. And all this time their child, whom they dearly loved, had never set foot beyond the beech- and holly-forests of her homeland. Nor did Thingol intend her to, while evil roamed the lands outside.

If events had moved differently, Thingol might have had his way; and he and Melian would not have been sundered at the last from their only daughter. But Fate did not so decree; and the coming of Melkor, which had been followed by the coming of the Noldor, was now followed by the appearance in Beleriand of altogether a new race: the Mortal Men whose awakening had long been prophesied. But though Morgoth was never able to pierce the Girdle of Melian (neither were the Noldor or indeed any other Elves), this new race possessed qualities which were not fully understood by the Quendi, or even by the Valar; and no enchantments were fully proof against them. The Edain entered the affairs of the time in dramatic fashion; and they aided the Eldar in their war; and many of them died in this cause; and at last one of them, Beren the son of Barahir of the First House, fleeing from the war-torn North, passed the Girdle, and entered Neldoreth, and the reencountered the daughter of Thingol of the Grey-elves. And from that instant their fates were joined.

The full tale of Beren and Lúthien, and their love for each other, and Thingol's bitter opposition to the match, and the vow made by Beren in response to the (ill-omened) challenge of Thingol, and the Quest of the Silmaril, and the fulfilment of the vow, and the death, in Neldoreth, of Beren, followed by that of Lúthien – and of their return to this life, by the grace of the Valar – is, of course, the subject of the *Lay of Leithian*, an exceedingly long poem composed during the First Age and subsequently recorded by the Hobbit Bilbo Baggins; in which form it has descended to us. This story appears in *The Silmarillion* (rendered into prose form), and thus requires no further re-statement. The Quest was successful, and the Silmaril was recovered (though it would have been better for all, especially Thingol, if it had not been); but Beren was slain by the Wolf of Angband; and Lúthien herself soon afterwards died of grief.

In the Halls of Mandos they might have been separated for ever, for the fate of Men is apart from that of the Elves; and theirs was the first union between the Kindreds – a union for which no precedents then existed. But for their goodness and valour and utter faithfulness this grace was granted to them: that Lúthien might be permitted, if she so wished, to exchange her Elven-life for the mortality of Men; and, moreover, if she so chose, that she and Beren would be granted a second lifespan in mortal lands. Lúthien did so choose, and she and Beren walked again in Middle-earth, in the green and secret country of Ossiriand; and there she bore Beren a son: Dior the Beautiful. And though in due course she and Beren died for the second time, it was also granted to Lúthien that her Line should never fail. Dior was the father of Elwing, who wedded Eärendil, who bore the Silmaril out of Middle-earth and brought succour to Elves and Mortals alike. And Eärendil's sons were Elros and Elrond. From Elros was descended Aragorn of the Dúnedain, and from Elrond Arwen Undómiel, who was said to walk in the likeness of Lúthien; and who, offered the choice of her Foremother, likewise relinquished her Eldarin immortality – for the love of a Mortal Man.

See also LINES OF DESCENT.

Lúva The Quenya or High-elven word for 'bow', but more properly, the title of one of the two primary brush-strokes upon which each of the Fëanorean Tengwar ('letters') were constructed. The *lúvar* could be both open and closed, and were doubled in certain letters.

See TENGWA, TENGWAR.

Notes

1 Book II Chap. 2.
2 'Sauron's hand . . . *was black and yet burned like fire, and so Gil-galad was destroyed*' (Book II Chap. 2).
3 Book II Chap. 2.
4 This prophecy is widespread among the cultural traditions of latter-day Men: notably the Norse and Jewish peoples.
5 There may be some connection with the name *Laurelindórenan*. See entry of that name.
6 Possibly the *Noldolantë*.
7 'Gift-of-words'; other details of this compositional method or style are unknown.
8 Book II Chap. 3.
9 *Ibid*.
10 Appendix B.
11 Cf. 'Lord of This World', an ancient title of Satan (Lucifer).
12 Appendix A I(iii).
13 Appendix III.
14 Appendix B.
15 Book I Chap 11.

Mablung 'Heavy Hand' (Sind.) One of the Sindar of the First Age; he was the chief captain of the hosts of Doriath. He attended the Feast of Reuniting (Year of the Sun 21) as one of the two emissaries of Thingol Greycloak, and was at the Hunting of the Wolf Carcharoth, in Neldoreth. A few years after this he and his companion-at-arms, Beleg Cúthalion, were granted permission to join the Union of Maedhros (though not to serve the Sons of Fëanor), and so came to be at the Nirnaeth Arnoediad, which both somehow survived, although fighting with the host of Fingon. Afterwards both these mighty Grey-elves became enmeshed in the Doom of the Children of Húrin; but though Beleg was slain, Mablung survived this episode. (He was the last living being to speak with Túrin Turambar.) Mablung then returned to Doriath, and was later slain guarding Thingol's treasury from pillaging Dwarves. Thingol himself had already perished.

Maedhros The eldest of the seven sons of Fëanor. He was born in Eldamar but, as is told in *The Silmarillion*,[1] joined his father's rebellion against the Valar, and took the Oath, and participated in the Kinslaying at Alqualondë, and came back to Middle-earth in exile. Maedhros is said to have opposed the burning of the ships at Losgar – for he was a great friend of Fingon, son of Fingolfin – but shortly after this event, the host of Fëanor and his sons was attacked by Orcs from Angband (see BATTLE-UNDER-STARS), and Fëanor was mortally wounded. Maedhros thus became his heir.

Yet he never became High-king of the Noldor in exile; for shortly after the Battle-under-Stars, he was captured by Morgoth, and tormented. But from this dreadful predicament he was rescued by

Fingon his friend. In his gratitude, and to show repentance for the abandoning of the host of Fingolfin, Maedhros himself proposed that the High-kingship be given to Fingon's father Fingolfin (though not all the brothers agreed with this).

The Noldor were now reunited, and in the years which followed the great among them chose realms for themselves, along the line of mountainous country which separated Beleriand from the North. Maedhros and the other sons of Fëanor were allocated the eastern sector of this 'front' (which was afterwards called the March of Maedhros); and Maedhros himself centred his realm on the Hills of Himring. On the tallest of these hills he built a great fortress. For many centuries he and his brothers did their part in the War; but there came the day of the Dagor Bragollach, and Dorthonion was captured, and the Pass of Aglon was forced; but Himring held. Yet after a decade or so, when the impetus of the Bragollach had spent itself, and the Eldar and their allies had begun to regain lost territory, Maedhros – who was the mightiest in war of all the sons of Fëanor – determined to do yet more.

He then formed the so-called 'Union of Maedhros', which was in reality an attempt again to unite the scattered Eldar, and defeat Morgoth in open battle. And although not all he summoned to the cause came to aid him (for the Sons of Fëanor had by now alienated many of their former allies, by their bad faith and by the general effects of the Oath, which was driving them to ever more evil deeds), a great army was assembled; and once more the Elves took the military initiative.

Too soon. Dorthonion was recaptured, and the passes to east and west of this highland; but in so doing Maedhros prematurely revealed the growing strength of the Eldar, and so Morgoth was prepared.

The day came of the great battle which Maedhros had so carefully planned. His own army was to manoeuvre provocatively on the desert of Anfauglith (formerly the grassland of Ard-galen) thus inviting attack from Angband – and this attack was itself intended to be countered by another Eldarin army, the host of Hithlum led by Fingon the High King. But treachery was at work in Maedhros' camp (SEE ULDOR THE ACCURSED), and from the beginning things went badly wrong. Maedhros himself was hindered from opening the campaign in the planned manner, and meanwhile Morgoth successfully decoyed the host of Fingon out on to the desert, where they became gravely embroiled in a losing battle. Then Maedhros arrived – and for perhaps an hour the Eldar were closer than ever before to winning the decisive victory which would have brought them within sight of regaining the Silmarils, and fulfilment of the Oath. But again treachery played its part, as it was doomed always to do, and the host of Maedhros was taken in the rear, and destroyed, though the Sons of Fëanor escaped; and an end was come of the might of the Eldar in Middle-earth. Himring was captured, and all Beleriand lay open to the Enemy.

For the remainder of his life in Middle-earth Maedhros had no fixed dwelling. He and his brothers wandered the Western Lands, bereft of all power to fulfil their dreadful oath, but driven still by the need to attempt it. During this time the sons of Fëanor comitted many grievous wrongs – among them the assault upon Doriath and the slaying of Dior Eluchíl, of Nimloth his wife, and of his two young sons. Maedhros had no part in this evil deed, and is said to have repented of the murders (the murderers themselves were slain); but soon afterwards he himself, having learned of the presence of the Silmaril of Doriath at the Havens of Sirion, like his brothers launched war upon other Elves in an attempt to regain the Jewels. But once more the Sons of Fëanor succeeded only in causing many deaths, and much anguish; and they did not gain a single Silmaril.

But also at this time Eärendil sailed into the West, and the Host of the Valar came across the Sea, and Morgoth was cast down, and the lands were broken and changed. Even now the last two sons of Fëanor, Maedhros and Maglor, attempted to seize the two surviving *Silmarils*, by force, from the keeping of the Valar. And at last they were successful, though only at the cost of more murders. Caught and trapped, they were, nonetheless, spared, and fled, each with a single Jewel. But the Silmaril that Maedhros had taken seared his hand, and he came to the end of his endurance, for he knew himself to be defiled. And he slew himself, in a deep chasm, bearing the Silmaril to his unknown grave.

Maeglin 'Sharp-glance' (Sind.) The only son of Eöl the Smith and Aredhel Ar-Feiniel the daughter of Fingolfin. In his youth he left the woods of Nan Elmoth, in East Beleriand where he had been born, and came to Gondolin, the Hidden City ruled by his mother's brother Turgon. And in Gondolin he was given lordship and powers of command, and wealth, and the love of Turgon besides; but in the end the evil that had been planted in him at his birth worked to its fulfilment, and Maeglin betrayed the city, and so came to be accursed in the memory of the Elves.

Maeglin's story is told elsewhere,[2] and this requires little more than summary in these pages. The evil that was in him was planted at his begetting, for his father, the Grey-elven smith Eöl, was an Elf of dark mood and secretive habits, jealous and misanthropic. But his mother was wilful, and feckless. The combination did not immediately show itself, for Maeglin, as a young Elf, was silent and shrewd; and he withheld his mind from all, even his parents. It was at this time that he first heard of Gondolin, and of Turgon, and of the power of the Noldor; and he determined to come there, and be adopted by Turgon as his heir.

And so it nearly came to pass. Ar-Feiniel secretly quitted Nan Elmoth, and took her son with her, and they were welcomed by Turgon; and Maeglin, even as he desired, was given great honour in the Hidden City, as a prince of the highest rank. But Eöl had followed the errant pair, and also came to Gondolin; and in the ensuing interview with Turgon Eöl slew his wife – in an attempt to slay his son, who had renounced him – and was himself slain, by being cast from the hill of Gondolin. Then Maeglin, as the only descendant of the dead Ar-Feiniel, was looked upon by Turgon with even more favour, and as he had wished he became the mightiest prince of Gondolin, after the King. But he was never named as Heir, nor did he succeed to this title while his life lasted. And after a long while, when it had at last become plain to him that this was being withheld from him, his ambition turned to jealousy, and his loyalty to malice.

Yet for all this Maeglin indeed served Turgon well and faithfully throughout most of his life; indeed, he was more assiduous in enforcing the ordinances of the King than Turgon himself. And he fought bravely at the Nirnaeth Arnoediad, for he was no coward – in battle. It was otherwise, however, when he was taken prisoner and threatened with torment (as indeed it might be with worthier folk); and Maeglin told all he knew about the hidden entrances to Gondolin, and promised to betray the city from within, in exchange for his freedom. And so he did. Gondolin was taken, and Turgon was slain – and Maeglin himself was killed, which was perhaps the better for him.

Why did he act thus, and throw away all his years of waiting and patient service? Because he had discovered that he would never become the heir of Turgon. For on the field of the Nirnaeth, Huor son of Galdor of Dor-lómin, spoke with Turgon and prophesied the mingling and continuing of their Lines of Descent. Maeglin overheard these words – and it must have been bitter indeed to learn that his service would thus go unrewarded (as he himself must have put it; for by now he had forgotten the love and honour that had always been his in Turgon's house). And it was this final quenching of his long hopes which made him susceptible to threats, of the kind employed against him by his captors. In the last battle, he was slain by Tuor (the eventual Heir of Turgon), and died in a manner like to his father before, by being cast from the precipice of Amon Gwareth.

Maglor The second of the sons of Fëanor; and the most renowned of all Elven-minstrels, save only for Daeron of the Grey-elves. He was the composer of the *Noldolantë*, the epic poem from which much of the material in *The Silmarillion* has been derived. Like his elder brother Maedhros, Maglor was less apt to evil than the other Sons of Fëanor – and yet he also took the Oath of Fëanor, and took part in the massacre of the Teleri at Alqualondë, and thus came under the Curse of Mandos; and he went back to Middle-earth in exile, as part of his father's host. And though he fought valiantly against Morgoth, in the end he too fell into evil, being constrained by the Oath; and he came to a bitter end. Yet he regained a Silmaril before he did so, and so came at least in part to fulfil his Oath before he died. (But whether or not he escaped that obliteration of the spirit which was the penalty of oathbreaking, none can now say.)

In Beleriand, Maglor ruled the weakest part of the Elves' northern front, strategically speaking: the area of open ground which lay between Himring and Mount Rerir and its foothills. Here were stationed many Eldarin cavalry, and Maglor commanded them. The region he thus defended became known as Maglor's Gap. But its weakness as a place of defence was always readily apparent, and many times the armies of Angband attempted to force it – sometimes with success. The Dagor Bragollach brought with it the eclipse of Maglor's realm, and the beginning of his wandering days in Middle-earth.

For the rest of his life in Middle-earth Maglor shared the destiny of Maedhros. They dwelled together on Himring, fought together – and lost – at the Nirnaeth Arnoediad; and afterwards found refuge where they might. Neither had any part in the slaying of Dior and the rape of Doriath, but in later years both led an equally reprehensible attack on other Elves, at the Havens of Sirion. (The reason, of course, was the presence of a Silmaril there – which their Oath demanded they seize from all who withheld it.) In this battle many Elves on both sides were slain, and Elros and Elrond, the sons of Eärendil, were taken prisoner (though well-treated, especially by Maglor); but the Silmaril escaped, and passed over Sea with

Eärendil and Elwing. Only two of the Jewels now remained in Middle-earth, and when these were taken from Morgoth, by the avenging host of the Valar, the two eldest sons of Fëanor again attempted to recapture the Jewels. And they succeeded. But it was too late, as Maglor had indeed suspected. Finding that he could not endure the touch of the single Jewel which was his portion, he cast it into the Sea, and both the Silmaril and he were never again seen in Middle-earth; though his fate is not known for sure.

Maglor's Gap The name given by the Eldar of Beleriand to the region of open country which lay between Himring and Mount Rerir: the abode and realm of Maglor, the second son of Fëanor. It was the weakest point in the line of the Siege. See also preceding entry.

Maggot See FARMER MAGGOT.

Magor One of the Edain of the Third House; he was the grandson of Marach, and the son of Malach Aradan, who led the Third House from Estolad into the north. However Magor, together with a large following, quitted the march west of Brethil and dwelt instead near the sources of the Teiglin. In later days his grandson, Hador Lórindol, led this House of Men back into the north, and became the first lord of Dor-lómin.

Mahal (Khuz.) The Dwarves' name for their Maker: the Vala Aulë.

Máhanaxar (Q.) The (untranslated) name given in the traditions of the Eldar for the Ring of Doom in Valinor: the place of assembly and lawgiving of the Valar, outside the gates of Valimar their city, and adjacent to the Mound of the Two Trees.

Mahtan One of the Noldor of Eldamar; the father of Nerdanel the wife of Fëanor. He was a mighty smith and craftsman, and the teacher of Fëanor in his youth.

Maiar The people of the Valar, likewise of the race of the AINUR but of lesser rank, and in greater number, than their Kings and Queens, the Valar. They dwelt, and dwell, for the most part in Valinor, though some came to Middle-earth, for reasons both good and evil, and thus have shared in the deeds of mortal lands.

Those names of the Maiar recorded in the traditions of the Elves are as follows: *Eonwë*, the Herald of Manwë; *Ilmarë*, the Handmaid of Varda; *Ossë*, *Uinen*, and *Salmar*, who serve the Lord of the Sea,

Ulmo. *Sauron*,[3] who served originally Aulë, but who fell under the influence of Melkor and so became evil; *Melian*, who was of the following of Vána and Estë, and who came to Middle-earth in the Elder Days and wedded a King of Elves, so passing on a strain of the Ainur among the *Erusën:* the mother of Lúthien Tinúviel; *Arien*, who also originally served Vána, but who was chosen to steer the Sun (Anar) through the Heavens; *Olórin*, a Maia of Nienna, the wisest and greatest of the Istari (Wizards) who came to Middle-earth in the Third Age (where he was known as Gandalf the Grey); and *Tilion*, of the service and following of Oromë, who afterwards became the Steersman of the Moon. In addition there are those lesser Maiar known in after Ages as *Valaraukar* (or *Balrogs*), spirits of fire who served only Melkor, the Maiar who were known in Middle-earth as *Curunír* and *Radagast*, and the (unnamed) remaining two of the five *Istari*, all of whom were Maiar of Valinor in their origins, though not all returned across the Sea.

See also *Valaquenta* (passim).

Malach Aradan The son of Marach, chieftain of the Third House of the Edain. While he was still a young man his people, last of the Three Houses of the Edain, crossed the Blue Mountains into Beleriand, and came to dwell in Estolad. Some years later, while his father was still hale and active, despite his age, Malach, for love of adventure and love of the Eldar, left Estolad and went to Hithlum to serve Fingolfin the High King, thus laying the foundations of a friendship and alliance between the kindreds which would reach its greatest glory under his descendant Hador Lórindol—and win its greatest renown in the days of Húrin and Huor. Malach dwelt there for fourteen years, and was named *Aradan* ('Royal-man'), but on his father's death returned to Estolad, and in after years led a great part of the Third House away into the North, to Hithlum. But his own son Magor instead passed south-west to dwell in East Beleriand, near the sources of the Teiglin. Not until the days of Hador did this last remnant of the Third House finally rejoin their kin in the North.

Malbeth the Seer Although the Elvish gift of foresight was in some measure bestowed upon all of the Dúnedain, ever and anon one would emerge whose talents in this direction far exceeded those of others among his race. Such a man was Malbeth the Seer, a King's Counsellor during the reigns of Araphant and Arvedui of Arthedain. Consequently, his foretellings were recorded in the annals of the North-kingdom and were long remembered by the Dúnedain.

Two of Malbeth's prophecies concerning the destiny of all the

Dúnedain are recounted in the Red Book. The first dealt with the fate of King Arvedui ('*Arvedui* you shall call him, for he will be the last in Arthedain . . .'[4]). Malbeth foresaw two possibilities for Arvedui: either he would be the last King of Arthedain *and* the first of the Reunited Kingdom of Arnor and Gondor – or he would perish, and the Kingship in the North would end with him. Arvedui duly laid claim to the Throne of Gondor when it fell vacant upon the death of King Ondoher (in 1944 Third Age), but the Council of Gondor refused this claim, choosing instead a victorious General, Eärnil. This choice of the Dúnedain eventually led to the failing of the Kingdom in the North, and the end of Arvedui.

Malbeth's second prophecy concerning the fate of the Númenorean race in Middle-earth remained dark and unexplained for a thousand years after his death:

> *Over the land there lies a long shadow,*
> *westward reaching wings of darkness.*
> *The Tower trembles; to the tombs of kings*
> *doom approaches. The Dead awaken;*
> *for the hour is come for the oathbreakers:*
> *at the Stone of Erech they shall stand again*
> *and hear there a horn in the hills ringing.*
> *Whose shall the horn be? Who shall call them*
> *from the grey twilight, the forgotten people?*
> *The heir of him to whom the oath they swore.*
> *From the North shall he come, need shall drive him:*
> *he shall pass the Door to the Paths of the Dead.*[5]

Malduin 'Golden-river' (Sind.) A tributary stream of the Teiglin; it rose in the most north-easterly part of East Beleriand, in the Ered Wethrin.

Malinalda 'Golden-tree' (Q.) One of the many names in the lore of the High-elves for the Golden Tree of Valinor, the Younger of the Two Trees: *Laurelin* as it was commonly known.

Mallor From 1029–1110 Third Age, the third King of Arthedain.

Mallorn, Mellyrn 'Tree-of-Gold' (Sind.) A species of tree found nowhere else in Middle-earth save the forest of Lothlórien. Indeed, the mallorn-trees gave the Golden Wood its name, for they were tall and beautiful, with trunks of silver bark, and their leaves were of deep gold, recalling to the High-elves (who had named the forest

Laurelindórenan) the 'Singing-Gold' of Laurelin the Golden, one of the Two Trees of Valinor.[6]

Unlike other trees of Middle-earth the *mellyrn* did not shed their leaves until spring, when the new leaves were already thrusting through. Then the Wood was carpeted and roofed with gold, and shaded with silver. In the tops of these trees dwelt the Elven people of Lórien, safe from their enemies upon high platforms or *flets*, called *telain* in the Grey-elven speech.

Note: in the Fourth Age a new mallorn appeared, the only one ever to grow outside Lothlórien. This was the tree grown in the Shire from a single mallorn-seed given to Samwise Gamgee by the Lady Galadriel herself. It was planted in the place where the Party Tree had once flourished, and soon became the wonder of the neighbourhood.

Mallos 'Snow-gold' (Sind.) A small, belled, golden flower which, together with the flower *Alfirin*, blossomed in the green fields of Lebennin during the early springtime.

M **Malta** The Quenya or High-elven word for 'gold', but more properly the title of the Tengwa number 18, used to represent the sound *m* in most cases.

Malvegil From 1272–1349 Third Age, the sixth King of Arthedain. After his reign, the Kings of Arthedain again claimed the rule over all ancient ARNOR (the Line of Isildur being extinct by this time in both Cardolan and Rhudaur); and in token of this claim, they all took the royal prefix *Ar-*. The first such King was Argeleb I, son of Malvegil.

Mandos In Eldarin tradition, the name given to the Vala *Námo* the elder of the two *Fëanturi* or 'Masters of Spirits'; more properly, the name of his domain, the Halls of Waiting in the Uttermost West of Valinor, where the spirits of the dead go, to linger according to due before passing on, with the consent of Mandos, to their long homes.

See also VALAQUENTA (passim).

'The Man in the Moon . . .' Two Hobbit-poems concerning the Man-in-the-Moon are recorded in the Red Book and have been published together as Nos. 5 and 6 in *The Adventures of Tom Bombadil*. And while the more serious of the two (No. 6) is actually thought to have had its origins in Gondor, both poems are good examples of the Hobbit taste for comic doggerel with a hint of moral to it. No. 5 was written by Bilbo Baggins and also appears in Book I Chap. 9, where it is recited by Frodo in front of the assembled guests at *The Prancing Pony* Inn.

Mannish Tongues The various languages developed by Men of western Middle-earth and Númenor during the First, Second and Third Ages. Though differing greatly from each other in a number of ways including their respective nobility, many of these tongues shared the same basic origin, being descended from the *Adûnaic* speech of the *Edain*, who emerged during the First Age.

Nothing is known of the pure Adûnaic spoken by the Edain before they came into contact with the Elves; and almost nothing is known of the way this language spread in Middle-earth as the early descendants of the Edain were gradually dispersed over the years.[7] However, at the opening of the Second Age, most of the tribes of the Edain left Middle-earth to found the distant island-realm of Númenor – and the broad development of Adûnaic in Númenor is better recorded.

Basically, although the Edain – or Dúnedain – of Númenor long preferred to use Elven tongues for all high matters, the Adûnaic endured as a vernacular speech (greatly enriched by Sindarin and Quenya), and eventually it replaced these Elvish tongues, when it was elevated for nationalistic and racial reasons late in the Second Age. Thus, in a renewed and nobler form, Adûnaic was ultimately carried back to the shores of Middle-earth with the Númenorean ship-captains and traders. There, mingled with the languages of lesser Men, it formed the base for a *lingua franca* of all the Westlands. This was the earliest form of the *Westron* or Common Speech.

Yet not long after this modified language began spreading throughout Middle-earth, the early (Númenorean) form of Adûnaic disappeared altogether. For the people of that island committed a great evil and their land was drowned under the Sea; and those few who escaped the Downfall were not users of the Mannish tongue. Therefore, by the very end of the Second Age, traces of the Adûnaic survived only in the Westron – and in the various tongues of Men descended from the few Edain (and their close kin) who had remained in Middle-earth and gradually become dispersed.

During the early years of the Third Age these remote descendants of the Edain were mostly settled in the northern parts of Eriador and Wilderland, and thus can be conveniently referred to as Northern Men. They ultimately included: Men from the Carrock and the vales of Anduin, Men of Dale and Esgaroth, the Woodmen of Western

Mirkwood and the Riders of Rohan. Other peoples who adopted the Mannish tongues used by these Northern Men were Dwarves, and Hobbits (who eventually abandoned their older Northern tongue for the Common Speech).

Of course, there were a number of other Mannish tongues known in the Third Age which were not even remotely akin to the Adûnaic-based Westron and the Northern language group, and these included one particularly mysterious tongue. This was the language of the Dunlendings, a secret race of Men who dwelt on the borders of Rohan. Although their speech was apparently never recorded, it was thought to be a degenerate descendant of the language spoken by their ancestors of the Second Age, the Men of the White Mountains. Some trace of this earlier language spread to northern Eriador with a tribe of their remote descendants, who eventually settled in Bree; and much later a tongue related to Dunlendish was carried to the Shire by the Stoors (Hobbits) who had once dwelt in Dunland. This accounts for some of the odd words and names found in Bree and Buckland in the late Third Age.

Of the other unrelated Mannish tongues mentioned in the Annals of the Third Age very little can be said. These included the strange speech of the Woses or 'Púkel-men' of Druadan Forest, as well as the tongues of the Haradrim and Easterling peoples. As the Men of Harad and the various tribes of Easterlings, though traditional enemies of Gondor, were so distant as to be almost unheard-of in the Shire, it is not surprising that little information about them was ever recorded by the Hobbits.

See also Appendix F; SPOKEN TONGUES.

Manwë Súlimo The noblest of the Ainur, and the brother of Melkor; afterwards Lord of the Valar (who were those Ainur who went down into Arda after the Creation, and dwelt there): the 'Elder King' of the World, who rules, together with his spouse Varda (Elbereth), from his high palace on the summit of the mountain Taniquetil, tallest of the Pelóri, in Valinor; the Lord of Winds (which is a meaning of the Quenya title *Súlimo*), and friend of birds, especially Eagles.

See also *Ainulindalë* (p. 19–21), and *Valaquenta* (passim).

Marach An early chieftain of the Edain of the First Age; the fore-father of Hador, Húrin and Huor, and leader of the Third House on the great journey from the eastlands into Beleriand. He and his people settled at first in Estolad, near the encampment of the People of Bëor (the First House), to whom they were akin; and Marach never left that region, ruling until his death. He was succeeded as Chieftain of the Third House by his son Malach Aradan, who quitted Estolad and led the House of Marach into the north and west of Beleriand.

Marcho and Blanco The two (Fallohide) Hobbit brothers who founded the Shire in 1601 Third Age. Year One Shire Reckoning was calculated from the day they led their followers across the Bridge of Stonebows from eastern Eriador.

See also Prologue 1.

March of Maedhros See MAEDHROS.

Mardil Voronwë From 2029–80 Third Age, the first Ruling Steward of Gondor. He eased the South-kingdom through a perilous transitional period after the presumed death of the last King, Eärnur, while simultaneously bringing great honour and renown to his own noble House, from which all the Ruling Stewards were descended. He was known as 'the Steadfast'.

As the name *Voronwë* implies, Mardil was the eldest son of Steward Vorondil (the Hunter); and on the death of his father in the year 2029, he took over the (hereditary) office of the Stewardship and served King Eärnil II for a number of years. After Eärnil's death the Steward likewise served his son Eärnur, until Gondor's last King rode away to Minas Morgul in 2050 and never came back. When no heir to the Throne could be found, Mardil took the rule of the South-kingdom upon himself with the approval of all, and governed the Realm in the name of the King until his own death. For almost a thousand years afterwards this Ruling Stewardship then passed to Mardil's heirs, although no Steward ever called himself King.

Note: Mardil is also remembered for introducing (in 2060, the tenth year of his rule) a series of minor innovations to the King's Reckoning calendar system then in use among the Dúnedain and other peoples of the Westlands – whereby a longstanding deficit of years was restored. This revised calendar became known as *Stewards' Reckoning* and, like its forerunner, it was eventually adopted by most of the Westron-speaking folk of Middle-earth.

Marigold Cotton The younger sister of the famed Samwise Gamgee. She wedded Tolman (Tom) Cotton, eldest son of Farmer Cotton and brother of Rose (to whom Samwise himself was wedded), thus further strengthening the links between the Cottons of Bywater and the Gamgee/Gardners of Hobbiton.

Marish The Marish of the Shire included all those marshy lands which lay on the western banks of the Baranduin (Brandywine) between the villages of Stock and Deephollow. Most of the Hobbits of this region were Stoorish in ancestry and, unlike all other Halflings, were accustomed to wear heavy boots in damp weather. The Marish was traditionally good farming country and, at the time of the War of the Ring, the choicest land in the area was that owned by Farmer Maggot.

Mark of the Riders A translation of the word *Riddena-mearc* (also rendered *Riddermark*); the name given to the country of Rohan by the Riders who dwelt there. They called themselves the *Eorlings* (orig. *Eorlingas*), 'Sons-of-Eorl'.

Mar-nu-Falmar 'Land-under-waves' (Q.) A name given in the High-elven tongue to (Downfallen) Númenor.

Master of Buckland The traditional, hereditary title borne by the head of the Brandybuck Family. This worthy was also sometimes called the 'Master of the Hall' (in reference to Brandy Hall, chief dwelling of the Brandybuck clan). His authority was fully acknowledged in the Buckland – and also across the river Baranduin in the Marish district of the Shire proper.

See also BRANDYBUCK; BUCKLAND; OLDBUCK.

Master of Esgaroth The title borne by the civic leader of the Lake-town on the Long Lake in northern Wilderland.

By the end of the Third Age, Esgaroth was, above all, a trading settlement, for much profitable water-freight was routed through it. Therefore, when the Dragon Smaug destroyed the neighbouring city-state of Dale – whose Kings the Lake-men had previously acknowledged – the Men of Esgaroth found it necessary to elect from among themselves a kind of Chief Merchant or Principal Burgess to conduct the bustling affairs of the settlement and regulate the tariffs. This official was known as the Master of Esgaroth. (As Bilbo Baggins reported in his narrative *There and Back Again*, not all such elected officials were worthy of the task.)

Master of the Hall See MASTER OF BUCKLAND.

Master-stone The eighth and mightiest of the *palantíri* or Seeing-stones made by Fëanor of the Noldor during the Elder Days. Alone of the *palantíri* it never left the Undying Lands, and was kept in the city of Avallónë in Eressëa. The seven remaining Stones were given by the Eldar of Eressëa to Amandil, Lord of the Faithful of Númenor, and by him to his son Elendil the Tall; so they came back to Middle-earth, and in the fullness of time were lost for ever. But the Master-stone abides still in the Far West.

Mat Heathertoes One of the 'Big People' of the village of Bree. During the War of the Ring he was killed in a skirmish between the Bree-people and renegades from outside.

Mathom A hobbit-term for an object of any value for which a use could not be found, but which the owner was not prepared to discard completely. (In the peaceful years of the Shire between the Battles of Greenfields and Bywater, most weaponry was classed in this way.)

Note: in the original (as opposed to translated) Hobbit-speech, the word for such an object was *kast*.

Mathom-house The chief museum of the Shire, where old un-wanted treasures or *mathoms* were kept. It was located in the town-ship of Michel Delving.

Matta In original (as opposed to translated) Hobbit-nomenclature, the name *Matta* (often shortened, Hobbit-fashion, to 'Mat') was normally given to male Hobbits.

Mauhúr One of the Orcs of Isengard; the leader of a patrol which, in February, 3019 Third Age, came to the aid of the Orc-band of Uglúk, encircled by the Rohirrim near Fangorn Forest when returning to Isengard with two prisoners (Book III Chap. 3). Un-fortunately for the trapped Orcs, this attack was insufficient to allow Uglúk's band to escape; and Mauhúr's Orcs were all driven off or slain like the others.

May Gamgee The fourth child of Hamfast Gamgee and the elder sister of Samwise. She was named after Hamfast's only sister.

Mayor of Michel Delving Although his power and importance did not compare with that of the *Thain* (or *Took*) and the *Master* (of Buckland) – hereditary titles borne by the heads of the influential Took and Brandybuck families – the Mayor of Michel Delving was at least the only official of the Shire ever regularly and properly elected, and the office did carry a certain amount of prestige. The Mayor was duly and democratically chosen at the Free Fair, which was held every seven years upon the White Downs. His chief duty was to preside at feasts, though his office was also nominally responsi-ble for the Shirrifs and the Messenger Service.

At the time of the War of the Ring, the elected title had been held by Will Whitfoot for some years; but he was unjustly imprisoned during the 'troubles' of 1419 Shire Reckoning (3019 Third Age), and his long stay in the unsavoury and cramped Lockholes weakened the poor old Hobbit greatly. Therefore, after his release, Frodo Baggins undertook his duties for the eight months it took to restore 'old Flourdumpling' to his former corpulent splendour. At the Free Fair of 1420 Mayor Whitfoot was re-elected for a further seven years.

However, the most famous Mayor in the history of the Shire was, of course, the illustrious Samwise Gamgee, who was elected no less than seven times (between 1427 and 1476 Shire Reckoning). In 1434 S.R. (Year 13 Fourth Age), King Elessar made the Mayor, the Master of Buckland (Meriadoc 'the Magnificent') and the Thain (Peregrin I) all Counsellors of the North-kingdom.

Mazarbul 'Records' (Khuz.) See BOOK OF MAZARBUL; CHAMBER OF MAZARBUL.

Mearas The name given by the Riders of Éothéod (and, later, Rohan) to their remarkable Line of Horse-princes – which they believed to be descended from an animal brought to Middle-earth by one of the Valar during the Elder Days. (See ARAW.)

The *Mearas*, most noble of all horses in Mortal Lands, would suffer none but the King or his sons to ride them, and did not take to bridle and bit. Indeed, the first of the *Mearas* to be recorded, Felaróf, threw his captor, thus causing the man's death – although the animal later attoned for this by surrendering his freedom to his captor's son: Eorl the Young, first King of Rohan. Felaróf understood the speech of Men and was as long-lived as his Master. His descendants, who ended with Shadowfax, were equally long-lived and immeasurably fleet of foot.

Mede See AFTERLITHE.

Meduseld This large and splendid Hall of the Kings was the greatest work of craft ever created in Rohan. It was known as the 'Golden Hall' of Edoras, for the roof and pillars of Meduseld were leafed with pure gold, and its hangings and tapestries were rich.

The Golden Hall was built by Brego, son of Eorl the Young, and at the feast held to celebrate its completion (in 2569 Third Age), his eldest son Baldor rashly vowed to take the 'Paths of the Dead'. Baldor never returned and his sorrowing father died the next year.

In later years all Kings of Rohan had their high seats in Meduseld.

Only once was it ever captured by foes: in 2758 Third Age, the rebel Wulf (son of Freca) took Edoras and slew King Helm's son Haleth at the very door of the Golden Hall. However, Meduseld was re-captured – and Wulf slain – within a year.

Mee 'Princess Mee' is the heroine (and title) of one of those poems originally scribbled in the marginalia of the Red Book and now collected and published under the title *The Adventures of Tom Bombadil*. Though seemingly Elvish in influence, it is plainly a nonsense-rhyme of the sort beloved by Hobbits, and is rich in (somewhat obvious) metrical tricks.

Melian 'Dear-gift' (Sind., from orig. Q. *Melyanna*) A lady of the Maiar, who alone of all the Ainur wedded one of the Erusēn: Elwë (Thingol) of the Telerin Elves. She came back to Middle-earth far back in the Elder Days, at the time when the Eldar were setting out on their Great Journey from Cuiviénen into the West; and in Beleriand, in the secret woods of Nan Elmoth, the sound of her voice sweetly singing was heard by a Lord of Elves, Elwë; and from that moment onwards his fate was linked with hers. It is not known whether or not Melian and Elwë defied any prohibition against wedding with one of lesser race, but wed they were, and Elwë, who had visited Aman by the Grace of the Valar – and who hitherto had sought only to return there – now lingered in Beleriand and, with the aid of Melian, made himself the greatest King of Elves in mortal lands. After the departure of the remaining Eldar they dwelled together in the land of Doriath, and Melian fenced the land with a Girdle of enchantment; and after a time she bore Elwë a daughter: Lúthien the Fair, who inherited her Mother's voice and beauty as well as her divine lineage.

Melian dwelled with Thingol for the remainder of the Age; but, as is told in *The Silmarillion*, the deeds of that time enmeshed her husband at the last, though against her design; and he was murdered. Then Melian withdrew from Middle-earth, and passed into the West, and never again left the Gardens of Lórien in Valinor.

See also *Silmarillion* pp. 55–6.

Melkor 'He Who Arises In Might' (Q.) The name given in the traditions of the Eldar to the firstborn of all the Ainur, the brother of Manwë and the mightiest of all their divine race. Melkor, alone of the Ainur envied his Maker, desiring also to be worshipped and adored. As is told in the *Ainulindalë*, he disrupted the Great Music with themes of his own imagining, but was rebuked by Ilúvatar;

and afterwards, in jealous rage, set himself for ever in opposition to the Creator and to the other Ainur, thus bringing into existence the qualities of Evil and Disharmony – with which his name will be for ever associated. In this way began his long rebellion, which has lasted for uncounted Ages of Eä and is not yet ended, though Melkor himself dwells now in the Void beyond Eä, shapeless and powerless. Of all the tragedies which have since afflicted the off-spring of Ilúvatar, this was the first, and immeasurably the greatest.

See MORGOTH.

Mellyrn See MALLORN, MELLYRN.

Men The younger Children of Eru – and, after the Elves, the noblest of all 'speaking-peoples' of Middle-earth – for whom the Gift of Mortality was expressly conceived as an alternative for life everlasting (the fate of the Elves); the possessors of immortal souls and conse-quent arbiters of their own destiny to a degree not experienced by other peoples; the race of Heroes, Mariners and 'Masters of Horses', who came comparatively late into the Middle-world, yet soon allied themselves with the other Free Peoples and became especial friends of the Firstborn, whom they were destined from their beginning to displace.

For long ages before their first appearance in the Middle-world the coming of the *Atani*, the 'Second People' (as opposed to the Firstborn, the Elves) had been prophesied among the Valar and the Eldar (indeed, this had been the subject of the 'Third Theme' of the *Ainulindalë*.) But not even the Valar knew for certain what form of body they would take. Yet at last the Second People awoke, in the land of Hildórien in the wide East, and this was in the very year that the Sun rose for the first time into the Heavens. For three centuries they wandered gradually away from their birth-place, in all directions save north; and at last the westerly vanguard came first into Wilder-land, and then into Eriador, and finally into Beleriand.[8]

These were the *Edain* (which is the Sindarin form of the more ancient Quenya name *Atani*), originally the term had been applied to the race of Men, but everafter the Elves of Beleriand used it specifi-cally for the Three Houses of the Elf-friends who fought alongside them in their wars against Morgoth, and who dwelt with them in allied kingdoms. Much is said of them elsewhere in this *Companion* (and far more in *The Silmarillion*). What must be emphasized here is the way that their providential contact with the Elves at such a crucial stage in their development singled out this people from all other Mannish races for elevation. Consequently, their direct descendants, the *Dúnedain*, eventually came to term themselves as a 'High People' – in comparison with other Men, whom they divided into 'Middle' and 'Wild' Peoples.

The 'Middle Peoples' shared the same origins and earliest histories as the 'High People', but their development was largely unaided by Elven-lore or fortuitous circumstance. For the ancestors of the Middle Peoples were those of the Edain (and their close kin) who did not pass west to Númenor after the end of the First Age,[9] remaining instead in Middle-earth, where they elevated their culture at a far slower rate. However, they greatly increased in number and by the end of the Second Age, their descendants were far more numerous than those of the Dúnedain who then came back to Middle-earth. Yet the kinship between the two peoples could still be discerned, for the Middle Peoples (who were primarily Northern Men, such as the Rohirrim) were capable of rising to great heights of nobility at need; and if their culture was lower than that of the High Men, then their histories were also untroubled by regret.

(In comparing the destinies of these first two groupings of Men, it is impossible not to find parallels with the 'High' and 'Middle' Elves, i.e., the Noldor and the Sindar, who were likewise separated at an early point in their history but were later reunited under circumstances both grievous and uplifting. Both 'High' groups were early singled out for exaltation beyond the measure of the rest of their kindreds, yet a large proportion of them rebelled against higher authority, and were exiled to Middle-earth as a consequence. And in both cases the 'Middle' race, which had freely elected to remain in mortal lands, found its culture greatly enriched by contact with the returning Exiles, while the higher kindred was obliged to diminish its own culture to some extent in order to lessen the gulf between the peoples.)

A further similarity in the divisions of Men and Elves lies in the third group, comprising those peoples who shared the same basic origins as the two 'Higher' groups but were soon sundered from them – and, as a result, pursued paths of almost totally separate development. For a comparison with the ennobled members of their races, both the Silvan Elves and the 'Wild Men' were rustic and primitive.

The various races of Men who were termed 'Wild' in the lore of the Dúnedain were not akin (except in the remotest possible sense) to the Edain of the First Age, and their subsequent histories display this basic difference. Included in this third grouping were: the Easterlings, the Haradrim, the Men of the White Mountains (and their descendants, men of Dunland), the Variags of Khand and, most alien of all, the Woses or 'Púkel-men' of Druwaith Iaur and (much later) Druadan Forest.[10]

The histories of these 'Wild Men' are all discussed separately elsewhere, and need not be repeated in this entry, which is primarily designed to consider their common origins (as well as some of the curious parallels in the destinies of Men). Unfortunately, their specific origins remain largely unknown: for these races became diverged from the main stream far back in the Elder Days, before any Men became known to the Elves and so entered the records of the time. Yet all the Wild Peoples were true Men, and thus were able, from their beginnings, to discern Good from Evil. And if they were often lured into follies or unthinking vices – by virtue of their ignorance and undeveloped potential – then they also had lesser aspirations and were for long content to live their lives as their forefathers had done, without the real desire for self-improvement which characterized the 'High' and 'Middle' Peoples.

Available evidence suggests that the first of these 'Wild Men' to wander into the westlands were peaceful aboriginal hunters later known as the 'Púkel-men'. During the Elder Days, they settled the regions around the western vales of the White Mountains, especially those lands south of the river Isen (*Druwaith Iaur*). However, early in the Second Age, another Mannish people, much better organized and far less peaceful, followed the hunters into the mountain-valleys and drove them out of their ancient homes. The 'Púkel-men' sought refuge in the southern forests, particularly Druadan, while their dispossessors occupied the fertile uplands and vales of the Mountains.

However, these newcomers eventually found their fortunes diminished by the first rise to power of Sauron of Mordor. For, while they continued to grow in craft, making many works of stone amid the high valleys, they soon fell into Sauron's power, being ruled by him during most of the Accursed Years. These were the 'Men of the Mountains' who built the Dunharrow and the labyrinth under the Dwimorberg – the purpose of which was never recorded – and who later swore an oath of fealty to Gondor which they afterwards broke with terrible consequences. After Sauron's first overthrow and the establishment of Gondor, their race was diminished; they abandoned the Mountains, and only the souls of the Dead remained to trouble the peace of the region.

Significantly, in their strange story and unhappy fate can be seen the seeds of the same destiny which overtook the very noblest of the 'High' People: the Númenoreans. For despite the vast gulf between them, both peoples experienced the same hunger for power un-matched by spiritual growth, and in both cases this resulted in an overreaching of ambition and eventual destruction. So, while the cultural differences among the Mannish peoples were (and still are) immense, ultimately, they were (and are) cancelled out by the great factors in common, most notably Free Will, the gift of all Free Peoples, and the possession of immortal souls tempered by Mortality, the Gift of Men.

Their common inheritance was realized by the wise even before the fall of Númenor had tied the destiny of Men irrevocably to Middle-earth. Indeed, the Third Age was as notable for the alliances forged among Mannish peoples as for the surviving enmities; and although Easterling and Southron peoples assailed the Western King-doms throughout the Age, the aftermath of the War of the Ring brought many signs of renewed hope that, one day, those hostilities might be eradicated. King Elessar (Aragorn) himself set the first example by pardoning and freeing all those of alien Mannish race taken during the War, and though it was not recorded that he achieved the lasting peace he sought, by his example he indicated the direction to be pursued. For all students of history will perceive that the ultimate fate of Man depends primarily upon his relations with his own race and the wise exercise of his Dominion in Middle-earth.

See also *Silmarillion* pp. 103–5.

Menegroth 'Thousand Caves' (Sind.) The name given by the Grey-elves of Doriath to the great underground fortress and Palace of their king Elwë Thingol, excavated and built (with the aid of the Dwarves of Belegost) early in the First Age. It lay underneath a stony hill in the centre of Doriath, and its doors were guarded by the river Esgalduin. Menegroth was said to be the strongest and the fairest of all kingly halls in Middle-earth, and long indeed it stood. But in the end, like all cities and palaces of the Eldar, it was sacked and defiled: on the first occasion by Dwarves (though not of the kindred which had assisted in its building); and on the second by Elves. Both groups of attackers were independently attempting to steal the Silmaril which was lodged there.

Meneldil 'Lover-of-the-Heavens' (Q.) From Year 2 to 158 Third Age, the third King of Gondor; the son of Anárion and grandson of Elendil the Tall. Meneldil was born in Minas Anor before the ending of the Second Age and remained there throughout the War of the Last Alliance. (In this respect he was not unlike his cousin Valandil, Isildur's fourth son, who became Arnor's third King, having remained safely in Rivendell during the War because he was too young to fight.)

Near the end of this War, in 3440 Second Age, Anárion was slain at the gates of the Barad-dûr; therefore after the Fall of Sauron in the following year, his brother Isildur was obliged to tarry in the South-kingdom, instructing his young nephew in the art of kingship. For two years Isildur acted as Regent before marching away to his own death at the Gladden Fields.

During Meneldil's long reign the South-kingdom was healed of many of the hurts it had sustained in the War against Sauron. His son Cemendur succeeded him.

Meneldor A swift young Eagle of the Misty Mountains and a close comrade of the mighty Gwaihir the Windlord. Together with his liege-lord and Gwaihir's brother Landroval, Meneldor rescued the Ring-bearers from certain death at the feet of the volcano Orodruin, when the completion of Frodo's mission brought about the final venting of the titanic forces which were imprisoned there.

Meneldur (**Tar-Meneldur**) The fifth King of Númenor and younger brother of Silmariën. Though the younger of the two children of Tar-Elendil (fourth King), he, rather than his elder sister, inherited the Sceptre. However, the Númenorean rules of succession were later changed so that the Sceptre descended to the eldest child, whether man or woman – and the descendants of Silmariën later carried the Númenorean succession back to Middle-earth.

See also the *Note* under LORDS OF ANDÚNIE.

Menelmacar 'Heavenly-swordsman' (Q.) The High-elven form of the Grey-elven name *Menelvagor*.

Meneltarma 'Pillar-of-the-Heavens' (Q.) The highest mountain of Númenor, situated in the middle of that island, most westerly of all mortal lands. From its hallowed summit the farsighted could make out the White Tower which marked the Haven of the Eldar in Eressëa, part of the Undying Lands – which lay even further West, forever beyond the reach of the Númenoreans.

Menelvagor 'Heavenly-swordsman' (Sind.) The Grey-elven name for the constellation known to later sky-watchers as *Orion*. The High-elves had two names for the Swordsman of the Sky: *Telumehtar* (the more ancient) and *Menelmacar*, from which the Grey-elven name was obviously derived.

Menelya 'Heavens'-day' (Q.) The fifth day of the *enquië* or 'week' in both the Elvish calendar and the ancient Númenorean system of Kings' Reckoning – which was ultimately adopted by most of the folk of Middle-earth who used the Common Speech. It was named after the Firmament (which to the Elves meant the Heavens themselves rather than that which they contained). The Dúnedain used the Sindarin form of this name, *Ormenel*; while the Hobbits used a translated form of the word, *Hevensday* or *Hensday*.

Men of Westernesse See NÚMENOR.

Mere of Dead Faces See DEAD MARSHES.

Meresdei An archaic form of the Hobbits' name for the sixth day of the week. The original name for this day was *Eärenya*, 'Sea-day' (Q.), given by Men of the maritime realm of Númenor, and established in their system of Kings' Reckoning, which was ultimately adopted by the Hobbits. The Shire-folk had, of course, no knowledge that the original (Elvish) week included only six days, and that the 'Sea-day' had been added by the Númenoreans. In fact, most Hobbits loathed the very idea of the Sea, and few ever gave thought to the origins of the (translated) names found in their calendar. By the end of the Third Age, *Meresdei* had been shortened to *Mersday*.
See also ENQUIË, ENQUIER; SHIRE RECKONING.

Meres of Twilight A translation of the Grey-elven name *Aelin-uial*.

Mereth Aderthad 'Feast of Reunion' (Sind.) The name given by Fingolfin, High King of the Noldor, to the great feast and celebration which he decreed in the 21st Year of the Sun; it was held near the sources of the river Narog in West Beleriand, at the Pools of Ivrin in the southern vales of the Mountains of Shadow. The occasion was to celebrate the reuniting of the Noldor with the Sindar – and of the House of Fingolfin with the House of Fëanor.

Merethrond The 'Great-Hall-of-Feasts' (Sind.) of the city of Minas Tirith, where Occasions of State were celebrated in the usual manner.

Meriadoc 'the Magnificent' Brandybuck One of the most renowned Hobbits of history, remembered in the Annals of the Shire not only for his deeds as a member of the Fellowship of the Ring, but for his deep interest in the origins of the Hobbits themselves, as shown by his many contributions to the sum of Hobbit-scholarship (made after the War of the Ring, during his years as Master of Buckland).

Meriadoc, more usually known as 'Merry', was born in Buckland in the year 2982 Third Age (1382 Shire Reckoning), the only child of the Master of the Hall, Saradoc 'Scattergold' and his wife, the former Esmeralda Took (sister of Thain Paladin II). Merry was therefore cousin to his great friend Peregrin Took and second cousin to his other good friend, Frodo Baggins. As his name implies, Merry's disposition was cheerful, even irrepressible; and like his cousins, he exhibited a strong strain of the Fallohidish 'adventurous' temperament.

Of course, the story of the great adventures which overtook these Hobbits, together with the other members of the Fellowship of the Ring, is set down in full detail elsewhere and needs no restatement here – so this entry will concentrate on noting Merry's considerable accomplishments after he and his companions returned to the Shire in the year 3019 Third Age. Before outlining some of the wide-ranging scholarly work which he later produced, however, it is worth recalling that even in the midst of his adventures Meriadoc occasionally showed signs of his developing interests. Of the two younger Hobbits of the Company he was undoubtedly the more mature, and unlike Peregrin, he took the Quest seriously from the first, characteristically spending a good deal of time in the libraries of Rivendell, studying maps of the lands which lay far beyond his knowledge. Since Meriadoc was later to become quite attached to one of these lands, Rohan, it is perhaps worth recounting just how his admiration for Théoden, the old King of the Mark, brought this to pass.

Being of 'aristocratic' Hobbit lineage, from the start Merry was able to express this admiration in the correct manner – by formally pledging his service to the King, a gesture which greatly pleased the aged ruler, though doubtless he continued to regard the Hobbit more as a ward than a warrior. Nonetheless, Meriadoc of the Shire did accompany the Riders of Rohan on their epic journey to the aid of Gondor during the War of the Ring. And in the Battle of the Pelennor Fields he stood by Théoden after the King was attacked by the Chief Ringwraith, and he courageously struck the Nazgûl, thus helping to bring about his downfall. For these deeds Merry won great honour and renown among the Rohirrim, who named him *Holdwine* in their language and gave him rank and much esteem in their land.

He later became a close friend of King Éomer and remained much attached to Rohan for the rest of his long life, visiting the Mark often and learning its language. For this tongue – a form of which was common enough among Men of the northern vales of Anduin – greatly interested Meriadoc, who fancied he could detect many names and words in it akin to his own Hobbit-speech. Therefore, after his return to the Shire, he made further study of the ancient language links between Hobbits and Northern Men, eventually producing at least one work upon the subject, a short etymological treatise titled *Old Words and Names in the Shire*.

Another subject which later captured the interest of this intelligent and widely travelled Hobbit was the calculation of years, and to this end he studied various forms of calendar reckoning used by some of the races of western Middle-earth. In fact, it is doubtless due to his researches that we have any records of these matters at all. (See Appendix D, which is in part an encapsulation of Meriadoc's *Reckoning of Years*, compiled in Buckland during the early Fourth Age.)

Finally, this accomplished Hobbit was also a fair botanist, with yet another scholarly work, *Herblore of the Shire*, to his credit on this subject. It seems quite likely that Merry's initial work in this particular field grew out of his great interest in (and fondness for) 'pipe-weed', the origins and history of which obviously held a special fascination for him. (See Prologue 2.)

Nonetheless, while all these varied academic accomplishments doubtless earned him respect, this could not compare with the great honour which Meriadoc's hereditary office and youthful heroics brought him in the eyes of the Shire-folk. For, although he arguably accomplished greater deeds on foreign fields of battle, it is certain that he was most esteemed by his fellow Hobbits for his adroit handling of the Scouring of the Shire, in which he captained the Hobbitry-in-arms with professional skill and admirable attention to detail.

At the age of fifty, in 1432 Shire Reckoning, Merry succeeded his father Saradoc as Master of Buckland. Two years later, after Peregrin had been made Took and Thain, King Elessar appointed the Thain, the Master and the Mayor of Michel Delving as Counsellors of the North-kingdom; and for some fifty years these old comrades continued to work together, shouldering the civic responsibilities of the Shire. Finally, in 1484 S.R. (Year 63 Fourth Age) Meriadoc and Peregrin took counsel together and resigned their offices. Handing over their chattels and estates to their sons, they rode away south, leaving the Shire for ever. The two Hobbits first travelled to Edoras in Rohan, where Merry saw his old friend Éomer for the last time (the King died that autumn). Then they continued their journey to Gondor, where they dwelt with King Elessar in great honour and splendour for some years before they, too, passed away and were laid to rest in the Hallows, in the House of the Kings.

Note: Meriadoc wedded Estella Bolger, and although no children are recorded for them in available genealogical tables, on the basis of the penultimate entry in Appendix B, one must assume that Merry had at least one son, who in turn became Master of Buckland.

See also KALIMAC.

Mering Stream The boundary between Rohan and Gondor. It rose in the Firienwood, on the edges of the White Mountains, and flowed north and east – separating the Eastfold of Rohan from the province of Anórien – before joining the river Entwash.

Merlock Mountains See 'THE MEWLIPS'.

Merry Brandybuck See MERIADOC 'THE MAGNIFICENT' BRANDY-BUCK.

Merry Gamgee The second son (and fourth child) of Samwise Gamgee, named after Meriadoc 'the Magnificent' Brandybuck.

Mersday See MERESDEI.

Messenger Service The system of communication most used in the Shire – since lettered Hobbits wrote continually to their friends, and expected prompt replies. The Messenger Service, which also included the Quick Post, carried all the mail plus any worthwhile news (which, to Hobbits, meant any news at all) among the four Farthings. The office of the Mayor was held responsible for its efficient functioning.

Methedras 'Last-Peak' (Sind.) The southernmost peak of the Misty Mountains. Below it, in a great cleft or fork, lay the coomb of Nan Curunír, the 'Wizard's Vale' of Isengard.

Mettarë (Q.) The last day of the year in both the Elvish calendar and in KING'S RECKONING: the system begun by the Númenoreans and later adopted, in one form or another, by most of the Westron-speaking peoples of Middle-earth. In the (Elvish) Calendar of Imladris, this day immediately preceded the opening of spring, while in the Dúnedain system it fell in mid-winter; however, in both, *mettarë* was an 'extra' day belonging to no fixed season or month.

'The Mewlips' An odd and decidedly disturbing poem found (as No. 9) in the Shire-collection published under the title *The Adventures of Tom Bombadil*. It is in the form of an eerie tale told for the unwary traveller, who is cautioned to avoid the path which leads

> *Beyond the Merlock Mountains,*
> *a long and lonely road,*
> *Through the spider-shadows and the*
> *Marsh of Tode,*

to the noisome pools – where the strange, cannibalistic Mewlips dwell. The verse might be said to encapsulate all the alien horrors ever heard of in the Shire.

Michel Delving The chief township of the Shire, located on the White Downs in the Westfarthing.

Mickleburg A rendering into Common Speech of the name given by the Edain of the First Age to the great Dwarvish city of BELEGOST. See also note 8 on p. 91 of this *Companion*.

Middle-earth A translation of both *Endorë* (Q.) and *Ennor*, *Ennorath* (Sind.). In all records of that Third Age, this expression means 'Mortal Lands', i.e., all the land East of the Sundering Seas and subject to natural laws.

Note: the far westerly island of Númenor was not considered part of Middle-earth, though it was still subject to mortal laws. Therefore, Elendil referred to Middle-earth as being apart from Númenor when he spoke the words:

> *Et Eärello Endorenna utúlien. Sinome maruvan ar Hildinyar tenn'*
> *Ambar-metta !*

('Out of the Great Sea to Middle-earth I am come. In this place will I abide, and my heirs, unto the ending of the world!')[11]

Middle Peoples An expression in the Dúnedain lore developed during the Third Age. According to the Dúnedain, the 'Middle Peoples' were those races of Men descended from the clans of the Edain who did not pass West to Númenor at the beginning of the Second Age. Of this type were the tall, blond, relatively uncultured but brave and noble Northern Men, such as the Rohirrim. The Dúnedain (the 'High People') accounted them as distant kin, and both loved and respected these 'Men of Twilight'.
See also MEN.

Midgewater Marshes An expanse of stagnant and treacherous bog which lay between Bree and the Weather Hills, to the north of the Great East Road. As their name implies, these marshes were infested with pestilent flying insects and other unpleasant creatures; consequently, they were usually avoided by travellers.

Midyear's Day See LITHEDAYS.

Milo Burrows The son of Rufus Burrows and Asphodel Brandybuck. Unlike most Hobbits, Milo was indifferent to the delights of personal correspondence and, as a result, was given a gold writing-set by Bilbo Baggins, when the elderly Hobbit departed the Shire for the last time in 3001 Third Age (1401 Shire Reckoning).

Mîm A Dwarf of the First Age, one of the so-called Petty- or Lesser-dwarves, the *Noegyth Nibin*, who wandered into Beleriand long before others of the Khazâd. It was this race who first delved the Caves of Narog, where in after years Finrod Felagund had his realm and city of Nargothrond. Another such ancient dwelling of the Noegyth Nibin was on the solitary hill of Amon Rûdh in West Beleriand (its Dwarvish name is unknown.) Mîm was the heir of those who had originally excavated Amon Rûdh, and together with his sons dwelt there for much of the First Age. But he was fated to become enmeshed by the Doom of the Children of Húrin, and so was destroyed. For Túrin Turambar, then the leader of an outlaw band, encountered Mîm and his sons not far from the western march of Brethil, and afterwards dwelt on the hilltop, together with Mîm and his small family. (See BAR-EN-DANWEDH.) But Mîm was captured by Orcs, and though he stipulated that Túrin not be slain, revealed the whereabouts of the outlaws' lair. The hill was attacked by Orcs. Túrin was captured, and all the outlaws save one were slain. Thus Mîm came once more into his own. But not many years afterwards, Túrin's father Húrin, released at last from Angband, came to Amon Rûdh, and there encountered Mîm, and slew him.

Note: in the preface to the selection of Hobbit-verse published as *The Adventures of Tom Bombadil*, an oblique reference is made to the 'Númenorean legend of Túrin and Mîm the Dwarf', in connection with the origins of poem No. 14, 'The Hoard'. The poem concerns, among other things, the fate of an ancient, solitary Dwarf of the First Age who inherited an Elvish treasure and lost it again (to a dispossessing Dragon).

Minalcar See RÓMENDACIL II.

Minardil From 1621–34 Third Age, the twenty-fifth King of Gondor. He was slain in battle with the Corsairs of Umbar (led by Angamaitë and Sangahyando, the great-grandsons of Castamir the Usurper), at Pelargir, during a raid upon Gondor's principal remaining naval base. His son Telemnar died during the Great Plague which followed two years later.

Note: in Appendix A I(iv), it is erroneously stated that Minardil was the son of Eldacar II, the twenty-first King, who was deposed by Castamir. In fact, Minardil was the son of Hyarmendacil II (Vinyarion), and was thus the great-grandson of Eldacar.

Minas Anor 'Tower of the [Setting] Sun' (Sind.) Originally a beautiful fortified city built shortly after the founding of Gondor at the end of the Second Age, Minas Anor was for years accounted one of the two principal fortresses of the realm; however, by the time of the War of the Ring, at the end of the Third Age, it had been renamed *Minas Tirith*, and had become the chief city and the only surviving stronghold of the diminished South-kingdom.

Minas Anor was founded in 3320 Second Age as the capital of the province of Anórien and the High Seat of Anárion, younger son of Elendil the Tall and conjoint King of Gondor. It was the twin of *Minas Ithil*, the 'Tower of the [Rising] Moon', High Seat of Anárion's brother Isildur and the capital of Isildur's province of Ithilien, which lay on the eastern shores of the Great River. Yet neither was accounted the centre of the South-kingdom, for Osgiliath, the Citadel of the Stars, lay in between the two, upon both sides of the Anduin; and it was no fortress but a large and populous city, created as the capital of the entire realm.

However, though never planned to be either the chief city or main fortress of the South-kingdom, from the beginning Minas Anor possessed a number of natural advantages which ultimately enabled it to endure. Chief of these was its position – upon the very knees of Mindolluin, easternmost of the White Mountains which were the backbone of the ancient realm. From its founding, Minas Anor was cunningly fashioned to make use of its unique position; and eventually it grew into a strong towering city, delved into the side of the mountain so that its rearmost walls were themselves the living rock of Mindolluin. Seven concentric walls it had and many towers, and the topmost circle of the City was built upon a great crag seven hundred feet high. At the summit of this mighty keep stood the Citadel of Anárion and the Court of the Fountain.[12]

Originally both Minas Anor and Minas Ithil were of equal royalty but, as is told elsewhere (see GONDOR), the Tower of the Moon was taken by Sauron of Mordor during the War of the Last Alliance, and although it was recaptured when Sauron was first overthrown at the very end of the Second Age, Minas Ithil afterwards became accounted an eastern outpost rather than a seat of Kings. In contrast, in the year 420 Third Age, Minas Anor was rebuilt by Ostoher, seventh King of the Line of Anárion, and it then became the summer residence of Gondor's royalty. Osgiliath survived as capital of the realm for a further thousand years – but in 1636, the Great Plague decimated the city and it remained partially deserted. Accordingly, in 1640, Tarondor, twenty-seventh King, removed the royal seat permanently to Minas Anor.

So by the middle of the Third Age Gondor's former westernmost fortress had become its new capital; and although both Osgiliath and Minas Ithil still endured, neither was ever again able to rival the Tower of the Sun. In 1900, Calimehtar, son of Narmacil II, built the White Tower at the highest point of the Citadel Rock. At the feet of this tower, the White Tree grew in the Court of the Fountain, while above it the banner of the Kings floated free in the wind, one thousand feet above the neighbouring plain.

Yet the days of the Kings were even then drawing to an end. During the reign of Eärnil II (who followed Ondoher, son of Calimehtar), the power of Mordor arose once more and Minas Ithil was taken by the Nazgûl. The Tower of the Moon thus became a place of dread: men of Gondor called it *Minas Morgul*, the 'Tower of Sorcery', and Minas Anor was then renamed *Minas Tirith*, the 'Tower of Guard' (the name by which it was known while the Third Age lasted). Shortly after this the last descendant of the royal Line of Anárion rode away to Minas Morgul and never came back, so the Banner of the Ruling Stewards replaced that of the Kings. And when, in 2475 Third Age, Osgiliath was finally ruined, Minas Tirith became the last surviving city of the realm as it had been originally ordered. Nonetheless, although Gondor continued her slow decline, hope endured and, in 2698, Ecthelion I, seventeenth Ruling Steward, rebuilt the White Tower of Calimehtar (which was ever after known as the Tower of Ecthelion). But few further additions were made to the City's strength, for the chief hopes of its inhabitants afterwards rested in its impregnable outer walls.

In the event, however, it was not these walls of stone which enabled Gondor to survive the War of the Ring; rather, it was the will of her people and the foresight of her rulers. For in the latter years of the Age the Stewards, being for the most part wise and far-seeing men, had assumed that sooner or later Gondor would be invaded in strength – and that no walls could long stand against the power of Mordor if other means of defence could not somehow be contrived. Therefore, they made alliance with Men of other races, and they strengthened the outer defences of the Realm. And so, when Sauron at last launched his attack, during the War of the Ring, Minas Tirith survived, even though the Great Gates were broken and the lower circles of the City were burned.

But all such damage was healed in the Fourth Age which followed the successful conclusion of the War. New and stronger gates were made for the City by the Dwarves of Erebor, and with the lifting of the threat from the East, many folk came from the seaward vales of Lebennin and Belfalas to dwell there. Best of all, the Kings of the Line of Elendil returned to Gondor and the Standard of the White Tree flew once more from the topmost tower of Minas Anor, last memory of vanished Númenor and the fairest City in the west of Middle-earth.

See also Appendix A I(iv).

Minas Ithil 'Tower of the [Rising] Moon' (Sind.) From its founding in 3320 Second Age until its final fall in 2002 Third Age, one of the two principal fortresses of Gondor, having been originally created as the twin of Minas Anor, the Tower of the Sun, and as the High Seat of Isildur, conjoint King of the Realm. After its capture by the Nazgûl, this once-fair city became known in Gondor as Minas Morgul, the Tower of Sorcery; it was cast down after the War of the Ring and never rebuilt.

Yet at its first raising, Isildur's city was fully as beautiful as Minas Anor, his brother Anárion's High Seat. It was also the repository of the White Tree, brought by the Men of Númenor from their drowned homeland, and one of the seven *palantíri* rescued by them was kept there as well. It was the capital of the fair province of Ithilien and stood in an upland vale in the Mountains of Shadow, on the very borders of Sauron's ancient realm of Mordor. For the builders of Minas Ithil believed that the Lord of Mordor had been destroyed in the drowning of Númenor.

But Sauron had escaped, and after a period of hiding in Mordor he unleashed war upon the Dúnedain; in 3429 Second Age his armies came over the Mountains of Shadow and took the Tower of the Moon in a savage surprise attack. Isildur managed to escape with the *palantír* but his city was taken and its White Tree burned. So began the War of the Last Alliance, in which the armies of Elves and Men at last had the victory, and the first overthrow of Sauron brought an end to the Age. Minas Ithil was then restored to the Dúnedain, but no King of Gondor ever resided there again. Isildur himself dwelt in Minas Anor for the two short years he lingered in Gondor, and his former capital became no more than an outpost of the Dúnedain. As such it endured the turmoils of the succeeding two thousand years.

By the end of the second millenium of the Third Age, Gondor had dwindled sadly from its frontier days of glory. Osgiliath, originally the chief city and capital of the whole realm, was partly desolate, and the South-kingdom was now ruled from Minas Anor. In the year 2000, the Nazgûl issued over the high pass of Cirith Ungol and laid siege to the Tower of the Moon; and although for two years their forces were unable to enter the fortified city, even so the siege was too powerful to be broken by Gondor, and no reinforcements were able to get through. In 2002 Minas Ithil fell at last and the Nazgûl themselves then inhabited it, together with many Orcs. Men of Gondor then began to call it *Minas Morgul*, the 'Tower of Sorcery', and Minas Anor was consequently renamed *Minas Tirith*, the 'Tower of Guard'.

Sauron was content with this gain, for by it he had dealt a heavy blow to the Dúnedain, who still revered Isildur's memory; moreover, he had acquired for his most faithful servants a foothold on the western side of the Mountains of Shadow; and he could afford to wait. The Nazgûl remained quiescent for some years (although in 2050 Eärnur, the last King of the Line of Anárion, was lured to this evil fortress and never returned). Not until the years immediately before the War of the Ring did the Lord of Minas Morgul finally come forth with his hosts to give battle to the Dúnedain. And even these skirmishes – in which Osgiliath was finally ruined and its last bridge broken – were no more than trials of Gondor's strength, undertaken to keep the Dúnedain off balance until the Dark Lord should unleash the great and final war long prepared.

This occurred in 3019 Third Age, when a mighty host came down from the mountains and captured West Osgiliath, pouring across the Great River in many boats. With all of the ruined city of Osgiliath in his hands, the Witch-king of Minas Morgul then advanced towards Minas Tirith, capturing the Rammas Echor and the Fields of Pelennor and besieging the last fortress of Gondor. Yet on March 15th, five days after leaving Minas Morgul, the Lord of the Nazgûl was himself destroyed – and the Morgul-host was also utterly overwhelmed – in the Battle of the Pelennor Fields. Minas Morgul fell once more into the hands of the Dúnedain, but it had been too long an evil place for any Man to dwell there, and by order of the King Elessar the once-beautiful Tower of the Moon was cast down and its foundations removed.

Minas Morgul 'Tower of Sorcery' (Sind.) The name given in Gondor to the fortified city of MINAS ITHIL from the time it fell to the Nazgûl in 2002 Third Age until its destruction at the end of the Age.

Minastan The second son of King Minardil of Gondor and younger brother of King Telemnar (who perished with all his children in the Great Plague of 1636 Third Age). After the death of Telemnar, Minastan's son Tarondor ruled as Gondor's twenty-seventh King.

Minastir (Tar-Minastir) The eleventh King of Númenor, and one of the mightiest warriors in her history. During his reign war broke out in Middle-earth between the Elves and Sauron, and news eventually reached Númenor that Sauron's armies were ravaging Eriador and threatening the borders of the Elven-land of Lindon, then ruled by Gil-galad. Accordingly, because he loved the Eldar even more than he envied them their immortality, Minastir despatched a great navy to the aid of the Elven-king in 1700 Second Age. With this reinforcement, Sauron was defeated and Gil-galad was able to contain the invasion and later mount a successful offensive, securing peace in Eriador for many years.

Note: Minastir's remarkable action appears, from available records, to have been the first renewal in the Second Age of the ancient alliance between Elves and Men which had preceded the founding of Númenor.

Minas Tirith 'Tower of Guard' (Sind.) In the First Age, the name given by the Elf-king Finrod Felagund to the fortress built by him on the strategic island of Tol Sirion, where he himself dwelt until the founding of Nargothrond, being succeeded there by his brother Orodreth (who also succeeded Finrod as King of Nargothrond). It was captured during the Dagor Bragollach, by Sauron, and was renamed *Tol-in-Gaurhoth*, the 'Island of Werewolves'.

The same name, Minas Tirith, was also given, in the Third Age, to the city of MINAS ANOR in Gondor, after its sister-fortress of Minas Ithil had been captured by the Ringwraiths (2002 Third Age).

Mindeb One of the smaller rivers of Beleriand, a tributary of the Sirion. The Mindeb rose in the Crissaegrim and flowed due south for twenty leagues before its confluence with the larger stream. It was accounted the eastern border of the land of Dimbar, and the western of Nan Dungortheb.

Mindolluin 'Towering-Bluehead' (Sind.) The easternmost of the White Mountains. Upon a spur of this great hill, Men of Gondor built the city of Minas Anor.

Mindon Eldaliéva '[Tall] Tower of the Eldar' (Q.) The loftiest of the towers of the city of Tirion the Fair, in Eldamar. It was built by the Vanyar, and is sometimes called the *Tower of Ingwë*. At its feet lay a great square or public place; and in its topmost chamber there burned a silver lamp, the Flammifer or Beacon of Eldamar. Its height is not known.

Also called The Mindon.

Minhiriath 'Land-between-the-rivers' (Sind.) The southernmost part of ancient Eriador, bounded upon the south by the river Gwathlo (Greyflood), on the north by the Baranduin (Brandywine), on the east by the old South Road, and on the west by the Sea.

At one time Minhiriath was peopled by folk migrating north and west from Dunland and the White Mountains. It was later incorporated into the realm of Arnor, and eventually formed the greater part of the lesser state of Cardolan. But Cardolan fell in the wars with the Witch-realm of Angmar, and the Great Plague of 1636 Third Age completed the devastation begun by the Witch-king. In the year 2912 this unhappy land was again overwhelmed – by great floods which followed the thaws of the Long Winter. It lay desolate throughout the remainder of the Age.

Min-Rimmon 'Towering-Rimmon' (Sind. & Mannish.) A beacon-hill which rose on the northern edge of the White Mountains, in the province of Anórien. It was part of a chain of seven such beacon-hills which allowed Gondor to communicate speedily with her ally Rohan in time of need.

Note: the name *Rimmon* is of pre-Númenorean (i.e. Mannish, but not Adûnaic) origin and belongs to a forgotten period in the early Second Age. There were several such names around the fringes of the White Mountains, doubtless a legacy from the race of Men who had originally inhabited the upper vales and mountain-plateaux of the range.

See also BEACON-HILLS.

Minuial 'Star-fading' (Sind.) The Grey-elven equivalent of TIN-DÓMË.

Minyatur 'The Founder'[13] (Q.) The High-elven title taken by Elros brother of Elrond, when he ascended the throne of Númenor as its first King (Year 32 Second Age). See ELROS TAR-MINYATUR.

Míriel Serindë A Queen of the Noldor in Eldamar; she was the first wife of the Noldorin High King, Finwë, and the mother of Curufinwë, whom Míriel named *Fëanáro* (Fëanor), by which name he was known ever after. Her own title *Serindë* ('The Seamstress') reflects the admiration in which she was held by the Noldor for her matchless skill in needlecraft.

We are told that the bearing of such a prodigious child as Fëanor so exhausted her both physically and spiritually – and filled her with such foreboding for the future – that she went into a decline and died: the first of all the Eldar to die while dwelling in the Blessed Realm (her husband Finwë was to be the second – though he did not fade and die, but was slain). Finwë afterwards wed again, though not without opposition. His second spouse was a princess of the Vanyar and a kinswoman of Ingwë: Indis the Fair. By her Finwë had two more sons, Fingolfin and Finarfin. But perhaps because of the great love he had borne Míriel, his favourite son was always the eldest: Fëanor.

Míriel (Tar-Míriel) The daughter and only child of Tar-Palantir (formerly Ar-Inziladûn), twenty-third King of Númenor. According to the Númenorean laws of succession, she should have inherited the Sceptre on her father's death, but her cousin usurped the Throne in her stead, taking the Númenorean title *Ar-Pharazôn* ('the Golden'). And at the same time, perhaps in an attempt to legitimize his reign, he forcibly wedded Míriel; she was then called, by the Númenoreans, *Ar-zimraphêl*. She was the last to perish in the Inundation of Númenor – her husband was the first.

See also LORDS OF ANDÚNIE.

Mirkwood A rendering of the Grey-elven *Taur e-Ndaedelos* (literally, 'Forest of Great Fear'); the name given during the Third Age to the mightiest surviving forest of western Middle-earth, formerly known as GREENWOOD THE GREAT. This renaming occurred at the end of the first millennium, after the raising of the evil tower of Dol Guldur, which then cast a shadow over the forest.

Mirrormere A translation of the Khuzdul (Dwarvish) name KHELED-ZÂRAM.

Miruvor (Sind., from the older Q. *miruvóre*) This High-elven word – believed by the Eldar to be derived from the language of the Valar – meant 'cordial', or perhaps 'nectar' (in the original Olympian sense). According to a note on the subject (see *The Road Goes Ever On*, p. 61), the Elves believed that the Valinorean drink came from the honey of the (undying) flowers grown in the Gardens of Yavanna, in Valimar; it was thought that the Valar dispensed this drink at their festivals.

The 'Cordial of Imladris', made by the Eldar of Rivendell, was doubtless prepared with similar skill, though the honeys from which it was distilled were less potent. Nonetheless, it was still an extremely warming and powerful restorative – which proved of great value to the Company of the Ring, trapped in a blizzard upon the heights of Caradhras (Book II Chap. 3).

Misty Mountains A rendering of the Grey-elven, *Hithaeglir* (literally, 'Mist Peaks'); during the Second and Third Ages, the greatest of all mountain-ranges in western Middle-earth, and a mighty barrier separating Eriador and Wilderland. Almost three hundred leagues these mountains ran, from Northern Waste to southernmost peak, in an unbroken chain, shrouded with the ever-present mist which gave them their ancient name. They were considered virtually unscalable, and the few routes across them could not be undertaken without great difficulty. For much of the Third Age (and doubtless the Second), the dangers of such a journey were increased by the presence of many Orcs of the Mountains who infested the high passes. Certainly an aura of evil clung to this great range of peaks: they were said (by the Eldar) to have been reared at the Beginning of Arda, by Melkor, as a barrier against potential foes (he raised the *Ered Engrin*, the 'Iron Mountains' of Angband, in the same epoch, and for the same reason).

Mithe The point, in the south-eastern corner of the Shire, where the outflow of the river Shirebourn ran into the Baranduin (Brandy-wine). The landing-stage there was called the Mithe Steps.

Mitheithel 'Grey-source' (Sind.) The river HOARWELL.

Mithlond 'Grey-havens' (Sind.) The chief harbours in Middle-earth, during the Second and Third Ages, of the Eldar. See GREY HAVENS.

Mithrandir 'Grey-wanderer' (Sind.) The name among Elves and Dúnedain for the Wizard known (to Northern Men) as GANDALF THE GREY.

Mithril 'Grey-brilliance' (Sind.) The most precious metal known in Middle-earth.

All folk desired it. It could be beaten like copper, and polished like glass; and the Dwarves could make of it a metal, light and yet harder than tempered steel. Its beauty was like to that of common silver, but the beauty of *mithril* did not tarnish or grow dim. The Elves dearly loved it . . .[14]

The Eldar were not the only people to desire this valuable metal, which was to be found only in a single great lode beneath the peak of Caradhras, deep in the Mines of Moria (discovered in the early Second Age). The Dwarves themselves valued it beyond price, and it was the desire of the Dwarf-miners of Moria for further supplies of *mithril* which led to their destruction and disinheritance. In 1980 Third Age, while seeking the mother-lode, far beneath Barazinbar (Caradhras), they disturbed an evil spirit of the Underworld, the Balrog, with consequences appalling for their people. In this way *mithril* was both the foundation of the Moria-dwarves' fabulous wealth and the means of their eventual downfall.

Note: mithril was also known as 'silver-steel' (in Bilbo Baggins' narrative, *There and Back Again*), as well as 'true-silver' and 'Moria-silver'. The alloy *ithildin* was a derivative of *mithril*.

Mithrim '[Home of] The Grey Ones' (Sind.) The name given by the Grey-elves of Beleriand to those of their kindred who dwelled in that region of the north which was afterwards named after them, together with its great Lake[15] and the mountains which bordered it on the west. Mithrim was the south-easternmost part of the (larger) land of Hithlum, bordered on south, east and west by mountain-ranges (the Ered Wethrin and the Ered Mithrim), and protected from the north by the great lake. Here the returning Noldor led by Fëanor made their first encampment in Middle-earth (Mithrim was thus the most ancient of the High-elven realms in Exile, though not the longest to endure); and here was fought their first battle against Morgoth, the 'Battle-under-Stars' in which Fëanor was slain. In the weeks and months following this battle Fingolfin, arriving at last in Middle-earth in despite of Fëanor, also camped beside the great Lake of Mithrim; and later took these lands as his realm. But after Fingolfin's death, Fingon his heir withdrew from the greater realm and concentrated his power into Mithrim, which then became the nearest of all Elf-kingdoms to Angband, and the vanguard-state of the Eldarin cause. But Fingon and all his people were slain in the

Nirnaeth Arnoediad, and Mithrim was afterwards occupied by Easterlings. It was never regained by the Eldar or the Edain.

Mode of Beleriand A *Tengwar* alphabet (based upon the Fëanorian system). It was developed by the Grey-elves of Beleriand during the First Age, but was maintained, curiously enough, by the High-elves of the Second.

In this mode of writing, the older system of diacritic marks (used to denote vowels) was replaced by a less stylized method. Unallocated *Tengwar* were incorporated as vocalic symbols with the full status of 'letters', and the *tehtar* ('signs') were either abbreviated or discarded. The grey-elven inscription on the Doors of Durin was written in this mode.

See ALPHABET OF FËANOR.

Mode of Erebor See ANGERTHAS MORIA.

Monendei An archaic form of the Hobbits' word for the third day of the week, being actually a translation of *Isilya*, 'Moon's-day' (Q.), the name for this day in the ancient Númenorean system of Kings' Reckoning. The week was the first part of this Númenorean calendar to be adopted by other peoples after it was taken to Middle-earth; and the Hobbits were probably using translated forms of the week-days by the end of the first millennium of the Third Age. By the time of the War of the Ring, *Monendei* had been shortened to *Monday*.

Moon-letters A form of secret writing created by the Dwarves, who desired privacy in all things. 'Moon-letters' were runes which were written with silver pens and which could only be read when held up before the light of the moon. The most cunningly devised moon-letters required the would-be cryptographer to illuminate the letters by a moon of the same phase and season – i.e., on virtually the same day of the year – as when they were originally drawn. Thrór's map, given to his grandson Thorin Oakenshield by Gandalf the Grey, was inscribed with runes of this type.

Morannon 'Black-gate' (Sind.) The heavily fortified entrance to the land of Mordor; an impregnable wall which ran from the western foothills of the Ered Lithui (Ashy Mountains) to the northern buttresses of the Ephel Dúath (Mountains of Shadow), barring the pass of Cirith Gorgor and the entrance to the vale of Udûn. Guarded at either side by the two Towers of the Teeth, Narchost and Carchost, the Morannon was in the form of a stone rampart, many feet high.

In it there was a single gate of iron, and upon its battlement sentinels paced unceasingly. Beneath the hills on either side the rock was bored into a hundred caves and maggot-holes; there a host of Orcs lurked, ready at a signal to issue forth like black ants going to war.[16]

Mordor 'Black-land' (Sind.) The Land of Shadow, realm of Sauron the Great throughout two Ages of the World and the heart of all his ancient might, once the most potent in Middle-earth. It was chosen by Sauron early in the Second Age (*c.* 1000) to serve him as a fortress-land, and its fortunes mirrored his own up to his final overthrow at the end of the War of the Ring (3019 Third Age).

Even before its adoption by Sauron, Mordor was a bleak and desert land, barren and infertile; its chief merits (from Sauron's point of view) lay in the enormous natural fortifications which walled it on the north, south and west: the *Ered Lithui* ('Ashy Mountains') and the greater range of the Ephel Dúath, the Mountains of Shadow. One hundred leagues the Black Land measured from northern wall to southern buttress, and one hundred and fifty from west to east (where alone it lay open to the world). In the far north-western corner the two mountain-chains met, enclosing the deep-shadowed vale of Udûn ('The Pit'); and in the very centre of the plain of Gorgoroth stood the fire-mountain Orodruin, amid the ruin of untold years of volcanic torment. South of this northern desert stretched the wider plain of Nurn, in the centre of which lay a great Inland Sea.

Such was Mordor during the early years of the Second Age – and to Sauron, newly arisen and not yet powerful, it must have seemed made especially for his purposes: for in those days his chief foes were stronger than he, and he desired above all a realm which could with little trouble be made secure. Accordingly, he took Mordor and fortified its passes, and upon a huge south-facing spur of the Ered Lithui he raised a mighty fortress, the *Barad-dûr*, the 'Dark Tower', to dominate the plain of Gorgoroth. Orodruin's fires he learned to harness to his own uses, and in a short time he had made himself master of the Black Land, which he filled with evil folk, bred to his service.

With the forging of the Ruling Ring in the middle years of the Age, Sauron finally gained enough power to send his hosts forth from Mordor to ravage the Westlands of Middle-earth; and for much of the remainder of the Second Age (see ACCURSED YEARS), his forces continued to threaten the southlands. Yet at the very end of the Age Sauron overreached himself, and the combined strength of the Elves and the Dúnedain cast him from his dark Throne and drove his spirit away in exile. Mordor then became desolate and uninhabited, except for a few garrisons from Gondor, stationed in fortresses built by the Dúnedain to watch over the passes and prevent any evil thing from entering. For many years the Black Land was quiet and Orodruin's fires were stilled. (It was at this time that the castles of Durthang, Narchost, Carchost and Cirith Ungol were built.)

But the fortunes of Mordor always mirrored Sauron's own, and by the end of the first half of the Third Age he was once more awake and plotting to regain his ancient realm – although for many years he did not dare to reclaim it openly. Instead, while himself continuing to dwell in Dol Guldur, he sent his chief servants, the Ringwraiths, secretly to prepare Mordor for his re-occupation. This they did before the end of the second millennium, while Gondor was fully occupied in holding off attacks from Easterlings (doubtless stirred up for this very purpose by his other agents). For the next thousand years the power of Mordor grew again – and was allowed to grow because there was no strength capable of obstructing it; and in 2951 Sauron himself again returned to the Black Land, after an absence of nearly three thousand years.

Yet even with all this careful preparation, and despite the boasted inviolability of Mordor's frontiers, in the final test the fearsome reputation and impassable mountain-walls were insufficient to keep the foes of the Dark Lord at bay. During the War of the Ring, while Sauron's attention was deliberately held elsewhere, his borders were passed by two enemies who bore with them the key to Sauron's survival or defeat. The success of their mission brought about the fall of Sauron and the final ruin of Mordor; and although the southern lands around Lake Nurnen were afterwards settled by emancipated slaves, the northern plains of Gorgoroth, Udûn and Lithlad were deserted and were never again made habitable. Mordor became once more a desert, but an empty desert.

Morgai A ridge of jagged hills in Mordor. It ran parallel to the Mountains of Shadow for some thirty leagues south of the Durthang Spur. Thus it was an inner fence of Sauron's realm (as opposed to the 'outer-fence' of the *Ephel Dûath*).

Morgoth 'Dark Foe [of the World]' (Sind.) The name given by Fëanor of the Noldor[17] to the eldest and greatest of the AINUR, Melkor the Mighty, whose fall from Grace during the Eldest Days initiated a series of lasting and profoundly tragic consequences for the World. From his very Beginnings, Melkor opposed himself to the wishes of the Creator and the Themes of the Great Music – for alone of the Ainur he envied Eru and desired to emulate (and surpass) him. And after the Making of Arda (the World) he desired to rule the 'Little Kingdom' for himself, brooking no equals. So began his rebellion, which waxed or waned according to his circumstances for many Ages of the World until, after bringing evil, war ruin and death to the Middle-world, he was cast out for ever by the Valar.

His first realm in Middle-earth, Utumno ('The Pit'), was made in the Far North; its westerly outpost was Angband. But in the Battle of the Powers Utumno was ruined, and Melkor was carried, a prisoner, back to Valinor. For three ages of the world he was held captive in the Halls of Mandos, but feigned repentance, and so was released, though not permitted to return to mortal lands. But Melkor secretly hated the Valar and the Eldar, and in furtherance of this hatred he poisoned the Two Trees – the Light of Valinor and Eldamar – and stole the Silmarils which had been made by Fëanor; and slew Fëanor's father Finwë; and then fled back to Middle-earth with his prize, to plan and build anew, dwelling everafter in Angband. And the Noldor followed him, to regain that which he had stolen. So began the war of the Great Jewels, in which *Morgoth*, as he was then named (and ever after known in Middle-earth) was ultimately victorious over the Eldar and the Edain.

It is known that Morgoth was discomfited at least once during the War of the Great Jewels – by Beren and Lúthien – yet apart from the loss of a single Silmaril, his victory seems to have been complete. His specially bred armies of Orcs and Trolls, augmented by Dragons and Balrogs, invaded Beleriand and captured the High-elven cities of Nargothrond and Gondolin. The Elves fled or hid themselves or were destroyed in the Great Darkness that followed Morgoth's victory.

Nonetheless, a single ship, bearing an ambassador from Middle-earth, eventually arrived on the shores of the Undying Lands, guided by the Light of the recovered Silmaril; and the representations which were then made brought about the mustering of the Valar and their intervention against the Enemy. The blow struck by this host against Thangorodrim obliterated that region and brought about severe disturbances of the land and seas, inundating a sizeable part of north-western Middle-earth. Morgoth was annihilated.

Yet his terrible example was to have lasting consequences, for not even the mightiest blow could destroy the evil now awake in Middle-earth. Although Morgoth's followers were for the most part overwhelmed with Angband, many of the creatures he had 'created' lived on, and at least one of his chief servants survived – later to become Sauron the Great, Lord of Mordor.

Note: also called *Bauglir* ('The Constrainer'), *Belegurth* ('The Great Death') and The Enemy.

See also *The Silmarillion* (passim).

Morgul 'Black-wraith' (Sind.) In the absence of clear information from surviving records of the Third Age, all hypotheses must assume the lesser stature of guesses; nonetheless, it seems not unlikely that *Morgul* was the name of the Lord of the Ringwraiths, the Witch-king of Angmar, who later became Lord of Minas Ithil, which his armies captured on Sauron's behalf in 2002 Third Age. The Tower of the Moon was then renamed *Minas Morgul*, and the vale in which it lay became known as *Imlad Morgul*.

Morgulduin The river which flowed through Morgul Vale (formerly Ithil Vale). It was given this name in Gondor after the Nazgûl captured Minas Ithil in 2002 Third Age; previously, it had been known as *Ithilduin*.

See also IMLAD MORGUL.

Morgul-knife A deadly, sorcerous weapon, doubtless devised by the Lord of the Ringwraiths and used by him in an attempt on the life of the Ring-bearer (Book I Chap. 11). So far as is known, it was intended to be used as follows: the blade pierced the heart of the victim, simultaneously taking his life and turning him into a wraith – like the wielder of the Morgul-knife, only of far lesser stature and power. If by chance the blade missed the heart, a fragment of the knife would remain in the wound and slowly work its way inwards. Like all such weapons of darkness, the blade (the bewitched part) wilted and turned to smoke when exposed to the rays of the sun; thus the dagger could only be used during the hours of night. It was an evil weapon.

Morgul Vale A translation of IMLAD MORGUL.

Moria Of all the mighty works of stone created by the Dwarves of Middle-earth, none was greater, nor more famed, nor more dreaded (in later days) than the vast underground city of the Dwarrowdelf, called by the Dwarves themselves *Khazad-dûm* ('The-Mansion-of-the-Khazâd'), and by the Elves *Hadhothrond* (a rendering of *Khazad-dûm*), but among themselves, in later Ages, *Moria*, the 'Black-pit'.

The story of Moria is a tale with an irresistible sense of destiny, of massive achievement, great power and royalty, of uncountable wealth and unsurpassed skill in stone-working, tunnelling, mining, delving and craftsmanship. It is also a tale of greed, self-satisfaction, obsession and final loss, brought about by the very factors which made the Dwarrowdelf the mighty achievement it was, from the Elder Days until the latter half of the Third Age.

Of all the names of this ancient realm, Khazad-dûm, the Dwarves' own term for it, was naturally by far the most venerable. *Khazâd* was the name this people had for their own race, the name they believed had been given to them by Aulë the Smith, the Craftsman of the Valar and their own demiurgic 'sponsor', who also gave them their ancient skills and singular nature. It was fitting, therefore, that their greatest accomplishment should be given the simple title 'Mansion-of-the-Dwarves' – for no other Dwarf-delving in Middle-earth, not even the First Age cities of Nogrod and Belegost, nor the dolven halls of Erebor, ever approached the sheer size and scale of Moria.

The name *Moria* itself is an Elvish (Sindarin) word and it was 'given without love; for the Eldar, though they might at need, in their bitter wars with the Dark Powers and his servants, contrive fortresses underground, were not dwellers in such places of choice . . . and Moria in their tongue means the Black Chasm'.[18] A vast and boundless chasm it was, from its very beginning, but it did not become black until after the Heirs of Durin fled, many thousands of years later; while the Dwarves dwelt in Khazad-dûm, 'it was not darksome, but full of light and splendour. . .'[19]

The beginning of the city lay far back in the Elder Days when, alone among the Dwarves' seven Fathers, Durin the Deathless awoke and came to the great vale of Azanulbizar (as it was afterwards named), on the eastern side of the Misty Mountains. There he received a sign of his great royalty (see DURIN THE DEATHLESS), and there he made his dwelling, in the caves about Lake Kheled-zâram (the Mirrormere). Many Dwarves then came and laboured there, transforming the rough-hewn caves into carven halls and passages, roads and tunnels, mines and pits. Great gates they built overlooking Azanulbizar and its lake; and all of Moria which lay on or above the height of these Gates was then systemized into *levels* – while the halls which were delved below (and these were many, and endlessly branching) were known as *deeps*.

Between the First and Second Halls (on the same level as the Gates) was a chasm so deep that even the miners of Moria were never able to sound it. Across this, in a single curving span, the Dwarves built a narrow bridge of stone which could only be crossed in single file; this was *Durin's Bridge*, an ancient defence against any enemies who might capture the Gates and the First Hall. High in the peak of Zirak-zigil the Dwarves carved a chamber with a ledge from which Durin (or his many successors of the same name) could view the wide lands of Eriador. This was Durin's Tower, and it was reached by an even more ambitious feat of stone masonry, the 'Endless Stair', which climbed in unbroken spiral from the lowest Deep to the very pinnacle of the mountain, in many thousands of steps.

Such was the Dwarf-city of Moria. Many of the Khazâd dwelt there, especially after the end of the First Age, when the cataclysm which overwhelmed Thangorodrim and most of Elvish Beleriand also destroyed the ancient Dwarf-cities of the Blue Mountains: Nogrod and Belegost. Thus many Dwarves from these cities came to Moria, bringing their skills with them, so that the Dwarrowdelf became a colossal city occupying much of the area beneath the three peaks of the Misty Mountains: Caradhras (called *Barazinbar* by the Dwarves), Celebdil (*Zirak-zigil*) and Fanuidhol (*Bundushathûr*).

Early in the Second Age the Dwarves of Moria made their greatest discovery, one which increased their power and wealth beyond all dream or design: below the lowest Deeps of Baraz, where miners had delved for many years in search of gold and silver ('the toys of the Dwarves'[20]) and iron ('their servant'[21]), they discovered a new ore, light and yet strong, beautiful and versatile. This metal became known to the world at large as *mithril* ('Grey-flame', a Sindarin word), for the Dwarves never revealed their own name for it. However, they traded their surplus willingly enough. For the Elves especially loved *mithril*, and it was the news of the discovery of the great lode under Moria which caused many High-elves of Lindon, descendants of the Master Craftsman Fëanor himself, to settle nearby, on the western side of the Misty Mountains. This Elvenland became known as Eregion, and a close friendship soon grew up there between the Elves and Dwarves. To further this friendship the Moria-dwellers extended their kingdom westwards to the far side of the Mountains, and the Doors of Durin, built there by Dwarfwrights, were etched and designed by the hand of no less an Elvencraftsmen than Celebrimbor, as a sign of the alliance between the two peoples.

Yet war came upon the Westlands before half of the Second Age had passed. The Elven-craftsmen of Eregion were overcome by the renascent forces of Sauron the Great – and doubtless Moria would also have been pillaged had the Dwarves not shut their impregnable doors in the face of the advancing hordes; they kept them closed throughout the remainder of Sauron's first dominion in Middle-earth. Thus Moria survived the Accursed Years; and though other races did not fare so well, the Dwarves grew ever richer and cared little for the turmoils which were taking place outside their Gates.

At the beginning of the Third Age Moria was therefore at the height of its power. The wars and alliances which had devastated other lands were of small concern to the Miners there, still busily extending their realm. But their nemesis awaited, slumbering deep under Caradhras. Towards the end of the second millennium the Miners were again busy following the *mithril*-lode down into the bowels of the earth; and in this search for yet more wealth, their picks and axes broke down the last wall of rock which imprisoned a Terror of the Ancient World. The Balrog of Morgoth, buried deep under the Mountains since the ruin of Thangorodrim nearly two Ages before, was thus unfettered; in two years it slew many Dwarves, including Durin VI and his son Náin I. The inhabitants of Moria then abandoned their ancient works and fled far away, leaving their vast halls dark and empty – except for that which continued to stalk the endless passages and lightless Deeps.

The loss of Moria proved the undoing of Durin's house. Without a secure dwelling, this people dwindled, and many were slain by the enemies the Dwarves always managed to acquire. Other Dwarf-kingdoms were founded – and some prospered, for a while – but always the Heirs of Durin's Line dreamed of returning to Moria. The first to do so was Thrór, disinherited King of Erebor, which had been sacked and occupied by the Dragon Smaug in 2770 Third Age. Some twenty years later Thrór, perhaps unbalanced by the mis-fortunes of his House, foolishly walked alone into the darkened realm. He never returned, though his decapitated corpse was later cast out on the steps. For a host of Orcs was now dwelling in Moria (although even they did not dare to seek the lower Deeps where the Balrog still prowled).

This atrocity brought about the great War of the Dwarves and Orcs, of which much is said elsewhere. Yet while, in the end, the Dwarves had the victory over the Orcs of Moria, they could not yet reclaim their ancient realm. For, as Dáin Ironfoot told Thráin, Thrór's heir, 'we will not enter Khazad-dûm . . . Beyond the shadow it waits for you still: Durin's Bane. The world must change and some other power than ours must come before Durin's Folk walk again in Moria.'[22]

The second attempt to reclaim this realm was better organized but equally foolhardy. In 2989 Third Age, Balin son of Fundin (and one of the twelve companions of Thorin Oakenshield on the Quest of Erebor), led an expedition to Moria from the Lonely Mountain. With him he took many companions, including Óin and Ori, Floi, Frár, Lóni and Náli. They effected an entry against the few Orcs who remained there, and managed to survive for some five years before a host of Goblins came up the river Silverlode and forced the defenders to take refuge in their last strong-point, the Chamber of Mazarbul. There all fell.

Such was the history of the great realm as briefly recounted in available Records of the Shire (which were no doubt derived from Gimli the Dwarf). It is not said whether the Heirs of Durin ever returned to Moria in the Fourth Age, but this is unlikely, despite their long-cherished dreams. For in the New Age all folk dwindled save Men; and those races which did not disappear altogether or depart (like most of the Elves) were gradually diminished and became rustic; and eventually they were either completely forgotten by Men or were made into figures of fun in legends and folk-tales. Such was the fate of the Dwarves. But even the most absurd of modern nonsense stories about them usually manages to credit the Dwarves with awe-inspiring skill in works of stone and metal; and if the Khazâd themselves have now completely disappeared from Middle-earth, at least records remain of their achievements. Of these the mighty city of Moria was unquestionably both the greatest and the longest to endure.

Moria-silver See MITHRIL.

Moriquendi See DARK ELVES.

Mormegil 'Black Sword' (Sind.) A *nom de guerre* of Túrin Turambar, awarded him by the Elves of Nargothrond during the years when he was that city's foremost warrior. Túrin was, of course, the wielder of the black sword Gurthang (formerly ANGLACHEL).

Morrowdim The Shire name for the period of twilight known to the Grey-elves as *aduial* and to the High-elves as TINDÓMË.

Morthond 'Black-root' (Sind.) One of the largest of the seven rivers of Gondor. It rose under the White Mountains and flowed down to find the Sea north of Dol Amroth in Belfalas. At its mouth were ancient elf-havens built by Silvan Elves of Lórien early in the Third Age.

Morthond Vale A large, fertile, well-populated valley, situated high in the White Mountains between the source of the river Morthond and the Hill of Erech. It was also known as the Blackroot Vale.

Morwen Eledhwen A princess of the Edain, the daughter of Baragund of the First House. She wedded Húrin the Heir of Dor-lómin, and bore him three children: Túrin, Lalaith (who died in infancy), and Nienor. But her life was unhappy, for she and hers fell under the curse of Morgoth.

Morwen was born in Ladros, in Dorthonion; but while she was still a child that region of the North was attacked, and captured, by Morgoth (after the Dagor Bragollach); and she was taken to safety in Dor-lómin, where the House of Hador still maintained a realm on the very frontiers of war. There she later wedded Húrin, and there their children were born. But when her eldest child Túrin was seven, there came the renewal of open war, and the Nirnaeth Arnoediad, in which Húrin was captured, having fought to the last. In the days which followed this catastrophe Morwen remained perforce in Dor-lómin, which was now subject to Morgoth; but she contrived to smuggle Túrin, now the Heir of Húrin and Hador, out of that oppressed land to safety, in Doriath. She herself, together with daughter Nienor, remained in Dor-lómin for a further twenty years. Then, taking advantage of a momentary easing of the power of Morgoth in that region, she fled, with Nienor, to Doriath, hoping to find Túrin still there. But he was gone. And soon afterwards came news of the sack of Nargothrond; and with it news of Túrin. Then Morwen quitted Doriath, in search of Túrin; and in an attack made upon her party by the Dragon Glaurung, chief instrument of Morgoth in the matter of the Children of Húrin, she was lost; and was never again seen by Elves or Men – save by her husband Húrin, whom she met again on the day of her death, years afterwards. She was buried with her son, at Cabed Naeramarth.

Morwen of Lossarnach A lady of southern Gondor who wedded Thengel, son of King Fengel of Rohan (in 2943 Third Age). This was the first recorded union between any of the Dúnedain and the Rohirrim, who were by then traditional allies of Gondor.

Thengel was old by the time he married, and he had dwelt for most of his life in Gondor, being at feud with his father Fengel (by all accounts a King of unpleasant personal habits and quarrelsome nature). While living in the South-kingdom, Morwen bore Thengel three children, including his only son Théoden. In 2980 Fengel died, and Thengel returned to Rohan to become its sixteenth King. There,

Morwen – whom the Rohirrim called 'Steelsheen' – bore him two more children, the last child being Théodwyn, beloved sister of young Théoden.

Théodwyn's own daughter Éowyn (who was later adopted by Théoden after he became King) was said to have 'a grace and pride that came to her out of the South from Morwen of Lossarnach.'[23]

Mounds of Mundburg The name given in Rohan to the burial-mounds of those who fell in the Battle of the Pelennor Fields (March, 3019 Third Age). The mounds themselves were not far from Minas Tirith ('Mundburg'), on the site of the great battle, near the river Anduin. Inside these long green barrows were laid all the warriors slain during the battle, both Dúnedain and Rohirrim – save only King Théoden himself. The story of the individual heroism of the fallen was celebrated in a lay, made in Rohan, which sings of the Mounds of Mundburg. (See Book V Chap. 6.)

Mountains of Aman The Pelóri.

Mountains of Defence The Pelóri.

Mountains of Lune The Hobbits' name for the *Ered Luin,* the 'Blue Mountains' which lay to the west of the Shire.

Mountains of Mirkwood A small range of broken hills that rose some distance north of the Old Forest Road which ran through the gloomy wood. In the Fourth Age they formed the southern boundary of King Thranduil's Elven-realm; the enchanted river which also guarded the Wood-elves' kingdom had its source in these mountains.

Mountains of Mithrim See MITHRIM.

Mountains of Moria The three great peaks which rose above the underground Dwarf-kingdom of Khazad-dûm: Caradhras (Bara-zinbar), Celebdil (Zirak-zigil) and Fanuidhol (Bundushathur). In the Westron or Common Speech they were known as Redhorn, Silvertine and Cloudyhead.

Mountains of Shadow A translation of the Grey-elven name *Ered Wethrin* (also 'Shadowy Mountains'); in the Third Age, a name given by Men of Gondor to the western wall of Mordor, closest to their realm (properly *Ephel Dúath* 'Dark [shadowy]-outer-fence').

Mountains of Terror A translation of the Sindarin name *Ered Gorgoroth,* given by the Elves of Beleriand to the southernmost heights and precipices of Dorthonion: a region of horror and dread.

The reason for the name, and for the fear in which this region of Beleriand was held, lay in the infestation of this range of mountains by evil creatures: spiders of monstrous size, descendants of Ungoliant (who in her origins was a fruit of the thought of Morgoth). There was no more dangerous place in Middle-earth, save Angband itself.

These creatures first appeared after the return of Ungoliant and Morgoth to Middle-earth; so rapidly did they breed that before long not only the Mountains of Terror but also the valley whose northern wall they were (Nan Dungortheb), had become their preserve; and as a result was avoided by all save the foolhardy, the ignorant, and the desperate. Moreover, at least one of these creatures somehow survived the ruin of Beleriand, and later came to Mordor, there to fatten once more upon the blood of Elves and Men. This was Shelob the Great.

It is recorded that the Ered Gorgoroth were successfully crossed once only: by Beren of the Edain.

Mountains of the East The *Orocarni* ('Red Mountains'), a range of mountains of unknown dimension which lay along the western shore of the Inland Sea of Helcar, a remnant of ILLUIN.

Mountains of Valinor The PELÓRI, the highest mountains in the World.

Mount Dolmed See DOLMED.

Mount Doom A translation of the Sindarin *Amon Amarth*, the name given in Gondor to the volcano Orodruin, when it burst into flame to herald Sauron's first assault upon the survivors of Númenor (in 3429 Second Age).

Mount Everwhite A translation of the Quenya name *Oiolossë* (also *Taniquetil*), highest of the Mountains of Valinor (the *Pelóri*).

Mount Fang A rendering of the Sindarin word *Orthanc* into the Common Speech or Westron. Orthanc was, of course, the great tower of Angrenost (Isengard), built by Gondor late in the Second Age. By curious chance, in the language of the Rohirrim, *Orthanc* translates as 'The-Cunning-Mind'.

Mount Gram A northerly peak of the Misty Mountains whose precise location has not been recorded. It was reportedly the dwelling place of the Goblins who, led by Golfimbul, attacked the Shire in 2747 Third Age (1147 Shire Reckoning) and were decisively defeated by Bandobras 'the Bullroarer' Took at the Battle of Greenfields that same year.

Mount Gundabad See GUNDABAD.

Mount Rerir See RERIR.

Mount Taras See TARAS.

Mouth of Sauron This was the self-awarded title of the Lieutenant of the Dark Tower, who conducted all his dark Master's embassies. In origin he was said to have been (like the Ringwraiths) a Black Númenorean, one of those renegades who settled the coastlands of Middle-earth during the Second Age. Whether or not he actually was of such great age cannot be told, for 'his name is remembered in no tale . . . and he himself had forgotten it'.[24]

Mouths of Anduin The Great River reached the Sea at Belfalas via a large and complex delta known as the *Ethir Anduin*, the 'Mouths of Anduin'.

Mouths of Entwash After passing through the flat, low-lying country south of the Emyn Muil, the river Entwash meandered into a wide marshy delta, actually greater in size than the Mouths of Anduin. It was a sad country with tall reeds and many birds, but no inhabitants. There were seven Mouths of Entwash, as much as thirty leagues apart, and all flowed into the Great River between the Emyn Muil and Cair Andros.

Mouths of Sirion The Sirion delta, in the Bay of Balar. (Possibly a translation of *Ethir Sirion*.)

Mugwort A family of Bree-hobbits.

Mûmak, Mûmakil The origin of this word is not known although it may be in the language of the Men of Harad. The *mûmakil* were pachyderms, giant war-beasts known to the Hobbits (in tales only) as 'Oliphaunts'.

Mundburg 'Guardian-fortress' The name used in Rohan for Minas Tirith, the great fortified city of Gondor.
See also MOUNDS OF MUNDBURG.

Mungo Baggins The eldest son of Balbo Baggins of Hobbiton, the father of Bungo and the grandfather of Bilbo the Renowned.

Muzgash An Orc-soldier of the Tower of Cirith Ungol, a member of Shagrat's company. Like his comrade Lagduf, Muzgash was shot by one of his own race, a member of the Orcs of Minas Morgul, who were in hot dispute with the Ungol-orcs over the possession of certain items of booty (see Book VI Chap. 1).

Notes

1 *Silmarillion* p. 83.
2 *Silmarillion* pp. 131–9.
3 Sauron's Maiarin name is not recorded.
4 Appendix A I(iv).
5 Book V Chap. 2.
6 See also LAURELINDÓRENAN.

7 It may have been taken back into Eriador by those Edain of the First and Third Houses (led by Bereg) who renounced the West and re-crossed the Blue Mountains before the Dagor Bragollach. See *Silmarillion* pp. 144-5.

8 *Silmarillion* pp. 103-5, 140-9.

9 Descended, it is said, from the House of Hador, see BEREG.

10 If indeed these were Men at all; at least, of our own species.

11 Book VI Chap. 5. *Ambar-metta* means 'Doomsday'.

12 A full description of the (later) city can be found in Book V Chap. 1.

13 Literally 'First-king'.

14 Book II Chap. 4.

15 Illustrated in *The Silmarillion Calendar* 1978.

16 Book IV Chap. 3.

17 See Note 12 on p. 107 of this *Companion*.

18 Appendix F II.

19 Book II Chap. 4. A politer name for Moria used by Elves was *Hadhodrond*, 'Halls-of-the-*Hadhod* [Khazâd]'.

20 Book II Chap. 4.

21 *Ibid.*

22 Appendix A III.

23 Appendix A II.

24 Book V Chap. 10.

Nahald In the original (as opposed to translated) Mannish tongues of Northern Wilderland, the personal name *Nahald* meant 'secret'. In translations from the Red Book this name has been rendered as *Déagol*.

Nahar The (onomatopoeically derived) name given in Eldarin tradition to the Horse of the Huntsman of the Valar Oromë. Possibly this great, silver-white steed was the ancestor of the *mearas* of Rohan.

Náin I From 1980–81 Third Age, the last King of Khazad-dûm (Moria), the great Dwarf-city under the Misty Mountains. His father was Durin VI. In Durin's time the Dwarves were again delving deep in their northern mines, seeking the mother-lode of the *mithril*-vein which had been the foundation of their wealth. Thus it came to pass that they released an evil spirit of the First Age, still slumbering far beneath the earth. This was the Balrog, who slew Durin, and drove the miners away from the great Deeps of Moria.

Nonetheless, under Náin I, their new King, the Dwarves held on to the upper levels of their ancient mansions – although it was only a year later that Náin himself was slain by the Terror that emerged from the Deeps, driving the Heirs of Durin from Durin's own Halls. Following Náin's death the Dwarves abandoned Moria and fled into the North.

Náin II From 2488–2585 Third Age, the King of the Dwarf-realm which had been established in the Grey Mountains (Ered Mithrin) shortly after the founding of Erebor. Náin was the last King of this once-thriving colony to die peacefully.

See also DWARVES.

Náin The son of Grór, first Lord of the Dwarves of the Iron Hills. In the year 2799 Third Age Náin led an army of his father's people to aid their kinfolk at the Battle of Azanulbizar, the final battle in the six-year War of the Dwarves and Orcs. The host of the Iron Hills did not arrive at the field of conflict until comparatively late in the day, when the Dwarves had already begun to give way in the face of great odds. But the grim warriors of the Iron Hills turned the tide, and soon reached the very gates of Moria, where Náin challenged Azog, the Orc-leader, to single combat. Azog, who had avoided all battle up to this point, was much the fresher and stronger and killed the Dwarf, although he was himself slain by Dáin Ironfoot, son of Náin.

Naith That part of Lothlórien lying between the rivers Silverlode (Celebrant) and Anduin. The Elves of that secret land looked upon the Naith as being in the shape of a broad spearhead (or *gore*) whose tip was at Egladil, where they themselves dwelt, near the confluence of the rivers.

Náli A Dwarf from the Lonely Mountain and a member of the gallant but ill-fated expedition to Moria led by Balin son of Fundin in 2989 Third Age. The colony failed five years later when overwhelmed by Orcs attacking from the east; together with his comrades Frár and Lóni, Náli fell while holding Durin's Bridge and the Second Hall.

'Namárië' 'Farewell' (Q.) A word of parting used among the High-elves and, more importantly, a name for the Lament of Galadriel in Lórien (called *Altariello nainië Lóriendesse* in the Quenya tongue). The verse was recorded and set down in the Red Book of Westmarch by Frodo Baggins, to whom it was originally sung, as a valedictory and parting benison (Book II Chap. 8).

The poem (or hymn) is in fact the longest single passage of High-elven speech to be recorded in surviving Annals of the Third Age. A full discussion of the context, grammatical structure and layers of meaning contained within the lines has no place in these pages: the compiler would indeed be glad of the leisure (and space in this *Companion*) to examine, in meticulous detail, the grace of the metre, the structure of the language employed – and, not least, the substance of the great matters briefly referred to in the stanzas; but since such a discussion already exists elsewhere, any sustained efforts in this direction would rightly be judged superfluous and indeed impertinent.

The reader is therefore unhesitatingly referred to Professor Tolkien's expert analysis of this beautiful verse, which may be found on pp. 58–62 of *The Road Goes Ever On*, a volume of Third Age verses arranged and notated for modern instruments. This book also contains translations of two Elvish hymns (*Namárië* and *A Elbereth Gilthoniel*), together with notes on their construction and meaning. However, as many readers will not have access to a copy of this excellent volume, a brief summary of the meaning behind the *Namárië* hymn becomes necessary.

Galadriel, exiled from her ancient home in Eldamar long Ages before the War of the Ring, addresses her song to Frodo the Ring-bearer, bidding him a fair journey and peace at the end of it. Simultaneously, she includes a veiled plea to Elbereth – who hears all words spoken in Middle-earth – asking her blessing on Frodo's mission and the acceptance of Frodo himself in the Undying Lands after the completion of his Quest. For Galadriel was the wisest of Elven women then living in Mortal Lands, and her foresight told her that if the Quest succeeded it would be at great personal cost to the Ring-bearer.

The verse therefore speaks indirectly of Galadriel's sorrow at her own long exile from the Undying Lands. There are many references to the high lore of the Elves – and many words in the 'personal' cases of the Quenya tongue, such as only one of the mighty among the High-elves would have felt entitled to use when addressing Varda (Elbereth). In the event, Galadriel's prayer (for such it was) was answered, and the Ring-bearer was granted the grace she sought for him; and for her own great acts of wisdom and unselfishness, Galadriel was herself finally forgiven by the Valar and permitted to return to Eldamar at the end of the Third Age.

Nameless Land An epithet used in Gondor for Mordor. During the latter years of the Third Age, after Sauron once again declared himself openly in Mordor, Men of Gondor and the Westlands frequently spoke of 'the Unnamed' and 'the Nameless Land', in order to avoid giving substance to what was a very real horror and ever-present threat on the borders of their lives.

Nameless Pass Because of the heavy omens associated with it, the Pass of Cirith Ungol, which lay above Minas Morgul, was spoken of with dread in Gondor – and therefore circumlocution was often employed to avoid naming it (see previous entry). 'If Cirith Ungol is named, old men and masters of lore will blanch and fall silent,'[1] reported Faramir when warning the Ring-bearer to avoid the place.

The inhibiting horror attached to this Pass was based on old tales dating from the days when Gondor kept a foothold in Mordor, when the Tower of Cirith Ungol, which guarded the Pass, was garrisoned by the Dúnedain. Their stories spoke of a living ghastliness which had long made its den in the highest peak of the Pass.

See also CIRITH UNGOL; SHELOB THE GREAT.

Námo 'The Judge' (Q.) See MANDOS.

Nan Curunír 'Valley of Saruman' (Sind.) Situated between the south-westerly and south-easterly spurs of Methedras, the 'Last-peak' of the Misty Mountains, the 'Wizard's Vale' was a large, well-guarded valley, in the centre of which rose the mighty Ring of Isengard – originally called *Angrenost* when the natural fortifications there were smoothed and strengthened by Men of Gondor late in the Second Age.

The Vale of Angrenost (as it was known before Saruman came to dwell there, late in the Third Age) overlooked the plain of Isen and the Gap of Rohan, and thus commanded an important strategic position.

Nandor 'Those-who-turn-back' (Q.) The name given in the lore of the Eldar to those of the Telerin kindred, hindmost on the Great Journey, who quitted the Journey while still east of the Misty Mountains, being overawed by the size of the range and moreover enamoured of the woods and falling waters of Wilderland. They were led by Lenwë. This was the first sundering of the Eldar. Lenwë led his people southward, out of the knowledge of the other Teleri, and little is known of what befell the Nandor afterwards. For they did not remain a united people, but scattered this way and that, wandering freely where the mood took them; and though they were of nobler origin than the wild and rustic Avari, in after years their lives were passed in similar fashion. Many remained in Greenwood; some passed south, to the Golden Wood, and so became the uttermost ancestors of the Galadhrim.[2] More still followed the Great River into the southlands, and came to its delta. And after many centuries and millennia, an adventurous vanguard circumvented the Misty Mountains, by way of the Ered Nimrais and Fangorn, and so came into the vast woods of Eriador. (In all probability these were those archaic Elves spoken of by Treebeard, for the Nandor were the first of the Eldar to encounter the Onodrim; at all events they seem to have left a lasting – and favourable – impression on the old Ent.)

This vanguard of the Nandor was led, not by Lenwë (whose fate is not recorded), but by his son Denethor. And it so chanced that their arrival in Eriador coincided with the release of Melkor from prison, and of the quickening of evil once more in northern Middle-earth. Eriador was fast becoming perilous. Therefore Denethor, hearing tales of Beleriand (possibly from Dwarves) and of its mighty King and Queen, decided to renounce the choice of his father Lenwë, and so gathering his people together, he crossed the Blue Mountains into Beleriand, last of all the Eldar to do so, and was reunited with a Telerin people – the Sindar – after more than two ages of separation. They were welcomed by Thingol, who gave them the Land of the Seven Rivers (Ossiriand) to dwell in, and there they spent their days. They still called themselves (and were called by the Sindar) *Nandor*, but the returning Noldor called them 'Green-elves' (or *Laiquendi*). Denethor was afterwards slain in the First Battle of Beleriand; and the green-clad Nandor came never again across Gelion, nor took any part in the affairs of the time, save when compelled to do so. Of the separate fates of the Nandor who remained in the east nothing more can be said.

Note: in the nomenclature of the Eldar, the Nandor are accounted *Moriquendi* and *Úmanyar*, together with the 'Western Nandor' (the Green-elves of Ossiriand) and the Avari.

Nanduhirion 'Vale-of-dim-streams' (Sind.) A name for that ancient place in the Misty Mountains known to Dwarves as AZANULBIZAR and to Northern Men as the Dimrill Dale.

See also BATTLE OF AZANULBIZAR.

Nan Dungortheb 'Valley of Dreadful Death' (Sind.) The sinister vale which lay between Doriath and Dorthonion, bordered in the east by the river Esgalduin and in the west by the Mindeb.

See MOUNTAINS OF TERROR.

Nan Elmoth A wood of East Beleriand, an outlier of the greater forest of Region, though separated from it by the valley of the Celon. It was shaped like the sickle moon, being three leagues broad and seven long. Its trees were the loftiest in East Beleriand. Here the Maia Melian came and sang alone under the stars; and here she was found by Elwë Thingol, Lord of the Telerin Elves. Here they plighted their troth. They afterwards made a realm in nearby Doriath; but Nan Elmoth was then taken as a dwelling-place by the great smith of the Grey-elves, Eöl. In this wood he met Aredhel Ar-feiniel of the Noldor (in a strange echo of the earlier and less ill-starred meeting), and here for many years she also lived, and bore Eöl a son: Maeglin.

Nan-tasarion 'Vale of Willows' (Q.) The more formal of the two High-elven names for the valley which lay about the confluence of the Narog with the Sirion, in East Beleriand (the other was *Tasarinan*). However, the name most in use was the Sindarin *Nan-tathren*, which is but an equivalent of the Quenya name and indeed carries the same meaning.

See also Treebeard's song 'In the Willow-meads of Tasarinan' (Book III Chap. 4 and *The Road Goes Ever On* pp. 11-17).

Nan-tathren See preceding entry.

Nár An aged companion of the Dwarf-king Thrór, who faithfully accompanied the exiled King on his last wanderings – which ended at Azanulbizar in 2790 Third Age. Against Nár's entreaties, Thrór proudly entered Moria alone; several days later, while waiting for him near the Great Gates, Nár heard a horn-blast and the beheaded corpse of the King was cast out on to the steps. Nár was mockingly called near by the Orcs inside Moria, who threw him a bag of worthless coins as weregild for Thrór's death and told him to take the tidings to his kin. He did so, and the news of the Goblins' act of desecration precipitated the War of the Dwarves and Orcs.

Narbeleth 'Sun-waning' (Sind.) Both an alternative name for the fourth of the six Elvish 'seasons' (see QUELLË), and the word used by the Dúnedain for the month more widely known as NARQUELIË.

Narchost 'Fire-fort' (Sind.) One of the two Towers of the Teeth, which flanked the Black Gate into Mordor. Both towers (the other was *Carchost*, 'Fang-fort') were originally built by Men of Gondor at the end of the Second Age, in order to watch over the borders of the Black Land and prevent the re-entry of evil there after Sauron the Great was first overthrown.

See also MORANNON.

Nardol 'Fire-head' (Sind.) A beacon-hill of Gondor; the third in the chain of seven such hills which ran from Druadan Forest to the Firienwood, enabling urgent tidings to be sent between Gondor and Rohan.

See also BEACON-HILLS.

Nargothrond 'Fortress-halls-of-Narog (an abbreviation of *Narog-ost-rond* (Sind.) The name given by the Noldorin king Finrod

Felagund to the great city he founded in the Caves of Narog, during the first century of his exile in Middle-earth. These were a honeycomb of delvings shaped originally by Dwarves (of the race of Noegyth Nibin), and called, by them, *Nulukkizdin*. Finrod learned of their existence from his kinsman Thingol of Doriath, and desiring to found a kingdom which would also be a hidden redoubt for the Eldar, he chose this ancient place as the site of his new realm in Middle-earth (hitherto he had dwelt on Tol Sirion in the North). The burrowings of the Dwarves were extended by Elf-masons and -miners, helped by more Dwarves, and although Nargothrond was never to be as fair as Gondolin or Menegroth, it was larger and more powerful than either of those cities, and the treasure which Finrod had brought out of Valinor and now stored in the vaults of his underground city made it the wealthiest by far. Three great portals it had,[3] and these opened on the brink of the swift-flowing Narog, and above on both sides of the river reared the sheer precipices of Taur-en-Faroth, which long ago the Narog had cloven in two with the force of its passage. Nargothrond as it was founded was therefore virtually impregnable, though its whereabouts were not long to be kept secret.

Nonetheless, the power of Nargothrond grew. During the Long Peace its people extended the influence of their city in all directions, and Finrod was accounted ruler of all the Elves of West Beleriand, save for the Falathrim of the Havens, who were of the Sindar and acknowledged only Círdan (and above him Thingol). But Finrod of Nargothrond they respected more than all the other Noldor, and the Havens became allied to Nargothrond, and profited thereby: for in these days of his power Finrod did all in his power to assist all Elves, and especially those who dwelt in the coastlands and so guarded the sea-ways. Thus he and his city acted as a bridge between the Noldor and the Sindar.

But these were days doomed to pass; war again broke out in the North, with frightening suddenness, and events were thereby set in motion which were to lead inexorably to the doom of Finrod – and ultimately to the fall of his city. Finrod himself barely escaped with his life from the Dagor Bragollach; but afterwards there came to Nargothrond a single warrior of the Edain, Beren son of Barahir (the saviour of Finrod), who bore with him the Ring of the House of Finarfin and claimed the aid of Finarfin's son on the Quest he had undertaken. Finrod did not refuse this aid, but his people were angry and confused at that time, and they (stirred up by the sons of Fëanor, then dwelling as Finrod's guests), deposed him. Finrod then passed away into the North and was never seen again in the Halls of Narog.

But the lordship of the city was given to his younger brother Orodreth (dispossessed of Tol Sirion by Sauron).

By this time war had at last penetrated into East Beleriand, and the Elves of Nargothrond now found themselves in constant contact with the forces of Morgoth. Perhaps for military reasons – and perhaps for reasons connected with their shame at the casting-out of Felagund – they now precipitately abandoned much of the greater realm of Nargothrond, and began to fight in secret ways: by ambush and swift escape. The bow became their chief weapon. It was at this time that the Fifth Battle of Beleriand was fought in the North, and the Eldarin cause ruined for ever. Even more did the people of Nargothrond now eschew open combat with Morgoth; the perimeter of their realm tightened further, and of the small host they had sent to the Nirnaeth, only one came back.

Now the doom of Nargothrond approached – in the person of the warrior Túrin Turambar of the Edain, who bore with him the Curse upon the Children of Húrin, a curse which never failed to ensnare and destroy those with whom Túrin shared his days. In the wild he had encountered the only survivor of those Elves of Nargothrond who had fought at the Nirnaeth: Gwindor son of Guilin escaped from the mines of Angband. And it was Gwindor who now brought Túrin to his former city. Túrin was a great warrior, more war-crafty than any Elf of Nargothrond (save Gwindor) and, moreover, apparently invincible in battle. He therefore assumed, by degrees, the military leadership of the hosts of the city; and by degrees his pride grew with this new station – and his new name *Mormegil* – so that he began to despise the methods of war which his forces had hitherto been accustomed to use. Against the advice of Gwindor, Túrin caused a great bridge across the Narog to be built, thus gaining the limited tactical advantage of being able to make swift sorties – in exchange for obligingly neutralizing the city's best single defence: for bridges may be crossed in two directions. And so it proved. There came a day when an army came out of the North, whose object was the destruction of Nargothrond – and Túrin caused the host of the city to meet this force in open battle, fifteen leagues north of the city, on the field of Tumhalad. There the Elven army was annihilated, and Orodreth the king was slain; for the host of Angband was accompanied by the Dragon Glaurung. And even before the fighting had finished, Glaurung and a force of Orcs which accompanied him had hastened south to the gorge of the Narog, had crossed Túrin's boastful bridge (Glauring was wingless and could not otherwise have entered) and had laid waste the city of Finrod. Nargothrond was destroyed, and never arose again.

Nárië (Q.) The equivalent of our June, being the sixth month of the year in Kings' and Stewards' Reckoning and the third in New Reckoning. The Sindarin name for this month (the name used only by the Dúnedain) was *Nórui*.

Narmacil I From 1226–94 Third Age, the seventeenth King of Gondor. He was the son of Atanatar Alcarin 'the Glorious', the shiftless heir of the great Hyarmendacil I; and although Gondor still seemed all-powerful by the time he came to the Throne, most of his family did little to preserve this power, being for the most part hedonists who surrounded themselves with luxury and ignored their first duty: to govern.

Such a man was Narmacil, who died childless, and so was his younger brother, Calmacil, who succeeded him. However, in 1240 Third Age, Narmacil appointed a Regent to take over his duties – and in this at least he showed good judgement. The man he chose was Calmacil's son Minalcor, who ruled on behalf of both his uncle and his father for over sixty years. After Calmacil's death, the patient, capable and honourable Minalcar was himself crowned King (as Rómendacil II), and he then ruled for another sixty years.

Narmacil II From 1850–56 Third Age, the twenty-ninth King of Gondor. His was a brief and unfortunate reign, for in his time a new enemy appeared on the eastern frontiers of the realm – which then extended as far as the Inland Sea. This was a tribe of Easterlings known as the Wainriders: a numerous, warlike people who travelled in huge wains or wagons while their khans or chiefs fought from chariots.

Inflamed by emissaries of Sauron, these Easterlings made a sudden, massive attack on the eastern pasturelands of Gondor in the year 1856. Narmacil led an army across the Great River to meet them in Rhovanion but suffered defeat and was slain. The Wainriders swept on as far as the Anduin, which became the new frontier in the east; and Rhovanion, traditionally friendly to Gondor, was enslaved. Narmacil's son Calimehtar took a delayed revenge in 1899, when he defeated the Wainriders, who were already in difficulty over a rebellion in Rhovanion.

Narn i Hîn Húrin 'The Tale of the Children of Húrin' (Sind.) The title given by a poet of the Edain, Dírhavel, to the long ballad or poem composed by him in the late First Age; it deals with the sad subject of Húrin of the Third House, and his children: Túrin and Nienor, accursed by Morgoth. (A prose extraction may be found in *The Silmarillion*, pp. 198–226.)

Dírhavel himself was slain in battle, shortly after the making of the Tale; for he dwelt at the Havens of Sirion, which were attacked by Maedhros and Maglor, the sons of Fëanor, and perished like many others in that fratricidal conflict.

Narog The longest river west of the Sirion; it had its source at Ivrin, in the southern vales of the Ered Wethrin, and flowed almost due south for ninety leagues, becoming swifter and fuller as it grew in size, until it reached the Sirion at Nan-tathren. It had one tributary: the Ginglith, which flowed into the Narog some twelve leagues north of the highland of Taur-en-Faroth. Where the larger river flowed through this upland, its passage had carved a deep gorge through the rock, and the action of the waters had also hollowed out caves on the western side. These caves were later extended by Dwarves, and still later by Elves of the House of Finarfin; and here was founded the great underground city of Nargothrond, whose moat and chief defence was the Narog.

Note: the name *Narog* may have some etymological connection with the Grey-elves' name for the race of Dwarves: the *Naugrim*.

Narquelië (Q.) The tenth month of the year in Kings' Reckoning, the system developed by the Dúnedain of Númenor in the early Second Age and introduced to the Westlands of Middle-earth by their descendants in the Third Age. This month was unaffected when the slightly modified system of Stewards' Reckoning superseded the old calendar in the last third of the age; however, when the New Reckoning was introduced at the very end of the Age, *Narquelië* became the third month of the new year (calculated to begin in spring). In all three systems this month had 30 days and was roughly equivalent to our October. It was used by the Dúnedain in the (Grey-elven) form *Narbeleth*.

Narrow Ice A poetic reference in the Elvish style to the great ice-fields of the far North, the HELCARAXË, where bergs and floes and pack-ice still grind everlastingly together. The Hobbit Bilbo Baggins, who used this term in his poem 'Eärendil Was A Mariner' (Book II Chap. 1), obviously employed it to indicate the northernmost latitudes that were navigable to Eärendil.

Narrows The 'waist' of the great forest of Greenwood (known in much of the Third Age as Mirkwood). After the conclusion of the War of the Ring, the Narrows came to mark the boundary between the domain of Thranduil in the north and Celeborn's realm of East Lórien, established in the south.

Narsil 'Red-and-White-Flame' (Q.) The Sword of Elendil, and one of the most renowned weapons in the history of Middle-earth. It was wrought by the smith Telchar 'in the deeps of time',[4] and passed to the Lords of Andúnië before the Drowning of Númenor (3319 Second Age), when Elendil the Tall, the son of Amandil, last Lord of Andúnië, bore it to Middle-earth.

In fashion Narsil was a long-sword, with a cutting edge that was extraordinarily keen – even as the Elves would reckon such things. In the hands of Elendil it was an irresistible weapon. During the War of the Last Alliance it shone on the field of battle alongside Aiglos, the Spear of Gil-galad (another famous and deadly weapon of the Age); and in the Battle of Dagorlad (3434) it proved too much for Sauron's soldiers to withstand. Yet in the final hand-to-hand combat with Sauron upon the slopes of the volcano Orodruin, in the last year of the Age, 'Elendil fell, and Narsil broke beneath him . . . although Sauron himself was overthrown'.[5] Elendil's son Isildur then took the hilt-shard of the Sword and used it to cut the Ruling Ring from the hand of the Dark Lord; and the Sword-that-was-broken was taken by the Dúnedain of the North back to Annúminas, where it was kept for many years as one of the chief heirlooms of the North-kingdom – 'for it was spoken of old . . . that it should be made again when the Ring, Isildur's Bane, was found.'[6]

It was not until the end of the Third Age that Isildur's Bane again came to light, and by that time the Bearer of the Sword-that-was-broken was the sixteenth Chieftain of the Dúnedain of the North, the Heir of Isildur, Aragorn II. After the Council of Elrond (3018 Third Age), in which it was decided to attempt the destruction of the Ring, Aragorn, believing that the time long prophesied had finally arrived, had the Sword reforged by the smiths of Elrond's House; and he gave it a new name: *Andúril*, 'Flame-of-the-West'. Aragorn bore the Sword Reforged throughout the War of the Ring and to final victory before the Black Gate.

Narsilion 'Song-of-the-Sun-and-Moon' (Q.) The name given by the Eldar to an ancient poem or rhyme (made most probably in

Eldamar) which deals, as its name indeed implies, with the raising of the Moon and Sun. It is one of the source poems of *The Silmarillion*.

Narvi The Dwarf stonewright who made the Doors of Durin: the West-gate of Moria which opened into the vast underground city from the neighbouring Elvish land of Eregion. The Dwarf's name was recorded for ever upon the Doors by the Elven-smith Celebrimbor, who engraved them. (See illustration in Book II Chap. 4.)

Narvinyë (Q.) The first month of the Kings' Reckoning, originated in Númenor in the early Second Age and eventually used in one form or another by most of the Westron-speaking folk of Middle-earth. After the year 2060 Third Age, the system was modified and the name was changed to Stewards' Reckoning, although *Narvinyë* itself was unaffected. Following the conclusion of the War of the Ring, the calendar was adjusted again and the year was calculated to begin in spring rather than mid-winter. *Narvinyë* thus became the tenth month of the New Reckoning; however, it still had 30 days and was roughly the equivalent of our January.

Although most of the peoples of Middle-earth who used the Dúnedain calendars preserved the original (Quenya, or High-elven) names for the months and days of the week, the Dúnedain themselves used the Sindarin (or Grey-elven) forms of these names. They therefore spoke of *Narvinyë* as *Narwain*.

Narwain The Sindarin form of the Quenya word *Narvinyë*. See previous entry.

Narya The Great The Ring of Fire, one of the Three Rings of the Elven-kings made by Celebrimbor in Eregion in the late sixteenth century of the Second Age. This Ring, adorned with its single stone as 'red as fire',[7] was originally given to Círdan the Shipwright, who kept it until the arrival of the Istari – or Wizards – from the Uttermost West (*c.* 1000 Third Age). Then, welcoming Mithrandir (Gandalf) at the Grey Havens, he surrendered Narya.

'Take this ring, Master,' he said, 'for your labours will be heavy; but it will support you in the weariness that you have taken upon yourself. For this is the Ring of Fire, and with it you may rekindle hearts in a world that grows chill.'[8]

See also THREE RINGS.

Nauglamír 'Jewel of the Dwarves' (Sind.) A rich and beautiful necklace of fine gold-work, set with many-coloured jewels, which was made for King Finrod Felagund by Dwarves of the Blue Mountains, at the time of the founding of Nargothrond. It was left behind by Finrod when he journeyed north with Beren of the Edain, never to return, and afterwards formed a part of the immense pillage of Nargothrond, gathered together in one vast heap by the Dragon Glaurung, the destroyer of the city. From this grim fate it was rescued by Húrin of the Edain, who took the Necklace with him to Doriath and gave it to Thingol Greycloak; who then had the Silmaril which he possessed mounted in the Nauglamír – and so brought his own doom upon his head. For the Dwarves who undertook this work also desired the Silmaril. When Thingol rebuked them, they murdered him. The Necklace and Silmaril were afterwards recovered from them, and eventually passed west over Sea, with Eärendil.

Naugrim 'Stunted People' (Sind.) The DWARVES.

Nazgûl 'Ring-wraiths' (Black Speech) See RINGWRAITHS.

Near Harad The northernmost region of the (undisputed) lands of Harad. It was bounded on the west by the Harad Road and on the east by the lands of Khand; to the north it stretched as far as the Mountains of Shadow, the southern boundary of Mordor.

Necklace of the Dwarves The NAUGLAMÍR.

Necromancer Shortly after the passing of the first millennium of the Third Age, the Istari (or Wizards) and the chiefs of the Elves of Middle-earth became aware that an evil force was emanating from Southern Mirkwood, from a stronghold afterwards known as Dol Guldur. For many years this Power was known to the inhabitants of the Anduin Vale simply as 'The Necromancer' (*Necromancer* meaning 'worker of black magic'). And for many long years, the sorcerer of Dol Guldur quietly hatched his plots and worked his evil, well content that his enemies remained unaware of his true identity: for the Necromancer was Sauron himself.

Needlehole A village of the Westfarthing of the Shire. It straddled The Water, to the north of Rushock Bog.

Neithan 'The Deprived' (Sind.) The first of the *noms-de-guerre* assumed by Túrin Turambar; he had just fled from Doriath, because of the death of Saeros.

Neldoreth 'Beech-forest' (Sind.; Q. *Taur-na-Neldor*). The name given by the Grey-elves of Doriath to the smaller and more northerly of the two forests which comprised the kingdom of Doriath, in central Beleriand (the name *Neldoreth*, we are informed, is derived from *neldëorn*, 'Three-trunked-tree', a word which refers to the greatest of all the beeches of Neldoreth, *Hírilorn*, which of course had three stems or trunks). Neldoreth was bordered on the south and east by the river Esgalduin, on the west by the Mindeb and the Sirion, and in the north by the dreadful valley of Nan Dungortheb. It was twenty-five leagues wide at its widest point. As the name suggests, it was comprised almost entirely of beech-trees of great height, though hemlock and *niphredil* also grew there.

Nénar One of the stars kindled by Varda (Elbereth) to bring light to Middle-earth at the Awakening, in Cuiviénen, of the Elves.

Nen Girith 'Shuddering Water' (Sind.) A later name for Dimrost, the 'Rainy Stair': the place where the Celebros stream joined the river Teiglin, to the west of the Forest of Brethil. It was so renamed because of the shaking fit which overtook Nienor, the sister of Túrin, when she first came near that place (see *Silmarillion*, p. 220).

Nen Hithoel This 'Lake-of-Many-Mists' (Sind.) was formed by the river Anduin after it rushed through the narrow Gates of Argonath. It was a long, pale, oval lake surrounded by the hills of the Emyn Muil, and at its southern end rose three hills which held especial associations for Men of Gondor: *Amon Hen* ('the Hill of the Eye') on the west bank, *Amon Lhaw* ('the Hill of the Ear') on the east, and in between, the tall island of *Tol Brandir*. After sweeping past these landmarks, the Great River poured in a mighty torrent over the falls of Rauros.

Nénimë (Q.) When the Númenoreans first divided the year into twelve months, early in the Second Age, *Nénimë* was the (Quenya) name that they gave to the second month, which had 30 days and was roughly equivalent to our February. Their calendar system, called Kings' Reckoning, was later preserved by the Dúnedain of Middle-earth and was eventually adopted by most of the other peoples who used the Common Speech – but retained the original names of the months and days of the week. The Dúnedain themselves used the Sindarin forms of these names, which in the case of *Nénimë* was *Ninui*.

Nenning A river of West Beleriand. It rose south of Nevrast, and flowed due south for forty leagues before finding the Sea at the Haven of Eglarest.

Nenuial The name of this beautiful northern lake was derived from two separate Sindarin elements: *nen*, meaning 'lake' or 'large-water', and *aduial*, the Grey-elven equivalent of the High-elven word for twilight, *Undomë* (literally, 'Star-opening'). *Nenuial* therefore means 'Lake Twilight', and it has been rendered in translations from the Red Book of Westmarch as 'Lake Evendim'.

Nenuial was situated in the north of Eriador, near the seat of the ancient Kingdom of Arnor, founded by Elendil the Tall before the ending of the Second Age. It lay open only to the east, being sheltered by the Hills of Evendim from the winds which blew from the north and west; and in shape it was like to the Mirrormere in faraway Dimrill Dale, being a spearhead thrust south-west into the hills. On its southern shore stood Elendil's fair city of Annúminas, capital of Arnor until the heirs of Elendil abandoned the Hills of Evendim and fortified themselves further east. In the Fourth Age Annúminas was rebuilt and the Kings of Gondor and Arnor again dwelt there beside Nenuial's deep blue waters.

Nenya The Ring of Waters, one of the Three Rings of the Elven-kings made by Celebrimbor in Eregion during the late sixteenth century of the Second Age. Nenya was the only one of the Three to remain with its original owner, for Celebrimbor himself gave it to the Lady Galadriel; and though it was necessarily kept hidden throughout the Second Age, Nenya was later used by her to heal such areas of Middle-earth as she still had power to influence. The Ring was made from *mithril* and the stone set in it was white and shone like a star; Nenya was also called the 'Ring of Adamant'.

See also THREE RINGS.

Nerdanel A princess of the Noldor of Eldamar; she was the daughter of the great smith Mahtan of Tirion, and the wife of Fëanor. Her sons were Maedhros, Maglor, Celegorm, Curufin, Caranthir, Amrod and Amras. Nerdanel was wiser than her husband, but gradually they drew apart as jealousy and fear grew within him; and she had no part in his rebellion, being among those of the Noldor who remained in Tirion under the rule of Finarfin.

Nessa One of the Queens of the Valar (the *Valier*); she was the sister of Oromë the Hunter, the patroness of deer, and the wife of Tulkas the Strong, youngest and mightiest of the Valar, whom she wedded at the Feast of the Spring of Arda, in Almaren, where the Valar then dwelt.

Nevrast 'Hither Shores' (Sind.) In ancient days, the name given by the Grey elves of Beleriand to the entire coastline of north-western Middle-earth; the coast of Aman, across the Western Seas, was termed, by them, *Haerast*, 'Further Shores'. However, in later days, with the expanding of the nomenclature of the Elves, the word *Nevrast* came to be applied more specifically to the enclosed seaward lands south of the Firth of Drengist, with the mere of Linaewen amidmost. This region became the first dwelling of Turgon of the Noldor, who after the Second Battle of Beleriand made a home for himself and his kin on the slopes of Mount Taras, in the halls of Vinyamar. But Nevrast was never thickly populated, and after Turgon removed to Gondolin it became an empty land. It fell under the domination of Morgoth after the Nirnaeth Arnoediad and the collapse of the lands of Dor-lómin and Mithrim, which had formerly protected Nevrast and the Falas from the danger to north and east.

New Age Each Age of Middle-earth was naturally called the New Age by those during whose lives it began. As the Red Book of Westmarch – from which all of the presently available records of Middle-earth have been translated – was mostly set down during the years immediately before, during and after the passing of the Third Age, the New Age referred to in these writings is the Fourth Age, which commenced in the year 3021. Significantly, the Hobbits, who are credited with setting down most of the information in the Red Book, had their own calendar, which was unaffected by the change of Age; therefore, in their own accounts, Fourth Age 1 remained 1422 Shire Reckoning.

The New or Fourth Age was also distinguished from the preceding three in that it was destined to become the Age of Men, and all the other 'speaking-peoples' of Middle-earth either departed or gradually declined during its span.

Newbury A village in the north of the Buckland, just above Crick-hollow.

New Reckoning Early in the Second Age the Edain of Númenor – who were accomplished mariners and therefore dependent on stellar and solar observation – devised a calendar system called KINGS' RECKONING, which was eventually brought to Middle-earth at the end of the Age. There, in the Númenorean realms-in-exile, Arnor and Gondor, this system survived unchanged until the latter part of the Third Age when, following the death of the last King of Gondor, a series of minor modifications were made by the first Ruling Steward.

This revised system became known as Stewards' Reckoning, and like its forerunner, the basic features of this calendar were gradually adopted by other folk of Middle-earth who used the Common Speech (or Westron).

At the very end of the Third Age, after the restoration of the Kingship, this system was changed again – to the *New Reckoning*, and in this form it presumably endured during the Fourth Age. In many ways the new system was a return to Kings' Reckoning, the major difference being that whereas Kings' Reckoning had followed the Mannish custom of commencing the year in mid-winter, the New Reckoning returned to the Elvish practice of beginning it in spring. Thus, while the names and order of the months remained the same, they now began with *Viressë* (the equivalent of our April), rather than with *Narvinyë* (January).

As in Stewards' Reckoning, each month had 30 days and there were five extra days not belonging to any month: three *enderi* ('middle-days') plus *yestarë* (the first day of the year) and *mettarë* (the last day). In leap years the feast-day known as *Cormarë* ('Ring-day') was doubled. Significantly, *Cormarë* was the birthday of Frodo Baggins, the Ring-bearer. More significantly, to honour the success of the Ring-bearers and celebrate the final Downfall of Sauron, the first day of the new year, *yestarë*, was made to fall on the old equivalent of March 25th, the date when the Ruling Ring was finally destroyed. (Thus each month now began some five days later than in the old system.)

The New Reckoning was adopted in all the lands of the Reunited Kingdom of Gondor and Arnor save in the Shire; and, like Kings' and Stewards' Reckoning, it may well have been picked up by the other Westron-speaking peoples of Middle-earth. It was begun in the middle of the year 3019 Third Age, and the Fourth Age was officially calculated as beginning two years later, on the anniversary of Sauron's fall.

New Row The name given to the former Bagshot Row after it was rebuilt by the Hobbits following the successful conclusion of the War of the Ring. This road – which led to the Hill of Hobbiton near the centre of the Shire, and housed among others Hamfast 'the Gaffer' Gamgee – was razed by agents of Saruman during the War. After their victories over these ruffians, the Hobbits rebuilt the neat row of cottages and called it simply New Row, although it was sometimes drily referred to as 'Sharkey's End' – a reminder of the way Saruman was finally slain by his own servant at the end of this road.

Nienna 'Lady of Mourning' (Q.) A Queen of the Valar, the sister of the *Fëanturi* Mandos and Lórien. In the traditions of the Eldar she is the Lady of Grief and Compassion, who dwells in the Gardens of Lórien but sleeps by day on the island in the middle of the lake Lórellin. Nienna is one of the three Valar Queens (the *Valier*) to be numbered among the seven *Aratar* (High Ones) of Arda. Although her title is somewhat doleful, her role is one of bringing peace of mind and bodily rest to the grief-stricken. She does this through the medium of dreams. (Olórin the Maia was of her following.)

Nienor 'Mourning' (Sind.) The birth-name of the maiden of the Edain afterwards known as *Níniel*, 'Tear-maiden'; for although she bore the earlier name for the first twenty years of her life, the Doom of the Children of Húrin overtook her in the end, and her life before that moment – or the memory of it – was taken from her, by bewitchment. Those who found her thus wandering named her Níniel and so she was called for the remainder of her short life.

Nienor was the third child of Húrin of the Third House of the Edain and his wife Morwen Eledhwen of the First House; the other two were Túrin Turambar and Lalaith (who had died in infancy before Nienor's birth). She passed her girlhood together with her mother in Dor-lómin (which had been occupied by Easterlings in the years following the Nirnaeth Arnoediad), but when Nienor was barely twenty Morwen took her and together they slipped secretly out of that country, intending to seek refuge in Doriath, whither Nienor's elder brother Túrin had been sent some years before.

In the event Morwen was never again fated to see her son; but Nienor's fate was different. Rebelling against her mother's commands, she wilfully left the safety of Thingol's kingdom and fled west: to be overtaken by recurring misfortune – and at length encountered by the arch-foe of her House and Kin: Glaurung the Dragon. This evil creature hypnotized her into forgetfulness, and so, wandering, she was found by some woodmen, Edain of the Forest of Brethil, who took her with them back their arboreal sanctuary of Ephel Brandir. Among these woodmen was her own brother Túrin, though neither of them knew it; for he had not seen her for many years, and she did not remember him. The tragedy unfolded itself with increasing speed. 'Níniel' wed Túrin, and became pregnant by him; and though Túrin slew the Dragon which had worked such evil, and thus partly avenged them both, Nienor, filled with horror – as she was when Glaurung withdrew his bewitchment and the memory of the days of her life came flooding back to her – slew herself in the river Teiglin.

Her brother also slew himself soon afterwards; and the following year their mother Morwen died in the same place.

See CABED NAERAMARTH.

Night-fearers A contemptuous term for Men, in use among some Elves (to whom the night was of course the holiest part of the day).

Night of Naught A poetic reference to the veiling cloak of Shadow which Elbereth, at her Lord's command, drew about the Undying Lands following the rebellion and flight of the High-elves from the Blessed Lands far back in the First Age.

See Bilbo Baggins' poem 'Eärendil Was A Mariner', which appears in Book II Chap. 1.

Nimbrethil 'Silver-Birch' (Sind.) The name given by the Elves of the Havens of Sirion and Arvernien to the birchwoods of that latter region of West Beleriand; these stood not far from the sea, and though not overly extensive, provided excellent wood for ship-building. Eärendil's ship Vingilot was built of this wood.

Nimloth 'White-flower' (Sind.) The name given by the Númenoreans to their White Tree, a descendant of Celeborn of Eressëa (and ultimately of Telperion, Eldest of Trees) which grew in the court of the King in Númenor. (*Nimloth* is etymologically identifiable with Q. *Ninquelótë*, a name for Telperion.) A fruit of this tree survived the Downfall[9] and was borne back to Middle-earth to become the chief heraldic emblem and holiest symbol of the Realms in Exile.

In an earlier age of the world, Nimloth had also been the name of the wife of Dior Eluchíl, a princess of the Sindar of Doriath; she was the mother of Eluréd, Elurín and Elwing. All save the last-named were slain by the sons of Fëanor, in Menegroth, as was Dior himself.

See also TWO TREES; WHITE TREE.

Nimphelos 'Whitefrost' (Sind.) The name of the great pearl from the Bay of Balar given by Thingol of Doriath as fee to the Dwarves of Belegost who had helped him in the building of his underground palace, Menegroth.

Nimrodel 'Lady of the White Cave' (Sind.) An Elf-princess, probably of the Galadhrim; she dwelt in Lothlórien but, with her lover AMROTH chose to pass over Sea at the end of the second millennium of the Third Age. It was at this time that the Dwarves of nearby Moria accidentally released the Balrog; the evil thus set free, added to that which already emanated from Dol Guldur, oppressed the lands between. Nimrodel and Amroth therefore prepared to flee from Lórien and pass to the sea-coast. But she, journeying separately from him, was lost in the passes of the White Mountains in the South, and was never found again.

Also the name of the cascading stream which flowed from the Misty Mountains eastward to join the Silverlode (Celebrant) inside the borders of Lórien. The Galadhrim believed that its clear running waters carried the voice of the maiden who had once dwelt beside it, and after whom the stream was named (or the other way about).

See also the segment of the Lay of Nimrodel, Book II Chap. 6.

Nindalf 'Swan-water' (Sind.) Known to Men as the Wetwang Marshes; a huge expanse of fen-country which lay on the eastern borders of the Anduin between the Emyn Muil and North Ithilien, whose own southern region was the Mere of Dead Faces.

Nine The RINGWRAITHS of Sauron, often called the Nine Riders or the *Úlairi* (or *Nazgûl*, in the Black Speech).

Nine Walkers The members of the Fellowship of the Ring; four Hobbits, two Men, one Elf, one Dwarf, and a Wizard.

Níniel 'Tear-maiden' (Sind.) See NIENOR.

Ninquelótë 'White-blossom' (Q.) See NIMLOTH.

Nínui See NÉNIMË.

Niphredil 'Pale-point' (Sind.) The name given by Elves to a small white flower of western Middle-earth, said to have come into existence in Doriath, on the instant of the birth of Lúthien Tinúviel. In later ages it also grew in Lothlórien.

Note: this flower is part of the design of the Heraldic Device or emblem of Lúthien.

Nirnaeth Arnoediad 'Tears Unnumbered' (Sind.) The name given in the lore and traditions of the Eldar to the Fifth Battle of Beleriand, or more properly the fourth day of that great conflict upon the desert of Anfauglith, when with great slaughter and terror the armies of the Eldar and their allies, the Edain, were overthrown for ever by Morgoth Bauglir of Angband, their ancient foe. (Also the first words of the Curse pronounced by the Valar upon the rebelling Sons of Fëanor, and on those who followed them into exile.)

A supreme irony lies in the fact that this battle, with all its appalling consequences, actually came about as a result of a renewed (and admirable) determination on the part of the Eldar to lure Morgoth into a conflict from which his forces could never escape. This new confidence and boldness was in turn the product of a string of military successes which the Eldar and the Edain – loosely grouped under the leadership of Maedhros, eldest son of Fëanor – had been winning, as the second decade since the Dagor Bragollach wore away and the shock of that defeat likewise diminished. Yet in the winning of these victories they had alerted Morgoth to their renascent strength, and so he was not unprepared (as seems to have been hoped by the Elf-captains Fingon and Maedhros). Moreover, by the adroit uses of treachery their Enemy learned of all their plans, and so was able to forestall them by a grand design of his own, which proved utterly victorious.

The conflict itself is described in a most vivid fashion in existing works,[10] and few will wish for more than a summary. Though there was great heroism, and deeds were done whose consequences outlasted more grievous results of the Nirnaeth, the Eldar and Edain, themselves lured into a gigantic trap, were virtually destroyed. But there was no rout, and Elves and Men – and Dwarves – fought as long as they were able. And because of this some survived: notably the Elf-host of Gondolin, led by Turgon, whose retreat was made only possible by the self-sacrifice of the Men of Dor-lómin, led by Húrin and Huor. But Azaghâl of the Dwarves was slain, and Fingon High King of the Noldor, and Huor together with all the Men of Dor-lómin (save Húrin only), and the Men of Brethil died, and the Elves of Nargothrond led by Gwindor son of Guilin were all slain. The realms of the sons of Fëanor were swept away for ever, though the brothers themselves survived. Mithrim was overrun, and Dor-lómin also. The armies of Morgoth penetrated even to the Falas, where they sacked the Havens of Eglarest and Brithombar. From here, as from other places now overtaken by disaster, Elves and Men fled to the Havens of Sirion, or here and there as they might. The black tide flowed around Doriath, Nargothrond, and Gondolin. But their days were doomed, and they also fell, in time, and those who survived joined the earlier survivors at the Havens. As the final stroke, they were then assaulted by others of their kin. After this internecine attack few indeed remained of the proud hosts who once had crossed over the Sea to wreak their will upon Morgoth and regain the Silmarils he had stolen. Before the Nirnaeth the Noldor of Middle-earth were a coherent military force, occupying and ordering many fair realms in north-western Middle-earth; but after that day they were a fugitive people, dispossessed of all they had held dear and bereaved of many of their close kin. The only hope of Elves and Men now lay in the West.

Nivrim The westernmost portion of the Forest of Region, separated from the main wood by the waters of Sirion; it was accounted Doriath's western march, and was protected by the Girdle of Melian. Nivrim was renowned for its oaks.

Noakes A family of Shire-hobbits, settled in Bywater.

Nob A Hobbit-servant of *The Prancing Pony* Inn in Bree at the time of the War of the Ring. His comrade Bob ran the stables; Nob looked after the guests and generally assisted the Inn-keeper, Barliman Butterbur.

Nobottle A village of the Shire, located in the northern part of the Westfarthing, not far from Needlehole.

Noegyth Nibin 'Lesser [petty]-Dwarves' (Sind.) A Grey-elven name (not altogether polite) for the strange, stunted race of 'speaking-people' who appeared in Beleriand early in the First Age, after the departure into the West of the Calaquendi but before the appearance of any other intelligent race. But their harsh speech was not understood, and their wizened appearance was misliked, and regrettably they were persecuted by the Sindar and the Green-elves. This drove them into hiding, where they nurtured grievances against Elves. It was this people who discovered and delved the first caves of Nulukkizdin (Nargothrond). They excavated other halls besides; one of these was on Amon Rûdh (MÎM was one of the last of this people). Not until other Dwarves had appeared in East Beleriand did the Elves cease their persecution of the Petty-Dwarves – but by then there were only a few left. (Mîm himself was actually slain by a Man, Húrin of Dor-lómin.)

Nogothrim 'Dwarf-folk' (Sind.) A Sindarin (Grey-elven) name for (the race of) Dwarves, more polite than *Naugrim* ('Stunted People'), though not as overtly complimentary as *Hadhod* or *Gonnhirrim*. Nogothrim is a collective plural. In the incantation first used by Gandalf the Grey when attempting to command the Doors of Durin to open into Moria, he chose the words *Fennas Nogothrim*, 'Gateway of the Dwarf-folk', which carried a distinct measure of respect: for no Dwarf-doors were likely to open to one using an impolite form of address. (Nonetheless Gandalf hedged his bets: he also addressed the gateway as *Annon Edhellen*, 'Door of the Elves' – no doubt taking into consideration that the Doors, though of Dwarf-make, were designed by, and for, Elves.)

Nogrod 'Hollow Dwelling' (Sind.) The Elvish name for a city of Dwarves in the east of the Blue Mountains, known to its builders and occupiers as *Tumunzahar*, and to Men as The Hollowbold. Its sister city was Belegost, seven leagues to the north. Dwarves of both cities had much to do with the affairs of the Elves in Beleriand during the First Age; but the memory of Nogrod is clouded for Elves, by the murder of Thingol Greycloak of Doriath, committed by Dwarves of this city out of desire for the Silmaril, which Thingol then possessed. For this reason the feud between the Sindar and the Dwarves of Nogrod was bitter. But both the Blue Mountains Dwarf-cities were destroyed in the inundation of Beleriand, and the survivors, chiefly from Belegost, afterwards went to Moria, in eastern Eriador, and settled there. Moria afterwards became the greatest of all Dwarf-cities; but Nogrod and Belegost lay ever after under the waters of the Firth of Lune.

ɳoldo (pr. *ngoldo*) 'Wise' The older form of the Quenya title for one of the Second Kindred of the Eldar (the *Noldor*), but more properly the name allotted to Tengwa number 19, which represented the sound *ng* (cf. Eng. Ki*ng*) in this older form. This *tengwa* ('letter') was later modified to the simpler *n* sound, and was accordingly renamed *Noldo*. In this later form Tengwa number 19 was inverted (see right).
See also NOLDOR.

Noldolantë 'Fall-of-the-Noldor' (Q.) The name given by Maglor son of Fëanor to the Lament he made at the end of the First Age, shortly before his death, whose subject was the ruin of his House and people. From it much of the material in *The Silmarillion* is derived.

Noldor 'Deep-elves' (Q.) The name given in the High-elven tongue (Sind. *Golodhrim*) to the Second of their Three Kindreds, the People of Finwë, the artisans and loremasters of the Elves, who came, together with the Vanyar, to the West of Middle-earth far back in the Elder Days, and then across the Sea to Eldamar, where for many ages they dwelt in ever-increasing bliss. Finwë was their first King; his sons were Fëanor, Fingolfin and Finarfin. The Noldor helped in the building of Tirion upon the Hill of Túna, and journeyed often into Valinor, and learned many things strange and wonderful, and developed their skills to ever greater heights of accomplishment.

And the knowledge they gained in this way and at this time enriched the lives of all dwellers in Aman, even the Valar. Yet before the Elder Days had passed, many of the Noldor, led by two of the sons of Finwë, rebelled against the Valar and exiled themselves from the Blessed Realm, returning to Middle-earth to wage war for repossession of their greatest treasure. In this War the Exiles suffered grievously; they never regained that which they sought, and in attempting to do so they unleashed ruin and desolation upon a Middle-earth hitherto innocent of such things. And even when seeking to undo the evil they had brought about, their destiny in mortal lands worked against them, so that only by their return into the Far West were they able at last to make amends.

The Noldor were the Craftsmen of the Eldar, and the many manifestations of the skill they developed in Eldamar were wondrous indeed. The greatest of all the Noldor in both crafts and lore was Fëanor, and the greatest of all his achievements were three marvellous Jewels, the *silmarilli*, which captured the blessed Light of the Two Trees within their translucent depths. So bright were the Silmarils that their beauty tempted one of the great Valar, afterwards known as Morgoth the Enemy – who stole the jewels from the Noldor and fled with them to Middle-earth. But this act filled Fëanor with such wrath that he proposed to follow Morgoth back to mortal lands, to wrest the Great Jewels from him by force; and although the Valar gainsaid this enterprise, a great part of the Noldorin Kindred then rose in rebellion and sailed away. In this way was brought about the Exile of the Noldor, and the introduction of war and sorrow into Middle-earth. And as the white swan-ships passed out of the seas of the Undying Lands, great shadows, summoned by Elbereth herself, passed across the face of the waters behind them, barring their return.

The full story of the hardships suffered by the Noldorin Elves in their long fight to regain the three Great Jewels is the subject of *The Silmarillion*; it can be sketched only briefly here. Led by Fingolfin, the 'High-elves' (as they became known in Middle-earth) established their many fair and extensive realms in the North, and in Beleriand, and for a while pressed their Enemy severely. But in the end Morgoth triumphed, and Nargothrond fell, and Gondolin was overcome; and then the Noldor retreated to the coast, or hid themselves in far valleys, while outside their hidden sanctuaries the Great Darkness rolled over Middle-earth. Finally, at the very end of the First Age, the Valar relented and sent a great host to the succour of the Elves and Men long oppressed by the Great Enemy.

At the beginning of the Second Age, which followed the casting-out of Morgoth, the Valar allowed all but the surviving leaders of the rebellious Noldor to return to the Blessed Realm, although 'many of the High Elves still remained. Most of these dwelt in Lindon west of the Ered Luin . . . [ruled by] Gil-galad, last heir of the kings of the Noldor in exile. He was acknowledged as High King of the Elves of the West.'[11] The story of Gil-galad's fortunes and those of his people may be found elsewhere, while the tales of the other individual Noldorin princes and nobles – and families and dynasties – may also be found under the appropriate entries. More pertinent here is the story of Eregion: the only High-elven realm to be founded during the Second Age, built on the very borders of Moria in the year 750. For it is in the story of the Elven-smiths of this land that the recurring ill-fortune of the Exiles once again makes an appearance.

The Elven-smiths were descendants of Fëanor, and they still possessed much of his ancient skill. Led by their lord, Celebrimbor, they determined to make amends for the evil wrought by their fore-father, and to this end they began the forging of the Rings of Power, all of which were designed to heal the ills of a Middle-earth still suffering from the effects of the War of the Great Jewels.

But the worthy plans of Celebrimbor were subverted by the treachery of Sauron of Mordor, servant of Morgoth in the First Age. The Rings of Power were turned against their owners, for the most part, and the knowledge obtained by Sauron from the Noldor of Eregion was put to evil uses: he forged the Ruling Ring to be the master of all other Great Rings and, in the middle of the Second Age, war broke out once more between the Elves and the servants of the Darkness. In this war Eregion was destroyed, and the Elven-smiths routed, and Celebrimbor himself was slain. And with the power of the One Ring Sauron of Mordor made himself unassailable in Middle-earth.

As a result of Sauron's rise to power, the end of the Second Age saw the outbreak of another great war which involved the Noldor. In alliance with the Dúnedain descendants of the Edain of the First Age, Gil-galad led the Elves of Lindon[12] to battle against Mordor; and in this war the last High-elven King of Middle-earth perished, together with many of the remaining Exiles, in combat with the Dark Lord. After that pyrrhic victory, the Noldor of Middle-earth 'attempted nothing new, living in memory of the past',[13] and through-out the Third Age white ships set sail at intervals from the Grey Havens, carrying High-elves and Grey-elves across the Sea once more to the Undying Lands. For the time was approaching when the

Dominion of Elves in Middle-earth would come to an end – and all the heroic labours of the Noldor had only hastened the onset of that day.

Those Exiles that nonetheless remained dwelt for the most part with Círdan the Shipwright at the Grey Havens, or with Elrond in Rivendell, or travelled the Westlands in wandering companies which made pilgrimages to the Tower Hills west of the Shire – where the Elves might gaze into one of the remaining *palantíri* (made by Fëanor himself far back in the Elder Days) to see Eressëa in the Far West. They took little part in the War of the Ring, for they were by then few in number, and their power had for the most part departed. Most of these remaining Exiles duly returned across the Sea at the end of the Third Age, together with the Three Rings wrought by Celebrimbor; and with the passing of the Three Rings the time was come for an end of the long and grievous history of that people in Middle-earth. 'They dwell now beyond the circles of the world, and do not return.'[14] The returning Exiles dwelt in Tol Eressëa within sight of Eldamar, but those of the Deep Elves who had never left Aman continued to dwell in their city Tirion, on the Hill of Túna.

Note: in the extensively-systemized Eldarin nomenclature, the Noldor are accounted both *Amanyar* and *Calaquendi*. In Middle-earth they were known as *Golodhrim* (or *Gelydh*) by the Sindar, as 'High-elves' (*Tareldar* in their own tongue) by most other folk of Beleriand, and (especially by the First House of the Edain) as *Nómin*, 'the Wise' (by chance or knowledge the meaning of the word *Noldor*).

Nóm (pl. *Nómin*) 'Wisdom' (Adûn.) The name given by the People of Bëor (the First House of the Edain) to Finrod Felagund of the Noldor; and (pl.) to the Noldor as a people, especially those of Finrod's House. This kindred of the Edain was the first of all their race to speak with the High-elves – with Finrod himself.

Nómin See preceding entry.

Nori One of the twelve Dwarves who accompanied Thorin Oakenshield on the Quest of the Lonely Mountain in 2941 Third Age. After the successful conclusion of the expedition, Nori remained in Erebor enjoying his rewards and much prestige.

North Downs A line of smooth hills in northern Eriador, lying to the east of the Hills of Evendim. After the division of ARNOR (861 Third Age), the heirs of Isildur removed their capital from Annúminas, beside Lake Evendim, and built a great walled burg on the southern slopes of these Downs. This was *Fornost Erain*, the 'Northern-fortress of the Kings' of Arthedain; it was later abandoned, and the ruins there became known as Deadmen's Dike, and were shunned by honest folk.

Northern Line The Line of Isildur. The royal Line of Descent from Elendil the Tall – founder of the Númenorean realms-in-exile, Arnor and Gondor – through his elder son Isildur, who inherited the North-kingdom of Arnor. This Line passed unbroken from father to son through all the Kings of Arnor and Arthedain and Chieftains of the Dúnedain of the North. The Southern Line, which provided the royalty of Gondor, was descended from Elendil's younger son Anárion. See also LINES OF DESCENT.

Northern Men During the Second and Third Ages of Middle-earth most of the Men inhabiting 'the northern region of the West-lands were descended from the *Edain* of the First Age, or from their close kin.'[15] By the latter part of the Third Age these Northern Men included: the Rohirrim (formerly the Éothéod), the Men of Esgaroth and Dale (the Bardings), the Men of the Carrock (the Beornings) and the Woodmen of Western Mirkwood. All these Men spoke tongues which were part of a Northern language group related to the ancient *Adûnaic* speech of the Edain, although many of them also knew the Common Speech (itself also partly based on Adûnaic).

See also NORTHMEN; MEN.

Northern Waste See FORODWRAITH.

Northfarthing One of the four quarters or 'farthings' of the Shire.

North Ithilien See ITHILIEN.

North-kingdom Arnor, later Arthedain.

Northmen In surviving Annals of the Third Age this name was used specifically to mean the inhabitants of the principality of Rhovanion, which stretched from the forest of Greenwood – later called Mirkwood – to the River Running. The Northmen were 'the nearest in kin of lesser Men to the Dúnedain (being for the most part descendants of those peoples from whom the Edain of old had come)'.[16] Consequently, after the first third of the Age, when Gondor began to decline in power, her rulers made alliances with the Northmen against recurring attacks of Easterlings; and in the middle of the Age, great numbers of Northmen migrated to the South-kingdom.

The Northmen who remained in Rhovanion continued to face new waves of Easterlings throughout the remainder of the Age.

Note: in the middle of the Third Age one notable branch of this proud people separated from the rest and migrated up and down the Anduin before eventually settling in the land later known as Rohan.

See also NORTHERN MEN; RHOVANION.

North Road The old North Road of Eriador; originally one of the two chief arteries of the ancient realm of Arnor. It ran from Fornost on the North Downs, through Bree (where it crossed the Great East Road), across the South Downs to join the main road from the Shire to Tharbad, on the southern border of the old North-kingdom.

After the fall of the North-kingdom (in 1974 Third Age), the road fell into disrepair and much of it became known as the Greenway, from the grass and weeds which sprang up between the stones. In the latter part of the Age, Bree-dwellers feared to follow the Greenway very far north, for it led to Deadmen's Dike, a haunted hill of mounds and old ruins of stone, where no one 'but a robber would go'.[17] These ruins were all that remained of Fornost Erain, the fortified capital of Arthedain.

North Tooks A Northfarthing branch of the Took clan of the Shire, founded by the illustrious Bandobras 'the Bullroarer' Took. The descendants of this huge and valiant Hobbit dwelled in Long Cleeve, near the scene of their forefather's greatest moment: his defeat of the Orcs, led by Golfimbul of Mount Gram, who invaded the Shire in 2747 Third Age (1147 Shire Reckoning). From this cadet branch of the Tooks was descended Mistress Diamond, who wedded Peregrin son of Paladin, one of the Shire heroes in the War of the Ring.

Norui See NÁRIË.

Nulukkizdin (Khuz.) The name given by the early Dwarves of Beleriand (the Noegyth Nibin) to the caves delved in the gorge of the swift river Narog, in West Beleriand. This complex of natural and dolven halls was afterwards occupied (and extended) by Elves, and called *Nargothrond*.

Númen The Quenya word for 'west' but more properly the title of Tengwa number 17, which represented the value of the sound *n* – apart from the weaker, 'semi-vocalic' *n* sounds such as *ng* and *nw*, for which there were other appropriate letters (nos. 19 and 20; see ŊOLDO; NWALME). The most common use for *númen* was to denote directional West (customarily shown at the top of maps made in the Westlands of Middle-earth). Thus the word and its sign were known even among peoples who did not use the *Tengwar*.

Númenor (Q., from the older *Númenórë*, 'People-of-the-West') Westernesse: the greatest realm of the world in the Second Age, apart from the Undying Lands. Founded by the *Edain*, at the very beginning of the Age, for three thousand years this realm continued to grow in both power and splendour until ultimately, the vaulting ambitions of the Númenoreans caused them to commit the most appalling act of sacrilege. As a punishment, the island-realm was thrown down and buried under the waves, with only a chosen few of the Faithful surviving to start afresh in Middle-earth.

At the end of the First Age the Valar, the Guardians of the World, desired to reward the Edain for the losses they had suffered by joining the Elves in their long and hopeless wars against Morgoth the Enemy. The Edain had previously dwelt among the Elves of Beleriand in the far north-west, but that land was drowned at the end of the Age in the catastrophe which the Valar brought down upon Morgoth. Therefore, so that the Edain, like the Eldar, might sail west over Sea to a land far removed from the turmoils of Middle-earth, the Valar gave them the great Isle of Elenna, the Land of the Star.

At the beginning of the Second Age, most of the Edain set sail into the Western seas and, following Eärendil's beacon-star, eventually reached this distant (star-shaped) island. Establishing their realm of Númenor in this most westerly of Mortal Lands, they then became known to the Elves as *Dúnedain* ('Edain-of-the-West'). Elros Tar-Minyatur, son of Eärendil the Mariner and the brother of Elrond, was chosen as their first King, and under his rule and that of his immediate descendants, the Númenoreans long continued to grow in wisdom and happiness as well as in power.

However, from the beginning a mighty prohibition had been laid upon them: the 'Ban of the Valar', which forbade the Númenoreans to sail anywhere near the Undying Lands, which lay tantalizingly close, just over the horizon to the West. These lands included Valinor, the home of the Valar themselves, as well as Eldamar and Eressëa, where dwelt those Elves who had forsaken Middle-earth. But while the Dúnedain were forbidden to go there, the Eldar of these lands were free to sail wherever they wished, and many of them paid visits to Númenor. During these visits the Elves freely gave much of their knowledge to the Dúnedain, who greatly benefited from Elvish wisdom and lore (from which, among other things, they developed a calendar system that was to survive for over six millennia).

After some time, however, the Númenoreans grew resentful of the Ban and jealous of the Elves, and eventually they became quite obsessed with envy of the Elves' immortality. For the natural restlessness and ambition of mortal Men, when combined with the long life span which the Dúnedain had been given – and the power and knowledge which they rapidly acquired – led to a great yearning in them for the unattainable. Nonetheless, for much of the Age, the more restless Númenoreans were able to avoid the forbidden waters of the West by turning eastwards instead. Within six hundred years of the founding of their realm, they were again sailing to Middle-earth and exploring its coasts. And they appeared in even greater numbers after the middle of the Age, following the reign of Tar-Minastir, who sent a military expedition there – to aid the Elves beleaguered by Sauron. But in the arrogance of their power over the 'lesser' Men of Middle-earth, a number of Númenorean mariners eventually began to seize their coastlands and harbours (see BLACK NÚMENOREANS; RINGWRAITHS). So Númenor entered its last, imperial and aggressive, phase.

As the years passed and their life span (once thrice that of other Men) began to lessen, the Númenorean Kings increasingly begrudged their mortality, the Doom of Men, and sought for life everlasting, in order to savour the mighty accomplishments and great splendour of their race. In 2899 Second Age, after the death of Tar-Calmacil, eighteenth King, the new ruler took his royal name in the Adûnaic tongue, calling himself *Ar-Adûnakhôr*, 'Lord-of-the-West'. In itself an affront to the Valar, this title also introduced a return to the use of Adûnaic: an ancient tongue of the Edain and the vernacular speech of the Númenoreans, who had always hitherto used Elvish tongues when dealing with high matters. This new nationalistic use of Adûnaic became so widespread that soon the old Eldarin tongues and traditions were preserved only by the Faithful, who dwelt in Andúnië, in the far west of the island. All the later kings followed the lead of Adûnakhôr; and although the penultimate King repented and changed his name from the (Adûnaic) Ar-Inziladûn to the (Eldarin) Tar-Palantir, this gesture only led to civil war. After his death the Sceptre was usurped by his nephew, the most powerful, the most ambitious, and the last of all Númenorean Kings: Ar-Pharazôn the Golden.

Pharazôn was able to fulfil his first military ambition with surprising ease when, in the year 3261, he landed at Umbar in Middle-earth, together with a fleet of incomparable power and majesty. Sauron the Great, Ruler of Middle-earth unchallenged throughout most of the Age, surrendered to him; and the King, satisfied of his victory, sailed away with the former Master of Middle-earth as his prisoner. However, Sauron soon gained his confidence and became the King's counsellor, eventually devising a scheme whereby his greatest enemies, both old and new, might be set against each other to the profit of neither. By degrees he lured the Númenoreans into great wickedness; and when the time was ripe he urged Pharazôn to renounce the Ban of the Valar and assault the Blessed Lands, forcibly taking his rights like all *great* Kings. In his overweening pride and unreasoning fear of approaching death, Ar-Pharazôn then spent nine years building the Great Armament and, in 3319 Second Age, finally broke the Ban of the Valar, attempting 'to wrest everlasting life' from them by force. But as soon as he reached their shores,

the Valar laid down their Guardianship and called upon the One, and the world was changed. Númenor was thrown down and swallowed in the Sea, and the Undying Lands were removed for ever from the circles of the world. So ended the glory of Númenor.[18]

However, as is told elsewhere, a number of the Faithful escaped this Downfall and, led by Elendil the Tall, sailed to Middle-earth to found the Númenorean realms-in-exile: Arnor and Gondor. Among the treasures of the realm which were rescued by them and brought away in their nine ships were: a seedling of Nimloth, the White Tree which had grown in the Court of the King and which was a descendant of the Eldest of Trees; the Sword of Andúnië (Narsil); the seven *palantíri*, the Seeing-stones made long before by the Master Craftsman of the Elves, Fëanor. The Ring of Barahir, a token of the great comradeship between the Elves and the Edain, dating from the First Age, was also salvaged and became a chief heirloom of the northern Kingdom-in-exile. The lineage of Elros, traced through Silmariën, eldest child and daughter of Tar-Elendil (fourth King) and founder of the House of Andúnië, was also saved from the wreck and brought to Middle-earth.

The Realms in Exile, although less imperial and magnificent than ancient Númenor, were thus no whit less royal; for many years both North- and South-kingdoms flourished in Middle-earth, before they were gradually diminished in various ways. Yet even at the end of the

Third Age much still survived in Middle-earth of the last remnant of Númenor, originally founded – with the full blessing of the Valar – nearly two full Ages before.

See *Akallabêth (passim)*.

Nurn, Nurnen *Nurn* was the name given to the greater part of the land of Mordor, comprising that region of the Black Land south of the central mountains and north of the lower range of the Mountains of Shadow. It was a dreary country, filled with endless acres of regimented fields, which were worked by Sauron's slaves to feed his numerous armies. In the centre of this drab plain lay a great inland sea, *Nurnen* ('Lake-of-Nurn'), whose waters were bitter and un-drinkable.

Nurtalë Valinóreva 'The Concealment of Valinor' (Q.) The poetic (Elvish) title given to the period of time immediately following the death of the Two Trees and the rebellion of the Noldor, when the Valar, determining to protect Valinor from the ravages of war in Middle-earth – and also to prevent any return of those exiled or banished – refortified their land, weaving webs of shadow and en-chantment in the Western seas. This labour was for the most part undertaken by Varda (Elbereth).

ᚳᚢ Nwalme The Quen yaor High-elven word for 'torment' (older form *Ywalme*), but more properly the title of Tengwa number 20, used for the sound *nw-* (or *yw-*) in those languages which required it.

Notes
1 Book IV Chap. 6.
2 A supposition.
3 Illustrated in *The Silmarillion Calendar* 1978.
4 Book III Chap. 6. Narsil was therefore of Dwarf-make.
5 Book II Chap. 2.
6 *Ibid*.
7 Book VI Chap. 9.
8 Appendix B 'The Third Age'.
9 Thanks to Isildur son of Elendil.
10 *Silmarillion* pp. 188–97.
11 Appendix B.
12 All Eldar, but of the mingled peoples of the Noldor, Sindar (the most numerous), Falathrim and some Nandor – chiefly a Telerin mixture, for the Noldor were greatly reduced in number.

13 Appendix B.
14 Appendix F II.
15 Appendix F I. See BEREG.
16 Appendix A I(iv).
17 Book VI Chap. 7.
18 Appendix A I(i).

Oatbarton A village in the Northfarthing of the Shire.

Oath of Eorl The name given in Rohan to the formal declaration of allegiance made in the year 2510 Third Age by Eorl the Young (last Lord of Éothéod and later the first King of Rohan) to Cirion, twelfth Ruling Steward of Gondor. The Oath bound the Riders of Éothéod to aid the Dúnedain at times of need; in return they were granted, in perpetuity, the former province of Calenardhon (Rohan). These reciprocal pledges formed the only basis for the alliance, yet the Oath was valiantly fulfilled many times during the ensuing five hundred years; and as a result both the Rohirrim and the Men of Gondor survived the turmoils of the Third Age and saw their pledges renewed in the Fourth Age which followed the overthrow of Sauron.

Oath of Fëanor This term refers to the great oath sworn, not only by Fëanor, but by his seven sons, in the Court of the King in Tirion, after the theft of the Silmarils by Morgoth. (Though the exact wording of the Oath is nowhere given, the dreadful terms in which it was couched are supplied in *The Silmarillion*, pp. 82–4.) It was this Oath which was the real cause of the misfortunes of the Noldor, for by it they set themselves beyond the Grace of the Valar and, moreover, it proved not an easy Oath to keep, although it constrained those who had taken it always to try. The Oath of Fëanor was the father of all the evil deeds which followed; and its corollary was the Curse of the Valar.

Ohtar The Esquire of Isildur and one of the three Dúnedain to survive the disastrous Battle of the Gladden Fields (Year 2 Third

Age), where Isildur and his three eldest sons were slain, together with many Dúnedain of the North-kingdom. Ohtar escaped with Isildur's sword (Narsil, the Sword of Elendil, which had been broken in combat with Sauron two years before). After long wandering he managed to cross the Misty Mountains and so come to Rivendell – where Valandil, the Heir of Isildur, had been anxiously awaiting news of his father and brothers. In this way the fate of Isildur became known to the Dúnedain of the North.

Óin From 2385–2488 Third Age, the King of the Dwarf-realm in the Grey Mountains. He was the grandson of Thorin I, who founded the colony, and his own grandson, Dáin I, was the last King of Durin's Line to rule there.

Óin A Dwarf of Durin's Line, the son of Gróin and brother of Glóin (the father of Gimli Elf-friend). Óin was also the cousin of Balin son of Fundin and, like Balin, he spent the greater part of his adventurous life engaged in honourable service to the Kings of Erebor in Exile: Thráin II and his son Thorin (II) Oakenshield. Thus, in 2941 Third Age, Óin, Glóin and Balin were among those chosen by Thorin – then a penniless exile – to accompany him on a desperate expedition to reclaim the treasure of Erebor, taken many years before by the Dragon Smaug.

The success of this Quest won its members great wealth and renown among the Dwarves of the reconstituted Kingdom Under the Mountain; however, after many years of prosperity, some of Thorin's former companions began to grow restless in Erebor, particularly Balin, Óin and Ori. Finally, in the year 2989, Balin assembled a small expedition including these two old comrades, and they set out with the declared aim of recovering Moria, greatest of all Dwarf-realms but lost to Durin's Folk centuries earlier. The fate of that expedition is well documented. Balin himself had reigned as 'Lord of Moria' for no more than five years before a host of Orcs overwhelmed the Dwarves and drove them to seek shelter deep within the ancient and desolate Dwarf-city. Óin was killed while attempting to find a way out on the western side, where he was taken by the 'Watcher in the Water'.

Oiolossë 'Mount-everwhite' (Q.) The highest of the Pelóri range of Valinor, and there the highest of all mountains in the World. Upon its summit stood the palace of Manwë, the Lord of the Valar, and his spouse, Elbereth.

Older Quenya names for this holy mountain were *Taniquetil*, 'High-white-peak', and *Elerrína*, 'star-crowned'. The Sindarin equivalent of Oiolossë was *Amon Uilos*. It was also called 'The Hill of Ilmarin'.

Oiomúrë The northernmost part of Araman, a land of swirling mists on the borders of the Helcaraxë.

Oldbuck An ancient family of Shire-hobbits, who acquired a position of ascendancy comparatively early in the history of the Shire, and later developed into one of its two leading dynasties.

The Oldbucks, who were largely of Stoorish blood, hailed originally from the Marish, a low-lying but fertile part of the Eastfarthing; and according to their own lore, they claimed descent from the first Thain of the Shire, a certain Bucca of the Marish. Indeed, the Thainship afterwards became a hereditary office among the Oldbucks and remained within the family until the year 2340 Third Age (740 Shire Reckoning), when Gorhendad Oldbuck led the clan across the Brandywine to settle the narrow strip of land between the river and the Old Forest. This was the area known as Buckland – and to commemorate the event Gorhendad renamed the family *Brandybuck* and began building Brandy Hall. That same year the family relinquished the Thainship, which then passed to the equally eminent Took Family.

See also BRANDAGAMBA; ZARAGAMBA.

Old Ford The chief fording place across the Great River in Wilderland, where the Great East Road descended from the Misty Mountains and, crossing the Anduin, passed further east into Mirkwood.

Old Forest The name given in the Shire to the area of ancient woodland which lay due east of it, between the river Baranduin and the Barrowdowns. Although the Hobbits were quite unaware of it, the name was not inapposite, for this forest was one of the last surviving tracts of the vast primeval woods of the Elder Days. As Elrond Halfelven once remarked, 'Time was when a squirrel could go from tree to tree from what is now the Shire to Dunland west of Isengard.'[1] The only wood of comparable age was Fangorn Forest.

The trees of the Old Forest were quite unlike other varieties known to the Shire-folk, except for the ancient willow-trees of the Withywindle valley. Yet this very river-valley was the centre of the mysterious power which filled the Forest, mysterious and malevolent, for chief among these trees was the Great Willow, whose 'grey thirsty spirit drew power out of the earth and spread like fine root-threads in the ground . . . till it had under its dominion nearly all the trees of the Forest from the Hedge [the High Hay] to the Downs.'[2]

Old Forest Road The Great East Road, where it passed through the forest of Mirkwood. Its eastern end – where the Road emerged at length from the vast gloom of Mirkwood by the banks of the River Running – became swampy and dangerous towards the end of the Third Age, and the Old Forest Road became as a consequence little used.

Old Grange The grain-storehouse of Hobbiton, Bywater and district. Unlike most buildings of the area, the Old Grange was constructed of brick and stone in the Mannish fashion. Sadly, this old barn was destroyed by agents of Saruman in 1419 Shire Reckoning (3019 Third Age).

Old Guesthouse The chief Inn of the city of Minas Tirith, situated on the main thoroughfare of the lowest circle, Rath Celerdain, the Street of the Lampwrights. It was constructed of old stonework, with a lawn enclosed on three sides by the building. The fourth side was open to the street.

Old Man Willow The chief peril of the OLD FOREST lay in the malevolent influence exerted over its trees by the Great Willow which, from earliest times, was able to dominate the Withywindle valley, and eventually came to control almost the entire forest. The rotten heart of the Willow placed a powerful spell over all creatures of the Wood (save Tom Bombadil and those under his protection). From the willow's sweetly-sung webs of sleep few escaped who once wandered down to the banks of the Withywindle, and in the Old Forest all paths, by some strange chance, led to the river.

Old Toby Tobold Hornblower; also the name given to a popular brand of Southfarthing pipe-weed named after him (other favoured varieties were 'Longbottom Leaf' and 'Southern Star').
   See also PIPE-WEED.

Old Took Gerontius Took.

Old Winyards An excellent variety of red wine from the Southfarthing of the Shire, strong in quality and flavour, with sound character and a notable bouquet. It was much praised by those (wealthy) Hobbits who drank it. (Hobbits, as a rule, were more partial to well-brewed ale than to wine, although the latter beverage was by no means unknown.)

'Old Words and Names in the Shire' An etymological treatise written by Meriadoc Brandybuck, Master of Buckland. This worthy Hobbit found many previously dormant interests greatly stimulated by his travels during the War of the Ring. Among other pursuits, he later took up the study of the origins of the language then used by the Hobbits of the Shire, discovering a definite kinship with the tongues of Northern Men. (Hobbits had originally dwelt in the upper vales of Anduin, whence these Mannish tongues had sprung.) Meriadoc guessed that the language formerly spoken by Hobbits was closely related to the Northern tongue still used by the Rohirrim, and his treatise attempted to show this, evidently with fair success (for example, he traced the origins of the word *Hobbit* to the Mannish word *holbytla*, 'hole-builder').

Later scholarship has indeed proved many of Meriadoc's assumptions correct. Like Dwarves, Hobbits always spoke the tongues prevalent in the lands where they dwelt. Therefore, in the middle of the Third Age, after settling in what was then a part of Arthedain, where the Westron was used, they adopted this Common Speech with ease. Yet many of the older names in their language, such as *smial* and *mathom*, long survived, as reminders from times when they had lived in Wilderland, a shy, quiet little people, unnoticed by all folk save their immediate neighbours but by no means averse to learning all they could, in their own elusive way.

See also Appendix F.

'Oliphaunt' A fine example of Hobbit comic bestiary lore, in the form of a short, somewhat terse, poem which can be found in Book IV Chap. 3 (where it is recited by Samwise, who evidently knew the verse well). *Oliphaunt* was the name given in the Shire to the great war-beasts of the Haradrim, known as *Mûmakil*. In fact, it is unlikely that any Hobbits had ever seen such an animal – until the War of the Ring.

Olog-hai 'Troll-race' (Black Speech) The name given by Sauron's servants to a great race of 'improved' Trolls which emerged in Southern Mirkwood and on the northern borders of Mordor towards the end of the Third Age. They were more cunning and fierce than other Trolls, and could endure the rays of the Sun. So marked were the differences between the Olog-hai and others of their kind that their enemies held them to be, not Trolls, but huge Orcs. This was, however, an erroneous assumption.

See also TROLLS.

Olórin The true name of that wisest and kindliest member of the Order of Istari (Wizards), who was known in Middle-earth as Mithrandir or Gandalf the Grey. *Olórin* is a name of Maiarin form.

Olvar See KELVAR AND OLVAR.

Olwë The younger brother of Elwë Thingol, and conjoint Lord of the Teleri, the Third Kindred of the Eldar, on the Great Journey. The Teleri were last on the line of march, and of their two hosts the one led by Olwë was the hindmost of all. But in Beleriand his elder brother Elwë was lost, and the time came for the Eldar to depart; but Elwë did not reappear, and the Vanyar and Noldor sailed away into the West; and the Teleri were left behind. Then Olwë became their king, and they dwelt by the sea-coasts. But after the passing of perhaps half an Age, the summons again came from Valinor, and this time most of the host of Olwë embarked, and was carried across the Sea, leaving Elwë and his people behind in Middle-earth. Olwë never saw his brother again.

We are told that Olwë's people did not come directly to Aman, but tarried in Tol Eressëa for a further Age; there they first learned and developed the craft of ship-building (in this they were instructed by the Sea-Maia Ossë), and only then did they complete the long Journey and set foot in Eldamar. On the northern shore of its Bay they made their new home, the city and port of Alqualondë, the Haven of the Swans. The other Calaquendi called them *Falmari*, the Sea-elves.

The name of Olwë's wife is not recorded; his daughter was Eärwen, who wedded Finarfin, the youngest of the three sons of Finwë. In this way the Teleri were allied with the Noldor. But this unhappily did not prevent Olwë's people from bearing the brunt of an insane attack launched upon them by the Noldor, in what has become known as the Kinslaying at Alqualondë. This, the most grievous of all the deeds of Fëanor, took place at the time of the theft of the Silmarils and the rebellion of the Noldor, when the Sea-elves led by Olwë denied the use of their ships to the Noldor. Nor would Olwë join Fëanor's revolt. Fighting broke out, and the Teleri were severely handled and many were slain; but their ships were taken from them, and used by Fëanor for his purposes, and afterwards contemptuously burned, by his order, on the shores of a remote bay in Middle-earth. In time the Teleri were able to restore their city and ships, but the loss in lives was made good only slowly. Olwë never again returned to Middle-earth, and dwells still in Alqualondë.

Ondoher From 1936–44 Third Age, the thirty-first King of Gondor. His brief (eight-year) reign was cut brutally short by a massive invasion of Wainriders, old foes of the Dúnedain. Ondoher led the main Army of Gondor across the Anduin to meet the Easterlings, and battle took place upon the ancient field of Dagorlad. The Dúnedain were defeated and Ondoher, together with his only two sons, was slain.

The passing of the King – and the death of his heirs – brought about two crises for the South-kingdom: an immediate military problem and a later constitutional dilemma. Both were resolved by the same man, Eärnil, Captain of Gondor's Southern Army at the time of the invasion. First, this able soldier defeated the Wainriders (see BATTLE OF THE CAMP), and so ended the threat to Gondor from the East for that time. Then, the problem of the Succession was resolved when the Council of Gondor awarded Eärnil Ondoher's crown. He was the penultimate King of the Line of Anárion.

Ondolindë 'Rock-of-the-Music-of-Water' (Q.) The High-elven name given by Turgon of the Noldor to the great and beautiful city he built on the hill of Amon Gwareth in the Hidden Vale of Tumladen; however, this city and refuge was more generally known under its Grey-elven name GONDOLIN.

One Ring The RULING RING of Sauron the Great.

Onodrim 'Ent-folk' (Sind.) The collective plural in use among Grey-elves for the race of ENTS. The standard plural was *Enyd*.

'O Orofarnë, Lassemista, Carnimírië!' A lament for the destroyed rowan-trees of Fangorn Forest, sung to the Hobbits Meriadoc Brandybuck and Peregrin Took by the Ent Bregalad (Book III Chap. 4). Bregalad (Quickbeam) was an Ent much attached to rowans, and the three trees named in this lament were especially beloved members of 'the People of the Rose' murdered by Orcs of Saruman. Forth is reason Bregalad was the first Ent to decide upon revenge against the Wizard.

Opening Hour In the traditions of the Eldar, the Hour before Hours: the first hour of the life of the Silver Tree Telperion, not reckoned into the Count of Time.

See *Silmarillion* pp. 38–9.

Oraeron 'Sea-day' (Sind.) The name given by the Dúnedain of Middle-earth to the sixth of the seven days in their week (see KINGS'

RECKONING). The original, Quenya name, used in Númenor during
the Second Age and by most Westron-speaking peoples of the late
Third Age, was *Eärenya*; Hobbits knew it as *Meresdei* (later
Mersday).

Orald The name given among Northern Men to the creature known
(to Buckland Hobbits) as Tom Bombadil.

Oranor 'Sun's-day' (Sind.) The Grey-elves' name for the second
day of their six-day week, and the name used by the Dúnedain of
Middle-earth for the second day of their seven-day week. This day
was known to the High-elves – and the Westron-speaking folk of
Middle-earth who used KINGS' RECKONING – as *Anarya*. The Hobbits,
who used their own idiosyncratic form of Kings' Reckoning, used a
translated form of the Elven names: *Sunnendei* (later *Sunday*).

Orbelain 'Day-of-the-Valar' (Sind.) One of the two Grey-elven
names for the sixth and final day of their week (*enquië*), being
equivalent to *Valanya* (Q.), the High-elven name. Its alternative
name was *Rodyn* in Sindarin.

This was the chief day of the week, dedicated to the Valar, or
Powers. It was later incorporated by the Dúnedain of Númenor into
their own calendar-system (see KING'S RECKONING), and the Dúnedain
of Middle-earth – many of whom spoke the Grey-elven tongue – used
Orbelain to mean the chief and final day of their seven-day week.

Orch (pl. *yrch*) The Grey-elves' name for the creatures known to
Men as *Goblins, Hobgoblins, svart-alfar* and many other names, but
in records of the First, Second and Third Ages as ORCS.

Orcrist 'Goblin-cleaver' (Sind.) One of a matching pair of Elven-
swords forged in the High-elven city of Gondolin during the First
Age, for use in the wars against Morgoth the Enemy. Its mate was
Glamdring. Both blades were fashioned at a time when Elvish smithcraft was at its height, and both were of marvellous workmanship,
with many curious properties. The swords were captured when
Gondolin was destroyed at the end of the First Age, and after two
full Ages they turned up in the lair of a band of Stone-trolls, in
eastern Eriador.

The swords were recovered from this unsavoury resting-place by
the members of Thorin Oakenshield's famous expedition to Erebor,
in 2941 Third Age; and Thorin himself chose to wear Orcrist
throughout the remainder of his adventures. He wielded the sword
to great effect in the Battle of Five Armies later that same year and

after he fell in that battle, his weapon was laid upon his tomb in Erebor, to give warning should enemies approach: for the blades of both Orcrist and Glamdring burned with a fierce blue flame if Orcs or Trolls came near.

See also GLAMDRING.

Orcs Any memories still preserved by Men of a far-distant time, when the world was both brighter and darker, are now almost buried in a morass of folk myth, and are thus easily dismissed by the sceptical as mere 'superstition'. And many of the denizens of age-old epic tales are similarly dismissed because our memory of them has become confused, and the feelings they once engendered in the breasts of Men have been forgotten or diminished. In this way the Goblins and Hobgoblins of an earlier time are now 'remembered' as diminutive creatures of malice who tease domestic pets, turn milk sour and – at their most malevolent – abduct human offspring while substituting their own progeny as 'changelings'.

Nonetheless the real, darker origins of these creatures may still be accurately traced. *Orc* is derived from the Grey-elven word *orch* (pl. *yrch*) and is today recalled somewhat in the Italian *Orco* or the French *Ogre*, both of which terms are classically applied to the blood-drinking, ferocious creatures whose appearance in even the most innocuous of folk-tales brings about a revival of ancient fears. As all will perceive, these are more accurate recollections of the foul and dangerous race of Orcs – no myth to dwellers in Middle-earth during the First, Second and Third Ages – than the mischievous sprites and kobolds of Celtic and (later) Germanic myth.[3]

Orcs were first bred by Melkor (Morgoth), far back in the Elder Days. They appeared in Middle-earth some time after the awakening of the Quendi in Cuiviénen, and were afterwards believed to be themselves descended from the Quendi, for their sires, it was said, had been abducted by Melkor and twisted and corrupted into this new race: evil, filled with his dark will, cannibalistic and cruel. They abhorred the light of the Sun from their Beginning, emerging from their lairs and caves to do battle for their Black Master only at nightfall. They were bred in Darkness, lived in darkness, died in the dark; yet although they were cowardly and unreliable, so long as the will of their Master animated them they were formidable soldiery, and the enmity between them and the Elves was bitter.

But at that far-off time the true Quendi were succoured by the Valar, who came back to Middle-earth in a great host and fought the Battle of the Powers against Morgoth. Their Enemy was captured, and his oldest stronghold, Utumno, was thrown down for ever. And his hosts of Orcs and Trolls (another of his counterfeits) were well-nigh destroyed. Yet some survived, sleeping under stone; and as the Ages of the Master's imprisonment wore away, and his will once again awoke in Middle-earth, they too awoke, and went out into the Night, and did evil; and increased in number, so that by the time Morgoth had once again rebelled against the Valar, and returned in triumph to Middle-earth, there were legions upon legions of dark soldiery awaiting his orders.

Yet these evil hosts were, in themselves, insufficiently adept (or valiant) to prevent the returning Noldor from inflicting defeat after severe defeat upon them. The Orcs were merely Morgoth's infantry in the War of the Great Jewels, his most expendable commodity, easily bred and easily led; and as fighters they were no match for the Elves, or their allies the Edain. Only when in overwhelming strength – or when accompanied by one of their Master's more terrible servants, such as Balrogs or Dragons – were they able to withstand their enemies, or attack them successfully. Nonetheless, they inflicted great loss on the Eldar and the Edain during the War, and after; and they remained the most numerous and often encountered of Morgoth's creatures. In the end sheer numbers told, and the Elf-realms and cities were captured and ground into the dust, by hosts of shrieking Orcs who were undeterred by enormous losses; and with this final defeat the Darkness rolled over most of Middle-earth. But the Valar at last took pity on the innocent, and themselves came with a great host to Mortal Lands, and Morgoth was cast out, while his innumerable servants were destroyed or scattered far abroad.

Yet the evil that was made in the First Age lived on in the Second in many of its ancient forms. Morgoth was destroyed, but those of his creatures which escaped the Breaking of Thangorodrim fled far and wide, and their prodigious breeding powers enabled them to spread. Hitherto the Orcs had chiefly been found in the Far North, in Angband, the land of Morgoth, but in the Second Age many tribes and bands made their homes in the Misty Mountains, and the Ered Mithrin, while others made lairs in the passes of other mountain-ranges, or delved tunnels from which to waylay travellers. And they began to diverge into different breeds, varying to some extent in size, colouring and minor details. Yet all were possessed of the same barbarous nature; and they were hideous, with jagged fangs, flared nostrils, tufted ears and slanting eyes which could see like gimlets in the dark – but which still feared the light of Sun as powerfully as in earlier times. They wielded spears and curved scimitars and bore shields of hide, and their weapons were often poisoned. All were filled with fierce, daemonic energy and had formidable strength; and they hated Elves and Men with an abiding hatred which reached back into their Beginnings.

In the Second Age which followed the Fall of Morgoth the Orcs spread far and wide throughout Middle-earth – and when the time came for the second arising of Sauron the Great, also a servant of Morgoth during the Elder Days, they were ready and apt to his hand, even as their ancestors had served Sauron's master. With their aid Sauron rapidly made himself Lord of Middle-earth (or of a great part of it), and their numbers swelled once more. Yet the defeats which Sauron suffered at the end of the Second Age were in part brought about by the basic untrustworthiness of his chief soldiers, and so he determined to improve the breed when the time came once more for his arising, in the Third Age which followed his defeat upon Orodruin.

Nevertheless, the first part of the Third Age was dominated by the Dúnedain of Gondor and Arnor, and the western reaches of Middle-earth were made unsafe for the Goblin-kind. At this time most of the Orcs which had survived the Last Alliance dwelled in their old lairs in the northernmost Misty Mountains, the chief stronghold of which was Gundabad, not far from the Grey Mountains. There they hid, and delved new tunnels to bar the passes, while others passed east to southern Mirkwood and entered the service of 'the Necromancer' operating from his new tower of Dol Guldur. In 1981 Third Age, after the Dwarves had fled from Moria, the ancient Dwarf-realm was occupied by Orcs of the mountains, and it was the brutal and obscene insult offered by these usurpers to the dispossessed Dwarves which led to the first organized attempt on the part of one of the Free Peoples to exterminate the race of Orcs. The six-year War of the Dwarves and Orcs led to vast numbers of Goblins being slain by the vengeful Heirs of Thrór, and at the Battle of Azanulbizar the surviving Goblins were practically annihilated. Those that managed to escape fled south.

Yet once more their powers of regeneration enabled the Orcs to repopulate all their old haunts before many years had passed. In 2510 the wife of Elrond, the Lady Celebrían, was captured by a band of Goblins in a high pass of the Misty Mountains. And although she was later rescued by her sons, from that date onwards the routes across the Mountains from Eriador to Wilderland became increasingly dangerous and hazardous because of these creatures. Only the Elves of Rivendell and the Men of the Carrock Ford made any attempt to combat the menace, with mixed success: in 2941 a well-armed party of thirteen Dwarves, one Hobbit and a Wizard was assailed and abducted by an Orc-band while attempting the crossing, and only presence of mind saved them from a terrible fate (see *The Hobbit*, Chaps. 4, 5 and 6).

Yet the Third Age closed, like both previous ages, with an overwhelming victory on the part of the Free Peoples over the Dark Powers, and the Orcs shared the downfall of their Master. The numbers who fell in battle – at the Hornburg, on the Pelennor Fields and in the final combat before the Black Gate – were never estimated. Doubtless the survivors fled north once more, to their ancient homes amid the crags of the Misty Mountains, but no records speak of this. It is certain, however, that the race was not extinguished, and soon increased its numbers once more to become the threat to the Free Peoples it had remained since the Great Darkness of its first creation.

Note: understandably enough, few Orcs have ever been mentioned by name in the records of their foes. *Azog* was the name of the Great Orc who slew King Thrór of the Dwarves, and who was himself dispatched by Dáin Ironfoot, later King Under the Mountain. Azog's son *Bolg* led the Orcs to the Battle of Five Armies (2941 Third Age), but was slain by Beorn the Skin-changer for his trouble. A certain *Golfimbul* led a foolhardy invasion of the Shire in 2747, and was killed by the Hobbit Bandobras Took at the Battle of Greenfields. During the War of the Ring the leader of the Uruk-hai of Isengard was named *Uglúk*, while the chieftain of the Goblins of Mordor was called *Grishnákh*.

Of this race of *Uruk-hai* something may be said here, The name is in the Black Speech of Mordor and means, more or less, 'The Orcs'. The breed was thought (by Men) to be the result of a blasphemous blending of the races of Orcs and Men on the part of Saruman the Wizard (others claimed the Uruk-hai had been bred by Sauron himself). Certainly the Uruks were larger in size than other Goblins, and were uncomfortably man-like in other ways; but they were nonetheless true Orcs (even as the Olog-hai, thought to be giant Orcs, were in actuality exceptionally agile Trolls). Yet the Uruk-hai were able to ignore the presence of the Sun, unlike all other Orcs, and they fought with swords which had straight blades, unlike the usual curved and jagged scimitars; and, they displayed more tenacity and courage than ordinary Orcs, and were as a consequence worthier foes. Most of them perished at the Battle of the Hornburg (March, 3019 Third Age).

See also BLACK SPEECH; Appendix F I.

Órë The Quenya or High-elven word for 'heart' or 'inner mind' but more properly the title of Tengwa number 21, which represented the sound of (untrilled) *r* in those languages which required it.

Orfalch Echor The name given by Elves of Gondolin to the narrow and secret pass through the Encircling Mountains, the hidden gate of their land. It was guarded at one end by a tunnel, and by the hidden door to the world outside, and throughout its length by seven more guarded gates, each of which had to be passed before the traveller at length passed out of the Orfalch and beheld, far off across the valley, the city of Turgon.

Orgaladh 'Tree-day' The Sindarin form of *Aldëa* (Q.), the name given by the Númenoreans to the fourth day of the week. The name *Orgaladh* was used only by the Dúnedain of Middle-earth, direct descendants of the Númenoreans. Most other folk of Middle-earth who used the Dúnedain calendar-systems retained the original (Quenya) names for the months and days; although the Hobbits used translated forms of these names. Thus their name for *Aldëa* or *Orgaladh* was *Trewesdei* (later *Trewsday*).

Orgaladhad 'Trees'-day' (Sind.) The Grey-elves' name for the fourth day of the Eldarin six-day week. Its High-elven equivalent was *Aldúya*, the name originally given in honour of the Two Trees of Valinor. In the later, Mannish system of Kings' Reckoning the Númenoreans created a seven-day week and the name *Aldúya* was replaced by *Aldëa*, 'Tree-day' – in reference to the (single) White Tree of the High-elves, of which a descendant, Nimloth, grew in the King's Court in Númenor. *Orgaladh* ('Tree-day') was therefore the Sindarin word for the fourth day of the Mannish week, while the plural form *Orgaladhad* referred only to the same day in the Elvish week.

See also previous entry.

Orgilion 'Stars'-day' (Sind.) The name given by the Grey-elves and the Dúnedain of Middle-earth to the first day of their respective weeks – the six-day week of the Eldar and the seven-day week of the Kings', Stewards' and New Reckonings used by the Dúnedain and many other folk of western Middle-earth. Its High-elven form was *Elenya*; the Hobbits' name was *Sterrendei* (later *Sterday*).

Ori A Dwarf of Erebor, one of the twelve companions of Thorin Oakenshield on the famous expedition of 2941 Third Age. After the successful conclusion of that mission, Ori lived for many years in peace and honour in the Lonely Mountain until, in the year 2989 he joined Balin's ill-fated expedition to Moria. It was Ori's hand which recorded (in the famous Book of Mazarbul) the last days of the doomed colony some five years later. He fell defending the Chamber of Mazarbul and Balin's tomb, one of the last to perish.

Orithil 'Moons'-day' (Sind.) The name used by the Grey-elves and the Dúnedain of Middle-earth for the third day of both the (six-day) Eldarin and the (seven-day) Númenorean week. The High-elven equivalent – also used by most of the Westron-speaking peoples of Middle-earth – was *Isilya*. The Hobbits' (translated) name for it was *Monendei* (later *Monday*).

Orkish Tongues See BLACK SPEECH.

Ormal See ILLUIN.

Ormenel 'Heavens'-day' (Sind.) The fourth day of the week in both the Elvish and Mannish usage, equivalent to *Menelya* (Q.). *Ormenel* was used by the Grey-elves and by the Dúnedain of Middle-earth, while the Quenya name was used by the High-elves, the Númenoreans of the Second Age, and most of the Westron-speaking peoples of the Third Age. The Hobbits used a translated form, *Hevenesdei* (later *Hevensday* or *Hensday*).

Ornendil The first son of Eldacar II, twenty-first King of Gondor. Civil war broke out in Gondor on Eldacar's ascension to the throne in 1432 Third Age, and eventually the rebels, led by Castamir the Usurper, gained the upper hand. For several years they besieged Osgiliath, the capital, and in 1437 finally captured it. Although Eldacar managed to escape, his son was taken by the rebels and, at the orders of Castamir, executed. His father later avenged him.

See also KIN-STRIFE.

Orocarni See MOUNTAINS OF THE EAST.

Orod-na-Thôn 'Pine-mountain' (Sind.) See DORTHONION.

Orodreth The second of the four sons of Finarfin; together with his brothers and sister (Galadriel) he came back to Middle-earth in exile during the First Age, and fought in the earlier battles against Morgoth. For the first four centuries of his exile, Orodreth was Finrod's warden, in the tower of Tol Sirion which the sons of Finarfin – under Finrod's leadership – had built; but at the Dagor Bragollach, and in the months afterwards, this tower came under siege, and it was captured by Sauron, and then Orodreth fled from the North and joined Finrod in Nargothrond (as did some other Elven-princes of those days). And when Finrod departed into the North with Beren, never to return, Orodreth succeeded him as King of Nargothrond.

The name of his wife is not recorded; nonetheless, Orodreth had one daughter, Finduilas, born in Nargothrond. She, formerly the betrothed of Gwindor son of Guilin, fell in love with Túrin of the Edain, when that warrior came to her father's city in the years following the Nirnaeth Arnoediad (at which Orodreth had not been present). But it was by the coming of Túrin that Nargothrond's fate was sealed. Bold and stirring though his leadership was (Orodreth virtually abdicated the generalship of the armies of Nargothrond to Túrin during this time), his counsels proved not all wise, and in the end he led the Elven-hosts to destruction, upon Tumhalad. There Orodreth was slain in battle. Finduilas, taken prisoner by the Orcs, was slain shortly afterwards. Túrin alone survived.

Note: also the name taken by one of the Dúnedain: the sixteenth (from 2655–85 Third Age) Ruling Steward of Gondor.

Orodruin 'Burning Mountain' (Sind.) The ancient name for the greatest active volcano in western Middle-earth, which thrust its smoking cone almost vertically up from the very centre of the plain of Gorgoroth in Mordor. The 'Fire-mountain' was the heart of the ancient realm of Sauron the Great, and the forge of his might; there he made the Ruling Ring during the middle of the Second Age.

Indeed, the existence of the volcano was undoubtedly a deciding factor when Sauron originally chose Mordor to be his stronghold (*c.* 1000 Second Age). To the east of the Mountain, upon a lofty spur of the Ered Lithui, he raised the Dark Tower; and a road he made from the Barad-dûr to the volcano, thrusting straight across the smoking plain to ascend the mountain's side in a great spiral. In the side of the cone he delved great chambers, the *Sammath Naur*, 'Chambers of Fire', and thereby gained access to the eternal fires which burned at Orodruin's heart.

But after his initial domination over the Westlands, during the Accursed Years, Sauron was finally defeated and taken prisoner by

Ar-Pharazôn of Númenor in the late Second Age, and in his absence the Fire-mountain became once more dormant. Nonetheless, before the Age had passed he returned to wreak vengeance upon the Dúnedain survivors of Númenor, and then Orodruin erupted once more, and was renamed in Gondor *Amon Amarth*, 'Mount Doom'. It was afterwards known by this later name.

Orofarnë See 'O OROFARNË, LASSEMISTA, CARNIMÍRIË!'

Oromë the Great The Huntsman of the Valar, one of the seven 'High Ones' (Aratar) of Arda, 'who alone of the Valar came often to Middle-earth in the Elder Days'; the Rider of the horse Nahar, and bearer of the great horn Valaróma; and first master of the Hound Huan. He is called by the Calaquendi *Oromë* (which may be ono-matopoeically derived, meaning 'blowing of horns'), and by the Grey-elves *Araw*.

During the First Age Oromë came many times to Middle-earth, and pursued the evil creatures of Morgoth to the death – for sport – and so he was the first of all the Valar to encounter the Firstborn Children of Eru. (At this time they named him *Tauron* and *Aldaron*, for they deemed [rightly] that the Huntsman was also a lover of trees.) It was he who bore three of their kings away to Valinor, so that they might see the Light which shone there with their own eyes, and so persuade their people to make the Great Journey; and afterwards Oromë himself led his first stage of the march from the East, as far as Beleriand. After that time he came to Middle-earth only as a member of the Host of the Valar.

Oromë's spouse was Vána the sister of Yavanna. His own sister Nessa was the spouse of Tulkas. See *Silmarillion* p. 29, also ARAW.

Oromet A hill of the province of Andúnië in Númenor. Upon this hill stood a tower which gazed into the West; it had been built by Tar-Minastir, he who 'loved the Eldar but envied them', and who sent a force to the aid of Gil-galad.

Orophin A Wood-elf of Lothlórien who, together with his brothers Haldir and Rúmil and other Elves, guarded the western borders of that land at the time of the War of the Ring.

Orthanc 'Mount-fang' [literally 'Forked Height'] (Sind.) The Tower of Isengard, built by Men of Gondor shortly after the founding of the Realms in Exile at the end of the Second Age. It stood within the Ring of Angrenost, and was constructed from four pinnacles of hard, glossy black stone, welded into a single tower five hundred feet high. Just below the summit, these pinnacles 'opened into gaping horns . . . sharp as the points of spears, keen-edged as knives. Between them was a narrow space . . . and a floor of polished stone, written with strange signs'.[4]

For many years after its completion the fortress of Angrenost with its impregnable Tower remained useful to Gondor; but by the middle years of the Third Age the South-kingdom of the Dúnedain had withdrawn its forces from an area so far north, and for many centuries the Tower remained locked while the Ring of Angrenost fell into disrepair. Yet secreted somewhere within Orthanc still remained one of the *palantíri* (Seeing-stones) of the South-kingdom, and it was the lure of the Stone which attracted Saruman the Wizard – who, by the closing years of the Age, was actively seeking independent power in Middle-earth. As is told elsewhere (see ISENGARD), in the year 2953 Saruman came to Rohan and made friendly overtures to the King of that land – and to Beren, Ruling Steward of Gondor, desiring that the custodianship of the fortress be given up to him. In need of a strong ally in this important strategic position, Beren gave Saruman the keys of Orthanc, which the Wizard then occupied.

In this way Saruman gained possession of one of the most powerful fortresses in Middle-earth. After much seeking he discovered the missing Palantír, and armed with this invaluable device he at once began to extend the web of his plots. Little by little he altered and strengthened Isengard, while secretly taking many evil creatures into his service. So it was that when the Ruling Ring of Sauron was once more discovered, Saruman turned the power of Orthanc against the Free Peoples in an attempt to seize the Ring for himself. In this he was unsuccessful: his armies were destroyed, his fortress-walls were torn down by the vengeful Ent-folk and he himself was expelled from the Order of Wizards and from the Tower of Orthanc, which then reverted to its rightful ownership.

Osgiliath 'Citadel-of-the-Stars' (Sind.) The capital and chief city of Gondor from its founding in 3320 Second Age until 1640 Third Age, when it was superseded by the fortress-city of Minas Anor. In the centuries which followed it was gradually deserted and lost all its former eminence, and by the time of the War of the Ring the city was little more than a vast ruin upon either bank of the Great River, whose eastern side was occupied by forces of Sauron.

Yet at its beginning the Citadel of the Stars had been a proud, vast and populous city, where was kept the chief of the four *palantíri*

(Seeing-stones) of the South-kingdom. It lay on both sides of the Anduin, where the road from Minas Anor to Minas Ithil crossed the river via a great stone bridge. But, like Minas Ithil, Osgiliath had been built at a time when Sauron of Mordor was still widely believed to have perished in the ruin of Númenor; and as a consequence it was unfortified, save for a few out-works, while its many bridges opened the way from the East into the heartlands of Gondor. Accordingly, when Sauron quietly returned to Mordor, and suddenly took Minas Ithil in a surprise attack at the end of the Second Age, Osgiliath lay virtually defenceless before his advance.

It has been recounted elsewhere (see LAST ALLIANCE) how Anárion son of Elendil defended East Osgiliath with desperate courage while his elder brother Isildur brought aid from the North. Sauron was overthrown in that war, and for many years afterwards the glory of Osgiliath grew with the ascendancy of Gondor itself: for the first thousand years of the Third Age the South-kingdom flourished and extended its bounds, and the Kings ruled from Osgiliath, where the Great River flowed through beneath the broad stone bridge. But in 1432 Third Age a terrible civil war, the 'Kin-strife', broke out, and in that war Osgiliath was besieged by the rebels; in 1437 the fugitive King Eldacar was forced to flee into the North, and Osgiliath was severely damaged by fire and sword: the Dome of Stars, beside the Great River, where the Palantír had been kept, was razed and the Stone was lost for ever in the waters of Anduin.

So began the decline of Osgiliath. Two hundred years later an even greater evil struck Gondor, when a foul pestilence came into the South-kingdom from the East. Osgiliath was sorely afflicted by the Plague, and most of its inhabitants died – save only those who fled north and west to spread the contagion elsewhere. King Telemnar and all his children perished and his nephew removed the royal seat to Minas Anor at the feet of the White Mountains further west.

Yet the city lingered on, partly ruinous, for another thousand years of Gondor's slow decline – until the year 2745, when a new race of soldier-orcs appeared on the marches of Ithilien and swept across the narrow land to capture Osgiliath. They were finally driven out, but in that war the city was finally destroyed and its great bridge was broken. The west bank of Anduin then became a frontier of war: fortifications were thrown up and Men of Gondor remained permanently on guard. The far bank was shrouded in shadow and was filled with watchful eyes of another sort. So the situation remained until the War of the Ring, when the ruined city was again attacked – once in June of the year 3018 (when the asault was thrown back by

Boromir son of Steward Denethor II), and again in March of the following year, when a great force from Minas Morgul forced the crossings and advanced towards Minas Tirith (Minas Anor). Although this army was decisively defeated at the Battle of the Pelennor Fields, and Osgiliath was recaptured, the city was never rebuilt and was afterwards allowed to fall peacefully into final ruin.

Ossë The Maia of the Sea, the chief servant of Ulmo. His spouse was Uinen. He came into the World at the same time as Ulmo, and ever after lived in the Seas, notably the eastern reaches of Belegaer. Here he came to know the Quendi, of the Telerin kindred, the minstrels of the Elves; this Kindred he loved always, and grieved when the time came for them also to pass into the West. At his prayer they halted their voyage while still in the mouth of the Bay of Eldamar; and for an age longer Ossë retained their companionship. But then for the last time the summons came; and as a final gift the Sea-maia taught the Teleri the craft of shipbuilding, so enabling them to come to the last shores. He was everafter their patron and friend.

Note: Ossë was known to the Sindar as *Gaerys*, 'the Awesome'.

Ossiriand 'Land of the seven rivers' (Sind.) The name given by the Sindar of Beleriand to all the country between the river Gelion and the Blue Mountains, south of, and including, the river Ascar, down whose northern shore the Dwarves first came into Beleriand. But Ossiriand was never a land of Dwarves, nor of Men (save one). Long empty, it was given by Thingol of Beleriand to Denethor lord of the Nandor (the Green-elves) who had come at length into Beleriand, last of all the Telerin peoples to make the journey to the West of Middle-earth. Here the people of Denethor afterwards dwelt, though Denethor himself was slain in the First Battle of Beleriand. But at the end of the Age, tumults and inundations overwhelmed most of Beleriand beyond the Ered Luin, and only remnants of Ossiriand and Thargelion (to the North) were left. Ossiriand was then re-named *Harlindon*, ('South-Lindon'), and so it remained. (*Lindon*, 'Land-of-Song', had been the name originally given by the exiled High-elves to all the Land of the Seven Rivers: a green and secret country into which none of them ever journeyed while the First Age lasted.)

Ossiriand was sixty leagues long by fifty broad (at its widest). Its northern boundary was the Ascar and its southern the Adurant with its island of Tol Galen, once the home of Beren and Lúthien. The Seven Rivers were Ascar, Thalos, Legolin, Brilthor, Duilwen, Adurant, and the Gelion, into which the first-named six all shed their waters.

Ost-in-Edhil 'Fortress-of-the-Eldar' (Sind.) The name given in tradition to the (fortified) city built by those Noldor led by Cele-brimbor who, in 750 Second Age, journeyed to Eregion near the Misty Mountains, to found a realm near the Dwarvish city of Moria. Ost-in-Edhil was the capital city of Eregion, and though its whereabouts have never been disclosed on available maps, it must have stood near Moria Gate. It was captured and razed by forces of Sauron during the War of the Elves and Sauron, in 1697 Second Age.

Ostoher From 411–92 Third Age, the seventh King of Gondor. It was this King who rebuilt the city of Minas Anor to make it a suitable summer dwelling of Gondor's royalty.

Otho Sackville-Baggins The son of Longo Baggins and Camellia Sackville, and the first of the short-lived Sackville-Baggins family. Otho is better remembered as the ill-tempered husband of the formidable Lobelia Sackville-Baggins, and as the father of the worth-less and unfortunate Lotho ('Pimple').

Outer Ocean See EKKAIA.

'Outsiders' The Shire-hobbits' term for any folk who suffered the misfortune of having originated elsewhere. To guard against un-warranted intrusion on the part of such 'Outsiders', Hobbits main-tained the custom of 'beating the bounds', thus ensuring that few intruders were able to penetrate the Shire-dwellers' rustic idyll.

Overbourn Marshes A low-lying area south of the Eastfarthing in the Shire, between the rivers Brandywine (Baranduin) and Shire-bourn.

Over-heaven The three separate aspects of the Creation were: Over-heaven, Middle-earth and the Underworld. Between Over-heaven and Middle-earth the Undying Lands of the West, home of the Valar and the Eldar from time immemorial.

Overhill One of the three villages of the Westfarthing which clus-tered close to the Hill of Hobbiton and the Bywater Pool. Overhill lay north of The Hill.

Overlithe The name given to Leap Year's Day in the Shire Calen-dar. Hobbits celebrated Leap Years by observing four Lithedays (instead of the usual three), of which the third, Overlithe, was an extra day in the calendar and did not normally appear. The four Lithedays were: 1 Lithe, Mid-year's day, Overlithe and 2 Lithe.

Notes

1 Book II Chap. 2.
2 Book I Chap. 7.
3 Although the *Svart-alfar*, the 'Dark-elves' of Norse epic, remind us of the ancient belief that these creatures were created at the Dawn, by dark powers, in mockery of the 'Light-elves' of Frey's *Alfheim* (Elvenhome).
4 Book III Chap. 8. *Orthanc* is also translated as 'Forked-height'.

Paladin (**II**) **Took** From 1415–34 Shire Reckoning (3015 Third Age – Year 13 Fourth Age), the thirty-first Thain of the Shire, father of the illustrious Peregrin Took. Paladin held office during the War of the Ring, at the time of the occupation of the Shire by agents of Saruman – and until the return of the Ring-bearers he was the only clan-leader to offer serious resistance to the ruffians. The Tooks indeed refused all dealing with the invaders, barring their folkland and shooting any who attempted to force entry. Thus, when the time came for a general uprising in the Shire, a sizeable body of armed and experienced Hobbitry was available for military purposes. Paladin then put all the forces he could spare under Pippin's leadership and sent them to take part in the Battle of Bywater, while he himself cleared the southern part of the Shire with the remainder of his forces. He held office as Thain until the year of his death, being succeeded by Pippin, his only son.

Palantír 'That-which-looks-far-away' (Q.) The eight Seeing-stones of Eldamar, made by Fëanor of the Noldor during the Elder Days, seven of which were given by his House to the Lords of Andúnië in Númenor during the Second Age. They were kept as heirlooms until the Fall of Númenor, after which the Seven Stones were brought to Middle-earth in nine ships carrying the Faithful, led by Elendil the Tall:

> *Tall ships and tall kings*
> *Three times three,*
> *What brought they from the foundered land*
> *Over the flowing sea?*

Seven stars and seven stones
And one white tree.[1]

Each of the *palantíri* was in fashion like a globe of crystal, in the heart of which flickered a tiny flame. One who gazed into the Stone saw this light expand until the surface of the globe became a mass of spinning colour, into which the mind might cast itself to be transported whithersoever the gazer wished, unrestricted by time or space. The Stones were all in accord with each other, and one was the master of them all. After their arrival in Middle-earth they were distributed throughout the Númenorean realms-in-exile, being kept at Annúminas, Amon Sûl and the Tower Hills in Arnor, and at Osgiliath, Orthanc, Minas Ithil and Minas Anor in Gondor. Each Palantír had different characteristics and performed according to the nature of the person who commanded it. Using the Seven Stones, the Dúnedain were long able to guard and unite the Realms in Exile; but with the passing of time, many of the *palantíri* were lost or were taken by enemies of the Dúnedain.

The Palantír of Osgiliath disappeared when the Dome of Stars was razed during the Kin-strife (in 1437 Third Age); the Stones of Amon Sûl and Annúminas were lost in the waters of the Ice Bay with King Arvedui of Arthedain in 1974; The Stone of Minas Ithil was captured by Sauron in the year 2002, when the Tower of the Moon was taken by his servants, the Ringwraiths; the Palantír of Orthanc fell into the clutches of the traitor Saruman (*c.* 3000); and finally, the Stone of Minas Anor (Minas Tirith) fell virtually under the control of Sauron (who used it to break the mind of Denethor II, last Ruling Steward). By the time of the War of the Ring, only the Palantír of the Tower Hills then remained untouched by evil. (Since it 'looked' only towards the Undying Lands, it was quite useless to those struggling for power, and it had long been in the keeping of the High-elves.)

As for the eighth of the stones, the 'Master-stone' or Chief Palantír, this had never left the Undying Lands; it stood in the Tower of Avallónë, in Eressëa, and was in direct accord with the Stone of the Tower Hills, which was the Master-stone of the Seven, though subservient to the Palantír of Eressëa.

During the War of the Ring the Ithil-stone, long before taken by Sauron, was destroyed in the Fall of Barad-dûr, and that of Minas Tirith rendered completely unusable (save by a person with an iron will). Only the Orthanc-stone, recovered from Saruman by a strange mischance, remained to the new King of Gondor for use during the

Fourth Age – for the Palantír of the Tower Hills was secretly put aboard Master Elrond's ship by Círdan the Shipwright, and so passed over Sea back to Eressëa at the end of the Third Age.

Palantir (Tar-Palantír) See INZILADÛN (AR-INZILADÛN).

P **Parma** The Quenya or High-elven word for 'book', but more properly the title of Tengwa number 2, which represented the value of the sound *p* in those languages which required it.

Parmatéma See TÉMA, TÉMAR.

Parth Galen 'Green Lawn' (Sind.) A swathe of cool greensward which lay between the river Anduin and the lower slopes of Amon Hen on its western bank, some little distance north of the Falls of Rauros.

Party Field The name given by local Hobbits to the large field which lay on the Hill of Hobbiton below the gardens of Bag End. In it stood a single tree, the 'Party Tree', beneath which Bilbo Baggins erected an imposing marquee for his 'private' dinner party on the day of his 111th birthday (see Book I Chap. 1). The field was partially dug up during the War of the Ring by agents of Saruman and the Tree was wantonly cut down. It was later replaced by a single shapely *mallorn* grown by Samwise Gamgee from a seed brought back from Lothlórien.

Party Tree See preceding entry.

Pass of Aglon The 'Narrow Pass' (the meaning of *Aglon*) which led from Himlad into Lothlann – or the other direction. On the west reared great sheer heights, the eastern walls of the Dorthonion Plateau; to the east the hills were lower. The Pass itself was some six leagues long. For obvious strategic reasons, this defile was a potential weak point in the chain of kingdoms created by the Noldor after the Battle-Under-Stars. The brothers Celegorm and Curufin, sons of Fëanor, therefore fortified the Pass and held large forces in Himlad, in a reserve capacity. Ten leagues to the east their elder brother Maedhros had his stronghold on the Hill of Himring, and beyond him Maglor's cavalry rode far out upon the steppe. Nonetheless, in the Dagor Bragollach all this great array was swept out of the North – for the time being. But Maedhros held out on Himring, which formed the nucleus in the East for a later re-grouping of the Sons of Fëanor and their hosts; and after a dozen years or so Aglon was again captured, and held for a while. Then came the Nirnaeth Arnoediad; after that battle the reconstitution of the realms of the Noldor in the North was no longer a possibility. Aglon, and all the lands of the North, fell under the domination of Morgoth and were never recovered.

Pass of Anach The seven-league ravine which descended from western Dorthonion to Dimbar and Nan Dungortheb. On the west the peaks of the Encircling Mountains towered above the pass; to the east loomed the Mountains of Terror. The upper reaches of the Pass of Anach were captured by Morgoth after the fall of Dorthonion, and soon afterwards armies began to come down into Beleriand by means of this route. It was briefly recaptured before the Nirnaeth, but lost again soon afterwards.

Pass of Light The CALACIRYA.

Pass of Sirion The five-league defile which led into Beleriand from Ard-galen in the north. It was walled on the west by the Ered Wethrin, and on the east by the sheer edge of the Dorthonion plateau. Through the pass, in a southerly direction, ran the great river Sirion (the action of whose waters had carved the defile in ancient days). For the exiled Noldor the Pass of Sirion was of immense strategic importance; for it was the veritable western cornerstone of their defence against Morgoth. It had additional value as a natural redoubt because of the Fen of Serech – deliberately never drained by the Noldor – which covered any sudden approach from the north. Further to fortify the Pass of Sirion, Finrod son of Finarfin built a tall watch-tower (called Minas Tirith) on the island of Tol Sirion, in the middle of the river and squarely in the neck of the pass.

Tol Sirion was captured shortly after the Dagor Bragollach, by Sauron the servant of Morgoth; indeed all the routes from north to south were taken from the Eldar at this time; but most – including the Pass of Sirion – were won back in the years immediately preceding the Nirnaeth Arnoediad. After which, of course, they were again lost, this time for ever.

Paths of the Dead The name given in Rohan to the Haunted Road under the Dwimorberg mountain which led from Dunharrow in the north to an unknown destination (actually the source of the river Morthond in the south). It was constructed – for what purpose none could say – early in the Second Age by the Men of the White

Mountains, and was part of the great megalithic complex known as Dunharrow.

See also Book V Chaps. 2 and 3.

Pelargir 'Enclosure-of-[Royal] Ships' (Q.) The most ancient port of Gondor, forty leagues upstream from the Mouths of Anduin, above the confluence with the Sirith. The haven was founded in the Second Age (2350) by mariners of Númenor and, though neither the greatest in size nor the most important, soon became the chief haven of those Númenoreans who called themselves the Faithful. Elendil himself landed there after the Downfall of Númenor.

For the first centuries after the founding of the realm of Gondor, Pelargir was allowed somewhat to fall into disrepair, and it was not until the reign of the first 'Ship-king' that Gondor attempted to regain any of her ancestral naval might. The second 'Ship-king', Eärnil I, repaired the ancient harbour and enlarged the basin to take the massive fleets that the Dúnedain then began to build: for to the south, the older and larger Haven of Umbar was filled with seafaring folk, unfriendly to the Dúnedain, and Eärnil had determined to end the threat they posed. Gondor indeed conquered Umbar, and held it, and for a while both harbours were filled with the warships of Gondor. The South-kingdom extended her influence along the coasts north, south and west, and soon reached the summit of her power.

Yet with the Kin-strife of the middle Third Age the navy of Gondor became rebellious, and Pelargir was then controlled by the disloyal elements who were opposed to King Eldacar. Even after these rebels had been soundly defeated at the Battle of the Crossings of Erui (1447) Pelargir still held out against the lawful King, and in the end the rebels took the fleets and sailed away to Umbar, which they made into a seafaring city-state opposed to the rule of Gondor. Nonetheless Pelargir remained the chief port of the South-kingdom – although its exposed position and rich commercial traffic made the harbour especially vulnerable to seaborne raiding from the Corsairs of Umbar. During the War of the Ring the Haven was once more assailed by these Corsairs – but in the nick of time they were defeated and their ships seized for another purpose. The port remained in Gondor's control throughout the War and, in the Fourth Age which followed, once again prospered in the manner of earlier times.

See also CORSAIRS OF UMBAR; KIN-STRIFE.

Pelendur A Steward of Gondor, descended from Húrin of Emyn Arnen and, in a sense, Gondor's first 'Ruling Steward'. It was Pelendur's lot to govern the South-kingdom during the one-year interregnum (1944–5 Third Age) following the untimely death in battle of King Ondoher and his two sons. The situation was further complicated by the strong claim to the Throne of Gondor made by King Arvedui of Arthedain (see ARVEDUI). In his capacity as temporary ruler, Pelendur was chiefly responsible for Gondor's rejecting Arvedui's claim, although his own choice seemed wise enough: Eärnil, a victorious General, of proven ability and acceptable antecedents. Eärnil duly became King – and his own son, Eärnur, became the last King of the Line of Anárion; after Eärnur's death (in 2050 Third Age), the descendants of Pelendur took office as (hereditary) Ruling Stewards, maintaining this weighty responsibility until the ending of the Age and the Return of the King.

Pelennor 'Enclosed-lands' (Sind.) The fenced townlands of Minas Tirith. See also BATTLE OF THE PELENNOR FIELDS.

Pelóri 'Mountains of Defence' (Q.) The Mountains of Valinor, tallest in the World and impassable save by a single ravine, the Pass of Calacirya, through which the ancient Light of the Two Trees flowed from Valimar into Eldamar and the long shorelands of the Blessed Realm.

The highest of the Pelóri was *Oiolossë* (older name *Taniquetil*, 'High-white-peak'), sometimes also called the Hill of Ilmarin. Upon its summit, at the roof of the world, stood the *Oromardi* ('High-halls') of the Lord of the Valar and his spouse, the Lady Elbereth (Varda).

People of the Great Journey The ELDAR.

People of Haleth The HALADIN.

People of the Stars A translation of the Quenya (High-elven) word ELDAR.

Peredhel (pl. -*edhil*) 'Half-elven' (Sind.) A term applied by the Elves to the brethren Elros and Elrond, sons of Eärendil (the Mariner) and the Lady Elwing the White; also, less specifically, to all those of mixed Eldarin and Mannish descent: Eärendil himself; Dior Eluchíl; Dior's children, Elvréd, Elvrín and Elwing; and Elrond's children, Elladan, Elrohir and Arwen Evenstar.

See also ELROND; ELROS TAR-MINYATUR; LINES OF DESCENT.

Peregrin Took From Year 13–63 Fourth Age (1434–84 Shire Reckoning), the thirty-second Thain of the Shire – and one of the most notable Hobbits of his day, being renowned also as a member of the Fellowship of the Ring and as one of the Captains who led the uprising of the Shire-folk against the agents of the Wizard Saruman at the end of the War of the Ring. Peregrin – more usually known as Pippin – later became a Counsellor of the reconstituted North-kingdom and remained a close personal friend of King Elessar (Aragorn II) throughout his life.

Peregrin was born in Tuckborough in the year 1390 Shire Reckoning (2990 Third Age), and was therefore only in his late twenties (having not yet 'come-of-age') when the great events of that time began to unfold themselves. As is recounted in the Red Book, both he and his kinsman Meriadoc Brandybuck learned somewhat of the Ring-bearer's plans before Frodo had even left the Shire, and thus were able to pressure him into accepting their company on the road East. At that time Frodo's plans led no further than Rivendell, and it must be said that his two young kinsmen did not particularly distinguish themselves during this part of the journey. Nonetheless, when the time came to allot the places in the Fellowship of the Ring – with an infinitely more dangerous journey ahead – Gandalf the Grey supported their inclusion in the Company. And later on both Pere-grin and Meriadoc came into their own, influencing great events far beyond their understanding at the time.

The story of Pippin's role in the War of the Ring is told in great detail elsewhere, and needs only brief recapitulation in these pages. Like his kinsman Meriadoc, he was separated from Frodo at Parth Galen on February 26th 3019, and thereafter his adventures took him across the plains of Rohan (in captivity to the Orcs of Saruman); to Fangorn Forest (as a guest of Treebeard the Ent); to Isengard (where he witnessed the destruction of Saruman's fortress); to Dol Baran at the southern end of the Misty Mountains (where he foolishly 'abstracted' the Palantír of Orthanc and inadvertently misled Sauron), and finally, in company with an exasperated Gandalf, to the city of Minas Tirith – where he swore allegiance to the Steward Denethor II and was made a Guard of the Citadel for his pains. While in Minas Tirith Peregrin witnessed the Siege of the City and was instru-mental in saving Faramir, Denethor's Heir, from an untimely death. He afterwards marched away with the Host of the West to the Black Gate and fought honourably in battle there, slaying a giant Troll-chief and thus saving his comrade Beregond son of Baranor from death under the Troll's claw.

Peregrin was knighted by King Elessar for his services to Gondor and afterwards returned to the Shire with his three original com-panions, playing a crucial role in the uprising which ensued. He personally rode through the night of November 2nd in order to bring reinforcements from his father, Thain Paladin II, and with this aid turned the tide at the Battle of Bywater the following day. For this feat both he and Meriadoc were afforded great honour among their kinfolk – and unlike Frodo and Samwise, they never really rejected any opportunities to parade around in fine style, wearing the arms and armour of Gondor and Rohan. Their splendid appearance (and their relatively enormous size, thanks to certain draughts quaffed while they had been guests of Treebeard the Ent) impressed the Shire-folk to a great extent, and of course both young Hobbits duly succeeded their fathers in positions of responsibility. Peregrin became Thain in 1434 Shire Reckoning, having already wedded Mistress Diamond of Long Cleeve (a descendant of Bullroarer Took, whom Peregrin had always greatly admired). That same year both he and Meriadoc (and Samwise Gamgee, now Mayor of the Shire) were appointed Counsellors of the North-kingdom.

The remainder of Peregrin's long life was happy and prosperous, and he became one of the greatest Thains in Shire-history. Like Meriadoc, he maintained the friendships he had made during the War, and rode often to Gondor, becoming something of an authority on the history of the Dúnedain (though it is not recorded that he ever actually undertook any historical writing on his own account). In Year 63 Fourth Age he handed over his Office to his only son Faramir (born Year 9 Fourth Age) and, together with his lifelong comrade Meriadoc, he rode away out of the Shire, to pass his last days in Gondor amongst old friends. He was laid to rest among the Great of Gondor, in the House of the Kings in Rath Dínen.

Perian, Periain 'Halfling' (Sind.) The several alternative spellings of this word and its plurals which appear in the Red Book doubtless indicate a word in the actual process of mutation from an antique form into a more colloquial, 'everyday' expression. For, when the events of the War of the Ring brought several 'Halflings' to the attention of the people of Gondor, they revived the old Sindarin name for them. The Grey-elven word for 'Halfling' was, of course, adopted by the Dúnedain of Gondor; the form given above was doubtless one of the newer versions. One Hobbit would be called *Perian* while a finite plural (e.g. two Hobbits) would earn the word *Periain*. However, Hobbits *as a race* were called *i Periannath* ('the Halfling Folk').

The older form of the word may be found in use during a 'ceremonial' occasion (Book VI Chap. 4, the Paean to the Ring-bearers), involving the antique *Ph* prefix: *Pheriain, Pheriannath*.

Periannath See preceding entry.

'Perry-the-Winkle' One of the humorous verses in the collection entitled *The Adventures of Tom Bombadil* (No. 8).

Petty Dwarves A translation of NOEGYTH NIBIN.

Pharazôn (Ar-Pharazôn) 'the Golden' From 3255–3319 Second Age the twenty-fourth and last King of Númenor. He was the son of Gimilkhâd, who was the younger of the two sons of Ar-Gimilzôr, an iron ruler hostile to the Eldar. Of the two princes Gimilkhâd took most after their father, while his elder brother Inziladûn (Palantír) took after their mother (Inzilbêth of Andúnië) in that he repented of the heretical ways of the later kings and desired the knowledge and conversation of the Eldar. And as he was the elder son, so he came in time to the kingship, and not Gimilkhâd. But the years waned, and Gimilkhâd's son Pharazôn grew to manhood, and Palantír waned. And Gimilkhâd died, and now it was Pharazôn who led the party opposed to the reforms of Palantír. This faction grew in strength throughout Palantír's reign, and on his death seized power, from Míriel, the king's daughter and the Heir of the Sceptre. Pharazôn proclaimed himself king of Númenor and, to make the bond final, forcibly wedded Míriel, even changing her (Eldarin) name to one of Adûnaic form, Ar-Zimraphel. He was now firmly in the seat of power, and was never to be challenged again during his reign.

Pharazôn had ruled for only six years when he made his first decisive move, setting sail with a great fleet to Middle-earth, where Sauron the Great reigned unchallenged. He landed at Umbar, determined to give battle for the mastery of all Middle-earth; but Sauron was unable to contest the power of Númenor, and instead abased himself, begging mercy from the King (and playing on his pride). So Pharazôn took Sauron 'prisoner' and proudly carried him back to Númenor, thus sowing the seeds of his own downfall and that of his people.

For, characteristically, Sauron was soon at work on the natural weaknesses of his foes, and it cannot have taken him long to discover the Númenoreans' obsession with the one prohibition ever laid upon them: the BAN OF THE VALAR, which forbade them from sailing to the Undying Lands, where the Valar, Guardians of the World, made their own home. Sauron, who almost from the first had ceased to be considered a 'prisoner', then seized on Ar-Pharazôn's constant pride and growing fear of Death, suggesting that the immortality which the Númenoreans always sought was still within their grasp.

And Sauron lied to the King, declaring that everlasting life would be his who possessed the Undying Lands, and that the Ban was imposed only to prevent the Kings of Men from surpassing the Valar. 'But great Kings take what is their right,' he said.[2]

In 3310 this false and evil counsel finally prevailed, for Ar-Pharazôn was then an old man and near death. He gave orders for the construction of the mightiest fleet the world had ever seen: the Great Armament, so huge and powerful that it took nine years to build and assemble. In 3319 the Host of Ar-Pharazôn embarked and went with war into the Western Seas, to contest the rule of the world – and the immortality which accompanied it – with the Valar.

It will never be known exactly what happened when the last King of Númenor set foot on the shores of Valinor, for none survived of that Host to tell the tale, and the High-elves did not come to Middle-earth in later Ages. Certainly no less than a change in the physical and metaphysical structure of the World was the result of Pharazôn's appalling sacrilege. The Sea rose in huge waves from the West and raged unchecked over Númenor, burying everything in a wall of black water which utterly destroyed the civilization of three thousand years (apart from a few who left in the nick of time, escaping to Middle-earth in Exile). And the Undying Lands were removed for ever from mortal seas, and so from further temptation.

Phurunargian 'Dwarf-delving' (West.) The name given in the Common Speech to the ancient city of Moria beneath the Misty Mountains. It has been translated from the Red Book as *Dwarrow-delf*.

Pickthorn A family of Big Folk (Men) of the Bree-land.

Pillars of the Kings A translation of the Sindarin word *Argonath*.

Pincup A small village of the Green Hill Country in the Southfarthing of the Shire.

Pinnath Gelin 'Green Ridges' (Sind.) A broad range of fertile green hills in the Anfalas coastal strip of Gondor.

Note: the suffix -*ath* indicates a collective plural; *gelin* is the plural of the Sindarin word *galen* 'green' (e.g. *Parth Galen* 'Green Lawn').

Pipe-weed Hobbits were, of course, aware that their 'Art' of smoking – of inhaling, without apparent discomfort, the smouldering leaves of the herb *nicotiana* – caused great amazement to other folk;

and for this reason they included throughout their various histories many accounts of the weed's singular properties, first discovery, and so on. Nonetheless, even in the Shire there were some who were more knowledgeable than others in the love of this Art, and of these the chief was Meriadoc Brandybuck, Master of Buckland from 1432–84 Shire Reckoning.

Meriadoc indeed incorporated all of his knowledge on this fascinating subject in his famous *Herblore of the Shire* (a remarkable work on the subject of comparative botany). He discussed the history of the weed, its probable route north from Gondor, where it grew wild, to Bree, and then to the sheltered gardens of the Southfarthing, and – most important – the horticultural *coup* on the part of one Tobold Hornblower which led to the herb's fulfilment of its natural role (as the Hobbits saw it).

He traced Old Toby's singular achievement (the first recorded growing of the true Pipe-weed) to the year 1070 Shire Reckoning. The weed had, of course, been smoked prior to that date but only in Bree. The importance of Tobold's raising of the herb was the vast improvement in quality brought about by the warmer climate of the Southfarthing (even Bree-dwellers confessed as much); Southfarthing pipe-weed was acknowledged by all to be immeasurably superior in aroma, strength, taste and overall quality. More importantly, it grew abundantly there and was as a consequence plentiful in the Shire (unlike the Bree-strain, which was often adversely affected by the climate of central Eriador).

So much for the general history and origins of Pipe-weed (further information may be found in Prologue 2). A more significant aspect in the history of the weed was the role its unofficial export (in 1418–19 Shire Reckoning) played during the War of the Ring. To find large consignments of the best weed in Saruman's fortress of Isengard may have been a revelation to the Hobbits Meriadoc and Peregrin (Book III Chap. 9), but it was no tribute to the Shire-dwellers' business acumen; nor did it bode well for the internal security of the Shire. Indeed, it was later discovered that it was through the leaf-trade that Saruman had initially acquired a controlling interest in the affairs of Lotho ('Pimple') Sackville-Baggins, and through Lotho that Saruman had come to dominate the Shire itself.

See also GALENAS.

Pippin Gamgee The third son (and fifth child) of Samwise Gamgee, born in Bag End in Shire-year 1429 (Year 8 Fourth Age).

Pippin Took See PEREGRIN TOOK.

Pool of Bywater 'The Water' was the nearest thing to a major river which passed through the Shire. From the northern part of the Westfarthing it flowed gently through the little land, eventually reaching the Brandywine (Baranduin) a little way north of the Bridge of Stonebows. In this journey (of about thirty leagues) it formed a middling-sized lake (also known, rather confusingly, as 'The Water') near Frogmorton, and a rather smaller tarn not far from the Three-farthing Stone, close to the villages of Overhill, Hobbiton and, of course, Bywater. This smaller lake was known locally as Bywater Pool.

Pools of Ivrin See IVRIN.

Poros A great river of southern Middle-earth, and the largest of the Anduin's eastern tributaries. It arose high in the stony vales of the southern Ephel Dúath (Mountains of Shadow) and descended through a wide valley to join the Great River some forty miles above its Delta. Thus it formed a natural barrier between South Ithilien and the Harad Lands, and was as a consequence often – especially during the late Third Age – a frontier of war between the kingdoms of Gondor and Harad. Luckily for the Dúnedain, the river could only be forded with safety at one point, the Crossings of Poros, and it was here that most invasions from Haradwaith were met.

See also BATTLE OF THE CROSSINGS OF POROS.

Powers A translation of the Quenya word VALAR.

The Prancing Pony The chief Inn of the Bree-land – which is to say it was the only tavern of any consequence (*The Forsaken Inn* lay a day's journey to the East and was little frequented as the lands grew wilder). *The Pony* occupied a prominent and convenient location within the village of Bree itself and was ideally situated to cater for the needs of travellers.

The Pony was an imposing building, built of timber on three storeys after the Mannish fashion, with two wings running back from the road into the hill behind, enclosing a courtyard equipped with stables. Nor had 'Little Folk' (Hobbits, of whom there were many in Bree) been forgotten: they were provided for by specially fitted chambers, close to the ground with round windows in the approved Hobbit manner.

The Innkeepers of *The Prancing Pony* were the family of Butter-bur, and the ale served by this prestigious Bree-family was highly regarded in the district; nonetheless the Inn's main attraction lay (for the locals) in the entertaining standard of conversation to be found in the public rooms whenever travellers stayed the night (as they frequently did). *News from Bree* was a Shire synonym for 'up-to-date' – and most Shire-news from Outside had its origins in the rapt, smoke-filled common room of *The Prancing Pony*.

Primula Baggins The mother of Frodo Baggins and the wife of Drogo. She was tragically drowned, together with her husband, in a boating accident when their son was only twelve. The orphaned Frodo afterwards went to live with his older cousin Bilbo Baggins.

'Princess Mee' One of the verses (No. 4) in the collection entitled *The Adventures of Tom Bombadil*. It was reportedly scribbled by an anonymous hand in a margin of the Red Book and cannot as a consequence be accounted one of the more important poems in the collection.

Proudfoot A family of Shire-hobbits, related to the Bagginses by marriage.

Prophecy of the North Another name for the CURSE OF MANDOS.

Puddifoot A family of Shire-hobbits, closely associated with the village of Stock in the Eastfarthing, and therefore probably of Stoorish descent.

Púkel-men The name given by the Rohirrim to the ancient graven statues which were to be found at each turn of the winding, pre-cipitous road which climbed from Harrowdale to the Hold of Dun-harrow many hundreds of feet above. These images had been carved by the mysterious builders of the Hold, which had been constructed at least an Age before the Riders came to Rohan. Who these builders had been none could state with certainty, although the forlorn, large-waisted, mournful, man-like creatures depicted in the statuary were not unlike the 'Wild Men' of Druadan Forest, which lay beyond the borders of Rohan. What their relationship had been with the stonemasons of the White Mountains during the Accursed Years was never discovered.

See also WOSES.

Notes
1 Book III Chap. 2.
2 Appendix A I(i).

Quarry A village of the Eastfarthing, situated near the village of Scary in the stone-cutting country of the Shire.

Quellë 'fading' (Q.) The name given by the High-elves to the fourth of the six 'seasons' – of fixed length – in the Elvish Calendar. The Númenoreans and the Westron-speaking peoples of Middle-earth used the same word to indicate the period of indefinite length which fell between the ending of autumn (*yávië*) and the onset of winter (*hrívë*). Its alternative Quenya name was *lasse-lanta* ('leaf-fall'), while to the Grey-elves it was known as *firith* (or *narbeleth*, 'sun-waning').

See also CALENDAR OF IMLADRIS; KINGS' RECKONING.

Quendi 'The Speakers' (Q.) The High-elven name for all Elvenkind (cf. *Quenya* 'the Speech'). The origins of this word are doubtless to be found in the Elves' age-old desire to communicate with other living things: they were the first of the 'speaking-peoples' to awake and wander in Middle-earth, and at that time the gift of speech was what set them apart from all other creatures. See *Silmarillion* esp. p. 309, also ELDAR; ELVES.

Quenta Silmarillion 'History of the Silmarils' (Q.) The title of a prose collection, itself a series of encapsulations and renditions of far older works, assembled and edited over the years by many hands, but most notably during our own century by Professor J. R. R. Tolkien (and his son Christopher). The *Quenta Silmarillion* forms the core of the published work known simply as *The Silmarillion*, though it is preceded in the text by the (more ancient) *Ainulindalë* and *Valaquenta*, and followed by the *Akallabêth* and by the (short version of the)

Tale of the Rings of Power. However, it is by far the largest of these five sections of text. The *Quenta Silmarillion* is almost entirely in prose form, and is divided into chapters which are arranged in chronological series. These chapters are derived from many different sources, others from single sources, as is made obvious by the many variations in style and tone.

The older works from which the *Quenta Silmarillion* is thought to be thus drawn, and of which it forms a *précis*, are as follows: the *Aldúdenië*, or Lament for the Trees; the *Narsilion* or Song of the Sun and Moon; the *Noldolantë*, or Fall of the Noldor; the *Lay of Leithian*; and the *Narn i Hîn Húrin*, or Tale of the Children of Húrin. It is assumed that these ancient works were copied out in their entirety – and thus rescued for posterity (and painstaking editorship) – by none other than the Hobbit Bilbo Baggins, during his long sojourn in Rivendell as Elrond's guest. Under the unassuming title *Translations from the Elvish* the collection was handed down, by various means, to the present day, and to its present benevolent custodianship.

Quenya 'The Speech' (Q.) The oldest of all recorded languages of the Elves, and thus of all peoples. Although it was first written down in Eldamar, after the Great Journey of the Eldar, the Quenya tongue was in fact descended virtually unchanged from the Ancient Speech once spoken by all the *Quendi*, and this accounts for its name.

Little is now known of the proto-Quenya spoken by the Elves before the separation of the Eldar (West-elves) from the other Silvan races. Certain changes had already begun to take place in its structure even before the vanguard of the Eldar crossed the Great Sea to Eldamar, far back in the Eldar Days. But in Eldamar, in the Undying Lands, the Eldar were unaffected by the changefulness of mortal lands, and after many years of the world outside they began to record their Ancient Speech in writing, using the *Tengwar* (Eldarin cursive letters) of Rúmil, and afterwards the Alphabet of Fëanor: a modified form of the same writing-system. Later still, the High-elves brought the Fëanorian alphabet and the (virtually unchanged) Quenya language back to Middle-earth, where both became known to the Grey-elves and to the Edain.

In fashion the Quenya was quite unlike the Sindarin tongue of the Grey-elves, to which it was of course distantly related (see SINDARIN). It was a stately and ceremonious language, with polysyllabic word-linkage and a comprehensive formal literature that was considerably more antique than anything the Sindar possessed. There are many examples of both tongues in the Red Book (and in this *Companion*), and the major differences between them are easily apparent. The Ancient Speech may be said (by some) to resemble Latin (to which it is quite unrelated), but it was far more inflected than any Mannish speech, and far more ancient. But if the introduction of Quenya into the culture of the Grey-elves can be said to have influenced the subsequent development of Sindarin (just as the Fëanorian Tengwar affected the Grey-elven runic alphabet), then the reverse is less true. The High-elves exiled in Middle-earth adopted for the most part, in daily speech, the language of the Grey-elves with whom they then dwelt, and the Ancient Speech was put aside as a 'High' language of ceremony and song (see NAMÁRIË).[1] It was therefore consciously preserved in its ancient form, and as a language of pageant it passed to the heirs of the High-elves in Middle-earth: the Edain of Númenor and of the Realms in Exile. In this way it was preserved unchanged.

The Edain indeed took the High-elven speech with them to Númenor, and in that land it also became a prized tongue, an 'Elven-latin' for ceremonial use (see KINGS' RECKONING). But for the most part the Dúnedain used the Sindarin or the Mannish tongues of their own early history, and little by little the Ancient Speech (and the Sindarin) became known only to those who held true to the ways of the Eldar. And so the two peoples walked further down different roads.

See also Appendix E; SPOKEN TONGUES; TENGWAR.

Quesse The Quenya or High-elven word for 'feather', but more properly the title of the Fëanorian Tengwa number 4, which was used (in Quenya) for the sound *kw-*.

Quessetéma '*Quesse*-series' (Q.) One of the four *témar* (series) which made up the complete Fëanorian Tengwar alphabet of letters. *Quessetéma* was used for the labialized sounds (*kw-*, *gw-*, *hw-* etc.), which occurred frequently in the High-elven speech.

See also TÉMA, TÉMAR; TENGWA, TENGWAR.

Quickbeam A translation of the Sindarin name *Bregalad*, adopted as a 'short' name by an Ent of Fangorn Forest.

Quick Post A luxury or emergency messenger-service, used in the Shire for the rapid conveyance of letters (a social service much in demand among Hobbits) from Farthing to Farthing. Its efficient administration was the responsibility of the Mayor of Michel Delving.

The mode of transport has not been recorded, but is likely to have involved the use of ponies.

Note

1 The use of Quenya was in fact prohibited in Beleriand by
  Thingol Greycloak.

Radagast the Brown A Wizard of Middle-earth, one of the Order of *Istari*, who arrived from the Undying Lands about the year 1000 Third Age. His special skills and responsibilities concerned the welfare of beasts and birds; his home was in Rhosgobel, in the southern vales of the Anduin, near the borders of the forest then known as Mirkwood. See also WIZARDS.

Radbug Reportedly the name of one of the Orcs in the garrison kept in the Tower of Cirith Ungol. According to the account of Samwise Gamgee, this unfortunate Goblin was slain for insubordination by one of his own sergeants, the villainous Shagrat, shortly after the fight between the Tower-orcs and the Morgul-patrol over certain items of booty (Book VI Chap. 1).

Radhruin One of the Outlaws of Dorthonion, a companion of Barahir. He was slain in an ambush, together with all his comrades (save Beren son of Barahir).

Ragnor One of the outlaws of Dorthonion; see preceding entry.

Rainbow Cleft A translation of the Grey-elven name CIRITH NINNIACH. See also ANNON-IN-GELYDH.

Rainy Stair A translation of the Grey-elven name DIMROST.

Ramdal 'Wall's End' The easternmost point of the *Andram* (Long Wall), a great escarpment which ran south-east from Taur-en-Faroth in West Beleriand and separated the populated north of Beleriand from the (largely uninhabited) south. At Ramdal the ground became level and the hills waned, and between here and the lonely height of Amon Ereb stood five leagues of open country. This region was ruled for a while by Amrod and Amras, the two youngest sons of Fëanor, but in later years Ramdal became the second line of defence for more of the Noldor.

Rammas Echor 'Encircling Walls' (Sind.) An outer defence-work of Minas Tirith, constructed by Steward Ecthelion II after the final loss of Ithilien (in 2954 Third Age). It was a great wall, over ten leagues in length, encircling the Fields of Pelennor, the hitherto defenceless townlands of the City. Nonetheless, the defensive value of the Rammas was open to doubt: for at its furthest point it was some four leagues from the City and thus could not be manned in strength, since the main defence of Minas Tirith lay in its city-walls and Great Gate. Moreover, defenders on the out-wall might find themselves cut off from retreat were a breach to be made and the gap stormed in strength. At best, the Rammas could only serve to delay unsupported cavalry forces or foot-soldiers without breaching tools.

See also BATTLE OF THE PELENNOR FIELDS.

Rána 'The Wayward' (Q.) A High-elven name for the Moon. See ISIL.

Rangers of Ithilien A guerilla force maintained by Gondor in North Ithilien, for the purpose of harassing the enemy and discomfiting his occupation of that land in the years leading up to the War of the Ring. These forces operated from secret bases (see HENNETH ANNÛN) prepared some years before on the orders of a far-seeing Steward, Túrin II. In later years the Rangers of Ithilien were led by Túrin's great-great-grandson, Faramir, the younger son of Denethor II.

Rangers of the North At the time of the War of the Ring it was the ironic fate of the Dúnedain of the North that, while their royal Line of Descent had been kept intact throughout the turmoils of three millennia, their Kingdom had been lost and their circumstances so grievously reduced that even their own kin in Gondor were unaware of their very existence.

The long process by which royal Arnor was first split into three smaller states and then overcome piecemeal is well detailed elsewhere (see ARNOR; ARTHEDAIN). After the fall of Arthedain in 1974 Third Age, the then stateless Heirs of Isildur passed into the shadows, emerging only as wandering strangers whose true identity was unsuspected by the inhabitants of Eriador, where they spent most of their days. The long wars launched upon them by Sauron and his servants had greatly reduced the Dúnedain in numbers, but their pride and sense of duty were intact: their task, as they saw it, was the continued protection of the Northlands, at whatever cost to themselves.

The labours they undertook in this worthy purpose were long, hard and yet not without result. Of course the Northlands were still threatened by groups of pillaging Orcs from the Misty Mountains, and the occasional cave-troll in business on his own account; but the hoped-for result was, by and large, attained, and the folk of Eriador were safely guarded, although they knew it not.

For the Dúnedain realized that Eriador could never be kept free from the Enemy if he once suspected that the Dúnedain – whom he had long hated – still survived there. And since Sauron never lacked for spies to serve him, the Rangers took great care to work in secret. The Elves of Rivendell were, of course, privy to the latent hopes and current duties of the Dúnedain Chieftains and their followers; indeed, the Eldar of Rivendell often rode with the Heirs of Isildur on their missions. But the Bree-dwellers and the Hobbits of the Shire were totally unaware of this long guardianship, and their names for the tough-looking, weatherbeaten Men who occasionally visited *The Prancing Pony* were anything but complimentary.

The first Chieftain of the Dúnedain was Aranarth, the son of Arvedui Last-king of Arthedain. In the intervening years there were a further fourteen before the last Chieftain, Aragorn II: the travel-stained Ranger who was known in Bree simply as 'Strider'.

Ranugad In the original (as opposed to translated) Hobbit-speech *Ranugad*, which meant 'Stay-at-home', was the name of Samwise Gamgee's father; in translations from the Red Book it has been rendered as *Hamfast*.

Rath Celerdain See LAMPWRIGHTS' STREET.

Rath Dínen 'Street of Silence' (Sind.) The central processional avenue of the Hallows of Minas Tirith, where the great men of Gondor were buried.

Rathlóriel 'Goldenbed' (Sind.) The name given to the river ASCAR in Ossiriand after the treasure looted from Doriath by Dwarves had been lost in its waters.

Rauros 'Roaring-spray' (Sind.) In the Third Age, the greatest waterfall of western Middle-earth, a stunning cataract whose roar could be distinguished many leagues away. It was located just south of Nen Hithoel, the lake on the Great River which was surrounded by the hills of Emyn Muil. In peaceful periods of the Third Age, the Falls of Rauros and the hills of Amon Hen and Amon Lhaw were places for the nobles of Gondor to visit on summer days, when the sound of the Falls and the golden light on their spray would provide a pleasant setting.

Ravenhill A small south-western spur of the Lonely Mountain (Erebor), where the Dwarves of that realm built a guardhouse and installed a small garrison. For some unaccountable reason, a family of ravens (headed by the wise and famous Carc) chose this place as their nesting-ground, thus giving the hill its name.

Ravines of Teiglin See TEIGLIN.

Ré (Q.) The Elvish 'day', which, unlike our own, was measured from sunset to sunset. Thus each *ré* began with the period known as *Undómë*, 'Star-opening'.

Realms in Exile See facing illustration; also ARNOR; GONDOR.

'Reckoning of Years' One of the better known works of that prolific Shire-chronicler, Meriadoc 'the Magnificent' Brandybuck, hero of the War of the Ring, Master of Buckland and Counsellor of the North-kingdom. In addition to an invaluable account of the Hobbit-calendars employed in the Shire and Bree, the *Reckoning of Years* included a comparative study of the reckoning-systems used in Rivendell, Rohan and Gondor, lands in which this widely travelled Hobbit was personally able to conduct his research.

Note: the *Reckoning of Years* was undoubtedly the primary source for the information which appears in Appendix D, to which readers are referred for a full analysis of the Elvish calendar and the other systems which sprang from it.

Red Arrow The traditional token used by Gondor when summoning urgent aid from her old allies, the Riders of Rohan. It was an ordinary black-feathered arrow except that it had a red-painted point. The summons it represented was of the most desperate kind, and the Red Arrow was not lightly dispatched.

Red Book of Westmarch The single most valuable surviving source of information concerning the War of the Ring, compiled during the late Third Age by the Hobbits of the Shire, in particular by the Ring-bearers, Bilbo and Frodo Baggins, and Frodo's heir

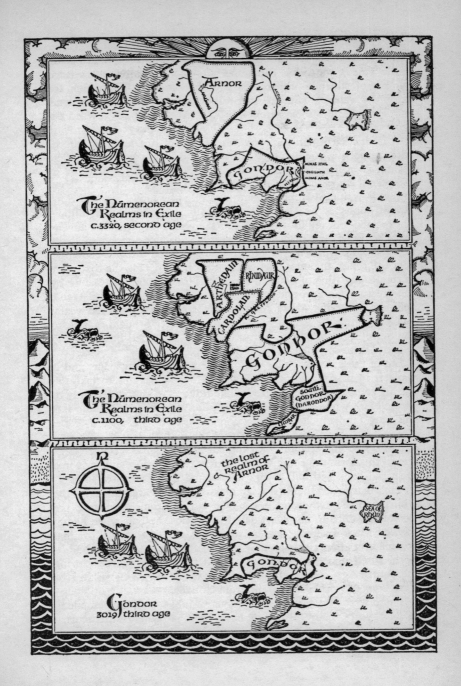

Samwise Gamgee. It deals with the heroic role the Hobbits played in the Tale of the Great Ring, and is further provided with a large number of addenda, appendices and annotations, all of which are extremely valuable sources of information concerning the Second and Third (and to some extent the First) Ages of Middle-earth long ago.

It is divided roughly into two main sections of unequal length, with supporting pages compiled by many different hands. The first section is in narrative form, and was written by Bilbo Baggins in the years between 2942–3001 Third Age (1342–1401 Shire Reckoning) at Bag End in Hobbiton, and was titled by him *There and Back Again* (published as *The Hobbit*). It deals in the main with Bilbo's unexpected journey into the East in the year 2941, with the adventures he underwent *en route*, and with his ultimate success and later homecoming. More importantly (although Bilbo did not recognize it at the time), this first part of the Red Book details the discovery of the Ruling Ring of Sauron, which had been found long before by the creature Gollum and had been kept by him in his miserable solitude under the Misty Mountains for over five hundred years. Bilbo acquired the Ring from Gollum, and later brought it back to the Shire, thus initiating a series of events which led in the end to Mount Doom and the Passing of Sauron.

But of these events Bilbo had of course no foreknowledge, and it was left to his young cousin (and heir) Frodo Baggins to take the further steps on that road. Frodo, like Bilbo (and almost certainly to please him), wrote his own account of the War of the Ring, and it is this later (and much larger) section of narrative (*The Lord of the Rings*) which forms the central part of the Red Book of Westmarch. Frodo wrote this account with the aid of his friends' recollections, and in this form the combined narratives (written in two hands in a great red book with tall covers) were handed to Samwise Gamgee, Frodo's heir, when the Ring-bearers passed over Sea at the end of the Third Age. Samwise added his own contributions, and gave the Book in his turn to his eldest daughter Elanor the Fair when he too passed West. Elanor's descendants kept custody of the original volume ever after, although they made certain annotations and additions, based upon information acquired from other sources during the Fourth Age, such as chronological material from Yellowskin (the Year-book of Tuckborough) and from Gondor.

There were also certain anonymous scribbles and rhymes added in later years, many of which have been published latterly as a separate volume (*The Adventures of Tom Bombadil*), part of the cycle of tales contained in the Red Book but not part of the main Tale of the Ring.

During the earlier part of the reign of King Elessar (Aragorn II), the King requested of the Shire-folk that they supply him with a copy of the Red Book which was even then being annotated by the Fairbairns and the Tooks. Thain Peregrin I accordingly commissioned scribes to draft a copy, and this volume, called in Gondor the *Thain's Book*, was taken by Peregrin to the King when he retired to Gondor in Year 63 Fourth Age. Over a century later, probably at the request of Eldarion, son of Elessar (who died in 120 Fourth Age), Findegil, a King's Writer of Gondor, again copied the Thain's Book, adding certain appendices and annotations (and corrections) of his own. This later volume was presented to the Hobbits, and it is this volume which has survived until the present day.

Redhorn A translation of the Sindarin word *Caradhras*, being the name given in the Common Speech to that great peak of the central Misty Mountains which was known to the Dwarves as Barazinbar. It was so named because the mountain seemed to glow with a blood-like tinge in the evening and morning sunlight. It had a cruel reputation and its high pass, the Redhorn Gate, was fraught with peril.

Redhorn Gate See previous entry.

Red Ring NARYA.

Redwater A translation of the Sindarin word *Carnen*.

Region 'Holly' (Sind.) The name given by the Elves of Doriath to the southern and larger of the two forests which comprised their silvan land. Region was indeed more than twice as large as its neighbour Neldoreth (being in places over fifty leagues long, and as much as fifteen leagues broad). In shape it was like a huge, reversed 'L', with much of its northern and western border formed by the river Esgalduin. Beyond the Esgalduin the beech-forest of Neldoreth marched away into the north. The southern boundary of Region was the River Aros; an outlier, Nan Elmoth, lay beyond the Celon, a tributary of Aros.

During the Elder Days Region and Neldoreth were both accounted part of Doriath, and were encompassed by the protective fence of enchantment, the Girdle of Melian.

Rerir A mountain of the northern Ered Luin. It was the tallest peak of a spur which thrust westward from the main range, enclosing

Lake Helevorn on three sides. Due north of the lake stood Mount Rerir. The Greater Gelion arose on its western slopes. This peak was accounted the northern border of the land of Thargelion.

Rethe The third month of the year (roughly equivalent to our March) in the calendars of the Shire and Bree.

Reunited Kingdom The name given in the Fourth Age to the realm ruled by King Elessar (Aragorn II), being the former states of Arnor and Gondor reunited for the first time since Elendil's day under Elessar's kingship.

Rhîw See HRÍVË.

Rhosgobel The dwelling-place of the Wizard Radagast the Brown, situated in the vales of Anduin near to the southern borders of Mirkwood.

Rhovanion This name has been translated on Third Age maps of western Middle-earth as 'Wilderland', and in this sense it refers to all the lands stretching east of the Misty Mountains to the River Running (Celduin), including the vales of Anduin and the forest of Mirkwood. However, in the appendices to *The Lord of the Rings* – and throughout this *Companion* – the name is used to indicate the principality of Rhovanion, which lay between the eastern eaves of Greenwood (later known as Mirkwood) and the River Running.

It was peopled by a loosely governed, vigorous race of 'Northmen', who were distantly related to the Dúnedain and were allied with Gondor often during the middle years of the Third Age. Sometime about the end of the first millennium, the kings of Gondor extended the boundaries of Rhovanion by ceding to the Northmen lands south of Greenwood – in the hope that these lands would act as a buffer state to protect Gondor from recurrent invasions by the fierce Easterling peoples. However, although this strategy was largely successful, eventually the favour shown by Gondor's nineteenth King Rómendacil II, towards the Northmen caused great jealousy in the South-kingdom. And the marriage of Rómendacil's son Valacar to the daughter of Vidugavia, the self-styled King of Rhovanion, ultimately led to civil war (see KIN-STRIFE). Valacar's son Eldacar was deposed and forced to seek refuge in his mother's land of Rhovanion; however, he was eventually able to regain his throne and restore peace, and during the remainder of his time he naturally showed great favour to the Northmen. At this time many of them settled in Gondor.

Nonetheless, contact between the peoples was not fully maintained; and, in the year 1856, the wide lands that had once been Vidugavia's were overrun by new hordes of invading Easterlings (called Wainriders). The Northmen were driven out or enslaved, and it was not until forty years later that they were able to start a rebellion which enabled Gondor to win a victory over the Easterlings.

At this point the peoples of Rhovanion pass out of available records for a while, although it may be assumed that most of them again moved north, out of the path traditionally taken by the Easterling migrations. In any case they are mentioned only once more, as allies of the Dwarves of the Lonely Mountain, after Durin's Folk returned to Erebor in the year 2590. Then, with the wealth and weapons produced by the Dwarves, 'the Northmen who lived between the Celduin (River Running) and Carnen (Redwater) became strong and drove back all enemies from the East.'[1]

Erebor was deserted some two hundred years later, following the arrival of the Dragon Smaug, and it is not known how the Men of Rhovanion then fared against the Easterlings (who made at least one more attack, at the very end of the Age). However, it seems probable that a people as vigorous and mobile as the Northmen of Rhovanion may somehow have managed to survive until the successful conclusion of the War of the Ring finally brought peace to their wide lands.

Note: at all events, one notable branch of the race of Rhovanion survived to play an important part in the history of the Age. For the valiant people known as the Éothéod 'claimed descent from kings of Rhovanion',[2] and the Éothéod rode to even greater glory in the last third of the Age, when they were known as the Riders of Rohan.

See also LINES OF DESCENT.

Rhudaur The name given by the Dúnedain of the North-kingdom to the easternmost of the three separate states formed by the partition of Arnor in 861 Third Age, following the death of King Eärendur. Its boundaries were the Misty Mountains, the Weather Hills and the Ettenmoors. Rhudaur was the most junior of the three Dúnedain realms (of which the other two were named Arthedain and Cardolan), and its lands were the wildest and least fertile; moreover, none of the three *palantíri* of Arnor had come into its possession. For these reasons Rhudaur's relations with the other two North-kingdoms were unfriendly from the first, and there was frequently strife between Rhudaur and Cardolan over possession of the strategically important Weather Hills and the chief Palantír of the North (which was kept in the tower of Amon Sûl, on the border of both realms).

By the thirteenth century the rivalry was intense, although the borders of the states still remained relatively unchanged. It was at this time that the evil Witch-realm of Angmar arose in the north-east, sharing a common frontier with Rhudaur; and from that moment the fate of the smaller state was doomed. In any case, the control of Rhudaur had already been seized from the remaining Dúnedain by a clan of renegades and wild men, and before many years these usurpers were themselves under the control of the Witch-king. Beginning with the battle in which King Argeleb I was slain (in 1356), there then ensued a centuries-long war waged by combined forces from Rhudaur and Angmar against Arthedain – with Cardolan falling a quick victim to the savagery of the onslaught. In the year 1409 'Rhudaur was occupied by evil Men subject to Angmar, and the Dúnedain that remained there were slain or fled west.'³ It never arose again, although the formal dissolution of the state was not held to have taken place until 1974 Third Age, the year of Arthedain's fall.

Rhûn 'East' (Sind.) A general name in Gondor for the lands beyond and including the Inland Sea.

Rhymes of Lore The name given by the Wise to the numberless collection of spells, benisons, charms, incantations and memory-aids recited and learned in order both to pass on knowledge and retain it.

Rían A princess of the Edain, the daughter of Belegund of the First House. She was born in Ladros before the Dagor Bragollach, but when Orcs overran Dorthonion, she and the other children were evacuated from the stricken land, and sent for safekeeping to Dor-lómin, where the House of Hador still defied the Enemy. There she came to womanhood, and wedded Huor the younger son of Galdor (her cousin Morwen Eledhwen, likewise a refugee from Dorthonion, was wedded to Huor's elder brother Húrin). Two months later came the Fifth Battle of Beleriand, the Nirnaeth Arnoediad, in which Huor was slain. Rían, already pregnant by Huor, fled from Dor-lómin into Mithrim, where she bore a son, Tuor, while in hiding among the Sindar of that land. Soon afterwards she gave Tuor into the keeping of her hosts, and went out into the wild, to die of grief on the mound called Haudh-en-Ndengin, the Hill of Slain, where her husband lay, together with all his kinsmen save one.

Riddermark (Older form *Riddena-mearc* 'Land of the knights') The name given by the Riders of ROHAN to their own land.

Riddle-game A time-honoured method of wagering for stakes, for testing another's sagacity and wit, or simply for passing the time. The practice was very ancient in Middle-earth, dating almost certainly back to the Elder Days, and all folk claimed the honour of having originated it. By reason of its ancientry alone the Riddle-game must surely be of Elvish origin: the Elves dearly loved tricks of word and meaning, and The Rules which informally governed the practice, being 'both ancient and just', bore all the hallmarks of early Eldarin thought.

Riders of Rohan The term used in Gondor for the armed and mounted men-at-arms of the country of Rohan, formerly the Dúnedain province of Calenardhon, which lay to the north of Gondor on the further side of the White Mountains. The Rohirrim were a Northern race, whose arrival in the southlands had proved fortunate for Gondor on one conspicuous occasion, and the 'Riders of Rohan' were spoken of with admiration and a good deal of respect: for the horses of Rohan were the finest then to be found in Middle-earth, and their riders were fully their match.

The mounted cavalry of Rohan were not a permanent standing force; rather they were horse-herders and -trainers, who wandered with the herds and studs throughout most of the year over the great grasslands of the Mark (as they termed their own land). Only in time of war or doubt were they mustered, for to assemble a host of Riders took many days. Nonetheless, they were fierce in war, for they were of proud northern stock and had learned the warrior code long before.

The basic military unit was the *éored*, a squadron of varying size raised from one particular lord or marshal's household and sworn to his service. The Mark itself was loosely divided into a number of regions, each of which had a Marshal nominally responsible for its defence. All were responsible to the King, who dwelt for the most part in the township of Edoras, a hill-fort on a foothill of the northern White Mountains.

The armour and weapons used by the Riders of Rohan were in essence those used by their ancestors in the North: long spears, bows, and long-swords. Most carried body-shields, painted on the toughened side to display a White Horse upon a field of Green.[4] Chain mail was not infrequent, and light metal helms were also worn. In war the Riders generally made good use of their superb horse-manship and the shock value of a massed cavalry attack; in other words, they had developed both light and heavy cavalry tactics to a remarkable degree. There were few formed infantry in western

Middle-earth who could withstand them unless safe behind defences or stone walls.

For these reasons the Riders of Rohan were greatly valued as allies by the men of Gondor, who had far fewer cavalry although their infantry was second to none. The Rohirrim indeed aided the Dúnedain (and were aided by them) on several different occasions, perhaps the most significant of which was during the War of the Ring, when the six thousand Riders led by Théoden King of the Mark lifted the siege of Minas Tirith and so set in motion the Battle of the Pelennor Fields, greatest military clash of the Third Age.

Rimmon See MIN-RIMMON.

Ringarë (Q.) The twelfth month of the year in Kings' and Stewards' Reckoning, and the ninth of the New Reckoning which followed the reuniting of Arnor and Gondor at the end of the Third Age. All three reckoning-systems were modifications of the old Númenorean calendar, and all were adopted by many Westron-speaking peoples of Middle-earth. The Sindarin equivalent of *Ringarë*, *Girithron*, was used only by the Dúnedain of Middle-earth.

Ringil 'Cold-star' (Sind.) The Sword of Fingolfin, the High King of the Noldor. It was the only weapon ever to inflict a wound upon Morgoth (see *Silmarillion* pp. 153–4).

Ring-inscription The series of Elvish letters engraved by some secret process into the surfaces of the Ruling Ring by its forger, Sauron the Great. The inscription was so fashioned that the writing remained invisible unless the Ring itself was first heated; when Sauron made this Ring, he was fair of bodily form, or so it has been recorded, and the inscription remained unseen, even by his close servants; but in later years Sauron's body grew black and hideous and burning hot, and the heat of his hand alone was sufficient to keep the inscription bright.

It is a curious fact that, although the Ring-inscription was in the ancient Black Speech of Mordor, the letters chosen for the writing were Elvish – the Fëanorian Tengwar. Some have held this to be proof of Sauron's own ancestry (see SAURON THE GREAT); others maintain that no other writing-system was sufficiently delicate for the minute engraving. The true reasons will never now be known.

The text of the Inscription, rendered from its Elvish writing-mode, is as follows:

Ash nazg durbatulûk, ash nazg gimbatul,
Ash nazg thrakatulûk agh burzum-ishi krampatul[5]

Translated into the Common Speech, this means:

One Ring to rule them all, One Ring to find them,
One Ring to bring them all and in the darkness bind them.

This, as will be recalled, was the final and operative part of the complete Ring-spell. Sauron spoke these words on the instant of his completion of the Ruling Ring itself. In setting the Ring on his finger and repeating the incantation, he activated the Spell and from that day forward his power waxed in Middle-earth, and he remained immortal until such a time as the Ring itself might be destroyed.

See also RULING RING.

Ringló 'Cold-flood' (Sind.) A river of Gondor, the major tributary of Morthond. It arose in the high vales of Lamedon, and was itself joined by the Ciril (or Kiril) some leagues south of the town of Calembel. The Ringló Vale was the valley watered by these two rivers.

Ring of Adamant NENYA.

Ring of Barahir The most ancient of the heirlooms of the House of Elendil. It was in origin an Elven-ring given as a token of friendship by Finrod Felagund, King of Nargothrond, to Barahir of the Edain, after the Dagor Bragollach, in which Barahir had saved Finrod's life. The ring itself was of gold, and bore the badge of the House of Finarfin.[6] Barahir bore it until his death on Dorthonion, and it was recovered from the Orc who had stolen it by Barahir's son Beren. The Ring remained in Beren's keeping for the rest of his life, and was passed to his son Dior Eluchíl, and by Dior to Elwing, who rescued it – together with the Silmaril and other treasures of the house of Thingol – from the ruin of Doriath, and took it with her to the Havens of Sirion. From her it passed to Eärendil her son, and from Eärendil to his son Elros.

In this way Barahir's ring survived the turmoils of the First Age. It was (presumably) given by Tar-Elendil, fourth King, to his eldest child Silmariën, and by Silmariën to her son Valandil, first of the Lords of Andúnië. In this way the Ring of Barahir became an heirloom of the Faithful, and so was brought to Middle-earth again when Númenor fell, late in the Second Age. It was then given by Elendil to his oldest son Isildur, and so became a token of the royalty of the North-kingdom.

For many years the Ring of Barahir was guarded at Annúminas, together with the other treasures of the North-kingdom, but in time the realm of Arnor passed, and then the Heirs of Isildur removed to Fornost Erain. Their kingdom of Arthedain survived until the end of the second millennium, but fell at last under the assaults of Angmar. Then Arvedui, last King of Arthedain, fled into the North to escape the wreck of Arthedain, bearing several of the treasures of Isildur with him. The two *palantíri* of the North were lost with Arvedui in the waters of the Ice Bay, but the ring was saved, for it had been given by the King to the Lossoth (Snowmen) of Forochel, as a reward for the aid they had rendered him during his months of exile. It was later ransomed by the Dúnedain and afterwards kept at Rivendell, together with the Sceptre and the Sword of Elendil, by Elrond.

Ring of Isengard See ISENGARD.

Ring of Doom The MÁHANAXAR.

Ring of Sapphire VILYA.

Rings of Power The greatest feat of craftsmanship performed during the Second Age was the making of the Rings of Power: the Three Rings of the Elves, the Seven Dwarf-rings, and the Nine Rings of Mortal Men 'doomed to die'. The greatest of all the Rings of Power was that One Ring wrought by Sauron of Mordor.

The tale of their making is a strange story of thirst for knowledge, combined with a pride in craftsmanship, being turned (albeit unconsciously) to evil purposes: an odd reflection of the tale of the Silmarils. The Elven-smiths of Eregion, the makers of most of the Great Rings, were themselves descended from Fëanor, who had wrought the Silmarils during the Elder Days. They were assisted in the task by Sauron of Mordor, who thus acquired great knowledge while pretending to dispense it. Together they made the Nine, and the Seven, and the lesser Rings of Power.

A mortal would have called these 'magic' rings, for like other Elvish devices their virtues were not merely those of adornment. Each ring had certain properties which were passed on to the bearer, like the gifts of foresight, protective power, and so on. But the Great Rings, the Nine and the Seven, had other qualities: they gave long life and many different powers of mind and hand. But Sauron's hand was also on their making (with the exception of the chief Dwarf-ring), and so these inherent powers were distorted far beyond what the Elven-smiths had intended; and they would all prove susceptible to the One Ring which Sauron planned to make.

But before he was to do so Celebrimbor, chief of the Elven-smiths, wrought the Three Rings of the Elven-kings, greater than all other Rings of Power, and Sauron had no part in their making. Celebrimbor did not desire power for Elves, merely the ability to make, heal and preserve; and Sauron never touched the Three, nor did he ever set eyes upon them. Celebrimbor completed the forging of the Three Elven-rings in or around 1590 Second Age, but Sauron had already learned all he needed for his own purposes; and ten years afterwards, far away in Mordor, in the Chambers of Fire within the cone of the volcano Orodruin, he set the newly forged Ruling Ring on his finger and repeated the Ring-spell which would bring his creation to life. On the same instant Celebrimbor became aware of the betrayal and swiftly hid the Three. But although these were saved, the Seven and the Nine were captured and distributed by Sauron.

The nature of the Ruling Ring was such that by its power Sauron was able to dominate and command the bearers of the Nine. With the Seven he was not so fortunate, for the Dwarves were 'made from their beginning of a kind to resist most steadfastly any domination ... and for the same reason their lives were not affected by any Ring, to live either longer or shorter because of it.'[7] Nevertheless, the potential beneficial effects of the Seven were lost to them and indeed their ultimate fall can be said to be due in part to the quality the Rings possessed of inflaming Dwarf-hearts with love of gold and wealth for its own sake – a trait towards which they were always only too partial.

The Three were never affected at all by the Ruling Ring, because their owners never wore them so long as Sauron retained the One. When it was taken from him at the end of the Second Age this restriction on the Elven-rings was lifted and their bearers were able to use them during most of the Third Age for the purposes originally intended by Celebrimbor. But when the Ruling Ring was found once more they fell again into great peril, for had Sauron recaptured his lost treasure, all that had been wrought by the Three during an Age would have been laid bare to him, and the minds of those that bore them – whether the Three were hidden or not – would have been revealed to his malice.

At the beginning of the War of the Ring Sauron thus controlled the Nine, and three of the Seven Rings of Power (four had been consumed – together with their hapless owners – by the Dragons). The Three he could ignore – for he needed only the One to make his already certain victory over the Free Peoples complete. How, despite his best endeavours, this Ring was denied him and destroyed in the teeth of his armed might, forms the substance of the Tale of the Ring, as recorded in the Red Book.

Note: it has been recorded that the Three Rings were named Vilya, Nenya and Narya. The names of the Nine and the Seven – if indeed they bore any – are not known. The Great Ring of Sauron also had no name, and was called simply the One Ring or the Ruling Ring.

See also RING-INSCRIPTION; RULING RING.

Ringwil 'Chilly-stream' (Sind.) A small stream which arose in the Heights of Faroth and fell into the Narog not far from the gates of Nargothrond.

Ringwraiths A translation of the name *Nazgûl*, a word meaning 'Ring-wraith' in the Black Speech of Mordor; being a name often used by enemies of Sauron for the slaves of the Nine Rings, Sauron's most terrible servants, the nine Mortal Men who were ensnared by lust for power during the Second Age and who were forced to linger in Middle-earth as undead creatures, totally subservient to their Master, unable to pass on or find rest.[8] They were filled with the evil essence of their Master, and thus implemented his will from afar and in his name during much of the Second and all of the Third Age of Middle-earth, falling at last when the destruction of the Ruling Ring released them from this fearsome bondage.

Yet it was always a measure of Sauron's true nature and of the rewards to be gained in his service that the most evil destinies invariably overtook those who served him most faithfully. The Nine Lords had once been proud rulers of great tracts of Middle-earth; and they had fallen into evil practices and deeds even before they began to worship Sauron, or he to plan their downfall. In the sixteenth century of the Second Age they individually accepted from him Rings of Power, made, so Sauron said, to give them power over all other Men and to give long life; and by this means he trapped them, for the Nine Rings of Power were so designed as to ensnare their wearers. The promised immortality of the Rings was revealed as a deadly and everlasting lengthening of days, so that life grew wearisome beyond belief yet the consolation of death was denied. Power they gained – the power of terror alone, for unable to relinquish their Rings, the Nine Lords became in the end wraiths, deathless spirits with no physical substance and no will to oppose he who wore the One Ring. It was a fearful doom, and it was to endure for over four thousand years.

The first recorded appearance of the Nazgûl in Middle-earth was in the year 2251 Second Age, although in what connection is not now remembered. They served Sauron faithfully for the remainder of the Age, becoming even then his most feared followers, and when he was temporarily overthrown at the end of the Age they went 'into the shadows' to await his return. When again he began to materialize – in the thousandth year of the Third Age – they also took shape again; and for many years, while he slowly grew to power once more, they made strokes on his behalf against the Free Peoples, sundered as these were and thus easy prey for the Nine.

Their Chief was known as the WITCH-KING (see also MORGUL). In the early fourteenth century he appeared in the barren lands north of the Ettenmoors and there founded a realm called *Angmar* ('Iron-home'). It lay in close proximity to the Dúnedain states of Arthedain and Rhudaur. And it grew so swiftly to power under the rule of its Sorcerer King that the Dúnedain themselves were unable to prevent its further expansion. But the Witch-king bided his time, using the days thus bought to bring about the fall of Rhudaur, his closest neighbour, by means of subversion; and when this was completed to his satisfaction he launched a great attack through the lands of Rhudaur, not at Arthedain, his more powerful foe, but at Cardolan, the weaker. And although Cardolan made desperate alliance against him with Arthedain, he captured the strategic tower of Amon Sûl and ravaged her lands far and wide. Thus Arthedain was isolated. And although she fought on for another six hundred years of intermittent war, in the end the Witch-king achieved his aim and Arthedain followed Cardolan and Rhudaur down into the dark.

But in 1975 Third Age Angmar was itself overthrown by a league of Elves and Men, such as had broken the power of Sauron two thousand years before, and the Witch-king was expelled from Eriador. South he came, to Mordor, and there assembled the Nine. And in 2000 he crossed the Pass of Cirith Ungol on the borders of Gondor and laid siege to Minas Ithil, one of the fairest cities of the South-kingdom. Two years later it fell to the Ringwraiths and their army, and was never again recaptured by the Dúnedain. Not content, the Witch-king later contrived to rob the Men of Gondor of the last King of the Line of Anárion (see EÄRNUR); and so he lessened their royalty and sowed the seeds of their downfall.

Yet having achieved so much on behalf of their Master, the Ringwraiths then fell quiescent while he began to plot and manoeuvre on his own behalf. Meanwhile the Nine Riders began to prepare Mordor against the day when he would return in power, and in 2941, after a millennium filled with defeats and temporary victories for the

Dúnedain, Sauron abandoned his lesser fortress of Dol Guldur and passed south to Mordor. Three of the Nazgûl he despatched to his older dwelling, while he himself set in motion the opening moves of the War of the Ring.

In this War the Ringwraiths, chief servants of Sauron, played a prominent part. As is told in the Red Book, all Nine were sent into Eriador in 3018, disguised as riders in black, to seek the Ring and to take it from the Hobbits who then possessed it. In this vital task they failed. Foiled in Eriador, they returned to Mordor and to Minas Morgul (Minas Ithil renamed) and they took to the air, mounted on evil flying beasts, and searched the lands for the fugitives, or carried their Master's messages across leagues of Middle-earth swifter than any bird could fly. Mounted on these beasts a number of them – probably four – accompanied the Host of Morgul in the attempt upon Minas Tirith in 3019; and when their leader was slain in that affray they retreated into the gloom-shrouded upper airs, shadowing the march east of the last Host of Gondor. But they took no part in the battle which followed, for upon the instant the armies clashed at the Black Gate, the eight remaining Ringwraiths were summoned with fierce urgency by their Master to fly south to Orodruin, where his Realm was in the greatest peril it had ever known. Once more they failed to arrive in time, and in the appalling eruption of the volcano which followed the melting of the Ring they were destroyed for ever, and so passed away at last.

Rivendell A translation of the Sindarin name *Imladris*, being the name of the dwelling of Master Elrond Half-elven in eastern Eriador, in the foothills of the Misty Mountains between the rivers Mitheithel (Hoarwell) and Bruinen (Loudwater). It was founded by Elrond and the Noldor in 1697 Second Age, following a perilous retreat from overrun Eregion during the War of the Elves and Sauron. Elrond dwelt there ever after (save a brief period at the end of the Second Age and a shorter one still at the end of the Third), maintaining the 'Last Homely House East of the Sea' as a refuge for all Elves and folk of goodwill. Most of the remaining Noldor dwelt there.

The House of Elrond lay beside a hurrying stream amid the pine-scented air of that deep vale (*Imladris* literally means 'Deep-cloven-valley'). House and Valley were guarded on two sides by the Bruinen's chief tributary and by the Bruinen itself. The Ford was under Elrond's power but 'the might of Elrond lay in wisdom not in weapons',[9] and the Power that dwelled in Rivendell desired only strength enough to defend itself.

See also KARNINGUL.

River Running The CELDUIN.

River-woman A poetic term for the river Withywindle, used by Tom Bombadil. See GOLDBERRY.

Rivil The most northerly of the many tributaries of the Sirion. It rose at Rivil's Well on the plateau of Dorthonion, and fell over the western edge of the highland into the Fen of Serech, at the southern end of which was its confluence with the Sirion.

Rivil's Well See preceding entry.

Roäc The Chief of the Ravens of Erebor, and the son of old Carc. The Ravens of the Lonely Mountain were traditionally friendly to Dwarves, and Roäc continued the alliance by rendering great aid to Thorin Oakenshield when the members of his expedition were besieged in Erebor by their foes (2941 Third Age).

Robin Gamgee The twelfth child and sixth son of Samwise Gamgee.

Robin Smallburrow A Hobbiton villager. Early in his life he was persuaded to join that fine body of official Hobbitry, the Shirriffs; but with the 'reorganization' of the Watch which followed Saruman's seizure of the Shire in 3019 Third Age (1419 Shire Reckoning), young Smallburrow found himself posted to Frogmorton, as part of the First Eastfarthing Troop.

Rochallor The steed of Fingolfin, High King of the Noldor. He rode this noble horse throughout the wars, and to single combat with Morgoth before the Gates of Angband during the Dagor Bragollach; but Rochallor's fate is not recorded.

Rodyn See VALANYA.

Rohan 'Land-of-Horses' (Sind. from Q. *Rochand*[e]) The wide and spacious realm which lay north of Gondor, upon the further side of the White Mountains. It was famed for its horses, which were unmatched for lineage, grace or beauty anywhere in Middle-earth, and for its leagues of grassland, rich and abundant, where the horses of Rohan ran free in great herds, watched over by their proud masters.

These were a people of Men, known in Gondor as the *Rohirrim*, 'Masters-of-Horses', traditionally friendly to the Dúnedain, and much respected in Gondor for their loyalty, bravery and nobility of soul.

The land of Rohan had indeed once been but a northern province of Gondor, called Calenardhon 'the Green Region'. Its borders were the Gap and the Fords of Isen (in the west), the river Limlight (in the north), the Mouths of Entwash (in the east) and the White Mountains (in the south). But the province became depopulated during the long wars of the Third Age, and by the twenty-sixth century few folk dwelt there. In 2510 Calenardhon was threatened from the east by a host of Balchoth and Orcs which crossed the Anduin north of the Limlight, and the Army of Gondor sent to contain the invasion was defeated and forced to retreat into an untenable position. But at the eleventh hour the Northmen of Éothéod, allies of the Dúnedain, arrived after a great ride down all the leagues of Wilderland and scattered the invaders with a great cavalry charge; for these Northmen were well mounted, and equipped as heavy cavalry, and their onslaught was too great for any Orcs or Easterlings to withstand. In gratitude for the Riders' heroism, the Ruling Steward of Gondor ceded Calenardhon which they had saved to the Riders; they named their realm the *Riddermark*, 'Land-of-the-knights' in their own Northern tongue. In Gondor it was called *Rohan*.

It was a fair and generous country, fertile and level for the most part, and ideal for the rearing and breeding of horses because of its grassland. The Riders were famed for their skill with their great steeds, and their herds and studs prospered in the years which followed the victory at the Field of Celebrant. The Rohirrim dwelt mainly in the West-emnet (the East-emnet was low-lying and marshy) and lived scattered in small settlements out upon the great wold, following the herds as they moved from pasture to pasture. Their chief town and capital was *Edoras* ('The Courts'), built in the days of their second King upon a green hill at the feet of the northern range of the White Mountains. There the Kings of the Mark dwelt, save in wartime, when the royal household moved to Dunharrow, an ancient fortress-plateau in the Mountains. The chief stronghold in the west of the land was the Hornburg.

Yet it was not a country easily defended against attack, not even by the valour of the Riders. The alliance with Gondor indeed benefited both realms alike, and on many occasions aid rendered by one to the other preserved both; for both countries shared the same enemies: Orcs, Easterlings, sea-pirates from the South, Wild Men of the hills and, of course, Sauron of Mordor. All of these at times invaded Rohan during the later years of the Third Age, and on a few occasions Rohan was gravely threatened. But its lack of centralization and its scattered people made the land difficult to occupy or subdue, and it is clear that Sauron himself judged Gondor the easier target. But during the War of the Ring the peril lay in the West, from the Wizard Saruman, and not in the East, where Sauron at first contented himself with physically severing the five-hundred-year alliance between the peoples; but Saruman was overcome and Sauron's armies were outflanked and the Riders of Rohan arrived in time to prevent the fall of Minas Tirith and the inevitable later destruction of their own land and its works.

In the Fourth Age which followed the Passing of Sauron the fair land of Rohan prospered and healed the ravages of war, and new links were forged between its people and the Dúnedain; for each realm, more than ever, valued the old alliance; and the peoples grew closer than ever before. The horses ran free once more over the plains, even as the White Horse upon Green floated in the wind above the hill of Edoras.

Roheryn 'Horse-of-the-Lady' (Sind.) The horse of Aragorn II, Chieftain of the Dúnedain of the North, brought to him in Rohan during the War of the Ring by his kinsmen. He had been given to Aragorn by Arwen Evenstar. See also HASUFEL.

Rohirrim 'Masters-of-Horses' (Sind.) The Riders of Rohan.

Rómen The Quenya or High-elven word for 'East', but more properly the title of Tengwa number 25, which was used for the sound of full (trilled) *r*. It was also used, as a symbol, to indicate the direction East, even among peoples who did not use the full Fëanorian Alphabet.

Rómendacil I From 492–541 Third Age, the eighth King of Gondor. His birth-name was Tarostar. He was the son of Ostoher, who rebuilt the city of Minas Anor, and during whose reign the South-kingdom was first attacked by Easterlings. Tarostar captained the armies which defeated the Easterlings (and which incidentally gained Gondor much territory beyond the Anduin), and as a result of his victories took the royal name *Rómendacil* ('East-victor') when he succeeded his father as King of Gondor. After a reign of 49 years he was slain in battle with an Easterling people, and was succeeded by his own son Turambar.

Rómendacil II From 1304–66 Third Age, the nineteenth King of Gondor; he was one of the greatest men in her long history. Born Minalcar, he was son to Calmacil who was brother of Narmacil, the seventeenth King. Both his uncle and father were effete men, weak aesthetes who were seemingly content to delegate (or abdicate) the onerous burdens of Kingship. When Narmacil died he was succeeded by Calmacil, and Minalcar served as Regent to both (from 1240–1304) before attaining the Silver Crown in his own right after the death of his father.

His first challenge came eight years after he assumed the Regency. Observing that fresh hordes of Easterlings were preparing to assault Gondor, he made alliance with Northmen of Rhovanion, and defeated the enemies in a great battle east of that land. He then took the name *Rómendacil* ('East-victor'). Learning that his alliance had not been as stable as he might have wished, he took it upon himself to improve relations between the Northmen and the Dúnedain, and to this end invited many of his allies to come and dwell in Gondor. This move caused a certain amount of unrest among the Dúnedain. At the same time the energetic Regent fortified the west shore of Anduin as far north as the Emyn Muil, and built the Argonath (the Pillars of the Kings) at the entrance to Nen Hithoel as a sign of Gondor's northernmost border.

Shortly afterwards, Rómendacil sent his son Valacar to Rhovanion, to dwell with the mightiest of their princes; for he had foreseen that Gondor needed to strengthen still further the alliance with the Northmen; he could hardly have foreseen that his son would marry a woman of that race. At all events, he came to the Kingship in his own right after the death of Calmacil and ruled for a further 62 years, leaving a realm with robustly fortified frontiers and a fatal seed buried in its heart.

See also KIN-STRIFE.

Rómenna 'East-home' (Q.) The chief eastern harbour of Númenor. In the days of the twenty-second King, Ar-Gimilzôr, this city and province was swelled by an influx of political exiles: the Faithful, uprooted by edict from their old homes in Andúnië and sent to the east of the land. (The most illustrious of these was Amandil, last Lord of Andúnië and kinsman of the king.) From the harbour of Rómenna the fleet of nine ships set sail on the day of the Downfall, to survive the wild waters and so come back to Middle-earth in exile. The quayside of Rómenna was therefore the last earth of Númenor trodden by any of the Dúnedain aboard those ships.

Roper A family of Shire-hobbits, descended, like the Gamgees, from old Wiseman Gamwich, who removed from the village of the same name to Tighfield in the Northfarthing, in the century preceding the War of the Ring. Wiseman's son Hob ('Old Gammidgy') adopted the trade of rope-weaving; and this craft had become well enough established a generation later for Hob's son Hobson to be nicknamed Roper Gamgee. The Tighfield Gammidges (now calling themselves Ropers) prospered in following years, with Hobson's son Andwise ('Andy') continuing the family trade.

It was doubtless on a visit to the Northfarthing that Samwise Gamgee, nephew of Andwise, learned all he knew of the craft; he was certainly deeply interested in it, though not enough to abandon either his own father or his father's trade (of gardening). These rope-making skills, acquired in Tighfield, came in handy on several occasions during the Quest – and so the Ropers of Tighfield may be said to have played their own small part in the successful conclusion of the War of the Ring.

Roper Gamgee See previous entry.

Rorimac 'Goldfather' Brandybuck From 2963–3008 Third Age (1363–1408 Shire Reckoning), the Master of Buckland. He was renowned for his wealth, as well as for his love of good food and wine. His grandson was Meriadoc Brandybuck.

Rose Gamgee The eldest daughter of Farmer Tolman ('Tom') Cotton of Bywater, and the wife of Samwise Gamgee, Hero of the Shire. She wedded Sam in 1420 Shire Reckoning and bore him thirteen children in the years that followed, of whom the eldest was Elanor the Fair. She died after a long and happy life in 1482 Shire Reckoning; a few weeks afterwards Samwise left the Shire and passed West over Sea.

Rothinzil 'Foam-flower' (Adûn.) See VINGILOT.

Rowlie Appledor A Man of Bree, murdered in a skirmish between Bree-dwellers and outlaws during the early part of 3019 Third Age.

Ruby Gamgee The eleventh child and sixth daughter of Samwise and Rose Gamgee.

Ruling Ring The Great Ring of Sauron the Great, Lord of Mordor; it mastered all the other Rings of Power. From the middle years of the Second Age, when it was made, until the end of the Third, when it was at last destroyed, it was the single greatest peril in a world full of dangers; and when it was consumed in the Fires of Doom its passing brought about the fading of the power of all other Rings. Apart from the Silmarils of the First Age, it was the most potent artifact ever wrought. Its maker was Sauron himself.

By strange chance most of the Ruling Ring's history is known – at least, its history after it was taken by force from Sauron's own hand at the end of the Second Age by Isildur son of Elendil. Isildur intended the Great Ring of the Enemy (which had burned him fiercely when he first seized it) to become an Heirloom of the North-kingdom of Arnor, but he himself lost it when ambushed at the Gladden Fields in Year 2 Third Age. In his hour of need the Ring abandoned him and it afterwards lay on a river-bed for over two thousand years, quiescent, while, in the world above, its Master slowly awakened to strength once more.

By the twenty-fifth century of the Third Age the Ring was no longer inert – stirred up, maybe, by the strengthening emanations from Dol Guldur – and it revealed itself to a simple riverside fisher, a creature of Hobbit-kind called Déagol. He was almost instantly dispossessed of it by a murderous crony, Sméagol (Gollum), who retreated with the precious object to a forlorn sanctuary deep in the bowels of the Misty Mountains. There he (and it) remained until the thirtieth century of the Age, for by that time it had become apparent that the Purpose was no longer being served by the degenerate creature. It then ensnared a passing traveller, another Hobbit of different race called Bilbo Baggins, who luckily took little harm from the encounter and returned with the Ring to the Shire of his home, unaware that what he bore in his pocket was the Peril of the world.

Bilbo continued to possess the Ring – although he seldom found use for its more obvious properties – for many years in the Shire; indeed his life was greatly lengthened by it. In 3001 he departed his homeland and (with some effort, for the Ring was beginning to wear him down) left the prized object to his nephew and ward Frodo Baggins, together with the rest of his estate. Frodo, already aware that all was not as it should be with this mysterious and wonderful ring, continued to guard it nonetheless until the year 3018, when for the first time the real history of his Heirloom was revealed to him.

Little more need be said of the Ring. It was borne into Mordor by Frodo and his companion Samwise, and there it was cast into the fires of the volcano Orodruin, where alone in Middle-earth it could be destroyed. With its passing its ancient hold over the other surviving Rings of Power was loosed, and the bond of their being was snapped. They faded, and with them all that had been wrought with them during an Age or more. This was the lasting achievement of the Great Ring, the One Ring, the Ruling Ring of Sauron the Great, Enemy of all Free Peoples.

See also RINGS OF POWER.

Ruling Stewards The name given in the lore of Gondor to the family of the House of Húrin, hereditary Stewards of Gondor and Counsellors to the Kings, who themselves ruled the South-kingdom from 2050–3019 Third Age after the failing of the Line of Anárion and before the restoration of the Line of Elendil (by Aragorn II). The first Steward to rule was Mardil Voronwë, son of Vorondil (the Hunter), who took office after the death of King Eärnur to prevent a clash among the Dúnedain over the succession.

Although none of the Ruling Stewards at any time claimed the Throne for the House of Húrin, after many years their formal Oath of Office – in which they swore to rule 'until the King shall return' – ceased to carry other than a symbolic meaning, and they acted as Kings in all but name. Their dynastic banner – a plain standard of silver with no device or distinguishing emblem – flew from the White Tower where once the White Tree of Elendil had fluttered, and the Stewardship passed from father to eldest son in the manner of kingly houses. The Heir of the Ruling Steward was habitually accorded the rank of Captain of the Host of Gondor, and as a token of his rank to come bore the chief heirloom of the House: a wild ox-horn worked with silver.

The Ruling Stewards of Gondor were: Mardil, Eradan, Herion, Belegorn, Húrin I, Túrin I, Hador, Barahir, Dior, Denethor I, Boromir, Cirion (the longest to rule), Hallas, Húrin II, Belecthor I, Orodreth, Ecthelion I, Egalmoth, Beren, Beregond, Belecthor II, Thorondir, Túrin II, Turgon, Ecthelion II and Denethor II, the twenty-sixth and last. After the passing of Denethor the rule of Gondor reverted to the King, although the Stewards continued to serve in their old capacity of hereditary counsellors and nobles of the Realm.

See also HOUSE OF HÚRIN; STEWARDS; Appendix A I(ii) and (iv).

Rúmil of Tirion One of the Noldor of Eldamar, a precursor of Fëanor. He was the first great Elven-poet, and is credited with the composition of the *Ainulindalë*. But Rúmil is perhaps better remembered as the sage who devised the earliest known system of writing, the *Tengwar* ('Letters'), which were later re-ordered and

-arranged by Fëanor, and so came to be more closely associated with him than with their original inventor.

Runes A translation of the Quenya word *Certar* (or of the Sindarin *Cirth*), referring in general to any incised forms of inscriptive writing, but in particular to the various alphabets developed by the Grey-elves (and later by other folk) during the First and Second Ages. The Eldarin runic system devised in Beleriand during the Elder Days was known as the ALPHABET OF DAERON or the *Certhas Daeron*, and was older by far than all the others, although less ancient than the cursive writing system originated in the High-elven *Tengwar* ('letters').

Note: a full and very clear description of the Elven runic system (as redeveloped by Dwarves of Moria and Erebor) exists in Appendix E II, which also contains something of the history of the runic alphabet as well as a detailed table indicating the various phonetic values of the individual *certhas*.

Notes
1 Appendix A III.
2 Appendix A II.
3 Appendix A I(iii).
4 The shield of the King, however, was of pure gold (for the Golden Hall).
5 Book II Chap. 2.
6 Described in *The Silmarillion* (p. 167).
7 Appendix A III.
8 Called also *Úlairi*, a hypothetical translation of which is 'undead'.
9 Book II Chap. 2.

Sackville-Baggins A family of Shire-hobbits which lasted for only two generations. See also LOBELIA SACKVILLE-BAGGINS.

Saeros One of the Elves of Doriath; but not of the Sindar, for he was one of those few Nandor, formerly of Ossiriand, who dwelt with Thingol in Menegroth. In Doriath he became mighty, and was accounted one of the king's closest advisers. Yet for all his supposed wisdom, Saeros was so foolish as to pass insulting remarks to Túrin of the Edain; and for this Túrin struck him. The following day Saeros attempted to take his revenge, by ambushing Túrin as he passed through Neldoreth on his way back to Dimbar (where he was fighting against the Orcs in company with the Elves and the Men of Brethil). Túrin, however, escaped this treacherous attack, and he pursued Saeros through the forest – and in his flight the Elf missed his footing and fell to his death in a deep ravine. Fearing condemnation, Túrin fled from Doriath, never to return – and so began his dreadful odyssey.

Sakalthôr (**Ar-Sakalthôr**) The twenty-first King of Númenor, and one of the (later) rulers who took a royal name in the Adûnaic tongue (as opposed to the Eldarin nomenclature of the earlier Kings of Westernesse).

Salmar One of the Maiar. He was of the service and following of the Vala Ulmo, and wrought the horns of the Sea-lord, the ULUMÚRI.

Sam Gamgee See SAMWISE GAMGEE.

Sammath Naur 'Chambers of Fire' (Sind.) The great dolven forges in the side of the volcano Orodruin in the land of Mordor. They were constructed by Sauron the Great early in the Second Age, and afforded him access to the volcanic inner fires of the mountain. At their heart lay the Cracks of Doom.

Samwise Gamgee There are few examples of loyalty, devotion and faithfulness recorded in the annals of the Third Age to equal those displayed by the illustrious Hobbit Samwise Gamgee, servant and steadfast companion of Frodo Baggins and honourable member of the Fellowship of the Ring. Throughout the many trials and hardships endured without complaint at his master's side, his purpose never faltered – to remain with Frodo wherever he might go, even to Mordor. And in the end he was rewarded richly: with honour, and many descendants, and a long life; and with a journey across the Sea at the end of it.

And yet Samwise – who later became Mayor of the Shire no less than seven times, and whose name was recorded in rolls of honour in Gondor and other lands – was born the youngest of three sons to a staunchly working-class family; and hist rade was the humble craft of horticulture, or gardening. In fact, the Gamgees of Hobbiton were renowned for conservatism and a lack of aspirations, yet these faults, if faults they were, sprang from respectfulness and a love for their gentle craft; and if they were less progressive and ambitious than other Hobbits, then all agreed they were worthy citizens (and the potatoes grown by Sam's father were locally much admired).

Sam's father Hamfast (known as 'the Gaffer') was the Gardener to the Bagginses of Bag End, the local squirearchy and the wealthiest Hobbits of the district. Yet neither of the Gaffer's two eldest sons chose to follow him in this trade, and it was his youngest, Samwise, born in 1380 Shire Reckoning, who remained with his ageing father and practised the craft of horticulture as Hamfast had taught him. In due course of time he succeeded the Gaffer in the position, though he continued to live with his father in Number 3 Bagshot Row (in close proximity to the extensive gardens for which he then bore the whole responsibility). He spent each working day weeding, clipping, digging, planting, seeding, cutting and anxiously tending the fruits, vegetables and flowers which grew in such profusion there.

Like other Hobbits of his own age, Sam spent many recreational hours in the local taverns (particularly *The Green Dragon*), being partial to a drop of well-brewed ale; and his companions at these establishments agreed that Sam was a likeable fellow, good with his hands, but a bit of a dreamer in his own way. In fact, Sam had spent much of his childhood listening (far more than was wise) to old Mr Bilbo, the then occupant of Bag End, and it had been Bilbo who taught the eager Hobbit-child his letters, simultaneously filling Sam's mind with fancies, stories and tales.

In due course Bilbo quitted the Shire for good, and his heir, Frodo Baggins, then became Samwise's employer. Sam continued to work for Frodo in much the same way that his father had worked for Bilbo – until one day in Shire-year 1418, when the trusting young gardener was recruited by two of his master's close friends (Meriadoc Brandybuck and Peregrin Took) into a 'conspiracy'. They had guessed at certain ideas even then taking shape in Frodo's mind, and Sam was instructed to learn what he could about the visits of Gandalf the Grey and other connected matters. But when caught eavesdropping one morning outside Frodo's study window, Sam's conscience reasserted itself, and no more information from his lips did the 'conspirators' receive.

The chief result of this incident (Book I Chap. 2) was that Gandalf chose Samwise Gamgee to accompany Frodo on a journey to Rivendell that was even then being planned. One may guess that the Wizard's motive was twofold: to keep the matter of the Ring a secret, and to ensure for Frodo a stalwart and useful companion on the road which lay ahead. In this Gandalf was more successful than he had perhaps foreseen, for of all the companions and friends Frodo encountered during his adventures, none proved surer than Sam, the first chosen for him.

The full tale of Sam's adventures at Frodo's side during their long and arduous quest from the quiet Shire of their home to the very walls of Mordor – and beyond – forms the chief section of the lay made in Gondor after the War of the Ring and known as *The Tale of Frodo of the Nine Fingers and the Ring of Doom*. For where Frodo went, there Sam also journeyed; and Frodo's tale is Sam's also. Together they entered Sauron's own land: two Hobbits from the simple countryside 'expected to find a way where the great ones could not go, or dared not go'.[1] And they survived the horrors that befell them to reach the very Cracks of Doom in the cone of the volcano Orodruin, there to make an end of the Ruling Ring and of its Black Master. Samwise was afterwards accounted, like his master, a Ring-bearer – indeed, he bore the Ring into Mordor, having been separated from Frodo by a sudden and treacherous attack. In a moment of supreme heroism, Samwise fought off the danger and later rescued his master from the nearby Orc-tower in which he had been imprisoned.

During this hour of trial Sam uséd the Ring (to escape from Orcs), and so for a while came to understand something of Frodo's burden. The Ring-spell worked on him so that he briefly saw himself as The Great Gardener, who might overcome Sauron by the force of his will and make a fertile garden bloom where once the reeking plains of central Mordor had smouldered. But his basic common-sense overcame the treacherous vision, and he renounced the Ring. In this way he too saved the Quest from disaster – and without his stout support Frodo would never have reached the Cracks of Doom.

For their deeds the two Hobbits were later honoured before the assembled Hosts of the West at the Field of Cormallen, and the King of Gondor himself bowed his knee before them (Book VI Chap. 4). Samwise later accompanied his master and his other companions back to the Shire, where further toil awaited them all; yet in the end the War of the Ring was brought to a conclusion, and the sturdy Hobbit was enabled to return to his beloved craft. Indeed, the Shire was much ravaged by the War and needed all his skills. To the astonishment of all, Sam's labours blossomed the following year (1420 Shire Reckoning) during a summer of extraordinary beauty, when every tree seemed laden with fruit, and the Shire was seen to be healed. For this accomplishment Samwise was revered among the Hobbits – and in due course his eldest son (Frodo) took the surname *Gardner*, in token of the achievement.

Sam lived to full age in the Shire, becoming Mayor seven times and dwelling in comfort (amid general esteem) at Bag End. For Frodo passed over Sea at the end of the Third Age, and to his former servant he left all he had 'and might have had'.[2] Sam thus became Frodo's heir. He married Rose Cotton, the companion of his boyhood, and she bore him thirteen children, of whom the eldest was Elanor, called the Fair. He lived at Bag End until 1482, Shire Reckoning. On September 22nd of that year – his 102nd – he rode away from Hobbiton and passed West to the Havens, last of the Ring-bearers.

Note: the name *Samwise* is actually a translation (into Early English, for contextual reasons) of the original Hobbit-name *Banazîr* ('Half-wise, simple'); *Gamgee* is likewise a rendering of *Galbasi* or *Galpsi* ('Game-village'). See also Appendix F II.

Sandheaver A family of Little Folk (Hobbits) of Bree.

Sandyman A family of Shire-hobbits, who owned and operated the Mill of Hobbiton. Neither the elder Sandyman nor his shiftless son Ted were much liked in the locality, and Ted eventually proved something of a bad lot: he threw in with the rogues of Saruman's employ during the War of the Ring and allowed them to 'remodel' his mill. The machinery ceased to grind corn and instead churned out a stream of filth into The Water. These matters were all attended to by the returning members of the Fellowship of the Ring.

Sangahyando 'Throng-cleaver' (Q.) See ANGAMAITË AND SANGA-HYANDO.

Saradoc 'Scattergold' Brandybuck The Master of Buckland from 1408–32 Shire Reckoning, and the father of Meriadoc 'the Magnificent'.

Sarn Athrad See FORD OF STONES.

Sarn Ford The last ford across the river Baranduin before it reached the Sea south of Harlindon. Sarn Ford was in fact the southernmost boundary of the Shire and the road which ran from Michel Delving to join the Greenway south of the river crossed the Baranduin at this point.

Sarn Gebir 'Stone-spikes' (Sind.) Fierce, dangerous shoals on the Anduin shortly before the Great River ran through the gorge of the Argonath and subsequently emptied into a wide basin in the Emyn Muil, called Nen Hithoel. These rapids were impassable to all river traffic, and travellers were obliged to take to the land if they wished further to descend the Anduin; for this purpose a portage-way was constructed early in the Third Age by Men of Gondor.

Saruman the White Also known as *Curunír*, the 'Man-of-Skill', the Chief of the Order of *Istari* (Wizards), leader of those five MAIAR sent to Middle-earth early in the Third Age (*c.* 1000) in order 'to contest the power of Sauron, and to unite all those who had the will to resist him'.[3] Saruman's knowledge was 'deep', and his hands were 'marvellously skilled', and he became Head of the White Council which alone moved against Sauron during the middle years of the Age. But his pride grew with his power, and little by little his true wisdom decreased as his fabled skills multiplied – and in the end he fell, bloodlessly, under Sauron's control, a victim of his own slow corruption. He died at the end of the War of the Ring, a shamed traitor, stripped of all power and lordship, and came no more to Valinor.

The manner of Saruman's passing is recounted by Frodo in some detail in his narrative; less well-documented is the story of the

Wizard's arising. For many years he wandered in the East of Middle-earth, acquiring arcane knowledge and learning many new skills. He then began to strengthen his will and so trained himself for eventual dominance, thus forgetting one of the chief injunctions of his Order. Yet many years of the Third Age were to pass before other members of the White Council detected his slow deviation from their common goal, and in due course Saruman succeeded in having himself declared Head of that same Council (the *Istari* and the Chief Eldar), in the service of which he bent all his newly acquired powers of mind and hand.

It was afterwards seen that Saruman had long desired to become a Power in himself, and that it was this weakness which was the beginning of his slow downfall. (For the other members of the Council, and of his Order, remained true to their original task, and did not seek to impose their will on others where it was resisted.) At all events, Saruman made his first deliberate move in this direction in the year 2759 Third Age, when he appeared at the Coronation of King Fréaláf of Rohan, successor of the mighty Helm Hammerhand. The Wizard brought with him rich presents, and declared himself the friend of Rohan and Gondor, and a little later was able to persuade Steward Beren of Gondor to grant him the Keys of Orthanc, the mighty Tower which, together with its fortress of ISENGARD, commanded the strategic Gap of Rohan. All thought this a welcome move.

For although Saruman's policies were already distorted and his aims self-serving, he long concealed his true mind. For many years he dwelt in peace with his neighbours – and all the time the Wizard was secretly searching the Tower of Orthanc for a long-lost treasure of the Dúnedain, the possession of which would immeasurably strengthen the power he craved. This was the Palantír of Orthanc, one of the fabled Seeing-stones of Gondor, and in the end he found it – and kept it – in some secret place high in the lonely Tower.

Nonetheless, his fascination with devices and objects of craft led the Wizard (like others before him) up dangerous paths. Long obsessed with the fate of the Ruling Ring of Sauron, and with the lost secrets of the Elven-smiths of Eregion, he suspected before anyone else that the Ring was indeed awake and seeking its Master (who was then dwelling in Dol Guldur). And when, in 2851 Third Age, the White Council met to consider ways of bringing about Sauron's downfall before he should again grow too powerful, Saruman, hoping that the Ring would expose its location if Sauron were left unharassed, deliberately overruled a strong recommendation (from

Gandalf the Grey, second of the Order) that Dol Guldur be attacked and its occupant destroyed or driven out. Saruman himself then secretly began to explore the shallows of the Gladden – for in his long search for information he had learned from the libraries of Gondor somewhat of Isildur's death. And when the Wizard discovered that Sauron was also seeking the Ring in that same area, he became greatly alarmed – but still he withheld his vital insights from his fellow Council-members.

Fourteen years later the White Council met for the last time under Saruman's leadership. Still he dissembled concerning the Great Ring, for by then he had begun to suspect that Gandalf the Grey was closer to its whereabouts than he. For this reason he began to spy on Gandalf, and he withdrew from the Council, and took Isengard and Orthanc for his own, rebuilding the fortress and gathering to him many Orcs and Wild Men. His mask of friendship towards the Rohirrim stiffened, and he began to meddle in their affairs, and to subvert their rule – for by this time Saruman was planning the destruction of Rohan as the first stroke of the war which he plainly foresaw. Fifty years later (*c.* 3000 Third Age) he dared for the first time to use the Palantír of Orthanc.

'Further and further abroad he gazed, until he cast his gaze upon Barad-dûr. Then he was caught!'[4]

For Sauron possessed the Stone of Minas Ithil, which his servants had captured nearly a thousand years earlier; and his will was greater than that of Saruman. Still the Master of Isengard believed that he would prevail – even in combat with the Lord of the Rings – if only the Ruling Ring were his. But, as is told in the Red Book, his efforts to secure it during the War of the Ring went badly wrong. Foiled in this, he attacked Rohan – but his great army never came back from Helm's Deep (see BATTLE OF THE HORNBURG), and in the end Saruman was himself assailed in Isengard and forced to seek refuge in the impregnable Tower of Orthanc. He was afterwards confronted by those he had made his enemies, and he was cast from the Order of *Istari* and from the Council of the Wise. Bereft of all true power, he was afterwards released to go where he might.

Yet Saruman had still some power left – the charm of his voice – and his malice was unabated. Northwards he journeyed, to the Shire (where his agents had long been at work) and from motives of pure malevolence he there awaited the return of the four Hobbits whose deeds (as he saw it) had robbed him of his own and brought him to a sorry pass. For the Shire had been ravaged by his orders, and Saruman wished to observe the Hobbits' grief and dismay.

It is recounted in the Red Book that Saruman was murdered by his own slave at the very doors of Bag End in the Shire; and so it came to pass that he who had once been a messenger of the Valar, he who had come to Middle-earth in hope and desire to aid lesser creatures afflicted by Sauron, he who had in his day possessed more knowledge than any other loremaster, whose voice was subtle and whose skills of hand were a byword, died in the dust like a vagabond, his throat cut by a poor mad wretch whom he had himself destroyed. It was not the least of the tragedies of the War of the Ring, and it did not go unmourned.

Sauron the Great The self-styled Ruler of Middle-earth and declared Enemy of the Free Peoples; servant of Morgoth in the Elder Days and supreme force for Evil throughout two subsequent Ages; Black Master of the land of Mordor, Eye of the Dark Tower, Seducer, Betrayer and Shadow of Despair; the Lord of the Rings of Power.

A discussion of Sauron's true nature would necessitate an enquiry into the intrinsic nature of Evil itself, since he later became – though he had not always been – the focus for all the greed, lust and terrible energy which was to be found in Middle-earth during the two Ages of his supremacy. All Evil gravitated to him, just as he himself became its ultimate source; and though he was, in the end, like Morgoth before him, cast into the void for ever, the mischief he had committed during the long years of his ascendancy could never be wholly unmade. And he has had his many successors.

'Yet nothing is evil in the beginning. Even Sauron was not so.' In his origins, he was one of the Ainur, of the race called Maiar; and he served the Vala Aulë,[5] and learned great craft from him. (*Sauron* is a later name given to him by the High-elves in their own language, and means 'the Abhorred', while the Grey-elves knew him as *Gorthaur* 'the Cruel'.) But in earliest times he relinquished his labours with Aulë the Smith, and transferred his allegiance to Melkor; and when Melkor first began to devise evil in Arda, long before the Elves awoke in Cuiviénen, Sauron was already his most accomplished, powerful and valuable servant. Great service he rendered to Melkor – and continued to render while Melkor ruled Middle-earth, acting as cruelly towards Elves and Men as his black Master had ever done, though at first with less power to command. His name first appears in records at the time of the Dagor Bragollach, when his armies of orcs and werewolves captured the tower of Minas

Tirith on Tol Sirion that Finrod had built; and here for a while he dwelled,[6] in Tol-in-Gaurhoth (as the island was re-named by the Eldar; it means 'Isle of Werewolves'), the Lieutenant of Morgoth (as Melkor was now known). Yet long before this he had been prominent in Middle-earth, as the first Captain of Angband. At the time of its building, this underworld realm was but a western bastion of Utumno, and Sauron was its castellain. But then the Valar came to Middle-earth and fought the Battle of the Powers against Morgoth, and took him, a prisoner, back to Valinor; but Sauron was overlooked, and escaped the doom of imprisonment. And by the time of the Bragollach he was become an evil lord of great power, second only in the world to Morgoth himself. Sauron it was who devised the ending of the outlaws of Dorthonion (see GORLIM THE UNHAPPY); but he is remembered by the Elves as the slayer of Finrod Felagund.

At all events, the Servant survived where the Master did not, and with the coming of the Host of the Valar the cause of Evil in the First Age was ended. So great was the destruction wrought among Morgoth's many servants that for a while the Eldar believed that Evil had been ended for ever. Morgoth himself was cast for ever into outer Darkness. But Sauron somehow survived the Breaking of Thangorodrim, though he remained in a deep sleep which lasted some five hundred years. Then he awakened and, as he began to formulate his plans, he became aware of the growing power of Númenor across the Seas, and of the hosts of his former enemies who still dwelt in the westlands of Middle-earth, a bar between him and his domination over mortal lands.

Alarmed by the strength of both the Elves and the Númenoreans, Sauron then began to seek for a land which he could fortify after the manner of Angband of old, where he could build a new Thangorodrim as a fortress of his might. Such a land lay empty, away to the south and east, behind impassable mountain-walls, and in its centre stood a mighty volcano, whose age-old fires had covered the plain round about with layer upon layer of dark ash. This forsaken land Sauron took for his own, and it was named *Mordor*, the 'Black-land'. There he built his Dark Tower, the Barad-dûr, and there he dwelt throughout the Second Age.

Although in later years Sauron's appearance grew hateful – so that his power then lay in terror alone – at the time of his rise he was still fair of aspect and form. Accordingly, he determined upon treachery and deceit as his chief weapon. Gil-galad, Elven-king of Lindon, whom Sauron first approached, nonetheless perceived his true nature and refused all dealings with him. Not so with other Elves: Celebrimbor of Eregion, greatest of surviving craftsmen, was less wise in these matters than Gil-galad and made a covenant with Sauron, whereby each provided the other with knowledge. Together they began to forge the Rings of Power.

It was by this means that Sauron of Mordor made himself supreme in Middle-earth for the remainder of the Second Age. He aided the Elven-smiths in their great task, and secretly wrought the One Ring to rule all the lesser rings – which then passed under his control, so long as their owners wore them. This brought at last the revelation of his true nature, and the Elves made war upon him. Too late: his strength was already greater than theirs, and Eregion was over-run, and Celebrimbor slain. Only Gil-galad held out – and even he would have been defeated had not aid arrived from Númenor in the nick of time. In this way the Edain of Númenor renewed their ancestral alliance with the Elves – and so gained for themselves the chief hatred of the Lord of the Rings. Sauron was forced to withdraw from Eriador and turn his interests eastward, for strong though he was, his power did not compare with that of Númenor, and he could wait.

Nonetheless, his writ ran throughout most of Middle-earth for the remainder of the Second Age, and many peoples endured the full weight of his tyranny (see ACCURSED YEARS). Yet all the time the island-realm of Númenor continued to grow in strength over the horizon, and the day of their second clash drew nearer. In 3261 Second Age the long-expected fleets appeared off Umbar, but so great was the power of the host led by Ar-Pharazôn the Golden that Sauron's own armies melted away and he was left defenceless.

Yet not all his skills deserted him. Perceiving that the King of Númenor was a vain man, Sauron humbled himself and appealed to the mercy (and the pride) of Pharazôn, who did not make an end of him but carried him back, a prisoner, to Númenor. There Sauron's old gifts for dominance and betrayal quickly reasserted themselves, and he made himself Pharazôn's chief counsellor. He had been captive less than fifty years when, at his instigation, an ageing Ar-Pharazôn gave orders for the assembly of the Great Armament. In 3319 this host put to sea and sailed into the West, to give battle for the Undying Lands.

In the ensuing downfall of Númenor, Sauron's mortal body was destroyed, but his spirit survived and fled back to Middle-earth, shapeless and vengeful. He was never again able to appear in a pleasing form, but instead became the Dark Lord, terrible of aspect, black and burning hot, with a single lidless Eye 'rimmed with fire . . .

glazed, yellow as a cat's . . . and the black slit of its pupil opened on a pit, a window into nothing'.[7] Hiding in Mordor for a while, he learned that a remnant of the Númenoreans had escaped him and were even then building mighty realms-in-exile upon his borders. Mustering his dispersed armies with furious speed, Sauron struck, purposing to sweep the newcomers into the Sea; in 3429 Second Age he came across the Pass of Cirith Ungol, capturing Minas Ithil and driving the Dúnedain back across the Anduin. But once more he had underestimated his foes: they made alliance against him and broke his armies, and laid siege to the Dark Tower itself (see LAST ALLIANCE); and in final combat with Gil-galad and Elendil, Sauron was cast down and his Ring was taken from him.

For the first thousand years of the Third Age Sauron slept and the westlands had peace from him. But slowly he began to take shape once more, though at this time he was too weak to recapture Mordor, which was essential to his greater purposes but which was closely guarded by the Dúnedain of Gondor. Instead he chose the smaller fortress of Dol Guldur in Greenwood the Great. There he began to hatch his plots once more: evil stirred in the Forest; Orcs and Trolls reappeared in great numbers, and wolves howled on its borders. Greenwood was renamed *Mirkwood* and the power of 'the Necromancer' of Dol Guldur was spoken of with dread.

In the meantime, desiring to strike at his enemies but seeing no hope at that time in an assault upon Gondor (then at the summit of its power), Sauron sent his chief servant, the Lord of the Ringwraiths, northwards into Eriador with the purpose of destroying the North-kingdom of the Dúnedain. How this task was faithfully carried through to a fearful conclusion is told elsewhere (see ANGMAR). Indeed, for most of the Third Age this most terrible servant worked assiduously on his Master's behalf, and Sauron's foes were frustrated by his capable hand. The eventual destruction of the North-kingdom freed Sauron and his servants to work for the downfall of Gondor, and the weakening of the South-kingdom allowed Mordor to be re-opened and occupied by the Nazgûl.

Yet throughout much of the Third Age Sauron continued to engage in policies of secrecy and concealment. He lay hidden in Dol Guldur, creating the grand designs while his servants harried his foes, growing ever more powerful even while the Wise debated whether or not he had awakened at all. Above everything else he desired to recover the Ruling Ring, for by the fact of his own existence Sauron knew it had not been destroyed; and to this end he bent all his guile during the remaining years of the Age. In the end he was driven from Dol Guldur before his spies could discover the Ring's whereabouts, and soon afterwards he came openly to Mordor once more and proclaimed himself. However, being cautious, and wishing this time to be certain of victory before striking, the Dark Lord forbore to attack his foes until the Ring should come within his grasp. But his enemies (who indeed, as he feared, possessed his Ring), made their own moves even while he hesitated; and in the final campaign that was made against him Sauron's armies were defeated in the hour of victory, his plans were brought to nothing, his servants were destroyed, the Dark Tower was cast down – and the Ruling Ring itself, the fount of all his hopes, was melted in the Fires of Mount Doom. So ended the Third Age, and so passed the power of Sauron the Great. He was cast into the void for ever and the fear of his domination was lifted from the World.

Sauron's Road The causeway which ran from the western gate of the Dark Tower across the reeking plains of Gorgoroth to Orodruin, the Fire-mountain, heart of Sauron's realm. It was built during the early Second Age to enable Sauron to gain access to the *Sammath Naur*, the 'Chambers of Fire' which he had delved into the side of the volcano's smouldering cone.

Scary A village in the Eastfarthing of the Shire, not far from the stone-quarries of the region.

Scatha the Worm One of the great Dragons of the Third Age, who dwelt in the Grey Mountains at the time of the Dwarves' expulsion from Moria (1981). Little is recorded of this Worm, save that, like all his breed, he was greedy, cruel; and he possessed a large hoard taken by force from the Dwarves. He was eventually slain by Fram son of Frumgar of the Men of Éothéod, who thus won himself great riches. Unfortunately, the subsequent disposition of Scatha's hoard became a source of bitter dispute between Fram and the Dwarves, who claimed the treasure. Fram insulted the rival claimants and they slew him in return.

Sceptre of Annúminas The chief symbol of the High-kingship of the Númenorean Realms in Exile. By the end of the Third Age, the Sceptre was the single most ancient object fashioned by Men's hands then in existence, being in origin the Silver Rod of the Lords of Andúnië in Númenor during the Second Age, and therefore over five thousand years old at the time of the War of the Ring. After the death of Elendil, who brought it to Middle-earth, the Sceptre was kept at his Northern capital of Annúminas beside Lake Evendim in Eriador; but after the final fall of the North-kingdom, it was given into the safekeeping of Master Elrond of Rivendell, together with the other treasures of Elendil's House. Elrond surrendered it to King Elessar (Aragorn II) after the War of the Ring, to be the symbol of the Reunited Kingdom.

Note: a Sceptre was also the supreme symbol of royalty in Númenor; this tradition was maintained in Arnor but not in Gondor, where the Kings' token was the Silver Crown.

Scroll of Kings The manuscript wherein was inscribed the list of the names of the Kings of Númenor; it was kept in Armenelos, the chief city of that land. By tradition, all writing on that scroll was in the High-elven tongue, even in latter days.

'The Sea-bell' An odd and decidedly distrubing Shire-poem, No. 15 in *The Adventures of Tom Bombadil* collection. It has been closely associated with Frodo Baggins, having been at some point subtitled *Frodo's Dreme* – though its dating seems to make it unlikely to have been composed by him. Nonetheless, the unknown verse-maker displayed surprising empathy with the Ring-bearer and the poem seems to provide an insight into the despairing dreams which visited Frodo during his last two years in the Shire.

It is, of course, quite possible that 'The Sea-bell' was actually written by Frodo, and that the manuscript was later discovered by a member of the Fairbairn family (who maintained custody of the Red Book of Westmarch during the Fourth Age), and subsequently copied directly into the Red Book itself. In which case the meaning of the poem becomes suddenly and chillingly more clear. The narrator takes a strange journey over Sea, where he finds to his anger that everything seems beyond his reach: he is unacceptable in the Undying Lands, and all flee at his approach. Tarrying there nonetheless, he grows old and mad – and still no one speaks to him. In the end, he forsakes the West, having found no refuge, and returns to mortal lands. But he has become a ghost, and has no substance in the world of Men; and so he is doomed to wander for ever, haunted and alone.

If Frodo was in truth visited by such dreams, then his final passing over Sea must have been blessed indeed.

Sea-elves The FALMARI.

Sea of Nurn See NURNEN.

Sea of Rhûn In the Third Age, the largest landlocked sea in Middle-earth, and as a consequence sometimes known as the Inland Sea. It lay far in the East, beyond Mirkwood and Rhovanion, over a hundred leagues south-east of the Iron Hills; and it was of vast dimensions, being over fifty leagues across at its widest point.

Seat of Seeing The name given in Gondor for the carven stone chair placed atop the hill *Amon Hen* ('Hill of the Eye'), above the Falls of Rauros upon Anduin.

Seaward Tower See TIRITH AEAR.

Second Age There were 3,441 years between the Breaking of Thangorodrim and the first overthrow of Sauron the Great. In the lore of the Elves and the Dúnedain this period was known as the Second Age of Middle-earth, and all later epochs were named and calculated accordingly.

These were the dark years for Men of Middle-earth, but the years of the glory of Númenor. Of events in Middle-earth the records are few and brief, and their dates are often uncertain.[8]

The Second Age followed immediately after the fall of Morgoth and began with the founding of the Elf-kingdoms of Lindon. Much of north-western Middle-earth had been destroyed or damaged in the terrible wars of the previous Age, and the Elves were much reduced in number, while their old realms lay under the Sea. Yet those Elves that chose to remain in mortal lands prospered for a while, wandering the Westlands and having commerce with other races. The Dwarves, too, flourished during this period, possessing the one invulnerable citadel (the realm of Moria) to be found in Middle-earth – save only the Dark Tower of Sauron. For this former servant of Morgoth awoke once more during the Second Age, and began to make himself a power in Middle-earth. And it was a measure of his success that the latter part of the Age was afterwards called the Accursed Years.

But for the Men of Númenor across the Western Seas the Second Age was the epoch of great glory and splendour. The land of Westernesse was founded in the 32nd year of the Age by the Edain, who were led at that time by Elros, called afterwards Tar-Minyatur; and he became their first King. While dispute and conflict raged to and fro in Middle-earth, the island-realm of Númenor grew ever more powerful until, by the last third of the Age, even the coastlands of Middle-earth itself were under its sway. In the end came the inevitable clash between Sauron and the Dúnedain of Númenor, a clash in which Sauron was temporarily defeated; yet ultimately he prevailed over them by treachery, and his evil counsels led most of the Dúnedain to destruction, when Númenor was cast under the Sea.

The Second Age ended with the events brought about by Sauron's discovery that his victory over Númenor was not yet complete. He suddenly attacked the Dúnedain Realms-in-Exile, but failed to conquer them with one blow as he had hoped, and the Last Alliance which his foes made against him overthrew his might, cast down the Barad-dûr and laid his realm in ruins. With his overthrow the Second Age of Middle-earth came to an end.

Secondborn MEN.

Second Line (of Rohan) The name given in the lore of Rohan to all the Kings of the Mark between Fréaláf Hildeson (tenth King) and Théoden Ednew (seventeenth King).

Second Music (of the Ainur) In the lore of the Eldar, the Ending of the World (*Ambar-metta*) and of the Universe; when a Great Music shall again be sung, but with different themes, and with the participation of the Children of Ilúvatar.

Second People A translation of the Quenya word *Atani*; the race of MEN.

Second Spring of Arda In the lore of the Eldar, the Years of the Sun, when light once again was brought to mortal lands. The (first) Spring of Arda had been long before, when the Valar dwelt in Almaren and the Lamps Illuin and Ormal had shone over the face of the world, stimulating growth and change. This archaic period, however, had been marred by Melkor, who destroyed Almaren and broke the Lamps, causing Darkness to fall over Middle-earth – a Night which was to endure for Ages upon Ages, until the raising of Anar (and Isil).

Secret Fire The Flame of Anor, also called the Flame Imperishable; the primaeval Life-force of the World and of *Eä*, the Universe. (The Order of *Istari* – Wizards – formally swore obedience to the 'Secret Fire'.)

Seeing-stones The PALANTÍRI.

Self-cursed An Elvish epithet for the race of MEN.

Serech See FEN OF SERECH.

Seregon 'Stone-blood' (Sind.) A flowering shrub with crimson blossoms which grew abundantly on the stony height of Amon Rûdh.

Serindë 'The Seamstress' (Q.) See MÍRIEL SERINDË.

Serni 'Stony' (Sind.) The major tributary of the river Gilrain in Gondor. Its source was in Lebennin south of the White Mountains. The Serni flowed south-west through the province to join the larger river some little distance above the town of Linhir.

Seven Fathers According to the lore of Dwarves, their race was descended in antiquity from Seven Houses, each of which had its own Founding Father. The eldest and most royal of these Seven Fathers was Durin I, widely called 'the Deathless'. The names of the other Fathers were not recorded in the Annals of Elves and Men.

Seven Rings The Seven RINGS OF POWER made for the (seven) Dwarf-kings during the Second Age by the Elves of Eregion working under the tutelage of Sauron of Mordor. Sauron's secret purpose was, of course, the making of Great Rings which would bring the Dwarves under his domination; but the Dwarves were a race that easily resisted all such spells, and the Seven proved useless as a means to this end. Accordingly, in the years that followed, Sauron bent all his will towards recovering the Rings: three he regained, while four were consumed (together with their owners) by Dragons. The last Ring to be recovered by Sauron was that originally given to Durin III of Moria by the Elven-smiths; it was taken from Thráin II, Durin's Heir, during his torment in the dungeons of Dol Guldur in 2845 Third Age.

Seven Rivers A translation of the Sindarin element *Ossir*; the Seven Rivers of Ossiriand were Gelion, Ascar, Thalos, Legolin, Brilthor, Duilwen and Adurant.

In the Second and Third Ages, this term was also applied to the (original) land of Gondor, which also had seven rivers: Lefnui, Morthond, Ringló, Gilrain (or Gilraen), Sirith, Erui, and Anduin.[9]

Seven Stars A heraldic emblem, used by the Dwarves of Durin's House and by the Dúnedain of Gondor, followers of Elendil. The Dwarf-emblems represented the constellation known as the Sickle (the Plough), while the Númenorean Seven originally stood for the (single) stars on the banners of the ships which bore the seven *palantíri* back from drowned Númenor to Middle-earth at the end of the Second Age. These Seven Stars were later incorporated into the

Heraldry of Gondor, where, together with the White Tree and the Silver Crown, they represented the Line of Elendil.
See also HERALDIC DEVICES.

Seven Stones The PALANTÍRI.

'Shadow-Bride' A short, disquieting Shire-poem, one of the lesser verses scribbled in the margins of the Red Book and subsequently published as part of *The Adventures of Tom Bombadil* (No. 13).

Shadowfax The name given in Rohan to the chief of the *Mearas*, Princes of Horses; the last descendant of Felaróf of Éothéod in the Third Age. Until approached by Gandalf the Grey, the horse was completely untamed, although he subsequently became a great comrade of the Wizard, bearing him into battle throughout the War of the Ring. At the end of the Age Shadowfax passed over Sea together with his master.

Shadowmere A lake or tarn 'beneath the Hill of Ilmarin'[10] (Oiolossë) in Eldamar. Beside it, say the Elves, stood the 'Great-watch-tower' of Tirion, and the lamps of the Elf city were reflected in the dark waters of the lake.

Shadowy Mountains A translation of *Ered Wethrin*; also a term (Third Age) for the Ephel Dúath, the west-wall of Mordor.

Shagrat An Orc of Mordor, captain or sergeant of the Guard of the Tower of Cirith Ungol at the time of the War of the Ring. He was afterwards described (by Samwise, who encountered him) as 'a large orc with long arms that, as he ran crouching, reached to the ground'.[11] Being the fiercest Orc in the Tower, he survived when his company and another Orc-troop fought for possession of certain items of booty (see Book VI Chap. 1). Shagrat subsequently escaped the carnage and carried the vital items to Barad-dûr, with nearly disastrous consequences (Book V Chap. 10).

Sharkey A nickname in the Shire for Saruman the Wizard. It was in origin the Orkish word *sharkû* ('old-man'), given to Saruman by his servants in Isengard and taken to the Shire by his other agents.

Sharkey's End A dry term, used only in Bywater, for the Hobbiton street known as New Row. The Wizard Saruman (known in the Shire as 'Sharkey') was slain at the end of the road on the last day of the War of the Ring (November 3rd, 1419 Shire Reckoning).

Shathûr See BUNDUSHATHÛR.

Shelob the Great The last of the Great Spiders of Middle-earth. These creatures infested the passes of the Mountains of Terror in Beleriand during the First Age, drinking the blood of all who came near, for they served no master but their own monstrous hunger. The first of these was named Ungoliant, and the last of her brood to survive was Shelob the Great.

Most of the evil creatures of Beleriand were destroyed when that Land of the Elves was drowned under the Sea at the end of the First Age, but by some chance Shelob escaped, and slowly made her way south, until she came at last to the Mountains of Shadow. There she built a lair in a high pass, afterwards called the Spider's Pass, and dwelt for many years, she 'who was there before Sauron, and before the first stone of Barad-dûr; and she served none but herself . . . for all living things were her food and her vomit darkness.'[12]

A full description of this loathsome creature may be found in Book IV Chap. 9; it is unlikely that any will wish for further details. She spun her webs of horror high in the Pass named after her for two full Ages, and Sauron tolerated her, for although his Orcs were eaten by her, she guarded his land better than he himself could have done.

See also Book IV Chap. 10.

Shelob's Lair The den of the Great Spider Shelob. It was a cavern of huge size, linked with other caves by many passages and tunnels, and it lay just below the summit of the Pass of Cirith Ungol on the western side. The road across the Pass had been tunnelled through solid rock at this point, and travellers were accordingly forced to use the outer passages of the Spider's Lair (*Torech Ungol*) on their way to and fro. For this reason the builders of the Tower of Cirith Ungol (which lay on the further side of the Pass) devised a 'back-door' passage which partly avoided the hazard.

See also Book IV Chap. 10.

Shepherds of the Trees The ENTS.

Ship-kings The period of Gondor's greatest maritime expansion took place under her 'Ship-kings', who ruled between the ninth and twelfth centuries of the Third Age. Their Númenorean ancestors had, of course, always been great mariners, whose argosies journeyed back to Middle-earth many centuries before the founding of the Realms-in-Exile; and the harbours at Umbar and Pelargir had been founded a full thousand years before Minas Anor or Osgiliath. This naval heritage was not forgotten in the South-kingdom, and when

Gondor began to prosper, the Dúnedain turned once more to sea power to realize their imperial ambitions south and west of their own coasts.

The 'Ship-kings' were the four rulers of Gondor most closely associated with this policy. The first was Tarannon, twelfth King, who constructed the first fleets and conquered the coastal areas south and west of the Mouths of Anduin; in token of his victories he took the name *Falastur* 'Lord-of-the-coasts'. He was succeeded by his nephew, Eärnil I, in 913 Third Age. Eärnil improved on Falastur's work, restoring the ancient Númenorean haven of Pelargir upon Anduin, and capturing the rival Haven of Umbar two years after his succession to the Throne. But in 936 he was lost at sea, and his own son Ciryandil, the third 'Ship-king', fared no better, falling in battle at Umbar defending the Haven from an attack of Haradrim (in 1015).

Ciryandil's son Ciryaher was the fourth and last of the 'Ship-kings', and he later became the most powerful ruler in Gondor's history. He set in hand a programme of fleet-building, all the while awaiting the most propitious moment for avenging his father; and when the time was ripe he crossed the Poros and descended upon the forces of Harad, which were still besieging Umbar, having failed to capture it despite their slaying of Ciryandil. At the same time the fleets of Gondor landed armies on the coasts to take the Haradrim in flank. Then the Southron besiegers were so severely defeated that not for several centuries were they able to recover their strength. To commemorate his great victory, Ciryaher took the royal name *Hyarmendacil* ('South-victor'). He was the mightiest of all the Kings of Gondor and reigned for 134 years. But with him died the line of the 'Ship-kings': his own son Atanatar (II) Alcarin proved little better than a vain spendthrift, and the great gains of the 'Ship-kings' were allowed to slip away.

Shire A translation (into Early English, for contextual purposes) of the Hobbit-word *Sûza*, the name among western Hobbits to the region of authority of their Thain, approximately speaking between the river Baranduin (Brandywine) and the Emyn Beraid (Tower Hills). These lands had previously been part of Arnor, and later Arthedain, but by 1600 Third Age had long been deserted, and although still rich and fertile were growing wild with disuse. At that time many Harfoots and Fallohides were dwelling in somewhat crowded conditions in and near the village of Bree in Eriador, and there was a strong desire to occupy the unused agricultural land west of the Baranduin. Permission was accordingly sought from King Argeleb II of Arthedain by the Hobbit-leaders Marcho and Blanco (both, incidentally, Fallohides), and when this was forthcoming a great multitude of Hobbits crossed the Bridge of Stonebows and took possession of the lands beyond.

As is told elsewhere (see Prologue 1), the King's conditions for the freehold of the Shire were not exacting, and the Shire-hobbits soon settled down to a quiet, peaceful and prosperous existence. Many of their kin joined them in the years that followed the Founding of the Shire (which took place in 1601 Third Age, or Year One of the Shire Reckoning), and all went well until thirty-six years later, when the Great Plague came into Eriador from the East and South. The Shire-folk suffered loss, but soon recovered in the years that followed and afterwards passed altogether out of the knowledge of other folk.

The long years of peace stretching from those days to the time of The War of the Ring brought about an understandable state of insularity among the Shire-hobbits. Their heroes tended to be selected from among those who had lived to particularly old ages, or who had sired the greatest numbers of children. It is true that Bandobras 'Bullroarer' Took was lauded for military prowess, but in general, warlike activities (like all 'adventurous' tendencies) were not much appreciated in the Shire. The countryside was fruitful and Hobbits grew steadily fatter – and echoes of growing danger from Outside did not cross the Baranduin.

Shirebourn A river of the Shire. It arose in the Green Hill Country in the Eastfarthing and flowed south and east to join the Baranduin (Brandywine) north of the Overbourn Marshes.

Shire-moot An emergency meeting of all landed Hobbits, summoned at times of doubt or danger by the Thain of the Shire. Such meetings were not a frequent occurrence.

Shire-muster An assembly of arms in the Shire, which was an even rarer occasion than the Moot (see previous entry). The only Hobbit with recognized authority to summon the Muster was the Thain of the Shire.

Shire Reckoning The calendar system adopted by the Hobbits of the Shire after the founding of their land. Though basically similar to the venerable KINGS' RECKONING of the Dúnedain, the Shire-system differed in one important respect: all years were reckoned from the Hobbits' first Crossing of the Baranduin (1601 Third Age,

Year One of the Shire), and the observance of Ages was not recognized in the Shire following that date. But although the Hobbits also had their own ancient names for the days and months,[13] the system they observed was still easily recognized as a variant of the same venerable Númenorean calendar, brought to Middle-earth by the Dúnedain.

Months were all of equal length – 30 days – and there were five 'extra' days (outside the months), which made up the chief feast days. Three of these formed a midsummer festival, known in the Shire as Lithe, the chief holiday of the year, the other – two-day – festival being at Yule. Leap Years were allowed for by adding an extra Lithe-day between Mid-year's day and 2 Lithe (see also the Shire Calendar in Appendix D).

Late in the Third Age (c. 1100 Shire Reckoning) the Hobbits made a further modification of their own to the calendar. This was called *Shire-reform*, and its purpose was to stabilise the names of the days and the dates on which these might fall from year to year. This was achieved, and

> the same date in any one year had the same weekday name in all other years, so that Shire-folk no longer bothered to put the weekday in their letters and diaries. They found this quite convenient at home, but not so convenient if they ever travelled further than Bree.[14]

Shire-reform See previous entry.

Shirriffs The Shirriffs (or 'Shire-reeves') were the chief law enforcement officials of the Shire. As most laws were observed to the letter, being after all based upon common sense and ancient tradition, the Shirriffs' task was easy, and the job was far more concerned with trespass and matters of property than with actual crime (which was almost unknown in the Shire). The office of First Shirriff was normally held by the Mayor of Michel Delving, while the main body was more commonly known as the Watch. There were twelve all told, three in each Farthing, and they were distinguished from other Hobbits by a feather worn in the cap.

The Shire also possessed a 'Special Constabulary' – whose size varied at need – for the purpose of patrolling the borders. These were known as 'Bounders'.

Sickle (of the Valar) A translation of the Quenya word *Valacirca*: the name given by dwellers in Middle-earth to the constellation of seven stars set in the sky by Varda (Elbereth) as a sign of the eventual fall of Morgoth; it is of course the same constellation known to later Men as 'The Plough' (or 'Great Bear', or 'Big Dipper').

Siege of Angband The name given by the Eldar to the period of four centuries – between the Dagor Aglareb (the Third Battle of Beleriand) and the Dagor Bragollach (the Fourth Battle) – when Morgoth was hemmed into the North by the chain of Elf-kingdoms reaching from Hithlum in the West to Mount Rerir in the East. Strictly speaking, it was not a true siege, for Morgoth was untrammelled in the North and North-east, and was always able to move his armies to and from Angband by these routes; the Siege only bore upon the south of his land. Therefore no real pressure could ever be inflicted upon him, and his real capacity for waging war remained largely unaffected: as was afterwards realized by the Eldar, in calamitous fashion.

Silent Watchers Two great stone statues, three-headed, with vulture faces and claws, which guarded the gate of the Tower of Cirith Ungol in Mordor.

> Each had three joined bodies, and three heads facing outward, and inward, and across the gateway . . . They seemed to be carved out of huge blocks of stone, immovable, and yet they were aware: some dreadful spirit of evil vigilance abode in them. They knew an enemy. Visible or invisible none could pass unheeded.[15]

It seems unlikely that these monstrous guardians were set in place by the original builders of the Tower, for the fortress had been raised in the early years of the Third Age by Men of Gondor, and its purpose had been the guarding of the route across the Pass behind. But the Tower was later abandoned, and Sauron returned to Mordor, and the fortress was strengthened by his slaves and filled with Orcs.

Silima The name given by Fëanor of the Noldor to the mysterious crystalline substance devised by him in Eldamar during the First Age, when the Two Trees still flowered and the craftsmanship of the Noldorin Kindred had not yet brought grief to the Valar and the High-elves. Silima was exceedingly hard, and possessed the gift of capturing light – and only Fëanor ever knew the secrets of its making. He wrought the three *silmarilli* ('Jewels-of-*silima*') from this substance.

Silmariën The only daughter and eldest child of King Tar-Elendil of Númenor. She was born in the year 548 Second Age, while Númenor was still young and its people uncorrupted. Although she was the eldest child of the King, after her father's death she was prohibited from receiving the Sceptre, for the laws of that time allowed only male heirs to rule in Númenor (this law was afterwards changed; see *Note* under LORDS OF ANDÚNIË). Her younger brother became King in her place, as Tar-Meneldur.

Nonetheless, it was through the Lady Silmariën that the House of Elendil traced its lineage back to Elros Tar-Minyatur and the still more ancient High-elven ancestry. Her son Valandil became the first Lord of Andúnië – a fair western province of Númenor – and from Valandil were descended Amandil and his son Elendil. From Elendil the Tall were descended all the Kings of Arnor and Gondor.

Silmarilli 'Jewels-of-*silima*' (Q.) The name given by Fëanor of the Noldor to the three Great Jewels wrought by him during the Elder Days, the mightiest works of craft ever made. So great was their beauty that none could behold it and be unmoved; so terrible was its effect that, because of the Jewels, grief and dissent, followed by rebellion, came to the Undying Lands, where the Silmarils had been wrought, and war and untold suffering to Middle-earth, where they were taken perforce. In the end they were lost for ever, in the Heavens, under the Earth, and in the deeps of the Sea.

The tale of the Silmarils is the story of the rebellion and fall of Fëanor, and the exile of those Noldorin Elves whom he led to Middle-earth. The Jewels were made, as is told above (see SILIMA), from a mysterious crystalline substance, exceedingly hard, which was somehow able to capture light and store it within its depths. The light was the ancient Light of the Two Trees of Valinor. But the glory of the Great Jewels overwhelmed one of the Valar, afterwards called Morgoth, who stole them from the Noldor and fled with them to Middle-earth, first poisoning the Two Trees so that their Light was dimmed for ever. This action grieved the Valar – whose land was plunged into eternal twilight – but it enraged the Noldor, who now regarded the Silmarils as symbols of the pride of their race. Fëanor led a great host of the Noldor back to Middle-earth against the wishes of the Valar, and so exiled himself and his people from the Undying Lands.

The war which the Noldor and their allies then fought against Morgoth in Middle-earth lasted for centuries, and at the end of it great destruction had taken place and many hitherto immortal lives had been lost – but the Silmarils were still in the possession of Morgoth (save one only, recovered by Beren of the Edain and Lúthien daughter of Thingol Greycloak of the Elves). In the end the Valar, taking pity on the innocent, themselves came to Middle-earth and crushed Morgoth in a titanic battle, in which his fortress of Thangorodrim was obliterated and Beleriand of the Grey-elves drowned under the Sea. The single Jewel recovered by the Eldar, which came back to the Undying Lands with Eärendil the Mariner, had already been set in the sky by Elbereth herself as a sign of hope to dwellers in Middle-earth. But the other two Silmarils were taken by force from Morgoth by the Valar – and were then stolen, at the very end of the Age, by the two surviving sons of Fëanor, Maedhros and Maglor. Indeed they were still constrained to attempt this deed, by the Oath they and their father had sworn on the eve of the rebellion long before in Eldamar. Yet by now their touch had become defiled, and they could not bear to keep or hold the Jewels; and Maedhros cast his into a chasm of the earth, and Maglor threw his into the Sea.

See also *Silmarillion* (passim); 'THE SILMARILLION'.

'The Silmarillion' The title given by its Translators, Editors and Publishers to the large and exceedingly ancient collection of songs and tales of the First Age assembled in Rivendell during the latter part of the Third Age by the Hobbit Bilbo Baggins (under the title *Translations from the Elvish*) and subsequently re-ordered, edited and anthologized by Professor J. R. R. Tolkien (and his son C. J. R. Tolkien). *The Silmarillion* proper is made up of five separately-originated works: the *Ainulindalë* or Music of the Ainur (composed by Rúmil of Tirion); the *Valaquenta* or History of the Valar and Maiar (authorship unknown); the *Quenta Silmarillion* or History of the Silmarils (derived from many sources); the *Akallabêth* or Downfall of Númenor (composed in Gondor during the early part of the Third Age); and *Of the Rings of Power*, which is a much-abbreviated version of *The Tale of Frodo of the Nine Fingers and the Ring of Doom*,[16] written, of course, by the renowned Hobbit Frodo Baggins, the Heir of Bilbo (though the authorship of the version which appears as the final section of *The Silmarillion* can almost certainly be ascribed to the celebrated Editors).

Silmarils See SILMARILLI.

 Silme The Quenya or High-elven word for 'starlight', but more properly the title of Tengwa number 29, which was used in almost all cases for the value of the sound *s*.

Silme Nuquerna A reversed form of the Tengwa number 29 (see previous entry), incorporated into the Fëanorian writing-system as letter number 30. Reversed letters of this type carried exactly the same phonetic value but were inverted for convenience of writing (i.e., when accompanied by one of the diacritic *tehtar*, 'signs'). The example shown above has an *a* tehta incorporated in order to illustrate this usage.

Silpion See TELPERION.

Silvan Elves Wood-elves. See ELVES; NANDOR.

Silver Crown The Crown of Gondor. It was made in the shape of an ancient Númenorean war-helm, with a high crown and long cheek-guards which fitted closely to the face. The original Silver Crown was said to be the actual war-helm of Isildur, but in the days of Atanatar (II) Alcarin ('the Glorious') this was replaced by a far more flamboyant crown, though still of the same shape. The Crown of Alcarin was made of pure silver, and was wrought with wings like sea-birds', and was embellished with seven gems of adamant studded at intervals in the Circlet. Above all was set a single great white jewel.

The Crown was the chief emblem of royalty in Gondor, but in Arnor (and in Númenor) the Kings wore only a simple diadem, and the chief mark of Kingship was a Sceptre.

See also SCEPTRE OF ANNÚMINAS.

Silverlode An (approximate) translation of the Sindarin name *Celebrant*.

Silver Rod See SCEPTRE OF ANNÚMINAS.

Silver-steel One of the names given to the metal MITHRIL.

Silvertine A translation of the Sindarin word *Celebdil*, being the name of that mountain known to Dwarves as *Zirak-zigil*. It was one of the three Mountains of Moria.

Simbelmynë 'Ever-mind' A type of small white grave-flower which grew only in Rohan, and which clustered thickly on the sides of the royal burial-mounds in the Barrowfield of Edoras.

Sindar 'Grey-elves' (Q.) The name given in the High-elven tongue by the Noldor of Middle-earth to the Elves of Beleriand and

Mithrim, in origin a subdivision of the TELERI. All these were the
subjects of Thingol of Doriath, and many dwelled with their lord
in Menegroth, his city beside the Esgalduin; but the classification
also included the *Falathrim* or 'Coast-elves' whose lord (under
Thingol) was Círdan the Shipwright; and also the various wandering
Telerin peoples who made their abode west of the Blue Mountains
during the First Age, save only the Nandor of Ossiriand, whom the
Noldor called *Laiquendi* ('Green-elves').

The manner of the sundering of the Grey-elves from the main
host of the Teleri is recounted elsewhere.[17] Here, it is enough to
recall that the love the Grey-elves felt for the lands of western Middle-
earth exceeded that which they bore for their kindred, or for the
Undying Lands which they had never seen; at all events, the 'Sea-
longing' did not at that time fully awaken in their hearts, and so they
lingered on the shores of mortal lands while the remaining Eldar
took ship into the Far West. The country in which they chose to
make their home was called Beleriand, a land of many forests and
mountains and the most westerly in Middle-earth. There the Grey-
elves were ruled by Thingol Greycloak, eldest and greatest of their
Kings, who wedded the Lady Melian of the Valar and dwelt agelong
in Doriath.

For years uncounted the Sindar dwelt in Beleriand in peace and
happiness – a state which, if less exalted than that of their High-elven
kin, far across the Sea, was a pleasurable mode of existence.
And even when evil began, slowly and almost imperceptibly, to
awake once more in Middle-earth, the Sindar at first were not greatly
troubled; for in those days they had the friendship of the Dwarves
of the Blue Mountains, and from them acquired arms and armour.
And indeed evil did not at first come into Beleriand, for the Grey-
elves were then a numerous people, hardy and valiant, noblest of
all Elves remaining in mortal lands; and the Orcs did not dare the
wrath of Thingol. But gradually Beleriand came under siege, and
raids began to be made deep into Thingol's domain (see FIRST BATTLE
OF BELERIAND); and shortly afterwards there came from the West a
mighty fugitive, one of the great Valar, who had turned renegade
and had committed a terrible crime against the peoples of the Undying Lands. His name was Morgoth, and with his return to Middle-
earth the long peace of the Sindar came to an end. In fear of the
pursuit which followed, Morgoth built[18] a mighty realm somewhat
to the north of Beleriand. The name of this place was Angband.

But before much time had passed a fleet of ships appeared on the
horizon: a great fleet, of white swan-vessels, with gilded sails and

many proud banners.[19] These were the Noldor, High-elves of Eldamar, coming in pursuit of Morgoth and desiring to recover that which he had stolen from them. Thus were the sundered Second and Third Kindreds of the Eldar reunited[20] after almost countless years, and so began the War of the Great Jewels which was to devastate western Middle-earth.

In those wars Morgoth was, at the last, utterly victorious. The High-elves were nigh on annihilated, and their allies, the Edain, were grievously reduced in number; and the Grey-elves also suffered, while their land of Beleriand was thrown down under the Sea by the cataclysm in which Morgoth was finally overthrown. Only a small coastal strip – Lindon – remained to them, and there the survivors dwelt in the Second Age which followed the defeat of Morgoth.

At that time the Grey-elves were ruled by lesser lords: Celeborn and Thranduil; for Thingol was no more. Celeborn ruled in South Lindon (Harlindon), but after some years he removed eastward to Eregion, and thence across the Misty Mountains to the inaccessible forests in the vale of Anduin (see LOTHLÓRIEN). Those of the Grey-elves who would accompanied him, or went further north with Thranduil; while those that remained in Lindon were ruled by Gil-galad of the Noldor, one of the few High-elven princes to survive the War of the Great Jewels.

As the Second and Third Ages passed, the waning years lessened the numbers of the once-numerous Sindar, and in the hearts of many the 'Sea-longing' awoke at last, and from the Grey Havens of Mithlond many grey ships put to sea, never to return. For with the passing of years the time drew nearer for the Eldarin kindreds to depart from mortal lands, and leave the Middle-earth to the Dominion of Men, their inheritors; and in the Fourth Age Celeborn finally abandoned Lothlórien to the Wood-elves and, together with his small retinue, returned to Eriador to dwell for a while in the House of Elrond, last of the Sindar lords to linger in Middle-earth. He passed west in the last ship to sail from the Grey Havens.

Note: it is important to emphasize that *Sindar* was the name given to this Eldarin race *by the Noldor*; their own term for themselves was *Edhil* 'Elves'. See also *Silmarillion* p. 348.

Sindarin The language of the Grey-elves. It was an ancient tongue of the Eldar, being descended, like the High-elven speech (Quenya), from the still more ancient root-language of all Elvenkind. But the long years of the Elder Days altered the Sindarin tongue, and although in basic structure it continued to resemble the Quenya, many other changes took place which affected the sound of this (phonetic) Eldarin speech. As these changes in spoken Sindarin largely took place before the Grey-elves devised methods of writing or inscription (SEE ALPHABET OF DAERON), one may assume that the sections of Grey-elven speech which appear in translations from the Red Book are in the tongue that was spoken in Beleriand during the rule of Thingol Greycloak in the First Age.

Sindarin was therefore to some degree less noble and antique than Quenya, for the High-elven speech brought back to Middle-earth by the Noldor was little changed from the original archaic Eldarin root-tongue, and in both spoken and written forms differed greatly from the language of the Grey-elves of Beleriand. Nonetheless, the Noldor Exiles put aside their own Ancient Speech and adopted instead the Sindarin tongue spoken by the (far more numerous) Grey-elves;[21] this then became the language of the Eldar in Middle-earth, and was later learned by the Edain, who kept it alive in Middle-earth long after the Eldar themselves had departed.

Indeed all the place-names in Arnor and Gondor that were given by the Dúnedain were in the Grey-elven tongue. The personal names of the Dúnedain themselves were also often in Sindarin, the exception being the royal names of Númenor, which had been in the more ancient High-elven language. Names of all the Kings of Gondor, and of all the Kings of Arnor (but not of Arthedain) were also in this Quenya speech (e.g. *Elendil, Ciryaher, Eärendur*). But rulers of Arthedain and Chieftains of the North invariably carried Sindarin personal names (*Aranarth, Arvedui, Aragorn*), and some of these were 'the names of Elves or Men remembered in the songs and histories of the First Age'.[22] And after the establishment of the Realms in Exile, the spoken Sindarin of the Dúnedain deeply influenced the (Mannish) Common Speech of the Westland, which afterwards became the most widely spoken language in both Eriador and Gondor.

See also SPOKEN TONGUES.

Singollo 'Grey-cloak' (Q.; older form *Sindacollo*) See THINGOL GREYCLOAK.

Sirannon 'Gate-stream' (Sind.) A river of Eregion. It originally flowed from an underground source near the West-door of Moria down into the flat lands of eastern Eriador, falling first over a gentle cataract (the Sair Falls) before wandering westward through the land of the Elven-smiths. But at an unknown date in the last millennium of the Third Age, the Gate-stream was dammed and formed a lake which sealed off the Doors of Durin from the surrounding lands.

See also Book II Chap. 4.

Sirion 'Mighty-flowing' (Sind.) The greatest river of western Middle-earth during the First Age (greatest in volume of water carried; the Gelion was actually far longer). It rose far in the North, on the eastern slopes of the Ered Wethrin (at the Eithel Sirion), and flowed south for 140 leagues before reaching the sea, and throughout its course was accounted the border between East and West Beleriand. It had seven tributaries, of which the Rivil, which had its source on Dorthonion, was the most northerly, and the Narog the most southerly. The Sirion reached the Sea in a great delta, the Mouths of Sirion – at which point this enormous stream was nearly a mile wide; and during its journey from Ard-galen to the Bay of Balar it underwent nearly every transformation a river can undergo, flowing through marshland, over mighty Falls – and even underground, for a distance of nearly ten miles.

Siriondil From 748–830 Third Age, the eleventh King of Gondor.

Siriondil The father of King Eärnil II of Gondor. Though not himself King, he was of royal blood, being the grand-nephew of Narmacil II, twenty-ninth King. This kinship was the constitutional basis of Eärnil's claim to the Throne of Gondor.

See also EÄRNIL II.

Sirith 'Flowing' (Sind.) One of the Seven Rivers of Gondor. It flowed south from a source high in the mountain-vales of Lebennin and joined the Anduin some little distance downstream from the port of Pelargir. Its chief tributary was the Celos (or Kelos).

Skinbark A translation of the Sindarin name *Fladrif*, which was borne (as a 'short name') by an aged Ent of Fangorn Forest.

'Slinker' See SMÉAGOL-GOLLUM.

Smallburrow See ROBIN SMALLBURROW.

Smaug the Golden One of the greatest *Urulóki* (Fire-dragons) of Middle-earth during the Third Age, a beast of cunning and cruelty whose first recorded appearance in the Annals of the Age was in the year 2770, when he came flaming out of the North to capture, sack and occupy the Dwarf-kingdom of Erebor east of Mirkwood. The attack was so successful that most of the Dwarves unfortunate enough to be caught inside the Lonely Mountain on that day were exterminated – and for good measure Smaug also destroyed the nearby Mannish town of Dale. After completing these labours, the Dragon crawled inside the Mountain and there gathered all the wealth of both Erebor and Dale into one vast heap, upon which he lay in contented slumber for nearly two full centuries.

So fearsome was the known wrath of Smaug that none came to challenge his ownership of the hoard for many years, and he grew complacent and vain. Yet in the end he was slain, for several reasons, the chief of which being his own Dragon-conceit. As is told in *The Hobbit*, Smaug's vanity accidentally led him to reveal the existence of a vulnerable unarmoured patch on his underside, and armed with this information the enemies of Smaug were able to pierce this spot with an arrow: Smaug was slain by the rightful heir of the Kings of Dale, Bard the Bowman of Esgaroth, in the year 2941 Third Age, and his bones ever after lay in the shallows near the ruined Lake-town. His destruction accomplished, the Kingdom Under the Mountain and the town of Dale were both restored to their rightful owners and the region had peace for many years.

Sméagol-Gollum Undoubtedly the most tragic of all the personal tales associated with the history of the Great Ring was that of the creature known as Sméagol, or Gollum. Originally a lowly member of a family of Stoors (Hobbits), he became an early victim of the malevolent power of the Ring, which he bore for nearly five hundred years of his long and miserable life, unwilling – and unable – to relinquish it. Yet in the end the Ruling Ring itself discarded him – and the loss of his greatest, indeed his only treasure proved the stimulus which finally caused him to leave his long-secret refuge under the Misty Mountains; and in recovering his Precious at the last, he brought about its destruction as well as his own, and so was reunited with it for ever.

The tale of Gollum's long and terrible odyssey has been recounted at length in the Red Book – in both of the major sections of narrative, for both Bilbo and Frodo Baggins encountered him during their adventures. This entry will accordingly confine itself to recording those details of Gollum's ancestry which lie outside the main tale. He was born in the twenty-fourth century of the Third Age and was in origin closely akin to Hobbit-kind, for his family were of Stoorish blood but had returned to the vales of Anduin after dwelling in Eriador, unlike most of their race (see STOORS). They dwelt at that time not far from the banks of the river Anduin, near the Gladden Fields.

This young Stoor was named *Sméagol* (orig. Trahald), which means 'burrowing-in'; and, like most of the clan, he made his living by fishing in the Great River. And it was while on a fishing expedition that Sméagol chanced to discover the Great Ring – or rather, his friend Déagol found the Ring on the river-bed where it had lain undisturbed for over two thousand years. The Ring-spell had an instant effect on Sméagol, who promptly murdered his friend to gain possession of the golden thing.

Taking it back to his little community, Sméagol soon discovered the Ring's more obvious properties, which he used in small, mean ways. He rapidly became unpopular among his kinfolk, not least for the habit he developed of making unpleasant glottal noises in his throat (from which he gained the name *Gollum*), and in the end his furtive ways and sneaking tricks brought about his expulsion from the family hole. Wandering north, alone and miserable, he chanced to follow a stream to its source deep under the Misty Mountains; for Gollum had always hated and feared the light of Sun and Moon, and it seemed to him that under the bowels of the Mountains he would be safe for ever from such things. In the underground caverns beneath the Orc-mines of the High Pass he made his home. And there he remained for many lives.

For from the first the terrible power of the Ruling Ring was on him, though to Gollum it gave power according to his measure: long life it granted, but little else (save the power of invisibility) and for many centuries he eked out a miserable existence, growing thin and unnaturally strong as his years lengthened beyond their natural measure – but never 'fading' or becoming a wraith, for in the endless darkness he found little need to wear 'the Precious' (as he termed the Ring). And so, although almost wholly ruined, Gollum was slow to fall completely under the power of the Ring.

Such was the misshapen, evil-minded creature encountered by Bilbo Baggins in the year 2941 Third Age, almost five hundred years after the finding of the Ring and the murder of Déagol; and with that meeting the Great Ring chose for itself a new bearer, for it was plain that as long as it stayed with Gollum it would never again leave the cave under the Misty Mountains. Bilbo acquired the Ring and Gollum was left desolate in the dark. But three years afterwards, his desire finally overcame his fear and he ventured forth into the world to begin his long search for the 'thief' of the Precious. During the next seventy years Gollum hunted the length and breadth of Wilderland, being captured at last by Sauron while prying on the very borders of Mordor. There he was put to the Question – and in this way the Lord of the Rings at last learned the truth concerning the whereabouts of his long-lost treasure. And so began the War of the Ring.

Released from Mordor with instructions to hunt for the Ring, Gollum finally located the Fellowship while they were passing through Moria (Book II Chap. 4), and from that time onwards he was almost continually within sight of the Ring-bearer and his burden, from Lothlórien down the length of the Great River, across the Emyn Muil and into Mordor itself. Yet it was later acknowledged by the Ring-bearer that, but for Gollum's self-serving treachery (oddly mixed with a genuine devotion to Frodo), the Quest could not have been achieved at all: for at the very last stroke, the power of the Ring overcame Frodo, and without the (ill-intentioned) intercession of Gollum at the brink of the Cracks of Doom, there can be little doubt that Sauron would have prevailed. In this way Gollum atoned for all the evils committed during his long life, and at last found the peace his trials had earned him.

Smial A translation of the original Hobbit-word *trân* ('burrow'), being the name given by Hobbits to the tunnels and delvings which were their most ancient (and most characteristic) form of dwelling-place. The practice of living in holes in the ground was indeed archaic, but by the time of the War of the Ring the custom had fallen somewhat out of use in the Shire, due to the shortage of suitable land; and thus it was 'only the richest and the poorest Hobbits that maintained the old custom'.[23]

Naturally enough, *smials* varied greatly in size and splendour. Some of the larger examples (such as Brandy Hall and the 'Great Smials' of the Tooks) were of vast dimension, with many branching tunnels and passages, while Bag End, the ancestral dwelling of the well-to-do Baggins family, was a well-preserved example of a 'manor-hole', or local squirearchical *smial*.

Snaga 'Slave' (Black Speech) A contemptuous name given by larger breeds of Orc (such as the Uruk-hai) to lesser Goblins.

Snowbourn A river of eastern Rohan. It rose in Harrowdale and flowed northwards as far as the hill of Edoras, after which it bent eastward to join the Entwash.

Snowmane The steed of King Théoden of Rohan. Snowmane bore his royal master throughout the War of the Ring and perished in battle on the Pelennor Fields (March, 3019 Third Age). The horse was slain by a dart from the Witch-king, and crushed Théoden beneath him when he fell. Snowmane was afterwards buried where he had fallen, in a mound later called Snowmane's Howe.

Solmath The second month of the year in the Shire and Bree Reckonings, equivalent to *Nénimë* in Kings' Reckoning and to our February.

Note: pronounced *Somath*.

Song of Parting The lament made by Beren of the Edain for his beloved, Lúthien Tinúviel daughter of Thingol Greycloak. (It is reproduced in entirety in *The Silmarillion* p. 178.)

Soronúmë 'Eagle of the West' (Q.) One of the constellations made by Varda (Elbereth).

South Downs A broad ridge of downland in Eriador, an eastern outlier of the Barrow-downs, which lay to the south of the Bree-land.

Southern Star A distinctive brand of Pipe-weed grown in the Southfarthing of the Shire.

Southfarthing One of the four quarters or 'farthings' of the Shire. The Southfarthing was the warmest and sunniest region of the Hobbit-land, and was rightly famous for its viticulture and its leaf-plantations. The chief family of the area was the Took clan of Tuckborough and district.

South Ithilien See ITHILIEN.

South-kingdom GONDOR.

Southlinch A variety of Pipe-weed grown in Bree, on the south slopes of Bree Hill. By all accounts this brand of weed was inferior to others grown in the Southfarthing of the Shire.

See also PIPE-WEED.

'Speaking-peoples' A name given in the lore of the Elves to the articulate races of Middle-earth – by which the Elves meant those of the Free Peoples able to converse with Elvenkind. The 'speaking-peoples' were: Ents, Hobbits, Dwarves, Men and, of course, the *Quendi* (Elves) themselves.

Spies of the Valar An epithet for the FAITHFUL or Elendili of Númenor, used only by the (heretical) royalists.

Spoken Tongues The accompanying diagram is intended to show, in as clear a manner as possible, the ancestry and development of the

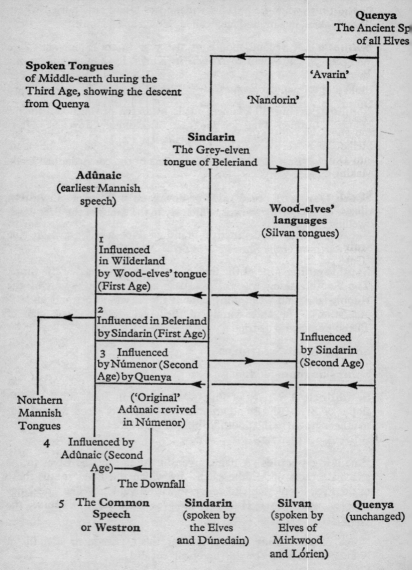

Quenya
The Ancient Sp
of all Elves

Spoken Tongues
of Middle-earth during the
Third Age, showing the descent
from Quenya

'Avarin'

'Nandorin'

Sindarin
The Grey-elven
tongue of Beleriand

Adûnaic
(earliest Mannish
speech)

**Wood-elves'
languages**
(Silvan tongues)

1
Influenced
in Wilderland
by Wood-elves' tongue
(First Age)

2
Influenced in Beleriand
by Sindarin (First Age)

3 Influenced
by Númenor (Second
Age) by Quenya

Influenced
by Sindarin
(Second Age)

Northern
Mannish
Tongues

('Original'
Adûnaic revived
in Númenor)

4   Influenced by
Adûnaic (Second
Age)

The Downfall

5 The **Common
Speech**
or **Westron**

Sindarin
(spoken by
the Elves
and Dúnedain)

Silvan
(spoken by
Elves of
Mirkwood
and Lórien)

Quenya
(unchanged)

various languages used by Men and Elves of Middle-earth during the First, Second and Third Ages.

Springle-ring A country dance common in the Shire. It was, by all accounts, somewhat vigorous.

Spring of Arda The name given in the traditions of the Eldar to the epoch at the very beginning of time, after the making of Arda (the World), when the Valar dwelled in Almaren and the two Lamps, Illuin and Ormal, shone out over the face of the Earth, giving Light. During this vanished time the first plants began to grow, and the first beasts awoke and walked in the wild. But the Spring came to a sudden and shocking end, with the launching of war upon the Valar – by Melkor. He overthrew the Lamps and Middle-earth was plunged into Darkness – a Darkness that was to endure for Ages, until the Making of the Moon and Sun.

Staddle A village of the Bree-land. It stood to the east of Bree village on the south-eastern slopes of Bree Hill, and was the main dwelling-place for the Little Folk (Hobbits) of the area.

Stair Falls An ornamental waterfall over which the *Sirannon* ('Gate-stream') of Moria originally flowed, on its way down to the lowlands of eastern Eriador. When the stream was dammed during the later part of the Third Age, the water ceased to flow over the Stair Falls in any measurable quantity.

Standelf A village of the Buckland, at the southern end of the track-way which ran northwards to meet the Great East Road near the Brandywine Bridge.

Standing Silence A moment of ceremonial silence observed by the Dúnedain at the commencement of each meal. All who were to dine faced west, 'towards Númenor that was, and beyond to Elvenhome that is, and to that which is beyond Elvenhome and will ever be'.[24]

Starkhorn The name given in Rohan to a great peak of the northern White Mountains. The Starkhorn overlooked the (southern) head of Harrowdale valley.

Star of Elendil A translation of the Quenya word *Elendilmir*, being the name of the royal diadem worn by the Kings of Arnor. In fashion it was a plain fillet of silver with a single diamond set over the brows.

See also SILVER CROWN.

Star of the Dúnedain The *Elendilmir*. See previous entry.

Star of the House of Fëanor The heraldic emblem of the Noldorin Elves of Fëanor's House. It was a Star of eight rays. An example may be found in the designs on the Doors of Durin (the Westgate of Moria), which were etched by the hand of Celebrimbor of Eregion during the Second Age. Celebrimbor was Fëanor's descendant.

See Book II Chap. 4; also HERALDIC DEVICES.

Steelsheen An admiring name given by the Rohirrim to the Lady Morwen of Lossarnach, wife of King Thengel of Rohan, mother of Théoden, and grandmother of Éowyn – who was said to have inherited her temperament from this noble lady.

Sterday A later form of the word *Sterrendei*, which was the first day of the week in the Shire Reckoning, equivalent to *Elenya* ('Stars'-day') in Kings' Reckoning and the Elven Calendar of Imladris.

Stewards of Gondor The chief counsellors to the royal Line of Anárion in the South-kingdom of the Dúnedain. They were traditionally appointed by the King from among his close advisers, but after the middle years of the Third Age the Stewardship became hereditary and all subsequent Stewards of Gondor were afterwards chosen from among the descendants of Húrin of Emyn Arnen, who had been Steward to King Minardil (1621–34 Third Age).

The waning of the Line of Anárion produced a corresponding strengthening of this hereditary Stewardship, and all holders of the Office after Pelendur, Steward to Ondoher and Eärnil II, received the Rod of Stewardship by virtue of being the eldest son. Pelendur was followed by Vorondil (the Hunter), and Vorondil by Mardil Voronwë, who officiated for both Eärnil and his son Eärnur. Mardil was later accounted the first of the Ruling Stewards, for during his period of office King Eärnur rode away to war and never returned; from that time onward the Stewards ruled Gondor in the name of the Kings.

See also HOUSE OF HÚRIN; RULING STEWARDS.

Stewards' Reckoning A calendar-system of the Dúnedain of Gondor, introduced by Mardil the Good Steward in the year 2060 Third Age to replace Kings' Reckoning. It was in essence the older system – which had already been adopted piecemeal by most of the inhabitants of the Westron-speaking area – updated and adjusted in order to eradicate the accumulated deficits of 5,500 years of the Númenorean calendar. Hador (seventh Ruling Steward) later added one day to the year 2360 to complete this adjustment process, but no further revisions were made during the Third Age. In the Fourth Age Stewards' Reckoning was replaced in Gondor by the New Reckoning, which represented a return to the older Kings' Reckoning adapted to begin the year in spring.

Stewards' Reckoning was the final form of Kings' Reckoning adopted by the Westron-speaking peoples during the Third Age (although the Shire- and Bree-dwellers continued to employ their idiosyncratic versions of the older system, together with their own nomenclature).

See also KINGS' RECKONING; NEW RECKONING; Appendix D.

Sting The name given by the Hobbit Bilbo Baggins to the short Elvish sword (or long Elvish knife) discovered by him in a Trolls' hoard during an early adventure in the year 2941 Third Age (see *The Hobbit*, Chap. 2). The weapon was forged by Elven-smiths of Gondolin during the First Age for the wars against Morgoth the Enemy, but fell into evil hands after that city was destroyed.

The sword's history throughout the Second and Third Ages is of course unknown, but one may surmise that it passed from hoard to hoard until it finally came to rest in a remote Troll-lair in eastern Eriador. The possessors of that hoard were slain by Gandalf the Grey (as is told in Bilbo's narrative), and shortly afterwards their intended victims were able to ransack the cave for wealth and weapons. Brought to light in the same cache were the Elf-swords Glamdring and Orcrist (borne afterwards by Gandalf and Thorin Oakenshield of the Dwarves).

Like all Elf-blades, Sting gleamed with a cold blue light if any servants of the Enemy were nigh at hand, and its cutting edge was sharper by far than any weapon made in later Ages. Bilbo used Sting many times during his adventure, and later passed the sword to Frodo, who bore it from Rivendell to the borders of Mordor. Samwise Gamgee bore it as far as the Cracks of Doom; after the War was over, Sting became an heirloom of the Gamgee family.

Stock The chief village of the Marish in the Shire. It lay near the river Baranduin (Brandywine), between the Great East Road and the Bucklebury Ferry.

Stockbrook A stream which arose in the Woody End of the Shire and flowed north-east to join the Baranduin a little way south of the village of Stock (after which it was presumably named).

Stock Road A trackway which ran from the Great East Road near the Three-farthing Stone and bent south and east in a wide loop through the Green Hill Country and Woody End to the village of Stock in the Eastfarthing.

Stone of Erech An enormous black spherical stone, some ten feet or so in diameter, which was said to have been brought to Middle-earth from Númenor in 3320 Second Age by Isildur, eldest son of Elendil the Tall. It was set by Isildur atop the ancient Hill of Erech in Morthond Vale as a symbol of the royalty of Gondor (and its kinship with ancient Númenor), and the Men of the White Mountains were required to swear fealty to the Dúnedain upon it. When the mountain-people later broke their Oath, it was to the Stone of Erech that they were summoned, a full Age afterwards, in order to fulfil their vow and so achieve rest at last.

Stone of the Hapless The grave-marker on the mound underneath which were buried Túrin Turambar and his mother Morwen Eledhwen, at Cabed Naeramarth. It was said in the lore of the Edain that no evil should ever defile this place, nor cause the stone to be thrown down.

See also TOL MORWEN.

'The Stone Troll' A comic verse composed by Samwise Gamgee. It has been preserved as part of Frodo Baggins' narrative in the Red Book, and may also be found (No. 7) in the collection entitled *The Adventures of Tom Bombadil*.

Stone-trolls See TROLLS.

Stonewain Valley A deep, hidden valley between Druadan Forest and the northern White Mountains. During the late Second Age it was used by Men of newly founded Gondor as a route between the quarries at Min-Rimmon and the cities of the Pelennor. In later years the quarries and the wagon-road fell into disuse, and were afterwards forgotten, and the forest drew a veil across the entrance once more. By the time of the War of the Ring, a full Age after the building of Gondor, only the ancient Wild Men (see WOSES) of Druadan Forest knew of the existence of the forgotten wain-road through the mountains; and when they revealed this secret to the Riders of Rohan, the Rohirrim were able to use the Valley to out-flank an army of foes which stood between them and the relief of besieged Minas Tirith.

See also BATTLE OF THE PELENNOR FIELDS; Book V Chap. 5.

Stoningland The name given by the Riders of Rohan to the land of Gondor; *Mundburg* ('Guardian-fortress') was their name for the city of Minas Tirith.

Stoors One of the three breeds or clans of Hobbits. The Stoors were larger and heavier in build than others of their race, and originated from the upper vales of Anduin, where they had once lived in close concord with the Men of that region of Wilderland. They were also the last Hobbit-tribe to leave those parts, eventually crossing the Misty Mountains westward in a great migration during the fourteenth century of the Third Age, after which they settled in Dunland or in the Angle between the rivers Hoarwell (Mitheithel) and Loudwater (Bruinen). But with the arising of the dread realm of Angmar the following century, a number of Stoors dwelling in the Angle re-crossed the Misty Mountains and went to dwell near the Gladden Fields. (A surviving family of this branch was still there a thousand years later; see SMÉAGOL-GOLLUM.)

In the meantime the Dunland Stoors remained where they were until shortly after the founding of the Shire (1601 Third Age), when they duly emigrated north-west to join their kinfolk west of the Baranduin. These latecomers settled mostly in the Eastfarthing, near the banks of the river, and later some of them re-crossed the Baranduin to dwell in the area known as Buckland (see OLDBUCKS).

The Stoors brought to the Shire many traces of the Dunlending culture unconsciously absorbed during the years spent east of the Greyflood. In this way their cultural influences were closely akin to those of the Bree-men (themselves descended from ancestors of the Men of Dunland), who likewise migrated into central Eriador during the Third Age. Even by the time of the War of the Ring a certain 'foreign' quality of the Eastfarthing- and Buckland-hobbits was easily remarked by other Shire-dwellers (who were mainly Harfoots, with Fallohide families in positions of prominence).

Straight Road The name given by Men, in the Third and later Ages, to the ancient route across the Sea into the Far West, by which Elves and those appointed could still make the journey to Valinor and Eressëa, even after the Drowning of Númenor and the altering of the World.

(The) Strangers MEN.

Strider The nickname given by folk of Bree to the Ranger of Eriador known (to his own people) as ARAGORN II, sixteenth Chieftain of the Dúnedain of the North.

See also TELCONTAR

Strongbow A translation of the Grey-elven name *Cúthalion*. See BELEG CÚTHALION.

Stybba 'Stubby' A pony of the Rohirrim, lent to Meriadoc Brandybuck during the War of the Ring by Théoden King of Rohan.

Súle 'Wind' (Q.) An alternative title for the Fëanorian Tengwa number 9 (normally known as *thúle* 'spirit'). The Sindarin equivalent was *Súl* (cf. *Amon Súl* 'Hill of Winds').

Súlimë 'Windy' (Q.) The equivalent of our March, being the third month in both Kings' and Stewards' Reckoning, and the twelfth in the New Reckoning of the Fourth Age. Although this month-name became adopted by most of the folk in the Westron-speaking area during the Third Age, the Dúnedain themselves, who had originally brought it to Middle-earth, used only the Sindarin equivalent *Gwaeron*. The Hobbit-name was *Rethe*.

Súlimo 'Lord of Winds' (Q.; literally 'Lord of the Breath of Arda') See MANWË SÚLIMO.

Summerdays The Bree-name for the period of midsummer known in the Shire as *Lithe*.

Sunday The later form of the word *Sunnendei*, the Shire-word for the second day of the week. (It was equivalent to – and in origin a translation of – the Quenya word *Anarya*, 'Sun's-day'.)

Sunlending The name given in Rohan to the province of Anórien in Gondor. (*Anórien* means 'Sun-land' in the Quenya tongue.)

Sunless Year The name given in traditions of the Eldar to the period of time between the death of the Two Trees and the raising of the Sun and Moon.

Sunnendei See SUNDAY.

Súrion (**Tar-Súrion**) The ninth King of Númenor.

Sutherland A translation of the Sindarin word *Haradwaith*.

Súza In the original (as opposed to translated) Hobbit-speech, this was the name given by Hobbits to the lands between the river Baranduin and the Tower Hills, the region of authority of their Thain, granted to them in perpetuity in 1600 Third Age (by King Argeleb II of Arthedain) and settled the following year. It has been translated from the Red Book as 'the Shire'.

Swanfleet The name given by Men of Eriador to the river Glanduin, a tributary of the Greyflood. (It is *not* a translation.)

Swarthy Men EASTERLINGS.

Sweet Galenas See GALENAS; PIPE-WEED.

Sword of Elendil See NARSIL.

Sword-that-was-broken See ANDÚRIL; NARSIL.

Notes

1 Book IV Chap. 3.
2 Book VI Chap. 9.
3 Appendix B. Saruman's Maiarin name is not known.
4 Book III Chap. 11.
5 Book II Chap. 2.
6 For the manner of his eventual expulsion from Tol-in-Gaurhoth, see *Silmarillion* p. 175.
7 Book II Chap. 7.
8 Appendix B 'The Second Age'.
9 Actually there were many more rivers flowing through Gondor – Anduin, Ciril (or Kiril), Celos (or Kelos), Serni, Entwash, Poros, and (disputably) Harnen. The term 'Seven Rivers of Gondor' applies strictly to *Old* Gondor (i.e. at the time of its founding).
10 'Eärendil was a Mariner' (Book II Chap. 2).
11 Book VI Chap. 1.
12 Book IV Chap. 9.
13 Derived or mutated from the original Quenya of Kings' Reckoning.
14 Appendix D.
15 Book VI Chap. 1.
16 i.e. *The Lord of the Rings*.
17 *Silmarillion* pp. 55-8, 91-7.
18 Or rather '*re*-built'; for Angband was first made long before the Elves awoke in Cuiviénen, but was razed during the Battle of the Powers.
19 One of these swan-ships is illustrated in *The Silmarillion Calendar* 1978.
20 But not for long: the deeds of the Noldor – and the tidings of their deeds in Eldamar – soon made alliance impossible so far as the Grey-elves were concerned.
21 The Noldor learned Sindarin perforce, for in Beleriand their language was proscribed. See also Note 20.
22 Appendix F I.
23 Prologue I.
24 Book IV Chap. 5.

Talan (pl. *telain*) The name given by the Galadhrim (Tree-elves) of Lothlórien to the dwelling-platforms (or *flets*) which they were accustomed to build amid the branches of the Mallorn-trees in their land. It is Sindarin in form.

Talath Dirnen 'Guarded Plain' (Sind.) The name given by the Elves of Nargothrond – and later by the Men of Brethil – to the region of empty moorland which lay between the rivers Narog and Teiglin, in West Beleriand. It was so-called because it was accounted the north march of the Realm of Nargothrond, and was accordingly frequently patrolled by Elves of that kingdom, in peace and war.

Talath Rhúnen 'East Vale' (Sind.) The oldest Elven-name for the land of THARGELION.

'The Tale of Aragorn and Arwen' A manuscript written in Gondor during the later second century of the Fourth Age by Steward Barahir of Emyn Arnen, who was the grandson of Faramir, Prince of Ithilien and Steward to King Elessar (Aragorn II). As its title indicates, the text deals chiefly with the life, hopes and eventual triumphs of Aragorn II, Chieftain of the Dúnedain of the North – who in his eighty-eighth year, became the first King of both Gondor and Arnor since Elendil himself – and with his long betrothal to the Lady who later became his Queen: Arwen Undómiel, Evenstar of her people and only daughter of Elrond of Rivendell.

The union of Aragorn and Arwen was of deep historical significance to both the Eldar of Middle-earth and their heirs, the Dúnedain of Arnor and Gondor. For by this means the two branches of the *Peredhil* (Half-elven) were reunited at last after more than five thousand years of separation (see LINES OF DESCENT). Moreover Aragorn, who at his birth was accounted merely sixteenth Chieftain of the Dúnedain, was later to become *Elessar Telcontar, the Renewer,* first King of the Reunited Kingdom. But the granting of Arwen's hand in marriage was made conditional on the securing of the High-kingship for his House, for reasons which are revealed in the *Tale* itself. He succeeded in this task and reigned in great glory and splendour until Year 120 Fourth Age; and his dynasty was firmly established in the kingdom of Arnor and Gondor.

The much-abbreviated section of *The Tale of Aragorn and Arwen* which appears in Appendix A was in origin added to the Thain's Book by scribes of Gondor after the Passing of the King, and was afterwards incorporated into the later copy of that famous volume made by Findegil, King's Writer, in the year 172 Fourth Age. The Thain's Book was a copy of the Red Book of Westmarch, made by the Tooks at the request of the King and presented to him by Peregrin Took in Year 63; and Findegil's copy (complete with authoritative correction and annotations) was presented to the Hobbits in return. In this way the *Tale,* in which Hobbits had played some part, came to the attention of Shire-scholars, and was after-wards incorporated in their Annals.

Tale of Grief An alternative name among Men for the NARN I HÎN HÚRIN (*Tale of the Children of Húrin*).

The Tale of Years A Chronology of the Third and early Fourth Ages – together with a much-abbreviated approximate chronology of the Second Age – which may be found in most translations from the Red Book of Westmarch in somewhat reduced form (see Appendix B). It was compiled on the orders of Peregrin Took, thirty-second Thain of the Shire, by his descendants (who maintained links with Gondor, from which most of the material contained in the chronologies was derived).

The chronologies also include plentiful information supplied by Meriadoc Brandybuck, who kept in close touch with Rohan and as a consequence came to learn much of the history of the House of Eorl. Meriadoc also visited Rivendell on several occasions, and doubtless it was from the libraries of Rivendell that many of the (largely conjectural) dates for the Second Age were derived; for in Rivendell, even after the departure of Elrond, there were many Elves whose memories reached back into those distant times.

Taniquetil 'High-white-peak' (Q.) One of the oldest names given by High-elves of Eldamar to that mountain known as *Oiolossë* or *Amon Uilos* (Sind.).

Tar- 'High [Royal]' (Q. from orig. *tára* 'lofty'; fem. *tári*) An ancient word-element in the High-elven tongue which was used as a royal name-prefix by all Kings and Queens of Númenor, excepting Vardamir (son of Elros) and five of the last six rulers (who took Adûnaic – *Ar*-prefixed – names). It also occurs in the High-elven form of the (Sindarin) name Elbereth: *Elentári* 'Star-queen'; it may likewise be found in many of the royal names taken by rulers of Arnor and Gondor (e.g. *Atanatar, Tarcil, Tarondor, Tarannon, Envinyatar*), and in many other names besides.

Note: those Kings and Queens of Númenor who took *Tar*-prefixed royal titles have all been alphabetized in this *Companion* under the main part of their names (e.g. SÚRION, ANCALIMË, CIRYATAN rather than Tar-Súrion, Tar-Ancalimë, etc.).

See also AR(A).

Tarannon 'Royal-gate' (Q.+Sind.) The birth-name of the twelfth King of Gondor; he was later known as *Falastur*, 'Lord-of-the-Coasts' (Sind.+Q.).

Taras The westernmost of all the mountains of Middle-earth during the First Age. It was a promontory in the south-west of Nevrast, and looked over the Sea. On its slopes Turgon of the Noldor built his first dwelling in Middle-earth, the halls of Vinyamar.

Tarcil From 435–515 Third Age, the sixth King of Arnor.

Tarciryan 'Royal-ships' (Q.) The younger brother of Tarannon (Falastur), who was twelfth King of Gondor and first of the fabled 'Ship-kings'. Falastur was the first ruler of Gondor to die childless, and Tarciryan's eldest son succeeded him (as Eärnil I).

Targon 'Royal-stone' (Sind.) A Man of Gondor. During the War of the Ring he was a member of the Third Company of the Citadel Guard of Minas Tirith; he was in charge of the butteries and store-houses of that Company.

Tárion (Q.) An alternative name for *Valanya*, the sixth and last day of the week in the Elvish Calendar of Imladris, and the seventh and last in the Kings' Reckoning of Númenor and Middle-earth.

Tark See following entry.

Tarkil The original (as opposed to translated) name given in the Common Speech (the Westron) to a member of the race of Gondor. It appears to be a worn-down form of the Quenya word *Tarcil*.

Note: the epithet *tark*, used by some tribes of Orcs, to mean a Man of Gondor, was doubtless a further debased version of *tarkil*.

Tarlang's Neck A narrow pass through a southern spur of the White Mountains, which opened the way from Morthond Vale to the province of Lamedon.

Tarmenel 'King-of-the-Heavens' (Q.) An Elvish poetic reference, possibly a term for *Oiolossë*, the highest of the Mountains of Valinor (the *Pelóri*). If this is so, then it may be assumed that the *Meneltarma*, highest mountain in Númenor, was named after this greater peak, as it bears a (subtly diminished) form of the same name.

Tarn Aeluin 'Blue-mere' (Sind.) The name given by the Grey-elves and the Edain to a small lake in the centre of the Dorthonion highland, at the entrance of the shallow pass which led to Ladros. This name was remembered by the Edain for its associations with Barahir, and his twelve comrades, who based their guerilla activities around this desolate place in the three years following the Dagor Bragollach.

Tarondor From 515–602 Third Age, the seventh King of Arnor. Also the name of the twenty-seventh King of Gondor who ruled from 1636–1798 Third Age, longest to reign of all the Line of Anárion. He succeeded his uncle Telemnar, twenty-sixth King, who was slain, together with all his children, in the Great Plague of 1636 Third Age; and to Tarondor fell the arduous task of reordering the Realm. As many folk had fled from Osgiliath – which had been particularly ravaged by the pestilence – he removed the King's Seat to Minas Anor, where he planted a seedling of the White Tree to replace that which had died during the Plague.

Tarostar 'Royal-forts' (Q.) The birth-name of the eighth King of Gondor, later known as Rómendacil I.

Tasarinan See NAN-TASARION.

Taurelilómëa, Tauremorna, Tauremornalómë 'Forest-many-shadowed, Forest-of-darkness, Forest-black-shadowed' (Q.) Three somewhat discouraging terms for the ancient Forest of Fangorn, used by Treebeard the Ent in various chants and songs which spoke of the Wood. They are all High-elven in form but Entish in style.

Note: the Quenya word-element *taurë* 'forest' may also be found in other names for woods, e.g. *Taur e-Ndaedelos,* 'Forest of the Great Fear' (Mirkwood), *Taur-na-Neldor* (Neldoreth), and *Taur-im-Duinath.*

Taur e-Ndaedelos See GREENWOOD THE GREAT; also preceding entry.

Taur-en-Faroth 'Forest of the Hunters' (Sind.) The name given in West Beleriand to the highlands which lay upon either side of the Narog, actually the westernmost outlier of the Andram. Deep underneath these tree-clad heights lay the caves of Nargothrond.

Also called *High Faroth.*

Taur-im-Duinath 'Forest-between-the-rivers' (Sind.) The name given by the Grey-elves of Beleriand to the immense region of scrub and woodland, largely uninhabited except by individual wandering Wood-elves, which lay between the Bay of Balar and the lower reaches of the Gelion. (The [two] rivers implied in the name are Gelion and Sirion.)

Taur-na-Neldor 'Forest-of-Beeches' (Sind.) See NELDORETH.

Taur-nu-Fuin 'Forest-under-Nightshade' (Sind.) See DOR-THONION.

Tauron 'The Forester' (Q.) One of the earliest names among the Eldar for the Vala OROMË THE GREAT. See also ALDARON.

Ted Sandyman The only son of the Hobbiton Miller, and by all accounts a rather ignorant and narrow-minded Hobbit. He was not over-friendly to Samwise and, during the War of the Ring and the Occupation of the Shire, was easily persuaded to abet the agents of Saruman. His eventual fate was never recorded, although there can be little doubt that his later relations with local Hobbits were somewhat strained, to say the least.

Teeth of Mordor The Towers of the Teeth, Narchost and Carchost.

Tehta, tehtar 'Sign' (Q.) The *tehtar* were an informalized series of diacritic marks used in the Fëanorian alphabet for many purposes, which differed according to the language or 'mode' of writing employed. The Fëanorian Alphabet (the TENGWAR) was, of course, fully phonetic, and vowels were held to be merely modifications of consonants; these modifications were shown by using the *tehtar* in conjunction with the necessary consonantal symbols. Later these marks came to stand for certain consonantal combinations, guides to stress and pronunciation, and as abbreviations for whole words or elements.

Note: for examples of the 'full' Fëanorian writing (i.e. incorporating the *tehtar* vowel-substitutes) see inscriptions on the title-pages of *The Lord of the Rings* and *The Silmarillion*, and the second inscription under the entry ALPHABET OF FËANOR in this *Companion*.

See also Appendix E II(i).

Teiglin One of the largest rivers of West Beleriand; it was a tributary of Sirion, rising from three sources in the southern slopes of Ered Wethrin. Like all the rivers of Beleriand, the Teiglin flowed southerly for many leagues before turning east, south of the Forest of Brethil, to join the Sirion. From source to confluence it was fifty leagues long. For the second half of its journey the Teiglin was a single great rapid, flowing through deep gorges called the Ravines of Teiglin. (The highest of these cliffs was CABED-EN-ARAS.)

Telchar A great Dwarf-smith of the First Age; he dwelled in the city of Nogrod in the Blue Mountains, most renowned of all the craftsmen of that city. He is chiefly remembered as the maker of the sword Narsil (Andúril) and the dagger Angrod (which Beren used to cut the Silmaril from the Iron Crown of Morgoth).

Telco The Quenya or High-elven word for 'stem', but more properly the title of one of the two primary brush-strokes upon which most of the Fëanorian *Tengwar* ('letters') were constructed. Each *telco* was vertical, and its size and position relative to the central line of the 'stave' indicated the *tyelle* or 'grade' of the letter, i.e. its phonetic series.

See also LÚVA; Appendix E II(i).

Telcontar 'Strider' (Q.) The dynastic name adopted by King Elessar (Aragorn II) after his accession to the Throne of the Reunited Kingdom in 3019 Third Age. Curiously enough, two of Aragorn's royal names – *Elessar* ('Elf-stone') and *Telcontar* – were chosen for him in their original forms by folk who were later to become his subjects, which may explain his later reluctance to abandon either of them. Aragorn was also known as *Envinyatar*, '*The Renewer*' (Q.).

Telemmaitë (Tar-Telemmaitë) The fifteenth King of Númenor.

Telemnar From 1634–6 Third Age, the twenty-sixth King of Gondor. He died, together with all of his children and many of his people, when the Great Plague swept across Gondor in 1636. His successor, his nephew Tarondor, removed the royal seat away from plague-stricken Osgiliath to Minas Anor.

Teleri 'Hindmost' (Q.) The name given by the first two kindreds of the ancient Eldar to the third of their peoples, formerly known as *Lindar* 'the Singers', during the Great Journey from Cuiviénen to the Sea; for this Third Kindred of the Eldar were always last on the line of march. But they were also the largest of the Kindreds. From the Teleri came many subdivisions of the Eldar. For the Vanyar (the First Kindred) and the Noldor (the Second) held together in a body throughout the Journey (although the Noldor later came to be divided into two peoples), but the Teleri journeyed more slowly, frequently fragmenting – so that by the time the Noldor had returned to Middle-earth, three Ages later, the Teleri had long become diversified into three quite distinct peoples: the Falmari of Eldamar; the Sindar (or 'Grey-elves') of Beleriand, and the Nandor of Wilderland and Eriador (with further subdivisions of the Sindar and the Nandor to reckon into the account).

At the outset of the Great Journey none of these divisions had yet taken place. The *Lindar* were led in those early days by two lords, the brothers Elwë and Olwë. But almost from the first they lagged, for one reason or another, despite Elwë's impatience to return to the Far West (which he had already visited by the grace of the Valar); and by the time the Host had reached Wilderland it had become sadly strung out and dispersed along the line of march. Hindmost of all was a large clan led by a certain Lenwë; these turned aside from the Journey while still east of the Misty Mountains, vanishing out of the affairs of the Eldar of Middle-earth and Eldamar. They were called *Nandor*, 'Those-who-turn-back'. (From them later came the *Laiquendi* or 'Green-elves' of Ossiriand.)

The second sundering of the Teleri came about in Beleriand. Having crossed the last mountain-range which lay between them and the Sea, the reunited Eldar of the Journey lingered for a while in this country, while their erstwhile Guide (the Vala Oromë), passed across the Sea to consult with the Aratar in Valimar. During this period Elwë was lost, as is told in *The Silmarillion*.[1] And soon afterwards the remainder of the Eldar, save only the Teleri, passed across the Sea, leaving the Third Kindred behind in Middle-earth. Olwë brother of Elwë then became Lord of all this people, and dwelled by the Sea. Still Elwë was not found, and once more the call came from Valinor, for the Teleri to forsake Middle-earth and join their kindred in the Undying Lands; and after delaying as long as possible, Olwë sadly led the greater part of his people across the Sea. But he departed without a portion of his kindred, those who would not be parted from Elwë, and who refused to believe him dead (see EGLATH). These were the *Sindar*, the 'Grey-elves' (as they were later called by the Exiles); and from them in time came the *Falathrim*, the Coast-elves whose lord was Círdan. But soon afterwards Elwë appeared again among his people, and he founded a realm in Doriath, and there most of the Grey-elves went and dwelled, save only those who pre-ferred the wandering life, or those who loved the sound of the Sea, and dwelled with Círdan in the Havens of Eglarest and Brithombar.

But the vanguard of the Teleri, led now by Olwë alone, passed safely across the Great Sea and came to the Bay of Eldamar; there they stayed their journey – at the plea of the Sea-Maia Ossë – and the island which had transported them was rooted in the waters of the Bay, and never moved again. This was now named Tol Eressëa, the 'Lonely Isle', and upon it the people of Olwë dwelled for many centuries, growing wise beyond all other Elves in the ways of the Sea. Only much later did they build ships and come to the shores of Aman, to be reunited at last with the Vanyar and the Noldor. Olwë afterwards made his dwelling at Alqualondë.

It will be appreciated that the Teleri therefore 'straddle' the Eldarin race-classification system. (Indeed, they created most of the differences which necessitated the devising of the system in the first place.) The people of Olwë, the Falmari of Eldamar, are accounted both *Calaquendi* and *Amanyar*; but the Sindar and Nandor are named *Úmanyar*, while the Nandor, alone of all the Eldar, are classed together with the Avari, as *Moriquendi*. For the greater part of this, people never came to Aman, and dwindled with the passing years to become 'a rustic folk of dell and cave'.[2]

Telperiën (Tar-Telperiën) The second Queen (and tenth ruler) of Númenor. Her son was Tar-Minastir, eleventh King, who sent reinforcements to the Elven-king Gil-galad during the War of the Elves and Sauron (1693–1701 Second Age).

Telperion The Eldest of Trees, one of the TWO TREES raised, by the Vala Queen Yavanna, on the Mound of Ezellohar at the Beginning of Days, to illuminate the land of the Valar.

Telumehtar The older of the two High-elven names for that constellation of stars known (to Men of later times) as Orion. Its later Quenya name was *Menelmacar* 'Swordsman-of-the-Heavens' (from which the Grey-elven word *Menelvagor*, which carried the same meaning, was derived). Also the name of the twenty-eighth King of Gondor, who reigned from 1798–1850 Third Age. He was the son of Tarondor (the longest to reign of all the kings) but he inherited a realm which, if internally somewhat stronger than in his father's day, was militarily weaker, due to the lingering effects of the Great Plague of 1636. By the time Telumehtar came to the Throne, enemies of the Dúnedain were already stirring once more, and the Corsairs of Umbar, led by descendants of Castamir the Usurper, were again attacking and pillaging the long and vulnerable coastlines of Anfalas and Belfalas. Indeed, these pirates had long gone unpunished for the death of King Minardil, which had taken place nearly two centuries earlier.

Accordingly Telumehtar assembled a great fleet and took Umbar by storm in 1810, and in that savage encounter the last descendants of Castamir were slain. Telumehtar afterwards took the royal title *Umbardacil* ('Victor-of-Umbar'), but Gondor was not to retain the Haven for long: before many years had passed it had fallen into the hands of the Men of Harad, who afterwards wielded all the sea-power of the Corsairs.

Telumendil The name of one of the constellations created by Varda (Elbereth).

Téma, témar The Quenya or High-elven word for 'series', but more properly the name used in the Fëanorian Alphabet (the Tengwar) for each of the four subdivisions into which all of the primary letters (nos. 1–24) were arranged. The Alphabet of Fëanor being of course fully phonetic, these groupings indicated point of articulation, and each had six separate (but related) consonant-symbols arranged according to 'grade'. Each of these carried a *lúva* ('bow') denoting the *tema* to which it belonged; for example, those in Series I (*tincotéma*) bore 'open' bows on the right of the letter-stem, while in Series IV (*quessetéma*) the bows, whether single or doubled, were all to the left of the stem and were closed by a horizontal stroke.

The names of the four *témar* were as follows: I (*tincotéma*), the dental series; II (*parmatéma*), the labial series; III (*calmatéma*), the *k*-series and IV (*quessetéma*), the labialized series. The High-elves also possessed a palatal series of sounds (*tyelpetéma*) which was not found in the Fëanorian Alphabet, so to indicate consonants of this sort they used the *quessetéma* (Series IV) reinforced with a *tehta* meaning 'following *y*'. Series III (the *calmatéma*) was then used for the labialized consonants (*kw-, gw-, hw-* etc.).

See also Appendix E II(i).

Tengwar The Quenya or High-elven word for 'letters' but more properly the name used for the cursive phonetic alphabet devised during the Elder Days by the Elf Rúmil and later revised and almost completely reconstructed by Fëanor of the Noldor.

Much information on this ancient and beautiful writing-system, the oldest in existence, may be found elsewhere: in this *Companion* (see ALPHABET OF FËANOR), and (much more comprehensively) in Appendix E, where a table of the letters arranged according to series and trade is also available to the serious student. Therefore this entry will attempt further to simplify those aspects of the Elvish writing-system in association with these other texts.

It is primarily essential to remember that the Tengwar were designed to form a fully phonetic system of writing when incorporated into a single alphabet, unlike our modern alphabets which are based for the most part on linguistic principles which are only partly phonetic. Using the Tengwar one may devise a system of lettering to fit almost any language which produces sounds by means of breath impacting upon vocal chords, and which articulates and controls those sounds by means of palate, teeth, lips and tongue.

Because of this very singular versatility, the Tengwar of Fëanor, which were brought to Middle-earth by High-elves exiled from the Undying Lands in the First Age, were adopted by other races, first being the Grey-elves, who made changes of their own (see MODE OF BELERIAND). Men also learned the system, afterwards taking it to Númenor, where it was greatly prized as an alphabet of high lore and ceremony. From Númenor the Tengwar were brought back once more to Middle-earth, and were used in houses of learning in both Gondor and Arnor during the Third Age. For the Elvish letters could always be adapted to the Mannish tongues of the westlands, and could be used even for Dwarvish speech. (Four individual *tengwar* indeed later came to symbolize the points of the compass, even on maps drawn by folk unfamiliar with the rest of the Alphabet.)

The Tengwar of Fëanor were 24 in number, with a further 12 'extra' letters of flexible purpose. The 24 were arranged in four 'series' (*témar*) of letters, cross-divided into six 'grades' (*tyeller*). The series represented degrees of 'voice' and the grades stood for modes and points of articulation. Each *tengwa* could therefore be located by means of phonetic principles, and furthermore bore a proper name or title, which often contained an example of the consonant in question. Vowels were indicated by means of *tehtar*, 'signs', written diacritically in association with the consonant to be modified.

The titles of the individual *tengwar* were as follows:

1 *tinco*	13 *anto*	25 *rómen*
2 *parma*	14 *ampa*	26 *arda*
3 *calma*	15 *anca*	27 *lambe*
4 *quesse*	16 *unque*	28 *alda*
5 *ando*	17 *númen*	29 *silme*
6 *umbar*	18 *malta*	30 *silme nuquerna*
7 *anga*	19 *noldo*	31 *áre* (or *esse*)
8 *ungwe*	20 *nwalme*	32 *áre nuquerna*
9 *thúle* (or *súle*)	21 *óre*	33 *hyarmen*
10 *formen*	22 *vala*	34 *hwesta sindarinwa*
11 *harma* (or *aha*)	23 *anna*	35 *yanta*
12 *hwesta*	24 *vilya*	36 *úre*

Not all the values of the letters have been recorded. Those that are known are as follows:

1 t	13 dh	25 (full) r
2 p	14 v	26 rd (Q.), rh
3 ch or k	15 zh or gh	27 l
4 k or kw	16 gh or ghw	28 ld (Q.), lh
5 d	17 n	29 s
6 b	18 m	30 s (with *tehta*)
7 j or g	19 ng	31 z
8 g or gw	20 nw or ngw	32 z (with *tehta*)
9 th	21 (weak) r	33 h
10 f	22 v (Q.), w	34 hw
11 sh or kh	23 cons. y (West.)	35 cons. y (Q.)
12 k or khw	24 Not known	36 cons. w

Naturally enough, many peoples who learned the Tengwar of Fëanor afterwards developed characteristic combinations of letters to suit their own speech (e.g. in the disposition of the *tehtar* in the Mode of Beleriand), while others reallocated some of the *tengwar* according to their own purposes. The system explained above was the most usual in Middle-earth during the late Third Age.

See also TEHTA, TEHTAR; TÉMA, TÉMAR; Appendix E.

Thain The title given to the titular chief of the Shire by the Hobbits who dwelt there. The role of the Thain was that of a Chief Executive appointed to hold the King's authority; at times of emergency, he also commanded the Shire-muster and the Shire-moot. In short, his authority began where that of the Mayor ended.

The first Thain of the Shire was Bucca of the Marish, appointed in 379 Shire Reckoning – five years after the fall of the North-kingdom – to represent the King's person. Bucca's descendants, the Oldbuck clan, inherited the title which afterwards became completely hereditary; but in 740 Shire Reckoning the Oldbucks migrated eastward across the Baranduin to found the Buckland, and the Thainship passed to the equally eminent Took family. The first Took to become Thain was Isengrim I; he was the thirteenth holder of the office since Bucca, and the first of a long and illustrious line of Took-thains.

At the time of the War of the Ring the serving Thain of the Shire was Paladin II, father of Peregrin Took, and the thirty-first to hold the Office since Bucca. He played a valiant role in resisting the occupation of the Shire by Saruman's agents, although such power as he possessed could effect little more than a stubborn defence of the Tookland. The return of his son Peregrin, together with his Companions, enabled Paladin to take the offensive in the Southfarthing against the stray gangs of Men who were to be found there, and these he dispatched to the borders with little difficulty.

Paladin was succeeded in 1434 Shire Reckoning (Year 13 Fourth Age) by Peregrin, who then became the thirty-second Thain of the Shire as well as The Took. Fifty years later, when Peregrin finally departed the Shire, he passed the thainship to his son Faramir, the last recorded holder of that office.

Thain's Book A copy of the original Red Book of Westmarch, made in Great Smials by Took-scribes of Thain Peregrin I at the request of King Elessar (Aragorn II). It was afterwards taken to Gondor by Peregrin when he retired there in Year 63 Fourth Age, and after his death received much annotation (and correction) by loremasters of Gondor. This revised copy was again copied, some fifty years after the Passing of the King, and the new volume was presented to the descendants of Peregrin, probably by King Eldarion, the son of Aragorn and Arwen. But the original Thain's Book was kept ever after in Gondor.

Note: owing to a typographical error in some editions, a certain amount of confusion has arisen over the actual date of Peregrin's (and Meriadoc's) retirement to Gondor. In his *Note on the Shire Records* which he appends to the Prologue of most editions, the Translator tells us this date is Year 64, Fourth Age; but in *The Tale of Years* (Appendix B) we are informed that the date is 1484 Shire Reckoning, i.e., Year 63 Fourth Age. As the Shire-folk are more likely to have recorded this date accurately, Year 63 has been chosen as the more likely estimate, and the other mention has been disregarded as a typographical or computational error.

Thalion 'Steadfast' (Sind.) See HÚRIN THALION.

Thalos One of the six tributaries of the river Gelion.

Thangorodrim 'Mountains of Tyranny' (Sind.) The name of the chain of grim peaks raised above the Gates of Angband by Morgoth, after the theft of the Silmarils and his return to Middle-earth. There were three such mountains, and they were constructed of the ash and slag brought to the surface by the delvers of Angband. Dark smokes hung about them; and they could be seen even from afar, an ever-present reminder (to the Noldor) of the menace which brooded in the North. Thangorodrim was destroyed and thrown down by the Valar, in the tumults of the Great Battle which overthrew Morgoth at the end of the First Age.

Tharbad 'Cross-way' (Literally *thara-pata*, Sind.) A town on the borders of Enedhwaith and southern Eriador, built (probably) during the earlier part of the Third Age when the climate was still friendly and the neighbouring kingdoms of Arnor and Gondor still strong. It stood upon either side of the river Greyflood (Gwathlo), where the road linking the two Realms in Exile forded the stream.

The town did not survive the wars of the Third Age. Arnor fell, and Gondor withdrew from north of the White Mountains, and the lands between Fornost and Isengard grew wild and desolate. Nonetheless, Tharbad was probably not altogether abandoned until after the Great Plague of 1636, the effects of which were especially severe in Enedhwaith and Minhiriath. But by the time of the War of the Ring the town was totally deserted and ruinous, and only folk who desired to ford the Greyflood ever went near the place. So far as is known, Tharbad was not rebuilt in the Fourth Age.

Thargelion 'Land-beyond-Gelion' (Sind.) The name given by the Nolderin Exiles to the region which lay between the river Gelion, the border of East Beleriand, and the Blue Mountains, bordered in the north by Mount Rerir and in the south by the river Ascar.

(Previously it had been known, to the Grey-elves of Beleriand, as *Talath Rhúnen*, the 'East Vale' of Thingol's domain.) Forty leagues separated the mountain in the north from the river in the south, and thirty leagues of open country, partially wooded, lay between the Gelion and the Ered Luin. Following the return of the Noldor, and the initial victories against Morgoth, this region was taken by Caranthir (one of the sons of Fëanor) as his realm, and accordingly became known as *Dor Caranthir*, 'Caranthir's Land'. It was at this time that the Dwarves of the Blue Mountains again began trading across the mountains into Beleriand, and it was through Thargelion that their caravans and trading-parties travelled. Caranthir was thus the first of all the Noldor to encounter the Khazâd; and though he did not love them, he was too avaricious to relinquish the chance of acquiring wealth in this way. Tolls exacted on the Dwarves by Caranthir enriched him greatly. But after the Nirnaeth Arnoediad all the Elven-realms of the North were swept away, and Thargelion became infested by servants of Morgoth. At the ending of the Age only a remnant of this land survived, renamed *Forlindon* ('North-Lindon') by the Eldar.

Tharkûn (Khuz.) The name by which the wizard Gandalf the Grey was known to Dwarves. (Those of Durin's Line called him *Gandalf* for the most part, for that was the old wizard's name among Northern Men, whose languages the Dwarves of Erebor habitually used.)

Thellamie A poetic invention in the Elvish style, though not in fact Elvish at all. It has been used (by Bilbo in his celebrated poem 'Errantry') as the name of a supposed Elf-kingdom.

Thengel From 2953–80, the sixteenth King of Rohan, the seventh of the Second Line of the House of Eorl. He was the youngest child and only son of Fengel, who was by all accounts a greedy and ill-tempered ruler, at constant loggerheads with his children. Doubtless because of Fengel's unpleasant temperament, Thengel left Rohan after coming of age and passed south to the land of Gondor, where he later won renown and honour in his own right.

In his thirty-eighth year he met and wedded a Lady of the Dúnedain: Morwen of Lossarnach. She loved the tall Northerner and while in Gondor bore him three children: Théoden, the second child, was the only son. They continued to dwell in Gondor for some years but in 2953 Third Age Fengel of Rohan died at last, and the Rohirrim summoned Thengel, last of the House of Eorl, to return to the Mark. Reluctantly he left Gondor and passed north to the land of his childhood, and there became King. He reigned for twenty-seven years, and during this time his wife Morwen bore him two more children, of whom Théodwyn, youngest sister of Théoden, was the last (born 2963).

However, during the reign of Thengel (which was for the most part wise and constructive, although the King made no secret of his affections for Gondor) a crisis came to the Mark, which Thengel was unable to resolve. Saruman the Wizard, long an ally of Gondor and the Mark, openly renounced his self-assumed Wardenship of Isengard and claimed the fortress as his own, even though he protested continuing friendship towards Rohan. This potential danger outlasted Thengel and grew to deadly proportions during the reign of his son, Théoden (Ednew).

Note: it has been recorded (in *The Tale of Aragorn and Arwen*) that Aragorn II, sixteenth Chieftain of the Dúnedain, disguised as a soldier of fortune, served Thengel of Rohan for some years as a captain of war. In this way Aragorn came to learn the language of the Rohirrim.

Théoden Ednew From 2980–3019 Third Age, the seventeenth King of Rohan, the eighth – and last – of the Second Line of the Mark. As is told elsewhere (see previous entry) Théoden was the only son of Thengel, and was born in Gondor before the death of his grandfather Fengel, whom he never knew. He was thus five years old when his father was summoned to rule the Rohirrim, and he was thirty-two when his own time came.

In his youth Théoden was said to have been tall and proud no less than the greatest of his forebears, but tragedy struck at him during the middle years of his reign and he sank into a decline (which was later exacerbated by evil counsels). Nine years after he came to the kingship, his youngest (and most beloved) sister Théodwyn had wedded a Marshal of the Mark: Éomund of Eastfold; and although she bore him two children – Éomer and Éowyn – she sickened and died shortly after the turn of the century, leaving the children orphaned (for Éomund had been slain by Orcs one year before).

Théoden already had a son and heir of his own: Théodred, born during the early part of the King's reign. But Théodred's mother, the Queen Elfhild, had died in childbed. Therefore Théoden took his dead sister's children under his care, calling them Son and Daughter. Yet while the sight of these children growing up might have rescued Théoden from the morass of his despond, the times were again growing perilous, and Saruman the White, the master of

Isengard, was beginning to prove troublesome to the Rohirrim.
Théoden he despised, for the old King was already defeated in spirit
– or so it then seemed to all – and accordingly Saruman won over a
certain man of Rohan, one Gríma son of Galmód, bidding him
ensure that the King's torpor and despondency continue. Gríma
made himself powerful in Meduseld through guile and flattery, and
during the years immediately before the War of the Ring played
Saruman's part and spoke with the Wizard's voice. Théoden sank
still further, and it seemed to those that watched that the days of the
Mark were doomed.

For now the peril of Saruman loomed closer, and at last in 3018
open war broke over Westfold. Théoden's heir Théodred was slain
at the first Battle of the Fords of Isen (February 25th), and although
Erkenbrand lord of Westfold continued to hold off the hosts of
Isengard, it seemed that in the end nothing could save Rohan if her
King would not. It is told elsewhere (see Book III Chap. 6) how, in
the very nick of time, Gandalf the Grey and his three companions
arrived at Edoras – on the very morning of the second battle at the
Fords, where Erkenbrand was defeated and the Westfolders scattered
in the darkness. But the power of Gandalf proved (not for the first
time) greater than the spells of Saruman, and Gríma the Wormtongue was exposed as a traitor to the King and banished from the
Mark. More importantly, Gandalf healed the aged King of his long
sickness of spirit – indeed, Théoden was shown how the imagined
feebleness of old age was, in his case, little more than a product of the
oft-repeated whisperings of a turncoat. So rapidly did Théoden
revive that later that same day he himself led the host of Edoras
westward to the help of Erkenbrand.

There is little which needs to be added to the story of the heroic
campaigns undertaken by the King of Rohan and his Riders during
the War of the Ring. The reverses at the Isen were atoned for by a
crushing victory over the armies of Isengard at Helm's Deep (see
BATTLE OF THE HORNBURG); and with the threat of Saruman eliminated
the King was freed to lead the greater part of his Host to the aid of
Minas Tirith in Gondor, besieged by her foes. Before he rode south
he named Éomer his heir, and himself led no less than six thousand
cavalry, with stores and spare horses, on the great ride through
Eastfold and Anórien which saved Gondor – and the West – from
destruction.

Indeed, the Battle of the Pelennor Fields, greatest military encounter of the Third Age, may be said to have commenced with the
classic cavalry charge executed by Théoden's Six Thousand at dawn,

March 17th, 3019 Third Age. The King personally led this onset – and was one of the first to fall; yet the account of his death (Book V Chap. 6) leaves no impression that Théoden was anything but content with the manner of his ending. Before he passed away in the midst of the battle, he hailed Éomer as King of the Mark, and so died.

> Out of doubt, out of dark, to the day's rising
> he rode singing in the sun, sword unsheathing.
> Hope he rekindled, and in hope ended;
> over death, over dread, over doom lifted
> out of loss, out of life, unto long glory.[3]

Théodred The only son of King Théoden of Rohan. He was born in 2978 Third Age, the King's Heir, and later became Second Marshal of the Mark. Yet he never came to the throne of Meduseld, for he was slain in his fortieth year while defending the borders of Rohan against attack (see previous entry).

See also BATTLES OF THE FORDS OF ISEN.

Théodwyn The youngest sister of Théoden King of the Mark. She died in the year 3001 Third Age, shortly after her husband Éomund, and was greatly mourned by her brother the King. Théoden afterwards adopted her two children, Éomer and Éowyn.

'There and Back Again' The title given (after much cogitation and indecision) by the Hobbit Bilbo Baggins to the narrative of his great adventure in the East, written by his own hand in the years following his triumphal return from Erebor. Bilbo completed the tale by the year 1401 Shire Reckoning, but contrived to keep his writings secret (except from his cousin Frodo) and took the manuscript away with him when he retired to Rivendell. He afterwards gave the complete work to Frodo – and the younger Hobbit completed the Tale of the Great Ring with a (longer) account of his own adventures.

There and Back Again has been published in several different editions over the last thirty-five years under the title of The Hobbit, for it was the first tale concerning this remarkable people to become widely known. (Nonetheless this Companion uses the former title more often for reference purposes, mainly because There and Back Again was the old Hobbit-scholar's own choice for a name.)

Thingol Greycloak The greatest King of the Eldar of Middle-earth during the First Age, the spouse of Melian the Maia, Lord of Doriath and High King of Beleriand; and father of Lúthien Tinúviel.

With his younger brother Olwë, he led the Host of the Teleri on the Great Journey from Cuiviénen to the West of Middle-earth in the Elder Days. For nearly three Ages afterwards he reigned in Menegroth, his capital, in great glory and splendour, the only one of all the Eldar to wed with the race of Valinor, being also accounted High King of all Elves East of the Sea; but in the end he became enmeshed in the Doom of the Silmarils, and disaster came upon his house, and he was slain in his own halls before the Elder Days had passed. But his Line survived; and though Doriath was ruined and Beleriand was drowned under the Sea, this descent passed on through many generations of Elves and Men, and indeed survived until the Fourth Age: for so it had long been prophesied.

His Quenya name was *Elwë* (*Elu* in the Sindarin tongue), but he was known in later days as *Singollo* (from the older form *Sindacollo*) 'Grey-cloak', of which the Grey-elven form is *Thingol*; and together with his brother Olwë, he was the ruler of the Third Kindred of the Eldar, the *Lindar* (later called *Teleri*) at Cuiviénen. As is told in *The Silmarillion*,[4] Elwë was one of the three Kings of the Eldar (the other two were Ingwë of the Vanyar and Finwë of the Noldor) who were taken to Valinor by Oromë, and afterwards persuaded their respective peoples to make the Great Journey out of Middle-earth. So began the march into the West, and though the Teleri were always last in the line of march, this was chiefly because of the great size of their host; and it is not recorded that Elwë was anything other than impatient to return to Valinor and once again behold the Light which shone over that distant and blessed land.

Yet he was fated never to come there again while his life lasted; for his fate was inextricably woven with that of Middle-earth itself. When at long last the Third Kindred came across the Blue Mountains into Beleriand – by now somewhat reduced in number – Elwë, wandering abroad in the unpeopled woods of that fairest of mortal lands, was lost to his people for a time; and during that time the other Eldarin kindreds forsook Middle-earth and passed into the West – without him, for they believed him dead. Yet it was not so: Elwë had not been in peril, but been under an enchantment of love; and after a while he came forth from the woods with his bride – to learn that most of the Eldar, including his own brother Olwë, had already departed into the West. Only a portion of the Teleri had lingered in Beleriand, and these were those who had not believed him dead. Thingol then renounced any desire to pass West, and made his domain in Beleriand, eldest and greatest of all Elves on Hither Shores. His followers dwelt for the most part with him, in Doriath – the great forested region in central Beleriand wherein he made his realm – or wandered the empty lands. But all acknowledged his lordship and obeyed his decrees; for of all of them, Elwë Thingol was the only one who had ever beheld the Light of Valinor, a memory of which now abode with him in Doriath.

Thingol's bride was the Lady Melian of the Maiar; and after a time she bore him a daughter, Lúthien; and his joy was complete. Never again while his life lasted was Thingol to reach such a pinnacle of bliss. For although Lúthien was the most beautiful of all the Elves, and although Thingol's people loved her as greatly as they revered Thingol himself, far across the Sea the will of Morgoth was once more awake after two Ages of imprisonment; and in Middle-earth sundry echoes of his dark thought were at work among the ruined strongholds of the North. At first little of this was felt in Thingol's domain, but Melian, sensing the evil, foresaw the dangers which must follow. Taking her counsel Thingol sought the aid of the Dwarves, who built him an underground city and palace, after the fashion of their own deep-delved homes. This hidden citadel of great strength (and beauty; for Elves also had a part in its making) was named *Menegroth*, the Thousand Caves; and it stood under a hill on the southern bank of the enchanted river Esgalduin, in the middle of Doriath. Then Thingol and his court and people went and dwelled there, and it became the fairest palace of any King of the Eldar east of the Sea.

An Age passed. Across the Sea, Morgoth's imprisonment came to an end; and the Valar released him from the Halls of Mandos. Almost straightaway he began to plot and scheme for the downfall of his former enemies; for his repentance was only feigned. And after a while he had struck a deadly blow at the Valar and the Eldar; and then he came flying back across the Sea to Middle-earth, to build anew his evil kingdom in the North; and with him he bore the three Silmarils of the Noldor. Immediately the evil creatures of Middle-earth were filled with new and deadly purpose, for they were now guided by a cunning hand. And before the ships of Fëanor had even set out in pursuit the armies of Angband had struck at Beleriand. Thingol, though not altogether unprepared for war, was hard put to it. But although he won a great victory over the Orcs (with the aid of allies; see DENETHOR) in East Beleriand, in the West he was less successful, and his people who dwelled on the coasts (the Falathrim) were besieged, while Thingol himself was forced to withdraw into his impregnable citadel of Doriath. This scattered affray was afterwards called the First Battle of Beleriand, and it was the only one of the five such battles in which the King of Doriath took any part. Nonetheless, West Beleriand was soon cleared of Orcs – but by the Noldor, who had now returned to mortal lands in pursuit of Morgoth. And it was the valour and swords of the High-elves which threw the armies of Morgoth back into the North with great loss, and kept them there for many centuries.

Nonetheless, the King of Beleriand was not overjoyed at the coming of the Noldor; but he gave them leave to make realms in the North, so long as they did not interfere in the affairs of the Teleri. It was the Noldor who now called his people 'Grey-elves', though their name for the King of the Grey-elves, *Singollo*, had been given to Elwë long before, in the days when, with Olwë, he was the Lord of the Lindar. (Doubtless there is a connection between the two names.) But as far as the hotheads among the Noldor were concerned, Thingol was merely King of Doriath; and though they did not at this time defy Thingol's writ, they resented his attitude and, moreover, considered him an ingrate; for it had been their arms which had liberated West Beleriand from the Orcs, and not those of the Sindar. In this way seeds of mistrust were sown between the Noldor and the Sindar. And worse was to come; for after a time Thingol learned of the evil deeds of the Noldor in Eldamar, and of the Kinslaying at Alqualondë – in which many of his kinsmen had been cruelly cut down; and then he proscribed the Quenya tongue, and barred all save his close kin among the Noldor from Doriath. And he never came forth from Menegroth while his life lasted.

For Thingol, wisest of the Eldar in Middle-earth – and, moreover, counselled by Melian – now perceived that a curse lay upon the enterprises of the Noldor, and he vowed to have nothing to do with the war for the Silmarils. The Sons of Fëanor he named as his enemies; and he forbade his people to aid or serve them. For he still hoped to ride the storm. Yet doom came to him in the end, in the person of Beren of the Edain, who sought the hand of his beloved daughter Lúthien. Of that tale much is said elsewhere.[5] By his own words, uttered in wrath and contempt, Thingol was ensnared in the trap of the Silmarils and brought under the Curse of Mandos: for he named them in desire, and in so doing set in motion a chain of events which ended in his own fall and in the ruin of his long-defended kingdom, oldest and fairest in Middle-earth. Against his every expectation, Beren succeeded in recovering a Silmaril from Angband, and it was brought to Doriath, and kept by Thingol in his hoard. And so his doom drew nearer. For, possessing it, his heart turned more and more towards it, and to its beauty; and in seeking to enhance this he made himself vulnerable to unforeseen perils. For although Thingol was of a great and noble kind, and would not easily have fallen into evil by his own acts, he was lured into displaying the Jewel before those whose resistance to such attractions was not so stern. They, falling under the spell, also desired the Silmaril – and slew Thingol to acquire it. So he died. And though his Heir Dior son of Lúthien and Beren succeeded for a time in restoring Doriath and Menegroth to its former splendour, this was to prove but a brief sunset. After a few years Dior and most of his kin were also slain, and Doriath was ruined for a second time – and again it was lust for the Silmaril which brought about the disaster.

But the Silmaril itself survived, and with it the Line of Thingol Greycloak of Doriath, noblest in Middle-earth. Mingled with the descent from the Noldor and all three Houses of the Edain, it was carried across the Sea to Númenor as well as continuing unbroken in Middle-earth: Two Ages after Thingol's death these two branches of his Line were re-united, in the wedding of Aragorn with Arwen daughter of Elrond – in whom, it was said, the likeness of Thingol's daughter Lúthien again walked the earth. But Elwë Thingol himself was never again seen East of the Sea, by Elves or Men.

Third Age The name given by the Dúnedain and the Elves to the period of 3,021 years between the first overthrow of Sauron the Great and the final Passing of the Three Rings, together with their Bearers, across the Sea to the Undying Lands.

The Third Age of Middle-earth was essentially an age of decline and transition, for after the victory of the Last Alliance the power of the Elves in Middle-earth was greatly reduced – and that of Men, their inheritors, greatly enhanced. Yet many Elves still lingered, especially in the North and in the great forests of Wilderland, while in the westlands the Realms in Exile grew to power.

For the first millennium there was peace in most lands, save for the expansionist wars fought by Gondor against her foes in the South and East, and it was not until the beginning of the second millennium that serious attempts were made to challenge the power of the Dúnedain. This period, from 1300 (the rise of Angmar) to 2002 (the fall of Minas Ithil), was grievous for the Númenorean Exiles, and although Gondor managed to withstand the many trials imposed upon her, the North-kingdom was swept away. Scant years after the fall of Arthedain, the ancient Dwarf-city of Moria was finally captured by evil creatures, and Durin's Folk were expelled from their ancestral home. Only the Elf-kingdoms survived the turmoils at the end of the second millennium, while Gondor lost some of her royalty and became an embattled state.

Yet the Third Age was also an age of great migrations and folk-movements. The Hobbits journeyed from Wilderland to Eriador and Dunland, while for many years successive hordes of Easterlings and Southrons attempted to occupy the fertile lands west of the Anduin. More ominously, the second millennium saw the reawakening of Sauron the Great, whom all had believed overthrown at the end of the previous Age; and the final years of the Third Age were dominated by his machinations.

Nonetheless the power of Gondor proved strong enough to withstand Sauron's return to power, and with a final effort the Free Peoples, working in league, were able to accomplish his downfall at the very end of the Third Age. In this way the Elves were able to depart from mortal lands in peace, and so pass on their inheritance at last to the 'Kings-of-Men', whose reconstituted realms formed the foundation on which the Dominion of Men in the Fourth Age was built.

Third House (of the Edain) The House of HADOR LÓRINDOL of Dor-lómin.

Third Line (of the Mark) All the Kings of Rohan after Théoden Ednew. Each time the direct line of descent (from Eorl the Young) was broken, a new line of mounds was begun in the Barrowfield of Edoras. Éomer, nephew of Théoden, was the first King of the Third Line.

Third Theme (of Ilúvatar) According to the traditions of the Eldar, the Third Theme of the Great Song was that which dealt with the race of Atani, 'the Secondborn' (i.e. Men).

Thistle Brook A stream of the Shire; it arose in the Green Hill Country and joined the river Shirebourn near Willowbottom.

Thistlewool A family of Big Folk (Men) of Bree.

Thorin I From 2190–2289 Third Age, the first king of the Dwarves of the Grey Mountains colony; it was he who led a great part of Durin's Folk away from newly founded Erebor into the North.

Thorin (II) Oakenshield From 2845–2941 Third Age, the King of Durin's Folk in Exile, and for a brief period in the last year of his life (2941) the King Under the Mountain. He was the leader of the renowned expedition in which Smaug the Golden was destroyed and the Lonely Mountain freed from the Dragon's dominion; and he was the last bearer of the Elf-sword Orcrist.

Thorin was born in Erebor in 2746, the son of Thráin son of Thrór the King, and was thus only 24 years of age when the Dragon descended upon the Dwarves in the year 2770. Together with his grandfather, his father, his brother Frerin and his sister Dís, he went to Dunland in exile; but the murder of his grandfather twenty years after the fall of Erebor brought about the War of the Dwarves and Orcs, and in this Thorin won great renown (not to mention his famous nickname). He was in the vanguard of the Dwarf-host which attacked the Orcs of Azog at Azanulbizar; this force was driven back by the Orcs, and Frerin was slain. Thorin's shield was broken and for a while he made shift with a handy branch of oak, for there was no time to acquire another shield. Even so he was wounded. Nonetheless Thorin survived the Battle of Azanulbizar – where many others did not – and afterwards went with his father and their kin to the Blue Mountains, where they founded a small and modest colony.

But in 2845 Third Age Thorin's father Thráin II was captured by Sauron, and Thorin became King of Durin's Folk in Exile. For many years he husbanded the strength of his people, until at last he felt strong (or angry) enough to attempt revenge on the Dragon and the recovery of the treasure of Erebor. In this project he had the unexpected aid of Gandalf the Grey. The story of that expedition, undertaken by Thorin and Gandalf together with twelve other Dwarves and a single Hobbit, has been told with admirable lucidity elsewhere (see THERE AND BACK AGAIN) and needs little elaboration here: by great good fortune the Dragon was slain and Thorin then became King Under the Mountain. But in the hour of triumph his heart, inflamed perhaps by the wealth of Erebor and the long injustices done to his House, turned towards pride and rashness. Rather than accord his erstwhile allies a fair share of the wealth won, he planned to deprive them of even this amount, and defied them at the Gates of Erebor. This ill-considered action nearly brought about a disastrous battle between Dwarves, Elves and Men; luckily, the opportune arrival of an Orc-host united the potential enemies in a desperate defence, and in this last fight Thorin came once more to his senses. He died heroically after slaying many Orcs and wolves, and was buried in a tomb of stone under the Lonely Mountain with the Arkenstone of Thráin upon his breast. He was succeeded in Erebor by Dáin Ironfoot.

Thorin (III) Stonehelm The son of Dáin Ironfoot and King Under the Mountain after the death of Dáin during the War of the Ring. Dáin was slain during the (second) Battle of Dale (March 17th, 3019 Third Age), in which hordes of Easterlings poured into Dale and drove the surviving Men and Dwarves to take shelter behind the Gates of Erebor. However, ten days afterwards news came north of the Passing of Sauron and, led by Thorin and his ally King Bard II of Dale, the besieged came forth and drove the Easterlings away.

Thorondir From 2872–82 Third Age, the twenty-second Ruling Steward of Gondor.

Thorondor 'King of Eagles' (Sind.) The greatest of all the Eagles of the Elder Days, and the ancestor of all the Eagles of the North. The Messenger of Manwë, who built his eyries high in the Crissaegrim during the First Age, Thorondor took many a part in the affairs of the time. He aided Fingon of the Noldor in his successful attempt to rescue Maedhros from torment upon Thangorodrim; and he took part in the combat of Fingolfin and Morgoth, rescuing the body of the fallen Elven-king from defamation by the triumphant Enemy; and Thorondor wounded Morgoth in the face with his great claws. At the same time two of his kin rescued Húrin and Huor from peril, and bore them to Gondolin, so initiating a series of events which were to end with the fall of Gondolin but the survival of the royal Line of Descent of that Elven-city. Thorondor himself rescued Beren and Lúthien from Angband, after the recovery of the Silmaril; and he warned Turgon king of Gondolin concerning the presence of the fugitive Húrin at his gates (though at this time Turgon did not act as the King of Eagles urged).

Soon afterwards came the long-prepared attack upon Turgon's city; and for the last time Thorondor came to the aid of the House of Fingolfin. His timely arrival enabled a party of survivors to escape from the stricken city. And by means of this deed another deed was enabled to come to pass: the summoning of the Valar from the Far West. In the battle which ensued Thorondor and the Eagles of the Crissaegrim played a notable part; but the ancient eyries in the Encircling Mountains were destroyed in the inundation of Beleriand, and in later years Thorondor's descendants dwelled in the high places of the Misty Mountains.

Note: the Quenya form of this name is *Sorontar*.

Thorongil 'Eagle-of-the-Star' (Sind.) The name by which Aragorn II, sixteenth Chieftain of the Dúnedain of the North, was known to

Men of Gondor, during the period in which he served Ecthelion II, twenty-fifth Ruling Steward, as a captain of war. Aragorn was, of course, highly incognito at this time and the origin of the nickname was the star-shaped brooch he wore on his cloak.

Thousand Caves See MENEGROTH.

Thráin I From 1981–2190 Third Age, the King of Durin's Folk; he led the exodus from Moria after the death of his father Náin I, and founded the Kingdom Under the Mountain in 1999 Third Age. There, in the 'Heart of the Mountain', Thráin discovered the great jewel, the Arkenstone, which afterwards became an heirloom of Durin's House.

Thráin II From 2790–2850 Third Age, the King of Durin's Folk in Exile; he was the son of Thrór and father of Thorin Oakenshield, Frerin and Dís. Together with his father and his family, he was driven into exile from Erebor in 2770 Third Age, and later still led the Dwarf-armies at the Battle of Azanulbizar (2799), in which epic encounter he was gravely wounded, losing an eye.

Thráin was the last of the Dwarf-kings to possess one of the Seven Rings, and it was by this means that Sauron later managed to ensnare him. For after the War of the Dwarves and Orcs, he became restless and unable to accommodate his spirit to the humble Dwarf-dwellings in the Blue Mountains; together with a few chosen companions, he left the Ered Luin and wandered far abroad. And slowly his footsteps took him ever closer to Mirkwood.

> Wolves pursued him, Orcs waylaid him, evil birds shadowed his path . . . There came a dark night when he and his companions were wandering in the land beyond Anduin, and they were driven by a black rain to take shelter under the eaves of Mirkwood. In the morning he was gone from the camp . . .[6]

For five long years Thráin endured the torments of Sauron in Dol Guldur, whither he had been carried after being captured. There, Gandalf the Grey found him while exploring the fortress of the Necromancer in secret (2850 Third Age). Shortly afterwards, Thráin died – but not before he had passed on to Gandalf the Key of Erebor and a secret map of the Lonely Mountain. In this way these heirlooms came to his heir Thorin Oakenshield; but the last of the Seven Rings was taken from Thráin by Sauron, who kept it ever after.

Thranduil A Lord of the Sindar and a kinsman of Celeborn of Lothlórien, and for at least two Ages of the World the Elven-king of Northern Mirkwood; his realm lay between the Forest River and the north-eastern eaves of the forest itself.

It has been recorded that Thranduil journeyed eastward across the Misty Mountains during the first part of the Second Age, after he and Celeborn had left their homes in Harlindon (South Lindon), together with a retinue of Grey-elves. Soon afterwards he came to Greenwood the Great, and passed north through the forest until he came to the abode of the Wood-elves. There he delved great halls under a hill (it is said that Dwarves 'helped in their making'[7]), from which a dark stream flowed swiftly south to join the Forest River.

Throughout the remainder of the Second Age Thranduil ruled the Woodland Realm – for if he and his court were of Sindarin (Grey-elven) race, the Silvan Elves of Greenwood were of the race of East-elves, among whom 'the Eldar were as kings'.[8] During the Third Age the Elven-king of the northern Forest continued to reign, although after the first thousand years of the Third Age had passed a rival power arose in the Forest, and Thranduil's borders were threatened by evil things. Nevertheless he resisted the forces of Dol Guldur till the end of his strength – and as a result the Wood-elves survived when all else in the forest was darkened.

In 2941 Thranduil's Elves encountered the errant Dwarves of Thorin Oakenshield's expedition, and the Elven-king (somewhat hastily) imprisoned them, for those were watchful days. Later that same year his people brought succour to the Men of Esgaroth afflicted by the Dragon Smaug, and Thranduil (with a score of his own to settle), sent a host to aid the Lake-men when they marched upon Erebor to demand compensation for their injuries from the Dwarves. Luckily, a fourth host – of Orcs and wolves – united the Wood-elves with both Men and Dwarves and in the end the allies had the victory. Thranduil and his people received rich reward from the Dwarves and they returned in peace to their woodland halls.

Yet although many Orcs and wolves were destroyed at the Battle of Five Armies, the lands were not freed altogether from peril and by 3018 Mirkwood was again an evil place. In that year Aragorn II, a friend of Elves, came to Thranduil's kingdom, and with him he brought the creature Gollum as a prisoner. The Elven-king agreed to lodge Gollum until it should be decided what was to be done with him, but that same year Gollum escaped – and then Thranduil sent his son Legolas to Elrond with the tidings. In this way Legolas was present at the Council of Elrond, and so came to be chosen as a member of the Fellowship of the Ring.

In the meantime Thranduil, alerted by the escape of Gollum, prepared for war. On March 15th forces of Dol Guldur made a great attack upon the Woodland Realm, but although many trees were burned and many Elves were slain, Thranduil succeeded in repelling the attacks. Dol Guldur was later destroyed and Thranduil returned to the North. He lingered in Middle-earth beyond the turn of the Fourth Age, and whether or not he eventually sailed over Sea has not been recorded in the Red Book.

Three-farthing Stone An obelisk erected by Hobbits of the Shire shortly after the founding of their land to mark the common boundary of the West-, East- and Southfarthings. It stood on the Great East Road, a mile or so south of Bywater Pool.

Three Houses The Edain.

Three Kindreds The Eldar.

Three Rings The three mightiest of the Rings of Power made during the Second Age by Celebrimbor of the Noldor and the Elven-smiths of Eregion. They were wrought for the purposes of 'under-standing, making, and healing'[9] by the Elven-smiths alone, and the hand of Sauron (who assisted in the making of all other Rings of Power) 'never touched them or sullied them'.[10] Unhappily the Smiths of Eregion were betrayed by Sauron, who forged a single Ring mightier than the Three; while this Ruling Ring remained in the world, the powers of the Elven-rings were limited by uncertainty, and when it was finally destroyed the Three were shorn of all potency.

The names of the Three Rings were: Vilya, the Ring of the Airs, mightiest of all, which bore a great blue stone and was originally possessed by Gil-galad, who gave it to Elrond at the end of the Second Age; Nenya, the Ring of Waters, with a single hard white stone of great beauty, which was always in the keeping of the Lady Galadriel; and Narya, the Ring of Fire, borne by Círdan the Ship-wright until the end of the first millennium of the Third Age, when he surrendered the Ring with its great red stone to the Wizard Gandalf the Grey. Gandalf wielded Narya throughout the remainder of the Age in pursuit of his sworn task: the uniting of the Free Peoples against Sauron the Great, Lord of all the Rings of Power.

See also RINGS OF POWER; RULING RING.

Thrihyrne 'Three-horned-peak' The name given in Rohan to the tall, triple-crowned mountain which lay to the south of Aglarond and Helm's Deep. The Deep was in fact a ravine in the northern face of the Thrihyrne.

Thrimich See following entry.

Thrimidge The Hobbits' name for the fifth month of the year (equivalent to our May). It corresponded to *Lótessë* in Kings' Reckoning. At the time of the War of the Ring it was most usually written *Thrimich* (an earlier form of the same word was *Thrimilch*).

Thrimilch See preceding entry.

Thrór From 2590–2770 Third Age, the King Under the Mountain, and from 2770–90, King of Durin's Folk in Exile. He was the Dwarf-king who led his people back from the failed Grey Mountains colony to Erebor (the Lonely Mountain) in 2590, following the deaths of his father (Dáin I) and younger brother the previous year. Thrór re-founded the dormant Kingdom Under the Mountain and ruled there in great splendour until the sudden appearance in the northern skies of the Dragon Smaug the Golden one hundred and eighty years later (2770).

Luckily Thrór and his son Thráin knew of a secret escape route from Erebor, and so were saved from the Dragon. Thrór then led the surviving Dwarves into exile in Dunland, but grew weary and dispirited in his straitened circumstances. Ten years after the beginning of his exile he left Dunland and went wandering in the wilderness, taking with him one old companion, called Nár. By ill chance he decided to enter Moria, long lost to his house and to his people; and in Moria he was taken and slain by Orcs. This murder – and the ensuing desecration of Thrór's body – brought about the brimming-over of the wrath of the Dwarves, who made war upon the Orcs. Thrór was eventually avenged, but at terrible cost.

Thúle The Quenya or High-elven word for 'spirit', but more properly an alternative title for the Tengwa number 9, which carried the phonetic value of *th* in Sindarin and Mannish tongues and *s* in Quenya. See also SÚLE.

Thuringwethil 'Woman of secret shadow' (Sind.) During the First Age a creature of Sauron's. To her care he would entrust messages for Angband. She flew the night-skies in the shape of a loathsome vampire-bat.

Tighfield A village of the Northfarthing, settled by a branch of the Gamgee family (after Wiseman moved there from the village of Gamwich). The Gamgees eventually settled in Hobbiton but the Tighfield branch remained in the Northfarthing to practise the prosperous family craft of rope-weaving. This family later became known as the Ropers of Tighfield.

Tilion One of the MAIAR, of the following of Oromë; he was a lover of the Silver Tree Telperion, and after the death of the Tree was granted the honour of becoming the eternal guardian of the last Silver Flower; and the Steersman of Isil (the Moon).

Timeless Halls *Eä*; the Universe.

Tinco The Quenya or High-elven word for 'metal', but more properly the title of Tengwa number 1, which represented the sound *t* almost universally among users of the Fëanorian Alphabet.

Tincotéma '*tinco*-series' (Q.) The first of the four self-contained 'series' of Fëanorian letters (the Tengwar). The *tincotéma* included all the letters (nos. 1, 5, 9, 13, 17 and 21) with a dental point of articulation (*tinco, ando, thúle, anto, númen* and *óre*). See also TÉMA, TÉMAR.

Tindómë (Q.) The name given by the High-elves to the period of twilight which came just before dawn, hence at the ending of the Elves' day. The Grey-elven equivalent was *minuial* (called *morrowdim* by the Hobbits). See also UNDÓMË.

Tindrock Tol Brandir.

Tintallë 'The Kindler' (Q.) The secondary title given by the High-elves to the Lady Varda (Elbereth). Its Grey-elven equivalent was *Gilthoniel*. Varda was also called, by the High-elves, *Elentári* ('Star-queen').

Tinúviel 'Twilight's Daughter' [i.e. a nightingale] (Sind.) A title of Lúthien of Doriath.

Tirion 'Great-watch-tower' (Q.) The name given by the Eldar of the Undying Lands to the beautiful city built by the Vanyar and the Noldor upon the Hill of Túna, at the entrance to the Pass of Calacirya which led into Valinor from Eldamar. Its walls were white, and its stairs were of crystal; and it had many tall towers, of which the highest was the Mindon Eldaliéva. At the feet of the hill of Túna upon the east lay a dark lake, the Shadowmere, and in the West the light from the Calacirya illuminated the city.

The first lord of Tirion was the King of the Vanyar, Ingwë, builder of the Mindon. But after an Age had passed he and his people departed from the city, and journeyed through the Calacirya to Valinor, and ever after dwelt on the western side of the Pelóri. The lordship of the city upon Túna then passed to Finwë of the Noldor, who ruled there until the release (from imprisonment) of Melkor (Morgoth), and his slow poisoning of the soul of Fëanor, Finwë's eldest son. With the rebellion of Fëanor – and the death of Finwë – Tirion was abandoned by most of the Noldor, and in after years Finarfin (the youngest son of Finwë) became its lord. He ruled over all those of the Noldor who did not join the revolt, and who never went into Exile. But those Noldor who journeyed to Middle-earth, and, surviving the wars, returned to the West, never again dwelled in the city their fathers had built, though they often visited it. But the Light that had illuminated its western walls in ancient days was now extinguished for ever; eternal twilight lay over Aman, the Calacirya was dark, and 'the lamplit towers of Tirion [were] mirrored in the Shadowmere'.[11]

Tirith Aear 'Sea-guardian' (Sind.) The watch-tower which stood atop the coastal promontory of Dol Amroth in Belfalas, ancestral dwelling and stronghold of the Princes of that tributary fief.

Tîw (alt. plural *tîwhin*) 'Letters' (Sind.) The Grey-elves' name for the alphabet of cursive characters invented by Rúmil in Eldamar and later modified – and brought to Middle-earth – by Fëanor of the Noldor. These letters were known to the High-elves as *Tengwar*.

Tobold Hornblower A Hobbit-gardener of the village of Longbottom in the Southfarthing during the latter part of the Third Age. 'Old Toby' was reportedly the first Hobbit to cultivate the herb *nicotiana* ('Pipe-weed') in the Shire (*c.* 2670 Third Age), and was afterwards immortalized for this accomplishment. See also PIPE-WEED.

Tode See 'THE MEWLIPS'.

Tol Brandir The Tindrock; a tall isle with precipitous sides which rose out of the Anduin in the centre of the stream between the hills of Amon Hen and Amon Lhâw, above the Falls of Rauros. It was said by the Dúnedain of Gondor that no Man had ever been known to set foot on its slopes. In the days of Gondor's power, the Tindrock marked the northernmost border of the South-kingdom.

Tol Eressëa 'Lonely Isle' (Sind.+Q.) See ERESSËA.

Tolfalas 'Coastal-island' (Sind.) A great isle which lay at the mouth of the Anduin, between the cape of Belfalas and the shores of Harondor (South Gondor).

Tol Galen 'Green Isle' (Sind.) The long, leaf-shaped isle in the midst of the river Adurant, in southern Ossiriand, the dwelling of Lúthien and Beren after the granting of their second mortal lifespans; and the birthplace of their son Dior Eluchíl.

Tol-in-Gaurhoth 'Isle of Werewolves' (Sind.) The name given by the Eldar and the Edain to the former island of TOL SIRION, after its capture by Sauron (from Orodreth of the House of Finarfin, who ruled there after Finrod, the builder of the fortress which stood upon the isle).

Tolma An original (as opposed to translated) Hobbit-forename; it has been translated from the Red Book as *Tom*.

Tolman Cotton Farmer Cotton.

Tolman Gamgee The youngest son of Samwise Gamgee.

Tol Morwen 'Morwen's Isle' (Sind.) The name given in the Second Age to the crag of CABED NAERAMARTH and the burial-mound which stood there, for this place was not buried under the destroying seas at the end of the Age, but stood above the waves as an offshore rock (in fulfilment of a prophecy spoken among the Edain). Underneath the mound were buried Morwen Eledhwen of the Edain and her only son Túrin Turambar.

Tol Sirion 'Sirion's Isle' (Sind.) The name given by the Eldar to the strategic island in the river Sirion,[12] which guarded the Pass of the same name against attack from the North. The island was first held by Finrod of the Noldor, who garrisoned it with warriors of his House (of Finarfin) and built there a watch-tower, called Minas Tirith. But after a while Finrod departed from the North, and went to dwell in Nargothrond, and the island – and the responsibilities which went with it – he gave to his younger brother Orodreth, in fief. Orodreth held Tol Sirion and its tower until the Dagor Bragollach; but although he held out during that battle, shortly afterwards Sauron, the servant of Morgoth, came against him with great strength, and the Elves fled, abandoning Minas Tirith and Tol Sirion to the Enemy. The island was then renamed *Tol-in-Gaurhoth*, the 'Isle of Werewolves'. But Sauron was not to retain this fortress for long: he was driven out, by Lúthien, Beren and Huan, and fled in his turn. No folk dwelled there afterwards, nor made any lasting stronghold in that region of the North.

Tomba An original (as opposed to translated) Hobbit-forename; like *Tolma*, it has been translated from the Red Book as *Tom*.

Tom Bombadil The 'Master of wood, water and hill', eldest of all living creatures in Middle-earth; he dwelt throughout the Second and Third Ages in the Old Forest east of the Shire, which was itself one of the last surviving reaches of the great primeval woods of the Elder Days, Bombadil's domain since the Beginning.

> 'Eldest, that's what I am ... Tom was here before the river and the trees; Tom remembers the first raindrop and the first acorn. He made paths before the Big People, and saw the Little People arriving . . . When the Elves passed westward, Tom was here already, before the seas were bent.'[13]

It was not recorded in the Annals of the Shire what kind of creature Bombadil was, but it seems certain from all available evidence that he was a unique being, 'oldest and fatherless' as the Elves deemed him. In the First Age he was known to the Eldar, who called him *Iarwain Ben-adar*, and acknowledged him as the oldest of all creatures. They considered him a benevolent spirit of the forest, a veritable incarnation of the ancient life-force present there, under no laws but his own, acknowledging no master.[14]

Of his history little is known, save only those brief and veiled allusions such as he revealed to the Hobbits under his protection (Book I Chap. 7). As the mighty woods of the Elder Days shrank with the passing of years, he too retreated until he finally took up his abode 'down under Hill' in the Old Forest. There he lingered, walking, weeding and watching the country – and so in due course became known to the Hobbits, especially the Bucklanders, who had many strange tales and songs concerning the old man of the forest. *Tom Bombadil* is in fact a Bucklandish name; the Dwarves called him *Forn*, and in the legends of Northern Men he was known as *Orald*. But only the Elves were aware of his true origins – and by the end of the Third Age even Elrond himself had forgotten that Bombadil existed.

See also *The Adventures of Tom Bombadil*.

Tom Cotton FARMER COTTON.

Tom Pickthorn A Man of Bree. Early in the year 3019 Third Age he was slain in a skirmish between the Bree-folk and the renegades led by Bill Ferny and Harry Goatleaf.

Took A rendering of the original Hobbit-name *Tûk*; more properly, an aristocratic and adventurous clan of Shire-hobbits, who from earliest days played a prominent part in the affairs of the little land. The head of the family was traditionally known as 'The Took', and ordered the doing of the clan from the family seat in the Tookland, a hilly region in the Westfarthing of the Shire.

Tooks were known to be descended from Fallohides, and were indeed far more adventurous than most of their kind; many younger sons vanished from the affairs of their fellow-hobbits because of this strange predilection. According to the family Genealogical Tables, Hildifons (sixth son of Gerontius 'The Old' Took) 'went off on a journey and never returned', while his youngest brother Isengar 'is said to have "gone to sea" in his youth'; and so on. However, the first Took to become prominent in the Shire at large was Isumbras (afterwards called Isumbras I), who in 740 Shire Reckoning (2340 Third Age) became the thirteenth Thain of the Shire and the first of the Took-thains. The Office remained in the family ever after (see also OLDBUCK).

It was Bandobras Took, the younger son of the eleventh Took-thain, who became the most renowned warrior and leader in Shire-history (until the War of the Ring). Not content with growing to greater stature than any other Hobbit, 'Bullroarer' also won acclaim as a military captain when, in Shire-year 1147, he led the Shire-muster which defeated an invading force of Orcs (see BATTLE OF GREENFIELDS). He also founded the North-took clan of Long Cleeve.

A third prominent Took was Gerontius, fourteenth Thain, who lived to the prodigious age of 130 years and accordingly became known as 'The Old Took'; his age was exceeded in all Shire-history only by Bilbo's score of 131, and his descendants were numerous indeed. Nonetheless, most of these continued to live in the ancestral mansion-smials in Tuckborough, and it was there, in 1390 Shire Reckoning, that the greatest and most renowned Took of all was born: Peregrin, son of Paladin, who jointly captained the Shire-muster which won the Battle of Bywater in 1419 – and who also outgrew the legendary Bullroarer. Peregrin later became the twentieth Thain of the Took line and was afterwards appointed Counsellor of the reconstituted North-kingdom of Arnor. He also wedded Diamond of Long Cleeve, a descendant of the Bullroarer, thus reuniting the North-tooks with their Southern kindred.

Tookbank A village in the Westfarthing of the Shire.

Tookland The area of the Shire chiefly settled by the Took clan, whose centre was the village of Tuckborough.

Torech Ungol 'Lair of the Spider' (Sind.) The name given in Gondor to the highest point of the Pass of Cirith Ungol, where the secret road ran through a dark, noisome tunnel past a foul pit. Here the spider Shelob the Great had her lair.

Torog (pl. *tereg*) See TROLLS.

Tower Hills A translation of the Sindarin name *Emyn Beraid*.

Tower of Cirith Ungol A great watch-tower and fortress constructed high on the inner, eastern side of the Mountains of Shadow by Gondor early in the Third Age. Its purpose – like that of Durthang, Isenmouthe and the Towers of the Teeth – was to guard Mordor against the entry (and exit) of evil creatures, and for many years it fulfilled this duty. Nonetheless by the end of the second millennium the power of Gondor was greatly diminished, and the Tower fell into the hands of Sauron's servants, who afterwards garrisoned the outpost on his behalf.

See also SILENT WATCHERS.

Tower of Ecthelion The highest tower of the city of Minas Anor in Gondor, originally built by King Calimehtar in the last century of the second millennium of the Third Age, and later strengthened and improved by Ecthelion I, seventeenth Ruling Steward, in the year 2698. It was three hundred feet tall in its completed form, and in its topmost turret the Palantír of Minas Tirith was kept.

Tower of Ingwë The MINDON ELDALIÉVA.

Towers of Mist A translation of the Grey-elven name *Hithaeglir*. See MISTY MOUNTAINS.

Towers of the Teeth Narchost and Carchost.

Town Hole The dwelling-place and Official Residence of the Mayor of Michel Delving in the Shire.

Trahald In the original (as opposed to translated) Northern Mannish tongue, this name meant 'burrowing-in'; it has been translated from the Red Book (into Early English, for contextual reasons) as *Sméagol*. See SMEAGOL-GOLLUM

'Translations from the Elvish' The name given by the Hobbit Bilbo Baggins to his greatest scholarly achievement: three bound red volumes compiled and annotated by him during the years (3003–18 Third Age) of his retirement in Rivendell. The books were later presented by Bilbo to Frodo, and by Frodo to Samwise, and were afterwards preserved together with the Red Book of Westmarch by the Fairbairn family.

Much of this work has recently been published under the title *The Silmarillion*.

Treebeard A translation of the Sindarin name FANGORN.

Treegarth of Orthanc The name given by the Ents of Fangorn Forest to the former valley of Isengard, after the area had been reforested following the victory of the War of the Ring and the eviction of the Wizard Saruman. The ancient walls of Isengard were, of course, destroyed by the Ents during the War, but instead of rebuilding them, they encouraged many wild and hitherto homeless trees to come and dwell there. Isengard ceased to exist as a fortress, but the Tower of Orthanc, being impregnable – even to the Ents – remained where it stood and reverted to the custodianship of Gondor.

Tree of the High-elves GALATHILION. See also TWO TREES.

Trewesdei An archaic form of the Hobbit-name for the fourth day of the week, corresponding to *Aldëa* in the Númenorean Kings' Reckoning system. A later form of the same name was *Trewsday* (equivalent to our Tuesday).

Trewsday See preceding entry.

Trolls A translation of the Sindarin word *Tereg* (sing. *torog*), being the name most widely used in Middle-earth for the giant, cannibalistic race of creatures which first appeared during the First Age and which remained to trouble the world for many Ages afterwards. Trolls were strong, fierce and exceedingly dull-witted, with hides of overlapping scales resistant to all but the most well-forged weaponry; and though brutish and ignorant, they were readily adapted by Morgoth the Enemy to serve the cause of Evil during the War of the Great Jewels. It was later said that Trolls were bred by Morgoth from an older, less dangerous race 'in mockery of Ents, as Orcs were of Elves',[15] and that ever after they proved apt to his will, and to that of his servants.

It is plain that this is the same race remembered in the folk-tales of Northern Men, although the years which lie between the Elder Days and our own are numerous and the memory has been accordingly diminished (which might also be said of worthier creatures). Yet one memory has lingered with especial clarity: the association of the Troll-race with stone, the substance of their being. Trolls bore the same relationship to stone as Ents did to wood; of stone they were made in their beginning, and to stone they returned if caught by the direct rays of the noonday Sun; for like the Orcs they were bred during the years of the Great Darkness of the First Age, and so the Sun was their enemy. To avoid this peril, therefore, many Trolls took to dwelling in caves and under stone, and so the breeds became diversified, resulting in Hill-trolls, Cave-trolls, Snow-trolls and Stone-trolls (the most common sort). Yet all were fierce if stupid creatures, with lumpen minds and brutal instincts, whose main value to Morgoth lay in their sheer strength – which, if less great than that of the Ents, was unmatched by any other living creature.

The disaster which overwhelmed Morgoth and his armies at the end of the First Age greatly decreased the numbers of Trolls, and as they were from the first slow to breed, they were not again a menace in Middle-earth until more than a full Age later, when a new race, called *Olog-hai*, appeared in Mirkwood and on the western borders of Mordor. This breed was at once perceived to be vastly more dangerous, being:

> a fell race, strong, agile, fierce and cunning, but harder than stone. Unlike the older race of the Twilight they could endure the Sun, so long as the will of Sauron held sway over them.[16]

Moreover, they were amenable to military discipline and could therefore be used as soldiery by the Dark Lord. They were also less dull-witted than other Trolls, for Sauron had 'improved' the breed to such an extent that many of their foes mistook them for huge Orcs. Many Olog-hai fought in the War of the Ring, on the Pelennor Fields; but in the last Battle before the Black Gate, most of them were slain with the fall of their Master and the consequent withdrawal of his animating will.

Trollshaws The dank, rocky and precipitous woodland which lay north of the Great East Road between the rivers Mitheithel and Bruinen. It was so named because the area was notoriously the abode of Stone-trolls wandering down from the Ettenmoors to the North.

It was in the Trollshaws of Eriador that Thorin Oakenshield's expedition had an unpleasant encounter with three members of this fell species (in 2941 Third Age).

True-silver One of the many names for the priceless metal *mithril*.

Tuckborough The chief village or township of the Took clan; it lay in the heart of the Tookland, in the Green Hill Country of the Shire. The 'manor-hole' of the village was called Great Smials, abode of the Tooks.

Tuilë 'Spring' (Q.) The first of the six seasons in the Elvish 'year' (the *loa*). It was of fixed length, having 54 days. The name was also used by the Númenorean compilers of the Kings' Reckoning calendar-system to indicate the first (approximate) season of their four. The Sindarin equivalent was *ethuil*.

Tuilérë 'Spring-day' (Q.) The name given in Gondor to one of the five 'extra' days in the Stewards' Reckoning calendar-system. *Tuilérë* fell between the third and fourth months (*Súlimë* and *Víressë*) and celebrated the advent of Spring. It was accordingly a holiday in Gondor.

Tûk The original form of the Hobbit-surname translated from the Red Book as *Took*.

Tulkas (the Strong) One of the Valar, the mightiest in battle and in deeds of strength. He is known also as Astaldo, 'the Valiant'. Tulkas was the last of the Ainur to enter the World, and he came at a time of war – the first conflict between Melkor and the Valar. The arrival of Tulkas turned the balance against Melkor, who withdrew from Arda for that time. Afterwards, Tulkas elected to remain in Middle-earth, and he was ever after accounted one of the Valar (though not of the Aratar). He wedded Nessa the sister of Oromë at the Feast of the Spring of Arda; and later fought in the Great Battle, as champion of the Hosts of the West. See also *Silmarillion* pp. 28–9.

Tumhalad The name of a shallow vale between the rivers Ginglith and Narog, in West Beleriand. For long it was accounted part of the Realm of Nargothrond; but Nargothrond was overthrown, in the great battle fought on this very plain. See TÚRIN TURAMBAR.

Tumladen 'Broad Valley' (Sind.) The name given (probably by Turgon of the Noldor) to the secret valley surrounded by the Encircling Mountains, in the middle of which stood the rocky hill of Amon Gwareth. Here was built the city of Gondolin.

Also (Third Age) the name of a valley in Lossarnach, a south-eastern province of Gondor.

Tumunzahar The Dwarvish (Khuzdul) name for the city known to Elves as NOGROD.

Túna See TIRION.

Tunnelly A family of Little Folk (Hobbits) of Bree.

Tuor One of the greatest chieftains of the Edain of the First Age, and one of the only three mortals ever to wed with the Elves. He was the husband of Idril Celebrindal, Turgon's daughter of Gondolin, and their child was Eärendil, afterwards called the Mariner, the saviour of Elves and Men. But it was afterwards said in the lore of the Eldar and the Edain that Tuor's path had been long appointed: through his own life and deeds to unite the kindreds of the Eldar and the Edain, and so prepare the way for the forgiveness of the Valar, and the casting-out of Morgoth. This Tuor did, and he survived the Wars of Beleriand, and at the end of his life he passed over Sea, and never came again to Middle-earth.

The story of Tuor, and of his high destiny, of course forms the substance of one of the major (closing) themes of *The Silmarillion*, and needs little beyond recapitulation in these pages. He was the son of Huor of Dor-lómin (the younger brother of Húrin Thalion), and of the Lady Rían of the First House of the Edain (she was the daughter of Belegund of Ladros). He was conceived shortly before the Battle of Unnumbered Tears – at which his father Huor was slain in defence of the Pass of Sirion – and born shortly afterwards, in the winter of that same terrible year, in Mithrim: a land now occupied by Easterlings allied to Morgoth. But Rían and Tuor did not at this time fall into the power of the North, for they were sheltered by the Grey-elves of Mithrim. But when Tuor was in his seventeenth year he was taken by the Easterlings, and endured three years of servitude at their hands. Then he escaped, and returned to the secret place where he had lived all his life (now abandoned by the Grey-elves) and waged a lone war upon the occupiers and des-poilers of his native land. But after three years he forsook this lonely and dangerous existence, and – moved by some impulse which he did not at that time fully understand – made his way, not south, but west, to the deserted land of Nevrast by the Sea. In time he came to the halls of Vinyamar under Mount Taras – and there he found the arms and armour which had been left there long before, by Turgon of the Noldor, at the bidding of Ulmo, the Sea-Vala. Truly Ulmo himself was the only one of the Valar ever to maintain contact with the exiled Noldor, and it was his intercession in this matter which was to prove the salvation of the Exiles – and his instrument, as would later be seen, was Tuor of the Edain. Now he appeared to Tuor in a vision, and revealed something of his purposes; and he instructed Tuor to seek for Gondolin, and to make himself known to Turgon, its lord, and there deliver a message.

Tuor then set out, now guided by an Elf of Gondolin (whom Ulmo had set in his path for this very purpose). Together they reached the hidden gate in the Encircling Mountain, and entered in, and so came to Gondolin where Turgon had reigned for four hundred years, last of the Noldorin princes of Middle-earth, and now High-king of all the Exiles. There Tuor discharged his message from Ulmo – and beheld for the first time Idril Celebrindal, Turgon's daughter. And Turgon loved Tuor for although he indeed had a great debt to discharge to Tuor's kindred – which would in any case have caused him to treat the son of Huor as his own son – he recognized this tall Man as the very flower of the Edain, and though unwise enough to reject the counsel of Ulmo, he perceived that Ulmo's will was at work in this meeting. So Tuor became a lord of the Gondolindrim, and Turgon made him his Heir, and seven years later his daughter Idril wedded Tuor, and one year later bore a son, Eärendil, thus fulfilling the prophecy made in the last day of his life by Huor, that a new star should arise from the joined Houses of Dor-lómin and Elven Gondolin.

But more wills than Ulmo's were at work in Gondolin during those later days. For high in the counsels of the king was an Elf, Maeglin, Turgon's nephew; and he had long desired to be named as Turgon's Heir, and to wed Idril. But Idril had not returned his attentions, and the words of Huor, spoken at the Nirnaeth, had disturbed him; and now they were made manifest. Maeglin, plainly, would never inherit the lordship of the Noldor, and the bitterness in his heart darkened to jealousy – and if he now hated rather than loved Turgon, even more did he hate Tuor.

With hindsight it can clearly be seen that if Turgon had followed the counsel of Ulmo, and had abandoned Gondolin, this rivalry might never have come to pass. But he did not do so, and so the evil worked its way deep into Maeglin's heart, and after a while he fell into the power of Morgoth, and agreed to betray all that which once he had loved. For like Tuor his rival Maeglin was but an instrument of a greater will – that of Morgoth, who did not desire the salvation of the Noldor, nor that any stars should ever again arise, but only the uncontested lordship of Middle-earth, and the annihilation of all those who opposed him. And refusing the advice of Ulmo Turgon had played – as he was bound to do – into Morgoth's hands. But in all this Tuor was blameless, and Idril also.

Seven years later, when Tuor was in his thirty-seventh year, there came the attack upon Gondolin, delivered with awful force and aided by the treachery of Maeglin. Turgon and many of his captains were slain, and the city was utterly destroyed by Dragons. Few escaped; those who did were led by Tuor (who had avenged Turgon by slaying Maeglin), Idril and Eärendil. After many perils, they came to the havens of the south, and there rested for a while, in the company and fellowship of the last surviving Eldar and Edain in all of Beleriand, now utterly defeated, one by one, kingdom by kingdom, and driven to this last refuge.

Thereafter for many years Tuor made his dwelling. His son Eärendil grew to manhood, and wedded Elwing, the daughter of Dior Thingol's Heir; and the royal Line of Descent of the Grey-elves of Middle-earth was thereby added to the Line of Gondolin and the descent of the Edain. But at about the time that his grandsons Elros and Elrond were born, Tuor determined to seek the West – he had by this time become a great mariner – and he and Idril built a vessel called Eärrámë, the Flower of Foam, and set sail. They were never again seen in Middle-earth, and their fate is not known for sure. But their line continued, and by their example they prepared their son Eärendil for the voyage that he too would one day make. And finally, at the very end of the First Age, the words of Huor came true, and a new star arose in the West to bring hope to Middle-earth.

Turambar 'Master of Doom' (Q.; Sind. *Turamarth*) The last of the many *noms-de-guerre* assumed by Túrin son of Húrin of Dorlómin. Also (Third Age) the name of the ninth King of Gondor, who reigned from 541–667. When his father Rómendacil I was slain by invading Easterlings (in 541), Turambar led the army of Gondor which avenged his father and defeated the intruders. As a result Gondor's eastern possessions were greatly increased.

Turgon 'Stone-master' (Q.) The High-elven name of the younger of the two sons of Fingolfin of the Noldor. He was born in Tirion before the passing of the Two Trees, and afterwards forsook the Undying Lands, together with his wife, his father and all their kin, and joined the rebellion led by Fëanor, and went into Exile in Middle-earth. There he came to be accounted one of the wisest and most far-seeing of the Noldor, and he built the renowned and beautiful city of Gondolin, in memory of Tirion the Fair; and in the end became High King of all the exiled Noldor, while Gondolin was the longest to endure of all the cities and realms made by the Noldor in Middle-earth. But it fell at last, and Turgon perished in its sack, but his daughter Idril, together with her spouse, Tuor of the Edain, escaped, and so came to the sea-coast. And their son Eärendil by his deeds enabled the Line of Turgon to be kept alive in Middle-earth, and much more besides.

Almost from the very first Turgon realized that the great enterprise of the Exiles was doomed to bitterness and failure (his own wife Elenwë perished even before setting foot in Middle-earth). Because of this, he held aloof from the remainder of his kin, sensing as he did that evil must follow them in all their deeds. Instead – for he was, nonetheless, committed to aid the enterprise as best he might – he determined to build a great city which would be at once a revered memory of Eldamar and a mighty redoubt against the power of Morgoth. (It was said that the Vala Ulmo put this thought in his mind, for Ulmo was a friend of both Turgon and Finrod son of Finarfin, and he knew that the heart of neither was fully set on recapturing the Silmarils. Both these High-elves indeed built great cities that were also great fortresses, and neither took a leading part in the Wars – until the end.)

At this time – the first few decades of his exile – Turgon was dwelling by the Sea, in the most westerly part of Middle-earth: Nevrast. Underneath Mount Taras he had built a great hall, Vinyamar; but very soon he began actively to search for a hidden place where his greater, still unbuilt, city might arise. But there was no immediate need for haste. It is told elsewhere how he came to find the vale of Tumladen in the Encircling Mountains,[17] and how he kept the secret for many years while he planned in secret and built with care. At the beginning of the second century of his exile he quitted Vinyamar, and together with all his people made his way to Gondolin, and entered in; and the gates in the mountains were shut, and thereafter for many centuries not even Finrod his friend knew where Turgon dwelt.

Much is said elsewhere of Gondolin, of its beauty and strength, and of its long stand against the evil of Morgoth, and of how it came to fall. For most of this time Turgon carefully husbanded his strength, and took little part in the Wars, not even in the great battle of the Dagor Bragollach. And all this time Gondolin grew still more fair; and within its bounds the High-elven tongue was still freely spoken in Middle-earth, and in the court of the King stood Two Trees. Few ever came there. Fewer still departed. The first of these was Turgon's own sister Aredhel Ar-Feiniel – and this was much against the liking of Turgon. That story (see MAEGLIN) indeed forms a great part of the tale of Gondolin's eventual fall, for by Ar-Feiniel's actions evil was allowed to enter Gondolin, though none realized it until the end. But others who came to the Hidden City while it stood were two princes of the Edain, Húrin and Huor; and *their* story, and what came of it, is also woven into the tale of Turgon and Gondolin, with happier results. But for the most part Turgon defended his land, and wrapped it in secrecy, and of all those beyond its mountain-walls, Elves and Men, only Huor and Húrin ever knew its secret; they and the Eagles of the Crissaegrim.

Turgon, however, never forgot his ancient belief that the real hope of the Noldor lay in the West; and always he looked to the Sea. After the Dagor Bragollach he sent messengers west, in search of Valinor, but one only returned, and that was years afterwards. And in the meantime the tide of war flowed to and fro across the northlands. At last Turgon could no longer hold aloof from the conflict, and he emerged from Gondolin for the first time in four and a half centuries, and brought his army to the Nirnaeth Arnoediad; and – despite great heroism – was defeated there. He and his host were saved from destruction, and enabled to make an uncontested retreat, only by the valour of the Men of Dor-lómin, led by Húrin and Huor. And though the days grew dark thereafter, Turgon never forgot this.

The last years of Turgon in Middle-earth were years of war and ravage in western Middle-earth, but a time of unreal bliss in Gondolin. Nothing had changed in Tumladen since the building of the city – and still no Elf departed from it, for Turgon now enforced his most ancient law with absolute determination.[18] And after a time there came a Man from the Sea bearing tokens, and Turgon knew him for a messenger from Ulmo (see TUOR). Yet on this crucial occasion his old wisdom deserted him – overmastered by his pride in Gondolin – and he ignored the counsel thus vouchsafed him; and in so doing brought about the fall of Gondolin. For evil was awake in the city. Yet if Turgon had followed the counsel of Ulmo, and had abandoned the City for the Sea, ruin might not have descended upon the last remnant of the People of Fingolfin. But Turgon would not relinquish the creation of his heart, and remained in Gondolin, and was betrayed, and perished in the sack. Yet this grace was granted, on account of his long piety, and as a reward for his repentance: that his Line should continue in the world after the ending of the Age, and that the memory of Gondolin should be preserved among Elves and Men until the latest days, unstained and fair.

Note: also the name of the twenty-fourth Ruling Steward of Gondor (Third Age), who reigned from 2914–53. Two years before his death Sauron the Great, Lord of the Rings, openly declared himself once more and re-occupied Mordor; and shortly after Turgon's death Sauron's ascendant rival, Saruman the Wizard, also rose to power, taking Isengard (which had been granted to him in fee by Turgon's ancestor Beren, nineteenth Steward) for his own and fortifying it.

Tûr Haretha See HAUDH-EN-ARWEN.

Túrin Turambar The most tragic of all the heroes of the Edain of the First Age. His life and deeds are the chief subject of *The Tale of the Children of Húrin,* longest surviving Mannish poem of the Elder Days (it is reproduced in edited form as part of the Quenta Silmarillion, and indeed forms a grim epilogue to the Nirnaeth Arnoediad). Túrin was perhaps the mightiest warrior of all the Edain (save only his father Húrin), and the last but one of the valiant House of Hador of Dor-lómin; but although he fought bravely all his life, and did deeds of prowess that won him the love and respect both of Elves and Men, he was of the Children of Húrin, and so accursed of Morgoth; and he brought only grief and disaster upon those whom he in turn loved, and in the end slew himself in despair.

Túrin was the son of Húrin of the Third House of the Edain and Morwen Eledhwen of the First House, born in Dor-lómin. When he was nearly eight years old his father and uncle and all the warriordom of their nation marched away to the Nirnaeth Arnoediad, and never returned. But Húrin had been taken prisoner, and had defied Morgoth; so Morgoth cursed Húrin and all his kin; and as the chief instrument of his will in this matter he chose the Fire-drake Glaurung. But first he sought Túrin – and at first he did not find him, for the boy had been sent soon after the Nirnaeth to Doriath, to be fostered in the care of Thingol; and Túrin came to early manhood in that secret, fenced land. And then he went to war, as the Heir of Dor-lómin, wearer of the Dragon-helm, and won renown on the north marches.

Slowly his ordained fate began to close in. A quarrel ended in tragedy (see SAEROS) and Túrin fled from Doriath, to eke out a miserable rogue's existence in the wilds beyond. But Thingol sent one of his greatest warriors, Beleg Cúthalion, to find the boy and, if necessary, protect him – if he could not first persuade him to return to Doriath. Beleg was unable to persuade Túrin to return, but he uplifted his life, and set the young man's mind towards nobler occupations than mere banditry. Together they waged war upon Morgoth in the lands about Teiglin in West Beleriand.

But this campaign was to be short-lived. Túrin and Beleg and their band of guerillas were betrayed (see MÎM), and Túrin was captured by Orcs, but afterwards freed by Beleg, whom he accidentally slew in the act. Crazed by grief for his dead friend, Túrin might then have fallen prey to the perils of the wild, but was befriended by Gwindor, an Elf, formerly of Nargothrond, who had escaped from Angband and was returning to his city. He it was who brought Túrin to Nargothrond.

Túrin's first comrades in the wild, the outlaw band of Amon Rûdh, and his oldest friend, Beleg Strongbow, were all dead. Now it had become the turn of Gwindor and the Elves of Nargothrond; for by succouring him and giving him their love – and later their respect and obedience – they too fell, as was afterwards seen, under the curse laid on Húrin's kin. For though a Mortal Man, Túrin was a hardier and more skilful warrior than any Elf of Nargothrond (though perhaps not quite so skilful as he thought himself); and by his valour and unbroken determination to wreak harm upon Morgoth was soon acknowledged – even by King Orodreth – as war-leader of Nargothrond. They called him *Mormegil* because of the Black Sword (once Beleg's) that he wielded with deadly effect (see GURTHANG). But Túrin scorned secret ambush, for long the practice of the Elves of Nargothrond. An understandable pride in being the only Man ever to command an Elven-host in the field perhaps affected his judgement. Disregarding an ancient tactical precept of Finrod, he bridged the Narog: to permit, as he explained, the swift sortie of armies – but ignoring the fact that he also thereby laid bare the doors of Nargothrond. And later, when a great host came from the North, an army which included the Dragon Glaurung, Túrin would not await their onset but went boldly out to meet them in battle. But the host he led to Tumhalad was destroyed; Gwindor was mortally wounded and Orodreth the King was slain, and most of the warriors of Nargothrond besides. But Túrin, as was his doom, survived – only to reap the full horror when he learned that Nargothrond, left undefended, had been sacked by the Dragon – and this had only come about because of the bridge he, Túrin, had made – and that the King's daughter Finduilas (who loved Túrin) had been taken prisoner by Orcs. And then, at the gates of Nargothrond, Túrin encountered the Dragon, who bewitched him. He fled north, crazed and anguished, seeking both Finduilas and his own mother and sister, for the words of Glaurung had put him in fear for their safety.

Now the curse hastened to its fulfilment. For in the meantime Morwen and her daughter Nienor, who were also accursed of Morgoth, had left Dor-lómin and had gone, like Túrin years before, to Doriath, hoping to find him there. But he, having now learned of the death of Finduilas, was at the same time seeking them in Dor-lómin; and so their paths crossed, Morwen never again set eyes on her only son. But she and Nienor came to Thingol's kingdom, and learning of Túrin's long departure determined separately to seek him in the wild; for they had also learned of the fall of Nargothrond, and of the Mormegil. So while Túrin dwelt in Brethil and made lonely war on the enemies of his kin, Morwen and Nienor were seeking him near Nargothrond. At this time Nienor also encountered Glaurung the Dragon, and was bewitched, and lost her memory. She was found, wandering witlessly in the wild, by Túrin – who did not recognize her, for she had been but an infant when he had left Dor-lómin. He comforted her, and took her with him to Brethil – where he was now dwelling, with the Haladin – and after three years he wedded her. And she conceived his child.

Now the doom was complete; but Túrin who now called himself Turambar ('Master of Doom'), still did not know of the evil he had unwittingly committed. And he gained no small revenge for his sufferings, by slaying the Dragon. But Glaurung spoke before he died, and lifted the bewitchment from Nienor and then she knew what was done, and slew herself. And when Túrin at last also learned the full truth, and realized the nature of the doom which had mastered him, he too now slew himself in despair, and was buried at Cabed Naeramarth, the place of his greatest victory and his greatest anguish. After the drowning of Beleriand, this crag still stood, as an island in the sea.

Such is the story of Túrin, the most grievous of all the tales of Men, in itself a monument to the vile wickedness of Morgoth. As a great warrior, slayer of the most terrible of all the Dragons of the Age, Túrin has great renown. But it is as a victim that the *Narn i Hîn Húrin* (or *Tale of the Children of Húrin*) depicts him. This very long lay was made some years after the events it describes in the Havens of Sirion, the dwelling of the poet, whose name was Dírhavel (he was slain soon afterwards). Copies of it were kept even by the Elves, for the story touched them deeply, and indeed they are not uninvolved in its fabric. But it is the copy kept by Elrond in Rivendell which probably forms the source of Chapter XXI in *The Silmarillion* (to which all readers are referred). For, as all know, the Hobbit Bilbo Baggins spent many years in the library of Rivendell, and he copied down the Tale of Túrin in its entirety. Chapter XXI is a prose version of the original poem (or 'ballad', since the verse was reportedly meant to be chanted or declaimed by a bard, rather than read in silence). Like the rest of Bilbo's work, it comes to us courtesy of the Fairbairn family of Westmarch in the Shire, the Heirs of Frodo and Samwise, and of Bilbo, and custodians of the records of their own, and earlier, Ages of the World.

Note: during his life Túrin assumed many *noms-de-guerre*. He was, after all, always aware of his mighty inheritance, and also that Morgoth was seeking for him, the last heir of Dor-lómin; and so he cloaked his identity under a series of titles. These, in chronological order, were: *Neithian* ('the Wronged'); *Gorthol* ('the Dreaded Helm'); *Agarwaen* ('the Bloodstained'); *Adanedhel* ('Elf-man') and *Mormegil* ('the Black Sword' – the only names awarded to him by others); 'Wildman of the Woods', and finally *Turambar* ('Master-of-Doom'). The circumstances surrounding these titles are more fully detailed under the corresponding entries.

See also BELEG STRONGBOW; MÎM; ÚMARTH.

Túrin I From 2244–78 Third Age, the sixth Ruling Steward of Gondor.

Túrin II From 2882–2914 Third Age, the twenty-third Ruling Steward of Gondor, and a farsighted strategian of his day. Early in his rule he received warning that the Haradrim, traditional foes of the Dúnedain, were again planning an invasion of South Ithilien; accordingly Túrin invoked the alliance between his people and the Riders of Rohan, sending the Red Arrow, most urgent token of war, to King Folcwine in Edoras. The aid sent by Folcwine enabled Túrin to defeat the invaders at the ford of the river Poros (see BATTLE OF THE CROSSINGS OF POROS).

Some years afterwards Túrin perceived that Ithilien was becoming untenable, due to the growing strength of Mordor; he therefore ordered built the secret refuges of that province (see HENNETH ANNÛN). At the same time he fortified the west bank of the Anduin, including the isle of Cair Andros, which guarded the province of Anórien. These farsighted fortifications were of great value to the Dúnedain a century later during the War of the Ring.

Twofoot A family of rustic Hobbits of Bywater and district.

Two Trees The Two Trees of Valinor, made at the Beginning of Days by Yavanna Kementári of the Valar. They grew on the mound of Ezellohar, near the western gate of the city of the Valar, and brought the first Light into the world since the extinguishing of the still more ancient Light of the Lamps Illuin and Ormal. The Trees were named *Telperion* (the elder) and *Laurelin*; and the one bore flowers which gave a silver Light, while the other had leaves of glistening gold. They were the most beautiful Trees that have ever been in the World, and they grew and flourished for Ages in the holiest place of Arda; but in the end Evil touched them, and they were poisoned, and died, and their Light was taken from the world – but not for ever, for some of it lingered in the three Silmarils which

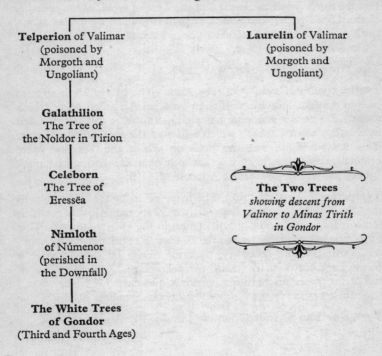

Telperion of Valimar
(poisoned by
Morgoth and
Ungoliant)

Laurelin of Valimar
(poisoned by
Morgoth and
Ungoliant)

Galathilion
The Tree of
the Noldor in Tirion

Celeborn
The Tree of
Eressëa

The Two Trees
*showing descent from
Valinor to Minas Tirith
in Gondor*

Nimloth
of Númenor
(perished in
the Downfall)

**The White Trees
of Gondor**
(Third and Fourth Ages)

Note: In addition to the direct Line of Descent of the Silver Tree there were the 'images' (of both Trees) made in Gondolin by Turgon: *Belthil* and *Glingal*, craft-replicas of Telperion and Laurelin. Both were destroyed in the sack of the city.

Fëanor of the Noldor had made. And, moreover, a scion of Telperion still grew in Tirion, a gift from the Valar to the Noldor; and a descendant of this Tree of the High-elves (*Galathilion,* as it was called), grew in Eressëa. This was *Celeborn.* In time a sapling of Celeborn's line found its way to Númenor (*Nimloth*), and a fruit of this Tree of Westernesse was taken to Middle-earth by Elendil and his sons, and in later days grew in Gondor.

A last descendant of this exceedingly ancient Line was still living at the beginning of the Fourth Age.

But Laurelin had no linear descendants in Middle-earth; and thereafter the Golden Light was to be perceived only in the mingled Light of the Evening Star. Yet it is said in the legends of the Eldar that the Sun is itself the last leaf of the Tree of Gold, borne eternally aloft on fixed paths; and that the Moon is the last Flower of Silver, similarly piloted through the heavens by untiring agency.

See *Silmarillion* pp. 38–9.

Two Watchers The SILENT WATCHERS.

Tyelle, tyeller 'Grade' (Q.) The name given by the High-elves to each of the six subdivisions of the Fëanorian Alphabet, all of which measured a certain mode of articulation and were further modified by the four *témar* ('series') which indicated the *point* of articulation. This cross-division was the basis on which the Tengwar were originally devised to function as a wholly phonetic writing-system.

See TENGWA, TENGWAR; also Appendix E II(i).

Tyelpetéma '*Ty*-series' (Q.) The name given by the High-elves to the *téma* ('series') in the *Tengwar* (the Fëanorian Alphabet) which indicated a palatal point of articulation in the Quenya tongue. This series was not normally part of the Fëanorian regulating-system, and was written, where necessary, by using Series IV together with a Fëanorian diacritic mark (*tehta*) for 'following *y*' (actually a pair of full points placed under the consonant in question).

See also TÉMA, TÉMAR; TENGWA, TENGWAR; Appendix E II(ii).

Tyrn Gorthad 'Dreaded Mounds' (Sind.) The Barrow-downs.

Notes

1 *Silmarillion* pp. 55–6.
2 Book II Chap. 7.
3 Theoden's Funeral Song, Book VI Chap. 6.
4 *Silmarillion* p. 52.
5 *Silmarillion* pp. 162–87.
6 Appendix A III.
7 Book II Chap. 8.
8 Appendix F II.
9 Book II Chap. 2.
10 *Ibid.*
11 Book II Chap. 1.
12 Illustrated in *The Silmarillion Calendar* 1978.
13 Book I Chap. 7.
14 His character and qualities are shared by the (much later)
   Arcadian nature-deity *Pan.*
15 Book III Chap. 4.
16 Appendix F I.
17 *Silmarillion* p. 115.
18 Or believed that he did.

Udûn 'The Pit' or 'the Underworld' (Sind., from Q. *Utumno*) The name given in the language of the Grey-elves to the first Realm of Morgoth, in the Far North of Middle-earth, destroyed in the Battle of the Powers when the world was young.

Also (Third Age) the name in Gondor for the deep vale which lay in north-western Mordor, between the Isenmouthe and the Morannon, the Black Gate.

Ufthak As recorded in the Red Book (by Master Samwise), this was the name of a miserable Orc, a member of the garrison of the Tower of Cirith Ungol, who was captured and afterwards devoured by the giant spider Shelob the Great. Through Sam we learn that this unhappy Goblin was, in fact, discovered by his fellow-orcs while still bound and uneaten; but in an act of almost unbelievable callousness, his 'comrades' declined to rescue him, not wishing to provoke the wrath of the monster.

Uglúk The leader of the raiding-party of Uruk-hai (Orcs) who slew Boromir son of Denethor II and captured the two young Hobbits Meriadoc and Peregrin, intending to carry them back to Isengard and his master Saruman the Wizard. Uglúk was afterwards described as 'a large black Orc'[1] with a deep, growling voice, and he was evidently a formidable warrior. At all events, he was no coward and seems to have commanded considerable loyalty from his own followers – though not, of course, from Orcs of other breeds, who doubtless resented the superior manner adopted by the Uruk-hai towards 'lesser' Goblins.

As is told elsewhere (Book III Chap. 3) Uglúk's raid, initially successful, was betrayed by fortune (and inattentive Orc-scouts) and the Uruk-hai, together with their reluctant allies (and their even more reluctant prisoners) were cut off by an *éored* of Riders of Rohan – led by Éomer, Third Marshal of the Mark – before they could regain the shelter of Fangorn Forest. And although Uglúk and his immediate followers remained disciplined to the last, in the end all the Orcs were slain by the Rohirrim. Éomer himself paid Uglúk the compliment of dismounting before killing him.

Uial 'Twilight' (Sind.) The Grey-elves' name for the periods of 'star-fading' and 'star-opening', which were moments of reverence for the Eldar. The word was incorporated in the Sindarin names for dawn-twilight (*minuial*) and eventide (*aduial*); these were known to the High-elves as *tindómë* and *undómë* respectively.

See also AELIN-UIAL; NENUIAL.

Uilos See AMON UILOS.

Uinen One of the MAIAR; she was the Lady of the Seas, the spouse of Ossë; and was revered for her powers of calming storms at sea.

See also *Silmarillion* p. 30.

Úlairi 'The Undead' (Q.)[2] The name given by the Númenoreans to those of their race, already given over to evil, who were ensnared by Sauron – by means of the Nine Mortal Rings – during the early part of the Second Age, and who afterwards came to be accounted his most terrible servants: the RINGWRAITHS (*Nazgûl* in the Black Speech).

Uldor the Accursed A Chieftain of the Easterlings during the First Age, youngest of the three sons of Ulfang the Black. His memory is accursed among Elves and Men – even of his own race – because of the treacherous part he and his brothers played at the Nirnaeth Arnoediad. It is no exaggeration to say that Uldor's actions were the single greatest reason for the catastrophic defeat suffered in that battle by the Eldar and the Edain – though perhaps that enterprise, foredoomed as it was, would have foundered on some other rock, at some later time, with consequences equally disastrous for all, even if Uldor and his kin had remained faithful.

Easterlings first entered Beleriand after the Dagor Bragollach. Many took service with Morgoth, but other clans, passing down the Dwarf-road, came to the March of Maedhros and enlisted in the armies maintained by the Sons of Fëanor in that embattled region. Two of these clans were led by Bór and Ulfang. The former chief took service with Maedhros and Maglor, and held The Gap; the latter clan, that led by Ulfang and his three sons, Ulwarth, Ulfast and Uldor, enlisted under the banners of Caranthir (who of all the Noldor was the least apt a judge of Men). But they were already under the secret command of Morgoth, and although for perhaps a decade they served with apparent faithfulness, they secretly reported all that was done by the Eldar to their Master in Angband, and on his orders made secret preparation to thwart the designs of Maedhros (see UNION OF MAEDHROS). So it proved. The set-piece battle which Maedhros had envisaged upon the desert of Anfauglith went badly wrong almost from the first. Certainly as a plan it was too elaborate and, moreover, the two armies of the Eldar were widely separated and messages were slow to arrive. Thus it was that when Uldor deceived Maedhros with false reports of a sortie from Angband, he was not able to initiate his part of the planned grand envelopment; and Fingon was too far away for messages to arrive in time. And besides, the Host of Mithrim had already become embroiled with the armies of Morgoth. Nonetheless, Maedhros managed to set forth in time to fall upon the rear of Morgoth's main host, and for a brief while the victory so long dreamed-of was within the grasp of the Eldar. But at this precise moment Uldor committed his second (and greater) treachery, and he brought on to the field of battle a great army of Easterlings friendly to Morgoth, who had been awaiting his order. He himself, with his brothers and followers, now fell upon the rear ranks of Maedhros. And though he (and his brothers) were straightaway cut down by those whom they had betrayed, the damage was done. The battle – and with it, the War – was lost.

Ulfang the Black A chieftain of the Easterlings of the First Age. See preceding entry.

Ulfast See ULDOR THE ACCURSED.

Ulmo 'The Pourer' (Q.) The Lord of Waters. One of the great Valar (the *Aratar*, 'High Ones'); King of the Sea.[3] In the traditions of the Eldar Ulmo is second in power only to Manwë: in his following are the Maiar Ossë, Uinen, and Salmar (who made for his lord the great horns of shell, on which Ulmo from time to time makes music on the shores of Middle-earth). Alone of the Valar, Ulmo did not entirely forsake the rebelling Noldor in their exile; for he dwells, not in Valinor, but in all the seas and rivers of the world, and has done so since the Beginning of Arda. And so he came from time to time to Middle-earth while the Noldor made war upon Morgoth, and learned of their doings, and from time to time offered counsel, in his own way, to those he deemed able to receive it. It was Ulmo who put the thought of building lasting refuges into the sleeping minds of Finrod, son of Finarfin, and Turgon, wisest of the children of Fingolfin. Indeed these two Elves he favoured above all; and when Finrod was slain Ulmo continued to play a part in the destiny of Turgon. And although the Vala's counsel was not always taken – or understood – in the end it enabled this at the least to come to pass: that the Line of Fingolfin and the memory of Gondolin should endure into a new Age of the World. But that was the most that even Ulmo could salvage from the wreck.

See also *Valaquenta* pp. 19, 26–7.

Ulumúri The horns of white shell made by the Maia Salmar and given by him to his lord, Ulmo King of the Sea. In Eldarin tradition, Ulmo will from time to time come to the shores of Middle-earth and make music on the Ulumúri: a music which carries with it a deep and profound enchantment of everlasting memory.

Ulwarth See ULDOR THE ACCURSED.

Úmanyar '[Elves] Not of Aman' (Q.) One of the divisions of the Elves; it applies specifically to those of the Eldar (all incidentally of the Telerin kindred) who never completed the Great Journey from Cuiviénen to Valinor while the First Age lasted, lingering instead, for various reasons – and having been sundered from their kinsfolk at differing times and in varying ways – in Middle-earth. Included under this classification are the *Sindar* ('Grey-elves') of Beleriand; a subdivision of the Sindar called 'Coast-elves' (*Falathrim*), led by Círdan, who dwelt at the Havens (while acknowledging the High-kingship of Thingol Greycloak); the *Nandor* ('Those Who Turn Back'), who quitted the Journey in Wilderland, never crossing the Misty Mountains; and a subdivision of the Nandor, the *Laiquendi* or 'Green-elves' of Ossiriand, allies and vassals of the Sindar.

Note: Úmanyar is *not* equivalent to *Moriquendi*; the latter term refers to all Elves, whether Eldar or Avari, who never came at all to the Far West, and instead lingered, dwindling, in mortal lands, as minor disembodied spirits. Obviously as a definition *Moriquendi* (a title depending on hindsight) came into being at a much later date than *Úmanyar*, which refers only to those who actually completed the Journey during the Elder Days. Confusingly, *Calaquendi* (the opposite of *Moriquendi*) *is* virtually synonymous with *Amanyar*; or rather, they are two separately conceived definitions of the same group of Eldarin peoples, and exclude all other Elves, even those of the *Úmanyar* who came, last of all, into the Far West. For this group there may be still another name,[4] of which we have yet to learn.

Úmarth 'Ill-fortune' (Sind.) 'The Bloodstained, Ill-fortune's child' is of course the somewhat dramatic pseudonym adopted by TÚRIN TURAMBAR when he first came to the city of Nargothrond, in company with the Elf Gwindor. Túrin had, of course, recently slain his greatest and oldest friend, Beleg Strongbow, by grievous mischance; and he was still deeply sorrowful and bitter about the incident. In such circumstances the slightly lurid quality of this short-lived *nom de guerre* can readily be forgiven him. After all, it proved an all-too-apt description of Túrin, who was destined to bring disaster upon all who loved him; for he was accursed of Morgoth, and though valorous beyond all other Men of his day, came to a bitter end.

Umbar The Quenya or High-elven word for 'fate',[5] but more properly the title of Tengwa number 6, which represented the sound *mb* in the High-elven speech, *b* in most other tongues. It was also the name of the great Cape and Firth on the coasts of Middle-earth, some seventy leagues south of the river Harnen. Umbar was first settled and fortified by Númenoreans returning to Middle-earth in the later Second Age, and by the year 2280 it was the chief haven of the Númenoreans outside their own land. Yet from the beginning the city lay under a spiritual cloud, and during the years of Númenor's moral decline it became a fortress of the King's Men, afterwards called the Black Númenoreans; some years later the Faithful of Andúnië founded their own haven of Pelargir further north.

Nonetheless Umbar was a mighty fortress, the greatest of its kind in Middle-earth, and it rapidly became a centre of the Númenoreans' sea-power. In 3261 Second Age the host of Ar-Pharazôn the Golden, last King of Númenor, disembarked there before marching out to offer battle to Sauron the Great for the supremacy in Middle-earth. But although Sauron was defeated and humiliated in that campaign, his cunning and deceitfulness later prevailed and Númenor was cast down under the waves; then for a while Umbar became the chief remaining fortress of Númenorean power in the world – until the Faithful of Andúnië, who had for the most part survived the Downfall, constructed their twin realms of Arnor and Gondor to the North of Umbar.

However, the Black Númenoreans of Umbar had also escaped the Drowning of Númenor, and from the beginning of the Third Age the rivalry between the two maritime states was intense. But in 933 Eärnil I, second of the 'Ship-kings' of Gondor, took Umbar by siege and held it, thus intensifying the rivalry and the hatreds. For many years the power of Gondor was unassailable, and Umbar became the southernmost harbour and fortress of the South-kingdom. On a headland the victorious Dúnedain erected a monument to Sauron's defeat at the hands of Ar-Pharazôn, and many ships were berthed in the harbour below. But in 1432 civil war broke out in Gondor, and her fleets mutinied against the lawful King; in the end the rebels were defeated on land, but they still controlled the ships and, in 1448, sailed away to Umbar to establish a breakaway Corsair state, at permanent feud with Gondor.

For nearly four hundred years the descendants of these renegades waged naval war against Gondor's coastlands, but in 1810 Telumehtar, twenty-eighth King, determined to stamp out the pirates and he took Umbar by storm. However, by the end of the second millennium of the Third Age the power of the Haradrim, allies of the Corsairs, had arisen once more, and shortly after Telumehtar Umbardacil's victory the Southrons captured the haven from the Dúnedain and so made its naval might their own. Haradrim seapower dates to this time. For the remainder of the Age the new maritime state (still called 'Corsairs' by the Dúnedain) continued to harass Gondor's coasts, often doing great damage (and furthering the cause of Gondor's foes everywhere). Counter-raiding by the fleets of Gondor failed to put an end to the menace, and by the time of the War of the Ring the seaborne threat from the South prevented Gondor's southern fiefs from sending more than a small proportion of their manpower to the defence of Minas Tirith. In that war the Corsairs indeed attempted landings in strength – at Linhir and Pelargir – but were severely defeated and lost most of their war-vessels to the Dúnedain, who used the ships as fast transports up the Anduin to the aid of Minas Tirith. The aid thus brought turned the tide of the war and the Haradrim were defeated. Accordingly, although Umbar remained in the hands of the Southrons, the sea-power of the Corsairs was greatly diminished; and in the peace which followed the victory over Sauron Umbar once again became a peaceful harbour and a centre of trade and commerce.

Note: the word *umbar* is said to mean 'fate' in the Quenya tongue as mentioned above, yet in the Red Book (Appendix F) we are told that the name is of pre-Númenorean (i.e. Mannish) origin. It is, of course, not impossible that both statements are correct, i.e. that they are two distinct names.

Umbardacil 'Victor-of-Umbar' (Q.) The royal title taken by King Telumehtar, twenty-eighth King of Gondor, after his great victory over the Corsairs of Umbar in the year 1810 Third Age.

Underharrow A village in Rohan, nestling under the mountains beside the river Snowbourn in Harrowdale.

Underhill A family of Hobbits of the Shire, with a distant branch in Staddle (in the Bree-land). This was the name chosen by Frodo Baggins as a travelling-name before he set out from the Shire in 1418 Shire Reckoning (he was incognito at the time).

Undertowers The 'manor-hole' of the Fairbairn family, descendants of Master Samwise, who settled the Westmarch early in the Fourth Age and built their home into the east-facing slopes of the Tower Hills (the *Emyn Beraid*).

Underworld An approximate translation of *Utumno* 'the Pit' (Q.; Sind. *Udûn*).

Undómë 'Star-opening' (Q.) The High-elven name for eventide; the Grey-elves' equivalent was *aduial* (called *Evendim* by the Hobbits).

Undómiel 'Evenstar' (Q.) The royal title borne by the Elf-maiden Arwen, daughter of Elrond Half-elven.

Undying Lands One of the many names given in the long traditions of Elves and Men to Aman, the Blessed Realm in the Ancient (True) West of Arda, set aside after the passing of the Spring of Arda as a home for the Valar and Maiar; and afterwards shared with those of the Quendi (Elves) who completed the Great Journey and so came to the last shores far back in the Elder Days.

It has been said that the Undying Lands are an abode of immortals; time as we know it does not pass there, and the waning of days in the world outside is not felt by those fortunate enough to dwell with the Valar in everlasting earthly bliss. At the Creation, and for long after, Aman was indeed part of the 'circles of the world', and could be reached by a long and arduous voyage across the Great Sea of the West. However, only the Valar were at first permitted to come there. This rule was later altered to include the Quendi, and later still to embrace a very few mortals, who had earned such a grace in some way during their mortal lives in Middle-earth. For the Quendi the Valar allotted a portion of Aman, the eastern shorelands surrounding the Great Bay; this was called, by the Elves, *Eldamar*, 'Elvenhome'. Beyond the tall Mountains in the West of the Elves' land lay the greater portion of Aman: the Land of the Valar and Maiar, called Valinórë. The Mountains which divided Aman from north to south were named *Pelóri*, the Mountains of Defence; they were raised as a barrier to Melkor (Morgoth), for the Valar had not forgotten that Aman had not been the first dwelling of their race in Arda. North of Eldamar stretched the wilderness of Araman, beyond which lay the misty waste of Oiomúrë – and beyond that the Grinding Ice, the Helcaraxë, in ancient times a physical link between Aman and Middle-earth, though a perilous one. To the south of Eldamar lay another cold wilderness, the region known as Avathar, a narrow shut-in land where the Valar and the Eldar did not go.

Eressëa, the 'Lonely-isle', was not originally part of the Undying Lands. As is told in *The Silmarillion*[6] it stood from earliest times in the middle of the Sea, a great island shaped like a monstrous ship, with a high prow looking westward. By the agency of the Valar this island was detached from the sea-bed and moved across the waves into the East; and then West. By this means the great hosts of the Vanyar and the Noldor were transported from Middle-earth to Aman (in those days the craft of shipbuilding was unknown to the Elves). Later the island returned to the Bay of Balar and again passed back across the Sea to the West, bearing this time the last of the Eldar destined to arrive in the Undying Lands while the Trees still shone, the Teleri led by Olwë. At the request of these lastcomers, the island was brought to a halt at the mouth of the Bay of Eldamar, and put down new roots, and never moved again. (A fragment – its easternmost region – had broken asunder, and still stood off the coasts of Middle-earth; this was the Isle of Balar.)

The Vanyar dwelled at first in Tirion, the fair city built by themselves and the Noldor in the mouth of the Pass of Calacirya, through the Mountains, from which flooded the Blessed Light of the Trees. But afterwards they removed and went further west, through the Calacirya, and dwelled evermore in Valinor itself. The Noldor continued to dwell in Tirion, and only abandoned it to return to Middle-earth – to their undying regret. The Teleri at first dwelled on Tol Eressëa, in the haven of Avallónë, but later came ashore to Aman and made a new haven and city for themselves at Alqualondë, north of Tirion. But the chief city of Aman was Valimar, or Valmar, the city of the Valar and Maiar, where stood also the Ring of Doom, or council-place of the Aratar – and, in ancient days, the fabled Two Trees upon their green mound. But the Lord of Arda, Manwë, and his spouse Varda, the Lady of the Stars, dwelled in a lofty palace on top of the highest of the Pelóri, from where they were – and still are – able to gaze out over Arda and mark all that passes therein, even though the Undying Lands themselves no longer constitute part of the physical world. As all know, in a later time the folly of the Númenoreans led to an actual assault upon Aman; and with the realization that their last sanctuary had proved, after all, violable, the Valar invoked Ilúvatar (The Creator), who altered the material (if not the spiritual) nature of Arda and removed Aman and Eressëa to another plane of existence, a plane which overlooks ours yet is not part of it. Thereafter the Undying Lands could only be reached by those specifically appointed to make the Journey; and so they remain.

Note: in this connection, it has become almost *de rigeur* to draw attention to the exceedingly widespread, but ancient, Mannish tradition concerning a vanished (but not unreachable) Paradise in the Mystic or Ancient West of the World. Indeed, an early meaning of the word *Paradise* itself refers to a kind of 'Half-way-house' between Middle-earth and Over-heaven, peopled by great Beatitudes who are Agents of The Creator; a home for those who deserve a blissful after-life but whose actual spiritual nature does not permit their entry to the Halls of Ilúvatar while Arda lasts. (The 'Garden of the Hesperides' and the 'Garden of Eden' are, in many traditions, similar places of bliss.) This myth is particularly strong among the Celtic Mannish peoples who (one is obliged to point out) were the most westerly of all the ancient Mannish peoples of the Old World. *Hy Braseal, Tir na nOg* are but two of their names for the Undying Lands. Celtic mariners have actually sought for these lands in historical times, and indeed there are still many among this race of Men whose Occidentophilia has a profoundly mystic quality, even in our own day.

See also AVALLÓNË.

Ungoliant The first and greatest of the Spider-race; a foul and dangerous monster, hideous to look upon, a worker of much evil and the begetter of many evil offspring. She was in origin an entity of the Outer Darkness, called into being by Melkor (Morgoth) at the Beginning of Arda, and thus the first of the Great Demons to invade the World, which she afterwards polluted. After the fall of Utumno she dwelt in Avathar, in the far, freezing south of Aman, where the Valar did not go; and she hungered after Light, devouring it as lesser spiders devour insect-prey. Here Melkor came to her, for he had fled but lately from Valinor, unmasked for the last time as irredeemably evil; and already he had a design for the discomfiture and grief of those he had made his enemies – the destruction of the Trees. Ungoliant, lured by his promise of a great and glorious assuaging of her hunger, joined him in this wicked action; and the Trees were poisoned by her venom, and so died. Together with Melkor, she then fled to Middle-earth, now swollen to huge size by her feasting yet still (for such was her nature) with hunger undiminished. And when Melkor, who by now was in fear of her, withheld the last – and to him, most precious – item of booty from the sack of Formenos, she attacked him (see LAMMOTH), and he barely escaped her fury. But he was delivered from her by others of his servants, and Ungoliant was herself put in great fear. She fled south, and made her dreadful nests thereafter in the dark glens and ravines of the mountains which were the southern wall of Dorthonion, in the North of Beleriand. (These mountains were afterwards called *Ered Gorgoroth*, the 'Mountains of Terror'.) Here she mated with lesser beasts of Middleearth. Her offspring were evil like herself, though of less stature (one of these was SHELOB THE GREAT). Her fate has not been recorded; and unless in the end she starved to death in some desert place[7] or was finally destroyed by a greater agency, she lives still in some hideous and forgotten cavern under the world.

Ungwe The Quenya or High-elven word for 'spider's-web', but more properly the title of Tengwa number 8, which stood for the sound of (hard) *g* (or *gw*) in those languages which required such a consonant.

Union of Maedhros The name given by Maedhros the eldest son of Fëanor of the Noldor to the grand alliance devised by him in the years following the Dagor Bragollach; an alliance, as he purposed, by which the Eldar and the Edain – and any others who would join them – were to be welded into one huge and irresistible force which, cleverly handled, would be large enough to annihilate the last armies of Angband: to the least Orc. But although grandly named, this alliance, to which not all proved willing to adhere (and not all of those who did proved faithful), was shakily-founded, and despite early successes of a minor (though fatally encouraging) nature, came to nothing – and worse than nothing – in the end. The result of the Union of Maedhros was the Nirnaeth Arnoediad, and the final defeat of the Elves in the Wars of Beleriand. No further alliances were ever contemplated, until the Host of the West came from over the Sea to put an end to the long and evil reign of Morgoth, and to deliver Middle-earth.

Unque The Quenya or High-elven word for 'a hollow', but more properly the title of Tengwa number 16, which represented the sound *gh* (or *ghw*) in those languages which required it.

Upbourn The name of a small village or hamlet in Rohan, which stood beside the river Snowbourn at the mouth of the Harrowdale valley.

Úre The Quenya or High-elven word for 'heat', but more properly the title of Tengwa number 36, which represented the sound of consonantal *w* in most languages; it was one of the 'additional' letters in the Fëanorian Alphabet.

Urimë The name given to the eighth month of the year in the Kings' Reckoning calendar-system. This month-name was retained in both Stewards' Reckoning and the New Reckoning of the Fourth Age. However, the Dúnedain of Middle-earth preferred the Sindarin equivalent *Urui*.

Urthel One of the Edain of the First House; a comrade of Barahir, slain on Dorthonion together with the remainder of the twelve-strong band shortly after the Dagor Bragollach.

Urui See URIMË above.

Uruk-hai 'Orc-race' (Black Speech) The name given by Sauron to a new strain of Orcs bred in secrecy by him in Mordor towards the end of the Third Age, and said (by his enemies) to have been created by the blending of the races of Orcs and Men. It is certain, however, that (so far as Orcs went) the Uruk-hai were a far superior breed, being taller and stronger, with great endurance, and an altogether higher level of intelligence. For these reasons alone they were greatly to be feared. They first appeared in 2475 Third Age, when a strong force attacked the outposts of Ithilien and captured Osgiliath; this army was later driven out by Boromir, son of Ruling Steward Denethor I.

However, the Uruk-hai did not remain exclusively in Sauron's service. By the time of the War of the Ring a great number formed the backbone of the Army of Isengard, and were trained and paid by the renegade Wizard Saruman the White. Most of this force was destroyed at the Battle of the Hornburg. Saruman himself attempted further genetic experiments with this race of 'Great Orcs' – with singularly unhappy results: creatures known as 'Half-orcs' which were said (by Saruman's enemies) to be the result of cross-breeding between the Uruk-hai and certain degenerate Men in his service.

Urulóki 'Fire-serpent'[8] (Q.) The name given by the High-elven exiles of the First Age to the terrible race of fire-breathing DRAGONS, bred during the Wars of Beleriand, by Morgoth, from an older stock. The first of these to become known to the Eldar and the Edain was GLAURUNG. The term *urulóki* includes flying dragons, when these are of the fire-breathing sort (as was SMAUG THE GOLDEN), but excludes so-called 'Cold-drakes'; these lesser beasts (one of whom, nevertheless, slew King Dáin of the Dwarves in the later Third Age) relied on strength and speed alone.

The Urulóki could only be withstood, in battle, by those specially armoured to face the fierce blasts of withering fire which were the Dragons' chief weapon. Best equipped in this fashion were the Dwarves, whose armour was the most durable in Middle-earth and who in addition wore masks, also of metal, to terrify their enemies. Thus protected, an armoured Dwarf – or Man, provided he was wearing Dwarf-armour – might approach near enough to the Dragon to bring a spear or an axe into play. But even then there was a formidable difficulty, in that the hide of all Dragons was almost impossible to pierce. On the whole, the Urulóki were best left alone, as many Elves, Men and Dwarves found to their cost, in the First and later Ages.

The Usurpers An Elvish epithet for the race of MEN.[9]

Uttermost West One of the many names among Elves and Men for the UNDYING LANDS of the Far (Ancient) West of Middle-earth. (Properly speaking, this term should apply only to the land of the Valar on the western side of the Pelóri range of mountains; but in some cases, it may refer to the still more westerly domain of MANDOS, for this was on the western shore of Aman itself, overlooking the Outer Sea.)

Utumno 'The Pit' (Q.) The Underworld (Sind. *Udûn*) The name given in Eldarin tradition to the first abode of Melkor (Morgoth) in Middle-earth, made by him far back in the Elder Days, when the

Valar, lately come to Arda, dwelt in Almaren. Utumno is indeed the origin of the ancient – and vivid – vision of Hell or the Underworld; and the characteristics commonly attributed to that awful place in many venerable creeds and religions are indeed those which obtained in Utumno of old. For it was deep under the earth that Melkor chose to make his first stronghold. In those days he did not wish the Valar, upon whom he had already made war, to guess that he had returned from the Outer Darkness, whither he had fled after his defeat. Nevertheless, he now put all his power into this great delving, and although it was at first concealed, afterwards it could no longer be hidden. Yet before its whereabouts were known to the Valar Melkor struck, and he destroyed their island of Almaren and cast down the Lamps Illuin and Ormal; and in the darkness thus brought upon the world, he escaped to Utumno in the North, and was not at that time brought to justice.

Thereafter he dwelled, for many Ages, while far off in the West, beyond his grasp, the Valar were making themselves a second home in Arda. This new dwelling-place they illuminated, but not Middle-earth; and the Darkness continued to mantle mortal lands: to Melkor's profit. Utumno was now at a pinnacle of power, and the later legends which shudderingly tell of endless branching tunnels, deep pits filled with fire, and countless evil creatures swarming to and fro – scenes of terrible, malefic energy and great heat – barely do justice to the vast and dreadful reality of Morgoth's first realm. It was at this time that he, fearing the Valar, decided to guard his western flank with another fortress, though of lesser size, for it was to be but an outpost of the Underworld, a lesser Hell. This was Angband; and its first captain was Sauron, Morgoth's chief servant.

But at this time another event occurred in Middle-earth: the Awakening of the Firstborn, according to ancient prophecy, in the east of Middle-earth. Using the Darkness as a cloak for his designs, Melkor moved covertly against the Quendi, for at first he did not understand what manner of creatures they were, nor did he know what powers they might have. But before he was able to take advantage of what he had learned,[10] the assault from Valinor – long-awaited but somehow still unexpected – broke upon the North; and Angband was levelled while Utumno, the greater and older fortress, was utterly destroyed, down to the last and uttermost pit. So complete was its destruction that Melkor was never again able to renew his work. Instead, when he returned again to Middle-earth after more than three Ages of imprisonment, he chose to centre his power upon Angband, which he made in the end into a great and dreadful place, the chief focus of all the sentient evil in Middle-earth. Yet even at the height of its power Angband was never as great, nor was it delved so deep, as Utumno.

Notes

1 Book VI, Chap. 1.
2 A tentative translation.
3 His characteristics, appearance and powers are recalled in the later (Mannish) deities *Poseidon* (Neptune) and *Dagon*.
4 The older term *Teleri* ('Last-comers') may well have been revived in this connection.
5 Cf. *Ambar* 'Doom' (Q.).
6 *Silmarillion* pp. 57–8.
7 As seems to be hinted in *The Silmarillion* (p. 81).
8 Cf. *Lóki*, the name of the God of Darkness in Norse (Mannish) mythology, and the widespread visualization of Evil Incarnate as a serpent (*lóki*, in Quenya, means 'worm').
9 And a somewhat unfriendly one.
10 Save only for his origination of the Orcs, from Elven-stock captured during this brief time from among the Quendi of Cuiviénen.

Vairë 'The Weaver' (Q.) One of the *Valier* (Queens of the Valar); the wife of Mandos. In the lore of the Eldar she is said endlessly to be engaged upon the task of weaving tapestries, the design of which records all things that have ever come to pass in Arda.

Vala The Quenya or High-elven word for 'Angelic Power' (i.e. one of the kindred of the VALAR, but more properly, the title of the Fëanorian Tengwa number 22, which represented the sound *w* in those languages which required it.

Valacar From 1366–1432 Third Age, the twentieth King of Gondor, and the unwitting instigator of the Kin-strife civil war which came near to destroying the South-kingdom. Valacar was the son and heir of Rómendacil II (Minalcar), who had won a great victory over the Easterlings with the aid of the Northmen of Rhovanion, allies of Gondor. Because of his regard for the Northmen, Rómendacil sent his son to dwell for a time in the court of Vidugavia, the mightiest of their Princes. However Valacar acquired an even greater regard for the Men of Rhovanion than had his father, and in due course wedded Vidugavia's daughter Vidumavi; the son she bore him was named *Eldacar* in Gondor, *Vinitharya* in Rhovanion.

As is told elsewhere, this mingling of the royal blood of Númenor with one of 'lesser' race caused a great deal of ill-feeling among the Dúnedain of Gondor, and when Eldacar came to the Throne this resentment turned to rebellion: many of the Dúnedain refused to accept Eldacar as their lawful King, and resisted his authority. The result was the Kin-strife civil war, in which great damage was done to the Line of Anárion and the Realm of Gondor.

Valacirca 'Sickle of the Valar' (Q.) One of the constellations; see SICKLE (OF THE VALAR).

Valandil The eldest son of the Lady Silmariën of Númenor, daughter of King Tar-Elendil, and the first of the Lords of Andúnië. He was thus the direct ancestor of Elendil, Isildur and Aragorn. Also the name of the third King of Arnor, who reigned from year 10–249 Third Age. He was the fourth son of Isildur, who was slain at the Gladden Fields (Year 2) together with Valandil's three elder brothers; Valandil himself had been left behind in Rivendell during the War of the Last Alliance, due to his tender age, and so escaped the massacre.

Valandur From 602–652 Third Age, the eighth King of Arnor.

Valanya 'Day-of-the-Valar' (Q.) The sixth and final day in the Elves' week and the seventh and final day in the week of Kings' Reckoning. In both calendars it was the chief or 'holy' day. Its alternative Quenya name was *Tárion*. The Grey-elves knew it as *Orbelain* (or *Rodyn*), while the Hobbits' name was *Highdei* (later *Highday*).

Valaquenta 'History of the Valar' (Q.) A short treatise, of unknown authorship, in which the natures and respective attributes of the VALAR and MAIAR have been detailed in due and proper order. It has been published as part of the collection entitled *The Silmarillion* but, like the *Ainulindalë*, is distinct from the larger work. Almost certainly the Valaquenta is of Eldarin origin, since the names of the various Powers, both Valar and Maiar, are in the Quenya tongue; and this in turn indicates authorship dating to the time when the Noldor (the chief loremasters of the Elves) were first dwelling in Tirion. How it came to survive until our own day cannot safely be ascertained: in all probability a copy of the work was kept in the library of Rivendell and consequently came to be 'acquired', or at least re-copied, by the famed Hobbit-scholar Bilbo Baggins – who, of course, is responsible for other literary acquisitions from the First Age. The *Valaquenta* can today be read in its entirety as part of *The Silmarillion* (pp. 25–32).

Valar 'Angelic Powers' (Q.) The name given by ancient Eldarin tradition to those of the AINUR, or Divinities created by The One before the Creation itself, who participated in the making of *Eä* (The Universe) and of *Arda* (the World) amidmost; and who, after the completion of this labour, departed from Eä and came to dwell in Middle-earth as Guardians of the World.

They did so because of their love and desire for the Children of God – Elves and Men – for whom they were to prepare the 'realm'. The future forms of Elves and Men had been revealed to them, though they had no part in their design or making, and the precise time of their appearance was not known.[1]

Much is said of the Valar in the *Quenta Silmarillion*; and even more in the *Ainulindalë* and the *Valaquenta*; and for a full account of the natures and powers of the individual Valar the enquirer is referred to those works, where he will find all that is known or recorded. Of more adjacence to this entry is the known history of the Powers since their arrival in the World, in a time so distant as scarcely to be within the comprehension of mortals. To prepare the World for the *Erusën* was all of their ancient purpose, but (as is told above in the quoted passage), even they did not know when this event would come to pass, and so for Ages uncounted they moved about the face of the earth, continuing their ancient 'demiurgic' labours, shaping the World, and peopling it with the first living things: the *olvar* and *kelvar*. Themselves beings of Light, they determined to bring Light to Arda, and for this hallowed purpose they made the great Lamps Illuin and Ormal; and Light shone on Middle-earth, and the *olvar* grew and flourished, and the *kelvar* wandered freely in the vast forests of that ancient time.

In those days (if 'days' is the correct word, since the count of Time had not yet begun) the Valar dwelt in the Isle of Almaren, together with their people, the Maiar, to whom they were as Kings and Queens. Almaren was their first home in Middle-earth, and the period of their abiding there under the mingled light of the Lamps is called by tradition The Spring of Arda. All things flourished. Yet evil befell them: the evil of Melkor, who in his origins had been the brother of Manwë Súlimo and the greatest of all the Valar. So mighty was Melkor that he envied even Ilúvatar (The One), and strove with Him even before the Creation. For this he had been rebuked; and from that time onwards he had withheld his aid, and had taken no part in the making of Arda, but had done much to mar it. One war he had fought already – and had lost it. Now he brooded in outer darkness; or so the Valar thought, for in those far-off times they were slow to comprehend the nature of Evil.

The result of their passivity was the secret, unhindered return of Melkor to Middle-earth, and the delving of Utumno, his great fortress in the North. Soon, by various signs, the Valar in Almaren were aware that he was once again at work; but before they could take steps against him he struck first. In a series of mighty blows he over-threw the Lamps, plunging Middle-earth into a Darkness that was to endure for Ages upon Ages, and in the convulsions engendered thereby Almaren was destroyed. The Valar had suffered their first defeat.

For that time they could not avenge themselves upon Melkor, being occupied with saving what they could from the ruin. And when finally the surface of the World had quietened, and the Equilibrium was once again in hand, the Valar decided to abandon Middle-earth to Melkor for a time, until they felt ready to reclaim it from him. For themselves they made a new home: Aman the Blessed in the Far West. At this time the Two Trees first grew and sent forth their Light; yet though Middle-earth remained dark for Ages to come, the Valar remained quiescent in Valinor. A city they built: Valimar. And on the highest peak of Taniquetil Manwë built his high halls, from which he oversaw and heard everything that came to pass, save in the darkened lands to the East.

So the slow Ages wound on. And in due course there came to the Valar news of the event they had awaited since the Dawn: the awakening of the Firstborn Children of Ilúvatar: the Elves. By this time the Valar were again grown powerful, and they, now fearing for the safety of the Quendi in darkened Middle-earth, determined to settle accounts with Melkor (it is worth noting that their motive in launching war upon him at this time was not revenge for Almaren and the Lamps, but pre-emption of any evil he might yet commit against the Erusën; after all, they were Guardians).

In the resultant Battle of the Powers (as it is called by the Eldar) Melkor was taken prisoner and Utumno was destroyed; but his lesser stronghold of Angband was only levelled, and by lurking deep under-ground, many evil creatures survived the wrath of the Powers. Nonetheless, the way was now clear for the Quendi to fulfil their destiny – if they so wished. For at this time the Valar themselves were confused. Evil, they now knew, might awake again in Middle-earth at some future time; for the Great Darkness still endured. So there were two apparent choices: to lighten Middle-earth once again, and so remove the fear of renascent evil and safeguard the Quendi (and the Atani who were still to come); or to summon the Quendi to Valinor, there to dwell with the Valar in bliss and everlasting life, in a land illuminated by the holiest Light that has ever been seen in the World. In making their choice, the Valar were guided by their experience; and this seemed to tell them that to lighten Middle-earth and leave the Quendi to dwell there might, in the end, prove disastrous. For who of the Valar had foreseen that Melkor would prove able to overthrow the Lamps Illuin and Ormal? Yet he had done this very thing. The safest course was to summon the Quendi to Valinor, for no evil could ever enter the Blessed Realm. Or so most of the Valar then believed.

(As was afterwards seen, this decision, though blessed with many fair consequences, also had its darker side; yet the memory of Almaren was strong, and the experience of Melkor's power for destruction had been profound; and unlike The One the Valar were not infallible in their judgements.)

Of the events which followed the summoning of the Quendi to the Far West much is said in the *Quenta Silmarillion*. For three Ages of Middle-earth Melkor languished, a captive, in the Halls of Mandos; while the Eldar who had completed the Great Journey from the land of their birth throve in Valinor and Eldamar, beloved of the Valar and Maiar. But still Middle-earth endured the Great Darkness, though this had now been enhanced by the stars created by Varda at the time of the awakening of the Quendi. Yet under that starlit Night the evil of Melkor still moved in Middle-earth, though directionless and impotent. And in the end the time came for the release of Melkor; for in this matter the Valar were bound by their word, and three Ages of imprisonment – no more – had been decreed for him, providing he showed repentance. This he did (though falsely), and was released. And before long his will had crossed the Sea and had entered the minds of his creatures in Middle-earth, so that they began to increase in number.

Finally, deeming himself (accurately) already under suspicion of falseness, and having worked what small evil he could in Valinor, Melkor fled. Powerless to repeat his first great blow, he nevertheless had power enough to strike another, equally grievous, before his flight. With the aid of the monster Ungoliant he poisoned the Two Trees and stole the Silmarils, slaying Finwë of the Noldor to do so. In this way the ancient hope of the Valar, that evil could never enter the Blessed Realm, was brought to nothing; and worse was to follow.

For Melkor's last and greatest rebellion led to the seduction into evil of many other creatures – and in time the Seduced themselves became Seducers so that a mighty consequence of Melkor's treachery was the rebellion of the Noldor and the War of the Great Jewels, with all the evil that entailed. And the process of corruption did not stop there – indeed it had been in process since the beginning of Arda, when many of the Ainur had gone over to Melkor's side. Evil followed evil – and perhaps the greatest evil of all was the rebellion of the Atani (the Númenoreans) and their assault upon the Undying Lands at the end of the Second Age.

But at the time of the rebellion of Morgoth and his flight to Middle-earth the Valar envisaged no such development. Rather than use force to prevent the revengeful Noldor from forsaking the Undying Lands in pursuit of the evil Vala, they merely ratified the High-elves' exile until such time as they should truly repent; yet after a while they could no longer stand aside from the affairs of Middle-earth, and when asked to do so they reluctantly took a hand in the War of the Great Jewels. The host they sent to Middle-earth at the end of the First Age was the greatest force that has ever been in the world; so irresistible was it that Morgoth – who had hitherto been almost totally victorious – was crushed and his evil realm of Angband destroyed in the cataclysm unleashed upon him. This apocalyptic event also destroyed the Grey-elves' land of Beleriand, and so changed for ever the destiny of Elves in Middle-earth.

Yet the Valar, Guardians of the World, were concerned above all with the innocent. The race of Men, which had appeared in Middle-earth during the later First Age, and which had fought unselfishly against evil with no thought of gain, seemed more deserving of reward than those of the High-elves who had survived the wars; and so the Valar gave to the Atani (Men) a land of their own, far out in the Western Seas and removed from the perils of Middle-earth. And yet this generous gesture, designed to repair in part the evils caused by Morgoth and Fëanor, led in the end to a disaster of even greater proportions: for an Age of the World Númenor grew in power and splendour and pride, and under the evil teaching of Sauron, servant of Morgoth, eventually rebelled, like others before, against the authority of the Guardians. This time the peril was too great for even the Valar to overcome unaided, and they 'laid down their Guardianship and called upon the One, and the world was changed. Númenor was thrown down and swallowed in the Sea, and the Undying Lands were removed for ever from the circles of the world.'[2]

After the Drowning of Númenor the Valar, chastened by their self-evident failure, determined to take no further direct part in the affairs of mortals. Instead, they sent messengers to Middle-earth to work against Evil – but these emissaries were themselves forbidden to use the awesome powers of their race; instead, they were made subject to the same laws which bound mortals (apart from lifespan). These were the beings known in Middle-earth as *Istari* or Wizards, and their individual successes and failures in their appointed tasks are recorded elsewhere in this *Companion* (see GANDALF THE GREY; SARUMAN THE WHITE). Yet it may be said that, in this final attempt to maintain the Balance, the Valar achieved a more lasting success than with all previous policies. For although they had not themselves originated Evil, it was one of their race who had done so – and they had failed to win him back to their side, in which cause he might have done mighty service. They had failed to foresee the blows he had struck against them, when the Lamps were cast down and their first realm destroyed (perhaps they were lulled by bliss, and by pride in their achievements). Determined nonetheless to fulfil their Guardianship, they had succeeded in ensuring the survival of the Firstborn – but they had failed to prevent evil from entering their second realm, with all its attendant consequences. Indeed, they had invited it in. And in caring overmuch for the West, they neglected the East, so that evil was not stamped out, nor has it ever been; and the Second People, when they arrived in the World, did so at a time of confusion and fear, which marred them ever after. All this was accountable to the Valar, though not directly, for indeed no evil had ever entered into any of them, save Melkor alone.

But with this new policy – of encouraging the Free Peoples to assist in the working of their own destinies, without placing direct pressure upon them – the Valar were at last rewarded by mortals' awareness of the ancient Balance, and of the need to maintain it. At the end of the Third Age they withdrew altogether from the affairs of Arda, in the knowledge that the infancy of the World was over, and their long Guardianship at an end.

Valaraukar 'Demons of Might' (Q.) See BALROG.

Valaróma 'Mighty Trumpet' (Q.) The hunting-horn of the Vala OROMË THE GREAT.

Vales of Anduin All the lands between the western eaves of Mirkwood and the eastern foothills of the Misty Mountains.

Valier 'Queens of the Valar' (Q.) The name given in the lore of the Eldar (see *Valaquenta*) to the seven most royal of the female VALAR, or Powers, corresponding to the seven Lords. The Valier are: *Varda* (Elbereth); *Yavanna Kementári*; *Nienna* sister of the Fëanturi; *Estë* the Healer; *Vairë* the Weaver; *Vána* sister of Yavanna, spouse of Oromë; and *Nessa* his sister, the bride of Tulkas. Varda, Yavanna and Nienna are in addition accounted *Aratar*, members of the innermost Council of the Powers.

Valimar 'Home of the Valar' (Q.) Also written *Valmar*. This name is applied in a general sense to the Land of the Valar, also called *Valinor*, but more properly to the City in the middle of that land. Little is known of it.

See also following entry.

Valinor '[Land]-of-the-Valar' (Q.; from older form *Valinórë* '[People] of the Valar') The name in the High-elven tongue for the second abode in Arda of the Valar or Powers; whose capital was *Valimar* or *Valmar* (see preceding entry). The term *Valinor* frequently refers to the Isle of Aman but in its later sense applies only to that part of Aman which lay west of the Mountains of Defence; in this form it is most commonly encountered.

(There is a certain amount of confusion between the terms *Valinor* and *Valimar*. This is best resolved by emphasizing that the latter name conveys a spiritual significance, while the former holds a geographical meaning. Both refer to the Far West, beyond the Calacirya.)

Valinor was founded after the destruction of Almaren, the first dwelling in Arda of the Powers. Its dimensions are of course not recorded, but it originally embraced the entire Isle of Aman; only later was the easternmost portion of this land set aside as a dwelling for the Eldar – being renamed *Eldamar* as a consequence – while the Valar and Maiar withdrew into the land west of the Mountains they had raised as a defence against Melkor. (In this connection Valinor is also sometimes known as the Guarded Realm.) Its chief – and only – city was Valimar (or Valmar) of the Bells; and at the western gate of Valmar stood the chief council-place of the Aratar, the Máhanaxar or Ring of Doom. Before the Máhanaxar stood the green mound Ezellohar; and upon the summit of Ezellohar, in ancient times, stood the Two Trees of renown. Elsewhere there were gardens and enchanted woods, and fields of grain, and orchards, and lakes: each the particular domain of one of the Valar or Valier, peopled by their servants and followers, the Maiar. The westerly boundary was the shore of the Encircling Sea, Ekkaia, where stood the lonely Halls of Mandos. North and south of Valinor the Valar and Maiar did not journey.

Valinorean The speech of the Valar. Little or nothing of this ancient language has been recorded, but doubtless it played some part in the enriching of the Quenya tongue far back in the Elder Days, and so therefore a certain resemblance between the two languages may be assumed.

Note: the words *aseä aranion* (Kingsfoil or *athelas*) were said to be in the Valinorean language.

Valley of Dreadful Death A translation of the Sindarin name NAN DUNGORTHEB.

Valmar See VALIMAR; VALINOR.

Vána A Lady of the Valar, accounted one of the *Valier* (though not among the Aratar). She was the sister of Yavanna, and shared many of Kementári's powers and characteristics, being especially attuned to both *olvar* and *kelvar*. Vána the 'Ever-young' (one of her titles), is the spouse of Oromë.

Vanimeldë (Tar-Vanimeldë) The third Queen (and sixteenth Ruler) of Númenor.

Vanyar 'Fair-elves' (Q.) The First Kindred of the Eldar, the 'Highest' of all High-elves. Led by Ingwë, their first and only King (Ingwë is also accounted High-king of all Elves), the Vanyar were foremost in the Great Journey from Cuiviénen to Aman, and tarried not at all in mortal lands, for they had been transfixed by the vision of Aman compellingly described for them by Ingwë, and sought only to come to the Uttermost West as speedily as possible. This they did, and never again yearned for Middle-earth – and never returned save on one occasion: as warriors of the Host of Valinor, come to wreak final justice on Melkor. Of all the Quendi the Vanyar were the most beloved of the Valar; and after an Age they forsook the fair and splendid city of Tirion – in whose building they had played a great part – and, seeking ever to come closer to the Light of the Trees and the society of the Valar, migrated through the Calacirya into Valinor and never came back, save as guests of their kinsmen.

The Vanyar were the least numerous of the Three Kindreds; and unlike all other Elves, their hair was golden (which accounts for their name). Few are mentioned by name in records. *Ingwë* the King was, and is, their Lord, and dwells with Manwë atop Oiolossë; *Indis* is the name of the Lady whom Finwë of the Noldor took as his second wife, after the passing of Míriel Serindë. From her the yellow hair of her kindred descended among the Noldor (in the House of Finarfin).

Varda 'The Exalted' (Q.) The High-elves' name for that Lady of the Valier known (to Grey-elves) as ELBERETH.

Vardamir The second King of Númenor, son of Elros Tar-Minyatur. He came to the Throne in 442 Second Age.

Variags A barbarous race of Men, dwellers during the Third Age in the remote region of Khand, to the south-east of Mordor. Like other Easterlings, they were apt to Sauron's will and did battle for his part during the War of the Ring.

Vása 'Heart of Fire' (Q.) A Noldorin name for ANAR (the Sun).

Veil of Arda The atmosphere.

Vidugavia The most powerful of the Princes of Rhovanion during the thirteenth century of the Third Age, and the valiant ally of King Rómendacil II of Gondor. His daughter Vidumavi wedded Rómendacil's son Valacar.

See also KIN-STRIFE.

Vidumavi See previous entry, also KIN-STRIFE; VALACAR.

Vilya (older form *wilya*) The Quenya or High-elven word for 'air' or 'sky', but more properly the title of Tengwa number 24. Also the name in Eldarin tradition of the Ring of Air, mightiest of the Three Rings of the Elven-kings made by Celebrimbor the Smith during the middle years of the Second Age. It was given by Celebrimbor to Gil-galad, High King of Lindon, and was later passed on by Gil-galad to Elrond Half-elven shortly before the final battle of the Last Alliance. Elrond bore it throughout the Third Age and carried it over Sea when he departed from Middle-earth in 3021. It was a ring of gold, and bore a large sapphire.

See also THREE RINGS.

Vingilot 'Foam-flower' (Q., from older form *Vingilótë*) The name given by EÄRENDIL to the ship he built of birchen planks felled in the woods of Arvernien, in which he and Elwing journeyed to Aman and besought the aid of the Valar against Melkor (Morgoth). The (later) Adûnaic form of this name was *Rothinzil*. Vingilot was after-wards set in the sky (or so the Eldar say) by Elbereth, to traverse the Heavens as the Evening Star.[3]

Vinitharya The birth-name of King Eldacar of Gondor, given to him by his mother Vidumavi, daughter of Prince Vidugavia of Rhovanion. The word is in the Northern tongue of the men of Rhovanion, and its meaning has not been recorded.

Vinyamar 'New Home' (Q.) The name given by Turgon of the Noldor to his first dwelling in Middle-earth during the years of his exile from Eldamar. Vinyamar was a great hall built upon the slopes of Mount Taras in Nevrast, the 'First Homely House' East of the Sea. But it was unfortified, and never more than a temporary dwelling. Turgon and his people afterwards removed to Gondolin, and dwelt there until the fall of that city, four centuries later.

Vinyarion The birth-name of King Hyarmendacil II of Gondor. It is Quenya in form.

Víressë The fourth month in Kings' Reckoning, equivalent to our April. The Dúnedain of Middle-earth, descendants of the Númenoreans, used instead the Sindarin equivalent *Gwirith*. The Hobbits' name was *Astron*.

Vorondil the Hunter From 1998–2029 Third Age, the Steward to King Eärnil II of Gondor. From him all subsequent Ruling Stewards (beginning with his son Mardil) were descended. He was renowned as a great huntsman, and the great ox-horn which was borne ever after by the Steward's eldest son was the result of a successful expedition on the part of Vorondil to the plains of Rhûn, where many of the fabled Wild White Kine were to be found.

Voronwë 'Steadfast' (Q.) One of the Noldor of the First Age, of the People of Fingolfin; he was one of those sent by Turgon of Gondolin into the Western Seas after the Nirnaeth Arnoediad, to beseech the pardon and the aid of the Valar. Seven ships set out, but of all that sailing only one Elf-mariner returned: Voronwë son of Aranwë; and this was many years later. It was afterwards said (by the Eldar) that the Vala Ulmo had played a part in this preservation, for Voronwë was cast ashore in a place where he would easily be encountered by Tuor of the Edain – another instrument of the King of the Sea – so as to furnish Tuor with a guide to Gondolin. Voronwë indeed led Tuor by the secret ways to Turgon's city, and so played his part after all in the great events which were to end the Age and bring succour to Middle-earth. His fate is not recorded.

Also the admiring title bestowed by folk of Gondor (Third Age) upon Mardil the Good Steward.

Notes

1 *The Road Goes Ever On*, p. 66.
2 Appendix A I(i).
3 Contradicted by Bilbo in his poem 'Eärendil was a Mariner' (Book II Chap. 1). '*A ship then new they built for him, of mithril and of elven-glass . . .*'

Wainriders See EASTERLINGS.

Walda From 2842–51 Third Age, the twelfth King of Rohan, third of the Second Line of the Mark. He had been King only nine years when he was trapped and slain by Orcs in the mountains near Dunharrow. His son Folca mounted a great campaign against the Orcs and succeeded in driving them from the Mark.

Wall's End A translation of the Grey-elven name *Ramdal*.

Wandlimb A translation of the Sindarin name *Fimbrethil* (literally 'slender-birch').

Wargs A Northern Mannish name for wolves, but more properly applied to the evil werewolves (*Gaurhoth*, Sind.), which appeared in Middle-earth during the First Age and remained to plague the wilderness ever after. Unlike real wolves, the Wargs were phantasms which only assumed real (and deadly) shapes after darkness had fallen; like Orcs, they were afraid of the Sun, which had the effect of nullifying their power.

War of the Dwarves and Orcs A bitter six-year conflict between two ancient races of Middle-earth, which represented the first attempt on the part of one of the Free Peoples to exterminate the Orcs of the Misty Mountains. It raged from 2793–9 Third Age, and reached a climax with the bloody Battle of Azanulbizar, in which the Dwarves gained a pyrrhic victory over their foes.

The full tale of this grim and attritive war may be read in Appendix A III; here it may suffice to say that the enmity was brought about by the Orcs of Moria and their murder of King Thrór of the Dwarves; the Dwarves of Durin's Line had fallen on evil times and had been driven from Erebor by the Dragon Smaug, and as a result their pent-up wrath overflowed when the news was brought to Thrór's heir Thráin II. He mustered all his people, 'and they were joined by great forces sent from the Houses of other Fathers; for this dishonour to the heir of the Eldest of their race filled them with wrath. When all was ready they assailed and sacked one by one all the strongholds of the Orcs that they could from Gundabad to the Gladden.'[1]

For six years the Dwarves pursued the fugitive Orcs the length and breadth of Wilderland, above and below ground, wreaking havoc among their foes and slaughtering all they could find. In the end they advanced upon Moria itself, and in the valley of Azanulbizar (the Dimrill Dale) they fought the greatest battle of the war against the Orcs. Many fell on both sides until in the nick of time reinforcements arrived from the Iron Hills; before the Sun went down the murderers of Thrór had been themselves slain, and those Orcs which had survived were fleeing south in terror and disarray.

The War of the Dwarves and Orcs was over, but the victorious Dwarves had themselves suffered cruelly in the final fight. Náin of the Iron Hills was slain, and so were Frerin son of Thráin and Fundin father of Balin. Thráin himself had lost an eye and Thorin had been wounded. Nonetheless, the Dwarves did not regret their victory, even while they begrudged its cost. They burned the bodies of their dead and marched away to their various homelands. And for over a hundred years no Orc dared show its face in the Vales of Anduin.

War of the Elves and Sauron The first great conflict of the Second Age, brought about by Sauron's betrayal of the Elven-smiths and his forging of the Ruling Ring, by which means he intended to make himself Ruler of Middle-earth. For the Elves, therefore, the War was a question of survival; and survive they did, though at great cost – and not without aid from an unexpected quarter.

The War commenced with Celebrimbor's discovery that he and his fellow Elven-smiths of Eregion had been deceived by Sauron of Mordor. Sauron had aided in the forging of most of the Rings of Power, but unknown to the Elves had secretly planned to use this very means to overthrow the Free Peoples. In 1600 Second Age he succeeded in forging the Ruling Ring – and upon the instant, across the leagues between Orodruin and Eregion, Celebrimbor 'was aware' of Sauron's treachery and of his intentions. The Elf immediately hid the Three Elven-rings and declared his hostility to the Lord of Mordor. In 1693 the first clashes between the Elves and Sauron's forces took place, but the Elves had waited too long and Sauron's power was greater than theirs. Two years afterwards he advanced into Eriador.

Although little is now known of the strategies of the War, it may be assumed that Sauron's initial advance into the North was made with the object of surrounding Eregion and (presumably) of seizing the Three Rings. Accordingly, he drove a great wedge between the Elven-smiths' land and Gil-galad's forces further to the north and west, and bent all his attention upon the siege of Eregion. Nonetheless, Gil-galad contrived to send reinforcements (led by Elrond) to Celebrimbor. Too late. In 1697 Eregion was captured and ravaged, and Celebrimbor was slain. The surviving Noldor retreated northwards beyond the Bruinen and founded the refuge of Imladris (Rivendell), and Sauron turned his attention to the Elves of Lindon, led by his oldest foe, Gil-galad of the Noldor.

Luckily the Elven-king had foreseen Sauron's treachery to some extent and so had not entirely been caught unprepared by the outbreak of war. Many Elven-warriors resisted Sauron's westward advance, yet by 1699 the armies of Mordor had overrun Eriador and were at the very borders of Lindon. All seemed lost – and then, just in time, a great fleet and host arrived in the Gulf of Lune, sent by King Tar-Minastir of Númenor to the aid of Gil-galad. Minastir's motives seem to have been somewhat mixed, for while he entertained great regard for the Eldar, he yearned for their immortality. Nonetheless, the help he sent was welcome indeed, and with it Gil-galad was able once more to mount an offensive against the Dark Lord. Sauron was defeated in Eriador in 1700 and, the following year, driven out altogether. So ended the War.

War of the Great Jewels The longest and most terrible war ever fought in Middle-earth, which lasted for many centuries of the First Age and brought grief, terror and unparalleled destruction to mortal lands. The War of the Great Jewels was begun for unworthy motives – and those who commenced it were, in the end, utterly defeated, together with their blameless allies. Only by the intercession of the Valar themselves, at the very end of the Age, was it finally brought to an end; yet its effects were far-reaching and lingered beyond the change of days. They are with us now.

The origins of the War of the Great Jewels lie far back in the Elder

Days, with the cult of craftsmanship perpetrated in Eldamar by the Noldorin High-elves, of whom Fëanor was a chief and the greatest in arts and lore. Pride in craftsmanship led to pride for its own sake, and eventually to possessiveness. Fëanor created the Silmarils, the 'Great Jewels' which were so marvellously beautiful that none could behold them without longing to possess them; and at last one of the great Valar, Morgoth, succumbed to this lure and stole the Jewels, which he carried back to Middle-earth.

As is told elsewhere (see FËANOR), the Noldor grew enraged at Morgoth's act, and resolved to follow him back to Middle-earth and wrest the Jewels from him by whatever means necessary. Against the expressed will of the Valar, they took ship and followed Morgoth; and almost immediately they were engaged in battle with his forces. Yet although this first clash resulted in victory for the Elves – and other victories were to follow, on an even greater scale – no real progress was ever made towards their ultimate objective: the overthrow of Morgoth and the recovery of the Silmarils. And in the end the tide of battle turned irretrievably against them, and they were defeated, and their cause was ruined.

The War of the Great Jewels is sometimes also known as the War of Beleriand. A glance at the map (supplied with *The Silmarillion*) shows why this was so. Beleriand was of old the heartland of the power of the Elves in Middle-earth; and although the purpose of the Noldor was, as has been said, the recovery of the Jewels, this war aim rapidly became identified with the holding of Beleriand against Morgoth; indeed, this alone was as much as the hosts of the Noldor were ever able to achieve.

But at the outset of the War the returning Noldor rapidly gained the initiative from the armies of Angband. An attack on their first encampment was swiftly rebuffed (see SECOND BATTLE OF BELERIAND), and Beleriand, which at that time was partially occupied by Orcs, was swiftly liberated. This initial series of successes was followed by the formulation of the governing strategy of the Noldor (see FINGOLFIN), in which the natural bastions of the north of Beleriand were occupied and fortified by the various Noldorin princes and their respective hosts, with the aim of erecting a permanent barrier against Angband, but with the ultimate intention of bringing Morgoth to battle on the open plains beyond: a battle which the Noldor, at this time, had no doubts whatever of winning. Then, and only then, did they envisage an advance upon Angband and a settling of accounts with Morgoth. But this conservative strategy left the initiative entirely in the hands of the Enemy; and in the fullness of time he took advantage of it, to his profit (being aided in this 'waiting game' by his knowledge of the precariousness of the alliance of peoples opposed to him, and of its inevitable – if prolonged – dissolution).

So it came to pass. And although in the end the alliance lasted for more than four centuries, Morgoth's strategy was proved correct. The Noldor quarrelled amongst themselves, and the Sindar withdrew their aid; and even the arrival of a new and formidable people in Beleriand, the *Atani* (Men), did no more than postpone the evil day. Yet a study of the various battles fought during this long period reveals a singular fact: that in defence the Noldor and the Atani were at their most formidable. Indeed, the only battles they ever won were those in which they themselves had been attacked (however they did not win all of these); and the greatest disaster of all came about as a result of a planned *offensive* against Morgoth. Yet the real military reason for their ultimate defeat lies in the fact that, in choosing to fight an attritive war (their only choice in view of the immense strength of Angband) they thus surrendered their best card – their matchless valour and superior weaponry – to the Enemy. For his armies, although less valorous and indeed clumsily led for the most part, were always far more numerous and indeed renewable; whereas from the day of their arrival at Losgar the Noldor began to decrease, and were never replaced. And the longer the War lasted the more the balance began to favour the Enemy.

Such was the pattern of events. Initial victories of the Eldar were followed by a defensive strategy; and this, successful at first (see THIRD BATTLE OF BELERIAND), was followed by the four-hundred-year Siege of Angband, the last two centuries of which are known as the Long Peace. But for reasons explained above, and elsewhere in this *Companion*, the Siege was at last overthrown by a sudden attack from Angband (the DAGOR BRAGOLLACH); and although for another decade or so the Noldor rallied valiantly, and indeed recaptured some of the territory lost during that battle, the tide had turned against them for ever. The Battle of Sudden Flame was followed by the Nirnaeth Arnoediad (the FIFTH BATTLE OF BELERIAND); in which a supposedly co-ordinated offensive went disastrously wrong – due to treachery – and brought about the all but total destruction of the last armies of the Eldar and the Edain. The northern front was overthrown and Beleriand was at last laid bare to Morgoth.

Yet the War of the Great Jewels was not yet over; for there were still isolated communities of Elves and Men who fought on – no longer in hope of overthrowing Morgoth, but because it was all that was left to them to do. But with frightening rapidity these islands were sundered one from the other; and the long-held (and immensely powerful) refuges of the Noldor, chiefly the cities of Nargothrond and Gondolin in Beleriand, were successively assailed and captured. For although they had been built by far-sighted Elven-princes in anticipation of just such a day, when the time came their powers of endurance were compromised by other forces now at work in Middle-earth: treachery not the least. Even the ancient coastal havens of the Grey-elves were sacked and destroyed; and now, in all Beleriand, there was only one Eldarin realm still standing: the Kingdom of Doriath, defended by the Girdle of Melian. Yet this, too, fell (though not to Morgoth) – and now all was over. Only in secret lairs at the Mouths of Sirion, and on the Isle of Balar, did Elves and Men survive. But there was no longer any thought (except in the minds of the Sons of Fëanor) of regaining the Silmarils or of defeating Morgoth. Indeed, it seemed only a matter of time before their Enemy discovered these last refuges and assailed them also, so making an end of the Eldar and the Edain.

But now the time had at last come for the Valar themselves to intervene. As long as the Noldor alone had been suffering destruction, they had held aloof; but now other peoples, guiltless of the crimes of Fëanor and his followers, had also been imperilled and had already endured great loss of life. The original reasons for non-intervention therefore no longer obtained – and the Valar, when informed of the change of situation (see EÄRENDIL), decided to take a part in the War. The host they sent from the West utterly obliterated Morgoth's land of Angband; and the Silmarils were at last regained – but not by the Noldor. The very last act of the long tragedy was the stealing of the two remaining Jewels by the two surviving Sons of Fëanor. But this in turn led directly to the destruction (or at least final loss) of the Great Jewels; and with the removal of the Silmarils from the reach of all who desired to possess them the War came to an end; and with it the First Age of the World. Morgoth was cast into the void and the Exiles (with one or two notable exceptions) were permitted to return to the Far West. The Edain – who had not brought the War about, but had bravely fought against Evil with great loss of life – were richly rewarded. But nothing could resurrect the dead, or restore the lost lands of Beleriand, or remove the stain of guilt from the sorrow-ful High-elves, whose rashness and pride had led to the War in the first place. Many indeed of the Noldor voluntarily continued their exile in mortal lands, for it seemed to them then that by labouring and healing they might in time come to atone for the great distress they had brought about. The product of this policy was the creation of the Rings of Power; and the result of that was the War of the Ring, two full Ages after the end of the War of the Great Jewels.

War of the Powers See BATTLE OF THE POWERS.

War of the Ring The name given in Gondor and the Shire to the great conflict which took place at the end of the Third Age between Sauron the Great, Lord of the Rings, and the Free Peoples of Middle-earth, acting in league. The object of the War was the possession of the Ruling Ring made by Sauron in the Second Age: the Dark Lord wished to regain it, and his foes to destroy it; in the end the Free Peoples prevailed and Sauron was himself engulfed in the wave of destruction which followed the melting of the Ring in the Cracks of Doom.

The War of the Ring is, of course, the very subject on which both Bilbo and Frodo have written so eloquently (and at such length) in the Red Book of Westmarch. That renowned volume indeed tells the story of the War from the point of view of the Hobbits, who had much to do with its successful conclusion, and there can be few who will expect to find it retold in these pages. By unprecedented heroism and great good fortune (as it is called) the Ring was carried to the Fire despite all Sauron's increasingly frantic efforts to recover it – and simultaneously his armed might was checked on the very point of victory by excellent strategy and impeccable timing. Defeated on the field of battle, Sauron was defeated in spirit and outguessed by his foes at every single turn; and although much damage was done and many lives were lost before all was over, in the end both Sauron and the Ring were removed from the world and an age-old peril was extinguished for ever.

War of Wrath The Name given by the Eldar to the final – and exceedingly brief – stage of the WAR OF THE GREAT JEWELS, in which the Valar, learning at last of the triumph of Morgoth and of the afflictions of Middle-earth, returned to mortal lands with a great host and, in a series of swift battles, achieved what the combined might of Elves and Men had been unable to accomplish in five centuries of bitter warfare. Angband was destroyed and Morgoth was taken captive; and the remaining Silmarils were, for a while, recovered. (See *Silmarillion* pp. 251–5.)

Wars of Beleriand The WAR OF THE GREAT JEWELS.

Watch The SHIRRIFFS.

Watcher in the Water A hideous and evil monster which, during the latter part of the Third Age, dwelled in a sinister lake at the West-door of Moria. The lake was itself created by the damming of the river Sirannon, and in this way the western entrance to the Dwarf-realm was sealed. For this reason it was afterwards guessed that the Watcher itself had been initially responsible for the damming of the river.

Watchful Peace The name given in Gondor to the period between 2063–2460 Third Age, when Dol Guldur was temporarily abandoned by Sauron (because of a desire to preserve his true identity from an increasingly inquisitive White Council).

The Water The chief river of the Shire (apart from the Baranduin). It rose in the north-west and flowed through Hobbiton, Bywater and Bridgefields to join the Baranduin (Brandywine) north of the Bridge of Stonebows. During this journey it formed two lakes or tarns: the Bywater Pool and a larger expanse (itself called, rather confusingly, 'The Water') north of Frogmorton.

Waybread A translation of the Sindarin words *len-bas* or *lembas*.

Waymeet A village in the Westfarthing of the Shire. It grew up around an ancient crossroads, where the road from Little Delving to Sarn Ford crossed the Great East Road. It was also called *Waymoot*.

Weather Hills See AMON SÛL.

Weathertop An approximate translation of the Sindarin name *Amon Sûl* (literally, 'Hill of Winds'). It was the tallest and most southerly of the Weather Hills.

Wedmath The eighth month of the Shire Reckoning, equivalent to *Urimë* in the Númenorean calendar (Kings' Reckoning).

Wellinghall A translation of the (unknown) 'short name' for an Ent-house used by Treebeard. It was on the south-eastern slopes of Methedras, not far from the source of the Entwash river.

Wells of Varda The great cisterns in Valinor wherein the Queen of the Valar, Varda (Elbereth), is said to have gathered and stored the luminescent dew from the Two Trees. They were emptied by Ungoliant after the poisoning of the Trees, and never again refilled.

West-elves The Eldar.

Westemnet The name given by the Rohirrim for that region of their land which lay to the west of the river Entwash.

Westernesse An archaic translation of the Quenya word *Númenórë* (literally, 'People-of-the-West').

Western Sea Belegaer.

Westfarthing One of the four quarters or 'farthings' of the Shire. It was bounded by the Tower Hills in the west, by the villages of Needlehole and Nobottle in the north, by the villages of Hobbiton and Bywater – and by the Three-farthing Stone – in the east, and by the township of Michel Delving in the south. Until the Fourth Age, it was the least inhabited portion of the Shire.

Westfold The name given in Rohan to the region between the river Isen and the northernmost White Mountains. Its chief stronghold was Helm's Deep.

Westfold Vale The low-lying central area of the Westfold, watered by the Deeping Stream.

West-gate (of Moria) The Doors of Durin. Early in the Second Age, during the years of Moria's greatest wealth and glory, many High-elves removed to the lands between the Swanfleet (Glanduin) and the Loudwater (Bruinen), to trade with the Dwarves. For their part, the Moria-dwellers extended their realm westward to enable this commerce to flourish. Where the Misty Mountains ended in a great vertical cliff the Dwarves constructed a door of marvellous workmanship, utterly impenetrable to those who did not know its secret. In return, the High-elves embellished the Doors of Durin with designs and writings in *ithildin*, a metal made from *mithril* which reflected only light of moon and stars. (The West-door is in fact illustrated in Book II Chap. 4.)

Westlands The name given (in a general sense) to all the lands west of the Misty Mountains and of the river Anduin.

Westmansweed The name given in the Common Speech (Westron) to Pipe-weed.

Westmarch A translation of the Grey-elven name *Nivrim*, being the western part of the Forest of Region in Doriath, the area of wood which lay beyond the Sirion. Also (Third Age), the name of a sparsely peopled region lying between the West-farthing and the Tower Hills, properly speaking part of the West-farthing itself. It was granted to the Shire-dwellers in perpetuity by King Elessar (Aragorn II) in 1453 Shire Reckoning (Year 32 Fourth Age), and was settled by many Hobbits from the other Farthings. Three years after its founding Fastred of Greenholm and his bride Elanor the Fair (daughter of Samwise) removed to Undertowers, on the eastern slopes of the Tower Hills, and Fastred was named Warden of Westmarch by the King. It was in Undertowers that the famous Red Book (of Westmarch) was afterwards kept.

See also RED BOOK OF WESTMARCH.

West Road The Great West Road. It joined Minas Tirith with Edoras.

Westron The COMMON SPEECH.

Wetwang See NINDALF.

White Company The personal guard of Faramir Prince of Ithilien, inaugurated after the War of the Ring by King Elessar (Aragorn II). Its first Captain was Beregond son of Baranor, formerly of the Citadel Guard of Minas Tirith.

White Council The Council of the Wise – the five *Istari* (Wizards) and the chief Eldar – formed in the late Third Age to co-ordinate policy against Evil in Middle-earth. It was summoned by the Lady Galadriel of Lothlórien and its first chief was Saruman the White. At the time of its founding (2463 Third Age), the chief enemy of the Free Peoples was the 'Necromancer' of Dol Guldur, and the over-riding aim of the Wise was the discovery of his true identity; for even at that time there were some who believed that the Necromancer was Sauron himself.

Nonetheless, this was not easy to ascertain. Sauron had, in his turn, perceived the Council from a distance, and had retired into the East to avoid a confrontation with his chief foes, for at that time he was not yet strong enough to challenge their combined might. And so the White Council abandoned their fruitless vigil, hoping that the more optimistic assessment of events was accurate. The second meeting was in the year 2851 – but this, too, was a fruitless experience, for the Council's titular head, Saruman the White, was then already falling into evil ways and he governed the doings of the Council with a firm hand and overrode a projected assault upon Dol Guldur (which had been proposed by Gandalf the Grey) for reasons of his own. Ninety years later the Council met again – and this time Saruman agreed to the attack (again for reasons of his own) and the assault of the Wise upon Sauron was made that same year. Too late. Sauron had meanwhile prepared contingency plans and when the attack came he merely withdrew from Mirkwood and re-entered Mordor long prepared for him.

And so the years drew on to the War of the Ring. In 2953 the White Council met for the last time, and once more Saruman lied to the assembled Wise, misleading most of them concerning the fate of the Ruling Ring. Yet by that time there were some among the Council who were beginning to cherish deep suspicions concerning Saruman himself – and so when the War of the Ring broke out in 3018 Third Age, they were not entirely unprepared for the rapid succession of events which followed, not the least of which was the open treachery of Saruman the White, for over five hundred years the leader of the White Council and during all that time the main reason for its singular lack of success.

White Crown See SILVER CROWN.

White Downs An area of downland in the Westfarthing of the Shire which sheltered the chief township of the region: Michel Delving.

White Hand The heraldic emblem chosen by the renegade Wizard Saruman the White after his renunciation of the White Council in 2953 Third Age and his subsequent fortifying of Isengard. It was borne by all his servants, including Orcs, as a device emblazoned on shield and helmet.

White Lady (of the Noldor) See AREDHEL.

White Mountain Oiolossë.

White Mountains A translation of the Sindarin words *Ered Nimrais*.

White Rider The name given in Rohan and Gondor to the Wizard Gandalf, formerly the Grey, reincarnated as the White.

White Tower An alternative name, used especially in Minas Tirith, for the TOWER OF ECTHELION.

White Tree The chief symbol of the royalty of Gondor. It was a direct descendant of Telperion, Eldest of Trees, through Galathilion[2] (the Tree of the High-elves in Tirion), Celeborn (the Tree of Eressëa), and Nimloth of Númenor. When disaster overwhelmed Númenor in 3319 Second Age, Elendil brought a fruit of Nimloth to Middle-earth, and planted it in Minas Ithil, where it grew and flourished for a while, being jealously guarded: for it was the token from afar of the Edain of Númenor and of their ancient kinship with the High-elves, and through the High-elves with the Valar themselves.

The White Tree of Gondor blossomed often, but only occasionally put forth fruit; each time it did so, the seed was planted elsewhere, in fear lest the Line of Telperion die from the world. In this way the Tree was preserved when Sauron attacked and captured Minas Ithil in 3429 Second Age; he burned the original Tree but a sapling had already been planted in Minas Anor, where it afterwards grew.

For over a thousand years this White Tree flourished in the Court of the Fountain in Minas Anor, until the Great Plague of 1636 Third Age, when it died. A further sapling was then planted (by King Tarondor) which survived until 2852; as no seedling could then be found, the dead Tree was left standing by the fountain. But after the successful conclusion of the War of the Ring the newly crowned King Elessar (Aragorn II) discovered a sapling growing wild in a high place above the city of Minas Tirith, and this he planted in place of the dead Tree. It blossomed almost immediately and grew to grace and beauty during the Fourth Age which followed.

Whitfoot A family of Shire-hobbits. See WILL WHITFOOT.

Whitfurrows A village in the Eastfarthing of the Shire, near the junction of the Quarry road and the Great East Road.

Whitwell A village in the Green Hill Country of the Shire, not far from Tuckborough.

Wídfara ('Wide-farer') A Man of Rohan, one of the scouts employed by King Théoden to reconnoitre the way through Anórien during the War of the Ring.

Wilderland An alternative name for the region of Middle-earth more usually known as *Rhovanion*. Its boundaries were approximate, but included the Misty Mountains, the river Celduin-Carnen, and the Grey Mountains.

Wildman of the Woods A name assumed by TÚRIN TURAMBAR, after his escape from the wreck of Nargothrond.

Wild Men See WOSES.

Willie Banks One of the Little Folk (Hobbits) of the Bree-land, unfortunately killed in 3019 Third Age in a skirmish between the Bree-dwellers and the robber band led by Bill Ferny and Harry Goatleaf.

Willowbottom A village in the Eastfarthing, near the southernmost reach of the Woody End.

Will Whitfoot The Mayor of Michel Delving during the closing years of the Third Age and (apart from a brief convalescence) the first seven years of the Fourth. He was reportedly a Hobbit of remarkable girth and great respectability, much liked by the Shire-dwellers; and he had a strong sense of responsibility. During the occupation of the Shire by agents of Saruman in 3019 (1419 Shire Reckoning), he bravely set out from Michel Delving to Bag End to protest against the unwarranted liberties taken by the invaders, but never arrived, being abducted while on the road and afterwards incarcerated in the Lockholes. He was released, much the worse for wear, by the returning Travellers later that same year and, after an interim of several months (in which he was deputized for by Frodo Baggins), he was re-elected at the Free Fair in 3020 (1420 Shire Reckoning). He retired from the Office in Year 7 Fourth Age (1428 Shire Reckoning) and was succeeded as Mayor by Samwise Gamgee.

'The Willow-meads of Tasarinan' A lament or chant sung by Treebeard the Ent (to the Hobbits Meriadoc and Peregrin), in which the old Tree-herd mourned the passing of the Elder Days, and the drowning of many wide lands that he had known and loved in those distant times. See Book III Chap. 4, also *The Road Goes Ever On*, pp. 11-17.

Wilwarin 'Butterfly' (Q.) One of the constellations created by Varda (Elbereth) at the time of the awakening of the Quendi in Cuiviénen. (Identified in *The Silmarillion* with Cassiopaeia.)

Wilya See VILYA.

Windfola A noble horse of Rohan, the steed of the Lady Éowyn (and shared by the Hobbit Meriadoc) for the journey from Edoras to Minas Tirith during the War of the Ring.

Windle-reach A long, clear reach of the lower Withywindle (between Grindwall and the weir).

Window of the Eye The topmost turret-room in Barad-dûr, so called because Sauron was accustomed to sit there, gazing out with his single Yellow Eye over the lands of his claimed Realm.

Window of the Sunset [of the West] A translation of the Sindarin name *Henneth Annûn*.

Winterfilth The tenth month of the year in the Shire Reckoning, equivalent to *Narquelië* in Kings' Reckoning (although the Hobbits believed that the name dated from the years before they had adopted the Númenorean calendar, when this month was the last of the year). Its Bree-equivalent was *Wintring*.

Wintring A Bree-adaptation of the (older) term *Winterfilth*. See preceding entry.

Wise The five *Istari* (Wizards) and the Chief Eldar. See also WHITE COUNCIL.

Wiseman Gamwich The son of Hamfast of Gamwich; he left the village of his family's origins and removed to Tighfield in the North-farthing.

Witch-king The Lord of the Ringwraiths, chief servant of Sauron the Great throughout the Second and Third Ages of Middle-earth and for much of the latter Age a great and evil Power in his own right, second only to his Black Master as a symbol of terror and despair. His were the policies and schemes which led to the founding of Angmar and the collapse of the North-kingdom of the Dúnedain; his were the armies which came from Mordor in 2000 Third Age to capture Minas Ithil from Gondor; his was the hand which slew the last King of the Line of Anárion; and his was the black host which emerged from the Tower of Sorcery during the War of the Ring to crush the Dúnedain for ever. He was a King and a Sorcerer, and he wielded great fear, and no warrior or army could withstand him; yet in the end he was slain by a Woman and a Hobbit, and his age-old power was brought to nothing, in fulfilment of a prophecy made long before.

Of his origins little has been recorded – even his true name is a matter of speculation. He was the mightiest of those renegades called Black Númenoreans, and in the later years of the Second Age he left Númenor and came to Middle-earth, where he became a lord of great power, working in league with Sauron of Mordor but not at that time one of Sauron's servants. But Sauron, being treacherous even to his allies, determined to bring the Númenorean renegades directly under his control, and to this end he forged the nine Rings of Power for Mortal Men. These he gave to nine powerful lords, of whom the Sorcerer King was the greatest; and they fell into his power for ever, becoming wraiths under the control of the Ruling Ring and of its Master.

The Ringwraiths served Sauron faithfully throughout the remainder of the Second Age, and when the Dark Lord was overthrown by Gil-galad and Elendil they passed 'into the Shadows' to await his second arising. After the first thousand years of the Third Age had passed both they and their Master were stirring once more, and in the fourteenth century the Ringwraiths openly declared themselves. Their chief came north, to the lands between the Ettenmoors and the Northern Waste, and there he established a realm, whose chief purpose was the destruction of the North-kingdom of Arthedain, last survivor of old Arnor. This evil realm was named Angmar, and throughout the second millennium the Witch-king (as he was known to the Dúnedain of the North) worked unceasingly for the downfall of his enemies (see ANGMAR). In the end he accomplished his chosen task, but at the cost of his own realm, and he was driven from the North by the combined forces of Gondor and Lindon.

> It was thus in the reign of King Eärnil . . . that the Witch-king escaping from the North came to Mordor, and there gathered the other Ringwraiths, of whom he was the chief. But it was not until 2000 that they issued from Mordor by the Pass of Cirith Ungol and laid siege to Minas Ithil. This they took in 2002 . . . and Minas Ithil became a place of fear, and was renamed Minas Morgul.[3]

In 2050 the Witch-king sent an insolent challenge to King Eärnur of Gondor (son of Eärnil, and the Captain whose army had destroyed Angmar). Eärnur had indeed been challenged by the Lord of Minas Morgul seven years earlier, on the day of his coronation, but at that time had been restrained from accepting it. But on this second occasion he furiously rejected all wise counsels and rode away to give combat to the Lord of the Ringwraiths. He never returned. In this way the Witch-king, having destroyed the Northern Kingdom, now extinguished the ruling Line of the South-kingdom: a mighty triumph indeed.

Yet having wrought all these strokes against his foes, the Lord of Morgul seemed content for many centuries to lie quiescent in Minas Morgul, for the time was not yet come when he would ride openly to battle against the most ancient foes of his Master. But by the end of the Age Sauron was against returned to power – and with the Dark Lord's return to Mordor the power of his nine servants waxed accordingly. On learning of the whereabouts of the Ruling Ring (from the prisoner Gollum), Sauron instantly despatched his trustiest servants, mounted on black steeds, into the North to seek the Shire; and as has been recorded elsewhere, one of these came to Hobbiton on the very evening of Frodo's departure. Led by their Sorcerer King, the Ringwraiths pursued Frodo and his companions across Eriador, but were foiled on Weathertop and at the Ford of Bruinen. Defeated, they returned to Mordor and to Dol Guldur – and to Minas Morgul: for the hour was approaching when Sauron would launch open war upon Gondor.

Chief among the Dark Lord's war-captains was the Lord of the Ringwraiths, King of Minas Morgul. Throughout the year of 3018 he mustered a great host and, in March 3019, led his evil army forth across the Morgulduin bridge and down to Osgiliath. So began the siege of Gondor, in which the Dúnedain, defeated at the crossings of Osgiliath, were driven back to Minas Tirith and forced to endure a two-day period in which the host of Morgul, led by their Black Captain, prepared to demolish the Great Gate of Gondor. This they accomplished at dawn on March 15th, and the Witch-king prepared to enter 'under the archway that no enemy ever yet had passed, and all fled before his face'.[4]

Yet in the instant of victory the initiative was snatched from the Witch-king. Foiled at the Gate by Gandalf, he discovered that his besieging armies were being overwhelmed by the Riders of Rohan, even while his black heart rejoiced in his triumph. And in attempting to stem this new tide of defeat, he was confronted by two warriors against whom all his ancient power availed him nothing. Two swords, wielded by a Maiden of Rohan and a Hobbit of the Shire, broke the ancient spell which knitted his sinews together, and he was cast down into the void at last. With his passing the armies of Morgul were left without a captain capable of assessing the true situation, and in the Battle of the Pelennor Fields which followed his fall they were utterly destroyed. None returned to Minas Morgul, which was later destroyed by the Dúnedain.

See also MORGUL.

Withered Heath A desolate region in the eastern range of the Grey Mountains, notoriously the abode of Dragons.

Withywindle ('Winding-willow-river') A brown river, bordered by many hundreds of ancient willow-trees, which arose in the Barrow-downs and flowed through the Old Forest to join the Baranduin at Haysend (the southern part of Buckland). Its central valley was known as 'The Dingle'.

Wizards The name given in western Middle-earth to the five members of the Order of *Istari*, who first appeared in the early years of the second millennium.

> It was afterwards said that they came out of the Far West and were messengers sent to contest the power of Sauron, and to unite all those who had the will to resist him; but they were forbidden to match his power with power, or to seek to dominate Elves or Men by force and fear.[5]

They were of the race called MAIAR; and the prohibition laid upon them at the commencement of their mission – that they should renounce all of their native-born power and conduct themselves within the limitations of Middle-earth itself – would seem to indicate a desire on the part of those who sent them to intervene in the affairs of mortals as indirectly as possible (see VALAR). But whether or not the five *Istari* were Maiar who sought to make amends for some ancient wrong, or who desired to discharge their duty to Middle-earth by long labour cannot now be discovered.

All that can be said is that the Wizards together formed an Order, sworn to the service of 'the Secret Fire'. They were five in number, 'graded' by means of coloured vestment (e.g. Saruman the White, Gandalf the Grey, Radagast the Brown), each of whom bore a Wizard's staff as a symbol of his membership of the Order. All were wise, and each had some speciality or particular interest, though their ways parted after their arrival and their ranks were sundered by time and the natural processes of Middle-earth.

See also GANDALF THE GREY; SARUMAN THE WHITE.

Wizard's Vale See NAN CURUNÍR.

Wold The name given in Rohan to the wide grasslands between Fangorn Forest and the Anduin, south of the river Limlight. Many horses and studs were kept there by the Rohirrim.

Wolf-riders Orcs of small stature who habitually rode into battle mounted upon Wargs.

Wolves See WARGS.

Wood-elves East-elves. See AVARI; ELVES; NANDOR.

Woodhall A village in the Eastfarthing of the Shire, at the north-eastern corner of the Woody End.

Woodland Realm See THRANDUIL.

Woodmen In the First Age, this term was applied solely to the Haladin of Brethil; in the Third Age, however, the name refers specifically to a tribe of Men, related to the Northern race of Middle-earth (like the Beornings and the Men of Dale), who lived in scattered settlements in western Mirkwood, making a living by forestry and other similar pursuits.

Woody End The largest forested area in the Shire, some fifteen miles broad at its widest point. It lay between the Stock-Tuck-borough road, the river Shirebourn and the Green Hill Country, and was the wildest part of the Shire.

Wormtongue Gríma son of Galmód, a Man of Rohan. He was a clever but mean-spirited person, and in the years before the outbreak of the War of the Ring was easily seduced by the Wizard Saruman into betraying his country. He afterwards worked secretly for Saruman, and by dint of guile had himself appointed King Théoden's chief counsellor. His task was to lull the King's fears concerning Isengard, and simultaneously to undermine the King's morale by constant emphasis on Théoden's age (actually a mere 71 at the time of the War of the Ring). For some years he succeeded in this task, although he earned the hatred of all those members of Théoden's house who saw beneath the mask; hence his name. In 3019 his coun-sels of despair came close to bringing about the downfall of the Mark. But his treachery, well-known to all except Théoden, was exposed to the King by Gandalf the Grey, and Gríma the Wormtongue was obliged to flee for his life.

Believing Saruman on the point of victory, he rode to Isengard, just in time to be captured by Treebeard and imprisoned (with his master) in the Tower of Orthanc. He later accompanied Saruman when the Wizard was expelled from Orthanc, and journeyed with him to the Shire. But Saruman's constant contempt and ill-treatment drove Wormtongue mad, and in the hour of the Wizard's expulsion from the Shire Gríma murdered Saruman in a frenzy of rage and despair. He was killed by the Hobbits as he attempted to flee.

Woses An Ancient race of aboriginal Men, the origins of whom have not been recorded, although various elements of their long and peaceful history may be detected in the histories and cultures of other peoples. From available evidence it seems that, in the late First or early Second Ages, they dwelt in the region between the river Isen and the westernmost spur of the White Mountains (this region was afterwards called *Drúwaith Iaur*, 'Old púkel-land', in maps made during the Third Age). In the first millennium of the Second Age they moved eastward into the vales of the White Mountains, driven perhaps by fear of the Númenorean mariners who were even then beginning to make settlements on the coastlands of Middle-earth. The Woses continued to live by hunting rather than agriculture or craft, and preserved their elusive and wary way of life for as long as they could. But in those years another race of Men came to the White Mountains, and these incomers drove the 'púkel-men' away from the high vales, although they made stone images of the curious, stumpy-bodied Woses to marvel at. Fleeing in terror from the Men of the White Mountains, the Woses came by mountain-paths to their last refuge: the ancient Forest of Druadan (as it was later called), at the very eastern end of the Ered Nimrais range. There they vanished into the Wood, and were afterwards hardly ever seen by unfriendly eyes.

Throughout the Third Age the Wild Men of Druadan Forest continued to dwell in the depths of the wood, hunting as they had always done and avoiding all contact with other Men. It seems certain that they suffered at the hands of the Orcs (when the Orcs could catch them), and on this account conceived a great hatred for the *gorgûn*, as they termed these creatures. They turned their weapons – bows and blowpipes – upon those who hunted them and took care to avoid the sight of all other living creatures; for they were 'woodcrafty beyond compare', and they learned the ways of the forest better than any other creature, save Elves. But by the time of the War of the Ring their uneasiness at the worsening taste in the wind which blew from the East led them to make overtures to the

Rohirrim, offering aid in return for a peaceful life; this offer of help was gratefully accepted, and led directly to the great victory of the Pelennor Fields (see STONEWAIN VALLEY). After the War King Elessar (Aragorn II) of neighbouring Gondor declared the Wild Men freemen of the Forest for ever, and he forbade any man to enter it without their leave.

Wulf The son of Freca, a renegade of mixed Dunlendish and Northern blood. After his father had been slain (for insolence) by King Helm Hammerhand of Rohan, Wulf made overtures to the Hillmen of Dunland, and in concert with other enemies of the Mark invaded Rohan in 2758 Third Age. This force was too great for the Rohirrim to withstand, and Helm was driven in retreat to the Hornburg fortress; Helm's son Haleth remained to defend Meduseld, and was slain before the doors of the Golden Hall by Wulf. The renegade then entered in and called himself King.

But meanwhile many of the Rohirrim had not been defeated, although they endured a siege of a whole winter (the Long Winter of 2758–9) in the Hornburg and Dunharrow. The latter fortress was occupied by Helm's sister's son Fréaláf, and in the spring he made a secret descent from the Hold and captured Meduseld, slaying Wulf with his own hand. With the death of their leader the Dunlendings were easily driven out of the Mark, and as Helm had perished during the winter Fréaláf then became King of Rohan. He was the first of the Second Line.

Notes

1 Appendix A III.
2 See Note 4 on page 265 of this *Companion*.
3 Appendix A I(iv).
4 Book V Chap. 4.
5 Appendix B 'The Third Age'.

Yale A village of the Eastfarthing. It stood between Whitfurrows and the Stock-Tuckborough road.

Yanta The Quenya or High-elven word for 'bridge', but more properly the title of Tengwa number 35, which represented the sound of consonantal *y* in most languages, *e* in the Mode of Beleriand.

Yavanna Kementári One of the great *Valier* (Valar Queens), the elder sister of Vána and spouse of Aulë the Smith. In the lore of the Elves she is accounted second only in might to Varda (Elbereth). Her powers are directly connected with growth and life, and it is said that she made the first *kelvar* and *olvar* (fauna and flora) in Middle-earth (at her prayer the race of Onodrim – or ENTS – was created by Ilúvatar, to protect from harm the trees of Middle-earth which were her especial love). But her most renowned accomplishment was the making of the fabled Two Trees, Telperion and Laurelin.

Yavanna means 'Giver of Fruits' (it is Quenya in form); her secondary title *Kementári* is translated as 'Queen of the Earth'.[1]

See also *Valaquenta* (pp. 27–8) and *Quenta Silmarillion* (pp. 35, 38, 40–41, and esp. 43–6).

Yavannië (Q.) The ninth month of Kings' Reckoning, equivalent to our September. Unlike the Númenoreans, the Dúnedain of Middle-earth used instead the Sindarin equivalent *Ivanneth*.

Yávië 'Autumn' (Q.) The name given (by the Elves) to the third of their six seasons, and (by Men) to the third of their four. In the

Elvish calendar this season was of fixed length (54 days), but in Kings' Reckoning was used in an approximate form. Both the Grey-elves and the Dúnedain of Middle-earth (who largely abandoned the Quenya names) used instead the Sindarin equivalent *iavas*.

Yáviérë 'Autumn-day' (Q.) The name given in Gondor to one of the five 'extra' days in the Stewards' Reckoning calendar-system. *Yáviérë* fell between *Yavannië* (September) and *Narquelië* (October) and heralded the advent of autumn. It was accordingly a holiday in Gondor.

Year-book of Tuckborough See YELLOWSKIN.

Year of Lamentation A name among Elves and Men of the First Age for the Year of the Sun 470 (see FIRST AGE): the year of the Nirnaeth Arnoediad.

Years of the Sun See FIRST AGE.

Years of the Trees See FIRST AGE.

Yellowskin The Year-book of Tuckborough, a large bound volume containing the Annals of the Took clan, begun in Tuckborough in about 400 Shire Reckoning (2000 Third Age), long before the building of Great Smials or the passing of the Thainship from the Old-bucks to the Tooks. It was accordingly the most ancient text preserved in the Shire, and many of its dates were incorporated into the Red Book of Westmarch. The Tooks undoubtedly had a certain reputation concerning the accurate compilation of chronologies (see THE TALE OF YEARS).

Yén, Yéni 'Long-year' (Q.) The 'true' Elvish year, equal to 144 *coranar* (solar years). See also CALENDAR OF IMLADRIS.

Yestarë (Q.) The name given by both the Elves and the Dúnedain (of Númenor) to the first day of the year, which in all calendar-systems was accounted separately from the rest of the months or seasons.

Yuledays The first and last days in the Hobbits' year. The Shire-folk accounted them separate from all the months (like the *Lithe* midsummer period).

Yulemath The Bree-name for the Shire-month of *Foreyule* (December).

Yuletide An ancient holiday-period or festival celebrated by Northern Men and adopted by the Hobbits during the early years of the Third Age. They continued to observe this six-day festival even after they had settled the Shire, much later in the Age, and by the time of the War of the Ring the period had been fixed to fall between 29th Foreyule (December) and 2nd Afteryule (January), with, of course, the two Yuledays in between.

Ywalme See NWALME.

Note

1 Cf. *Elentári*, 'Queen of the Stars', the secondary title of Varda (Elbereth).

Zaragamba The original (as opposed to translated) name of the Hobbit-family from the Eastfarthing, hereditary Thains of the Shire, who passed on the office to the Took (Tûk) clan and removed to the strip of land between the Baranduin and the Old Forest. It has been translated from the Red Book as *Oldbuck*.

Zimraphel (**Ar-Zimraphel**) The (Adûnaic) royal title assumed (under duress) by Míriel (Tar-Míriel), daughter and rightful heiress of Tar-Palantir, penultimate King of Númenor, after her forcible wedding to the usurper of Palantir's throne, Ar-Pharazôn the Golden.

Zimrathôn (**Ar-Zimrathôn**) The twentieth King of Númenor, the second to take his royal title in an Adûnaic (rather than Eldarin) form.

Zirak-Zigil The Dwarvish (Khuzdul) name for the centremost of the three great peaks of Moria, known to Men as the Silvertine and to Elves as Celebdil.